Jump Cuts, Tracking Shots, and Scherzos

Jump Cuts, Tracking Shots, and Scherzos

Writings on Film, Music, and
Contemporary Culture

David Sterritt

Sticking Place Books
New York

Contents

Part 2: Articles and Essays

Preface and Acknowledgements

I've been writing on film, theater, and music for more decades than I care to think about, and certainly more than I expected when I started down this path. During much of that time I was film critic and cultural correspondent at *The Christian Science Monitor*, a self-described international daily newspaper that boasted more prestige and esteem than actual readers; although for some of those years the *Monitor* had a news service reaching other papers with a combined readership of many millions, I never had the kind of audience that writers for larger outfits reached. I once asked the great dancer and choreographer Merce Cunningham how he managed to become so firmly established while creating such resolutely avant-garde work, and he told me that by sticking to his guns over the long haul he'd simply become a part of the landscape. Without likening myself to that towering artist I'll say that my story is somewhat similar; by faithfully marching off to screenings and performances, hanging out with valued colleagues, writing for numerous publications, and participating in the ongoing arts-world dialogue to the best of my ability I found that I'd fashioned a career in the field(s) that mattered most to me. I've been fortunate to serve as a reviewer and critic, a film programmer, a university professor, a radio and TV commentator, and a few other things along the way. It's been challenging and it's been fun.

This collection contains a small portion of my writing for the *Monitor* and other outlets. In compiling the material I've made almost no editorial changes (even when refining or polishing might have been a good idea) and I should note that my choices of Monitor articles have been limited by the near impossibility of acquiring pieces published there before 1980 and in some cases more recently than that. Revisiting reviews and essays I wrote in bygone times has been an interesting, sometimes harrowing, and occasionally enlightening experience. I guess I've occupied a modest little spot in the cultural landscape, and I'm pleased with this opportunity to share a few snapshots of the terrain I've explored.

Turning to acknowledgements, my thanks go first to Paul Cronin for inviting me to join the remarkable group of cineastes and cinephiles whose writings are making Sticking Place Books a major resource for anyone with a serious interest in the advancement and preservation of film culture. I first met Paul around twenty-five years ago, when he came to my apartment in lower Manhattan to film me for his 2001 documentary on Haskell Wexler and *Medium Cool*, and I'm delighted to be involved in his latest exciting venture. Thanks also to the many periodicals, publishers, editors, and others who have ushered my articles, essays, reviews, and interviews into print over the past several decades. The Christian Science Publishing Society has generously allowed me to republish a goodly number of Monitor articles, and the esteemed Gary Crowdus has done the same with numerous essays and reviews from Cineaste, the most valuable film magazine on the planet. And finally, a zillion thanks to my ever-supportive sons, Jeremy and Craig, and a zillion more to my personal and professional partner, Mikita Brottman, whose insights and intelligence have been propping me up as long as I've known her.

PART 1
REVIEWS AND INTERVIEWS

Don't hate me, I'm just a movie critic: Our reviewer responds to the deluge of mail after he panned *Lord of the Rings*

The Christian Science Monitor, February 6, 2004

Keep those emails and letters coming, folks! But can we correspond about something besides *The Lord of the Rings* for a while? I've riled up a lot of moviegoers with my lukewarm reviews of the trilogy—and they've let me know, with a vengeance. Here's a small sampling.

"When one is the lone voice of dissent, it's often the case that the dissenter simply has poor taste in films," says one of the more respectfully written missives.

"Do your [paper] a favor and post reviews by a real critic like Ebert or maybe even a small monkey," writes a reader who seems a tad more peeved. "You are trying to get a name for yourself by dissing this movie," says another, raising a possibility—getting a name for myself—that hadn't occurred to me.

"Your movie critic is an idiot," says a correspondent who doesn't mince words.

"Booooooooo," writes someone who minces them even less. One asks me if I grew up near a toxic-waste dump, and another inquires about mistreatment I may have suffered as a child.

Now you know why we movie critics tell our editors we deserve hazard pay. I answered as many emails as time allowed, and along the way I realized some raised issues worth writing about in return. For example: "You praise all the stupid movies either nobody's heard of or were really dumb and boring, then give bad reviews to all of the popular, well-liked, box office hits… I strongly suggest you end your job as a critic."

What's interesting here is the idea that a critic's function is to echo the tastes of some hypothetical average moviegoer. I enjoy popular, well-liked movies—why, last month alone I gave good reviews to pictures like *Torque* and *Win a Date With Tad Hamilton*, which ought to suggest I'm not exactly a cinema snob. But a critic's job goes further than that. We're supposed to form our own opinions and then articulate them in a sort of long-distance dialogue with our readers.

Of course, I have my prejudices. Nothing pleases me more than a movie that gives my own imagination a workout, asking me to interpret and ponder its contents for myself. Nothing pleases me less than a picture that dishes up knee-jerk formulas, making me feel like one of Pavlov's trained puppies. But readers can easily spot my idiosyncrasies and take them into account when reading my reviews.

I suspect many of my correspondents saw my *LOTR* reviews on websites for Tolkien and fantasy fans, rather than in the Monitor itself, since "we" crops up more often than "I" in the most aggressive (sometimes unprintable) messages. Most of the emails can be grouped into a few basic categories. Many come from people who feel I've hopelessly misunderstood author J. R. R. Tolkien and filmmaker Peter Jackson all my life, and want to set me straight. Others complain I'm just snooty and want to flaunt my supercilious airs. Still others take genuine pity on me, and want to enlighten me so I can love the movies too.

The idea that I simply found the movies less than sensational doesn't seem to have crossed many of their minds. I came to *LOTR* with high hopes, as a Tolkien admirer who's read all the books more than once. Most of the trilogy disappointed me with wooden acting, unconvincing settings, and more emphasis on dazzling effects than real emotions. The series got better as it went along, but I've seen no reason to revise my response, which is based more on the letdown I felt as a moviegoer than any high-minded ideas I might cook up as a critic.

And hey, I'm not the lone voice of dissent. There are folks out there who agree with me! "I'm very pleased to see someone looked past the surface of this series," wrote one of them, "and saw that the 'adapters' have cut the heart out of this epic masterpiece... My inner fan boy cries out for something more."

Another wrote, "I believe these movies appeal mainly to those who were Tolkien readers first and now enjoy seeing the stories 'fleshed out' in gloriously computer-generated images. You may be in a minority of film critics, but you have at least one bleary-eyed, mentally numb supporter." Said another, "I left the theater marveling that despite having given Peter Jackson more than nine hours of my life, he had somehow failed to engage my emotions for more than 10 or 15 minutes."

Such support notwithstanding, I know I'm in a small minority, even among my movie-critic colleagues. And I reluctantly predict an *LOTR* sweep of the Oscars this year. So remember, all you critic-critics, you're definitely winning this skirmish. And that's fine with me, as long as we keep open minds and hearts when we debate the next epic blockbuster coming to a theater near us all.

Days of Heaven and Waco: Terrence Malick's *The Tree of Life*
Film Quarterly 65:1, Fall 2011

Call it coincidence or call it Providence, but Terrence Malick's eagerly anticipated epic *The Tree of Life* debuted at Cannes less than a week before the Rapture was to occur, according to a California evangelist whose prophecy was widely reported at the time. What's interesting here is not the prediction but the fact that a delusional nonagenarian could make international headlines with a claim that apocalyptically minded preachers have been making since the dawn of the Christian era. Americans are oddly vulnerable to this sort of nonsense—witness our eagerness to inject religion into debates over gay rights, stem-cell research, abortion, and other issues relating more to the flesh than to the spirit. Adding more fuel to the ideological fire is the Christian narcissism that courses through large segments of the United States, less belligerent now than in the Reagan era or the aftermath of the September 11 attacks, but still festering in the national unconscious.

I start my discussion this way not to sound contentious or unholier than thou, but to indicate from the start my reservations about the theology Malick embraces in *The Tree of Life*; while he does brilliant things with his narrative materials, they tap into a kind of American religiosity that specializes in affirming static traditions and shoring up reactionary mindsets. Certain tropes in the film, such as the glowing crystal that apparently symbolizes God, come perilously close to the vague "spirituality" and hazy mysticism of so-called New Age gurus. Other sequences are religious in old-school Christian ways, and some of the imagery recalls the kind of fundamentalist recruiting pamphlet you find on park benches and subway seats. From the prayers at the beginning to the sermon in the middle and the vision of heaven at the end, Malick's film is wrapped in a religiosity that secular humanists will find nostalgic and naïve. When the movie visits a cemetery, a thuddingly symbolic name—Gracy, as in grace of God—looms on the biggest gravestone, and when a scene set in heaven shows a bird flying over the ocean, you can only hope it isn't Jonathan Livingston Seagull trying for a comeback.

In just about every other way, however, *The Tree of Life* seems to me a stunning achievement. And despite my reservations about its religious notions, I'm impressed by the courage Malick shows in organizing such an ambitious, personal film around themes that Hollywood rarely bothers to sniff at, much less explore, except in superstitious fantasies like *The Da Vinci Code* (Ron Howard, 2006) and propaganda screeds like *The Passion of the Christ* (Mel Gibson, 2004). It's easy to write off the film's sketchy, impressionistic narrative, and it's even easier to scoff at what one reviewer called its "cosmic woo-woo." It's far more interesting, though, to look beyond the surface layers of story, characters, and milieu, taking Malick's evocation of the supernatural not as a stab at timeless truth but rather as a distinctive cinematic matrix upon which he weaves an intuitive web of meaning and emotion that makes up for its shortage of theological sophistication with large amounts of aesthetic ingenuity.

The film's driving force appears to be Malick's conviction that he can invoke a sense of divine wonder by artfully juxtaposing an autobiographical bildungsroman with sublime artifacts chosen from the visual, verbal, musical, gestural, and architectural treasures that Judeo-Christian thought has generated during its long history. Viewed as an exercise in the Hollywood genres it borrows from—psychological drama, domestic melodrama, coming-of-age tale, family romance—the film is often as muddled as its less imaginative critics have claimed. But they miss the point. *The Tree of Life* puts genre elements into play for the purpose of exceeding and transcending them, using them as building blocks for a risky, resourceful tour de force that moves from earthly, psychological concerns to heavenly, sacramental ones in a manner that might well have pleased one of Malick's heroes, Martin Heidegger, who believed that modern philosophy's most important task is to dig out from under the traditional metaphysics that has long dominated Western thinking.

Before going further into this, some words about the story and the production are in order. *The Tree of Life* takes place in the 1950s in Waco, Texas, one of the places where Malick, born in 1943, grew up. The movie begins with a prologue introducing its allusive, associative structure and the central themes of love, death, grief, and humanity's existential choice between "the way of nature" and "the way of grace" as the right path to redemption and salvation. Malick's trademark voiceovers come and go over a far-reaching montage of microcosmic and macrocosmic images that eventually jell into a fairly linear, if highly unconventional, narrative.

The plot centers on the O'Brien family, whose new proximity to mortality and mourning is established when bad news comes to Mr. and Mrs. O'Brien (Brad Pitt and Jessica Chastain) in a telegram.

We then go back in time, seeing the early days of their marriage, the birth of their first son, and the arrival of two more offspring who complete the household. More family history emerges from bits of information scattered throughout the film—the hardship of losing their home when Mr. O'Brien is forced out of his job, a welcome rebound thanks to patents he registered years earlier, the physical comfort they've achieved by the time the sad telegram sets the story in motion.

One of the three O'Brien children, Jack (Hunter McCracken), becomes the focal point of the film, which vividly depicts his experiences on the brink of adolescence. Although he spends much of his time with his brothers and friends, Jack's life is primarily defined by his relationships with his parents. His mother is warm, sympathetic, and fun to be around; his father is the disciplinarian of the house, forever laying down rules (sit on the front of your chair; pull weeds out by the roots; call me father, not dad) and sometimes flying into fearsome rages when he's disobeyed. Logically concluding that his father hates him, Jack naturally hates him back, and he's at his happiest when the patriarch goes away on a business trip, leaving mom in charge and sparking the film's most idyllic family sequences. Only in the fullness of time does Jack realize that he and his father are very much alike, led as much by instinct as by reason and crisscrossed with contradictory impulses. Meanwhile, tragedy strikes when one of Jack's brothers abruptly drowns in a community swimming pool, the pivotal event around which the entire film can ultimately be seen to revolve. In a sense, the most important figure in the story is the one we see least often: Jack many years later (Sean Penn), a prominent professional coping with a midlife crisis that brings memories of these bygone events—and intimations of a higher power that guards and guides him—flooding into his mind and heart.

By all accounts, the making of *The Tree of Life* was as curious as the film itself. According to Peter Biskind's 1999 *Vanity Fair* article "The Runaway Genius," after Malick finished the high-romantic drama *Days of Heaven* in 1978 he pursued a project called "Q," which was to begin by illustrating the origins of life. That imposing topic soon became the subject of the entire film, and Malick used his connection with Paramount Pictures to get cameras rolling around the globe, filming everything from volcanic activity at Mount Etna to ice shelves tumbling into Antarctic waters. Malick himself labored on the screenplay, which was described by an associate as "pages of poetry, with no dialogue, glorious visual descriptions." Paramount grew impatient for a workable script, and one day Malick simply dropped the project, moving on to *The New World*, his sweeping historical romance of 2005. Or so it seemed, but he may have reshuffled and recycled "Q" instead: parts of *The Tree of Life* deal directly with the origins of life, seen in cosmic montages where specks of rock and strands of DNA make momentous contact with planets in outer space and ova in the nascent biosphere, producing an array of cataclysmic blasts, planetary lineups à la *2001: A Space Odyssey* (Stanley Kubrick, 1968), and other cosmos-making miracles. Eventually dinosaurs arrive, looking like extras from *Jurassic Park* (Steven Spielberg, 1993); there's an inscrutable little scene where a big one puts its paw on a small one's head, as if to crush it, then ambles benignly away—perhaps the birth of altruism in the world. Finally human-kind enters the scene.

Simultaneously with *The Tree of Life*, according to *IndieWire*, Malick has also been making an IMAX film called *Voyage of Time*, narrated by Pitt and depicting the first stirrings of life and consciousness, the rise of humanity, and finally the end of ever thing. If and when it's released, its content may have direct connections with *The Tree of Life*, which was also shot partly on IMAX film. [Note: The 44-minute IMAX film *Voyage of Time* was released on September 20, 2016.] The vicissitudes of casting these projects are a saga in themselves, so I'll just mention reports that "Q" would have starred Mel Gibson along with Colin Farrell, who worked well with Malick on *The New World*, and that Heath Ledger was set to play Mr. O'Brien in *The Tree of Life* until Ledger burned himself out by racing directly from Christopher Nolan's *The Dark Knight* (2008) to Terry Gilliam's *The Imaginarium of Dr. Parnassus* (2009), the last movie he finished before his untimely death. There's little point in wondering how different actors might have influenced the outcomes of these ventures, but these days it's a good idea to keep Gibson at a distance.

A factor distinguishing *The Tree of Life* from other Malick projects is its strong autobiographical component; going back to Biskind's account, it's clear that young Malick resembled young Jack in numerous ways. Malick was the oldest of three brothers, fought often with his father, and felt extremely close to his mother. His youngest brother was a gifted classical guitarist whom the great Andrès Segovia took as a student, but once in Spain he had a breakdown, destroyed his hands, then died in an apparent suicide. In another tragedy, the middle brother was horribly burned in a car accident. In the film, Jack relates to his parents much as Malick related to his in reality, attached to mom and at odds with the patriarch. Jack's youngest brother has precocious skills on the guitar and dies, appreciated by few, in the swimming accident. A voice-over tells us that the second brother also died quite young, reiterating the lost-sibling motif, and we occasionally glimpse a neighborhood boy whose head was partly disfigured in a fire.

As bildungsroman, *The Tree of Life* positively sparkles. I've never seen a film that more richly limns not just the characteristic occurrences of growing up but also the ephemera, the fleeting perceptions, the quicksilver moods, the endless ambivalences and indeterminacies that make up both the constitutive bedrock and the ungraspable core of a blossoming personality that's already formed in some respects, still ambiguous and amorphous in others. The overflowing energy of childhood surges through a number of briskly presented scenes, as when Jack and another boy have a whole conversation while running down a back road at top speed, or when the neighborhood kids fire a homemade rocket into the air, then gaze in bafflement when it refuses to come down where they expect. Fleeting views of youngsters talking through tin-can-and-string telephones and standing on paint-can stilts seem to symbolize their dim awareness of the possibilities for connection and exaltation that the world reserves for humans just like them. Other examples abound, one of the most resonant being a sequence where Jack slightly injures his brother, then apologizes in ways so delicate and inconspicuous that they're hard for an outsider to fathom.

These sequences get much of their power from the cinematography by Emmanuel Lubezki, who also photographed *The New World*, and from the editing by a five-person team during three years of postproduction. The shots in the domestic scenes are brief and mercurial, and the camera is on the move as incessantly as the kids it photographs; yet the predominant effect is less flighty and distracted than dynamic and precise, blending the transitory and the enduring, the breathless and the timeless. From the standpoint of eternity, Malick poetically suggests, the feeling of an instant and the meaning of a lifetime are interwoven parts of a seamless whole.

Malick captures the locales in Waco with equal sensitivity, steeping them in the moods and appearances of lower-middle-class 1950s suburbia. This is partly a matter of story and dialogue: Mr. O'Brien grumbles about neighbors who "have money," for instance, and dreams of the musical career he longed for but never had. As for the physical environment, Malick makes it ring true not by dwelling on drab surroundings, worn-down possessions, or economic anxieties, but by making every house, yard, dusty street, and commercial strip look flawlessly nondescript, allowing the poetry of the ordinary, the rhymes and rhythms of the run of the mill, to settle gently over the film. The technique is simple, subtle, and as different as can be from the heroically grand style Malick applies to the film's cosmological and theological material.

The sequences in Waco and other earthbound milieus are nonetheless charged with Malick's sense of life's inherent mystery, expressed through visual markers familiar from his earlier work. Boundaries between outdoors and indoors are blurred in various ways—a room has no solid walls, a glass building mirrors the sky—and voiceovers speak of the "shining" of the world, a term from Heidegger that Malick virtually patented with *The Thin Red Line*, his philosophical World War II epic of 1998. The camerawork is crucial in this regard, continually gliding, swooping, soaring, and traveling with the characters as they go about their daily rounds. The film's quick cutting and spirited camera movement have led some reviewers to think of Stan Brakhage's boldly kinetic style, but if you're acquainted with Brakhage's work you'll see there's approximately zero resemblance between the luminous precision of Lubezki's photography for Malick and the radical lyricism of most Brakhage films, which are even more subjective and spontaneous than *The Tree of Life*. The one strikingly Brakhage-like touch I do detect is the God-symbolizing crystal, which recalls *Text of Light* (1974), an essay in articulated luminescence that Brakhage made by photographing a glass ashtray over many months. (Nor do Jordan Belson's nonfigurative works have much in common with the occasional abstract interludes in Malick's film, although the thought did cross my mind.)

One of my strongest impressions regarding *The Tree of Life* is that no filmmaker has ever come closer to creating an authentic *Gesamtkunstwerk*, a work of art that incorporates all the arts on an equal and interactive basis. Of course the term derives from Richard Wagner, who was first and foremost a composer, and despite his ideal of equivalency among the arts, music is first among equals in his masterpieces. Visuals have the same privileged place in cinema, and Malick approaches the *Gesamtkunstwerk* ideal via his truly Wagnerian orchestration of framing and composition in conjunction with poetic language and dialogue, verbal and gestural performance, source music and underscoring, costume, architec-

ture, and décor. Critics and scholars will be analyzing the extravaganza for years to come, so I'll note only that if dynamic imagery
is its greatest single asset, majestic music is a very close second.
The original score was written by Alexandre Desplat, my nominee
for finest movie composer working today. The rest ranges from
harmonic chants by David Hykes and sound collages by Arsenije
Jovanovic to funerary music by Zbigniew Preisner and selections
from the classical hit parade by Gustav Mahler, Hector Berlioz,
and Gustav Holst, plus an arresting excerpt from Bedrich Smet-
ana's *Ma Vlast* with brisk dotted rhythms we've heard a million
times before, joined here to exhilarating images that set the musical
warhorse galloping with renewed vigor. These are some of the
ingredients that justify ranking *The Tree of Life* not too many
notches below Wagnerian opera; and while there's no Wagner
on the soundtrack, remember that *The New World* opened with
Wagner's prologue to *Das Rheingold*, itself the prologue to *The
Ring of the Nibelung*, his magnum opus.

Also like a Wagnerian opera, *The Tree of Life* is a mythopoetic
work. The cosmological sequences sketch out a scientistic creation
myth, while the family scenes trace Jack's growth along classic
Oedipal lines, following the mythos of classical psychoanalysis:
strong attachment to his mother accompanied by sharp conflict
with his father, which is eventually resolved. Malick's use of the
Oedipal scenario is not as one-dimensional as some commentators have implied, though. At the film's Cannes press conference, Pitt said he was somewhat reluctant to play an "abusive
father," and many journalists have picked up on this, describing
Mr. O'Brien as a veritable household ogre. They and Pitt should
have watched the finished film more carefully, since while Jack is
looking through Oedipalized eyes, most disinterested folks would
agree that Mr. O'Brien falls well within normal limits as a dad. At
one point, for instance, we hear a string of Jack's resentments on
the soundtrack—father lies; he makes up stories; he says don't put
your elbows on the table but he puts his on the table—yet what
we see on the screen is Mr. O'Brien goofing around with the kids,
all of them having a terrific, playful time. Even a scene showing
Mr. O'Brien exploding with rage at the dinner table is less the
stuff of Dickensian nightmare than a portrait of a well-intentioned
but all-too-human man who falls short of his own standards in
any number of departments. Malick delicately conveys this. He
also portrays sibling rivalry extremely well, as when Jack plays
"trust me" games with one of his brothers, sometimes fooling or

betraying him in little ways, then taking care to calm the waters afterward. In an episode that beautifully captures Jack's wobbly position between childhood and adolescence—another blurry, wavering borderline—he sneaks into a neighbor's bedroom, steals a slip from her drawer, and runs to a nearby river where, driven by an ill-understood combination of fear and desire, he hides it on the bank and then puts it in the current, which carries it swiftly out of sight and mind. The scene superbly encapsulates the scary, exciting, mystifying advent of maturity.

Malick's films are always pervaded by philosophy, most notably that of Heidegger, which Malick studied, translated, and taught during his academic years. Heidegger's presence in *The Tree of Life* is as plain as the "shining" affirmed in the voiceovers, recalling resonant words from *The Thin Red Line*: "Darkness and light, strife and love, are they the workings of one mind? The features of the same face? Oh my soul... look out through my eyes. Look at the things you made, all things shining." This is not the telepathic "shining" explored in the eponymous film by Stanley Kubrick, another director with a restlessly moving camera and a taste for philosophical subjects; to Malick shining is not anomalous but universal, not amoral but a sign of God's goodness and mercy. More emphatically in every new film he makes, his goal is to evoke the shining of the world with reverence and awe, showing that the way of mortal nature is a misleading, ultimately illusory detour from the abiding way of immortal grace. The filmmaker who shot parts of *The New World* on 65mm film and parts of *The Tree of Life* in IMAX is something of a cinematic alchemist, hoping that an expansive, fine-grained film emulsion might absorb not only the light but the very essence of the people, places, and things in God's creation. This is the very essence of Malick's art: movie technique as revelation, cinematography as theophany.

As engrossing and often stirring as these aspects of Malick's creativity are, his new film's passage from philosophy to theology—and specifically to theodicy, arguing for God's goodness despite the evidence of a fallen, iniquitous world—eventually lets me down, as I said at the beginning. *The Tree of Life* opens with a quotation from the Book of Job, and dead center in the story an Episcopalian priest delivers a sermon on the sufferings of that virtuous man; yet the film presents us with a strangely bloodless version of suffering, so reticent about physical agony and psychological affliction that giving birth seems effortless, characters hardly seem to age, and dying is over in a flash. In the end Mrs. O'Brien can give up her son with contentment because she knows he is in God's hands, and has been all along, and they'll be happy together in heaven before long. O death, where is thy sting? Not in this movie.

Near the beginning and again near the end, Malick fills the screen with a large field of beautiful sunflowers, the great mono-theists of the plant kingdom. While it's a glorious image, I couldn't help reflecting that like their fundamentalist Christian counter-parts, sunflowers have both the blessing and the curse of facing forever in a single shared direction. This unchanging uniformity makes them a dubious metaphor for the spirituality Malick aims to celebrate. What this flawed, fascinating film needs more of is the boundless contingency of the human spirit, faced with unyielding pain as well as needed solace, and greater recognition of the power we humans have to remake and rejuvenate the myths, philosophies, and theodicies we invent to make sense of ourselves. Instead the film gives us those obedient sunflowers and the dutiful worship-pers they symbolize, transfixed by a radiance that out-glows and often veils the horrors of the world, but does not prevent them from recurring no matter how soothingly, suggestively, spellbind-ingly it shines.

Howl

The Journal of American History 98:1, June 2011

The Beat Generation has not fared well at the movies. The short film *Pull My Daisy*, directed by photographer Robert Frank and painter Alfred Leslie in 1959, has become the consensus choice for Beat motion picture par excellence, featuring horseplay by such luminaries as Allen Ginsberg and Peter Orlovsky accompanied by Jack Kerouac's semi-improvised narration. A handful of other avant-garde productions aside, the Beat filmography manifests little of the high-voltage creativity that characterizes Beat literature at its best: Roger Corman's sardonic *A Bucket of Blood* (1959), David Cronenberg's plodding *Naked Lunch* (1991), a few other commercial follies, and assorted documentaries of varied quality. After many false starts, Francis Ford Coppola's film adaptation of Kerouac's novel *On the Road*, directed by Walter Salles from a screenplay by Jose Rivera, is scheduled for completion this year, but there's no telling whether this will break the jinx. The Beats exerted considerable influence on the history of literature, social thought, popular culture, and spirituality between the end of World War II and the early years of the twenty-first century, and it is a minor scandal that cinema has fallen so short in its occasional efforts to keep their memory alive.

Given the failure of fiction movies, biopics, and documentaries to capture the Beat spirit so far, it's heartening that the enterprising filmmakers Rob Epstein and Jeffrey Friedman have now tried a more audacious strategy, grafting all three approaches into a cinematic hybrid that capably accomplishes its Beat-friendly goals. Its title is *Howl*, borrowed from Ginsberg's eponymous poem, which was written in 1955, published in 1956, pronounced obscene in 1957, and cleared in a courtroom later that year. The film's most noteworthy antecedent is *The Source*, a 1999 compilation film in which director Chuck Workman mixes documentary material—talking-head interviews, clips from movies and television shows—with renditions of Beat poetry and prose by actors portraying the group's core writers: Johnny Depp as Kerouac, charismatic and intense; Dennis Hopper as Burroughs, volatile and eccentric; and John Turturro as Ginsberg, scruffy and freewheeling.

Howl takes genre mixing a step further, using four different formats to explore the poem, the poet, and the trial that made them famous. Ginsberg, marvelously played by James Franco, speaks at length to an unseen interviewer about how "Howl" came to be written; the obscenity trial of "Howl" publisher Lawrence Ferling-hetti is reenacted by an impressive Hollywood cast; animated segments illustrate some of the poem's more vivid passages; and connective sequences fill out the picture with archival footage and reconstructions of other moments in Beat history, such as Gins-berg's anguish over his mother's suffering and the beginning of his love affair with poet Peter Orlovsky, his lifelong companion. According to the filmmakers, about ninety-five percent of the dialogue comes straight from the historical record, gleaned from trial transcripts and interviews that Ginsberg gave at various points in his career.

I find that many of today's students (and many of their elders) have little idea of what the Beat Generation stood for, if they recognize the term at all, so some background is appropriate here. Founding members Ginsberg, Kerouac, and Burroughs met in New York City in 1943. Kerouac embraced the label "Beat Generation" in 1948, taking it to mean existentially worn out and beaten down but also spiritually beatific and musically on the beat, as in the bebop jazz that influenced his writing. Later milestones include a 1955 poetry reading in San Francisco that made Gins-berg, presenting "Howl" for the first time, into a rising literary star; the publication of Kerouac's novel *On the Road* in 1957, six years after he typed it on a 120-foot scroll in a three-week writing marathon; and the publication of Burroughs' novel *Naked Lunch* in 1959, followed by its exoneration on obscenity charges in a 1966 case that proved to be the last such prosecution in an American court of a verbal (as opposed to pictorial) artistic work.

Ginsberg, Kerouac, and Burroughs were the most influen-tial Beats, and their proudly antiauthoritarian stance attracted a widening circle of writers, artists, iconoclasts, and sociopolitical malcontents. Generalizations about them can be deceptive, but they shared a powerful impulse to attack the deadening, repres-sive values of American society in the cold-war era. In their eyes, anomie, alienation, and anxiety had become raging epidemics, growing steadily worse even as terms such as "rat race" and "orga-nization man" and "lonely crowd" bespoke inchoate uneasiness about the conformity, conservatism, and consumerism that accom-panied the postwar economic boom. This disaffection catalyzed the Beats' search for more artistically and spiritually attuned ways of thinking, often inflected by Eastern religion and inclining toward rootlessness, introspection, and improvisation. Their ethos of freedom and spontaneity reached out to many other artists as well, from Norman Mailer and Amiri Baraka to Bob Dylan and Patti Smith.

Ginsberg's became the most widely visible Beat writer, thanks initially to "Howl," which became an anthem for aggrieved American youth. As the *Howl* movie shows, he dedicated the poem to Carl Solomon, a troubled young man he met during a brief stay in a New York mental hospital. Searching for an original poetic voice, and seeing evidence of society's spiritual decay in its uncaring treatment of Solomon's travails, he wrote a wail of protest couched in a heightened vernacular idiom, beginning with one of the most frequently quoted poetic lines of its day: "I saw the best minds of my generation destroyed by madness, starving hysterical naked/ dragging themselves through the negro streets at dawn looking for an angry fix..."

The poem has a respectable literary pedigree, rooted in William Blake, Walt Whitman, Hart Crane, and William Carlos Williams; but its graphic references to illegal drugs and illegal sex — in a deeply homophobic era, Ginsberg's uncompromising candor about his homosexuality was genuinely courageous — spurred the charges that landed publisher Ferlinghetti, himself a leading Beat poet, in the San Francisco courtroom of Judge Clayton W. Horn, who heard extensive testimony before deciding that the poem had "redeeming social importance" and was therefore not obscene under the law. Ginsberg stayed home, waiting for Ferlinghetti's pro-bono defense attorney, Jake Erlich, to phone him with the verdict.

The trial provides the most riveting scenes in *Howl*, with dialogue that is all the more fascinating for its adherence to transcripts of the proceedings. A college professor argues that Ginsberg's poem is a pale imitation of Whitman, which deprives it of merit because "enduring literature always creates its own form for every significant occasion." One wonders if William Shakespeare's plays are likewise valueless, since the Bard didn't invent iambic pentameter. "In content... anything that can really be classified as literature [has] some moral greatness, and I think this fails to the Nth degree," says another teacher, undermining her credibility as a witness when she adds, "I didn't linger on it long." The chief prosecutor, Ralph McIntosh, challenges Mark Schorer, a celebrated University of California professor, to explain one of the poem's more extravagant formulations — "angelheaded hipsters burning for the ancient heavenly connection to the starry dynamo in the machinery of night" — and Schorer answers, "You can't poetry into prose. That's why it is poetry." And so on, in a series of crisply constructed scenes.

The filmmakers' choice of prominent actors to play these personalities is distracting at times, and the picture's realism would be more robust if the characters' faces were as little-known as their names. They handle their parts with conviction and aplomb, however, and Franco is a revelation as Ginsberg, soaring above his performances in the likes of *127 Hours* and *Eat Pray Love* (both 2010) to establish himself as a definitively mature and accomplished screen actor. Defense lawyer Erlich is played by Jon Hamm, whose stardom in the TV series *Mad Men* gives him the shiniest 1950s credentials in show business today. David Strathairn's talent for buttoned-up concentration serves him well as prosecutor McIntosh, and well-selected character players—Jeff Daniels, Mary-Louise Parker, Treat Williams—are consistently persuasive as people on the witness stand, backed up by Bob Balaban as the presiding judge. The courtroom scenes in *Howl* are docudrama, not documentary, and these seasoned players make up in dramatic authority what they lack in historical authenticity.

Howl has been promoted as a breakthrough picture for Epstein and Friedman, marking their narrative-film debut after many years of work, separately and together, in such ably crafted documentaries as *Word Is Out* (1984), *The Celluloid Closet* (1995), and *Paragraph 175* (2000), which also deal with gay-related subjects. In some respects, *Howl* is a continuation of their nonfiction work by other means, restaging historical events in ways that would transgress accepted norms if employed in a conventional documentary. In other respects, it is a foray into historical fiction, using techniques of narrative cinema to evoke and interpret past events and personalities while staying true to their sociopolitical era. The portions of the film that elude these categories—and have drawn rebuke from some literal-minded critics—are the animated sequences, based on illustrations created by former Ginsberg collaborator Eric Drooker for a new edition of the poem called *Howl: A Graphic Novel*. These scenes are pure cinema, having little to do with the official record but everything to do with the free-flowing spirit of the Beat Generation, which Ginsberg and "Howl" synecdochically represent. City buildings loom like child-devouring pagan gods; copulating couples float ecstatically in the air; organization men trudge lifelessly to work; the urban scene pulses with aggression, creation, energy, and mystery. These are not the most instructive episodes in *Howl*, but during their moment-to-moment rush across the screen they are among the most enthralling. History is a matter of moods and feelings as well as events and personalities, and I think these atmospheric passages rank with the film's most lasting contributions to Beat historiography.

Stalker
Cineaste 43:1, Winter 2017

Andrei Tarkovsky's amazing *Stalker* takes place mainly in the Zone, a mysterious patch of countryside called "the greatest miracle of miracles" in a brief text seen at the beginning. *Stalker* itself has a touch of the miraculous, and the same can be said of the film's very existence, given its extraordinarily troubled production history. It's a history so tangled that different veterans of the project, some of whom reminisce via extras in the Criterion Collection's new Blu-ray and DVD edition, have different versions of what went on.

Before getting to that, here's a brief refresher on the film's content, bearing in mind that the 1979 masterpiece is less a story to follow than an environment to inhabit. The prologue states that in the wake of some unfathomable occurrence, inscrutable in its nature but inestimable in its effects, a region of an unnamed country has become detached from the normal laws of space and time. The authorities first responded by sending in troops (shades of the Fifties flying-saucer genre) who promptly vanished into thin air. The area was then declared forbidden territory, its borders cordoned off and rigidly policed.

Now its only visitors are travelers drawn by reports that the heart of the Zone contains a wondrous Room in which one's deepest desire will come true, either on the spot or afterward. Despite its bucolic appearance and enticing legend, however, the Zone is a sort of supernatural minefield, so replete with invisible snares, inexplicable traps, and lethal pitfalls that only devoted explorers of the area, known as stalkers, can hope to traverse it safely. The film traces the journey of three generically labeled men—a Stalker, an Author, and a Scientist—through the Zone and toward the Room, which they ultimately reach but fail to enter, perhaps by choice, perhaps not. The film's tone is meditative, otherworldly, and so radically unhurried that its characters occasionally look almost dead, as if putting into practice André Bazin's theory of cinema as a form of mummification. Yet all this notwithstanding, comedy (a barely avoided tumble through the Room's doorway) and melodrama (the Scientist has a nuclear device in his knapsack) sneak in occasionally as well.

The fascination of the tale lies in the manner of its telling. As a pioneer of what's now called slow cinema, Tarkovsky cultivated a contemplative technique that privileges style over story, mise-en-scène over montage, and philosophical thought—about love, memory, family, and above all time, which comes to seem as physical and fluid as the water that pervades so many of his shots—over everything. His hallmarks include distanced camera placements that deemphasize personal psychology, irrational cuts that divide the indivisible and connect the unconnectable, and long takes that allow him to "sculpt in time," to paraphrase the title of his eloquent 1986 book about cinema, art, and poetry.

Tarkovsky was also a religious filmmaker, not a bet-hedging "spiritual" or "mystical" sort but a thoroughgoing Russian Orthodox believer who put questions of faith, salvation, redemption, and resurrection at the heart of every film, however much trouble this caused with Soviet cultural commissars. (He emigrated to Italy after completing *Nostalghia* there in 1983.) Discussing the 1966 biopic *Andrei Rublev*, cultural scholar Nariman Skakov has maintained that its dazzling conclusion—it ends with reverent close-ups of icons by the fourteenth-century painter—is an effort to make the divine actually present on the screen, since the purpose of icons is to body forth Godhood in a literal, unequivocal way. *Stalker* has a theologically geared finale of a less traditional kind, extending the Zone's supernatural influence into the fallen world outside by showing the Stalker's disabled daughter moving objects by telekinesis. Here again Tarkovsky aims to evoke the invisible sublime by cinematic means. And this film too displeased the Soviet establishment, standing as a strong political statement as well as a religious one.

In a leaflet essay for the Criterion release, Mark Le Fanu cites diary entries by Tarkovsky suggesting that the science-fiction format of *Stalker* and the earlier *Solaris* (1972) offered a way to broach religion without running too far afoul of Soviet censors. Writing several years before *Stalker* reached the screen, Tarkovsky mused about the 1972 novel that inspired it—the entertaining *Roadside Picnic* by Arkady and Boris Strugatsky—in strikingly metaphysical terms, envisioning a "totally harmonious" film graced with "unbroken, detailed action, but balanced by a religious action, entirely on the plane of ideas, almost transcendental, absurd, absolute." This is an uncannily prescient anticipation of the film he went on to make.

And quite a task the making proved to be. Preliminary problems arose when the shooting location in Soviet central Asia was laid low by an earthquake. Filming was switched to Estonia, whereupon conflicts erupted between Tarkovsky and Georgy

Rerberg, his enormously esteemed cinematographer. When about a third of the picture had been shot, a great mass of footage was deemed unusable, forcing a long hiatus, during which Tarkovsky fundamentally revised his concept of the film and fired Rerberg, replacing him briefly with Leonid Kalashnikov and then permanently with Alexander Knyazhinsky, with whom he started the whole picture over again. He also dismissed Alexander Boim and became his own production designer. According to an interview with set decorator Rashid Safiullin on the Criterion disc, the state-owned Mosfilm studio agreed to the restart but refused additional funds, exacerbating the pressures weighing on the project. Safiullin adds that no prior elements of the décor or the action were repeated when the film was reshot from the beginning.

On top of these and other problems, the shooting locations were often physically insufferable. While filming in a defunct refinery, for instance, Le Fanu says "the crew had to stand for hours on end up to their knees in stinking puddles of oil, while the effluent discharged, upriver, from a paper processing plant enveloped the set in a fetid miasma." And so it went, for month after excruciating month, in circumstances as perilous as the Zone itself. Several key participants—including Rerberg and actor Anatoly Solonitsyn as well as Tarkovsky and his wife Larissa, an assistant director on the film—subsequently died "before their natural term," as Le Fanu diplomatically puts it. Tarkovsky's health was generally less than robust, and it would be exaggerating to say that shooting *Stalker* killed him, but it certainly took a toll on his colleagues and himself.

Not all aspects of the production are so readily tracked down. A particularly tantalizing question concerns Rerberg's contribution. He had photographed Tarkovsky's great autobiographical film *Mirror* (1975) to wide acclaim, so what accounts for the piles of purportedly unusable film that led the director to shut down *Stalker* when nearly half was supposedly in the can? According to Rerberg's testimony in Igor Maiboroda's absorbing *Rerberg and Tarkovsky: The Reverse Side of "Stalker,"* a Russian documentary of 2009, the film stock was faulty from the beginning, spoiling numerous takes and retakes despite changes of lens, lighting, and vantage point. Safiullin tells a somewhat different story in his Criterion extra, though, saying the first year's footage was photographed on an "experimental Kodak" that may have been inherently defective, in which case one wonders why months passed before anyone noticed, but might instead have been incompetently developed, perhaps botched up on purpose (!) by saboteurs whose motives Safiullin does not specify.

Then again, Le Fanu reports that those who saw Rerberg's original footage (stored by film editor Lyudmila Feyginova but destroyed in a 1988 fire) found it "extraordinarily beautiful" despite whatever damage (if any) had occurred in the factory or the processing lab. Evidence for that claim is the single Rerberg sequence included in Tarkovsky's final cut, showing marshy terrain roiled by a surface disturbance of some kind; it's a sublime moment, but so are nearly all the sequences shot by Knyazhinsky after Rerberg's departure. The bottom line is that Rerberg and Tarkovsky both had big egos, that both were heavily into vodka a great deal of the time, and that the regrettable loss of Rerberg's footage is mitigated by the manifest excellence of Knyazhinsky's camerawork in the finished film.

Another missing link in the *Stalker* chronicle is Tarkovsky's initial conception of the film. Gestated to some extent from his thinking about Fyodor Dostoevsky's grand novels and W. T. A. Hoffmann's phantasmal yarns, the concept existed more as a set of ideas and intuitions than as a detailed screenplay, and Tarkovsky drastically reworked it—clashing with the Strugatsky brothers, writers of the source novel and (nominally) the script—during the interruption in filming after the first months. The most important change involved the title character, originally meant to be a rogue or bandit who swashbuckled through the Zone in search of fun, profit, and adventure. He emerges in the finished film as a profoundly earnest figure who regards the Zone as a site of ineffable discovery and the Room as an infinitely tempting holy grail.

His nature comes out most clearly near the end. Hunkered down just outside the Room with his endlessly squabbling, hopelessly indecisive fellow travelers, the Stalker contrasts the hope offered by the Zone with the failed promises of modernity. In the everyday world, he says, everything has been taken from him. "All I have is… in the Zone," he continues. "My happiness, my freedom, my dignity, everything." Like the Christ figure he increasingly resembles, he longs to bring others into his fold ("I lead the same as me in here, unhappy ones, suffering") and sees the cynical worldliness of the Writer and the Scientist as anathema to his mission. "It's the only place one can come if there's no more hope," the Stalker argues as his companions dither and equivocate on the Room's threshold. "You came here, didn't you? Why are you destroying the faith?" His thoughts clearly mirror those of

Tarkovsky, who likewise felt cheated and betrayed by a material-istic society unable to meet the deepest needs or highest aspirations of its people.

While the video quality of the Criterion release is superb, the extras are fairly insubstantial. The interview with Safiullin is brief, a visit with Knyazhinsky is briefer. Better is an interview with the film's composer, Edouard Artemyev, who neatly sums up Tarkovsky's attitude toward film music, saying the director didn't want or need it, but felt a small amount helped advance the new art of cinema by linking it with the older, more established arts.

The longest supplement is a video talk by Geoff Dyer, and I was eager to see whether he still sustains the frenzied enthusiasm for *Stalker* that gushes through the 230 pages of his 2012 treatise *Zona: A Book About a Film About a Journey to a Room*. He does! His ecstasy has mellowed a bit, though, and nothing in the video matches his book's wildest huzzahs for *Stalker*, such as the decla-ration that its ending "redeems, makes up for... all the stupidity in every film made before or since." Wow. I can't push my admiration quite that far, but my Blu-ray encounter with Tarkovsky's tour de force leaves me as much in awe of its magnificence as ever.

Mirror
Cineaste 47:1, Winter 2021

Andrei Tarkovsky's semiautobiographical *Mirror* reached American theaters in 1983, eight years after its extremely limited release in the Soviet Union, and on first viewing I found it all the things the publicity for the new Criterion Collection edition says it is: poetic, richly textured, mystical, and above all elusive, as intense yet ungraspable as a multilayered dream. Seeing it again, though, I was surprised by how lucid, coherent, and articulate it had come to seem, even though I hadn't done any deep thinking or studying up in the interim. It's a profoundly personal and radically nonlinear film, to be sure, but its mercurial structure has an intrinsic logic and its images and sounds are as enchantingly beautiful as they are meticulously crafted. I have spent many hours with it over the years, and I've spent a few more with Criterion's fine digital transfer and extensive extras package, and today I find the movie less mystifying but more mysterious than ever—less mystifying because familiarity makes its codes easier to crack, more mysterious because what underlies the codes is a sense of reality rooted in metaphysical enigma rather than everyday rationality. Tarkovsky was a bold and innovative stylist, moreover, pioneering and exemplifying the so-called slow cinema espoused by such deliberative directors as Lav Diaz, Béla Tarr, Tsai Ming-liang, and Alexander Sokurov, the chief inheritor of Tarkovsky's legacy. Among its many other virtues, *Mirror* gives you time to contemplate its conundrums even as they're unfolding on the screen.

The title *Mirror* has multiple meanings, including the notion that culture and media reflect the inner lives of the artists who make use of them. Tarkovsky used them to explore his own psychological concerns, and more important, to seek out the larger spiritual forces he regarded as the all-pervading matrix of human existence. Not even the forthrightly religious *Andrei Rublev* (1966) outdoes *Mirror* in exemplifying his belief that faith, salvation, redemption, and renewal are the most imperative subjects an artist can investigate. Although some critics with secular worldviews write off his interests as hazily "spiritual" rather than pointedly religious, Russian Orthodox Christianity informs every one of his major features, very much including *Mirror*, and the distaste this aroused in Soviet bureaucrats at the Mosfilm studio was a chief cause of his emigration to Italy after filming his 1983 masterpiece *Nostalghia* there. *Mirror* doesn't dwell on the traditional iconography celebrated in *Andrei Rublev*, and its elliptical narrative, grounded in Tarkovsky's own memories, dreams, and experiences, is less otherworldly than the stories of *Solaris* (1972) and *Stalker* (1979), the science-fiction epics made just before and after it. But no film better embodies his conviction that cinema is the best possible medium for connecting ordinary mortals with an awareness of the invisible sublime. Many of its perplexities stem from his refusal of taken-for-granted boundaries that lend order to our thinking but reduce its nuance and complexity; as film scholar Nariman Skakov showed in his 2012 book on Tarkovsky's work, *Mirror* blurs countless borders between past and present, fiction and documentary, private and public, and society and individuality, transforming the world into a numinous realm that exceeds and confounds the cause-and-effect continuity of conventional cinema. Hence his love for visual perspectives that defamiliarize places and personalities, incongruous cuts that scramble time and space, and lengthy takes that enable the "sculpting in time" at the heart of his practice.

Mirror begins with a scene that paradoxically combines documentary realism with dreamlike obscurity: a boy switches on a living-room television set, the TV image expands to fill the movie screen, and we see a woman in a clinical smock cure a young man of stuttering by means of hypnosis. Neither the hypnotist nor the patient is seen again, but the boy watching the TV turns out to be Ignat, the son of Alexei, the surrogate for Tarkovsky in the film. The opening titles follow, after which the main body of the narrative commences with a serendipitous meeting between a rural woman named Maroussia and a physician going someplace or other with his medical bag. As they part, the man glances back at his new acquaintance, and a sudden gust of wind rushes through the tall grass between them (a delicious effect facilitated by an off-camera helicopter) suggesting an ephemeral link between the two. Evidently suffering some deep sadness, the woman goes on to a string of activities that are both mundane and oddly cryptic, such as watching a barn burn down during a rain shower and washing her hair in a black-and-white interlude as ghostly and surreal as any J-horror imagery.

These sequences introduce one of the three levels of time that converge and diverge over the course of the movie. The first takes place in the years preceding World War II and centers largely on Maroussia, whose husband has run off and left her with their young children. The second transpires during the war, often revolving around the young Alexei, who converses with an unidentified and evanescent visitor, goes through some poorly implemented military training, visits a neighbor with his mother, and reunites with his father. In the third, set about 25 years later, the adult Alexei argues with his estranged wife, Natalie, about who will have custody of Ignat and moves toward his own death from an unspecified cause. The movie ends with Maroussia smiling through tears while seeing her children walk through the countryside with what appears to be a much older version of herself. These are only a few of the film's incidents; others are dramatically emotional, as when Maroussia panics over a possible mistake in her work at a printing plant, and still others—easily the most memorable—are utterly oneiric, as when workers tend a massive hot-air balloon at some vertiginous height above the earth, or when Maroussia, after reluctantly agreeing to slaughter a neighbor's rooster, inexplicably levitates and hovers in midair, as if the material world had relinquished its hold for reasons neither she nor we can ever understand. The film oscillates between color and black-and-white footage, most of it shot by the gifted and eccentric cinematographer Georgy Rerberg and some gleaned from vintage newsreels, such as an astonishing view of Soviet troops slogging across a lake in wartime, which Tarkovsky likened to the Exodus of Old Testament times.

Along with its protean array of periods, settings, and characters, *Mirror* contains a tremendous wealth of allusions to works in other art forms; one needn't be a certified art historian to enjoy its visual quotations from Pieter Bruegel the Elder's *The Hunters in the Snow* (1565) or Johannes Vermeer's *Girl with a Pearl Earring* (1665), or to ponder the references to Fyodor Dostoevsky and the Book of Revelation, or to appreciate the verses recited on the soundtrack by Arseny Tarkovsky, the filmmaker's father, a respected Russian journalist, translator, and poet (who once came perilously close to execution after dissing Lenin in some teenage doggerel). These are signs of the devotion Tarkovsky felt toward the likes of Johann Sebastian Bach, Leonardo da Vinci, Leo Tolstoy, Robert Bresson, and perhaps above all William Shakespeare, whose *Hamlet* was "clearly the most important and poetic work ever created," as Tarkovsky opines in the documentary *Andrei Tarkovsky. A Cinema Prayer*, directed by his son, Andrey A. Tarkovsky, and included in the Criterion edition. In that film Tarkovsky describes the giants he most admires as "holy fools" and "lunatics" who didn't "belong to this world" and were "possessed" by their art. "People like that frighten me and at the same time inspire me," he says. "Their work is absolutely impossible to explain… Miracles can't be explained. A miracle is God." Beyond signaling his reverence for these figures, Tarkovsky's allusions indicate his belief that while cinema is the newest and youngest art, it can summon unconscious resonances in viewers' minds by incorporating materials from bygone eras in every other art. This point is made in two other Criterion extras, a British documentary called *The Dream in the "Mirror"* (2021) by Louise Milne and Seán Martin and a video interview with Eduard Artemyev, the film's composer. Not that Artemyev exactly composed the score. As he says in his interview, Tarkovsky told him he he didn't need a composer since he had Bach at his disposal, so Artemyev's job would be creating sounds that could serve as subliminal characters in the film. Artemyev did just that, and his explanations and descriptions on the Criterion disc opened my ears to dimensions of the soundtrack I'd never perceived before.

Other extras in the Criterion edition include brief TV interviews with Tarkovsky, a TV documentary about Rerberg, and a video interview with Alexander Misharin, who cowrote the film, along with a preliminary treatment and early draft of the screenplay (when "Confession" and then "A White, White Day" were the working titles) in a nicely illustrated booklet. With ancillary aids like these now available, *Mirror* should find a wider audience—and a more informed and comprehending audience—than ever before. Its reputation as an exercise in incorrigible puzzlement has surely dissuaded many people from engaging with it, and it's a little comforting to know that making it was hugely puzzling for Tarkovsky, who struggled mightily with the editing and often feared it would never come coherently together. In the end, he succeeded so well that *Mirror* stands up brilliantly not only as a discrete work but also as a thematic capstone to the string of masterpieces he created in the Sixties and early Seventies. He says in *A Cinema Prayer* that *Mirror*, the relatively straightforward wartime story *Ivan's Childhood* (1962), the period epic *Andrei Rublev*, and the science-fiction drama *Solaris* all partake of his "desire to develop and delve into characters who exist in a state of extreme tension, who are going through an intense spiritual crisis in which they must either break down or finally get their footing… in terms of being faithful to their ideals and true to their principles." Rudimentary though that formulation is, it offers a helpful clue to what this complex and introspective artist saw as a basic tenet of a key period in his career.

Soviet authorities hated *Mirror*, restricting its release to a small handful of out-of-the-way Russian theaters, and Soviet critics lambasted it. But what mattered to Tarkovsky were the letters he received from everyday moviegoers who felt personally touched and intimately understood by a filmmaker they'd never met. In the documentary by his son, he quotes a remark made by a cleaning woman during an audience debate after a screening: "The film is very clear [and] very simple," she said. "A man fell very ill and thought he might die. He remembered all the terrible things he'd done to others and wanted to apologize. That's all." To which Tarkovsky adds, "The many film critics present hadn't understood a thing, as usual. The more they talk, the less they understand. And that simple woman explained it all."

I wouldn't take that anecdote too literally; no matter how you slice it, *Mirror* is a knotty, gnarly film, and while a naïve viewer with fresh eyes may well have interesting ideas to offer, there's obviously more to it than the meandering regrets of a repentant sinner on his sickbed. To make a broad generalization about my own relationship with it, I find *Mirror* as challenging and invigorating as various other high-modernist and postmodernist works I've thought of during recent viewings, such as James Joyce's *Ulysses* and *Finnegans Wake*, Arnold Schoenberg's *Moses und Aron*, and Stan Brakhage's *Sincerity/Duplicity* (1973-80) series. These achievements, like Tarkovsky's, tantalize the mind as much as they beguile it. Fathoming the depths of *Mirror* is a labor of love and an unending pleasure. Cinephiles can warmly welcome the new Criterion edition for its technical excellence, its generous array of additional resources, and the encouragement it offers for diving ever deeper into a unique and extraordinary film.

The Pervert's Guide to Cinema
Cineaste 34:3, Summer 2009

Thinking about Slavoj Žižek always raises the same question—where to begin? He's published more books than I care to count, pops up constantly in the media, has an entire periodical (*International Journal of Žižek Studies*) devoted to commentaries on his work, and contributes to more disciplines than most of us managed to study in college. A list of his official and unofficial occupations would include author, professor, philosopher, psychoanalyst, political scientist, sociologist, media theorist, lay theologian, former presidential candidate in the Republic of Slovenia, film critic, and up-and-coming movie star.

The last-named credential comes from Žižek's appearance in several films over the past few years, sometimes as the leading man. *Žižek!* is a documentary about his life and work directed by Astra Taylor, who skillfully balances admiration for his prodigious mind with awareness of his propensity for taking over every situation he finds himself in. *Slavoj Žižek: The Reality of the Virtual* is a Žižek lecture filmed in London by Ben Wright, whose minimalist camerawork is a good complement to Žižek's high-octane speaking style—he exudes more intellectual energy just sitting at a table than other scholars do when they pace around, wave their arms, and shout. So far, however, the Žižek movie to beat is *The Pervert's Guide to Cinema*, a two-and-a-half-hour opus directed by Sophie Fiennes (the sister of Ralph and Joseph) and "presented by" the celebrated thinker himself.

For those unfamiliar with Žižek's ideas, a quick run-through of them—or rather, the small fraction of them that space allows—is a good way to introduce *The Pervert's Guide to Cinema*. After studying philosophy in his native Yugoslavia he went to Paris and steeped himself in Jacques Lacan's brand of psychoanalysis, which amounts to a revised and expanded version of Sigmund Freud's work. Žižek is still affiliated with the University of Ljubljana in Slovenia, but he spends much of his time jetting around Europe and the United States, where his first English-language book, *The Sublime Object of Ideology*, put him on the intellectual map in 1989—and take note of that title, which points to Marxist theory, Kantian philosophy, and Luis Buñuel's last movie in just five words. To sum up Žižek's specialties with similar economy, they are psychoanalysis à la Lacan, philosophy à la Hegel, politics à la Marx, and film theory à la himself.

The Pervert's Guide to Cinema is in three parts, which is fitting, because psychoanalysis is fond of that number. Freud wrote about the id, the superego, and the ego, which stand for irrational desire, irrational guilt, and conscious reason; Lacan came up with the Imaginary, the Symbolic, and the Real, which represent free-flowing fantasy, the constraints of language and paternal law, and a primordial core of mental something-or-other. Žižek's favorite category is the Real, which can't be imagined or symbolized because it's outside all of the psyche's categories. When we stumble on it in our mental lives, the results are ecstasy and trauma—remnants of an unfathomable "enjoyment" we felt in the earliest days of our lives. Films are partly Imaginary, with their incessant fantasies, and partly Symbolic, with their socially coded stories; but Žižek is fascinated most by their connection with the Real, which accounts for his fascination with films of horror and the uncanny, where what can't be *thought* can be sensed, felt, and—in that special meaning of the word—*enjoyed*.

Žižek's intellectual personality surges through *The Pervert's Guide to Cinema* from the very first moments. The soundtrack hums with the noise of a whirring projector; Rorschach inkblots materialize on the screen; and Žižek appears in a quick series of simulated movie settings—first *Psycho*, with shadows swinging across his face in Mrs. Bates' fruit cellar; next *Mulholland Dr.* with a blood-red theater curtain behind him; and then *Blue Velvet*, where he's watering a lawn. "There is nothing spontaneous, nothing natural about human desires," he declares, introducing his central theme. "Our desires are artificial. We have to be taught to desire." Then, gazing down at us from the top of a deep well, he speaks the aphorism that gives *The Pervert's Guide to Cinema* its title, which fans have been quoting all over the internet since the film's premiere: "Cinema is the ultimate pervert art. It doesn't give you what you desire, it tells you *how* to desire."

Unpacking those two sentences would require a side trip into Žižek's way of re-spinning psychoanalytic language, but the gist of the statement is reasonably clear, at least from a Lacanian standpoint. What movies give us, generally speaking, are vivid encounters with desirable things. What they don't give is any satisfaction of our longing, which is why we *keep* going to movies (and other sources of fiction and fantasy) in the impossible hope of filling the emotional gaps our yearnings open up. This endless circulation of desire, as Žižek and Lacan call it, lends illusory structure to our mental lives. But it's interrupted or sidetracked when some fragment of the incomprehensible Real gets caught in the circuit, knocks the psyche for a loop, and brings on symptoms of shock and wonder. Is this bad? Not necessarily. Freud saw symptoms as problems to be overcome, but Lacan's different view is conveyed by Žižek's cleverest book title: *Enjoy Your Symptom!*

The Pervert's Guide to Cinema is a tour through some of the films that give Žižek and the rest of us enjoyable symptoms, even when the material itself, objectively considered, should bring the opposite of enjoyment—outside the movies it would be pretty awful to watch Melanie almost get pecked to death, as in *The Birds*, or to see Ripley discover her malformed, still-born clones, as in *Alien: Resurrection*, or to see Erika painfully *mis*-learn how to desire in a pornography store, as in *The Piano Teacher*. The picture's main tools are excerpts from famous films and Žižek's nonstop comments on them, delivered in the imitation movie settings mentioned earlier. Piloting a speedboat across Bodega Bay, he explains how the birds in *The Birds* rip the fabric of reality. Standing next to an ancient redwood tree from *Vertigo*, he explains why "its... extra-large distortion embodies something that comes out of our inner space: libido, the excessive energy of the mind." Sitting in the bathroom of *The Conversation*, he speaks of the toilets in that film and *Psycho* as gateways to a "netherworld" where "hidden forces run the show" and chaos "threatens to explode... and engulf us." This is the return of the repressed, Freud might say, with a vengeance.

A good example of Žižek's method is his analysis of the nightmarish scene in *Blue Velvet* where Frank (Dennis Hopper) forces Dorothy (Isabella Rossellini) through a ritual act of sado-masochistic sex while Jeffrey (Kyle MacLachlan) watches and listens from a closet. Žižek describes Dorothy's apartment as "one of those hellish places which abound in David Lynch's films... where all moral or social inhibitions seem to be suspended" and we are confronted with "the deepest level of our desires that we are not even ready to admit to ourselves." He then offers three interpretations of the scene from the perspectives of all three characters. For the voyeuristic Jeffrey it's what Freud calls the "primal scene," when the child witnesses or overhears the parents having sex; since Jeffrey's father was felled by a stroke at the beginning of the film, Žižek says Jeffrey might be imagining Dorothy and Frank as a "wild parental couple" who fill in for "the lack of a real paternal authority." Looking into Frank's motivations, Žižek suggests that his shouting, cursing, and overacting add up to "a ridiculously violent spectacle" set up by a pathetic father figure to hide his impotence. In his most provocative statement, Žižek points to Dorothy's passivity and asks if Frank might be *her* fantasy—if his loony behavior is actually "a ridiculous but nonetheless effective attempt to help Dorothy, to awaken her out of her lethargy, to bring her into life?" There's no need to choose one of these readings over another; the "strange, mutual interlocking" of all three fantasies, Žižek concludes, is what generates the "strange reverberations" of this horrible yet memorable scene.

Film studies have moved in various directions over the past few decades—into auteur theory, semiotics, historiography, and so on—and one of the most interesting has been the so-called philosophical turn, pioneered by the likes of Stanley Cavell and Gilles Deleuze and now epitomized by Žižek, who like them is a philosopher writing about film rather than a film theorist borrowing from philosophy. His work moves across highly porous borderlines among many fields, so keeping up with his breathless ideas is always an invigorating mental workout. I've seen *The Pervert's Guide to Cinema* several times, and I've found something new with each viewing. This doesn't mean Žižek's ideas are always in crisp focus, though. Sometimes he uses a movie scene merely to illustrate a philosophical point he wants to make. Evocative clips are sometimes almost swamped by the torrent of words, words, words he submerges them in. He can be intellectually self-indulgent and even downright silly—comparing the three Marx Brothers with Freud's structural model of the psyche, for instance, he asks us to take Groucho as a superego figure! And the countless cameo-style appearances do less to enliven Žižek's arguments than to underline the point that Hitchcock is own Freudian father figure. (They also make me suspect that the fabricated film stills of artist Cindy Sherman loom larger in his thinking than he likes to let on.)

In all, however, *The Pervert's Guide to Cinema* is an ingenious exercise in filmmaking as film criticism, highly recommended for anyone who finds thinking about cinema as engrossing and entertaining as watching it. More such guides will reportedly arrive in future years—one about opera is said to be next—and if they're as strong as this one, Žižek's movie-star ambitions will continue to pay off. [Note: Only one subsequent "guide," *The Pervert's Guide to Ideology*, has arrived. The opus on opera never materialized.]

The Pervert's Guide to Ideology
Cineaste 39:1, Winter 2013

Several years have passed since I reviewed *A Pervert's Guide to Cinema*, the previous collaboration between philosopher Slavoj Žižek and filmmaker Sophie Fiennes, and my first question before watching their follow-up production, *A Pervert's Guide to Ideology*, concerned the title. Far more than a mere film critic, Žižek is a psychoanalyst, sociologist, cultural theorist, political scientist, one-time presidential candidate in the Republic of Slovenia, and leading man in a handful of documentaries centering on him and his ideas. He wears all of those hats in *A Pervert's Guide to Cinema*, an illustrated lecture about everything from Sigmund Freud and Stephen King to reality and fantasy, the death drive and the undead, violence and masochism, voyeurism and ventriloquism, toilets and totalitarianism, and why cinema is "the ultimate pervert art" because "it doesn't give you what you desire, it tells you *how* to desire." No matter how far afield his monologue wanders, he invariably has a film clip up his sleeve to clarify or illuminate each intellectual point.

I expected something different from *A Pervert's Guide to Ideology*, which has a slightly weightier title, recalling *The Sublime Object of Ideology*, the 1989 study of Freud, Karl Marx, and Immanuel Kant that propelled Žižek to intellectual superstardom. It made me think the new film might be more strictly philosophical, analytical, or conceptual than its predecessor. I should have known better, of course, since whatever else he may be, Žižek is the most reliably entertaining theoretician around. His new movie turns out to be a continuation of the earlier film, equally generous in the film-clip department and no less witty in the many ways he finds of inserting himself into the excerpts, be they from *Titanic*, *The Sound of Music*, or *Brazil*. With these things going for the picture, it's disappointing to find some of Žižek's arguments and ideas considerably less persuasive than in the previous installment, or in the best of the academic and journalistic writing that he produces at record-setting speed.

True to form, Žižek begins the show with a truly unexpected Hollywood excerpt: a scene from *They Live*, John Carpenter's 1988 rehash of the *Invasion of the Body Snatchers* narrative. It's not much of a movie, but it's terrific for Žižek's purposes, ushering in his main theme with a flourish. *They Live* posits that Earth has been colonized by aliens who control us through secret messages in advertisements, TV commercials, and the other media bombardments we undergo every day. The hero, George Nada (Roddy Piper), stumbles on a cache of magic eyeglasses that let him view the concealed content; where others see a bikini-clad woman in a travel poster he sees the command "Marry and Reproduce," for instance, and where others see colorful magazine covers he sees phrases like "Consume" and "Obey Authority." Forcing his skeptical buddy Frank Armitage (Keith David) to try out the specs in a garbage-strewn back alley, Nada barks out a threat: "I'm giving you a choice! Either put on these glasses or start eating that trashcan!" But instead of a reverse shot to Armitage we now see Žižek in the alleyway, instantly interpreting the scene. "I already am eating from the trashcan all the time," he announces. "The name of this trashcan is ideology." The same goes for everyone, he continues, and there is no escape from our garbage-eating destiny. The tragedy of the human predicament, Žižek tells us, is that our dreams and fantasies enslave us as insidiously as our so-called realities do.

With this established, Žižek proceeds to opine on filmic fantasy and fiction for the next couple of hours, veering down all sorts of detours but mentioning ideology often enough to keep his nominal theme from slipping away entirely. And some of the film's most compelling insights arise when we're on one of the detours. Žižek is a spirited music lover, for instance—the Royal Opera House in London has actually commissioned four operas inspired by his work, due in 2020—and at one point he engages with the "Ode to Joy" choral movement of Beethoven's Ninth Symphony, showing how its capacity to inspire and excite has been appropriated by political entities that despise one another in every other way, from Hitler's Germany and Stalin's Soviet Union to Mao's China, Guzmán's Peru, Ian Smith's Southern Rhodesia, and the European Union today. It seems that the music is an empty container into which an infinite variety of ideological feelings and convictions may be projected. Yet as Žižek then points out, a neutral container is never as neutral as it appears. The all-embracing "Ode to Joy" is not *all*-embracing, as Stanley Kubrick demonstrates in *A Clockwork Orange* (1971) by associating the misanthropic Alex with passages that are carnivalesque and even vulgar when contrasted with earlier portions of the movement. In this composition Alex's beloved Ludwig Van accomplishes what Žižek rightly deems a difficult task: "practicing... in a purely musical work the critique of ideology."

Žižek crowns this part of the film with an analysis of the *West Side Story* song "Gee, Officer Krupke," in which merry juvenile delinquents display their mastery of "root cause" discourses ("I'm depraved on account of I'm deprived!") that automatically excuse any transgressions they care to perpetrate. And he's in top form again when he connects the main action of John Ford's *The Searchers* (1956) and Martin Scorsese's *Taxi Driver* (1976) not just to each other (which many critics have done) but also to the geopolitical arrogance that causes warrior leaders of the United States to insist on "rescuing" countries and cultures that don't want rescuing any more than Jodie Foster's underage hooker or Natalie Wood's abducted girl.

There is no particular segment when the film's intellectual level starts to decline, but the slide becomes apparent around the half-hour mark. Turning from the existential horrors of *Taxi Driver* to the crafty mechanics of Steven Spielberg's *Jaws* (1975), Žižek cites Fidel Castro's admiration for the latter film as proof that its true symbolic subject is the voracity of modern capitalism—hardly a penetrating observation about *Jaws*, and potentially applicable to every monster movie ever made. Similarly obvious points occur from here on out, tangling lines of thought that are otherwise smart and original. We don't need Žižek to tell us that Coca-Cola ads are designed to convey a "mysterious something more" than ordinary refreshment, or that faux-charitable marketing (part of every dollar goes to save the rain forest) makes you feel good about consuming Starbucks while making you pay for the good feeling by boosting the price. Additional truisms pile up as the film proceeds. Movies usually end with the production of a couple. Dictators like Lenin and Stalin habitually present themselves as nice folks who love cats. "If you posit or perceive or legitimize yourself as a direct instrument of the divine will," Žižek says over footage of the World Trade Center attacks, "then of course all narrow, petty, moral considerations disappear." This is self-evident in the post-9/11 world. (Here Žižek adds useful context, though, noting that if you replace "divine will" with "historical process," you see that the twentieth century's Marxist despots weren't all that different from today's global terrorists.)

The film's biggest weaknesses show up when Žižek jumps into the ring with religion, approaching it by way of Scorsese's admirably devout, profoundly imperfect 1988 hagiopic *The Last Temptation of Christ*. "The contrast between Judaism and Christianity is the contrast between anxiety and love," Žižek declares, wearing essentialism on his sleeve. In the Jewish tradition, he explains, nobody knows what God wants, so when catastrophes occur the outcome is terror and meaninglessness. In the Christian tradition this dilemma is resolved, since "by sacrificing his son God demonstrates that he loves us." So goes the conventional view, Žižek continues. But in Scorsese's film, the crucifixion of Jesus is more radical, representing "the disintegration of the God which guarantees the meaning of our lives." God is dead, in other words, and that's good news because it sets us free to make our own meanings of our world, our lives, and ourselves. Yet at the same time, Žižek puzzlingly adds, Christ is actually present every time believers get together and form a community. In the end, Žižek claims, "the only way to really be an atheist is to go through Christianity," which is "much more atheist than the usual atheism" because it teaches us that there is "no point of reference which guarantees meaning."

Hmm. If I wanted to become an atheist, I doubt if my first step would be signing up at the nearest Presbyterian church. But by this point Žižek is positively sermonizing, and the peroration is in sight. He concludes by exhorting us to sort out our fantasies, distinguishing "the right dreams," which point beyond the reigning ideologies, from "the wrong dreams," which reproduce and reinforce those ideologies. "This is the basic lesson of psychoanalysis and fiction cinema," he summarizes: "We are responsible for our dreams." We are also responsible for the world our dreams create. The future is not determined by a train of history that simply carries us along. "It depends on *us*. On our *will*!"

And with that *The Pervert's Guide to Ideology* glides to a close, ending with a final joke: Žižek slips from a *Titanic* lifeboat into the sea, then raises a clenched fist through the water in a sign of solidarity. Solidarity with the future? Or with Christian atheism? Or with the triumph of our will? It's not exactly clear. And that's one of the troubles with this stimulating, exasperating film. Žižek has been many things during his prodigious career, but rarely has he sounded so much like a pesky superego, nagging us to put on our ideology glasses, forget about reference points, and squelch those "wrong dreams" so the right future can come to pass. I'm very fond of Žižek the thinker, Žižek the writer, Žižek the entertainer, and Žižek the pervert's guide. But Žižek the preacher, not so much.

The Tales of Hoffmann
Cineaste 48:1, Winter 2022

The Tales of Hoffmann, the 1951 phantasmagoria made by
Michael Powell and Emeric Pressburger under the banner of the
Archers, their enterprising production company, has acquired
some surprising enthusiasts over the years. Martin Scorsese and
George A. Romero, auteurs with emphatically dark streaks in their
filmographies, came upon it as children, watched it repeatedly on
New York television's long-gone *Million Dollar Movie* program—
in black and white!—and later studied a 16mm Technicolor print
available from a Manhattan rental outlet. In a video interview for
the Criterion Collection's sparkling new Blu-ray edition, Romero
says he must have rented that copy 50 times, and when he didn't
have it, chances were that Scorsese did. In the audio commentary
for the Criterion release, Scorsese says he was "obsessed" with
the picture, which is one of the films, along with *Black Narcissus*
(1947) and *The Red Shoes* (1948), that led him to seek out Powell
as a collaborator some years after the scandalized response to
the 1960 horror opus *Peeping Tom* had put a stop to the British
auteur's once-thriving career. Powell and Pressburger too had dark
streaks in their filmography, and while it's tempting to exempt *The
Tales of Hoffmann* from that judgement, so inexhaustible are its
melodies and so exuberant are its colors, macabre undertones are
never far away.

Which is what one should expect from a movie named after
E. T. A. Hoffmann, the 19th-century Romantic who wrote the
three stories that Jacques Offenbach adapted as opera and Powell
and Pressburger as film. Hoffmann doesn't appear as a character
in these tales, but he has an important role in the adaptations,
helping to unify their otherwise separate episodes. The movie
adds a prologue of its own, "The Ballet of the Enchanted Drag-
onfly," introducing Hoffmann (Robert Rounseville) as a young
poet attending a dance performance and receiving a love letter
and key from the prima ballerina, Stella (Moira Shearer, sung by
Dorothy Bond), whose gifts are intercepted by the evil Councillor
Lindorf (Robert Helpmann, sung by Bruce Dargavel), a villain
with multiple identities who will dog Hoffmann throughout the
film. Going to a tavern for drinks during the ballet's intermission,
the poet regales a group of students with three love stories. In the
first, where Hoffmann is himself a student, he falls prey to the
puppet maker Spalanzani (Léonide Massine, sung by Graham Clif-

ford) and the optician Coppelius (Helpmann again), who extort money from him by passing off the automaton Olympia (Shearer again) as a real woman deserving of his love; the scheme falls apart when Hoffmann's check bounces, Olympia's wiring goes berserk, and the angry scammers pull her body to pieces, all of which keep right on dancing. In the second tale Hoffmann is a traveler, duped by Dapurtutto (Helpmann yet again), a collector of souls, and Giulietta (Ludmilla Tchérina, sung by Margherita Grandi), a courtesan who helps imprison Hoffmann's soul in a magic mirror; he escapes after vanquishing the underling Schlemil (Massine, sung in this episode by Owen Brannigan) and retrieving the elusive key. In the third tale, Hoffmann is in love with Antonia (Ann Ayars), a tragically ill soprano who knows she will die if she sings again but is beguiled into the fatal act by Dr. Miracle (Helpmann once more) and expires at the climax of her aria. In a brief epilogue, Hoffmann acknowledges that the loved ones in his stories have all represented facets of the sublime Stella, but when she arrives in the tavern and finds Hoffmann plastered and oblivious, she promptly strolls off with Lindorf.

The film's three-part structure is not remarkable for a release from this period, when (as Scorsese points out) there was a fashion for anthology pictures grouping multiple episodes derived from a single author, such as *Quartet* (1948), from W. Somerset Maugham, and *O. Henry's Full House* (1952), from the eponymous American writer. *The Tales of Hoffmann* fits this pattern, but many of its other elements are highly unusual. For one thing, it's an opera film, and while these have been made since the silent era—see Phillips Smalley and Lois Weber's *The Dumb Girl of Portici* (1916) for an early example—this was the first movie, according to Bruce Eder in the audio commentary he shares with Scorsese, to transform an opera into purely cinematic form instead of simply capturing a performance on celluloid. Beyond this, it's one of the most scrupulously choreographed narrative films ever produced, coordinating subtleties of framing and camera movement with meticulously balletic body movements. ("Even Helpmann's eyes are choreographed!" Scorsese exclaims at one point.) Powell and Pressburger thought of it as a "composed film" where the actions of performers within the frame, the mobility of the frame itself, the décor, the rhythms and harmonies of the music, and other elements coalesce into a continually changing yet perfectly integrated whole, putting me in mind of what Richard Wagner called the *gesamtkunstwerk*, or total work of art. Powell and Pressburger had moved in this direction with *Black Narcissus* (1947) and especially *The Red Shoes*, a glorious mélange of music, dance, and melodrama, and as Scorsese observes, *The Tales of Hoffmann* brought them closest to fully realizing their ideal.

What made this possible was Powell and Pressburger's inspired decision to shoot the entire film to a prerecorded score, conducted by Sir Thomas Beecham, a towering musical figure and longtime lover of this opera. (Beecham had conducted the big ballet in *The Red Shoes*, and he also composed this film's opening ballet music, using Offenbach themes.) With the whole soundtrack already in the can, the filmmakers could photograph the action without worrying about microphones, outside noises, or the enormous blimps that normally dampened the whirr—and thwarted the free movement—of bulky Technicolor cameras. Taking full advantage of this, the directors and cinematographer Christopher Challis worked on a stage originally built to create special effects for William Cameron Menzies' 1936 science-fiction epic *Things to Come*; it didn't matter that the stage had no soundproofing, and its vast size—maybe the largest ever built, Challis said—allowed for extravagantly large backdrops, huge pieces of painted scenery, and what Eder describes as "miles of gauzes" that could be freshly adapted for each new scene. With the Offenbach music wafting through the air, *The Tales of Hoffmann* was shot like a silent movie, and Powell once told Eder that it essentially *was* a silent movie. Powell and Pressburger had started their careers in the silent era, and Pressburger had worked at Germany's legendary UFA studio during the Expressionist heyday. *The Tales of Hoffmann* offered a splendid opportunity to disregard dramatic realism, foreground gesture and mime, and play with allusions to classics like Robert Wiene's *The Cabinet of Dr. Caligari* (1920) and Fritz Lang's *Metropolis* (1927). Challis could even vary the camera speed at will, further enhancing the film's dreamlike atmosphere. The result is as proudly artificial as anything Kenneth Anger or George Kuchar ever confected, and its artifice is essential to its charm.

Several key contributors to *The Tales of Hoffmann* were veterans of *The Red Shoes* and had dazzling reputations outside the movie world as well: Shearer was a rising ballet star, Tchérina was an international prima ballerina, Helpmann and Massine were world-class dancers and choreographers, and Frederick Ashton, who choreographed the film and dances two secondary roles, was a ballet superstar. Another returning artist was production designer Hein Heckroth, who had won an Academy Award for the oneiric settings of the grand ballet in *The Red Shoes* and went further still in *The Tales of Hoffmann*, associating each character with a dominant color—yellow for the antic Olympia, red for the sensual Giulietta, dark blue for the melancholic Antonia—and devising ingenious *trompe l'oeil* effects, as when Hoffmann and Antonia race down a colossal staircase that's actually a stripe-covered carpet spread on the stage's floor. Eder notes that Heckroth had designed three German productions of this opera between the world wars and was second only to Beecham in intimate knowledge of it. His imagination is apparent in the everything from the outlandish costumes to the eccentric puppets (each controlled by as many as 15 wires) that serve as the opera's chorus. He and the other artists comprised a truly outstanding creative team.

As interesting and impressive as these particulars are, *The Tales of Hoffmann* is more than the sum of its visionary parts. In my 1980 interview with Powell and Pressburger, they stressed the centrality of morality in their films; before thinking about plot or characters when starting on a new project, they said, they usually began with a moral idea or theme, which the film would then illustrate or illuminate. Its otherworldly atmosphere notwithstanding, *The Tales of Hoffmann* has at least one of its terpsichorean feet planted in the real world. In a self-reflexive flourish at the end, Beecham is seen conducting the final strains, laying down his baton, and closing his printed score, whereupon a hand enters the frame and stamps a large "Made in England" on the back cover. This is a witty reminder that the country was back in business after years of horrific war, which the Archers had directly confronted in pictures as different as *The Lion Has Wings* (1939), *49th Parallel* (1941), *One of Our Aircraft Is Missing* (1942), and *The Life and Death of Colonel Blimp* (1943). Seen in this context, *The Tales of Hoffmann* is a purposeful affirmation of art and imagination, saluting them as productive and provocative forces that enrich and oppose the conventional world in which so many ills abound. It is also an introspective venture, setting forth an "elemental statement about the fate of the artist," embodied by the character of Hoffmann, who must "fight to retain his soul and his sanity in a world of malevolence and seduction, before accepting that the muse of poetry demands complete devotion," as film historian Ian Christie eloquently puts it in the Criterion leaflet essay (although the artist's weakness for booze suggests that his devotion to the muse might not be altogether complete). This is a moral theme of the loftiest nature, and it's ironic that in their one subsequent opera film—the relatively frivolous *Oh… Rosalinda!!* (1955), an updated version of Johann Strauss II's *Die Fledermaus*—the Archers operated on a far less philosophical level.

I'm a very active operagoer, with subscriptions to the Met and two other companies, and I too used to watch a 16mm print of *The Tales of Hoffmann* at home. Yet for reasons I've never quite pinned down, it has never been one of my Powell-Pressburger favorites on a level with *The Life and Death of Colonel Blimp* (1943), *A Canterbury Tale* (1944), *A Matter of Life and Death* (1946), *The Red Shoes*, *The Small Back Room* (1949), or Powell's solo effort *The Edge of the World* (1937). The diversity of their work makes comparison a tricky business, of course, but I'll add that even a few other opera films surpass *The Tales of Hoffmann* in my eyes and ears, most notably Jean-Marie Straub and Danièle Huillet's *Moses und Aron* (1975), Ingmar Bergman's *The Magic Flute* (1975), and Hans-Jürgen Syberberg's *Parsifal* (1982). Broadly speaking, though, *The Tales of Hoffmann* is as resourceful, innovative, and adroit as almost any movie of its day, and my reservations are basically just quirks. Criterion's superbly rendered 4K edition restores footage that has been missing through most of the film's history and supplements the feature with eye-filling stills of Heckroth's artwork and a short West German film of *The Sorcerer's Apprentice* that Heckroth hired Powell to direct in 1955. Opera connoisseurs and opera neophytes should make a beeline for this splendid disc.

The Caretaker
Cineaste 44:4, Fall 2019

Trying to pin down the unconventional artistry of Harold Pinter, critics have linked him to movements as different as the Angry Young Men and the Theater of the Absurd, notwithstanding the former group's penchant for kitchen-sink realism and the latter's predilection for howls against the existential void. So distinctive is Pinter's writing that important qualities of his plays do incline toward each of these disparate camps, but the term "comedy of menace," first applied to Pinter by a British critic in the late Fifties, best sums up his aesthetic. It certainly describes *The Caretaker*, the play that placed him on the international map when it opened in London in 1960 and on Broadway the following year, earning Tony nominations for actor Donald Pleasence, director Donald McWhinnie, and the play itself. The movie adaptation, directed by Clive Donner from Pinter's screenplay, was filmed in 1962 and premiered in 1963 at the Berlin International Film Festival, winning the Silver Bear, a runner-up award. It reached American theaters in 1964 under a new title, *The Guest*, because its distributor feared audiences might confuse it with Hall Bartlett's melodrama *The Caretakers*, a 1963 release with no detectable similarity except an interest in mental illness. With its rightful title restored, *The Caretaker* is now available in a dual Blu-ray/DVD edition from the British Film Institute, accompanied by a number of creditable extras.

Pinter is thought of mainly as a playwright, but in addition to his forty-plus stage and television dramas he wrote poetry and fiction and racked up around twenty screenwriting credits, a mix of art cinema (Joseph Losey's 1966 *Accident*, Karel Reisz's 1982 *The French Lieutenant's Woman*) and commercial products (Michael Anderson's 1965 *The Quiller Memorandum*, John Irvin's 1985 *Turtle Diary*) as well as screen versions of some of his plays, most notably *The Birthday Party*, directed by William Friedkin in 1968, and *The Homecoming*, directed by Peter Hall in 1973. Chillier and more austere than the Friedkin and Hall films, *The Caretaker* was shot by the great Nicolas Roeg in black-and-white tones perfectly suited to the minimalist precision of the dialogue and the slow unveiling of characters who seem ever more mysterious as their pretenses, facades, and self-delusions are ostensibly but never actually stripped away. *The Caretaker* presents the essence of the comedy of menace—a sense of psychological enigma, emotional danger, and philological non sequitur that endures and increases via three attributes Pinter gives to each of his three characters: eccentric language; perplexing gesticulation; and a strenuous yet utterly unreliable sincerity.

The characters, all male, have equal weight in the bare-bones narrative. Aston (Robert Shaw) is a soft-spoken, introverted man living in a rundown house with Mick (Alan Bates), his loquacious and mercurial brother. Aston has just rescued a raggedy homeless man named Davies (Donald Pleasence) from a pub fight and brought him to the house for a respite from the freezing winter weather. After some rambling conversation, Aston invites Davies to spend the night on one of the beds in his crazily cluttered attic room. Mick arrives later, aggressively questioning and goading Davies but going along with Aston's idea of giving the slovenly, irresponsible guest the job of caretaker in their home. The drama has two moments that might be called climaxes, neither causing a turning point in the action but both marking a peak in its psychological intensity. One is Aston's long, affectless description of a mental breakdown, psychiatric hospitalization, and electroshock treatment he underwent as an adolescent; the other is Mick's abrupt and violent smashing of a small Buddha statue stored in the junk-filled bedroom. Eventually the brothers, understandably fed up with Davies' awful habits and constant complaints, tell him to leave. At the finale he's still around, and the ending recalls that of *Waiting for Godot* by Samuel Beckett, one of Pinter's inspirational figures. Movement is called for. Nobody moves.

This outcome is foreshadowed by the many unrealized plans that run through *The Caretaker*, which also recalls Anton Chekhov's *Three Sisters*, about women whose romantic dream of moving to Moscow will never come true. Aston, a former factory hand, dreams of building a shed in the backyard. Mick, something of a hustler, dreams of refurbishing the rundown house with his idea of splendid accoutrements. Davies' dream is to get to a neighborhood called Sidcup and reclaim his identity papers from someone or other who has hold of them. Given the personalities involved, these aspirations are both modest and impossible. Stuck in perpetual holding patterns, they buzz through the minds of characters whose idea of decisiveness is to wait and see if the weather is better tomorrow. Sidcup is hardly Moscow, but it's just as unreachable.

Despite his inclination for oblique narratives and perplexing dialogues, Pinter was a fiercely political thinker with a proud history of supporting human-rights causes. The politics of *The Caretaker* operate on more than one level, starting with its language. While progressive filmmakers like Mike Leigh and Ken Loach have created characters whose lack of agency comes across in their bondage to clichés and bromides, Pinter presents figures who don't hesitate to vocalize and speechify but crash against a constant failure to connect one thought to another, much less to the practical problems at hand. What's really at issue in all the verbiage is power, and the measure of that power is mostly the quantity, not the quality, of the words hurled heedlessly about. Aston's monologue about his psychiatric travails is the flip side of the same coin, very earnest and deliberate but delivered only to Davies, who uses it as a cudgel to beat up Aston's battered psyche even more. Such is language in a culture where words and ideas have come unglued and miscommunication is omnipresent.

On a more explicit level, the destitute and obnoxious Davies may be a flamboyantly "politically incorrect" character, as producer Michael Birkett says in the BFI audio commentary, but he has a long pedigree in films by mavericks like Luis Buñuel and Arturo Ripstein, who likewise portray the dehumanizing results of the dehumanizing treatment inflicted by callous societies on their poorest and weakest members. Pinter sympathizes without sentimentalizing, and when Davies rails against the Indian immigrants next door, the fatuousness of his bigotry speaks more loudly than the clamor of his splenetic tone. Pinter also puts property and identity into question, using the house's cramped geography as the occasion for numerous squabbles, and equipping Davies with two names—he lives under a pseudonym, for no imaginable reason—that can't be verified by his tantalizingly inaccessible papers. Davies is both a victim and a victimizer, and so are the brothers who impulsively take him in and engage him in power games incomprehensible to all of them.

Anyone familiar with Pinter is familiar with Pinter's famous pauses, which come in three flavors: ellipses (…) for short ones, stage directions ("Pause") for longer ones, and more emphatic stage directions ("Silence") for those longer still. *The Caretaker* abounds in these, and besides underscoring Pinter's view that inchoate language mirrors inchoate ideology, they are strong determinants of rhythm and tempo. Donner's film adds an effective counterpoint to the linguistic rhythms, punctuating key moments with electronically distorted sounds derived from actual noises— footsteps, closing doors, water dripping into a bucket from a hole in the ceiling—in the world of the story. Like the three kinds of Pinter pauses, these sounds come in three varieties, as Donner notes in a 1973 interview on the BFI disc: steady, to point up Aston's impassivity; busy, to accentuate Mick's constant bustling; and chaotic, to echo Davies' slapdash crankiness.

Further enhancing the original play, Donner and Pinter have opened it up with a small number of outdoor scenes showing Aston shopping, Davies panhandling, Mick silently smoking in his car, and other such ephemera, placing the generally hermetic action into the context of a larger social world without compromising the claustrophobic ambience in which the characters live, brood, bicker, and almost suffocate. In the most memorable outdoor sequence, Mick drives up to a curb where Davies is sitting on a bench, offers to drive him to Sidcup, then takes the bewildered tramp on a quick trip around a traffic circle and deposits him exactly where they started a moment earlier. This is Pinterism at its purest, simultaneously funny, ridiculous, unnerving, and thoroughly integrated with a motif of circularity (another Beckett legacy) that runs through the film, most uproariously when Davies and the brothers have a three-way scramble for possession of a shabby bag that's not worth having in the first place.

In addition to the extras already mentioned, the BFI release includes two videos by Pinter biographer Michael Billington, both informative if not very probing, as well as a brief on-location report made for British television in 1962, a booklet, a nicely done stills gallery, and a six-minute animation called *Last to Go*, excerpted from the 1969 TV special *Pinter People*, written by Pinter, directed by Gerald Potterton, and voiced by Pleasence and the playwright. The most illuminating extra is the audio commentary by director Donner, producer Birkett, and star Bates, all of whom get somewhat beyond the everyone-was-so-great-to-work-with reminiscence to which this genre is prone. There's useful information about the production's funding—studio support fell through so the filmmakers and actors turned to celebrities like Elizabeth Taylor, Richard Burton, Peter Sellers, and Noël Coward, all named in the opening titles—and about Pinter's readiness to open up the play and shorten it by half an hour. Donner praises the ingrained grayness of the film stock so brilliantly handled by Roeg, and he discusses the gradual brightening of the visual tone as the film proceeds, a counterintuitive effect that (for me) further heightens the uncanny atmosphere. Pinter isn't part of the audio commentary but others have interesting things to say about him. This was the playwright's first experience with theatrical filmmaking, and having a few TV productions under his belt, he was surprised Roeg had only one camera. It's also fascinating to learn that one of the added outdoor scenes, showing the brothers standing by a forlorn little backyard pool, was Pinter's favorite in the entire movie.

With the film as with the original play, and to some extent with nearly all of Pinter's work, the everlasting question is what in the world it all means. Pinter had little interest in clearing up the mystery, and Donner says in his 1973 interview that he did his best to set forth the drama as neutrally as possible, imposing no interpretations on the material. Proposing interpretations is the purpose of life for critics, however, and many have risen to the occasion. Reviewing the play's initial London run, for instance, the illustrious Harold Hobson declared that the characters represent Jesus and the two thieves condemned to crucifixion with him, while the equally illustrious Kenneth Tynan decided that they stand for the psychoanalytic id, ego, and superego. I saw the same cast in the original New York production of *The Caretaker* in the early Sixties, when it was promoted as the second "avant-garde" show to reach Broadway, following Eugene Ionesco's galumphing tragicomedy *Rhinoceros* a few months earlier. What thrilled me then and thrills me now is precisely the sense of impenetrable yet alluring mystery that permeates every word and gesture, from Aston's uninflected sentences and Mick's mercurial mood swings to the way Davies' hands incessantly collide as he grapples with the anarchic impulses and puerile emotions that carom off the fuzzy borders of his sadly inadequate mind. Donner's film preserves this mystery in all its darksome splendor.

The Red Riding Trilogy
Cineaste 35:3, Summer 2010

It's no secret that some of the most invigorating American cinema in recent years has been produced for television series—not just *The Sopranos,* which I find overrated, but also such original and intelligent programs as *The Wire, Big Love, Mad Men,* and *Six Feet Under,* the richest of them all. Similar things have been happening in Europe, with more emphasis on movies that can be exported to theaters as well as broadcast.

The Red Riding Trilogy is something of a hybrid, comprising three feature films that you need to watch sequentially, like a five-hour miniseries, if you want to decipher the intricate story and tease out its deeper meanings. The production was financed by British film and television sources including Channel 4, LipSync Productions, Revolution Films, which is co-owned by producer Andrew Eaton and director Michael Winterbottom, and the regional media agency Screen Yorkshire, which deserves a heap of credit for funding three movies that will make many viewers vow to never, ever, go anywhere near Yorkshire.

The three films are based on four novels: *The Red Riding Quartet*, published one book a year between 1999 and 2002 by British author David Peace, who grew up in Yorkshire, lived abroad from 1991 to 2009, and returned to England not long ago. (He also wrote *The Damned Utd*, the 2006 novel that inspired last year's movie *The Damned United*.) Each book is named after the year when it takes place—*Nineteen Seventy-Four*, *Nineteen Seventy-Seven*, *Nineteen Eighty*, and *Nineteen Eighty-Three*—and the movies are similarly called *1974*, *1980*, and *1983*. All take place in Yorkshire, and the umbrella title Red Riding refers to the county's division into three districts—the West Riding, the North Riding, and the East Riding—while associating them with the redness of blood and rage, and perhaps with "Little Red Riding Hood," an archetype of the menaced children who abound in the novels and films.

The plot is crowded and elaborate, so I'll give only a brief outline here; this paragraph and the next contain spoilers, but they might come in handy as you follow the movies' labyrinthine storylines. The protagonist of *1974* is Eddie Dunford (Andrew Garfield), a young journalist covering two depressing cases. One is the murder of prostitutes by the so-called Yorkshire Ripper, a real-life serial killer convicted in 1981 and still imprisoned in the high-security Broadmoor Hospital for psychiatrically impaired criminals. The other is a string of disappearances of little girls, one of whom is found with a pair of swan's wings stitched into her dead body. Dunford's investigation leads to romance with a missing girl's mother (Rebecca Hall) and to grave suspicions about a business wheeler-dealer (Sean Bean) who's putting together a grandiose project in the area. All of them meet unpleasant fates. Neither heroes nor villains fare well in these films.

1980 centers on Peter Hunter (Paddy Considine), a constable brought from Manchester to lead a police Super Squad and jump-start the stalled Ripper investigation, mightily annoying the York-shire force, whose failures are highlighted by his arrival. Hunter is a good cop but an unhappy man, and he's unhappier still when his colleagues turn against him, his wife (Lesley Sharp) sinks into despair, and someone burns his house down. Eventually a mentally stunted man with the Dostoevskian name Michael Myshkin (Daniel Mays) is arrested in the Ripper case and tortured into confessing. He turns out not to be the Ripper, though, and Hunter ends as badly as Dunford before him. *1983* combines new story threads with existing ones, revolving around malevolent cop Maurice Jobson (David Morrissey), gay hustler and everyman BJ (Robert Sheehan), and lawyer John Piggott (Mark Addy), a sagging, burnt-out man whose reluctant decision to file a legal appeal for Myshkin leads to a great deal of misery before a conclusion that's considerably less downbeat than the end of the eponymous book.

Peace's novels have been likened to the thrillers of James Ellroy, whom Peace has cited as an influence, but they're more complex and experimental than anything I've come across in Ellroy's work. An enormous number of characters come and go, many of them appearing *à la* Balzac in more than one book; multiple storylines leap with abandon through time and space; the prose becomes ever more eccentric and obsessive. Conversations and interior mono-logues are brutally obscene; episodes of torture and slaughter are obscenely brutal. Although the fact-based narratives focus on supposedly decent people hunting child tormenters, abductors, and murderers, the cops are often as crooked and sadistic as their prey. This is savage stuff, but Peace seems to think he's writing with old-fashioned British understatement. For the real deal on the period's rampant corruption, criminality, and sleaze he suggests reading nonfiction such as Tony Bunyan's *History and Practice of the Political Police in Britain* (1977).

Pared down from four novels to three films, evidently for budget reasons, *The Red Riding Trilogy* has a density and concentration not often found in mass-audience movies. It also has a sharp political edge, taking unambiguous stands on contentious issues. The narrative's time period, 1974 to 1983, overlaps with Margaret Thatcher's reigns as leader of the Conservative Party, starting in 1975, and Prime Minister, starting four years later. British readers and viewers surely recognize the connection between *Red Riding* and the state of their nation during the early Thatcher era, when unemployment soared, inflation festered, and organized labor seethed. Similarly, the trilogy's American viewers will (or should) remember the urban crises of the Seventies and the right-wing regression that brought Ronald Reagan to the presidency in 1980 and encouraged his policies of busting unions, lowering millionaires' taxes, flushing billions down the military drain, and so on and so on. While the period's economic insecurity and civil malaise brought waves of vicious crime and violence to both sides of the Atlantic, these were exacerbated in northern England by decadence and incompetence in the political and law-enforcement establishments, which *Red Riding* mercilessly depicts as object lessons in the amorality of unchecked police power. (John Stalker, an assistant chief constable in northern England in the early Eighties, told *Radio Times* in London that the trilogy is "the most shocking portrayal of a named force" he has ever seen.) *Red Riding* also indicts the role of capital in enabling, producing, and prolonging egregious abuses. One of its most insidious villains is Yorkshire's chief constable, Bill "Badger" Molloy, who raises his glass in a toast that summarizes his modus operandi — "To the North, where *we do what we want*" — and another is his mate John Dawson, a "construction magnate" whose plan to build Europe's largest shopping complex in the region feeds and enlarges the old-chap network of fraud, greed, ruthlessness, and narcissistic cruelty. Demented evildoer that he is, the Yorkshire Ripper takes a back seat to these guys and their rancid cronies, toadies, and apprentices. And although the last *Red Riding* novel was published before the terrors of Abu Ghraib and Guantanamo became public, the films were completed just last year, and their depictions of brutal interrogations and forced confessions serve as indirect but scathing denunciations of those atrocities.

The Red Riding Trilogy has so many intertwining plots and subplots that even British critics have admitted difficulties in following it; the reviewer for *The Telegraph*, for instance, wrote after watching the first installment that elements of the story "remained somewhere between sketchy and inexplicable." And that's before things get *really* complicated in parts two and three. The trilogy pays good dividends on the time and effort it requires, however, thanks first of all to the producers (Eaton, Wendy Brazington, and Anita Overland) who devised an unusual filming protocol for this unusual project. The screenplays were all written by Tony Grisoni, whose hard-driving style is way too obvious at times but lends the series a sense of cohesion it might otherwise lack. Countervailing the centripetal energy of the scripts, meanwhile, is the centrifugal energy resulting from each film having a different director and screen format. Julian Jarrold shot *1974* in Super-l6mm, opening the series with a grainy, subtly abrasive look that sets exactly the right tone; James Marsh chose standard 35mm for 1980, partly because of its suitability to low-light conditions; and Anand Tucker filmed *1983* in anamorphic widescreen, which well accommodates the rush of converging plotlines as the trilogy gallops to a close. (The directors favor the same color scheme, though, which Jarrold describes as "slightly brownish and muted," in keeping with Yorkshire's grimness at the time.)

Beyond cinematic style per se, the three directors and formats produce nuanced variations in matters of tone, psychology, and narrative point of view, which remain fluid and unpredictable as characters wax and wane in importance along with the stances and attitudes they embody. More broadly, Peace's novels and Grisoni's adaptations play off one another in ways that indicate some of the possibilities and limitations currently operating in popular literature and mass-market film. The quartet shows a definite evolution from the first book to the last, always preoccupied with visceral ferocity but growing less hysterical (fewer scenes are marred by over-the-top emotionalism) and more impressionistic, conveying events and feelings through increasingly primal means based on repetition, variation, and almost ritualistic transformations of words and phrases. The novels also become steadily more invested in a quality that crime fiction frequently neglects—an abiding compassion for the victimized, which becomes the main driving force in some portions of the quartet. The makers of the trilogy seem to be using their unconventional production setup to achieve a corresponding sense of anxiety, insanity, and incipient chaos lurking in every dismal nightclub, rain-soaked landscape, and police-station torture chamber to which the story takes us. And they succeed, creating a claustrophobia and paranoia you could cut with the Ripper's knife.

Translating the quartet's volatility and instability into cinematic terms has drawbacks, including the narrative confusion I mentioned earlier; although much of it is temporary, it's discombobulating while it lasts. Regarded from another angle, however, this can be taken as one of the trilogy's most daring and effective moves, giving up linear-film conventionality to hammer out a blood-red critique of both sociopolitical dysfunction and the tendency of "normal" television to present corruption and violence as entertainment that distracts its audience from the actual evils of the world. I wish the filmmakers were even more unsparing, and I suspect that some of their decisions—truncating the revelation of a pedophilia den, for instance, and downgrading the Reverend Lawes character (Peter Mullan) from a uniquely horrifying madman to just another nasty weirdo—were prompted by fear of putting more on the screen than today's TV traffic will bear. But for the most part *The Red Riding Trilogy* is conceptually solid, culturally progressive, and aesthetically audacious. Now let's see who outside England is brave enough to produce a politically outspoken movie that requires conscientious viewing of three dense, demanding installments and offers generous intellectual rewards to those who make the effort.

What does video art look like? Sometimes it can be a sculpture
The Christian Science Monitor, May 17, 1982

Until recently, "video art"—the art of the television tube—was a minor offshoot of the avant-garde. A medium for tinkerers and experimenters, it was so new that nobody had quite figured out how it worked, much less what to do with it. In the past couple of years, though, video art has done a lot of growing up. The novelty has faded, the grammar has been worked out, and significant work has emerged. The dominant figure of this activity has been Nam June Paik, a Korean-born composer, artist, and performer who switched from music to video in 1963 and hasn't looked back since. His current exhibition at the Whitney Museum of American Art—perhaps the most prestigious American showcase for major video work—makes a compelling case for this new, blossoming form.

What does video art look like? Generally speaking, nothing like *Mork and Mindy* or *Life on Earth*, or even the video games that have sprouted like weeds lately. Most video artists—including Paik—work in a poetic vein, expressing ideas and feelings in a personal and subjective way. Image and structure tend to be more important than story or character. Visual imagination is the highest priority. The results may be videotapes that look like TV poems. Or video may be used as a plastic form, like painting or sculpture, in works nicely suited to galleries and museums. As this trend continues, video is gaining recognition as a versatile and malleable medium. After all, as long as the electricity stays on, a video work is as permanent as any other. And despite its complicated circuits, it's no more heterogeneous than the mixed media of, say, a Joseph Cornell collage or a Robert Rauschenberg "combine painting."

Paik's exhibition focuses on video as a sculptural element. In some cases, the video tube contains the work of art like a picture frame. Good examples are the "Magnet TV" pieces, with images bent into shape by simple magnets placed on television consoles. In other cases, the video tube becomes part of a larger construction. The most striking case is "Video Fish," in which tropical-fish aquariums are lined up in front of 15 TV monitors jumping with kinetic pictures of blue skies, zooming airplanes, imposing buildings, and yes, more tropical fish. Isolated in its own dark corridor, such a work isn't just a sculpture, it's an environment. The same goes for "Fish Flies on Sky," which invites viewers to lie on the floor and watch TV monitors dangling from the ceiling. "Laser Video" fills a wall with bright green images of Merce Cunningham, the dancer (in a superb videotape by Charles Atlas), punctuated with frantic beams of pure red light. Other environmental works build a quieter atmosphere. The dazzling "TV Clock" presents an array of slanted lines on a gently curving string of 23 monitors. "Moon Is the Oldest TV" displays the lunar phases. A less impressive piece called "Imagine There Are More Stars on the Sky Than Chinese on the Earth" projects round, blurry images onto otherwise bare walls and ceiling

Imposing works, every one. Yet there's a sense of whimsy lurking here—after all, the dominant motif is tropical fish! As it happens, Paik is a joker as well as a thinker, and he was a dadaist before he became a technologist. A sly sense of humor shines through much of his activity: There's a photograph of him in his music-student days, slumped over a keyboard in solemn slumber. There's his "TV Chair," a gloriously impractical invention. There's the "Violin With String," a bedraggled instrument to be dragged along the ground, and the "TV Cello," built of working picture tubes.

Then too, Paik is not entirely a rampaging modernist. Tradition threads through his work, along with a wry nostalgia for nature. The fabulous "TV Garden" surrounds upended monitors with a lush roomful of green plants. Another work features a video image projected on a huge glass egg—giving a touch of the farmyard and a hint of three-dimensional television. The meditative "TV Buddha" is a stone statue contemplating its own "live" image on a monitor buried in dirt, while nearby a small copy of Rodin's "The Thinker" gazes at a tiny Sony screen. "Real Fish/Live Fish" juxtaposes more of those ubiquitous tropical fish with their own televised ghosts, in a punning comment on the word "live.' More radically yet, the wonderful "Candle TV" dispenses with electronics completely, replacing the picture tube with a lonely candle burning brightly in an empty console. Another piece contrasts a traditional sculpture with a fire-damaged TV set. Even a static work like "Life Ring 66"—a beat-up old electromagnet—reflects a healthy demystification of technology.

It seems clear that Paik is steeped in science, art, and nature, all at the same time. Some of his most expansive works are intimately tied to the computer age, from his friendly-looking robot (named K-456) to his babbling tower of TV tubes, the "V-rymid." Yet touches of sea, sky, and earth are never absent for long. It's this balance of the timeless and the timely that puts Paik at the forefront of the burgeoning video-art movement. Firmly rooted in the real world, and swarming with tropical fish to prove it, his antic technologizing has a great deal to tell us.

The exhibition of works by Nam June Paik will continue at the Whitney through June 27. In conjunction with it, a selection of Paik videotapes will be shown on Channel 13 in New York each Sunday evening through June 20. The museum will sponsor a panel discussion of Paik's art on May 21, and performances by Paik and cellist Charlotte Moorman will take place on June 2 and 3. After closing at the Whitney, the exhibition is tentatively scheduled for the Museum of Contemporary Art in Chicago, the National Gallery in West Berlin, and the Museum Moderner Kunst in Vienna.

All sounds can make music for radical and influential composer John Cage
The Christian Science Monitor, May 3, 1982

Let us now celebrate John Cage—honorary grandpa of today's experimental music, and a revered guru to avant-garde artists in every field—one of the 20th century's most influential composers.

Tributes to Cage are flourishing lately, in anticipation of his 70th birthday in September. A festival called New Music America, to be presented in Chicago this July, will be dedicated to him. An exhibition called *John Cage: Scores and Prints* has just completed a stay at the Whitney Museum of American Art here and will travel to the Philadelphia Museum of Art and the Albright-Knox Gallery in Buffalo. Further events will focus on Cage's contributions to music, graphics, and other fields.

Perhaps the most heroic tribute, however, took place at Symphony Space in Manhattan not long ago, where a marathon "Wall-to-Wall" concert presented 14½ hours of continuous music by Cage and friends, without a single break long enough to be called an intermission. Attending the entire event was a challenge, and also a joy—dispelling any doubts over the diversity, imagination, energy, and sheer friendliness of Cage's work. It was a day to win over the skeptical, and to give the receptive listener an unforgettable dose of Cagean magic.

Cage's most enduring legacy is probably his concept of "indeterminacy" and "chance" as integral parts of music. Using elaborate—and sometimes very amusing—methods, he has developed a creative style that bypasses the personality of the composer, and sometimes the performer as well. Convinced that his own choices and decisions are likely to limit a work, rather than liberate it, Cage would rather rely on the flip of a coin or the whim of a computer. A devotee of the visual as well as the sonic arts, he seems happiest when his work spills freely into the domains of theater, drawing, and dance, appealing to the eye and mind as well as to the ear. And he has always insisted that all sounds should be treated with equal respect, from the reverberations of the concert hall to plain, everyday "noise." Thus the pitches of *Études australes* are based on tracings of star maps, while the *Concert for Piano and Orchestra* uses imperfections in the paper it is written on. Cage's instrumentation is equally unexpected. *Child of Tree* calls for "amplified plant materials," while *Inlets* uses water-filled seashells. "Living Room Music" is scored for household furniture.

Not surprisingly, performers of Cage's music often face unusual tasks. The player of *Music for Carillon No. 5* studies the grain of a plywood board to determine what notes he should sound; the soloist of *Water Music* must be a master of numerous instruments including piano, radio, whistles, and deck of cards. The player of the composition entitled *4'33"* ("four minutes, 33 seconds")—arguably Cage's most famous work—sits at the piano without touching the keys, while the audience enjoys the silence. Inevitably, such works have been roundly and regularly attacked. Many musicians regard them as mere stunts, lacking musical or aesthetic interest. Some resent the very basis of Cage's philosophy, with its emphasis on chance composition and its eagerness to heighten rather than hide the accidents of performance. Even admirers of Cage's career sometimes suggest that his attitude is more important than his actual music, and that his freewheeling ideas will last longer than his individual pieces.

Cage keeps right on thriving, however, influencing whole generations of musical experimenters while refusing to tone down his cheerfully outrageous forays. It's important to note that his work is rooted in concepts few would quarrel with: the notion of strict discipline (despite his "indeterminacy" theory), and the love of sound for its own sake. True, his discipline is employed in unorthodox ways, and his enthusiasm for sound is uncommonly broad. Still, these are positive and affirmative values, and they inform every inch of Cage's best work—as well as his sunny personality, which has been an essential element in his life and career. His influence has extended beyond the world of music to the fields of theater , dance, art, and literature. His own works are often theatrical in nature, with musicians honking horns and kicking drums, parading around the concert hall with blaring radios, or pounding tricky rhythms on TV sets and filing cabinets. As a permanent collaborator with the Merce Cunningham Dance Company, he has played an important role in contemporary dance, too, sharing Cunningham's enthusiasm for "different things happening at the same time."

As the current Whitney Museum show proves, Cage's scores also make provocative art, with their extravagant graphics, unheard-of notations, and occasional bright colors. And he is an inventor, the "prepared piano" being his most notable credit—a modified piano with objects placed among the strings to alter their sound. Even the world of words has come into Cage's career, as he collects anecdotes, publishes lectures, and performs his own variations on earlier works by such admired authors as Thoreau and Joyce.

Though many attempts have been made, no record or tape can encompass the vitally theatrical quality that infuses most of his work. Moreover, every performance of a Cage piece is different, because of the crucial "chance" element. Recordings betray this spontaneity, by their very nature. Hence it's essential to hear Cage's compositions in their natural habitat, which is almost anywhere except on records—from the concert hall to the street corner. Cage relishes the humor and theatricalism that flow from much of his work. When a Cage composition ends and he takes a bow, he grins and sparkles as if some wonderful joke had come off flawlessly well. An intense composer as well as a prolific philosopher, he approaches his work with a seriousness devoid of solemnity. Savoring every sound, he seems to find laughter the most delightful noise of all.

Gibson's *Passion* Has Little But Suffering on Its Mind
The Christian Science Monitor, February 25, 2004

Few things breed controversy more readily these days than a movie on a religious topic. *The Passion of the Christ*, directed by Mel Gibson, reminds us of this with a vengeance. Tabloid columnists and cable-TV pundits have been raising a ruckus over it for months, starting long before the picture was even finished. Now the movie is here, and whatever else one might say about it, Mr. Gibson has clearly tapped into the uneasy, often troubled mood of the early 21st century. As the advance buzz indicated, it's an exceedingly violent movie, reenacting the torture and crucifixion of Jesus with a ferocity unknown in traditional film treatments. It also offers a dubious depiction of the Jewish community's role in Jesus' execution—not actively supporting anti-Semitic interpretations, which Gibson has publicly disavowed, but leaving that door open for viewers already tainted by an anti-Semitic bias. Pontius Pilate is shown as a rueful believer in realpolitik, for instance—an ancient Henry Kissinger, you might say—while the Jewish mob is portrayed as yowling for death with no hint of reason or rationality.

Measured on the more mundane scale of motion-picture craftsmanship, *The Passion of the Christ* is expertly made, thanks largely to Jim Caviezel's fervent portrayal of Jesus and Caleb Deschanel's skillful camera work. But the film contains little to learn from, unless one is unfamiliar with basic Christian history. And it presents even less to be inspired by, unless one regards Jesus' earthly suffering as momentous for its own sake, rather than a precondition for his triumph over death, which occupies only the last few seconds of the film. The highly selective screenplay includes only a few of Jesus' words, spoken in occasional flashback scenes.

Gibson has said making *The Passion of the Christ* was a religious mission for him, and I'm sure that's true. The logo of his company, Icon Productions, includes a small section of a religious painting, and several close-ups of Caviezel's face unmistakably mirror this image, suggesting that the picture of the suffering of Jesus has long carried deep meanings for Gibson himself. The single-mindedness of *The Passion of the Christ* bears this out. Still, it's important to note that while Gibson is a versatile actor and director, he has shown a recurring penchant for violence in his projects, from the *Mad Max* and *Lethal Weapon* series through more ambitious pictures such as *Braveheart*, the Best Picture winner that climaxes with

Gibson's character being tortured at harrowing length. Looking at this motif in a positive light, one could say Gibson has always been fascinated by suffering heroes—characters who serve as Christlike figures in secular surroundings. Considering it more skeptically, one could conclude that Gibson has a morbid fascination with agony and affliction, and that *The Passion of the Christ* gives him an ideal opportunity to indulge this in extreme terms. This may explain why it sometimes seems as much like a horror movie as it does a serious biblical film. The opening is strikingly similar to the eerie, mystically tinged scene-setters of countless supernatural thrillers. At times, Gibson approaches the greatest artistic challenge of the story—how to keep jolting moviegoers already subjected to awesome quantities of blood and gore—by throwing in uncanny visions that could have been borrowed from *The Exorcist* or *Hellraiser*. While this doesn't refute Gibson's serious intentions, it does imply that he's willing to take low roads as well as high ones to make a bruising impression on his audience.

That's what makes *The Passion of the Christ* different from most previous treatments of biblical topics. In bygone decades, Hollywood steered clear of controversy by imbuing major religious figures with movie-star charisma (think of Charlton Heston's majestic Moses in *The Ten Commandments*) or keeping them largely off the screen (the barely glimpsed Jesus of *The Robe*). Those days ended with *The Last Temptation of Christ*, which infuriated many people in 1988, and *Dogma*, which did the same in 1999. The angriest protesters of those movies were Christians trying to dissuade viewers from seeing them. By contrast, the most prominent Christian voices in media coverage of Gibson's movie have encouraged audiences to view it, notwithstanding its extraordinary violence and Jewish anxiety regarding its possible anti-Semitic undertones. Times have indeed changed when church representatives vocally support a film that focuses so literal-mindedly on the physical suffering of Jesus' body rather than the metaphysical meanings this suffering helped convey to humanity.

Gibson says he based *The Passion of the Christ* primarily on the Gospels, and some theologians contend that the diversity and incompleteness of those books purvey a crucial insight in themselves: that the full spiritual wisdom of Jesus' revolutionary thought cannot be contained in recorded words and deeds. Gibson evidently disagrees, seeing so much meaning in the blunt spectacle of Jesus' tormented body that he finds it unnecessary to depict almost anything else.

The Passion of the Christ is at once a well-crafted film, a merciless excursion into motion-picture ultraviolence, and a regrettably cramped historical account that stays doggedly on the surface of its overwhelmingly important subject.

Einstein on the Beach: a masterly revival. Robert Wilson's sensitive staging shapes production
The Christian Science Monitor, January 9, 1985

Like most operas, *Einstein on the Beach* is identified most closely with its composer. Yet this particular opera is a special case, shaped from the beginning by director Robert Wilson in tandem with composer Philip Glass. It's easy to see why this has been overlooked. Glass' reputation has soared among American listeners—boosted a lot by the recorded *Einstein on the Beach* score itself—since the show had its American premiere in 1976. By contrast, Wilson has worked largely in Europe during the past decade, forfeiting the "exposure" that American audiences demand from their cultural heroes.

One purpose served by the superb revival of *Einstein on the Beach* this season (in the "Next Wave" series at the Brooklyn Academy of Music) was to enhance Wilson's reputation in his own country by recalling the visual majesty of this astonishing production. It's not an easy work, running nearly five hours with no story, dialogue, or intermission. Yet its indelible imagery and transfixing rhythms carry it to heights of theatrical splendor that I've rarely seen matched in more conventional settings—the Broadway hit *Sunday in the Park with George* is a pale echo by comparison. And while music is the motor that propels it, stagecraft is the magic at its heart.

In place of plot and characters, *Einstein on the Beach* focuses on images that go through slow, unexpected changes. Near the beginning we see a locomotive in profile; later we see the train receding from us at night; in the last act it has turned into a large building. Similarly, we twice see a flying saucer hovering over a field full of dancers and are transported miraculously into the "spacemachine" at the climax. What does it all mean? Not much, if taken literally. But critics who call the work shallow miss the essence of Wilson's art, which is to explore, in visionary terms, pervasive tensions between order and disorder. Simply put, the content of *Einstein on the Beach* is rooted in elements of disorder: randomness, irrational connections, the subtraction of information. Yet these elements are contained within a tightly designed structure marked by painstaking, even obsessive, artistic discipline. What might have led to chaos leads to harmony before our very eyes! And the effect is as gorgeous as it is unexpected.

The three courtroom scenes make a vivid example of this process, beginning with bizarre juxtapositions and ending with elegant simplicity. First we see the room decked out for a trial, with a huge and improbable bed standing in the center. Later, half the room and half the bed vanish, to be replaced by a prison. In the last act everything is gone except the bed, seen only as a long rectangle of white light which, in an inspired 20-minute scene, is silently hauled from the floor until it disappears into the heights above the stage. The more we watch, the less we see and the more we sense the strange but palpable rightness of Wilson's exquisitely crafted plan.

To stress the importance of Wilson's achievement in *Einstein on the Beach* is not to belittle Glass' score, still the pinnacle of his career, which has veered in more conservative directions lately. Wilson's contribution is felt in the sounds of *Einstein on the Beach* as well, however, since the spoken portions reflect the director's yen for eccentric texts by such nonwriters as dancer Lucinda Childs (the rigorous choreographer of the revival) and performance artist Christopher Knowles. Indeed, the combination of Glass' music and Wilson's words is a first-class collaborative achievement even without their visual counterparts.

Einstein on the Beach may be ahead of its time even now, almost a decade after it first appeared. Its run at BAM did not sell out, as had been hoped, and a planned United States tour has been shelved because its projected cost outweighs its likely income. But its reputation may continue to grow as new audiences ease into the insinuating rhythms of Wilson's career. I was flanked at a BAM performance by two early teens who found *Einstein on the Beach* fascinating. The recording is a fine document of its sonic dimension. This is truly "a landmark in 20th century music theater," as a critic remarks in *Robert Wilson: The Theater of Images*, a highly readable book just published by Harper & Row. Its revival, more intense in my view than the original production as seen at the Met, was an aesthetic coup par excellence by the bold-as-brass Brooklyn Academy.

Seeking (and Finding) Brakhage
Quarterly Review of Film and Video 40:3 (2023)

Stan Brakhage was one of the most gifted, most prolific, and most scandalously underrecognized artists in cinema history. His hundreds of films range from a few seconds (*Eye Myth*, 1967, eight seconds) to several hours (*The Art of Vision*, 1965, 260 minutes) in length; their formats range from 8 mm and super-8mm to 16 mm and 35 mm, and a handful are in IMAX or the short-lived Polavision process; most are silent, but some contain music or spoken words; and while most consist of photographed imagery, in many the visuals are painted or scratched directly on the film stock, and the 1963 classic *Mothlight* was made by arranging insect wings and bits of plants between strips of clear perforated tape. In addition to his vast filmography, which began with *Interim* in 1952 and culminated with the *Chinese Series* in 2003, Brakhage wrote several books on cinema, displaying a keenly poetic style exemplified by *Metaphors on Vision*, published as a special issue of Jonas Mekas' enterprising *Film Culture* magazine in 1963 and subsequently republished in book form. Its opening words have been quoted countless times by countless critics, theorists, and philosophers of film, myself included, but they convey the essential concerns of Brakhage's esthetic so vividly that they deserve to be quoted yet again:

> Imagine an eye unruled by man-made laws of perspective, an eye unprejudiced by compositional logic, an eye which does not respond to the name of everything but which must know each object encountered in life through an adventure in perception. How many colors are there in a field of grass to the crawling baby unaware of "Green?" How many rainbows can light create for the untutored eye? How aware of variations in heat waves can that eye be? Imagine a world alive with incomprehensible objects and shimmering with an endless variety of movement and innumerable gradations of color. Imagine a world before the "beginning was the word." (Brakhage, 1963)

Connecting the insights expressed in those words with the specifics of filmmaking practice, the incomparable Brakhage exegete Fred Camper writes in his magisterial new book, *Seeking Brakhage*, that in Brakhage's photographed works "the filmic appearance of [an] object is meant to represent the act of perception itself. Brakhage's imagined world is a world of continually intruding perception; not something that you can lose yourself in directly, as if it had a life of its own, but rather something which is a dynamic, continuing process. An object never has a fixed meaning which can be 'identified with' by the viewer: it is rather, only, an element of perception. In this sense Brakhage speaks not directly to our imaginative sensibilities but rather to those sensibilities only as reached through perception" (Camper, 2022, 254). In this passage Camper is discussing the long cycle of *Songs* that Brakhage made in (mostly) 8 mm between 1964 and 1969, but the principle is true of virtually all his films. One of Brakhage's great enemies is "picture," an image that can be rapidly absorbed and easily inserted into the standardized meaning systems we use to navigate through our everyday environments and intellectual activities; another great enemy, not mentioned by Camper, is what he called "clutch," the ability of narrative movies (which Brakhage enjoyed watching, incidentally) to seize and hold attention by means of strategies that his own films vigorously foreclose. Camper's analyses rightly emphasize the distinction Brakhage drew between "picture" and "active eyesight," as well as his replacement of "what one knows" with exploration of "that which one does not know," an "extreme" artistic choice that "expresses ambivalence about everything [Brakhage] has lived through, including his own self" (161–2).

Extreme, indeed. As are the aesthetics of pretty much everything in Brakhage's voluminous filmography. I've been watching and pondering his work for more than half a century, and today as always, their primary effect for me is one of speed—speed of camera movement, speed of editing rhythm, speed of shifts among shapes, colors, and juxtapositions, and speed of allusion to the teeming wealth of worldly knowledge, psychological speculation, and spiritual intuition that underlie the astonishingly dense manifestations of the films themselves. Camper has an astonishing talent for perceiving, registering, comprehending, and connecting even the most fleeting of forms, textures, colors, and edits, and his interpretive intelligence is equally sharp, relating individual films, sequences, and frames to the larger contexts of Brakhage's artistic philosophy as it evolved over the long span of his career. While the book is not biographical, Brakhage's cinema was intensely personal—a great many films use his home, his first wife and their five children, and himself as subject matter, raw material, or both—

and details of his life occasionally filter into Camper's discussions. Some of the details involve fateful matters, as when Brakhage stopped painting on film after learning that the coal tar in his paints may have caused the bladder cancer that killed him in 2003. Other details may be mundane, as when Camper runs through possible reasons for Brakhage's turn from 16 to 8 mm in 1964 (he was low on money, someone stole his 16 mm camera, he wanted his films to be as easily purchased as paintings are). And some are unexpected, as when Brakhage says that a major influence on his style is the imperfect vision caused by his slightly defective eyes: "… much of what you and others have described as my experimentation is just my scrambling to come to an understanding of how you achieve sight" (160). On the latter point, Camper admits he was momentarily disappointed with the seemingly reductive nature of Brakhage's comment, but then realized that the filmmaker's description of how he sees is also a description of how he thinks, "the images standing for a thought process that never ceases to move, and hence, never reaches a conclusion that might feel like a resting point, or suggest a statement translatable into words" (164). Precisely.

Seeking Brakhage offers limitless opportunities for discussion, so I'll quote a few passages to suggest the depth and breadth that characterize the book.

On politics and the failure to "save the world" by means of art: "Make a work with specific references to political and moral battles… and you are forced to deal directly with issues of power and persuasion… Follow Brakhage's path, and few viewers will see commentary on current issues. Indeed, few viewers will see your film at all. And yet, in his attempt to create a new viewer consciousness separate from that fostered by mass culture, his films could not be more relevant." (151–2)

On antipathy for symmetry: "Symmetry is… a kind of knowing. It knows that left and right, or top and bottom, are identical. It represents a predetermined pattern. It is a cousin to knowing objects by their names. It is complete in itself, while Brakhage is a poet of continually unfolding incompleteness. His alternative to symmetry is a collection of temporary imagined sought-for nightmares and paradises, in which the viewer is as untethered as the filmmaker, always adrift in a world whose glory is that it cannot be fully represented or mapped or explained." (164)

On exploration: "[T]here should... be a place for experiences that take us out of dailiness, the world of what we already know, that which is already familiar, even that which has been made familiar through repetition within the structure of a film, offering instead visions of what we have not yet experienced, of what we had not imagined seeing, of what the artist himself admits, in the very structures of his unparsable and untranslatable films, he does not know." (173)

On the eponymous object in My Mtn. Song 27 *(1968):* "The mountain is not a real mountain, nor is it a mountain in Brakhage's imagination; it is a shape of imagined perception. The mountain is not unlike the specks of paint in some of Brakhage's other films which [he] says have to do with an attempt to render 'closed-eye vision.' This may be part of the reason for the strange distance that always seems to exist between the object and the viewer: it is like the distance of the everyday senses from the kind of shapes you see with closed eyes, or dreaming. The gulf between viewer and mountain is the gulf between sensual perception and unsensual imagination." (218–19)

On the lasting nature of art: "All art exists for the consciousness of the viewer, of course, but less rewarding art dies in a single instantly-transmitted mood, affection, or statement, the consumerist delivery of a triggered pleasure, while the best has an almost infinite life as an ongoing experience." (275)

In the interests of disclosure, I'll note that I knew Brakhage for the last 25 years or so of his life, and I've known Camper for more than twice that long. I initially met Stan when I interviewed him for the first of many articles I wrote as film critic of *The Christian Science Monitor*, and I first encountered Fred via screenings at the Massachusetts Institute of Technology, where he was a student and ran the MIT Film Society in the 1960s. Brakhage was wonderful about keeping in touch over the years, and while my ongoing friendship with Camper has surely predisposed me in favor of his new book, my admiration for it is carefully considered and based on very long familiarity with Brakhage's unique cinema. Nor is my approbation of the volume blind to the venial imperfections I've spotted here and there. It may be true, for instance, that the "tiny lights" in *Song 11* (1965) "can be seen as clearly (during a careful watching of the film) if one closes one's eyes" (267), but it seems to me that closed eyes and "careful watching" are mutually exclusive categories. At another point, the phrase "kind of," a hazy locution in any case, appears three times in one paragraph.

More broadly, Camper sometimes falls prey to hyperbole, especially when evoking the high blood pressure aroused in him by certain films: some in-and-out movements in *Song 9* (1965) are "terrifying" (265); *Song 11* is "deeply terrifying" (267); close-ups of a dog's corpse in the sublime *Sirius Remembered* (1950) are "horrifying" (295); *The Wold-Shadow* (1972) presents a "terrifying vision" (301); *Fire of Waters* (1965) contains "terrifying" fragments (82); *Delicacies of Molten Horror Synapse* (1991) contains "utterly terrifying" images (324); the *Arabics* are "terrifying" (333); and so on. I don't mean to impugn Camper's accounts of his own feelings, but I have watched many a film with him, and since I do not remember him trembling with fear or fleeing the auditorium even once, I think his language in these passages may be a bit too strong. Then again, he may be describing uncommonly deep emotional resonances with an accuracy and candor rarely found in critical writing. When he states that his viewings of one film "have shaken the very foundations of my existence in the world" (280), and says of another that no film "has involved me more in its watching, terrified every fiber of my being, totally deranged my perception, and more deeply, everything that I've come to think of as my thought processes" (282), he appears to be expressing literal truths about experiences so intense that I can only envy him for having them.

Finally, some brief words about the structure of *Seeking Brakhage*, which came into being at the suggestion of its publisher, Eyewash Books, and consists of diverse material; some was written as far back as Camper's days at MIT, when his program notes were invaluable guides to challenging works by Brakhage and others, and some was penned as recently as the essay "Still Seeking Brakhage," written expressly for this book. Since it is a compendium of essays and articles written at different times for diverse purposes, some repetition and duplication are inevitable, but for me the book reads smoothly and engagingly throughout. Stills made from short film-strips punctuate the text, which begins with an introduction by film scholar P. Adams Sitney, probably the most prominent scholar of avant-garde cinema in general and Brakhage's great contributions in particular; his comments on Brakhage's intersections with artists in other fields (especially poets as various as Dante, William Blake, Robert Duncan, and Charles Olson) complement Camper's occasional invocations of painters (Paul Cézanne, Clyfford Still), composers (Olivier Messiaen, Johann Sebastian Bach), and choreographers (Merce Cunningham, Martha Graham) whose influence makes any comprehensive Brakhage study an interdisciplinary study. No critic, scholar, or cinephile is better qualified than Camper to keep Brakhage's messages alive and make them alluring, not to mention comprehensible, for new generations of viewers. Reading his book is very different from watching a Brakhage film, but it too is an adventure in perception. Camper writes that he is still seeking Brakhage; for me, he has come remarkably close to finding him.

Works Cited
Brakhage, Stan (1963), *Metaphors on Vision* (Film Culture).
Camper, Fred (2022), *Seeking Brakhage* (Eyewash).

With Borrowed Eyes: Abbas Kiarostami
Film Comment, July-August 2000

Abbas Kiarostami deserves more credit than any other single director for fueling the recent rise of Iranian cinema, arguably the most dramatic film development of the past dozen years. The excitement started when his slyly reflexive *Close-Up* reached the international circuit in the early Nineties, and crested when his extraordinary *Taste of Cherry* shared the Palme d'Or at Cannes in 1997. While a handful of his Iranian colleagues have also achieved a fair share of Western recognition—including Mohsen Makhmalbaf and Jafar Panahi, both of whom have collaborated with him—he has remained the most highly visible figure, thanks to films like the so-called Koker trilogy (*Where Is the Friend's Home*, *And Life Goes On*, *Through the Olive Trees*) that have earned ecstatic reviews and drawn enthusiastic art-house audiences in Europe and the United States.

All of which explains why a touch of Enthronement Syndrome has crept up on Kiarostami, with the worshipful attitude of some devotees sparking a backlash from others who question whether this emperor is wearing as impressive an outfit as his admirers claim. A surprising amount of debate surfaced over the ending of *Taste of Cherry,* wherein the film's fascinatingly discursive story—centering on a man's long discussions with three strangers about his wish to end his life—is followed by a video epilogue showing the actors and filmmakers preparing their final take in the pleasant hillside location where the suicide scene is set. Supporters saw this as a bold extension of Kiarostami's self-referential complexity, detractors labeled it a confusing cop-out that dodges narrative issues instead of resolving them. The latter group was back in action when *The Wind Will Carry Us* screened at the Toronto Film Festival last fall, complaining that its reliance on familiar moves—driving scenes, front-seat talkathons, God's-eye views of Iranian countryside—prove the director is literally spinning his wheels.

Such arguments notwithstanding, it's plain to anyone who has seriously engaged with Iranian film in general or Kiarostami's work in particular that *Taste of Cherry* and *The Wind Will Carry Us* are full-fledged masterpieces, and that the master who created them deserves any throne he might choose to occupy. Far from repeating a series of trademarked gestures, *The Wind Will Carry Us* finds Kiarostami weaving one of his most suggestive philosophical webs around the deceptively simple tale of a filmmaker who barges into a rural town, hoping to record a folk ritual that will take place after an old woman's impending death. One of the movie's feet is planted firmly in the earthbound world of the village and its inhabitants, while the other roams as freely as the protagonist's ever-present cell phone—which isn't so freely, it turns out, since the phone refuses to function unless he climbs into his Land Rover and races to the top of a distant hill. There he chats with a ditch-digger whose face is never seen and finds a human bone that becomes his talisman, signaling that while the wind may carry us, the earth remains our home and our destination.

The Wind Will Carry Us takes its title and a small but crucial point of its screenplay from a poem (reprinted on pg. 75) by the late Foroogh Farrokhzaad, an Iranian feminist and poet of the modem Persian style. This is fitting, since the cultivation of a deeply poetic cinema has been a driving force behind Kiarostami's career, as he acknowledges in the following interview. I first met Kiarostami at Cannes three years ago, and caught up with him again at the San Francisco International Film Festival this spring. He speaks some English but preferred to conduct our interview in Farsi through interpreter Nazli Monahan, listening closely to her translations and occasionally jumping in with corrections.

Since you're in San Francisco to receive the Akira Kurosawa Award for lifetime achievement, do you feel a particular kinship with Kurosawa's films?

No, but I think a filmmaker of a certain mold can enjoy movies by a filmmaker of a very different mold. For example, one of the movies I really like and enjoy is *The Godfather*, and people are shocked by that.

"If you make movies like you do, how can you enjoy a movie like that?"

But that's the beauty of it! *[laughs]*

Is it still appropriate to speak of national cinemas today, or has film become too internationalized for that kind of labeling?

Each movie has an ID or birth certificate of its own. A movie is about human beings, about humanity. All the different nations in the world, despite their differences of appearance and religion and language and way of life, still have one thing in common, and that is what's inside of all of us. If we X-rayed the insides of different human beings, we wouldn't be able to tell from those X-rays what the person's language or background or race is. Our blood circulates exactly the same way, our nervous system and our eyes work the same way, we laugh and cry the same way, we feel pain the same way. The teeth we have in our mouths—no matter what our nationality or background is—ache exactly the same way. If we want to divide cinema and the subjects of cinema, the way to do it is to talk about pain and about happiness. These are common among all countries.

Often your films don't provide us with complete information about the characters or the story, and you've been quoted as saying that one reason is because the viewer is part of the creative process. It's up to us to make sense of the material, and each of us will do that differently. How does this idea—each individual coming to his or her own understanding of a film—match with the idea that we're all basically the same since we share a common humanity?

It's a difficult question. People do have different ideas, and my wish is that all viewers should not complete the film in their minds the same way, like crossword puzzles that all look the same no matter who has solved them. Even if it's "filled out" wrong, my kind of cinema is still "correct" or true to its original value. I don't leave the blank spaces just so people have something to finish. I leave them blank so people can fill them according to how they think and what they want. In my mind, the abstraction we accept in other forms of art—painting, sculpture, music, poetry—can also enter the cinema. I feel cinema is the seventh art, and supposedly it should be the most complete since it combines the other arts. But it has become just storytelling, rather than the art it should really be.

There are some filmmakers who say what you just said and proceed to make films that don't tell stories—that really are abstract, with form and color and movement but without pictures conveying a narrative. Has that approach ever interested you?

Every movie should have some kind of story. But the important thing is how the story is told—it should be poetic, and it should be possible to see it in different ways. I have seen movies that didn't attract me or make a lot of sense while I was looking at them, but there were moments in them that opened a window for me and inspired my imagination. I have left many films in the middle because I felt I already had an ending. I felt quite complete and fulfilled with the movie, and if I stayed longer that feeling would be ruined, because it would keep telling me more and forcing me to judge who is the good guy, who is the bad guy, and what's going to happen to them. I prefer to finish it my own way!

Much of what you say describes how poets work more than how novelists work. It's interesting that your most recent film, The Wind Will Carry Us, *draws its title and some of its text from poetry. Are you trying to move farther in that direction—toward cinema as poetry rather than cinema as novel?*

Yes. I feel the cinema that will last longer is the poetic cinema, not the cinema that is just storytelling. In my library at home, the books of novels and stories look brand-new because I just read them once and put them aside; but my poetry books are falling apart at every corner, because I have read them over and over and over! Poetry always runs away from you—it's very difficult to grasp it, and every time you read it, depending on your conditions, you will have a different grasp of it. Whereas with a novel, once you have read it, you have grasped it. Of course, this doesn't encompass all novels. There are stories that do have a poetic essence to them, just as there are poems that are much like a novel. The poetry we had to memorize at school was all that kind—dialogues between a caterpillar and a spider, and that sort of thing. They weren't trying to teach us poetry in the true sense, they were trying to train us and develop us through poetry.

One of the differences between a film and a poem is that most people assume they can see a film once or twice and "get it." Will there always be problems reaching audiences with a poetic form of cinema, since people aren't accustomed to returning to a film again and again? Do you expect people to see a given film of yours many times, or do you at least hope they will?

I would be too selfish if I said everyone should see my movies more than once. To say that would mean I'm just marketing my work! I can't really say why I make movies this way, it's just the way I know how. When I'm in the process of making a movie I'm not thinking about the finished result, and whether people have to see it once or more than once, and what the reaction to it will be. I just make it, and then I live with the consequences, some of which may not be as pleasant as I'd like! I know one thing, however. Many viewers may come out of the theater not satisfied, but they won't be able to forget the movie. I know they'll be talking about it during their next dinner. I want them to be a little restless about my movies, and keep trying to find something in them.

You're one of a small group who—by consistently making films according to certain principles and ideas that you believe in—are educating your audience, teaching them how to appreciate a more challenging kind of cinema. With each movie we understand a little better how to engage with your work.

I believe the chance that exists for this type of cinema today did not exist 20 years ago. Audiences are tiring of the kinds of movies they see nowadays, and they're wanting to see something different. Of course, in Iran this [poetic] type of cinema is shown in only one theater, and [in the U.S.] it's shown in two theaters. But I'm satisfied. Most people want simplicity, they want to get excited, cry, laugh… and we can't expect the same level of enthusiasm for [poetic] cinema. I'm not comparing my works with theirs, but if you had the paintings of Kandinsky or Braque or Picasso on auction in a park, how many people would buy them, even at $100 apiece? One must have a realistic expectation for art that is real art, as opposed to what is entertainment. The general public won't pay for a picture if they can't quite understand what's in it and what it says.

I sometimes think of this issue in terms of works that close off thought—like the poetry we had to learn in school, which hands us the answers and ideas it wants us to have—as opposed to works that open thought and serve as a place for us to start our own thinking.

I agree. The poetic film is like a puzzle where you put the pieces together and they don't necessarily match. You can make whatever arrangement you yourself would like. Contrary to what the general public is used to, it doesn't give you a clear result at the end. And it doesn't give you advice!

Turning to The Wind Will Carry Us, *one theme that interests me is a striking tension, or dialogue, between that which is physical, material, rooted in the earth, and that which is ungraspable in physical ways. This operates on a number of levels, but to choose one, we have communication within the village—where people speak to each other and give things to each other—and opposed to this we have the cell phone, which is carried on the wind, so to speak. I'm interested in your view of how the abstract or ungraspable relates to the limitations of our physical lives—to the fact that we are material, mortal beings. Is there a tension in your film between what we might call the physical and the spiritual?*

I haven't really seen the movie yet. I looked at it as a technician for a year, and I'm still too close to it in that way, so I can't really judge it. But one of my viewers told me it's about souls, about people who are gone, who don't exist—for example, the man digging the ditch, or the old woman who is dying. We don't see their lives. Just as you said, the movie does have a physical essence to it, but it also has a nonphysical or spiritual side. We don't see some characters, but we do feel them. This shows there is a possibility of being without being. That's the main theme of the movie, I think.

Being without being? Would you elaborate on that?

With this type of movie, we as viewers can create thing according to our own experiences—the things we don't see, that aren't visible. There are eleven people in this movie who are not visible. At the end you know you haven't seen them, but you feel you know who they were and what they were about. I want to create the type of cinema that shows by not showing. This is very different from most movies nowadays, which are not literally pornographic but are in essence pornographic, because they show so much that they take away any possibility of imagining things for ourselves. My aim is to give the chance to create as much as possible in our minds, through creativity and imagination. I want to tap the hidden information that's within yourself and that you probably didn't even know existed inside you. We have a saying in Persian, when somebody is looking at something with real intensity: "He had two eyes and he borrowed two more." Those two borrowed eyes are what I want to capture—the eyes that will be borrowed by the viewer to see what's outside the scene he's looking at. To see what is there and also what is not there.

*Who are some other filmmakers you feel might be working on a
similar wavelength?*

Hou Hsiao-hsien is one. Tarkovsky's works separate me
completely from physical life, and are the most spiritual films I
have seen—what Fellini did in parts of his movies, bringing dream
life into film, he does as well. Theo Angelopoulos' movies also
find this type of spirituality at certain moments. In general, I think
movies and art should take us away from daily life, should take
us to another state, even though daily life is where this flight is
launched from. This is what gives us comfort and peace. The time
for Scheherazade and the King—the storytelling time—is over.

> *THE WIND WILL CARRY US*
> by Foroogh Farrokhzaad (1935–1967)
> Translated by David Martin
>
> in my small night, what mounting regret!
> wind has a rendezvous with the trees' leaves
> in my small night, there is terror
> of desolation
> listen! do you hear
> the wind of darkness howling?
> I watch breathless
> -ly and wondrously this alien happiness
> I am addicted to my own hopelessness
> listen! listen well!
> can you hear the darkness
> howling?—the dark hell
> —wind scything
> its way towards us?
> in the night now, there is something passing
> the moon is red restless and uneasy
> and on this roof—which fears
> any moment
> it may cave in—
> clouds like crowds of mourners
> await to break in rain
> ruin
> a moment and then after that, nothing.
> behind this window, night shivers
> and the earth stands still

behind this window an unknown
something fears for me and you
O you who are green from head to toe!
put your hands
like a burning
memory into my loving hands—lover's hands!
entrust your lips—your lips
like a warm sense of being!—
entrust!—your lips to the caress of *my*
loving lips—lover's lips!
the wind will carry us with it
the wind will carry us with it

The main character of Taste of Cherry *seems to want a total escape from the physical, the material. A conventional director would make this into a psychological tale, but I don't think that's what your movie is, because we don't understand the way this man thinks any better at the end than at the beginning. So this film also seems to concern a quest to somehow get beyond the physical, even if that means having to be very negative, and it relates again to the tension between the material and the spiritual.*

Different viewers have different opinions about that movie. Committing suicide is forbidden in Islam, of course, and is not even spoken of. But some religious people have liked the film because they felt that, just as you said, it shows a quest to connect with something more heavenly, something above physical life. The scene at the end, where you see cherry blossoms and beautiful things, has that message—that he has opened the door to heaven. It wasn't a hellish thing he did, it was a heavenly transition.

Did Taste of Cherry *run into difficulties with the censors because of its subject?*

There was controversy about the movie, but after I talked with the authorities, they accepted the fact that this is not a movie about suicide—it's about the choice we have in life, to end it whenever we want. We have a door we can open at any time, but we choose to stay, and the fact that we have this choice is, I think, God's kindness. God is kind because he has given us this choice. They were satisfied with that explanation. A sentence from [a Romanian philosopher] helped me a lot: "Without the possibility of suicide,

I would have killed myself long ago." The movie is about the possibility of living, and how we have the choice to live. Life isn't forced on us. That's the main theme of the movie.

One more question. You are known for working not from a screenplay but from an outline of perhaps a few pages, and for making up much of the acting and dialogue at the last minute. What's the advantage of working this way?

On-the-spot creation of dialogue has been necessary because it's the only way I could work with people who are not professional actors, and some of the moments you see in my movies have surprised me as well as others. I don't give dialogue to the actors, but once you explain the scene to them, they just start talking, beyond what I would have imagined. It's like a cycle, and I don't know where it starts and ends: I don't know whether I'm teaching them what to say, or they're teaching me what to receive!

Time Destroys All Things: An Interview with Gaspar Noé
Quarterly Review of Film and Video 24:4 (2007)

Gaspar Noé was born in Argentina in 1963 but has lived in France since the middle seventies. He studied filmmaking in his teens, then turned to philosophy, although he recalls being a far-from-conscientious student. He entered the French film industry as an assistant director of shorts, then made his directorial debut in 1991 with the forty-minute *Carne*, about a misanthropic butcher who takes revenge on the wrong man for molesting his autistic daughter and goes to prison for it. Noé further explored these characters in his 1998 feature *Seul contre tous* (*I Stand Alone*), in which the butcher opens up a new shop in the suburbs with his mistress, then reunites with his daughter and contemplates the prospect of ending their lives in a murder-suicide.

Both films raised a critical ruckus, but the 2002 debut of *Irréversible* went farther still, reportedly inducing physical illness at the Cannes film festival and leading a normally unshockable *Village Voice* reviewer to denounce it for aiming to inflict "nausea [and] moral indignation" on its viewers. Especially controversial were the film's frequent uses of expletives directed at homosexuals and women, and a several-minute scene in which the character played by Italian actress Monica Bellucci is anally raped.

Irréversible, which tells its story in reverse chronology, consists of about thirteen long, apparently unbroken shots. The first is a brief prologue featuring the butcher who appears in both of Noé's previous films, rehashing his sordid past. The camera convulsively swoops and gyrates throughout the scene, providing only fleeting moments of clarity. The camera then plunges into the bowels of an underground gay nightclub called The Rectum, where two men—Marcus and Pierre, played by Vincent Cassel and Albert Dupontel –are determined to find and kill a male prostitute known as Le Ténia—The Tapeworm—who has raped and tortured Alex, the current girlfriend of Marcus and former lover of Pierre. Thinking they've found their quarry, Pierre smashes his skull with a fire extinguisher—only it isn't Le Ténia at all, but a hapless bystander. The camera's constant movement mirrors the chaos and violence of the situation. Moving back in time, we next see Marcus harassing a taxi driver and a transvestite hooker as he searches for The Rectum, while Pierre pleads with him not to be so violent. Moving back in time again, we see Alex walking into the dark subway underpass where she is raped and beaten. We then see the situation preceding the rape—a party, at which Marcus plays around with other girls, leading Alex to walk home by herself. Eventually a less obtrusive directorial style comes into play, and we see Marcus and Pierre as pleasant young men who joke around with Alex as the three of them head for the party. Then comes a romantic sequence in which Marcus and Alex indulge in love-play and play-fights. The film ends with Alex, newly pregnant, surrounded by children and families as she relaxes in a park. Here the camera soars free of its moorings in a different way, flying into a gyroscopic spin that turns the scene into a swirling hallucination of dizzying, delirious intensity. This gives way to a stroboscopic barrage of black-and-white frames and a printed repetition of the film's motto, first articulated by the butcher in the opening sequence: "Time destroys all things." This was the film's working title, gleaned from Ovid's *Metamorphoses*.

Critics in general dismissed the film at Cannes, and many despised it, although it was better received at the Toronto International Film Festival a few months later. I interviewed Noé at the Toronto festival in 2002, using questions provided by Mikita Brottman in addition to my own.

In Cannes, I spoke with a lot of people who were very shocked and upset by Irréversible. But here in Toronto, the people I'm talking with mostly seem to like the film very much.

Have you found anybody who actually hated the movie in Cannes and likes the movie now?

No, I don't think so, although there probably are such people. My first question is about the J. W. Dunne book, An Experiment with Time, that we see in the film.

I don't remember much about his series [of books]. I read three books by him years ago... The main thing I remember is that he would note his dreams every morning.

Yes.

And then he would find out that there were a lot of things he'd note from his dreams of the previous night that would happen during the day. The whole series said the future is already kind of written by yourself, and all the elements around you. And you have a precognition of important things that you are in contact with in your own brain, a few hours later, or a few days later–big events in your life, like deaths, accidents, and so on.

And is that central to the concept of the film? That idea of precognition?

Yes. For example, I wanted to add many more symbols to the movie, on the way to this tragedy. I thought I would put more elements that would, like, announce things that would happen later, because you know what is going to happen later. Then you would see a symbol, on a wall, or in the paper, or just people saying something. Then you would see these things happen. Because you know what's going to happen, and then you say, well, people don't even read the signs around them. That would make the whole movie much more paranoid. But on the set, finally, we didn't put in many elements of that kind. Specifically, for example, at the end of the movie when she's waking up, after having sex with her boyfriend, she says, "Oh, I had this weird dream. I was in a red tunnel and the tunnel broke," but she doesn't pay too much attention to what she had been dreaming.

And her boyfriend Marcus can't feel his arm.

Yes, he can't feel his arm. Also, some [elements in the film] were not done purposely. For example, Marcus says [to Alex in the bedroom] at one point, "I want to fuck you in the ass," and because I shot the rape scene [quite a while] after that scene, I didn't know [yet] that she would be sodomized. But just the day before the [bedroom] shot, I said, do you mind if he says, "I want to fuck you in the ass," and you say, "No, no"? Now when you see the movie and he says that at the end… it suddenly brings you back to the scene of the rape, and makes you think that also Marcus is a potential rapist, maybe. There are many elements that have resonances at other points in the movie.

Yes, absolutely. Would it be true to say that the film itself is an experiment in time, in that the reverse chronology is not just a trick, but an essential element in terms of what you're saying about cause and effect?

Yes. Someone asked me recently, "What's the difference between a drama and a tragedy?" It's that in a drama, dramatic things happen, and in a tragedy, they unfold. In a tragedy, you cannot change the events. In the way [*Irréversible*] is told, the characters cannot change their future, because you've already seen what's going to happen next. So all you can ask is, "What happened before?" But yes, there is something that is close in its structure to the writings of Dunne.

So you feel that what happens to the Irréversible *characters, in terms of cause and effect, is fixed? Are things simply fated to happen, or is there some way out?*

I think they could have escaped it. But… the way it's told, it seems that they cannot escape it, because you already know where they're going to. If you [told] the same story in a normal way, you would feel like their power of will could bring them somewhere else than where they go. But if you tell it backwards, you know where they will go.

What's your idea of fate and destiny? Do you feel we actually have freedom to control our lives?

I think we have present freedom. But you're not free from your genes. You have a genetic code that brings you to things, above anything your brain can tell you. So in a very general way, no, you're not free. You're drawn by your guts. You're not free from fighting for your survival, and the survival of the species, all the time. And seen from a softer point of view–questions like, "Should I take coffee, should I take tea? Should I take this one or should I take the other one?" Yes, you can choose, but your freedom is very limited.

Why did you then choose to tell the story in this way—backwards?

Because I thought it would be more melodramatic. And maybe because my two previous movies were very linear. When I've seen non-linear narratives—for example, [in] Tarantino or Christopher Nolan's *Memento* [2000], or other movies—I thought they were more amazing than linear narratives. Also, you experience things in a linear way, but when you reconstruct them with your mind, they're not linear anymore. Your remembrance of your own past is not linear. It's just emotions, and moments, and they're in a chronological disorder. If you want to write a diary of what you did, like, three years ago, it will take you a long time to remember in which order the events took place. You just remember faces, moments, doors, rooms.

In a way, Irréversible *is linear, though, because it's directly backwards.*

Yes. It's more conceptual, you see. It's linear, and it's not linear. There was an article in France where they said it was a Rubik's Cube. You could take it to pieces and put it together the other way. In that sense it's a bit childish, because it would have been more ambitious if it could have been made not only backwards but more going back and forth.

Maybe that would have been too much for an audience to take in?

Yes. Because it's like a game. I think after the third scene, people understand the rules of the game, and they want to play with you and try to understand it. You could do something more complex, but it's true that it would get people lost. *Mulholland Drive* [David Lynch, 2001] is more complex than my movie, from a structural point of view.

Your three films are Carne, Seul contre tous, *and this one. I'm a big admirer of* Carne, *especially. I think it's a wonderful film. And they're all very, very dark. Are you very, very dark?*

I don't think they're dark. They're very visceral, but not dark.

They are visceral, and visceral things can be joyful, but these are not joyful films, right?

They're joyful. For me, *Los Olvidados* [Luis Buñuel, 1950] is a funny movie, dealing with visceral subjects. It's a joyful movie. You can tell that the movie's joyful when there is energy on the screen. I think bitterness doesn't bring you too much energy.

Bitterness?

Yes. I have problems, for example, with Ingmar Bergman. There is something very dry and bitter in his movies that is not joyful. And I think my movies, even if they're much more violent, graphically, are much more life affirming than Bergman's movies. There are some movies by Bergman that make me want to commit suicide. [Michael] Haneke is not that funny either. They are very sentimental. Some people are very sadistic and sentimental at the same time. They're not sadistic in real life, but when it comes to directing movies, maybe it brings out their sadistic, sentimental part. Be mean, but be gentle at the same time.

Very interesting, because when I think of Seul contre tous, *for example, I certainly think of the main character as a very bitter man, but I guess at the end of the film, he kind of chooses life. Is that accurate?*

He's more of a lost dog. You know, those dogs in the street, they don't have anybody to take care of them, so you don't know if they'll end up being killed or whatever, they're just lost. And for me, the character in *Seul contre tous*, he's just a lost dog.

How do you relate to this lost dog? How does that affect how you view the character?

I could be like him, but I have many friends to take care of. I'm a dog, but I am not lost!

Back to Irréversible, *would you agree that this is an apocalyptic film? Do these characters represent "the way things are"—in society, in France, maybe in human life itself? Is this film a metaphor for the human condition?*

The movie's not that ambitious. It's not *2001: A Space Odyssey* [Stanley Kubrick, 1968]. It's more obsessing about someone you love, losing someone you love, and reproducing yourself with someone you love. It's much more unpretentious than that. All the structure is funny, the camerawork is full of energy, but it's more about losing someone you love. And that was already the subject of *Carne*. I mean, in *Carne*, the father thinks that his daughter gets raped by someone, and then [seeking revenge] he stabs the wrong person. So it's quite close to this movie, but the structure is just the opposite. I am very sentimental, and you can see that.

So you see this, then, as a very personal, intimate kind of film?

Yes. It's an intimate film.

How did you shoot the movie in terms of chronology?

I shot it in chronological order. Not completely–for example, we didn't shoot the park scene at the very beginning of the movie. We shot the apartment scene first, then the park scene, then the next Monday we shot the subway scene, then the party scene. But we shot them in chronological order apart from one or two scenes. The last week was the gay bar, and the opening scenes were shot at the beginning.

And was the film very tightly scripted, or storyboarded?

No, no, no storyboard. I did the camera, so we were improvising with the camera. We improvised with everything—the dialogue, the camerawork, all that on the set. The whole script when we started shooting the movie was three or four pages long.

How did the movie come about?

It was financed on the names of Monica Bellucci, Vincent Cassell, and mine. We all had six weeks to prepare the shooting, and then we were shooting, and I knew I wouldn't have time to write the dialogue, so we just did the best lines that came on the set. I don't know if they're the best lines, but they're very realistic. They make sense, not because they're deep, but because they come out in a natural way. We would shoot a scene two times, three times, up to twenty times, and usually we would keep one of the last takes, because the first ones were a lot shorter, and the best ideas came when we were shooting. People would make comments–the assistant director, the camera assistant, the actors—like, "Oh yeah, that part was good, you should do that again." We had two or three days for each scene. There is nothing really interesting that is said, but the way things unfold is interesting. It's not a very verbal movie. *Seul contre tous* was a very verbal movie. You could cut the images and just listen to the soundtrack, like a radio show, and you'd get the whole movie. In this case it's the opposite. You could turn off the sound and just watch the images.

How many scenes are there?

I think the whole movie has maybe thirteen scenes.

It was a fairly quick shoot, then. You didn't take a long time.

Five weeks and a half.

And in terms of editing, once all the scenes were shot? Was it just a question of splicing them?

Yes, it was a question of choosing the best take. Also, we did a lot of digital post-production. Some takes are actually made of two takes, and we made a morphing in the middle to go from one take to another. For example, the scene in the gay club–that looks like one take, but it's made of maybe thirty different pieces. There's a lot of dark, and you can cut in the dark, and make a match with another take.

Was this how you did the head being broken?

Yes, that was a lot of work. The guy who was responsible for it took care personally of that special effect. He was working with that for something like three months. It was a mix of many things– many different takes, some with a dummy, some with a real actor... it's a mix of many different techniques.

It's extraordinarily successful.

We had as a reference a documentary of a guy who was executed in Lebanon. They shoot the guy, and the rifle destroys just half of his face, and the other part of his face keeps screaming for something like a minute. So he's a person with half of his head missing, and still screaming. And when I saw it, I was really... I felt like vomiting, because, you know, in movies, people get killed very quickly. But here you see so much suffering, for a whole minute, and he's screaming, and he knows he's going to die, and he cannot die because his brains keep on working. And that really shook me, so I said, "Well, if we show these crimes in this movie, let's do it in a way that would be closer to that documentary, and not to what we usually see in a fiction movie."

I assume the rape scene was one continuous take?

No, there is one cut. When she comes out from the party, we follow her, and she goes into the tunnel, and there is one cut there. It's when the camera goes to the [sign over the tunnel reading] "passage" and comes back. It's like in the beginning of *Snake Eyes* by Brian De Palma [1998], where there are many invisible cuts. There's one invisible cut there, and then we go to another take, where she gets raped.

And the rape itself is all one continuous take.

But still there are some special effects in that scene. For example, when the rapist comes out, you can see for five seconds his erect penis. That was added in post-production, because [the actor's] zipper was closed. We added the penis, with some blood. So it looks much more realistic, and people were thinking, when they saw the movie, maybe they were having sex during the whole scene, and how could Monica take it? But no, we added that, and also we added some blood on her face at the end of the scene.

It's all completely convincing. But it gets us back to the darkness of the film. I'm curious about two things that are related—your motivation in making the scene so incredibly difficult to watch, and whether you were concerned that this might simply send people out of the theater.

I didn't think it was bound to send people out of the theater. In fact, in France, one person out of ten did walk out, and still the movie was a commercial success. Word of mouth was very positive—even from people who were coming out saying, "I can't take it, it was too violent," because that would excite other people to see it. But no, you don't do a movie to make people walk out. You just say, "I want to do the violent scenes really violent." That's the only useful way to do it. I walked out when I saw *Straw Dogs* [Sam Peckinpah, 1971] when I was seventeen, and still, I think it's a great movie. I saw it again on DVD later on, but I know that the day I first saw it, I walked out during the rape scene. And I almost walked out the first time I saw *The Texas Chain Saw Massacre* [Tobe Hooper, 1974]. It's just that you get scared. If you see people walking out—some people even fainted in Cannes at my movie, in the film festival—I don't think it's bad that they feel this way. As long as people know what they're going to see, they get prepared.

I'd still like to hear more about why you made the rape scene that incredibly brutal—so long, so close, so anal. It's a painful scene!

That's the thing. I could not think of doing a rape scene that would not be painful. Otherwise, you're not [thinking about] what you're shooting, what you're representing. The thing is, you really are emotionally linked to the victim, and not the rapist. In many movies, you get linked to the rapist, because it's shot from a subjective point of view, the guy coming at the girl with a knife, and so on. But in this case, it's evident that you are linked to the victim, and not for one second to the aggressor.

Let's move to a different subject. You're from Argentina originally?

I was born there, yes.

And when did you come to France?

When I was twelve. Because my father had to run away from the country, for political reasons.

How did you get involved with filmmaking?

When I was seventeen, I went to a film school, which was a very good one. I finished there when I was nineteen. I was supposed to start working, but I was too young. So just to avoid working, I started studying philosophy, but I was not a very serious student, so I would never go to the lectures or anything like that. Then I started working as assistant director on some shorts and things like that.

Why did you want to become a filmmaker? Had you always wanted to be an artist?

No, no, no, no. I don't think if you're making things you're doing art. If you're making, you're making. If you enjoy doing it, it's a lot of fun. It's a lot of pressure, it's a lot of suffering if you don't get the financing and you get lots of debts. But still, you're working with a team of people, and you can choose the people you work with, and it's very exciting. It can be art as many things are—as creating furniture is doing art, and even politics is doing art. You're inventing, or reinventing, a lot of things. But sometimes the word "art" is very pretentious. When people claim they are artists, usually it's because they are not.

But you did want to do some kind of creative work?

Yes. But many things are creative. Maybe the scientist is much more creative in what he's making.

It doesn't have to be a contest. [laughs]

[*laughs*] But I don't like the word "artist" because people say, "Oh, I'm a poet," like people say, "I'm crazy." If someone comes to you and says, "I'm a crazy guy," don't believe him. He may be just the most square person in the world pretending to be crazy.

Well, your own films to date are obviously from a very distinctive personality—that is, they're not the kinds of films other people make.

I saw one movie this year that I really thought—well, it was not close to mine, but there was some energy in it, so I really feel sort of linked to it. That is *City of God* [Fernando Meirelles, 2002], a Brazilian movie. It's so well shot. When I saw it, I thought this is a movie and a script that I would have liked to shoot myself. Maybe there would be some differences—for example, there was a rape scene that he shot, and then he cut it, and so there was not any reason to really show that rape. In my case I would say no, if you shoot the rape, you show it. But still, it's maybe the movie this year that I come the closest to. Some people complain that it was a bit of a pop video, and I don't think so at all. It's full of visual ideas, but it's not a pop video… I think there are a lot of people who hate things that are too visual. Also, in my case some people say, "The filmmaking is pretentious because you move your camera and use cranes." Why not? Should you always put the camera on the same level and shoot flat?

How did you do the camerawork for Irréversible, by the way?

Hand-held camera.

Do you go to the movies a lot?

Not when I'm shooting. The rest of the time, yes, I will see a lot of movies. But when you're shooting a movie you just sort of forget about it.

When you go to films, what do you like to see?

I liked *Mulholland Drive*. I liked *City of God*. There's one movie I discovered lately that I love. It's an old movie called *The Thief* [Russell Rouse, 1952], with Ray Milland playing a Russian spy, who's stealing documents for the Russian government. It's made in the fifties, and the whole movie's silent. There's not one sentence in the whole movie.

Oh, I have seen that, yes. There's sound, but no dialogue.

Yes. And it's great, it's really scary. It's one of the best suspense films I've ever seen. From time to time, you discover these old movies you haven't seen. Like *I Am Cuba* [*Soy Cuba/Ya Kuba*, Mikheil Kalatozishvili, 1964], that's another.

Yes, I agree.

Maybe that was my main inspiration for this film.

Really? I Am Cuba?

Yes.

It is a very visual film. And in ways, a very non-linear film.

Yes. I mean, dialogues don't come that much, it's more how the face is represented, and so on...

And yet you said earlier that Seul contre tous *is a film which is very verbal. It has a visual element, but...*

It's a sort of radiophonic movie.

Yes, yes. So do you see yourself moving much more in a visual direction now, or...

Not so much. I just didn't want to try the same movie. As soon as you go far one way, you say, "Let's go another way." Still, there are a lot of similarities between *Irréversible* and *Seul contre tous*. But I suppose the next movie is going to be even less talkative than this one.

Can you tell me a bit about that?

I'll just say that it's experimental, and hallucinogenic.

Does it have a title?

Yes, but I'd rather not speak about a movie that might come out in two years.

Okay. Can you see yourself making a comedy?

Sure. But I think I would rather do a black-humored comedy. Still, I think *Irréversible* is funny.

There's some funny stuff in it.

I think Seul contre tous *is funny. It's black humor. I was thinking one day of doing a kids' movie.*

Really?

An Andersen tale, or something.

Why?

Because I think there's a big audience in it. You're much less rational when you're a kid, and I think if you respect kids for what they are—future adults—sometimes I think they're more intelligent than adult people. Your vision of life might be much more square when you're forty, fifty than when you're six, because [young people are] just drinking, drinking, drinking all this energy. For example, *2001: A Space Odyssey* was much more popular with kids than with older people. I remember, I saw it when I was six, and it was just like, it was giving me an ecstasy trip. I felt like, "Well, bloody hell, what is all this? What does it represent? I don't understand!" But I noticed that I liked the movie much more than my parents, although I was six years old. I think I will go at least once in my life for a general-audience movie.

You've mentioned filmmakers like Kubrick and David Lynch and Buñuel. Do your tastes tend to run toward art films, toward more serious kinds of personal cinema, or do you enjoy Hollywood movies as well?

2001 is a Hollywood movie.

Yes, but a very peculiar one.

Yes, yes. [I like] those kinds of movies. But Hollywood scripts are getting worse and worse. *The Matrix* [Andy Wachowski, Larry Wachowski, 1999] is an ambitious script inside the Hollywood system. But besides *The Matrix*...

Do you tend to think a lot in visual terms? I know you said you studied philosophy for a while, even though it wasn't seriously. Do you think of yourself as a verbally oriented person as well, or do you think that your imagination works in pictures?

Well, I think I'm much more visual than verbal... I'm not a drug addict but I'm addicted to rushes. I feel like every two weeks I have to be afraid of something, to motivate me.

To be afraid of something?

Yes. I like it when things get out of control, when I'm out of control, when I don't control things. For example, doing a movie, when you're shooting, and you say, "Well, improvise the dialogue," you're not controlling things. You've put yourself in a position where you're just guiding people, you're not controlling them. Some people are control freaks. I'm not a control freak at all. I like to put my brains in a closet and see what happens in front of my eyes. I love going to roller coasters and things like this, with people screaming. From time to time you just need to have a big rush of fear, like jumping with a parachute... I like the idea of putting yourself in a position where you might die. When you're dead, your fear of death is over, so you start laughing.

You said earlier that Irréversible *did well in French theaters.*

It did very well.

Was it well received by critics?

Not so much the critics. But it's weird, because it was shown in competition at Cannes, and the president of the Cannes film festival didn't want us to show it to the daily press before we had shown it to some big magazines. And so a lot of journalists were hating the movie because they were not invited to see it. And when it came to their turn that they should talk about the movie, I had 100 percent of the daily press against it. It's weird, because a lot of cheap, popular magazines were raving about it. So the people [whose reviews] came out [just as it opened] were hating it because they were not invited to the party before. It was funny, because when the movie opened—the day following the official screening—all the newspapers were saying, "Oh, this is a piece of crap," and you could not take them seriously. It was not a real point of view on the movie.

That's an embarrassing thing about some film reviewers. But have you read articles about any of your movies that you've felt were smart, and that maybe you've been interested in?

Sometimes. The review can be good or bad, but sometimes they put their finger on things that are really interesting. It's funny, there was one good review of the movie, and the guy was saying it was a Christian movie. I never had any religious background in my life, I never went to church, whatever. I couldn't take it as a positive thing… to say it's a Christian movie. I said, "No, no, it's not a Christian movie!"

That reminds me of another question. I mentioned the other day [after a screening of Irréversible *at Toronto] that when I saw your movie at Cannes, it ended with the words "Time Destroys All Things" on the screen. The words weren't there at the end of the print shown here, and you seemed surprised that they had been removed.*

I just found out that [the words] hadn't been removed, but the projectionist just stopped the movie. The screen is black for eight seconds, and then you have this title afterwards. Maybe he just saw a black screen and thought the movie was over, so he stopped it. But at the beginning [of the production] the first title I had for the movie was "Le Temps Detruit Tous," which is a famous sentence of Ovidius, this Latin author, from the *Metamorphoses*. I thought it would be a good title for the movie, but then I found *Irréversible*, which sounded better. Still, at the beginning the butcher from *Seul contre tous* [who appears as a character in *Irréversible*] says, "Time destroys all things." So I'm not really sure you need it again. So yesterday, when they cut the film before the title card came up, I thought, "Well, it's okay without it."

"Time destroys all things" sounds like a very negative statement, a very pessimistic statement. Still, what happens in your film is that we start with all this horror, but at the end of the movie's running time, in the last scene, everything's light and pleasant and happy. So in a way, time has destroyed the ugliness we see at the beginning of the film. It reminded me of Dante. The Divine Comedy *starts off in hell, but ends up in heaven.*

Also, you have an architecture in *Metropolis* [Fritz Lang, 1927] kind of close to the one in my movie. There you have the gutters of the city with the poor people fighting in an underground world [against privileged people living above]. And the people in [*Irréversible*] live in the top of a building, and they seem quite rich, or maybe they have money from a rich family. Alex seems to be living a little bit on her money. Also, the rapist is a bit of a visionary—he says, "Who do you think you are, you rich bitch, because you're rich you have everything." So there's a little bit of rich and poor, up and down, light and dark.

Like Metropolis *and other films. So, in a way, it is a film that has social commentary built into it.*

Not really, because it's so binary that I couldn't say it's a commentary. It's just that there's joy and there's danger. If you value something, you have to protect it, because things can happen to you. Unless you have a bodyguard!

And then you have to worry about the bodyguard. Do you feel that way? You say you like to let control go, but you don't seem to be a fearful person.

No, no, I'm not fearful, but there are some situations that I wouldn't put myself into... I don't do illegal things, although I appreciate it when other people do them!

The Music Man: Ennio Morricone

Moviemaker, October 15, 2007 (updated January 31, 2023)

When you interview Ennio Morricone, the first thing you learn is what to call him. Do as the Romans do—he's Maestro Morricone to just about everyone, although you can take a chance on just Maestro once he's at ease with you.

If anyone deserves that honorific, Morricone does. The list of moviemakers he has worked with reads like a who's who of world cinema: Pier Paolo Pasolini, Elio Petri and Bernardo Bertolucci in Italy; Pedro Almódovar, Roman Polanski and Jerzy Kawalero-wicz elsewhere in Europe; and Americans from Mike Nichols and Warren Beatty to Oliver Stone and Barry Levinson.

As for sheer diversity, the Maestro is unsurpassed. He has scored horror films for Dario Argento and John Boorman, science-fiction for Brian De Palma and John Carpenter, action-adventure for Don Siegel, comedy for Edouard Molinaro and Shakespeare for Franco Zeffirelli—not to mention genre-benders for Liliana Cavani and Samuel Fuller.

He's garnered five Academy Award nominations over the past 30 years—for Terrence Malick's *Days of Heaven* (1978), Roland Joffé's *The Mission (1986)*, De Palma's *The Untouchables* (1987), Levinson's *Bugsy* (1991) and Giuseppe Tornatore's *Malèna* (2000). Like such overlooked luminaries as Alfred Hitchcock and Howard Hawks, he never got to take an Oscar home. But earlier this year the Academy made amends, giving him an honorary statuette for "magnificent and multifaceted contributions to the art of film music."

To say the least, the Maestro is... well, the word "prolific" doesn't quite describe his prodigious output since he earned his first screen credit with the comedy *Il Federale* in 1961. One source lists no fewer than 480 titles, not counting two—Tornatore's war epic *Leningrad* and De Palma's prequel *The Untouchables: Capone Rising*—that the 79-year-old composer is preparing for next year.

Born in Rome, where he still lives and works, Morricone studied composition before becoming an arranger for studio recordings by the likes of Chet Baker, Charles Aznavour and Paul Anka. When he began scoring films in the early 1960s he was already a seasoned music producer, composer and conductor. He made his movie score breakthrough with the legendary *Dollars* trilogy by his compatriot Sergio Leone, starring Clint Eastwood as "The Man With No Name." It's ironic that Eastwood's laconic gunslinger actually has a name in each of the installments—the no-name label was a PR gimmick—while Leone and others appeared in the credits of the first picture, *A Fistful of Dollars* (1964), under pseudonyms designed to hide the movie's Italian origins from Italian audiences who'd grown tired of viewing westerns made in their own country. Morricone thus released his first important score under the unassuming moniker of Dan Savio, although he reclaimed his own name in the follow-up films, *For a Few Dollars More* (1965) and *The Good, the Bad and the Ugly* (1966).

The trilogy reached American screens in 1967, building an instant fan base for the Maestro, whose soundtrack albums were bestsellers. While his earlier scores had been fairly conventional, Leone let him draw on his pop music experience for effects that were new to the western genre. The timbres and textures of his scores—fleshed out with ocarina, chimes, whistling, twangy electric guitar, electronically altered voices and other offbeat sounds—gives them a unique, immediately recognizable flavor.

Along with his extraordinary film career, Morricone remains an active composer of classical music, where he expresses his keenly progressive (and often avant-garde) sensibility in pure, uncompromising ways. There are few areas of contemporary music that the Maestro's talent hasn't touched, and interviewing him was an uncommon pleasure. His answers, made through an interpreter, were direct and to the point, sharing the no-nonsense practicality that has facilitated his creative work for almost half a century. I suspect he was itching to leave the interview chair and get back to his latest score.

I'm curious about how you work with directors. Do you see a cut of the film before starting on the music?

There's no rule about what comes first. It could be anything. The director may decide to call after the film is edited or before he's started to shoot it. If the movie hasn't been shot yet, we can talk and the director can explain what kind of movie it will be and what the images will be like. If not, I may be able to read the screenplay and discuss it with the director before starting the score.

Are some directors unable to discuss music articulately?

That happened to me just recently—a director told me he didn't know how to say what he wanted. In a case like this the composer has to work on his own, which is a huge responsibility.

If a director is musically literate, is there more danger that a clash of wills might develop between the two of you?

That has happened to me, and at those times I bowed out of the project. Almost for sure, when a director asks for something special, it's because he has a memory of some music he's heard before and he doesn't have the musical creativity to understand what [new musical ideas] we could use... The director certainly has the right to express his own ideas for his own movie, but we have to reach an agreement. If that isn't possible—if I have to be the slave of somebody else's ideas—I prefer to just walk away.

How much of your composing is inspired by the subject and mood of the film, and how much by the musical ideas that interest you at the moment?

Both are important. The story is important, the acting is important, the psychology of the characters is important and so forth. But if the director and composer are good ones, the composer can respect the story and characters and still put his own style into the music.

Do you have a favorite movie genre for which to compose?

My favorite music is the absolute music I compose for concerts, outside the cinema industry. In cinema, I have fun doing all of them.

Do you ever feel a sense of "culture shock" when jumping from one genre or director to a very different one?

It isn't a problem. The important thing is that I take into account the different places or cultures where different films are made— what the society and music there are like. When a director in Japan asked me to do a film, I said, "I can do the film for you, but I can't do Japanese music. That's not me. I can do my music." The director said that was fine.

I take it that you do research for some of your scores then.

Certainly. An example is when I did *The Mission*. I had to learn the kind of music that was being played and studied in South America in 1750. This was very important because that particular movie had so many elements—the different instruments, what the missionaries were teaching the Indians and so forth—and it was necessary for me to examine all of this. Sometimes a film requires that.

When composing for movies, is it ever frustrating not to have firm control over how your music will be used in the film?

That can be frustrating, I have to admit. But sometimes when a director moves a piece of music from one part of the film to another, it can prove to be very [effective] and well done. So sometimes it's a nice surprise for me!

How much control do you have over the CD recordings of your scores?

One hundred percent.

In the movie Amadeus, the emperor criticizes Mozart for writing "too many notes" in a piece he's just heard. Nobody would accuse you of that, but you are amazingly prolific. What's the average amount of time it takes to write a score?

If my mind is clear and I know what I've got to do, I can write a score in two weeks... If my mind isn't clear and I don't have a good idea of what I have to do, I can't predict how long it will take.

I'm sure you have opportunities for many more projects than you have time to do. How do you choose which projects to accept?

The first consideration is how much time I have available. The second is how much I like the director, and I must also be interested in the story. But in some cases I just say yes because I want to; it's a leap of faith and I go with it.

You compose your music in the most thorough possible way, right down to writing out the orchestrations. Why not take advantage of assistants to do the more mechanical parts of the job?

For me, those who don't do their own orchestrations aren't real artists; they're half-composers.

I suppose that's one of the things that allows you to create such distinctive music—one knows "this is a Morricone score."

I can only say that it's my music because it comes from me. Everything affects this—the ideas I have for the score, the orchestrations, the counterpoint, the simplicity or complexity of the chords and other things. All of these together are what make my style… and the one thing I never do is deny my own style because of what the director wants. I always put my own personality into whatever I do. I couldn't do anything else.

Ever since Max Steiner in the early days of sound film, most composers have used some kind of leitmotif system—associating a particular theme with each important character or story element—to help the audience follow the narrative. Your music seems to rely more on timbres and textures than on conventional melodies.

Yes, but everything is useful, including leitmotifs, because they help the audience.

Music usually supports the mood or action of a scene, but sometimes your music creates a contrast or counterpoint to the words and images. What's the purpose of this?

It serves to underline the psychology of the actor and the character instead of just following the action. You can't do this all the time, but you can do it once or twice in a movie. It's usually something the composer suggests, not something the director thinks of. If the director doesn't accept it, you have to do something else.

Glenn Gould once said that horror movie music would get people so accustomed to dissonance that they'd become more receptive to atonal music as a result. Based on your experience, can music heard in films unconsciously affect the kinds of music that people will be able to accept and enjoy?

Of course! That kind of music can only be used for certain kinds of scenes, but I sometimes compose very strong avant-garde music for scenes where it's appropriate, and getting audiences to accept this kind of music is my goal. I wouldn't do it otherwise.

Do you watch your movies with audiences to see how they react? Do you care about what critics say?

Of course. I'm very interested in what audiences and critics think about my music.

Do their responses affect what you do in later scores?

Not at all!

There's an excellent book, Unheard Melodies, *which says that the audience should be emotionally affected by the music without being consciously aware of it. Do you agree?*

I say that when there is music in a scene, the rest of the film shouldn't interfere with it!

Ralph Bunche, An American Odyssey
An Interview with William Greaves
williamgreaves.com

This is a splendid piece of work. It's extraordinarily clear and compelling and dramatic in its presentation of an enormous amount of factual material and historical material, which can easily become non-compelling and non-dramatic.

Oh, that's a big problem for a documentary filmmaker.

But this is engrossing, beautifully put together, the variety of visual materials. I think it's one of the rare cases where a documentary — or a nonfiction film, if you prefer — manages to combine a really powerful presentation of material with an appealing and engrossing approach so that it's actually fun to watch. It's an entertaining movie, but at the same time, it's a very serious and informative movie.

That's what we were hoping to accomplish. We knew the viewer had to become involved viscerally as well as intellectually, in the content. However, in this case, the problem was compounded by the fact that we were doing a film about a scholar, a diplomat who thinks and speaks in abstract terms, and film, needless to say, is a visual medium. Moreover, viewers are programmed — conditioned — to think of film in entertainment terms. So it was a real challenge.

How did this project get started? Why Ralph Bunche?

In part it was sheer serendipity. I was jogging in Central Park one day and just happened to run into Lloyd Garrison, an old friend of mine who was working at the Ford Foundation. We stopped and chatted, and in the course of our conversation he said, "Do you know anything about Bunche?" I said, "Not as much as I should but I've always been very interested in him." And he said, "Well, if you are really interested, you might want to pitch the idea of doing a film about him to Ford. They seem to be interested in him." Well, I also found out that Brian Urquhart had an office at the Foundation and he had just finished writing a biography of Ralph Bunche. So I pitched the idea of doing a film based on Sir Brian's book. The Ford Foundation went for it and that's how it got started. But even though I'd always been intrigued by Bunche I didn't know very much about him. I mean he had been world-renowned, but who was he really? How could a Black man, in pre-civil rights America, attain this level of prominence? And then somehow be forgotten. He was a mystery. He seemed to have functioned, in a sense, "behind the veil." As a diplomat and international civil servant at the UN, certainly, he became the consummate insider. He didn't always show his hand and, of course, that's what made him so effective. But how do you do a film about this kind of inscrutability, about a reality that is largely subtextual? What's going on between the lines? This really fascinated me about Bunche. And, as we got deeper and deeper into his story, we realized that he was moving with remarkable assurance in the direction that he wanted to go, apparently without anyone being aware of it.

Is there any particular phase of his life or career that was your entry point, that you thought was the most fascinating part for you? I mean, he was a scholar, he was a diplomat. His work with the United Nations was hugely important. Near the end of his life he was a civil rights activist and so forth. Obviously, they're all important, and obviously you deal with all those. Was there any one that was the entry point for you, that was the quintessential Ralph Bunche?

I suppose I'd have to say that it was the whole anti-colonialist, anti-imperialist, anti-fascist thrust of his life that was the trigger for me. It's true a lot of people struggle against these forces, but from the outside. They march, protest, sign petitions. All this is well and good. It helps to marshal public opinion, but public opinion usually doesn't have much impact on those who are inside the citadels of power. Sure, once in a while there's a French Revolution, or an American Revolution, but holding up placards and handing out leaflets rarely alters the course of world history or changes the biography of a country. Bunche took another approach. He understood how power worked and how self-interested it was, and found ways to negotiate that kind of terrain. He went inside the citadels of power. That I found fascinating, that he could have the audacity—the chutzpah—to move into this area and see what he could do to effect change, to nudge and prod things along a path of social, political and international progress. So that was very interesting to me. Also, I have to admit, I connected with the fact that he was a high achiever both academically and in sports, and that he overcame so many barriers, racial, social and economic. He succeeded against the odds. You have to say he had a competitive personality and he seems to have gotten it from his family. Like Bunche, I was brought up in a family that valued competition and excellence, so I guess I identified with this aspect of his personality. As a kid in Harlem I loved sports, boxed at the Y, played basketball, competed in track and won medals in all three. Went to Stuyvesant High School, the most competitive high school in New York City, where I was in the top 10 percent of my class, and then went on to win featured roles in Broadway hits and in movies, auditioned for the Actors Studio and was admitted as a member. Psychoanalytically speaking, I suppose it's a neurotic need to succeed. But there was a certain resonance between my background and Bunche's except, of course, he's Ralph Bunche, and I'm poor old Bill Greaves. [*laughs*]

Pretty important, too, just a different field.

Well, somehow this resonated with me. However, even though I admired his commitment to excellence, I was even more impressed with his concern for humanity. Bunche combined intellect and idealism with action. Very rare combination. He had a tremendous sense of responsibility and a need to be of service to others. I mean, it was a very strong thing with him, and my feeling was that a film about this kind of social consciousness might serve as a road map, a manual for other gifted and talented individuals to do more, not only for themselves but for society. The premise, of course, is that in working for others you're ultimately helping yourself, which, I think, Bunche understood very clearly. So it was my hope that the film could be—I don't want to say educational—but a motivator—especially for young people, and if it achieves that, that would be just great. There are many, many talented young people out there but the big question is will they use their knowledge, intelligence, and creativity to help raise human consciousness and work for the improvement of the human race?

Something else that really fascinated me in the film—and I'm just wondering about your observations on this, as perhaps our leading authority on Bunche, or one of our leading authorities on Bunche, and as a filmmaker who had to assemble the movie—the fascinating interaction between the man who is Ralph Bunche, with his extraordinary talents and abilities and motivations, and the huge historical forces that he's operating within. How do you go about capturing the interaction between the individual and this huge, complicated midcentury world situation, which is his field of operations?

Well, you put your finger on the crux of the problem. How do you get a symbiosis or a dialectic going between Bunche and the sprawling world scene? We wrestled with that a great deal, and the trick, of course, was to find the underlying connecting links. This was the bridge—the glue—that would connect the individual to the historical events and them to him. Of course, we had to stay focused on those events in which Bunche was involved, be it philosophically or politically or psychologically, or hopefully, all three. But even within this framework, we still had to let go of a lot of important stuff. For example, we don't deal with the atomic bomb, which affected not only Bunche's thinking but was a major factor in the postwar world. Time was a constraint, too, I should add. Actually, when we started out doing the research, and we began to discover more and more about Bunche, it gradually dawned on us that we had underestimated this man's importance. Here's a story that's never been told and there's a huge historical canvas, and it's very relevant for the 21st century. We realized this material deserved a more extensive, in-depth treatment. It cried out for a series treatment. In fact, we wondered how we could do justice to Bunche, even in a six-hour series. But there were problems getting the completion funding for such a series so, in the end, we had to cut it to two hours in order to finish it and get it on television as a PBS prime-time special. But for a long time we just kept trying to complete it as a series.

We were lucky that the funders all stood by us as we wrestled with the material, trying to get it down to a shorter length, once we realized that we weren't going to get the funding to put it on television as a six-part series. In the final analysis, the film was put through several completely different versions, a six-hour rough cut, a four-hour [cut], and a three-hour fine cut. But getting the story down to two hours was brutal. The interesting thing is that the film works very well at this length! Which proves, I guess, that there's probably a creative solution for every problem, if you work at it hard and long enough. And I have to admit that the two-hour version gets to the essence of Bunche. Once in a while we get a complaint that a piece of the story is missing. But most audiences are amazed at the amount of information we did manage to convey. On the other hand, we know what was left on the cutting-room floor and we are planning to finish the four-hour version, assuming we can get the completion funds for it. It will tell the Bunche story in greater depth because it will include some very important material that doesn't appear in the current version at all. For example, it will not only include the atomic bomb but will show Bunche's role in the setting up of the International Atomic Energy Agency, which attempts to find peaceful, rather than destructive, uses for atomic energy. It will look at the Vietnam War, Bunche's role in the passage of Eleanor Roosevelt's Universal Declaration of Human Rights, his immense contribution to the [Gunnar] Myrdal study of the ugliness of racism in America and its destructive impact on Black America which resulted in the landmark book *An American Dilemma*. I don't know if I've answered your—

You have. You certainly have. What do you think ultimately was Bunche's most important contribution? It's a little different from what I asked before about what the entry point was for you.

Well, he is probably best known for his successful negotiation of four armistice agreements between Israel and her Arab neighbors, the thing that got him the Nobel Peace Prize in 1950. This was a milestone for the United Nations and, as a result, Bunche came to personify the spirit of the United Nations and the aspirations of all people for a peaceful world. In his Mount Tremblant, Quebec, speech he talked about the right of all people, irrespective of caste, class, religion or race, to "walk with dignity along the world's great boulevards." He came to be called "Mr. UN" because he worked consistently and effectively to empower the United Nations and advance its mission in the world. The most important contribution was probably the key role he played which helped to facilitate the peaceful transition of much of the colonized world into politically independent states. As the Director of the UN Trusteeship Division, he set up the procedures that helped to make this possible and, even before that, he was instrumental in drafting the chapters of the UN Charter that laid out the basic principles of self-determination of all peoples. That document formed the legal groundwork for the decolonization of more than one-third of the world. He is also considered to be the father of UN peacekeeping, because of the principles and techniques he pioneered in peacekeeping and in conflict resolution and peacemaking are still in use today by the United Nations and other international groups.

    If I can add one more major contribution made by Bunche, it would be the fact that, in facilitating the emergence of the developing world as players in the international scene, and infusing some of the principles of the American Bill of Rights and the Declaration of Independence into the UN Charter, he helped to create a climate worldwide which was sympathetic to the American Civil Rights movement and permitted leaders like Malcolm X, Stokely Carmichael, Martin Luther King, Fannie Lou Hamer and others to function with a degree of impunity. This international pressure, with the eyes of the world focused on what was going on in America and its widespread racism, meant that civil rights could no longer be ignored by the federal government. America had to show the world, and especially the newly independent nations of the third world, that it was a reasonably democratic nation, one that they could deal with when they started talking trade with these nations. So this pressure certainly encouraged America to live up to its stated creed. I hope I've said enough.

To switch gears a bit, how does one go about planning, organizing a production like this, not just in logistical terms, but in conceptual terms— "We're going to communicate so and so... and at the end of this whole process we're going to have a film which conveys this information." How does one go about planning and organizing all this?

Well, it's a daunting task. One resigns oneself to very hard work. It's all uphill. From start to finish. The research alone was an immense job. Fortunately, Sir Brian Urquhart's new biography on Bunche was invaluable. I don't see how we could have handled such complex political, diplomatic and historical material without this extraordinarily well-documented book and, of course, access to Urquhart himself, who was our chief advisor on the project, for crucial advice. In addition, we had a great team of scholars who met with us in person and went over the script with a fine-tooth comb. But no matter how much work goes into the scripting phase, and this is especially true of a documentary, it's just a guide. I call it a bible. At best, we hoped to find a throughline, a basic theme or premise for the film. Frankly, a documentary film is put together in the editing room. That's the real world. After all is said and done, what audiovisual materials do we actually have to work with? What archival footage, photos, newspaper clippings, maps did we find? How did the various interviews turn out? What's the photographic quality of these various elements? There's an infinite number of variables, permutations and combinations of images and sounds that you can use or not use. So you experiment and look for the most creative solutions. But in the final analysis—this is my personal experience—having tried various alternatives and reflected on the results, agonized over them and lost a considerable amount of sleep trying to solve what in effect are a series of differential cinematic equations, one has to pull back, relax, take a deep breath, and just go with your intuition. You know what I mean? Forget the intellectualizing—does this montage go with that sequence, or do we cut from here to there? Put Eisenstein and his excellent theories of film montage aside. You have all the information you need stored in your brain. How do you feel about it? Where are the mountain peaks? What is really paramount here? Which shots affect you on a visceral level? For example, the shot of Bunche's grandmother, a very proper-looking lady, standing with her coat and hat on. Then we cut to the long shot of Bunche, a teenager holding a basketball, and he's annoyed about being discriminated against in a scholastic contest. You know, he's on the verge of quitting school and his friends are waiting for him on the basketball court. But his grandmother stands there and you know she wants him to go back to school. And she stops him in his tracks. I mean, that's the metaphor that I'm using for this sequence. The right visual metaphor will help you understand what's happening on a subtextual level. So here is Bunche with this basketball, and there is Nana standing there—this is Eisenstein here—and intercutting between these images, the confrontation between the two of them is intense. That moment in the Bunche story of his grandmother stopping him from quitting school moved me tremendously, and I said, "If I can set up the action and the events that lead up to this encounter, it could be quite dramatic, powerful." We were able to arrange the sequences that immediately preceded it in such a way that you are really depressed that this talented kid is going to give up his studies, but then you see this determined, wise woman who stands in his path.

William Greaves produced, wrote, and directed Ralph Bunche: An American Odyssey.

An Interview with Andrew Sarris
Quarterly Review of Film and Video 30:1 (1995)

Andrew Sarris, who died in New York on June 20, 2012, at eighty-three years old, was easily the most influential film critic—on other critics, if not on the public at large—of the past half-century. His primary berths were the *Village Voice*, where his protégés included J. Hoberman and Tom Allen, and later the *New York Observer*, where he shared movie-reviewing chores with Rex Reed, a very different critic but a cinephile all the same. At both publications Sarris evaluated new releases and old favorites with a blend of auteur-oriented analysis and personal commentary that sometimes bordered on the confessional. He also wrote several books, including *The American Cinema: Directors and Directions 1929–1968*, which remains an indispensable guide to midcentury Hollywood film and to the theory and practice of auteur criticism, which Sarris singlehandedly imported from France in the early 1960s, turning the *politique des auteurs* devised by future members of the French New Wave into a valuable tool for assessing and organizing films and filmmakers on the basis of directorial style.

Sarris' contemporary and occasional sparring partner, Pauline Kael of *The New Yorker*, had a flashier prose style and a more ironbound following; her famous Paulettes were a gaggle of strategically positioned reviewers whom she often led on critical crusades, especially during yearend award seasons. Sarris was more doggedly individualistic, and he certainly made a more lasting impact. Auteurism remains the dominant paradigm for critics, and even for the many film historians and academics who find that its practical value outweighs the theoretical arguments levied against it by Kael and others over the years.

Andy was a respected member of the organizations (the New York Film Critics Circle, the National Society of Film Critics) that I've chaired over the years. He was also my colleague on the Film Studies faculty at Columbia University, where he taught for decades. And he was a friend. Molly Haskell—his wife, and equally influential as the first and greatest proponent of feminist film criticism—has been all of those things as well, and I trust she will remain so for a long time to come.

Hearing the news of Andrew's death reminded me of an interview I conducted with him in Montreal in 1995, when he won the Maurice Bessy Award for excellence in film criticism. We did it mostly for fun, and I never published it, but I think it captures something of his spirit at a time when his career, his energy, and his cinephilia were at their most mature. I offer it here as a tribute to my friend and colleague.

Looking back on the early years of auteur criticism, why did it become so controversial so quickly?

Because the fun and games about American movies were over. From here on they'd have to be taken seriously. Particularly genre movies—westerns and noir films and gangster films and musicals. These were all on the same level as Ingmar Bergman and Federico Fellini now. That was bad news, because a lot of people—particularly intellectuals—insisted that these foreign films were the serious cinema, and American movies were just fun.

But the attacks were so vituperative!

People said I had added a pretentious note to film criticism, and that upset them. But there were three main attacks on auteurism after the early days. One, that it was all nonsense. Two, that film is collaborative—which I knew, because I obviously knew there were actors and lots of people involved! I was only making the point that the director is the most important person, not the only one deserving credit. And three, that there was nothing original in what I said, because the French had all said it and I was only copying them. So people attacked on every possible front, even though the different attacks were inconsistent. But what I was really doing all this time [in the early auteurist period] was trying to make a living. I was basically a movie reviewer!

Your most famous polemical move in The American Cinema *was to rank directors according to their relative merit, and to place them into whimsically named categories—The Pantheon, The Far Side of Paradise, Strained Seriousness, Less Than Meets the Eye, and so on—that set off instant alarm bells in people who disagreed.*

All the people I liked in *The American Cinema* have stood up. The big mistakes I made were the people I didn't like. I grievously underrated some of them. I think it's human nature: when you respond to somebody, you find out more about them, and when you dislike them, you don't. It took me a long time to come to terms with Kubrick, for instance. My first reaction was that he was cold and inhuman. But once I figured out that he had no unconscious—that he just builds elaborate edifices, like Brecht—then I had a way to approach him, and when something like *Full Metal Jacket* came along, I was free to admire it for what it was.

The more sophisticated auteurists, including you, take account of various factors that intersect with directorial style in determining the ultimate value of a movie or a director's [body of] work.

There's been a lot of modification of writing on movies [because of auteurism] and now I think it's gone too far! I look at reference books, and with movies from the '30s to the '50s, they've stopped mentioning studios. And also, you can't find screenwriters in most of them. I think they both should be mentioned. Studios and writers are both interesting parts of it, particularly writers.

So the focus on auteurs has become too intense for the king of auteurists! You've clearly won the battle that Pauline started all those years ago.

People say I won, but no one ever wins these things. I still feel I haven't reached the point where I can say I could really define the theory. There's something always eluding me, something I haven't quite reached. And that keeps me going!

Your essay "Notes on the Auteur Theory in 1962" is still the best explanation and defense of auteurism ever written, but Pauline's response in "Circles and Squares" [originally in Film Quarterly *for Spring 1963] is a clever polemic too, vicious though it sometimes is.*

Someone said you can only argue with someone with whom you're in fundamental agreement. I believe that. With people like [John] Simon and [Stanley] Kauffmann, I feel we could never agree on things, because we're different types of critic. But with Pauline, we both came out of the little magazines, and we're both movie buffs. I'm officially an academic, but I'm like her—a polymath, an autodidact, constantly filling in all kinds of gaps. I think I'm getting to the essence of what works and what doesn't, and why it does, and it comes down to something Tolstoy said—the transmission of feeling. That's what I'm always looking for. I've always been bound by a kind of good faith with my reader. I would never say anything that I did not feel myself.

I know you're writing a history of sound cinema. [Note: You Ain't Heard Nothin' Yet: The American Talking Film, History and Memory, 1927–1949 *was published by Oxford University Press in 1998.]*

I've been working on it for fifteen years. I was born about the same time as the sound film [Sarris came into the world on Halloween in 1928] and I have all kinds of memories about it. I've always kept them in a kind of balance with the objective history of it, and now it's possible to check on these memories [through video and television]. The book isn't exclusively about directors, like *The American Cinema*—it also deals with genres and adaptations and actors. And it's personal. It's not the history, if any such history is possible, which I don't think it is.

Do you think changing tastes and new technologies will alter the movies beyond recognition one of these years?

The cinema's always dying, film criticism is always dying. But the reason cinema will never really die… is that it's infinitely renewable, because we'll always want new people, young people on the screen. Even if the stories are stale and repetitious, there are new driving forces carrying them on. And the world itself changes, everything is changing. Film records this change. That's why even old films—the most naïve of the old films made around the [beginning] of the [twentieth] century—are so heartbreaking. The people aren't thinking about dying, they're bursting with life, and we're watching that. It's gone and yet it's here, it's alive, and it exists for itself without needing anything else. It's always going on. Certain genres are going to die, like the musicals did—the western has morphed into different forms, but the musical is as dead as the mummies in Egypt, and you'll never have another *Singin' in the Rain* or *The Band Wagon* or *Swing Time*. So you can only watch and marvel at the talent, skill, life, and vitality that went into all that stuff!

This article first appeared with the title "A Previously Unpublished Interview with Andrew Sarris."

I conducted countless interviews over several decades for The Christian Science Monitor, *and have selected the ones presented here partly on the basis of availability. I have tried to find various 1970s interviews to no avail. Such are the vicissitudes of the internet in general and the* Monitor *archives in particular.*

Even with that limitation, there are hundreds of interviews I could have chosen. Most of the ones below date from the 1980s because I had a fair amount of freedom in choosing interview subjects at that time, and also because the worlds of film, theater, and dance were rife with new and exciting developments that I wanted to explore by talking with some of the period's artistic prime movers. I've spoken on multiple occasions with Steve Reich, Philip Glass, Errol Morris, Jonas Mekas, Neil Simon, John Adams, and some of the others included here, but these early interviews capture something of that very fecund era as well as the thoughts of the particular artists involved.

I've left the articles unchanged except for minor alterations: reformatting paragraphs, deleting superfluous words, and so on. Readers should note that newspaper journalists hardly ever write their own headlines. The pieces have been placed in chronological order rather than by category, since jumping around among different art forms and media is true to the spirit of the epoch under consideration.

T-Rex: Is this the musician of mystery
Interview with Marc Bolan, November 22, 1972

Marc Bolan is T. Rex

Look at his face, gazing wistfully from an album jacket: Beautiful, nearly feminine. The features are so delicate one fears the whole assemblage might crack, break.

But T. Rex is a popstar, and rock'n'roll is not delicate. T. Rex records, tours, sings, plays, dances, leaps into the air, his hands wresting joyful shrieks from amplified strings. In its rock'n'roll context, the T. Rex face projects a tension through its very fragility, its sensitivity. Millions of rock'n'roll-lovers are moved to delight by the sight and sound of it.

"We've seen our Master's face/It's young and gold And silvery old." So says T. Rex in "The Children of Rarn." A rare comment on faces from a man whose face is a significant part of his fortune.

In T. Rex's hotel suite Marc Bolan shakes hands, smiles, has a good time talking. The face, in person, is masculine, expressive, cheerful. One strains a bit to remember that this is indeed the musician of mystery, the marvelous child-man who sang of "Dragon's Ear," "Ballrooms of Mars," "Fist Heart Mighty Dawn Dart," "The Wizard," "Summer Deep." Whence does the awesome imagery spring?

"From my imagination, not from experience," answers Marc. "But I don't know the difference between what's real and what's not real, do you?"

A promising start from the musician of mystery. Yet spoken with the good-natured matter-of-factness of a man who knows exactly what he's doing—even if he sees no point in pinning down too closely the stuff of his poetry. And as a performer, one soon discovers, Marc is more concerned than ever before with communicating directly with his audience.

"I am a warrior," says the star whose first American smash was an LP titled *Electric Warrior.* "If an audience doesn't react when we're working hard, working really hard, I'll stop a number and ask them why." But Marc is increasingly anxious to meet his listeners halfway. In the early days, for example, the band was known as Tryannosaurus Rex, "because I liked the name." It was shortened to T. Rex because the old name was too long. "I wasn't media-conscious then, but 1 am now, I have to be."

So he's fighting to talk to people through those strange, likable songs. Yet without pretending to understand all the nuances of his own delicately nuanced works. He mentions the one called "Metal Guru": "I don't know what a metal guru is. Except something godlike. And my idea of being godlike is being all alone without a telephone. I never answer the phone because it's an intrusion on my life. And sitting in a big metal chair might increase the feeling of power." He's adrift in an age of media and technology. But he's in control.

"I was dancing when I was twelve / I was dancing when I was aaah" sings the British "Cosmic Dancer" in his hotel room. Marc has done a lot of things since he was 12. He was once "washup" in a hamburger bar, now says he's England's best-selling poet with a book called *The Warlock of Love*. From his early teens he's been acting on television, in the theater, working as a mod model. "I've never been one of the crowd, I've always been a phenomenon... I'll continue with T. Rex as long as it's fun—I mean when it stops being a process of growth, I'll stop doing it."

The non-Bolan constant in T. Rex has been sideman Mickey Finn, who works with sundry other backup musicians. But Marc says T. Rex is really just himself. He uses a group name because "there are much better psychological connotations with a group." He has used music as a means of growth in various directions. He finds recording and touring "both very stimulating" and prefers neither over the other. His latest project is a 75-minute film made with Ringo Starr, "a documentation—though not a documentary—of T. Rex. It should be seen as strictly a rock'n'roll film."

One asks about *The Slider*, the latest LP, mottled with oblique allusions to the hazily defined title object. A person slides from one experience or emotion into another, is the ready explanation. At the end of a sad time, it's good when one can slide into another way of feeling. "It's like a kid's slide, that's the image."

A remarkably straightforward answer. Why isn't it included somewhere on the album?

"It's not a book, full of explanations. And I don't want to impinge on your mind. They're your—their—songs as much as mine."

Mr. Bolan becomes more accessible by the moment. A questioner asks if he is in danger of being demystified—an important query to present to a man who is one of Europe's more worshiped rock idols.

"Oh, no!" protests Mr. B. "There's too much mystification. When someone says 'a pane of glass is made out of sound,' what does that mean? I don't know, and neither does anyone."

But isn't the Rexian persona built on mystery?

"I'm a child," says the voice of T. Rex. "Everything blows my mind."

So that's it. The key, it seems, is not mystery after all, but playfulness. No arch psychedelia, no hidden runic answers, even in the ongoing unity that is the Bolan corpus of lyrics. Rather a real good time, a playful wielding of the casually bizarre ideas and allusions that lie at the core of T. Rex's rock'n'roll art. A fun so deeply felt that its rocking manifestations can even glide gallantly into poignancy.

"Girl I'm just a jeepster/For your love" sings T. Rex that evening from the stage of a crowded Boston theater, his rock-age-evocative words obscured, underlined, surrounded by a haze of heavy, hard rock sounds. Then just a little later, to his own brittle acoustic strumming: "I'm just a man/I understand the wind/And all the things that make the children cry."

Marc Bolan is "The Slider."

Quiet, Gentle, Candid, but at the jazz piano percussive, complex
Interview with Dave Brubeck, May 1, 1973

"We're breaking down the walls!
We're marching round and round!
Like Joshua at Jericho, we'll crumble walls with sound."

These words are thundered out by a "militant revolutionary" rock group during Dave Brubeck's jazz-rock-classical cantata, *Truth is Fallen.*

Brubeck himself seems to believe in the value of building, rather than tearing down. He pours musical, emotional, and spiritual energy into compositions that, he hopes, will help dissolve walls between people, generations, and even cultures.

Brubeck's conversation—quiet, candid—fits nicely in with his gentle, casual manner. But his talk differs greatly from his music.

At the piano he favors precise, swinging melodies. These often build into pounding, percussive chords, transforming linear tunes into complex blocks of musical power.

In relaxed conversation over dinner, one feels a sense of melody as Brubeck recapitulates the main themes of his life and work—especially when his soft-spoken humor pads slyly out. One glimpses the "percussive" aspects only at the roots of his nature, in the persistent energy and forthright commitment that underlie it.

Brubeck, born in California, is a remarkable man from a musical family. His mother was a classical pianist, his father a cattle-raiser. Two older brothers became musicians, "so my father claimed me as his last chance for a son in the cattle business."

It was, of course, not to be. Brubeck started school hoping to become a veterinarian. "But I discovered that music was easier than chemistry and zoology and the things I was studying." So he followed the path of his brothers. One of them, Howard, now is Dean of Music at California's Palomar College. The other, Henry, is head of the music department at the Santa Barbara public schools.

Brubeck's music has specific roots in childhood experience. Consider, for example, his fascination with odd rhythms and time signatures—which revolutionized jazz during the '50s.

When asked how this began, Brubeck says he really doesn't know. But when he was very young, his mother felt that children should be taught to tap out different rhythms, and even to walk, to them.

Later, there were days when he would ride a horse for eight or ten hours, herding cattle. There was little to do, "so I'd listen to the horse's cadence and think other rhythms against it. I'd do the same thing when I started the gasoline engines that pumped water for the cattle. You should have heard the crazy rhythms those things came out with!" Brubeck, it seems, was a boy on whom nothing was lost.

An early interest in jazz came from one of the older brothers, a jazz drummer and "legit" violinist. His band played dance music, Dixieland, some current popular tunes—and Dave listened attentively to their at-home rehearsals.

When his own career began, Brubeck joined a band playing dances in northern California gold-mining towns. They had to shift gears constantly, from hillbilly music and dance tunes to swing and popular songs. "The dances would start at 8. You'd play until midnight, then take a break and play till 4. You'd try to quit at 4—but you'd have to fight your way out. Everybody wanted to dance until they dropped."

Not all of Brubeck's musical training was so spontaneous, however. He earned a degree in music at the University of the Pacific. And most important, he went on to study composition at Mills College, Oakland, with classical composer Darius Milhaud—after whom the oldest Brubeck son is named.

Today, Brubeck sees Milhaud as his most important personal influence. Indeed, this goes back to the days when he was still learning from older brother Howard—who was the first of Milhaud's male students to earn a master's degree at Mills, which was primarily a girls' school.

Brubeck promptly and easily names the three jazz-world figures most important to him. Art Tatum, "the all-time greatest jazz pianist technically, and the most advanced harmonically," Fats Waller, "for the joy he expressed when he played and sang." And Duke Ellington, "for composition, and for his ability to keep a band together." This leadership ability "compares with what a great general knows how to do."

Waller's name comes up again when Brubeck discusses his own experiments with jazz time values. "One jazz waltz was recorded" before his work in that field, he says: Waller's "Jitterbug Waltz." But Brubeck never heard it until his own explorations were under way. Other similar experiments also took place, he reports, "but none of us knew the others were doing them... Ours were the ones that caught on with the public, so ours eventually had the greatest influence."

These days, Brubeck's most daring work outdoes even his time innovations in complexity. The jazzman has turned serious composer. It all began with a lengthy "Oratorio for Today" titled *The Light in the Wilderness.*

Brubeck sees the oratorio form as "very free, with sectionalized pieces." In his next major work, *The Gates of Justice*, he "tied the thematic material together more, into a cantata form." Then came the most recent composition, *Truth Is Fallen*. Its dedication is "to the slain students of Kent State and Mississippi State, and all other innocent victims, caught in the cross-fire between repression and rebellion."

The composition and premiere of *Truth Is Fallen* were guided by unusual circumstances. They illustrate Brubeck's closeness with his audience. The commission came from the Midland Symphony Orchestra, which wanted a piece for the dedication of the Midland Center for the Arts in Midland, Mich. It was first performed there under Don Th. Jaeger's direction in 1971.

The Midland center sought a work that would utilize local talents. Brubeck complied, incorporating a wide variety of musical elements. Hence the piece's heady mixture of jazz, symphonic, and rock elements—which represent the entire spectrum of a community's musical interests.

The composer's family was also deeply involved. As with all three major compositions, Brubeck's wife Iola helped adapt and write the text. When the work was recorded by the Cincinnati Symphony Orchestra, the New Heavenly Blue rock band was on hand, with leader Chris Brubeck also playing all trombone solos.

And, of course, Dave himself sat at the piano.

Brubeck is now composing a work based on Christmas music. It will reverse the trend toward more musical mixing. "As it develops," the musician says, "I see it will include less rock, less than all three others." Why? "I don't know. I never can say what I'm going to do next."

He sees the new piece, however, as "simpler, without the built-in problems of doing rock and jazz with an orchestra and conductor." America, he feels, "should move in the direction of mixing jazz, rock, and classical music. Because that's what we are, and you should try to reflect your culture." But there is a practical problem involved here. "That style of music depends on musicians being familiar with things they haven't done until that performance."

So Brubeck, seems relaxed, for the moment, working in a less eclectic framework. Yet he shows no sign of abandoning insights from various musical spheres. "People speak of pure music, and I never know what they're talking about," he says. "People blindly believe in 'musical tradition,' even when it takes a wrong turn. Like classical music did when it abandoned improvisation. Maybe that's why they're where they are today."

Brubeck still sees jazz at the center of American musical life. "Jazz came and said you could be more human and free. And this had a tremendous influence on art—painting, poetry, dance… Jazz is also the most important influence to stop all the over-intellec-tualization going on. Though most symphonies can't improvise any better than some of us can write a strict 12-tone serial piece without looking foolish"

Today, Brubeck insists, "We don't need to grow into new areas as much as to consolidate, to look into the past, A small percentage of the audience should always be challenged by the avant-garde; what survives will come into the language and be understood by everyone. But we're in a position now to utilize things from other cultures, that are fresh and new to us."

Does Brubeck see the jazz world as being healthy today? Brubeck-the-socially-conscious answers: "Art is not healthy any place in the world where there's been a war recently. So we've had an unhealthy period for quite a few years. We're in a hard period that expresses protest. That's not one of my favorite things to hear in music, though I've done it myself. I'd rather hear joy, and I hope we can get back to that soon."

Brubeck feels an attitude of protest in today's art, even when it is not specifically political. "An individual artist can't help but reflect what's going on, unless he totally cuts himself off." Yet he has a humble view of his own music's effect.

"It changes the heads of those in the orchestra and especially in the chorus. They are reached by it. The audience only hears it once. We hope they're reached by it, but most people never even hear of it…

"Still, you never know if a piece will have a longer life." All three major Brubeck projects "have had more performances than I, anticipated. They are a reaching-out to at least a small number of people."

Are the new, large pieces as artistically successful as the well-known Brubeck jazz? "For me, they're about equally important. But they're completely different. Both communicate with audiences. During the first performance of *Light in the Wilderness*, there were 500 in one chorus alone, plus 100 college students and the orchestra. Just that we all stood up together was really something. But they actually became inspired, and sang difficult music beautifully after only one rehearsal.

"That total momentary commitment to music is found more often in jazz than in symphonic situations. But it did happen there. That's what I'm looking for—inspiration, communication, and a oneness between ourselves and the audience, with no negative thoughts to interfere."

Characteristically, the Brubeck future looks busy. He had planned on a "refining period" starting about now. "I was going to get off the road more and re-examine past pieces I played, recorded, and then never played again." But new directions are calling: Now, for the next year or so, he wants to concentrate on the recently inaugurated "Two Generations of Brubecks" concerts, featuring veteran sidemen and young family members.

The ambition to look back and refine still holds strong, though. And it receives a new impetus from the Brubeck sons. Chris's rock group has a recent record called *Pegleg*, played in a rare 35/4 time signature. Those new rhythmic feats "still hold the old fascination," reports Dave. "And Darius will write something and ask, 'Did you ever hear a theme like this?' 'I'll say yes, and realize that he's discovering extensions of areas I once wanted to go into. Now I can go back to areas like these, and look at them again."

Brubeck's evident pride in his family reaffirms an old Emersonian distinction. He is not just a musician. He is a man making music—a sensitive and fully rounded man, whose family life means as much to him as anything. A talk with Darius, the eldest of the younger Brubecks, confirms this.

Darius's first ensemble started in 1969. Since then his musical work has become "a serious and steady thing." When one asks his father how he feels about this, Brubeck says, "It's fine. But it's a rough life." Darius, however, emphasizes that his famous father always wanted him to go his own way.

"I never thought I would, or wouldn't, be a musician," the up-and-comer reports. "It was never an issue. I was a religion major at Wesleyan University in Connecticut. And I studied music and instruments far from jazz—Indian classical music most extensively. I grew up during the whole 'folk' thing, and that was fine with Dad.

"But my family made it easy for me to go in the direction of jazz. The scene was set... I was influenced-by-my-father, but in indirect ways. I can't really be objective about it. His influence on a whole generation has been persuasive, broad, and deep. Everyone's playing in 5/4 time now. I haven't been singled out to be a receiving point for this influence. He's shaped music now. I was just influenced by a force of history."

Why have two other Brubeck children, as well as Darius, headed into musical lives? Darius's remarks are revealing.

"For us, music was always a primary way of recreation. To pick a really off-the-wall example, do you know anything about the music of Java? Their music is outasight, and everyone participates. There is no conception of what we call art. The feeling is, 'We have no art, we just do everything well.'"

"Brubecks don't do everything well. But we make a lot of music, communicating and participating. 'Art' doesn't become an issue until you're old enough to think of a career. It's a way of participating and belonging."

Has Darius been influenced by social, political, and religious thoughts as his father has? "I've been active politically, but as politics. I haven't expressed polities in music. Religious thinking has been a principle of inspiration—a source you can get in touch with, that makes meaningful things come out.

"Music is for me a spiritual activity. That's deep and parallel with both of us... Dad has reached his conclusions, though. For me religiosity or spirituality is more a feeling than a philosophy."

Predictably, Dave's role as mentor has been more fatherly than professorial. "If I asked a direct question, he'd tell me," reports Darius. "But he wouldn't say 'Do this' or make suggestions... Though he does help, like with programming, format, and so forth. Craft know-how things, not aesthetic direction.

"It's never been a 'superiority' thing... And I think that's really laudable. At an earlier age, I might have fallen into that."

Under this benign guidance, Darius's career has already blossomed considerably. Besides playing the "Two Generations" concerts with his father's trio, he leads his ensemble, featuring younger brother Danny on drums. He has also written film scores, and released an album. His 20-year-old brother Chris, leader of the New Heavenly Blue rock group, has two discs to his credit. He is also a bass-trombone major in college.

Two other Brubeck children, Michael and Catherine, have stopped playing music, but are artistically inclined. Catherine studies art and teaching. Michael is concerned most with poetry and—that other family interest crops up again—horse training.

There is another Brubeck child, named Matthew. When Brubeck mentioned his name, I remembered an old composition written "in a burst of joy" at his birth, and said, "That must be 'Charles Matthew Hallelujah.'"

The proud father burst into a grin and made a quick gesture of delight. He seemed pleased that the song was still remembered. But more, he seemed suddenly to recall the deep happiness that had inspired it. The Brubeck's strong musical kinship seems firmly related to this warm, deeply felt sense of family.

Federico Fellini: Filmmaker who hates going to movies
Interview with Federico Fellini, January 29, 1975

La Dolce Vita, *8½*, *Juliet of the Spirits*, *La Strada*, *Nights of Cabiria*... the list goes on and on, crammed with feisty Italian blockbusters. Their maker, Federico Fellini, might well be the most famous, and admired, and simply enjoyed movie director in all the world.

Since his work is behind the scenes, most Fellini fans have little idea what their favorite artiste looks like. At best, they may have an image of Marcello Mastroianni floating hazily about their minds, since Mastrolanni has starred in some of the best-known Fellini works (including the autobiographical *8½*). In fact, the filmmaker himself is a large, jovial, plain-featured man, more robust than his onscreen alter ego—with a scrupulously deadpan expression to abet the deep humor that strides forth with remarkable regularity.

Like most other film artists, however great, Fellini must occasionally bow to the pressures of the movie publicity mill. Often, this means travelling—galumphing from city to city, from country to country, explaining, explicating, soliloquizing, and generally calling attention to oneself and one's work. Such a tour recently brought Fellini to New York, a city he sees as a very Fellinian place—"that mixture of decadence and science fiction, carnival and cemetery, macabre and innocence, energy and oldness...

The purpose of the trip was to tout the latest Fellini epic, *Amarcord*—a colorful, eccentric, whimsically picturesque voyage into the boyhood memories of a provincially bred Italian. It's a deliberately unusual film, serving up large dollops of vintage Fellini imagery, yet wallowing lengthily in its own self-indulgent caprices. For myself, I appreciated it more at a second viewing, when the meanderings of its characters seemed less important than the sheer beauty of images. For Fellini, he seems delighted with it, and is openly pleased that many American critics agree with him.

After introducing me to his interpreter—"She helps with my English When I am lost, which is always"—Fellini began to expound on the curiously personal nature of his movies, which are compounded of fictional and autobiographical elements.

"In part, *Amarcord* is something that I have remembered. In part it's something that I have invented. But that means the same thing, because there is no difference between what has happened to me and what I have thought, or what I have dreamed." The important thing is not to determine if this is "the real life of Mr.

Fellini," he goes on, but to respond to the "very personal, autobiographical point of view" of the film.

Amarcord wheels along freely because "every fantasy asks the author to be told in a certain kind of way," and this particular fantasy demanded an "open" and "difficult" structure. Yet Fellini insists that it is a "conventional" movie, since after all "everything is conventional."

People, says the filmmaker, "are always seeing things in a very conventional way. We are afraid of news. We don't want to be open. We want to hear what we know, to see what we have seen, to read what we have read, to know what we know. We defend ourselves about new things; we don't accept. That is why real art is always revolutionary. It is against the old conventional laws. Real art is always very offensive because it offends our stupidity, our nearsightedness, our fear. We want to live in safety, we don't want to be disturbed. In many ways—in a political sense, a religious sense, an art sense. We don't want to know; we don't want to be free."

If "real art" must make people uncomfortable, why are Fellini films among the most popular ever made? "I don't think my pictures are very revolutionary," explains the director. "After all, I am not a very revolutionary type. I just try to communicate, and I feel I am using the normal, conventional, very recognizable way." Yet, he notes, his movies were not popular a few years ago. His first was "a flop" in Italy, and even the much-lauded *8½* was widely accepted only after years of "critics and explanations."

Fellini does not consider his audience when working on his films. "What is the audience anyway?" he asks, saying that all he can imagine is "an abstract image of a crowd." The real problems of filmmaking are practical, he notes—"The realization of your work... which color to put into this sequence, what kind of shoes to have this character wear, what kind of slang will he speak, what is the rhythm of that scene, how can I express life and dreams... To those very serious problems, if you add the problem of 'Will I be understood by the people of Boston or Beirut,' you will be lost... If you really want to communicate something, you will."

Fellini's communicative career has passed through many stages. He began as a cartoonist, and still acknowledges cartoons as an influence on his art. Among his favorites he lists *Popeye*, *Krazy Kat*, and *Dick Tracy*. "You should be very proud of this kind of art," he tells his American interviewer. "It will be valued." He also mentions the underground cartooning of R. Crumb. And he admires the early animation work of the Walt Disney studios, in which he finds something "macabre."

During the first stages of his moviemaking life—after a stint as an actor—Fellini was identified with the neorealist movement, which sought to return emotional realism to a romanticized Italian film tradition. Today Fellini reaffirms the importance of "reality" in movies.

"The most honest neorealist is the visionary, because he honestly talks about things that he knows very well—his own reality... He talks about life."

As to the personal side of his work, Fellini waxes, brief— "I just make pictures." He professes no interest in "why and when and how" his films are made. He works "with spontaneity," just for "the joy, not worrying about the results." Consequently he never looks at his own past movies, saying that he wants to go on, not to look back. "I have reasons to be disappointed with myself 10,000 times a day," he explains with tongue in cheek. "Why add another reason more?"

He never goes to anyone else's movies, either. Not for any complicated artistic reason, just because sitting and staring at a screen doesn't appeal to him. He admits no interest in the directors who claim to have been influenced by him (which include Mike Nichols, Paul Mazursky, and others). He lives in blissful ignorance of "the damage I have done."

In contrast with his dislike of moviegoing, Fellini feels comfortable in nearly all moviemaking situations. He has become such an effortless technician that "The camera does not exist" for him: "The problem is what you put before the camera—the vision, and how to express the vision." He further holds that all directors must feel inflated, even godlike, while working. "You must believe that the world was built for you, everything was put there for you, all the skyscrapers and everything has been done for you. That is craziness, exaltation, drunkenness. But you need it... and your co-workers must be people who have chosen to represent *your* fantasy."

Fellini goes on to state that there is a prime element in cinema, more important than actors or story or anything else: "Light... light came first... light gives the film..."

He is happy with his work and his life. His wife, actress Giuletta Massina, still travels with him often—she is a silent presence in the room as I interview Fellini—so that he feels no break between "home and studio, professional and private life." He writes in conjunction with his directing work (he co-authored a rambunctious but effective novelization of A*marcord*), but most of all he still loves making movies. "I am 54 years old now," he says, "and still joking with puppets. Everything is all right."

"I watch, I think, I am conscious of everything"
Interview with Michelangelo Antonioni, May 30, 1975

Michelangelo Antonioni. Even his name calls up visions of monumental art. But unlike his namesake, this latter-day Michelangelo paints no ceilings and carves no stone. He creates his frescoes on celluloid.

During the past two and a half decades he has fashioned a sweeping and wholly personal commentary on man and his world that couldn't have existed before the age of movies. In the process he has inspired (a) whole books of admiring prose, and (b) angry attacks from befuddled critics. And he has sold a mighty pile of tickets to a mighty horde of loyal film fans.

The latest Antonioni epic is *The Passenger*, a thriller gone mystical. In it Jack Nicholson plays a world-weary newsman who exchanges identities with a man he scarcely knew. Response from reviewers has been favorable indeed, with special praise for the director's bold conception.

Most Antonioni films have been similarly applauded. *Blow-Up* became an overnight legend with its eccentric whodunit (or who-dunwhat) story, on-target performances, and unabashed philosophizing. Other hits have included *L'Aventurra*, *La Notte*, and *Eclipse*. An Antonioni documentary about China has appeared on American network TV, and now the filmmaker's first feature — *Story of a Love Affair* — a has been imported for a belated U.S. premiere.

As the wave of Antonioni's popularity hit yet another crest, I visited the slight, graying director during his most recent stay in New York. I found him tired after several days of nonstop chatter about movies, movies, movies, but good-humored and eager to discuss his life and work. Antonioni stands firmly behind his movies — his famous fictions, and the occasional documentaries that he makes as a way of staying "in shape."

"All my films come out of reality," the director explains. "I get some moments, characters, a situation, events, etc. So I think that to keep ourselves trained to look at reality is very, very useful… I like it… I can't get away from this. That's why I never made a 'costume film,' a historic film. I can't look back. I can only look at the present or at the future."

Why this insistence on the here and now? "I don't know. I think because we have a certain number of years in front of us, and these are the most important for us. Not what has happened, but what is going to happen." As a young man, however, Antonioni had no idea that he would become a filmmaker. When I was a student in my native town—Ferrara, a small town not far from Venice—I started to do things on the stage. I directed many plays, and I wrote some, and so on... And then I started as a critic for the local paper. Then I went to Bologna, to the University, and then to Rome."

But even at this early stage, Antonioni "wasn't satisfied with theater. I remember that I was fed up with the fact that I was forced to use only one 'shot,' this 'long shot' which is the stage... When I directed someone on the stage, I would sit in the audience part of the theater, and I would have just that one shot. But as soon as I got up and approached the actor to tell him something, I would see another shot. But I couldn't do it. So I got bored with this."

Eventually the young artist began to work in the movies, and has been happy ever since. As for his basic leaning toward artistry instead of some other field, "that's nature—it pushes you toward one way instead of another. It is nature and will. Nature creates the will to be someone... I remember when I was very young, I thought of myself as becoming a diplomat. But," he chuckles, "it would have been such a mistake!"

The most famous quality of Antonioni's films is probably their leisurely, unhurried pace. But, says the director, "I realized that my films had that pace when someone told me. Until then. I didn't know it."

Antonioni is pleased about the present state of world cinema. But he maintains that in the future "cinema has to change quite a lot. I'm getting bored with these... technical limits," he says, echoing more and more major directors. "We need to do something more to be more violent to the reality, to the limits...

"I think when we are able to shoot with tape instead of film, that will be a good help... in the development of the medium... Now we are still tied to some techniques which are very old... Our cameras are more or less the same as 20 years ago..."

What does he mean by "doing violence to the limits" of cinema? "If I could tell you, I would be a writer. I am a director. I only came to show you something."

Many Antonioni fans have traced a thread of messages running through his work, tying his films together thematically. Asked to comment on his themes and philosophies, he acknowledges being "conscious about these feelings in between films. As soon as I finish one film and before starting another, I am conscious of everything. I watch, I look, I think, I read. I have a lot of experience.

"But I don't think that this influences—at least consciously—what comes to me in the way of invention, fantasy. I try to forget everything. I think it is kind of store. You put in everything, and then something comes out... I try to store everything I see, everything I observe, everything I think, everything I feel. And then as soon as I get an idea for a film I forget everything."

For Antonioni, the most important part of filming is the actual shooting. But every aspect is important in its own way, including the editing process. As for the script, "for me it" a kind of notebook, an introduction to shooting with the camera... I try to put everything in the script... But it will be known that afterwards I am going to cut some of it..."

On the set "I have control of everything as much as I can... Nothing is done without my approval, of course... The others must do what I need... They can be creative within the boundaries of what I want, what I need."

As for actors, Antonioni has worked with such stars as Jack Nicholson, Maria Schneider, David Hemmings, Vanessa Redgrave. and long-time collaborator Monica Vitti. Yet performers "are not as important as the director or the photographer or the art director..."

Antonioni says that he chooses stars in the same way that other filmmakers do, according to "very, very common procedure. There are two ways to look for actors. One is to prepare the script having someone in mind. This is the best way. The other is to look for an actor as close as possible to what you have in mind... For *The Passenger* I knew that I would have Jack Nicholson and Maria Schneider. So it was easy."

As he travels about discussing his latest film, Antonioni seems most bothered by his uncertain command of English. Actually he speaks the language fairly well. "But I have to simplify everything," he complains. "I think my interviews must seem very poor because I can't tell in English what I want... Brecht used to say, 'In English I only say what I can say, not what I want to say.' That's the problem."

Yet Antonioni appears to enjoy the life he leads. "I must amuse myself doing films," he muses, "otherwise why would I do them? I can't imagine another kind of life... Yes... I like it."

Woody Allen: His serious side is funny too
Interview with Woody Allen, May 4, 1977

Before he started work on his latest comedy, *Annie Hall*, Woody Allen was asked why he makes movies.

"Every young person in America wants to direct films," he explained, "and I can. People actually give me money to create motion pictures! So I guess I'd better do it, or I might regret it some day.

Woody is not the most eager cinéaste in Hollywood. In fact, he isn't even in Hollywood—he lives in New York, has returned to making his films here, and spends a good part of his new film *Annie Hall* venting hilarious spleen at southern California. He finds film-making hard work, works hard at it, and generally behaves like a sensible fellow.

In short, he's a far cry from the lovable loser he plays on-screen. He worries about being "too cerebral" in his daily life. He acknowledges that the literacy and seriousness of his films may keep him from ever gathering a truly huge following. And he dreams of making more sober and introspective projects in the future.

If you didn't already know it, this straight-talking comedian is a major movie artist with a bright and challenging future.

Interestingly, the two most important makers of American comic films—Allen and the more raucous Mel Brooks—share a freewheeling interest (despite their many differences) in stretching the limits of screen comedy. Brooks breaks all the rules and shoots a farce in black-and-white (*Young Frankenstein*), then gets even bolder and fashions a film with no dialogue (*Silent Movie*). Allen's films include a zany documentary (*Take the Money and Run*), a scrambled Japanese adventure with bizarre English dubbing (*What's Up, Tiger Lily?*), and now *Annie Hall*, a fascinating comic exploration involving every cinematic device from subtitles to split screens.

This visual adventurousness is one of Allen's pet preoccupations. "Years ago," he explained to me a few days before *Annie Hall* opened, "when Buster Keaton and Charlie Chaplin were making films, the world was very physical. Chaplin would be working on a conveyor belt; Keaton would be taking a locomotive across the country. Now things are electronic, not so physically oriented. The conflicts have moved from the exterior to the interior.

"What's interesting are psychological conflicts. The problem is finding a vocabulary to express inner psychological states in a visual way. In serious films, Ingmar Bergman has found ways to express deeply personal psychological states in a very visual way he uses revelatory cinematic devices.

"In *Annie Hall* I tried to do a psychological comedy, in such a way that we didn't just talk and make jokes. The playing area has moved from outside to inside. We have to find good ways of dealing with this in comedy—we need a vocabulary tantamount to the slapstick vocabulary of years ago."

Allen's current ambition is to make increasingly "serious" films. "I've done a certain amount of comedy that was strictly for laughs," says the former nightclub comic and writer of sardonic essays for *The New Yorker* magazine and other publications. "It was thin, amusing if you liked it, and that's all. In order to grow, I knew I'd have to deepen the work—to use comedy in the service of ideas, or more genuine satire, or emotional exploration. It's an attempt to develop."

That's why Woody feels he's going to be "more and more of a challenge" to his fans. I hope I can at least maintain the basic audience I've established, even if it doesn't grow. I hope they're willing to go with me through my serious comedies and serious films—as long as I don't do anything stupid, which can happen with comedians, because you're never quite aware of what a fool you're making of yourself. I could think I'm doing *Long Day's Journey Into Night* when actually I'm doing *Edge of Night*.

According to Woody's wisdom, "If you do a comedy and get serious now and then, it's creepy." So his "serious comedy" would be largely drama. "It would have to be about real people—essentially a serious story with comedy in it, with humor based on situation and observation, confronting a subject of some profundity."

Ultimately Allen would like to fashion a true tragedy, in the Eugene O'Neill vein. "I'd like to try that psychological, personal style," he says, "as opposed to a social drama, a *Dog Day Afternoon*, or a *One Flew Over the Cuckoo's Nest*."

He admits it might take the public some time to get used to this idea, and knows for sure that he would never appear in such a picture.

Allen agrees that cinema is a difficult medium to use for personal communication, within a commercial framework, and that "only a few guys" have been able to "elevate it to art." Film, he says, "is the only art form where big money is one of the creative tools of the artist. A painter or composer can sit home and work, and it doesn't cost him that much. For me, to make even a low-budget film, I have to go and ask for $3 million!"

Allen continues to try, despite the difficulties, and to succeed as few other comic film-makers. He readily gives credit to the predecessors who have influenced him: He adores Chaplin, has called Groucho Marx "the greatest comedian," and still reminds himself of Bob Hope in some scenes. Many Allen admirers are surprised at his love for Hope, but Woody staunchly defends the major Hope movies of 20 years ago and more, recalling that "as a teenager I used to pretend I was Bob Hope before I went on a date…"

Conversely, "in terms of developing a cinematic style," he has been influenced by such serious artists as Fellini, Truffaut, Bergman, and Godard. Inspired by such worthy models, Woody Allen expects to plunge ever deeper into moviemaking. As his works grow still more thoughtful, remember that directing is no great joy for him, and that he always feels "disappointed" in his work.

"When you conceive of something," he sighs, "you have idealized, grandiose ideas. Then you write it, and it's a little less funny than you had imagined. Then you film it, and it's a lot less funny. By the time it ends up on the screen, you're down to 50 percent of that brilliant idea. So you always think, if only you could have seen it as it appeared in my mind."

New Directions in American Theater
Interviews with Robert Wilson and Spalding Gray, May 3, 1979

Robert Wilson's productions have the logic of a dream; he's more interested in "patterns" than in traditional plots, and his performances have gone on for as long as seven days without intermission.

Spalding Gray, dissatisfied with having to "play-act" fictional roles and mimic make-believe emotions, has gone into "autobiographical theater" in which he is the main character and the star of his own productions.

Scene: uptown, at the Metropolitan Opera House. Event: a bold new kind of American theater.

Einstein on the Beach, an opera by Robert Wilson and Philip Glass, flows across the stage for five hours without a break. Its words consist of numbers and solfeggio—"one, two, three..." and "do, re, mi..." Its movements are utterly nonrealistic, yet planned and timed down to the tiniest detail. The evening has the logic of a dream: a cutout locomotive inches on and off the stage: a baggy-pants Einstein plays obsessively on a violin; a huge fluorescent bed is hoisted into the invisible stratosphere over an improbable courtroom.

Elsewhere, another scene: downtown, in a converted garage on a narrow Soho street. The event: another bold new kind of American theater.

Sakonnet Point, a dancelike piece by Spalding Gray and Elizabeth LeCompte, dangles a string of free associations across the stage for approximately an hour. Its words are few, its gestures are spare and minimal. The evening has the logic of a reverie: a man in bathing trunks flies a toy airplane over a miniature village, his voice howling the "aaaaaaaa" sound of the engine; unidentified people hang sheets on clotheslines, obscuring the performers from view; an actor shines a flashlight on tiny houses in the distance, conjuring a sense of hushed nostalgia beneath a suddenly starry sky.

Wilson, Glass, Gray, and LeCompte are just a few of the artists who are gradually expanding the boundaries of theater in directions undreamed of before they came along. They take their inspirations from a thousand sources—from the theatrical traditions of India and the dramas of Thornton Wilder; from Chinese opera and electronic "modular music; from dreams, accidents, books, improvisations, and meaty dramaturgical problems like "How am I going to get off the stage with that big hunk of scenery in the way?"

Sometimes they even inspire one another, though they form no deliberate school or movement. Indeed, their views on a given question can be diametrically opposed. Wilson, for example, insists on spacious and technically sophisticated theaters for his massive works. By contrast, Gray and LeCompte cheerfully make the most of a barnlike Performing Garage in lower Manhattan, cherishing their freedom from the large and entertainment-hungry audiences they might encounter in a fancier setting closer to Broadway.

What they have in common is audacity. Robert Wilson cares little for "manageable" durations, letting his plays run on for hours or even days. Spalding Gray prefers to avoid the veneer of fiction usually applied to "autobiographical theater," and serves as the main character as well as the star of his recent works. Similarly, composer Glass cares more about repetition than modulation, and director LeCompte designs "environments" for her shows that have only slight resemblances to traditional theatrical spaces.

These and other breaches of convention earn hearty scorn from some theatergoers, standing ovations from others. Even the play-makers are sometimes uncertain what effect their latest extravaganza will have on a living, breathing audience. Since they are working on the brink of the untried, surprises are always in store.

Robert Wilson is the best-known practitioner of today's "experimental" theater. *Einstein on the Beach* proved phenomenally popular in its two-day engagement at the Met in 1976, and the Met hopes to present a new Wilson opera later this year: *Death Destruction and Detroit*, which recently premièred in West Berlin. *A Letter From Queen Victoria* played on Broadway — Wilson likes to think of his avant-garde work as being in direct competition with shows like *The King and I* — and acclaim has been accorded such Wilson plays as *Deafman Glance*, *The Life and Times of Joseph Stalin*, *The Life and Times of Sigmund Freud*, and *The $ Value of Man*.

At five hours, the popular *Einstein* was practically a quickie by Wilson's standards — *Stalin* lasted 12 hours, and one Wilson play presented in Iran lasted seven days without so much as an intermission. When Wilson does manage to keep the length down to a "normal" time, the title seems to expand. His last New York show was called *I Was Sitting on My Patio This Guy Appeared I Thought I Was Hallucinating*. Wilson casts range from two performers (*Patio*) to about 500 (in Iran). Sound effects range from seven hours of silence to five hours of nonstop music.

Ironically, the creator of these massive works had a massive dislike for theater in his younger days. "I hated it," he told me during an interview at his lower-Manhattan loft. "And I didn't know anything about it.

"In fact, I still hate it. I love ballet—Balanchine, Merce Cunningham, and all—but even there, I just like the architectural arrangement and the music. That's enough for me. I don't like the stories, and I never could get involved in Shakespeare and Tennessee Williams and all that stuff. It requires too much thinking. I just like to see a pretty picture or arrangement."

This attitude has roots deep in Wilson's past. "I'm visually concerned, not literarily," he says. "As a child, I was always concerned that the drinking glass was here instead of there. I don't know why. When I was six or seven. I'd wake up in the middle of the night and go to my parents' kitchen and rearrange all the glasses on the shelf, because it was driving me crazy that the tall one was in this spot, and the short one in that spot. Other directors were reading books, or something, but I was busy discerning these patterns."

Wilson got into theater "by accident." A painter who had studied architecture, he started teaching in various institutions during the mid-1960s, and doing welfare work with the handicapped, the very young, and the very old.

"Somewhere toward the end of the '60s," he recalls. "I started bringing people together from all the different communities I was working in, and started making plays with them. I was a sort of forum for bringing together people who wouldn't normally get together. Everyone contributed something. It was like making a dinner together—everyone did what they could do. The plays required no special gifts or talents, but used what people could do naturally. They were architecturally arranged, not literary structures. The main concern was how things were arranged in time and space."

Eventually Wilson "phased out" of this "communal" work but continued using a wide variety of people in his plays. He also kept his visual and temporal interests in the forefront, infuriating audiences who were not prepared for his slow and storyless art.

Today, Wilson finds that his work goes over much better in Europe than in the United States. "Europe is much older, and there's more cultural awareness." he says. Though he has threatened in recent months to boycott the US—fed up with restless, coughing spectators and insensitive entrepreneurs—the forthcoming run of *DD&D* indicates some softening on this issue, and the event will be a welcome homecoming in the eyes of his many ardent US fans.

Spalding Gray has had a very different kind of career, though he acknowledges Wilson's influence on his work with the Performance Group in New York. Trained in traditional acting techniques, he became increasingly dissatisfied with the "job" of playing fictional roles and mimicking make-believe emotions.

"I was constantly having to express things I hadn't felt in my life," he said during a conversation in his lower-Manhattan loft. "I felt that if I did express them, and managed to convince people, then where did that leave me? All I can compare it with is prostitution. It was a very empty feeling because there was no emotional root."

Bit by bit, hampered by having no "model" to follow, Gray developed his own solution to the dilemma. He began to do improvisations based on his own responses to memories, spontaneous ideas, and props found in sidewalk sales or five-and-dime stores. Eventually he asked some fellow actors to join him — not "following the leader," but bringing their own perceptions and ideas to bear. One of these colleagues was Elizabeth LeCompte, who later dropped out of the improvisations and became an "outside eye" that could observe, make critical judgments, and cull the moments that worked from the ones that didn't.

The result was *Sakonnet Point*, which Gray describes as being "like a collage or a dance or a silent poem. It's like having a long day with nothing to do, where small movements mean a lot… It's an abstract piece, really like a dance."

The title was chosen when the piece was complete: it recalls a Rhode Island location where Gray spent summers a child. "I wanted the title to refer to a physical place," explains Gray. "I wanted something that would bridge the gap between the community which I've left behind and the art I've chosen in its place. The title *Sakonnet Point* is like an iconographic gesture in Buddhism, where the Buddha touches the earth with one hand and raises his other hand toward the sky. By choosing the Indian name of Sakonnet Point, I was touching the earth. But I was reaching to the sky with my spaced-out new theatrical piece."

The work of Gray (star, main character) and LeCompte (director, designer) became more controversial when they decided to expand *Sakonnet Point* into a trilogy called *Three Places in Rhode Island*. In an unprecedented play called *Rumstick Road*, they developed improvisations around tape recordings of Gray's real-life family, dealing mostly with the suicide of Gray's mother some years earlier. Some spectators were deeply moved by the work's haunting sincerity and theatrical brilliance. Others were offended by its undisguised autobiographical elements—amounting to full-scale invasion of privacy, some felt—or by its irreverent references to such subjects as religious belief and psychiatry.

"We were questioning the validity of memory." Gray remarks. "Jorge Luis Borges speaks of memory as a stack of coins: You have only the top coin to deal with, the present thing, because you can only remember in the present. The play is about memory. not about suicide. Still, I was interested in the confessional angle... and I regarded the family tapes as sociological documents."

In the third *Rhode Island* piece, called *Nayatt School*, Gray and LeCompte launched a monumental exploration into the nature of sanity. the role of socialization in shaping personality, the cultural functions of medical practices, the ambiguous boundaries between "acting" and "performing" and "real life," the co-option of children by adults, and T. S. Eliot's *The Cocktail Party*. Again response to the show was mixed, but audiences steadily grew as the show continued its engagement (and its evolution) over several months and a couple of tours.

Gray and LeCompte now are developing a "footnote" to the *Rhode Island* trilogy, to be called *Point Judith*. After the extensive feminine imagery of the trilogy, which dealt largely with Gray's mother as a character and a guiding image, the new work will explore masculinity. Once more, the show is evolving bit by bit through extensive improvisations—visions and revisions, initiated by Gray and presided over by LeCompte.

"Looked at from one angle," says Gray, who has taught "autobiographical theater" at New York University. "I'm not playing myself at all. In a sense, Liz LeCompte invented the character of 'Spalding Gray' just as Cézanne invented something new when he painted a portrait of his wife. I bring the themes we work with, but she is the structuralist of the team. When people write about our work. they always split our functions into separate things. Actually, our work—she as director, me as performer—intersect much more than they would in regular theater."

It is an unorthodox way of developing plays. Though the influence of other theater artists shows in their work occasionally (such as Robert Wilson and Meredith Monk in *Sakonnet Point*, Eugene O'Neill and T. S. Eliot in the other plays), cinematic metaphors also come readily to mind when assessing the trilogy. The indelible images of *Rumstick Road* recall Stan Brakhage's artistic revivification of a deceased pet in *Sirius Remembered*—coincidentally, an original theme of *Rumstick Road* was the death of childhood pets—while the fractured time and space of *Nayatt School* recall the intense concentration of experience in Jean-Marie Straub's *Not Reconciled*. These films are not direct influences on the trilogy: yet similar artistic preoccupations have a way of surfacing simultaneously in different places at the same time, just as scientific discoveries do.

For himself, Gray distrusts a medium (cinema) that presents an "image" with no real substance attached. "The presence of my body gives me real *connection* in the theater," he says. "I'd like to write poetry, too, but I connect more with the spoken word than with the written word. My body is my medium. I see myself as a theater poet, and 1 want to develop that. When I finish an evening. I'm very full, because I've been with an audience and given that gift—that presentation—for the evening. I have an enormous desire to make these pieces and then show them. And I'm happier now than I've ever been."

Other theatrical artists are working in equally new equally unexplored areas. For example: Meredith Monk explores conundrums in music, form, and movement in her acclaimed *Education of the Girlchild*; Joan Jonas (a star of *Nayatt School*) offers an eccentric, deeply personal interpretation of a fairy tale in *The Juniper Tree*; Bob Carroll offers a manic one-man biology lesson, vaudeville show, and power-to-the-people tract in *The Salmon Show*; Richard Foreman is famous for cramming more visual astonishment into a Soho loft than many directors conjure up in huge Broadway theaters.

Such visionary stuff does not lead to smash hits, movie contracts, and TV talk-show appearances. Yet the influence and ingenuity of these uncompromising experimenters is being felt—and will be felt increasingly in the years to come.

Strange, provocative look at Hitler's world
Interview with Hans-Jürgen Syberberg, March 5, 1980

By any measure, *Our Hitler—A Film From Germany* is one of the most massive movies ever made. More than seven hours long, it poses physical as well as intellectual challenges for its audience. It's a film of almost intimidating proportions: an epic monologue that sweeps across nearly every aspect of the Hitler phenomenon, inventing a new kind of cinema language in the process. Since it was completed about two years ago, director Hans-Jürgen Syberberg has traveled with it around Europe, showing it at film festivals, universities, and enterprising theaters. Not long ago it attracted the attention of Francis Ford Coppola—best known as the director of *Apocalypse Now* and the *Godfather* pictures—who brought it to the United States. Response has been strong in the cities where it has been shown so far; and Syberberg is ready to screen it anywhere public demand crops up. And he was mightily pleased with the reception given *Our Hitler* during a large showing at Lincoln Center here. He made notes on the audience, "like a critic," and gathered that most spectators were following the film closely and intelligently. This has reinforced his hope that "a new aesthetic" may develop in film, to replace the popular entertainment represented by the TV series *Holocaust*, which he cordially despises.

In terms of style, *Our Hitler* is a unique experience—slow, fascinating, pretentious, inescapable. It takes place entirely on a stage, which partly accounts for its claustrophobic atmosphere. The actors and the camera move slowly and deliberately about the playing area, which is littered with mannikens, dummies, and ostentatious props. On the rear wall we see huge slide projections, representing the places in Hitler's life. Sometimes their effect is almost realistic, making it appear that an actor is strolling through one of the dictator's old haunts. More often, the effect is expressionistic—evoking feelings and impressions without pinning us down to particular biographical or historical facts. Within this setting, a small company of actors (generally seen one or two at a time) launches a seven-hour torrent of talk. Using little in the way of dialogue or off-screen narration, Syberberg prefers to have his characters speak directly to the camera, occasionally using ventriloquists' dummies as intermediaries. *Our Hitler* is a movie that moves very little. Its aim is contemplation, not action.

Yet this is very much a film, not an illustrated lecture. Just as slide projection is one of its key visual devices, the concept of projection is its main metaphor. Did Hitler project his will on the German people? Or, as Syberberg suggests, did the Germans project their unconscious needs and desires onto their leader? Even more outrageously, was all of World War II a massive media event—a loathsome spectacle concocted by Hitler to ensure his immortality in films assembled by his ever-busy crew of movie-makers? In a sense, all of *Our Hitler* is a passionate response to the Führer's own noxious misuse of the film medium. This helps explain some of the unorthodox choices made by Syberberg in planning the work. To use conventional characters and plot devices, for example, could have been as manipulative (though in a more constructive way) as Hitler's propagandistic ploys. Above all, Syberberg has sought to avoid any vestige of sensationalism— what he calls "left-wing concentration-camp pornography." As it turns out, *Our Hitler* is so "pure" in this regard as to become almost abstract. Yet it remains an uncommonly provocative film.

Over lunch recently in New York, I asked Syberberg if his film could be seen as a compendium of the same forces that converged at an earlier time to form Hitler himself. Syberberg agreed, remarking that "Hitler was not a man of the right or the left, in the usual sense. His genius was that he didn't invent. Rather, he drew together different things from different areas of history, tradition, ideology, and technology. And he turned all these things to his own purpose. I used the same system, putting things together in another way, for another purpose—to oppose him. Like Hitler, I use Wagner. But my use is quite different." The soundtrack of *Our Hitler* throbs with music of Wagner, Verdi, Beethoven, and other great composers. It also contains long passages from archival recordings, dating back to the Third Reich. The use of these recordings blends well with the film's dense audiovisual texture, providing a rich historical flavor without the intrusive imagery that inevitably clings to the occasional newsreel footage that is also included. In many instances, however, it was budgetary considerations that prompted the use of sounds where sights would have been preferable. According to Syberberg, less money was available to make *Our Hitler* than was used by Ingmar Bergman to run tests.

The shooting schedule was also uncommonly short—about three weeks, though this was preceded by four years of planning. Through it all, Syberberg hoped to make a film that would not just be not just be about politics, but would be a political act in itself. The result is a major statement about the Hitler period, with special reference to two controversial subtopics: the continuing reverberations of Hitler's mentality in the world today, and the potential dangers of the democratic form of government which allowed Hitler to achieve his power through legal electoral means. Syberberg is pleased that audiences are provoked and stimulated by his meditations on these subjects. "Art must always be in motion," he says. "When it becomes quiet, it's dead. And the same goes for politics. But in art the aim is not always to climb up, so we reach the top of some mountain. The movement can be backwards, or in the direction of meditation. I don't know how much hope there is in other things, like politics, but art is healthy as long as it keeps moving."

Syberberg wasn't sure what response *Our Hitler* would find in the United States. "Coming to the country of Hollywood," he says, "I expected to find the difficulties that might be encountered by an enemy of this kind of aesthetic. People here are brought up with the idea of entertainment, box office, and quick-moving stories, with lots of crime and sex. The early Hollywood had a lot of power—Griffith and Stroheim and such filmmakers—but today people use TV as a substitution for life. And on top of that, I am very different from Fassbinder and the other German directors who are known by Americans. I am far from the European and German cultural traditions. How could I expect people to follow me?

"Aesthetics are connected with morals," he insists. "Something like *Holocaust* is immoral because it is a bad film. Bad art can't do good things. In many ways, Leni Riefenstahl was a good director in the films she made for Hitler, and maybe she was quite avant-garde, too. But we know her work was not done for good purposes." In his own case, Syberberg's purity of purpose may be less debatable than the actual products of his imagination and his camera. Perhaps the virtues and shortcomings of *Our Hitler* will be easier to assess when the screenplay is published soon in book form, with an introduction by Susan Sontag, who is an avowed admirer of the film. On the printed page, for example, we may see more clearly the film's maddening lack of specificity in some areas—its reliance on allusion. One is reminded of Nietzsche's references to "intimation" in his work *The Case of Wagner*, particularly the wry suggestion that intimations are often a substitute for thought. "Nothing is more compromising than a thought," wrote the philosopher in a sarcastic mood.

Syberberg's film is full of thought, and it dearly desires to provoke thought in its viewers. Yet there is something here of "infinity, but without melody," to quote Nietzsche again. One feels that Syberberg might have accomplished his task in far less time, and with far less bother, if he did not so fiercely champion art — and artifice — as the predecessor and protector of intellect and analysis. In proclaiming its own artfulness, *Our Hitler* protests too much. And rambles about in the process. Still, one must heartily admire Syberberg's insistence on noble motivations inextricably coupled with noble deeds. What's his opinion of second-rate film that seeks to lead people in a beneficial direction? "Even that is no good," he answers, "because you are moving the audience only by quick excitement. Afterward they feel regret, and unhappiness. And then you are in a worse situation than before."

New sound—and a new world—for George Shearing
Interview with George Shearing, April 20, 1980

For many years, the George Shearing Quintet was a mainstay of the jazz world, specializing in its own brand of crisp, sophisticated sound. At its center was Shearing himself, a dedicated craftsman who traveled to the United States from his native England in 1947 and has been heard from continuously since. In recent times, Shearing has moved to a more intimate musical profile, disbanding his quintet and appearing with only a bass player to share the spotlight. His reputation has continued to ride high, and he has felt freer than ever to explore the depths of his sound and his style. He has also kept up his strong interest in classical music, playing with symphony orchestras around the United States, and experimenting with music that blends jazz and classical idioms. He is something of a TV personality, too, having appeared on a wide selection of talk and variety shows; and he has devoted a great deal of time to teaching at jazz schools and workshops. Shearing now records for the Concord label, which carries his latest album, *Blues Alley Jazz*, a potpourri ranging from new material to "Up a Lazy River." The following interview was conducted at Shearing's apartment in New York.

On your latest album, you do some singing. Isn't this a fairly new direction in your career?

I've been singing for just a few years, professionally—that is, on records and on the air. You have to listen to yourself a lot first, to learn how consistent you are, and how good your intonation is. You have to learn a lot of things about yourself.

Self-examination is an important part of jazz, then?

Your performance depends on your mental and physical attitude. If you have a feeling of well-being, and technical ease as well, you'll come out fine. And that goes for any movement, whether it's walking or conversing, or whatever. What counts is: Have you been taking care of yourself? Or are you carrying around extra physical and mental baggage? That's why I never like to argue before I perform. And the same goes for downers like alcohol.

Lately you have been working in a duo, with just a bass player at your side. Why did you disband your quintet?

It comes back to mental attitude. For the past few years, the quintet was on automatic pilot. Just coasting along. You see, the larger the group, the more you must be fettered by preconceived arrangements—and the less chance there is for on-the-spot creativity... Of course, the members of the quintet were always playing choruses and going into improvisation. But if a member of the audience requested something one of us didn't know, we couldn't comply. Now I work with a bassist who has very good ears, and can sight-read anything you put in front of him. If the tune is of a fairly simple nature, and doesn't go on for five years, chances are he'll pick it after the first time. So I have nobody else to worry about... And, of course, the logistics have an ease and lack of complexity. I have a greater opportunity to address myself to the task of being a pianist, rather than a bandleader.

Your greatest hit is probably "Lullaby of Birdland," written in 1952. Is it true you composed this classic in ten minutes?

Yes, over a steak in my dining room in New Jersey. But I always tell people, it took me 10 minutes and 35 years in the business. Just in case anybody thinks there are any totally free rides left, there are none!

How did you start in the music world? Were you gifted at an early age?

Yes, I think so. When I was about three or four years of age, I used to toddle over to the piano and pick out the tunes I'd just heard on the old crystal set.

A lot of parents wish their children would approach the piano so enthusiastically.

Success usually comes from personal incentive somewhere along the way. We get mixed up between parents who want their children to play, and parents who assist their children with lessons. Of course, I don't know anybody who loves to practice. But there's a difference between kids you have to carry over to the piano and those who toddle over by themselves.

And you were one of the toddlers.

Yes. Also, while there are many activities of play that the blind can involve themselves in, it must be fewer than those available to the sighted. So if there's any kind of musical incentive at all, it is automatically increased by the slight lessening—however slight—of other available activities.

You weren't just interested, though. You were talented.

For as long as I can remember, someone could play a ten-note chord, and I could play it right after them—they never had to spell it out. I have that kind of ear. Natural ability like this is born; the degree to which one can utilize it can be cultivated. Certain things within the ear can be cultivated.

Did you take lessons at that time?

From age five to age 12, in a kind of day school. The supervision there was less close than in the residential school I attended between 12 and 16. When anyone was watching, we'd play Liszt or whatever the teacher wanted. But then we'd get permission to use the piano for half an hour, and we'd play tunes of the day, or jazz. I'd even use some of my practice time for that, if there was nobody around to police me. But always, it was a desire to do something at the piano. It wasn't a matter of "how can I get out of it."

So you always leaned to improvisation?

Oh, yes. My teacher would give me eight bars to learn by the next lesson, but I was a terrible Braille music-reader. I'd come back with only two bars learned. The teacher would call me a silly fool and play the other six bars.

Did you have to be a sort of childhood rebel, to be able to play more and more of your kind of music?

I never looked at it like that, in those days. You see—I could pontificate on this subject for hours—discipline is necessary. It disturbs me considerably when an 18- or 19-year-old comes to me, before ever having met me, and addresses me as George. I am bothered by the assumption that no degree of seniority is necessary to gain equality. That leads to the attitude of, "Who says I have to abide by the rules?" And it potentially leads to a kind of lawlessness. In terms of music, it leads to people asking, "Who says a consonant chord is 1-3-5, and a dissonant chord is 1-2-3 or 1-2-4? What is consonance and what is dissonance?" When you ask questions like these, nothing is taken for granted and accepted without examination. After this, all kinds of rules can be questioned, including social rules. Where does it end? What are the consequences, in terms of one human being having respect for another, and doing what the other would like—including a parent who wants the children home at a reasonable hour?

But in jazz, isn't it good to experiment—to question all the assumptions, to challenge the old concepts?

Within reason. But if everyone did it, we'd have nothing traditional—only freedom jazz. Jazz has its Bach, too, in the traditionalists. There's a traditional bass line, and so forth.

To return to your professional history, when did you start playing in public?

I left school at 16. I could play enough piano to earn my living. I wasn't a high-standard professional, but I got a job in a neighborhood pub, for the princely sum of about $5 a week, and a box on the piano for gratuities. I did that for a year. Then I joined a semi-professional band, and then an all-blind band that did Ellington and Lunceford arrangements… And the drummer of that band introduced me to [critic] Leonard Feather. He got BBC and recording dates for me. Then I started winning trade-magazine polls in England. I became more jazz-oriented all the time.

Was your immigration to the United States a professional move?

Yes, very much so. The second world war was over, and I felt I'd gone about as far as I could. I was married, and we came to the US for a three-month vacation. Then we went back, sold our home, and returned. I had been encouraged by fine American jazz musicians I'd met during the war—Fats Waller, Glenn Miller, and others—and I thought I'd come here and just lay everybody out! But people weren't really interested in my ability to play like Tatum and Waller, even though they often expressed it that way.

They really wanted to hear what I had that was mine. So when the quintet came out, I established my identity. And I established what I was going to offer at the end of the frantic, frenetic bebop period. People wanted what I did, so I was able to sell it to them. We abided by the strictest tradition in playing the melody. But what happened after the first statement was anybody's guess, until we finally returned to the first chorus.

Have your own tastes in jazz — as a listener — evolved and changed over the years?

Oh, yes. I've loved Art Tatum, Teddy Wilson, Fats Waller. And I haven't disposed of these people; I still enjoy listening to them. But I've added to them — Bill Evans, Chick Corea, Herbie Hancock. I love Bach, Delius, Ravel, Debussy. And I've added to them Bartók, Hindemith. and I still love Mozart.

Overall, is jazz in a healthy state today?

Yes. There's a healthy integration between jazz, folk, rock. I like that merging of categories, as long as it's not too blurred. I also like the idea of mixing jazz and classical music and crossing those barriers. I like an ever-increasing search for something different, as long as one is constantly conscious of the necessity to obtain permission for the search — by maintaining the musically traditional, and thus some degree of sanity.

A "shadow warrior" from Japan heads for America
Interview with Akira Kurosawa, October 23, 1980

It was a good idea when they asked Akira Kurosawa to direct the *Shogun* miniseries for TV. In the West, he is easily the most famous of all Japanese filmmakers, with a long line of hits including *Rashomon*, *Yojimbo*, and *The Seven Samurai*. But Kurosawa turned down the offer, for a fascinating reason. He looked at the story, examined the characters, and promptly declared he couldn't involve himself with a project that had so little to do with the actual facts and spirit of Japanese history. As the director of many historical films, as well as contemporary subjects, Kurosawa knows the necessity of ending stories and ordering events for dramatic purposes. Yet he also has a sharp sense of where to draw the line. In all his pictures that deal with the past, he has worked to convey the essence of two visions: what it was like then and what we can draw now.

Kurosawa's 27th picture, now playing in the United States, is an epic called *Kagemusha*. It shares the vast scale of his last movie, *Dersu Uzala*, which won the 1975 Oscar for best foreign-language film. But this time there's also a period setting, a welter of action scenes, and a cast of thousands (it looks like thousands, anyway) that has made *Kagemusha*, the most expensive production ever undertaken in Japan. Some of the cost was underwritten by Twentieth Century-Fox in a rare display of big-studio confidence. American directors George Lucas and Francis Ford Coppola are credited as executive producers of the subtitled "international version."

The hero of *Kagemusha* is a "shadow warrior"—a man who impersonates the leader of his clan to confuse their enemies. Only in this case the "warrior" is a condemned thief who has been forced into his new role, and the deception is aimed not just at enemies, but at members of the clan itself—whose loyalty must be maintained after the real chief has gone insane and died.

In a recent conversation with Kurosawa—assisted by translator Audie Bock, who is currently rendering the filmmaker's autobiography into English—I asked what interested him in the *Kagemusha* story. He replied that he had been researching another project when he ran across historical accounts of the battle that ends the film. "I couldn't find any parallels to it in the rest of Japanese history," he said. "All the generals on one side died, a whole clan was decimated. And on the other side, no one died.

That peculiarity fascinated me." Kurosawa decided to dramatize this unusual event. Yet he couldn't deal with it too braodly—he needed a focus for the tale. "I had to find a narrower angle through which to view the whole thing," he says. "That's when I discovered that this warlord had doubles, who impersonated him by his own command. I hit on the idea of seeing the battle, and the events that led up to it, through the eyes of one of these men."

Most Japanese samurai films take place during the Tokugawa shogunate, which began in the early 17th century. Yet most of Kurosawa's period movies (leaving out *Yojimbo* and *Sanjuro*) take place during the time of civil war before that, in the 16th century. "When the Tokugawa shoguns took over," he says, "they set up a rigid class structure. The samurai were one of the four classes, and their freedom was completely gone—the purpose of the shogunate was to keep them in line. But during the civil war before that, very interesting warlords vied for power all over Japan. The competition was fascinating. Also, these were very distinctive and energetic characters. One of them, for example, was a farmer. Because of the strength of his personality and his energy, he took over a good part of the country, and for a time he held sway over the whole place. That wasn't possible later, when the class system was established."

Kurosawa's interest in these matters is not isolated or detached. Rather, he sees a strong relevance to contemporary life in chronicles of the past. "The Tokugawa period was very bureaucratic, with a very rigid structure," he says, expressing his personal viewpoint on the subject. "I feel Japan today is also very bureaucratic. And I don't like that situation. I'd like to see Japan closer to the way things were during that time of civil war. I only wish we had politicians in Japan today who were as strong as Nobunaga," he continues, referring to a *Kagemusha* warlord. "And unless we get them, I don't feel there is much hope for Japan."

Of course, Kurosawa isn't looking for civil war to break out. "But I would like to see more free competition in Japan," he says. "The situation now is most uninteresting. If we could get our leaders from more different sources, it would be much better." Not that *Kagemusha* is a "message movie" about the dangers of bureaucracy in Japan. "That's not the reason I made the picture," he says. "I did it because I found the people and the subject interesting, and I wanted to transform them into a film people throughout the world could enjoy. That's all."

Still, Kurosawa feels other resonances between the era of *Kagemusha* and today. "I've always been drawn to the splendor and energy and power of that time," he admits. "It's not the politics and warfare that fascinate me. The warlords competed culturally, as well, and influenced the taste of the whole country during their times of power. Look at the things they had: their arts and letters, their magnificent castles, the clothes they wore, the utensils and dishes they ate with. We don't have anything like that in Japan today, nothing of that quality. I'd like to show that again, to people all over the world."

In his long and detailed book on *The Films of Akira Kurosawa*, Donald Richie tells many times of the lengths Kurosawa goes to in ensuring the rightness and authenticity of his images—building an entire town as the set for *Red Beard*, for example, complete with century-old roof tiles. This kind of attention is integral to Kurosawa's vision. "It does appear to me that the further back you go in history," he says, "the better things were, and the objects were connected with how the people were—the more wonderful the objects, the more wonderful must have been the people who prized them. Today, not only in Japan but all over the world, the only thing that has really advanced is that technique of killing people. Throughout the world, the spiritual values of human beings have decayed with time." In his films, Kurosawa is battling this tendency. They are never flawless—*Kagemusha* goes on much too long in its spectacle scenes, and its human relationships seem rather tortured at times. But everywhere you can see the care Kurosawa lavishes on telling details, right down to the freely flowing clothes worn by the women, so much less restricting than the rigid get-ups fancied in the Tokugawa period.

In his book on Kurosawa's films, Richie repeatedly finds a theme running through the picture: Good people are always in a state of becoming, or growth, while bad or misguided people have become rigid and inflexible. The same goes for *Kagemusha*, where the hero must learn new kinds of courage and resourcefulness, even though his efforts are doomed. And something similar goes for Kurosawa, who says that "the older you get, the easier it is to keep with the same formal construction in your films. I try to change things consciously," he adds. "I try to keep it new, to keep it interesting for myself."

Yet cinematic form is only part of the situation. Kurosawa feels other things matter, such as the director's personality, and the cultural framework in which he works. for Kurosawa, this has very much to do with being Japanese. "I feel there is something essential that the best Japanese films have in common," he says. "It can't be expressed adequately in words, and you shouldn't look for it only in the form of the pictures. Rather, it comes from what's in the heart of the director. I hope people will look for that, in other people's films as well as mine. it's the most important thing, this element of the heart."

Tradition re-seen: composer Steve Reich
Interview with Steve Reich, October 23, 1980

Steve Reich is among the dominant figures of today's most popular
and influential "New Music." He and his ensemble have been
cheered at Carnegie Hall, praised by major critics, and recorded
by prestigious labels. In the meanwhile, his work has continued to
evolve, and controversy over his techniques has remained active.
Along with such kindred composer as Philip Glass, Terry Riley,
and LaMonte Young, Reich began his career in a "minimalist"
vein. One early piece, "Four Organs," took all its notes from a
single chord played over and over; another planned composition, "Slow-Motion Sound," couldn't be played at all because the
necessary technology didn't exist. Over the years he has moved
away from tape and electronic music, preferring to work exclusively with acoustical instruments and vocalists. His pieces have
also become more dense in structure and more lavish in instrumentation. His interest in pulsing rhythms and sensuous timbres
has earned great popularity for his compositions, even among
listeners not schooled in classical tradition. Non-Western influences have played a strong part in his development as a composer,
as has his own past experience as a listener, a student of the human-
ities—he almost chose graduate studies in philosophy instead of
composing—and a professional jazz drummer. He spoke with me
in the Manhattan loft where he works and lives.

*Your work has gathered a lot of momentum lately, in terms of
popularity. Are you concerned with the widespread acceptance of
your music?*

Yes, I am. I believe that music does not exist in a vacuum. One
mode of feedback I rely on most is the popular, naive reaction.
No offense intended, but a critic is often politically biased, for or
against a composer. A review may virtually exist before the critic
even attends the concert! So the public reaction can be a better
weathervane of the music's basic health.

Why has your music flourished so well in the past few years?

The reasons are probably simple. The music has a steady pulse, and
it uses tonal materials. You can whistle fragments of a tune, and
the general patterns will stay in your head. It wasn't written to be

accessible; it was written because that's the way I am. But this turns out to be accessible!

How does this contrast with other contemporary music?

A lot of music by people like Boulez, Cage, and Stockhausen was not rhythmical, not tonal. It was quite difficult to get a handle on what was going on. New Music was a kind of bitter pill—you had to take your culture with your cod-liver oil. My work, and that of Glass and Riley, comes as a breath of fresh air to the New Music world. A listener can come because he wants to come, and enjoy it. You can like some pieces, and not like others.

Is this a major new trend?

I feel there is definitely a movement in the music community at large—not so much toward my style, but toward working with traditional musical material. Sometimes this is called the New Romanticism or the New Classicism, though this doesn't describe what I'm doing. Some of this work may not be very important. But the basic feeling is very healthy. It's a feeling of moving back—away from a recondite and isolated position, toward a more mainstream approach. It's a matter of working within an accessible musical tradition, whether this purely Western or influenced by non-Western sources.

Many of your pieces are based on strict musical procedures that are clearly audible in the music itself. You even wrote an essay called "Music as a Gradual Process," expressing your enthusiasm for slow and steady musical development that allows the listener to detect every nuance. How did this interest come about?

I wrote that essay in 1968, when there was a lot of interest in "chance techniques" and free improvisation, as opposed to structure. If you did anything structured, you were regarded as a kind of fascist. It was almost un-American to write composed music! I felt this was basically wrong and unfair. I also felt it was inhuman to ask someone to give up a lifetime's experience in playing music that was written, not to mention lopping off several hundred years of considerable importance. So I made a point of saying that the musical process should be perceptible. It was a personal statement, in distinction to people like John Cage—who used nonmusical devices to make music, perhaps with philosophical overtones, although this isn't such a concern anymore.

In seeking to avoid chance elements, you might have stayed with electronic music, where you can have total control over every detail. Why do you work with live musicians, instead?

Let's say you're playing a piece of traditional music, like a Beethoven concerto. No matter how careful the conductor is, no matter how good the musicians are, there are going to be imperfections in tuning, variations in tempo, and changes of nuance from one performance to the next. But those are what give the work its life and its character!

What about the possibilities offered by music synthesizers?

If I really wanted my work perfect, I would synthesize it. But there are two reasons I don't. First, I don't like the sound of synthesizers. Second, here's why I don't like it. Take a synthesized tone, run it into an oscilloscope, and you'll see a steady wave form on the screen. But ask a violinist to play the same note similarly — with no vibrato and no inflection whatsoever — and you see the tone on the oscilloscope dancing and jumping all over the place! Now go into the room blindfolded. In about three seconds you can hear and feel that it's live music. It's that microvariation in a "perfect" ensemble that gives the music its life. Also, there are the incredible complexities in the human voice. Even when you're working in a "controlled" structure, the material itself is so vibrant, and so beyond your control, that a tension exists. So I don't feel it's necessary to seek out the aleatory, or "chance," element. I feel this is a part of life. Human control is over a certain domain, and to go further than that is demonic and inhuman. Then again, I'd rather not relinquish control, either. There's a balance in the basic thrust of Western music, and I agree with this. I'm willing to try to continue it.

This reminds me of a conversation I had with Michael Snow, the experimental filmmaker. I asked him about the small technical imperfections in celebrated works like Wavelength *and* Back-and-Forth. *He said these gave the films their character — a totally smooth zoom shot is less "human" than a zoom with little lurches and hesitations, which give evidence of the hand guiding the shot.*

Michael Snow is a good friend, and *Wavelength* is as fine a film as has ever been shown. I agree all the way.

Still, your work tends to be precise, even rigorous. Is it as satisfying to play as more traditional music?

It's different from playing the piano solo in a romantic concerto, but it's not that different from playing baroque music, which is also precisely notated. If it weren't satisfying to play, why should the same musicians work with me for 10 or 15 years?

It is a repetitious kind of music, though.

Yes. But the only time it's difficult to play is the rare occurrence when we're not having a good performance. Repetition is only a bore when you're not "on." When we are "on," I literary feel energy flowing up my arms. And I feel full of energy after a performance—so much that it's difficult to sleep.

Is performance "self-expression"?

No, not for me. But it's incredibly enjoyable. For me, performance is playing the music, whatever the music may be. And when it's mine, I want all the musicians to love playing it.

How did your tastes develop? How does your work relate to other musical trends, past and present?

Tradition is the key word. I'm an American, not a European. Therefore I live in a racially and religiously mixed society. And that's very valuable—it makes us off from more homogenous societies. For example, jazz is obviously a derivative of black culture. Yet for anyone not to listen to jazz in America is like being a cultural ostrich, with your ears in the sand. As a child, I heard Beethoven and Wagner and Schubert, but none of it made a great impression on me. I also took piano lessons, but it was the middle-class John Thompson-type course, where you did watered-down versions of Mozart and Haydn. What really made a dent on me was at the age of 14, when I heard—within a few months—the Brandenburg Concertos of Bach, *The Rite of Spring* by Stravinsky, and the jazz of Charlie Parker and Miles Davis. That whole family of music had an enormous influence on me: baroque music, Stravinsky's and that of Bartók shortly thereafter, and jazz from around 1950 up to the end of John Coltrane's life. I decided then and there to study drums. And to this day, my tastes are a combination of these influences—tonal music with a steady pulse and a certain vitality.

Did you continue to listen to a lot of jazz when you were heavily involved in classical studies?

Yes. While I studied privately, and when I was at Juilliard between 1958 and 1961, I went to jazz clubs all the time. I loved Coltrane's modal period, when he did "My Favorite Things" and pieces like that. It was just two chords, basically, and that drew me like a magnet. It's very full-blown, very sophisticated music based on a very limited harmonic vocabulary. But the jazz that followed Coltrane went in another direction, in which I had no interest whatever—music that really doesn't have a tonal base. Ornette Coleman, and so forth. I admire it, but I don't care for it.

How about rock-and-roll? Your most famous colleague, Philip Glass, has demonstrated a strong interest in rock. And rock might be called a stepchild of jazz.

I never became that involved with rock-and-roll, because it happened later on. It was an interesting sociological phenomenon, and I liked a couple of tunes by the Motown groups and very early Bob Dylan—"Maggie's Farm"—but since that time I've had minimal contact with rock-and-roll.

So you missed rhythm and blues in the '50s?

Yes. I was into Charlie Parker, so I had no use for the likes of Chuck Berry!

How about your frequent use of amplification? Are you reaching for the sense of presence and volume often associated with jazz?

The use of amplification in some of the pieces is not to make the music louder, but to create certain balances that would be impossible otherwise. for example, if you play piano in the upper register, and a xylophone at the same time, the xylophone will completely obliterate the piano. By amplifying the piano, you can create a balance between them. Then, too, though a piece like the Octet can be played acoustically, I have amplified it to help it hold its own on a program of much larger works, in a large place like Carnegie Hall. Also, mixing all the instruments through one source will make them blend even more. I'm not aiming at a separation of sources. I'm aiming at a sort of glorious monophonic sound, putting everything together.

Besides such Western influences as baroque and jazz, non-Western music has also played a large part in your work.

Yes, I heard African music for years, on recordings. I admired it, and it swung, and it was very exciting. But I had no idea how it was put together, and back in the '50s I had no serious idea how I could find out. Also, I had heard Balinese gamelan music, which I thought was unbelievably beautiful. Eventually I was able to study these musics, through books and teachers and correspondence, and I traveled to Africa for some firsthand experience. But I had studied drums long before I heard an African drummer, and I had a predisposition to African music long before I took a trip there. Going to Africa was more like an enormous pat on the back—a confirmation of directions I had been travelling in for some time. It was like a seal of approval to some basic instincts I had. It was thrilling to go to a culture where the "art music," the religious music, the most serious music was made with percussion, was acoustical, was organized primarily on a harmonic basis, and swung!

Have there been any other major influences on your work?

Yes, after a while, I started thinking about the fact that I'm not Balinese or African. I'm Jewish. So I became interested in my own backyard. From a personal and musicological standpoint, I became curious to pursue my own ethnicity, which is Western and non-Western at the same time. I studied cantillation, and even learned Hebrew at age 37.

All these influences notwithstanding, your music always has a sound all its own.

I hope so. If I use materials found in Bartók, it doesn't sound like Bartók, any more than my other music sounds African or Balinese. I would like to learn from the structures of these sources, without imitating their sound. Some composers do borrow directly—for example, by putting a sitar in a rock band. But I don't think this is the best way to use non-western music.

In one of your essays, you call this "the old exoticism trip."

Yes, and I don't like it very much. After all, sounds are very personal and ethnic. They're things you grow up with. I grew up with the piano scale in my head, and playing in the "cracks" doesn't come naturally. Most non-Western scales are really foreign to us. They're exotic and attractive, and I feel a sort of reverential, hands-off attitude toward them. Ultimately, scales and instruments come out of a certain place and a certain time, and have their own way to go. That's why I feel most at home with a percussion instrument I buy on 48th Street. I like to know it was made in Chicago and is tuned to the piano scale, and it's mine, and I can do what I want with it!

Still, you have gone into fairly unusual territory at times, particularly in your early tape pieces.

What got me into tape was an interest in working with speech. I had an interest in American poetry during the 1950s—especially William Carlos Williams, Ezra Pound, Robert Creeley, and Charles Olson. This group of poets drew their inspiration largely from American speech rhythms, which have a broken, irregular quality. I tried setting their poems to music, but it was unsuccessful: it robbed them of exactly they acquired by quoting phrases of jargon or slang or informal speech. Tape opened up the possibility of taking "found objects" of speech and using them as the basis—the musical subject—of the piece. Later, I became fascinated with the idea of changing the synchronization of two pieces of tape, creating new patterns through the changing "phase relationships" of the sounds. Later I carried this idea into live music, which I much prefer.

Today your work is a great amalgamation of the ideas we've talked about, and a few others, besides, Journalists and critics have come up with various terms to describe your music—which is often linked with that of Philip Glass and Terry Riley—but I find most of them unsatisfactory. Do you have a name for your work or your style?

No. In fact, I don't know of any composer who did. True, Schoenberg wanted to call his music "pantonal," but everyone else called it "atonal" or "12-tone." Nor do I wish to name my music. After all, it keeps changing. I've seen labels come and go. The one that strikes me as particularly absurd, though, is "trance music." This is the most unrealistic and sensational, in the cheap sense. There's no intent on my part to create anything like a trance. A lulling into unconsciousness would be the worst possible result. What I hope my music summons up is more attention to detail… A listener will listen the way he wants to, but if you ask me what an ideal listener is, I'll say someone who's as wide awake as possible.

Recalling Hollywood at the height of the cold war
Interview with Victor Navasky, January 2, 1981

At the height of the cold war, Hollywood found itself in hot water. Convinced that Communist influences had penetrated the movie business, the House Committee on Un-American Activities— loosely nicknamed HUAC—opened a massive investigation into the motion-picture community. Some witnesses cooperated, while others refused and found themselves on an employment blacklist, unable to get work because their patriotism was suspect. Communists, non-Communists, and anti-Communists wrestled with their consciences. Cool debates and hot arguments took place over the legal and moral ramifications of "taking the Fifth," "taking the First," or telling all. Some careers were ended, some reputations were ruined, some lives were shattered, and Hollywood has never forgotten the trauma—which is still being rehashed in such books as *Scoundrel Time*, by Lillian Hellman, and such movies as *The Front*, with Woody Allen.

Now Victor S. Navasky, editor of *The Nation*, has issued a stunning account of those difficult years called *Naming Names* (published by the Viking Press). For the first hundred pages or so, it's a meticulous though dry account of what happened to whom. Then the book catches fire, as Navasky devotes nearly 400 pages to a scrupulous investigation of the moral and cultural implications of the HUAC probe and the blacklist that grew out of it. It's a moral detective story, tracing what Navasky calls the "informer principle"—the idea that informing on one's colleagues, or "naming names," is not just good idea but a "litmus test" of patriotism and decency.

Though he examines all sides of the question, Navasky sides with those who resisted naming names. He contends that the HUAC hearings were a kind of "degradation ceremony" with little meaning, since "the committee had all the names anyway, and called witnesses only as a social ritual." He also explores the idea that the blacklisters and the blacklistees were equally victims of their time, critically examining the proposition that suffering was evenly distributed among all involved. In the process, he details the physical and intellectual history of the HUAC hearings and the blacklist. And he illustrates an enduring line from Jean Renoir's film *The Rules of the Game*, in which a character says, "… in this world there is one awful thing, and that is that everyone has his reasons…"

I met with Navasky recently and asked some questions about his investigation and his book.

A lot of people feel the United States has "swung to the right" lately. Do you feel the old Communist probes might return?

Last year, I was frequently asked: Why are you doing this now, 30 years after it happened? But ever since the election in November, the first question is: When you started this seven years ago, how did you know it would be so timely?! But I don't think it will happen again, in the same way—partly because of the example set by so many people who resisted and prevailed against the temptation to name names, putting themselves on the line. And there's a counterexample, too: the negative way our culture has come to regard those who did name names. No matter what one's politics are, the big consideration is, how does it look 20 years later?

What originally interested you in the topic?

I had a lot of friends whose parents had been hit by the blacklist. Also, I've always been interested in the whole subject of police informing. The Hollywood period had the highest per-capita number of informers, including people informing on their friends.

As you pursued your investigation, what was your approach?

I went at it almost a mystery story. Why did all these decent people behave indecently? Why did so many inform, though they had been brought up to think that's not the right thing to do—and there was no obvious national-security reason, since the names were already known by HUAC? Once I was into it, I just followed the material where it led. It's interesting that almost everybody who went through the days of the blacklist seems to judge himself— and others—not by how they are I've noticed that people who survived the blacklist are still eager to talk about the experience. I discussed this with Woody Allen when he starred in *The Front*, and he had noticed the same thing. The blacklist was tragedy. But if you survived it, the stigma was eventually removed, and one was proud of having resisted... It's a difficult area, and the moral issues are complex. I try not to pass judgment on people's motives.

Can you give an example?

Some people named names because they had been Communists, and later they felt they had contributed to the existence of Soviet-death-lists, and they had to make up for that.

In any event, you feel that naming names has profound social implications.

The whole notion of community is based on trust. If someone informs, it means you can't trust this other member of your community, and the impossibility of trusting your fellows. During the days of HUAC and the blacklist, the state took the willingness to betray one's friends, and made this the measure of civic virtue: That's how you proved you were cooperative. Totalitarian cultures do that all the time, but we're not supposed to do that there. so it reflects on our national state of mind…

Do the movies still carry a mark from the days of HUAC and the blacklist?

The movie business may have gone through enough structural changes to transcend the residue of values from the blacklist episode. But television is different: Shows are still half an hour, you still have sponsors, ad agencies still play an important role, the networks are still there. The same structure is in place, even though there's more independence. I have a feeling that the unwritten laws governing the TV business are not entirely attributable to the millions of dollars at stake. I'm talking about the obsession with ratings, the rules about what you can and can't put on, the great fear that seems to infect some of the people who work in TV. I think these things are partly attributable to the fact that TV was born as a mass medium during the cold war years…

Your book focuses on people during the cold war, who were faced with the question of informing against Communist Party members and sympathizers. But in the process, you paint a portrait of the party itself—and to my eyes, the portrait isn't flattering. How could intelligent people have complained about "thought control" from HUAC while putting up with the obvious "thought control" of their own party? Was their idealism that strong?

The cultural commissar in Hollywood was John Howard Lawson, and I talked to him before he died, about why he never criticized the Soviet Union. It's because he thought of himself as a humanist and a socialist, and he believed it was wrong to criticize the revolution—because socialism is still the only hope for mankind, and a certain amount of discipline is necessary to achieve this glorious goal. That was his reasoning. Of course, there are other factors, too—bureaucratic factors, and personal or self-serving ones. As Murray Kempton pointed out, it was the only way a $500-a-week writer could socialize with a $2,500-a-week writer: at a party meeting! And the religious analogy is real, also. Like some religions, you accept a set of dogmas as part of your faith, because of the ultimate virtues of the system. You turn over your conscience to the party, because they know better. In the same way, the witnesses turned over their consciences to the state. Or they just wanted to work, and it wasn't a matter of conscience. They violated their consciences.

Though you examine all sides of the question in your book, your sympathies are clear. Still, I think your approach is basically fair.

You know, the Communists did a lot of awful things. And they didn't hire their enemies, any more than the blacklisters did. But they weren't part of an organized system that denied work to anyone who took the Fifth Amendment at a hearing.

And it fascinates you that the government did catalyze such a system.

Yes. I wanted to deal with some of the key questions raised by that episode. For example, is there a statute of limitations on moral crimes?

Philip Glass—hard work and no compromises
Interview with Philip Glass, March 4, 1981

For many listeners, Philip Glass is the reigning king of the "new music" world. Certainly his range is impressive. What other musician has premiered his second opera and produced his first rock record within the space of a few weeks?

Though his work attracts a varied audience, Glass comes from strict classical background. His first "hit" was the four-and-a-half-hour *Einstein on the Beach*, directed by Robert Wilson, which proved enormously successful when it reached the Metropolitan Opera House in 1976. Since then Glass has toured widely, written several new works, played for capacity audiences at Carnegie Hall and elsewhere, and received a huge Rockefeller Foundation grant for general support of his career.

Glass' music is unique, with unusual instrumentation—largely saxophones and organs—and rigorous structures based on repetitive melodies and cyclical rhythms. Gradually he is building a wide following comprising classical and pop fans alike. This year will see the first American performances of his opera *Satyagraha*, his chamber opera *The Panther*, and perhaps a new dance work. He is also completing a third opera called *Akhenaton* and is scoring a film "about technology and the decay of the cities." [*Koyaanisqatsi*, directed by Godfrey Reggio, premiered in 1982.]

The following interview took place in his West Side apartment and in a taxi to his rehearsal hall, where a concert performance of *Einstein on the Beach* was in preparation.

More and more people are listening to your music these days. Why is it catching on at this particular time?

It's partly because of the vacuum created by the new-music world in general, which is very insular. But also, people want a concert music that goes along with the popular culture of their time. There's a lot of good pop music these days, but people want a high-art kind of music, too. They get tired of hearing the Rolling Stones and the B-52s. And my music touches quite a few bases. Even the amplification is part of the appeal. There's a fair amount of intellectual content in the pieces, and lots of fancy writing that musicologists can look at. But I don't talk about that much. The music doesn't depend on that to be appreciated.

What do you want to accomplish in your music?

To make it a very physical and immediate experience, for one thing.

You have gone to some lengths in that direction, with forceful rhythms and assertive dynamics and textures.
Yes. It's a reaction to the very cerebral and theoretical way that the academic composers like. You can prove the academic pieces are beautiful, but you can't make them moving. Schools of music don't make music. They just make trouble, as far as I'm concerned!

What have your tastes been?

In the old days, I was interested in the American school of (William) Schuman and Vincent Persichetti, and then the more dodecaphonic American school that began with Charles Ives and led into people like Elliott Carter. But I was always interested in the maverick people like Harry Partch and Moondog. And I've always had a strong interest in jazz, though I've never played it.

Besides your classical composing and performing, you recently produced a pop record by the group Polyrock. Is the pop world alive and well, in your opinion?

Oh yes. The most interesting music is the new wave/punk music. The Raybeats are real favorites of mine, for instance.

I don't think they're very well known.

A lot of these people don't even record. I'm talking about noncommercial pop bands. They don't make records, and even if they do, they don't sell in the hundreds of thousands. You see, they've found a noncommercial way of dealing in the world of popular culture. They are serious and dedicated to their work. They are more honest than a lot of people who are writing so-called experimental music.

What are some other examples?

I've liked the Lounge Lizards for a while. I also like the Talking Heads and the B-52s. Those are well-known bands. They're trying to strip popular music to very basic ingredients. It's similar to what

I did in classical music, in a way—going back to something very basic and readily acknowledgeable.

But your main path has been in classical music. Has that path been smooth?

At a very early stage, I decided I was going to make a living by playing and writing music—not teaching music, like most of my colleagues. But it didn't happen overnight. In fact, until a couple of years ago when I was 40, I wasn't self-supporting as a composer. I had other jobs which took up a lot of my time—driving a cab, moving furniture—the usual things people do to get by. Things you can drop whenever you want to and go on a tour. No ties at all, but a fast cash turnover, so you can keep going.

Did you enjoy those years, or was it distracting?

I didn't mind it much. I didn't become bitter or angry. Two weeks after my first opera appeared at the Met, I was out working again, and it didn't concern me. I like being in the street. I like street life. Of course, there were other things I could have done: writing film music or jingles. I just decided I didn't want to. I wasn't so anxious for an audience that I would change what I was doing. And now an audience has emerged so I can spend more time writing and doing what I really want to. The turning point came when I realized I could make more money just doing my music. You see, I have a very deep commitment to this music. It's more than liking or loving it. It's been part of me so long that it's the natural thing to do. It would never occur to me to give it up or change it in any way. I've had offers to do other things. But I'd rather have it my own way, no matter how long that takes. And to be honest, I'm surprised it didn't take longer. I was prepared for a longer haul than I've had to go through.

So you would have gone on with your ideas indefinitely, even if an audience didn't develop?

Well, I never thought it would be forever. I could tell there would be an audience, from the responses I was getting. Even when I was down in SoHo, the experience of the audience was so real, so authentic. It was just a question of dissemination. Now that an audience has emerged, it must feel good to devote all your energy to your music, with no time siphoned off to mundane jobs. It turns out I don't spend more time composing, after all! I just do different things—talking to people like you, for example. I'm a real activist in my work. I play all my music, and publish it, and get involved in lots of activities.

What's your background?

Very academic. I started music when I was about eight, at the Peabody Conservatory in Baltimore. At 15 I went to the University of Chicago, got a liberal-arts degree, and studied music there. Then came Juilliard, from age 19 to 24. Then I got a Ford Foundation grant, wrote music for the Pittsburgh public schools, went to Paris, studied with Boulanger. So for 20 years I was in music school. I really had a dose!

What sort of music did you write when you were younger?

I didn't really have a music of my own. I was learning from other people. I studied their work, and wrote about 70 pieces in the style of my teachers: straight, middle-of-the-road American music.

Then what happened?

Something unexpected. In 1965 I put all the music in a box, and said I wouldn't write that any more! I just turned my back on it, overnight.

So you rejected the influences on you to that point. How did you find your own voice?

I was hired to be Ravi Shankar's assistant on a movie score. Through him, I got in touch with a whole different world: non-Western music. I traveled in North Africa, central Asia, India. I became aware of traditions that had nothing to do with my background. I was inspired by it. I saw there were other powerful ideas and ways of organizing music. I got involved with it, and tried to invent things. It sounds pretentious, but it was more desperate. It was like I really didn't know what else to do.

What was your approach in this "inventing"?

I had to start somewhere, so I started at the beginning. Looking back, it seems almost arrogant: to put aside 400 years of music, and say I'm not going to do that anymore! But there was no other way—I had to do something very radical. So I reduced my music to the style you find in my early pieces, where there's just one line of music that gets longer and richer all involved with the rhythmic profile. Then I found out nobody would play this music!

Did that distress you?

It was a big shock, because my earlier music had always been played. I showed the new pieces to people, and they were offended, they laughed at it. But looking back, the surprising thing is that I was so surprised. I should have known—weird, though it didn't seem so to me.

Basically, your starting point was a radical simplicity.

That's true. And it was a real reaction to what I perceived as a sterile and uncommunicative new-music situation.

From those basic starting points, your work has evolved and changed a great deal. It certainly sounds richer and more sensuous than it used to.

I've noticed that, too. I like it, actually. It's kind of a pendulum effect. I started with things that were so severe—no fat, just muscle and bone. Then gradually, I've brought in all this other stuff.

You have brought your music to some unlikely audiences, or at least unlikely places—rock clubs, for example.

Yes, and we were the first to do some of these things, like playing new music at the Bottom Line. You see, there are these hidden, unspoken rules of behavior, and I simply decided I was going to ignore them and do whatever I wanted.

Do you know what will come next in your development?

It's hard to predict. I like surprises. I like to surprise myself. When I know what I'm doing, I'm so bored that I don't want to finish the piece. So I tend to go into projects without any idea of what I'm going to do. And so sooner or later, we all find out.

Anthology Film Archives is like a world headquarters: the world of independent cinema—and its guardians

Interview with Jonas Mekas, July 9, 1981

If there is a world headquarters for independent cinema, it's probably Anthology Film Archives in New York. Led by Jonas Mekas, a filmmaker himself, this feisty organization is a museum, a library, and a movie theater all in one—championing every kind of noncommercial, non-narrative, non-Hollywood film and video. Among its activities are frequent screenings of hard-to-see movies, acquisition of film-related research materials, and maintenance of a "repertory collection" that sets the standard for classic "experimental" film.

Now the 11-year-old Anthology has launched a new adventure. In 1979 it purchased an unused courthouse building on the corner of Second Avenue and Second Street and announced plans for a major expansion. When renovated, the new quarters will contain three theaters—one for repertory screenings, one for video, and one for special events. The largest will be equipped for videotaping and transmission, like a small cable-TV station, and will be available for public uses such as neighborhood meetings and conferences on the arts. And that's not all. According to Mr. Mekas, the building will also house "the most up-to-date film preservation vault on the East Coast, and maybe in the whole United States," complete with temperature, humidity, and air-chemical controls. In addition, a library space will hold "the country's largest collection of material on avant-garde film." Filmmakers will be invited to deposit original materials, on paper or celluloid, and rooms will be available for research over periods of days, weeks, or months.

Even in its present cramped quarters at 80 Wooster Street, in the downtown SoHo district, Anthology has been a major force in the world of non-Hollywood film. Scholars, researchers, and student groups have used its screening facilities and its collection of about 3,000 movies, plus documents and photographs. And its reach has been wide. "Just this week," Mekas said recently, "the head of the Austrian Film Archive is coming familiarize himself with recent avantgarde works and make some purchases. Then someone is coming from a New England college to see some films of Dreyer." Not to mention the regular Anthology screenings, which provide a major showplace for noncommercial movies. Yet fundraising for the new project has not been easy. According to Mekas, the organization is relying on a variety of sources, from private patronage to a federal Urban Development Action Grant, and—the latest hope—sale of impressive portfolios especially prepared by leading artists and photographers. Corporate support is hard to come by, Mekas says, for two reasons. First, it has already been tapped by larger, more established outfits. Second, "the foundations and corporations like to support projects that immediately benefit larger numbers of people" than Anthology traditionally deals with. Still, he says, the project will continue "no matter what," and the corporations "will come around after we've actually moved and shown what we can do." At worst, the vaults and library spaces will be postponed until after the opening of the new theaters. "We will succeed," says the ever-confident Mekas, who went on to answer questions about Anthology in particular and independent film in general.

Your plans for the new building are ambitious, and very encouraging for people who care about independent film. Why is fund-raising so hard?

Everybody asks, how many people will you serve? They'd like to hear it will be millions. But we work on a different principle—we go for quality and selectivity. It's a very compact, nuclear kind of situation. And it has strong results: If you serve scholars and researchers, you eventually do reach millions, indirectly.

Just on a local level, I imagine your presence will have a good effect on your new neighborhood.

The area has been deteriorating. Our venture will help revive the area, just as we assisted in reviving SoHo when we started the first cooperative here. We're already helping to set up coops in buildings near the courthouse that haven't been used for years.

What brought Anthology Film Archives into existence?

Around 1960, a large movement started among independent film-makers, which grew and even exploded during the '60s. For a while, most universities and other institutions ignored this. Then another pattern developed. In the late '50s, perhaps 10 large universities offered one or two film courses apiece. By 1970, according to a survey by the American Film Institute, more than 1,000 colleges and universities were teaching film. Today about 1,600 are teaching film—with more than 10,000 courses.

How did you enter the picture?

Around 1968 and 1969, as film teaching increased, educators kept coming to me and a couple of other people—P. Adams Sitney and Stan Brakhage, for instance—who were known to be authorities in the field. Every year, we got calls and letters asking for information about what was happening, and guidance in programming films. If you live in New York or San Francisco, the films are available to you. But in small university towns, information is harder to get. If you are teaching a course, and you need to assemble three or four representative programs of independent film, what do you choose? So we spent a lot of time, and wasted a lot of time, serving each case as it came up. Then we decide to get together and stop relying on individual taste. We formed a committee of five people that could preselect films. We wanted to reduce the thousands and thousands of titles and names to a more manageable list.

It was really in the thousands?

Oh, yes. In the New York Film-Makers' Cooperative alone, there are now about 700 members, and the Canyon Cinema cooperative in San Francisco represents another 600 or 700. So there alone are about 10,000 titles.

Just what did you and your associates do?

We screened films, and argued and argued and argued. And we tried to reduce the field to a list of about 300 titles. It was controversial, and some felt it was unjust, but what choice did we have? If a professor writes from a university and asks for one program of films, you simply have to make choices. Anyway, 300 titles by 30 or 40 filmmakers is still a large number.

What is the guiding principle of this collection?

To cover all directions and styles, show their development, and represent every major achievement and filmmaker. Some are not there, true. But the collection is not a closed project. The repertory collection of Anthology Film Archives is a tool, a means of criticism. We constantly reevaluate the field and add new titles. And a title is never removed: If it was included once, there was a reason for it at that historical moment, so it stays for good. And new works keep joining it.

Who is on the committee now?

P. Adams Sitney, a film scholar. Peter Kubelka and James Broughton, who are noted filmmakers. Ken Kelman, a playwright and film theoretician. And myself. We haven't met for four years now, so we will have a meeting around the time of the move to our new quarters. And there may be changes in the committee at that time. The filmmaker Stan Brakhage used to be on it, but left because of a dispute over veto power. Now we are sometimes reproached for having no women on the committee, and that may change, since there are some women film scholars now.

You maintain a collection of nonfilm material, too.

Yes. Besides giving guidance to films and titles, we provide reference materials—scripts, letters, clippings, photographs, and so forth.

Will independent film, of the type championed by Anthology Film Archives, ever reach a truly large audience? Or will it remain a minority art?

That's a relative question, because "mass appeal" is a relative concept. Look at the nature of avant-garde film—the content, the techniques, the forms. In general, it represents exploration in the nonnarrative forms. The language is more concentrated that that of most narratives. But it's not so different than in literature, where we have both prose and poetry—and one form reaches many more people than the other. The analogy with literature is very good. Few poetry books sell a lot of copies or are read by many people. Yet poetry is taught in schools, so most people know at least a little about it and it continues to have outlets through some publishers and publications. It has little mass appeal, but it carries on. It's the same in film. Cinema has matured in the past two or three decades—branched out, strengthened, and developed nonnarrative forms. Not all avant-garde film is nonnarrative; we have very condensed forms of narrative, too. But I don't think any of these works can reach a huge number of people, even though every filmmaker—like every poet—wishes for a large audience. That sort of thing is possible only in a country like the Soviet Union, where the government controls things. And they you lose freedom and creativity, and also standards: You go just because you are told to go.

So you are resigned to a limited, though surely a growing, audience.

The nonnarrative, avant-garde cinema will always attract a limited number of people. But how limited? Around 1950, there were only about 40 film societies across the US. A film by Maya Deren or Sidney Peterson could reach only 300 or 400 people. Then Maya Deren started traveling to universities and pushing avant-garde film, and she managed to open some universities, so her films could be seen by thousands. Then in the '60s, because of both good and bad publicity, more universities opened up to us. Now the Film-Makers' Cooperative has a card list of more than 6,000 users who rent films. And Stan Brakhage can say that his *Dog Star Man* [1964] has been seen by more than one million people in this country. In 1950, only a commercial film could do that. Even in the avant-garde, though, some works must be more popular than others. There are many outlets for important avant-garde filmmakers who make an impact on cinema and on the audience: George Landow, Bruce Baillie, Stan Brakhage, Michael Snow, Ernie Gehr. There are gradations—Ernie Gehr is still very difficult for many people, so he has less exposure. But for some of these people, the audience can be counted in the hundreds of thousands. And some Hollywood films are seen by no more than that. Of course, being seen by as many people as a Hollywood movie doesn't make an avant-garde film "commercial." Our films tend to deal with feelings and content that are not everyday stuff. Bruce Baillie may get excited about some red roses on a fence and make a very ecstatic little haiku film about them. This isn't everyday emotion. Narratives, with plots and protagonists you can identify with, will always appeal to larger audiences. But in arts, somebody has to deal with those areas that are not everyday matters. This is part of the human condition. Art that doesn't cover the whole human experience— art that covers only entertainment, or strong and dramatic needs and feelings—would not be a full art.

Has avant-garde film had much impact on commercial cinema?

It's hard to determine. The main impact is that certain film-makers are by nature more poets than novelists. Once, they would have turned to the novelistic, dramatic, commercial cinema, and destroyed themselves. Now they have a choice: They know they don't have to go into commercial, Hollywood, narrative film. They can stay in the independent area that suits them best, and work within those forms. Then too, there are times when a commercial filmmaker wants to use some technique that has been used in nonnarrative film. But usually it fails—it doesn't work, doesn't stick. It's the same thing that often happens when a novelist decides to be "poetic." It's watery, and we say he should have stuck to the basics!

What is the status of avant-garde film today?

It comes in waves. It was very strong in the '40s, and again in the '60s. The forms of "structural film" developed in the '70s and the semi-"punk" super-8 movement are still going on. Meanwhile, the movements of past decades are continuing, and have developed into classical forms. Such classic filmmakers as Brakhage, Snow, and Ken Jacobs are still continuing their work, while new notes come in at the same time. But right now we're at a pause. We need more perspective on the work of the '70s, and we must review the '60s. So much has been produced! In 1955 or 1965, I could sit in New York and have a good overview of the whole situation. But that's impossible today. We simply don't have proper perspective on what's been done in France, in London, in Tokyo, or even across the US. So the future will be? We have planned two years of surveys at Anthology: the avant-garde in Britain, in France, in the smaller Eastern countries as well as Japan… And then, of course, video comes in! We need to have a much better idea of where we are, and what has been done. In general, this is not an exciting time for new film and video. It's a time for consolidation, for review. I feel the new Anthology quarters can help a great deal—helping young artists to see what has been done, to review their predecessors for their own inspiration. And to preserve the best of the past, for the future.

Veteran director challenges today's films—and audiences
Interview with Sidney Lumet, August 13, 1981

In the center of a rustic living room, Michael Caine sits behind a desk. Christopher Reeve holds a pistol to his head. With menacing calm, Reeve explains the next step of his evil plan, backing slowly from his victim and out of the room. As he exits, a smallish man behind a large movie camera yells "Cut!" and jumps to his feet with a delighted smile. Another scene from *Deathtrap* is wrapped up and in the can.

Like most Hollywood movies, *Deathtrap* is built mostly of illusions. The lightning that flashes during Reeve's monologue is generated on cue by a busy special-effects man, and even the living room is no rural retreat but a carefully constructed set on a New York City soundstage. Like the plot of *Deathtrap* itself, nothing is what it seems. And it's the job of the director, that furiously concentrating man behind the camera, to lead us through the labyrinth so artfully that we enjoy both the illusions and the story that they serve. Since the director is Sidney Lumet, there's a strong chance that *Deathtrap* will prove as popular on-screen as it is onstage. Despite a plot that's too tricky for comfort, it has been running for years on Broadway, with a variety of stars in the leading role of a playwright who gets snarled in one of his own whodunit schemes.

Lumet is one of the most versatile filmmakers in Hollywood today. A veteran entertainer who insists on treating his audience and his material with equal respect, his work ranges from *12 Angry Men* [1957] and *Long Day's Journey Into Night* [1962] to *Dog Day Afternoon* [1975] and *Network* [1976]. He was attracted to *Deathtrap* by its wit and literacy, scarce qualities on the current movie scene. Before it goes into release, however, Lumet will be represented by another picture of a very different kind, which opens later this month: *Prince of the City*, an epical study of crime and punishment based on the real-life story of a New York cop who sparked a major probe of police corruption and connections with organized crime. On the surface, it sounds like a reprise of *Serpico* [1973], an earlier Lumet hit. But this is no cunningly contrived "biopic" with a photogenic Al Pacino grabbing all the attention. *Prince of the City* is a long, relentless melodrama without a single movie-star face to conjure its many plots and subplots into a neat celluloid package. Though it periodically loses its way among cardboard characters and stereotyped scenes, it deserves hefty credit for attempting more than the average movie dreams of accomplishing.

Over sandwiches in a modest Manhattan office, Lumet recently discussed his latest ventures and the Hollywood scene in general.

What appealed to you about Prince of the City?

It's a classic tragedy: A guy steps into a situation thinking he can control circumstances, and circumstances end up controlling him. I wanted the chance to do that time-less subject in modern times.

Why is it such a long picture—nearly three hours?

I thought it would be even longer. The story covers several years, but that's not the main reason. We needed a lot of time because everything in the story must reverse itself sooner or later. Everyone who starts out looking good has clay feet revealed. Everyone who starts out low has moments of magnanimous behavior.

Why?

Because I wanted no rubber-ducky psychological stuff about why people did things. I won't know why so-and-so did what he did, and he probably doesn't know either. And it doesn't matter. All that matters is what happens.

That's similar to what Raging Bull *tried to do, avoiding "motivations" and showing people in all their rawness and ambiguity. But this goes against the old Hollywood tradition, where everything is carefully worked out and explained.*

Yes, and people like me are largely responsible for that old tradition. In Hollywood, and back in the so-called "golden age of television," we'd always wrap things into a neat package. But I've gotten to the point where I can't stand that. I know it's not true. Those are the two good things about *Raging Bull*—it doesn't try to make the main character sympathetic, and it doesn't try to explain him. It will be interesting to see the reception *Prince of the City* gets from the critics, because it's their responsibility to point out the approach I'm taking. But I can name four critics right now who won't like it, because we don't explain everything. It's all there, of course, but you have to work for it. It's not laid out in psychiatric terms. There's a restless quality in many of today's movies.

Even frivolous films like *Raiders of the Lost Ark* [Steven Spielberg, 1981] and *Superman II* [Richard Lester, 1980] have unsettled conclusions that don't tie all the loose ends into a neat knot. It's not artful ambiguity—it's real indecision, or a shameless priming of the audience for sequels that are still years away.

What's going on?

Something very distressing is going on. The reason for that unsettled quality is that the movies have gone brainless. And what scares me is that it's probably the audiences' fault—not Hollywood's, because Hollywood is just catering to a taste. It's depressing and alarming. In the final analysis, it doesn't matter how brilliantly a *Raiders of the Lost Ark* is done... I don't care how respected the homage is, it's a homage to idiocy. There's nothing wrong with anyone's childhood. But... many of today's filmmakers appear to be gearing their work directly toward the teenage and early-20s audience, who have the most time, energy, and money to spend on movies. The movie executives worry about falling grosses, yet they're abandoning a whole audience. Maybe the older people won't come to the movies anyway these days, but a vicious circle has been created. The youth thing—the "me" thing—took over in the '60s and '70s. Young people became a major part of the audience. Then the studios began catering to it more, out of their insecurity. Older people stopped going, more young people started, material kept getting more banal.

You seem quite unhappy about this situation.

I've been distressed about it for well over a year. This fall and winter, during the season when serious pictures should have been visible, only two movies really made money. One was *Stir Crazy* [Sidney Poitier, 1980]. The other was *Nine to Five* [Colin Higgins, 1980], with a stupid script badly directed. Even Jane Fonda was bad for the first time in her life. And the corollary is that drama gets dissipated too. Ultimately, *Ordinary People* [Robert Redford, 1980] is a banal piece of work, a soap opera from the *Good Housekeeping* set.

For anyone who agrees with your observations, this is sad commentary on the current scene.

It all reflects a childish inability to pay attention. There's a cut every seven seconds in the *Raiders* style of picture—you have to keep jazzing the audience, constantly giving them something new to look at.

How does your work fit into this bleak picture? What about the scope of Prince of the City *and the literacy of the* Deathtrap *project?*

I don't know. I'm very nervous about *Prince of the City*. I hope it gets good reviews, which it'll need to even get launched. As for *Deathtrap*, it's an old-fashioned and literate comedy thriller. I don't know if they'll sit still for all that talk. But I love plot, and *Deathtrap* has the best plot since *Murder on the Orient Express*.

Your films offer some alternative to all the adolescent hits, regardless of what the specific critical response and box-office figures turn out to be.

I'll be fascinated to see what happens to my new ones. You see, I don't deplore all the pictures we've been talking about. What I deplore is that there are no other kinds. And by the way, as much money as those idiotic pictures make, they've lost a lot, too—a comedy like *1941* [Steven Spielberg, 1979] that didn't do very well, and a drama like *Heaven's Gate* [Michael Cimino, 1980] that was a disaster.

Ivan Passer, who directed Cutter's Way *[1981], thinks the "art of film" may rebound because so many bright young people are studying it in schools and colleges. They could become the core of a serious audience that wants to support serious movies.*

I hope he's right, but I don't think he is. When a picture like *Deathtrap* costs $9 million, there's no such thing as a "smaller audience" any more: A "smaller audience" won't pay that picture off! When the ordinary budget is $10 million… Also, I doubt if seriously young people will be seeking out movies to any great extent. They aren't entering the political arena lately, and those things always go together. In terms of my own career, when I became so successful in the '70s with so many hits in a row, I think it had a direct connection with the politically active generation that had emerged. They wanted to see the kind of movies I made. The success or failure of that kind of film is directly in line with what's happening politically in the country. As for older people, maybe they've been driven away from the movies permanently. It's the TV syndrome you find everywhere today. I don't even like to go to movie theaters anymore, because people just talk and smoke—they think they're in their living rooms! I won't see movies under conditions like that.

You began your career in television. Might you return there someday?

I started in the early days of television. And I never left TV—it left me, to follow a course I wasn't interested in. Some of the TV movies lately have been pretty good. By contrast, I've read a lot of film scripts recently—firm projects looking for a director—and they're all rotten. But I don't think I'll go back to TV… And unfortunately, that big screen hasn't been filled with much inspiration in recent times. Pictures don't even have endings anymore! When there's no mind behind a movie to begin with, there's nothing to resolve at the end. It's like the "feelie" in *Brave New World*—we have movies designed totally for momentary sensation. They're just supposed to blind you for two or three hours. Fortunately, though, a few thoughtful films are due in the near future—*Ragtime* [1981], from the E. L. Doctorow book, and *Reds* [1981], the big movie from Warren Beatty. We'll find out a lot from the reception those pictures get. Whatever else you can say, we're entering a very interesting time. I can't wait to see how things turn out.

**Interview with the writer: That Neil Simon hit-after-hit touch—
what makes it so successful?**
Interview with Neil Simon, October 1, 1981

Neil Simon doesn't always want to make us laugh. Some of his
works are meant to be downright serious, beneath the one-liners
and comic digressions.

One such is his latest movie, *Only When I Laugh*, based on
an earlier play called *The Gingerbread Lady*. It's the story of
an actress (Marsha Mason) coming to terms with her teen-age
daughter (Kristy McNichol) while recovering from an unhappy
romance and a drinking problem. The situations are adult, the
language is just rough enough to earn an R rating. And the characters are just complex enough to transcend the farcical dimensions
of, say, *The Odd Couple* [1968] or *Murder by Death* [1976]. In
sum, it's unusually weighty Simon work, though the dialogue is
sometimes flat and the characters have the annoying Simon habit
of communicating largely through wisecracks. Fleshed out and
"opened up" from the confines of the stage, *Only When I Laugh*
works better on-screen than *The Gingerbread Lady* did in the
legitimate theater.

Besides writing the screenplay, Simon served as coproducer of
the film—a first for him, though he has often filled a similar function "unbilled" by taking an interest in the casting and production
of his shows. The director was Glenn Jordan, making his movie
debut after years of stage and TV experience.

What's it like directing a film under the watchful eye of the
author and producer, combined? "It was great," said Jordan
during a recent interview. "Neil cooperated in every way, without
imposing his own views.'

Simon himself was happy working with Jordan, and delighted
working again with Marsha Mason, who happens to be his wife.
"I wrote the screenplay two years ago," he said during a recent
talk in a New York hotel room—not quite a Plaza Suite, but close
enough—"and showed it to Marsha last year. She read it and said,
"I have to play that lady!" Which she did. Simon went on to
discuss *Only When I Laugh* in detail, and make observations on
his work in general.

Only When I Laugh *seems more serious than many of your earlier
works.*

The seriousness was there before, only I didn't deal with it as much. There was the subject matter of *The Prisoner of Second Avenue* [1975], for example, or *The Sunshine Boys* [1975]. These were basically serious plays—not fluffy, light entertainment like *Barefoot in the Park* [1967], where nothing is really at stake. Also, I go back and forth between the light stuff and the more serious work like *Chapter Two* [1979]. That may mix up people's minds about what it is I actually do. I'm not like a Tennessee Williams or Arthur Miller, who always write serious work. In between, I'll do something frothy like *Seems Like Old Times* [1980].

How does Only When I Laugh *fit in?*

It's different from many of the other plays, because when I deal with a serious aspect of the theme, I stay with it—I don't suddenly break away to something funny. The funny things come out of the enjoyable moments in the story, like when the girls go shopping. When they actually come to grips with their problems, the tone of the writing is quite different.

As an essentially comic writer develops—a Woody Allen, say—the work sometimes tends to become darker. Do you agree?

Yes, the dark side does creep in, because more dark things creep into your life: losses and so forth. But it's also connected with the need for new challenges. You want to expand your work. Not necessarily to make it better—my most lasting play is probably *The Odd Couple* [1968]—but to do something different. So I wouldn't be interested in writing an *Odd Couple* or *Barefoot in the Park* now. I think I'm more perceptive than I used to be, and I want to get into my characters more deeply. Laughs were very important to me, back then—they were the only contact I had with the audience, the only way I could get them to listen to me. And I wasn't so prepared to probe deeply. But one expands, one grows. I don't mean ever to give up comedy. My next picture with Marsha is a comedy, though a rather exotic one, with Jason Robards. As for the darker areas, I don't know how dark they'll get. My next play, *Brighton Beach Memoirs*, has seven characters; only one is at all funny, and that's only when he comments on the play as narrator. So it's dark and light at the same time. I think I'll always write that way. I'm never going to be Ibsen, and I don't choose to write that way. I don't see things that way.

You wouldn't write an Interiors [1978], *as Woody Allen did, that was quite tragic?*

I admired *Interiors*, because I thought the theme was excellent — a middle-aged couple being divorced, and the grownup children being affected. But Woody purposefully stayed away from any kind of humor.

To return to Only When I Laugh, *the subject matter has held your interest for many years, from the original play eleven years ago until now. How would you describe it?*

It's about a mother and a daughter, the lack of self-esteem, and friendship — including the kind of friends who pull you down rather than lift you up.

When set you down this particular path?

I never quite recall the point of inspiration for anything I've written. It just sticks in there one day, and starts to develop by itself, and by then you've forgotten what the initial moment was.

Why did you focus on a daughter-mother relationship?

I have observed this. When I first wrote the play, my own daughters were little girls, but now they are teen-agers and above. I have been through some rough times, especially when my first wife was ill. My daughters were so supportive, and dealt with things in such a grown-up way, that some of this crept into the story. Two of the characters are a playwright and an actress who have been close to each other, and he writes a drama based on their experience.

Are there echoes of your own Chapter Two *here, since that play treated your relationship with Marsha Mason in fairly autobiographical terms?*

Sure, there must be echoes, though not consciously. All my serious works are about things that have happened to me in the past, are happening to me now, or that I sense will happen to me in the future.

You don't seem uncomfortable about revealing yourself in your plays.

A writer inhibits himself by not telling the truth. I read many biographies of creative people, especially writers and painters and musicians. If you don't reveal yourself, you're lying somewhere along the way, and it will come out in the work. You don't have to be graphic, but you have to be truthful.

The autobiographical aspect is quite important to you, then.

Yes. And it's a very mysterious process, because you don't realize it's going on. You have to be careful, too, because you should be explicit only up to a point. I try to be honest about the other characters, also, and not just the character who represents me. But there are certain things you leave out. I could never write something like *Mommie Dearest* [1981] about somebody close to me. When I was a kid, especially a teen-ager, I went through some really rough times. What went on at home was really ugly. My new play, *Brighton Beach Memoirs*, talks about that time—but I try to show the parts of those people that were loving. They aren't loving all the time, and they aren't heroes. But I am kind to them, and show their better aspects, because that's the impression they left me with. As you grow older, you become more forgiving, because you see you have the same faults in yourself.

Still, you didn't have to be forgiving in Brighton Beach Memoirs. *You could have chosen a gloomier portrayal in the interests of the "dark side" we were talking about.*

I don't mind making the gloomy choice if it will serve a purpose. There is an essence of life that I would like to pass along. If I put down everything these people did in their weakest moments, they would emerge so villainous that we would learn nothing from them. We would walk out and say, who wants to be with people like that? Yet I certainly don't whitewash them.

The end of Only When I Laugh *is also upbeat.*

Maybe. Or maybe it's just a good day for the main character, and tomorrow she'll be down again. I would never impose a view of what happens after the movie ends. This is connected with one of the main purposes I have in writing. It's something I found out in my own life, and when I discovered it, life became better — when I found out I had choices. The people who are trapped in life are the ones who feel they have no choices. They say, "That's the way I am," like Felix Unger in *The Odd Couple*. He wants to wallow in self-pity. But when you have choices, there are options to lead your life in a different way. So there's no sure way to tell what happens after the end of a film like *Only When I Laugh*. People like happy endings, so they make them up for themselves, but they aren't necessarily true. It's characters that interest me, and that's what I want to write about.

How does your family feel about showing up in your work?

They have responded well. For instance, I've portrayed my brother in five or six plays. The other night, he said he's been the central character of more plays than Julius Caesar or Cleopatra!

Only When I Laugh *is another step in your working collaboration with Marsha Mason. This has become a regular partnership.*

It isn't because she's my wife. It's because she's superb. I practically married her because I had such respect for her ability. And this implied to me how intelligent she was. I have enormous respect for her, besides loving her for all her other qualities. Among other things, she is one of the most vulnerable actresses I have ever seen. Yet she can make a human being out of any character — even someone like the girl in *Cinderella Liberty* [1973], who was as unlikable as anyone you'll ever find.

When you begin to develop an idea, how do you decide whether it will be a movie or a play?

That's a good question. I'm never quite sure what happens. The only film that could have been a play first was *The Goodbye Girl* [1977], because the apartment was a central character in that piece. Generally, though, the idea seems developed as a play or film when it first comes to me. If it's going to be a play, I try not to think of it as a film, because it pushes me in other directions. Lately, though it's been sneaking up on me; my more recent plays have more visual aspects than the earlier ones. For example, they don't have a single set — like *Chapter Two*, which has two apartments on the stage. And my new play, *Brighton Beach Memoirs*, has five rooms at the same time. So my movie experience is creeping into the playwriting craft.

When Chapter Two *was on Broadway, it seemed extremely cine-matic—maybe because Herbert Ross directed it, using his own movie experience. It actually had dissolves, just like a film.*

Yes, it was very much like a movie. And I like that. The theater needs change.

Will you continue to move between the two media of stage and screen?

I'll never give up the stage, because I consider myself essentially a playwright. I was brought up with the stage, and I love it. But I made a decision after 14 years of doing a play in New Haven each season and seeing all these 40- and 45-year-old people come in, and seeing all these 16- to 24-year-olds lined up for the movie across the street. I wanted to reach that young audience. There were things I wanted to say to them. So I decided to get into films more seriously, rather than just adapting *The Odd Couple* or *Barefoot in the Park*. So I'm serious about working in films. I want to go back and forth, doing both movies and plays.

Some people feel the movies are geared exclusively to kids nowadays.

Well, I never had children in mind, exactly. I can't write that way—even *Murder by Death* is sophisticated, to some degree, though it's geared to a younger audience. When I write, I don't have a specific group in mind. I have myself in mind. I wonder if I'd have a good time seeing this. If not, there's no chance it's going to work.

In films, you have more control over the final result. In stage work, a lot depends on the specific production.

A woman from the Midwest once came up to me and said she had never liked my work. I told her she was entitled. But she said she was a convert. I asked why. She said she had read my plays.

A conversation with Paul Newman
Interview with Paul Newman, December 3, 1981

In his new movie *Absence of Malice*, Paul Newman plays an unusual hero: Michael Gallagher, a blue-eyed but hard-boiled businessman whose only crime was having a bootlegger for a father. Normally, his parentage would pose no problems. The police are investigating a complicated case, though, and they think Gallagher might know some answers. So they plant an incriminating story in the local newspaper, hoping this will irk him into spilling some beans. And that's where the love story comes in. To plant their bait, the cops dupe a hotshot reporter, who happens to be played by the winsome Sally Field. Skullduggery or no, it isn't long before she and Gallagher are gazing wistfully into each other's eyes, wishing this movie were a plain old romance instead of an ambitious look at the responsibilities of the press in a free society. It's the kind of role Newman loves to play—a strong character in tough but dramatic circumstances. And this time, he said during my recent interview with him, it was more than just a meaty part with a good script and director. It was a chance to make a statement on a subject that has concerned him a lot lately: the proprieties of the newspaper business.

Newman had an unpleasant brush with the journalistic world during his last project, *Fort Apache the Bronx* [1981], a film that angered some New Yorkers by its image of their city as a battleground between heroic white cops and vicious minority thugs. It wasn't the opinion of the local citizenry that bothered the star, though. It was reportage by newspapers, some of which he claims was blatantly false. Little wonder he was pleased when his next enterprise turned out to be *Absence of Malice*, which turns the tables on the press-worshipping attitudes of *All the President's Men* [1976], pointing out the damage a careless or irresponsible "investigative reporter" can do.

"I was savaged by some papers after *Fort Apache the Bronx*," says Newman. "I was most offended by the *New York Post*," which he claims misrepresented events surrounding the location filming of the picture. "But journalists and newspapers protect each other, like doctors do. They won't name the paper that did these things. They'll only say, 'Mr. Newman has attacked a New York newspaper.' That's too bad, because if some papers are not accurate in their news stories, and report events that didn't occur, it damages the credibility of all papers, through guilt by association. It's unfortunate when responsible newspapers won't take the irresponsible ones to task. So I felt I'd like to do a picture about media abuse."

Though his feelings on the subject are clearly strong, Newman insists that *Absence of Malice* is not "an indictment" of the press. Rather, he maintains, "It's simply a cautionary tract that says, 'Look around.' Of course, I expect the chief violators will be most offended by the picture, because their arrogance is so great. But I wanted to call attention to the situation.' Ironically, the movie might have been more "cautionary" and more effective if it had gone about its own business more singlemindedly. *Absence of Malice* is an unusually thoughtful film, by current standards, requiring a fair amount of brain-power just to follow its convoluted plot, much less meditate on its meanings. But besides raising a few hackles and raking a bit of muck, it wants to be a glossy Hollywood entertainment, too. Inordinate time and energy are diverted into the love angle, which is goopy despite tasteful treatment by the filmmakers. Too little care is spent on the reporter character: You wonder how anyone who means so well could do everything so badly, and how she wangled herself into a big-time newsroom in the first place. And then there's poor Melinda Dillon, dragged into the plot solely to suffer a tragic fate, in a potentially devastating segment that seems rather academic under the solid but uninspired guidance of director Sydney Pollack.

Still and all, despite its considerable flaws *Absence of Malice* is a movie to be grateful for at a time when few films offer anything in the way of social relevance or inner integrity. Newman is proud of the picture's cerebral slant, stating that its challenging story line and refusal to give easy answers were entirely conscious choices. Will audiences approach the picture with the necessary concentration, though, or have too many childish movies dulled the appetite for hard issues and ambiguous conclusions. "We'll see," says Newman with a smile. "Nobody can second-guess an audience, and I wouldn't have the arrogance to try. It's true audiences get seduced by easy movies they don't have to put anything into. And it's true the viewer has to work in this film. But somewhere along the line, there has to be a screaming protest against all the junk. Somewhere out there, there must be people who are fed up with baby food and want to work a little. They want something a bit more challenging. They can handle it, if it's interesting and good."

What does Newman look for when he's considering a script? "Who knows?" is the laconic reply. "I wish I could pin it down, but I've never been able to." Then he thinks for a moment and waxes a bit more philosophical, pointing out that "there are only a few plots in the world, anyway. All that changes are the characters you can play, because a few new ones are added by technology from time to time—astronauts, for example, or certain kinds of doctors that didn't exist a few years ago. For the rest, it's just a question of presenting a basically familiar story in some new way. What I look for is a new envelope to put the same old letter in."

Over the years, Newman has found a lot of provocative envelopes, from *Hud* [1963] to *The Hustler* [1961], from *Cool Hand Luke* [1967] to his Tennessee Williams collaborations. It's been a fairly diverse career, peppered with great successes and a few fascinating flops, such as *Buffalo Bill and the Indians, or Sitting Bull's History Lesson* [1976] and *Quintet* [1979], his Robert Altman puzzlers. Says the star, musing on it all, "It would have been a lot simpler to always look for one kind of hero image, and at times I wish I had. But it would have been a lot lazier, too." In all, he seems pleased with his various accomplishments and delighted that he found a few real gems—in his opinion, at least—along the way. *Slap Shot* [1977], for example. "What a deeply original film that was," says Newman enthusiastically. "I mean, nobody had ever seen anything like that: a movie about a second-rate hockey team!'

Newman has also distinguished himself by moving beyond his acting career and into the director's chair. *Rachel, Rachel* [1968] was his first (and highly praised) effort along these lines, followed by *Sometimes a Great Notion* [1971], in which one scene—featuring Richard Jaeckel, Newman himself, and a rising river—must be among the most suspenseful episodes ever filmed. And don't forget *The Shadow Box* [1980], a rather shallow but definitively offbeat drama that Newman directed for television. Not surprisingly, one of the toughest tasks for a complete performer/director like Newman is hunting out worthy material. "I used to spend 85 percent of my time reading," he says. "Now I spend 85 percent of my time reading for business," looking for scripts that might make feasible projects. "I think my perceptions about film are pretty good," he continues. "But the fact is, there simply isn't much good stuff around. So what's an actor to do? You can stop working. But you have to keep the instrument tuned. So you take the best there is and hope for the best. And you always start with the idea that it's going to end up pretty good."

The only sure thing is that a serious actor's job is never a simple matter. "You may start with a pretty bad script and make it into a pretty good movie—not a blockbuster, but reasonable. Or you may start with a good script and fail to improve on it. So which do you give yourself the greater credit for? The great script might have been a great film no matter what. But your achievement on that 'pretty good' one was significant."

Then too, Newman likes different kinds of "envelopes" to put his work into. For a pair of contrasting examples, he mentions *The Sting* [1973]—calling it "a plot movie"—and his own *Rachel, Rachel*, which has "very little plot, but gives penetrating perceptions and comments on the human condition." How about his latest, *Absence of Malice*? As he sees it, "the character moves inside the plot. The film is propelled more by the story than by the character development alone, but the characters are important too. And that's okay. You can do some very interesting acting under those conditions."

Miloš Forman and the tricky business of filming *Ragtime*
Interview with Miloš Forman, December 10, 1981

It's hard to imagine a more American novel than *Ragtime*, by E. L. Doctorow, which takes place around New York in 1906. Many of its characters are familiar figures in the myth and history of the United States, from showman Harry Houdini to anarchist Emma Goldman. Others are fictitious, but seem just as typical of their time and place—from the immigrant Tateh, who almost literally makes riches out of rags, to the black Coalhouse Walker Jr., whose wounded pride leads him to acts of violent revolution. It's a colorful book, and its popularity made it a natural for Hollywood treatment. But it posed considerable problems for would-be filmmakers. Its plot is complicated, its characters are numerous, its narration is digressive and occasionally raunchy. Robert Altman, master of the overstuffed American myth-movie, wanted to bring it to the screen, but the project fell through. Miloš Forman then took charge—a native of Czechoslovakia whose credits include such quintessentially American films as *One Flew Over the Cuckoo's Nest* [1975] and *Hair* [1979].

It is probably too late to hope Forman will return to the exquisitely intelligent and delicately understated style he developed in his best Czech and early Hollywood work, such as *The Firemen's Ball* [1967] and *Taking Off* [1971]. In his subsequent (and best-known) movies, he has sold out artistically—retaining his energy and technical command but turning his attention toward plot pyrotechnics rather than character development. Commenting on Forman's earlier work, his colleague, writer Buck Henry, recently praised it for capturing "behavior" rather than "acting." The same can't be said for *Ragtime*, big and brassy as it is. Yet it's the most consistently crafted and earnestly inspired Forman project in quite a while, and that is cause for celebration, if not unbounded joy.

The screenplay, by Michael Weller, is a substantial achievement in its own right, incorporating a remarkable number of the book's threads and themes, and largely cleaning up the yarn in the process, except for a few rough words and a brief nude scene. The hand of Hollywood can be clearly felt in the adaptation of the story, however. While the movie has received some critical praise for its social awareness and political consciousness, most of Doctorow's strongest sociopolitical points have been excised. Emma Goldman is nowhere to be found. Tateh is on board, but his radical socialism is barely hinted at, and we never hear of the bloody New England strike that is one of the novel's most dramatic episodes. It's not that these people and causes need to be sung and celebrated in what is basically an entertainment movie. But they were part and parcel of their period, and their omission from the film reduces a potentially sweeping tapestry to something more like mere nostalgia. Only the drama of Coalhouse Walker Jr., the embittered black man, remains to sum up the nastiest nuances of the Northeastern United States in the early 20th century. Still, considered as pure Hollywood, *Ragtime* has plenty of solid surprises. The cast is a wonder to behold, beginning with the return of James Cagney to the screen as Rheinlander Waldo, the police commissioner who has a final showdown with Coalhouse. Walker himself is played by Howard E. Rollins in a promising movie debut. Also on hand are Brad Dourif as the eccentric Younger Brother, Mary Steenburgen as Mother, James Olson as a toned-down but surprisingly effective Father, Mandy Patinkin as Tateh, and Kenneth McMillan in a fine portrayal of the coward Will Conklin, who precipitates much of the action.

Discussing the film in a recent interview at his New York apartment, Forman told me he was unfamiliar with Doctorow's novel when the project was first put before him. He promptly read it, and was impressed "mostly with the story, but also the characters and the whole ambiance." He felt it was "the most exciting and intelligent piece of literature I'd read in a long time," and decided he'd be happy to make it a motion picture, as long as he could retain final approval of the screenplay. "I don't mind getting involved in a risky project," he says, "as long as I don't have to stay married to it if the script turns out lousy." Forman started his career as a writer, so he hates to squabble with writers when he works with them. Before embarking on *Ragtime*, he met several times with Doctorow, who created the tale from a meandering mixture of whimsy, historical fact, and literary license—borrowing not only from real life, but from other books, including the Heinrich von Kleist novella *Michael Kohlhaas*, which inspired the character of Coalhouse Walker. Eventually, the novelist gave permission for the filmmakers to play as fast and loose with the book as he had played with his material. "I wanted to use the novel as a source," says Forman, "and create my own vision. Just as Doctorow did when he invented the story."

It was clear from the beginning that many characters and episodes would have to be abandoned. Forman and Doctorow met several times, reaching "95 percent agreement" on the general outline of the screenplay. This was then handed to Weller, who had collaborated with Forman on *Hair*, and the two thrashed out the final script in four months of daily work. "The way one perceives a book and a film are totally different," says Forman. "You read a book in the privacy of your room. You are the boss; you set the pace and rhythm of your reading. In the movie house, you can't do that. When you make a film, you realize that the audience will be powerless to stop it, or flip back to refresh their memories, or skip the boring parts. They are at the mercy of your storytelling. If you want to keep their attention for two and a half hours, you have to follow the story. Whatever doesn't contribute to the main plot line has to be sacrificed. You make the choices instinctively. Only then do you analyze them rationally." A lot of Tateh's story was cut because it doesn't intertwine with the rest of the action. Similarly, the filmmakers tried hard to keep Emma Goldman in the script, but Forman claims that her scenes "stopped the flow of the action." Anyway, the director says, "those scenes are in the book to tell you about the class structure of the society then."

Theme and image are close in "Ragtime," and that's a key to Forman's brand of filmmaking. It's also a reason, he thinks, for his success with international audiences. "Themes are more universal than you'd expect," he says, maintaining that *One Flew Over the Cuckoo's Nest* was watched all over the world, while *Hair* was twice as successful abroad as it was with American audiences. As for *Ragtime,* the director feels it has "a very universal theme," especially in the sequences that deal with Coalhouse, the black musician whose mistreatment by bigoted whites drives him into a sweeping and murderous revenge. As filmmaker Forman sees it, "the basic drama of Coalhouse is not a racial problem. Rather, it's a man's pride being hurt. Because he's black, everything is much sharper, and that's good for the drama. But this kind of problem always exists, regardless of race. It has to do with a big dilemma, which every civilized human being faces: What do you call people like this, revolutionaries or terrorists?" Though this may sound like a side issue to readers of Doctorow's freewheeling novel, it's at the heart of the story as far as Forman is concerned. "I'm not talking about hired hands," he says. "They are terrorists, and there's no excuse for them. And I'm not talking about people who choose violence when they could achieve a goal by peaceful means. There's a sadistic aspect to that behavior. As for myself," Forman continues, "I am absolutely against any violence. But what about basically honest people—not criminals—who are turned to

violence after their pride is hurt? I can't call certain people terrorists, because I understand and feel strong compassion for a frustration that goes past certain limits, past what a person's pride can
hold. Problems like this pose disturbing dilemmas for all of us."
Forman is not condoning any violence; indeed, he emphasizes his
opposition to violent acts. But he is concerned with the proper label
for people who are driven to desperation, and feels that "terrorist"
is too broad and imprecise a term to be universally applied. In part,
Ragtime is an exploration of such moral and philosophical questions. But does the director feel it will actually trigger new thought
and discussion among audiences?

"As always with art," he says, "the answer is no for the
majority, but yes for a few. It's very individual." Is it possible for
the filmmaker to shape his work so it will communicate serious
ideas—and stimulate serious thought—in more rather than less of
his audience? "I don't think so," says Forman, "because if you get
too deep, people just won't come to your film. The movie *Pixote*
[Hector Bebenco, 1980] shows that," he continues, referring to a
very responsible but very brutal Brazilian film of recent vintage,
dealing with juvenile delinquency. "It's very well done, artistic,
and personal. But it's obviously a political statement, and people
are staying away from it. I'm sure the people who do come have
their thinking stimulated. But how about all the people who are
being kept away?' Is it impossible for popular films to be truly
provocative, then? Forman answers: "The main effect must be
entertainment... When someone puts up $22 million, I can't tell
them to get lost because I'm doing this for my friends!'

This doesn't imply any cynicism toward Hollywood on
Forman's part, though. In fact, he says, Hollywood is "relatively
the healthiest place in the world for films. It's way ahead of Europe,
where an ambitious, good, meaningful film is a rare bird nowadays.
American films are reaching in more intelligent and redeeming
directions than any others.' But there's nothing to be smug about.
In the aftermath of the *Heaven's Gate* [Michael Cimino, 1980]
disaster, Hollywood may abandon serious filmmaking if certain
movies—such as *Prince of the City* [Sidney Lumet, 1981], *Reds*
[Warren Beatty, 1981], and *The French Lieutenant's Woman* [Karel
Reisz, 1981]—don't fare well at the box office. "The executives of
Hollywood will panic if these flop," Forman says, "and they won't
put any more money into ambitious projects for the next two or
three years. So I'm keeping my fingers crossed for all these films
to succeed."

As long as the studios stay active, Forman feels, there will always be a place for movies, even in the age of super-cable TV and home video that's supposedly around the corner. "People will always want that community experience of watching a good film in the company of others," he says. And one suspects he will always treasure that community experience of making ambitious films in the company of movie folks who share his own enthusiasm. He relished the shooting of *Ragtime*, especially when it meant fulfilling an impossible dream like working with the legendary Cagney — who is still such a pro that he needs little in the way of directing, according to the director. And it was fun discovering fresher talent, too, at which Forman excels. From conception to casting, he seems to relish every aspect of the filmmaking process. If his enthusiasm proves infectious, *Ragtime* should fare very well indeed.

Pioneering a new kind of stage magic
Interview with Elizabeth LeCompte, December 14, 1981

When her picture appeared on the cover of *New York* magazine not long ago, nobody was more surprised than Elizabeth
LeCompte herself. As leader of the Wooster Group, an Off-Off-
Broadway theater company, she has earned a growing reputation
for her ground-breaking artistic explorations. Yet her fame and
following have remained modest—partly because of the originality
of her work, and partly because critics have a hard time fixing
labels on her. Nowadays, pinning her down is harder than ever, as
she turns her talent to different media, including films and video.
Her latest major work, *Route 1 & 9 (The Last Act)*, now running
at the Performing Garage in New York, includes a movie and two
videotapes, all directed by LeCompte, as well as performances
by members of her troupe. Her last show, *Ray Whitfield and the
Johnsons in Hula*, was a dance piece incorporating elements of
burlesque, Hawaiian dancing, and old-fashioned charades. Earlier
works have blended film, slides, dance, music, literary classics,
and performance into multimedia extravaganzas. And there is no
telling what her next production, scheduled to open next month,
will look like.

"I consider myself an entertainer," LeCompte said during a
recent interview in the SoHo neighborhood where she lives and
works. "I don't mean my work to be difficult or obscure. It's
meant to be enjoyed." Still, many viewers find her work challenging. When the powerful *Rumstick Road* was presented at an
Off-Broadway theater, several blocks uptown from the troupe's
usual turf, a large number of spectators were openly befuddled by
its lack of conventional plot and characters. While this bothered
LeCompte, she noted that audiences seemed to catch on as the
engagement continued. In any case, she has not compromised her
style. Her future work promises to be as complex—and, she hopes,
as enjoyable—as her past shows.

In terms of subject matter, there is nothing esoteric about
Wooster Group productions. Indeed, one theme in particular has
fascinated the troupe since the beginning: American family life,
of the everyday middle-class kind. *Sakonnet Point* was a string of
daydreams based on fragmentary childhood memories. *Rumstick
Road* was a pitchblack comedy about an ordinary family under
extreme stress. *Nayatt School* combined these elements into a
phantasmagorical study of stagecraft, society, and sanity itself.

Point Judith carried this exploration a step further, with a view of human experience as an explosive mixture of psychodrama and slapstick. The troupe's technique is based on "layering," which is LeCompte's word for combining different artistic elements into a single experience. "Every element has equal importance," she says, "and I am totally serious about creating each one, even if it ends up with a minor place in the finished show." The group may travel to distant areas, study research materials, and develop lengthy improvisations, all for one "layer" that will eventually be overlain and underlain by various others.

The troupe's last major show, *Point Judith*, illustrates this method. The first section was a play by Jim Strahs, about three men and a boy on an offshore oil rig. The second part was a slapstick condensation of *Long Day's Journey Into Night*, accompanied by taped dialogue and the Roman Carnival Overture of Berlioz, with a film projected on the stage area as the performers went through their paces. The third section also mingled film and performance, including the projection of an image onto the face of a live actress. All these layers underlined the themes of the work—the turbulence of family relationships, the pervasiveness of memory, the ambiguity of attitudes toward masculinity. Clearly, such complicated and precisely crafted productions are "director's events"—that is, the skill and personality of the director are always dominant aspects of the show. LeCompte agrees with this observation, but reluctantly. One of her chief complaints about critical response to her work is that the dedicated Wooster Group performers rarely receive enough individual credit. "As performers, they need recognition and attention," she says, "and they certainly deserve it. But they get overlooked because their contributions are so thoroughly integrated into the work as a whole."

At least one performing member of the group has built a flourishing reputation of his own, however: Spalding Gray, whose life and dreams were the basis for the company's first four shows. A believer in "autobiographical theater," Gray supplied the materials for such works as *Sakonnet Point* and *Nayatt School* from his own experience, sharing his past with the audience in a startingly (and, some feel, unsettlingly) direct way. The collaboration between LeCompte and Gray has flourished partly because they have complementary artistic personalities. She has an Apollonian talent, meditative and painstaking, willing to spend six or eight weeks developing a 20-minute segment for a new production. Gray is a Dionysian sort, working on impulse and instinct, happiest when he can confront his spectators directly, without even a script between them and himself.

Discussing her own background, LeCompte stresses her lack of conventional theatrical training. After studying art and graphics, she came to the stage through a community theater in upstate New York, where she stepped into roles whenever a need arose. "It was always a last-minute thing," she recalls, "and I wouldn't even know the lines. I'd walk onstage and fake it, sometimes reading directly from the script. Nobody seemed to mind, and I enjoyed it.' After moving to New York City, she joined the highly regarded Performance Group, headed by director and theoretician Richard Schechner. Working as his assistant, she gradually moved into directing on her own, starting with a restaged edition of *Commune*, a show originally developed by Schechner and the entire company. Then came *Sakonnet Point*, the first production to be created wholly by Gray, Ron Vawter, Libby Howes, et al, under LeCompte's guidance. Three shows later—including the composite trilogy *Three Places in Rhode Island*—the troupe became an entity unto itself, dropping the Performance Group name and adopting their own Wooster Group identity, named after the street on which their theater is located.

Distinctive as her methods and results may be, LeCompte maintains a fresh and unjaded attitude toward her work. Her shows often refer to earlier plays—*Nayatt School* quoted liberally from *The Cocktail Party* by T. S. Eliot, while *Point Judith* and the new *Route 1 & 9* incorporate Eugene O'Neill and Thornton Wilder, respectively. Yet these are not authoritative musings from an old theatrical hand, LeCompte insists. "I don't really know these plays until we start exploring them for our own purpose," she says. "I'm discovering them for the first time, right before your eyes.' It's a risky process, but a fascinating one, with results so volatile that they often seem to shift and change from one performance to the next. They have made the Wooster Group one of the most invigorating presences on the current theatrical scene, marking LeCompte as one of the fresh talents able to combine the emotional impact of traditional stagecraft with the conceptual rigor and formal innovation of today's most advanced theatrical thinking.

Laughs and deep themes—a talk with *Time Bandits* maker
Interview with Terry Gilliam, January 7, 1982

"Actually, we're pretty childish. It would be nice to say child-like, wouldn't it? But no, childish it is!' The speaker, with a broad smile on his face, is Terry Gilliam—writer, director, and member of the Monty Python comedy troupe. He's referring to himself and Michael Palin, a fellow Python who teamed with him to create *Time Bandits*, one of the most popular movies of the holiday season. It's not surprising that a children's film should be successful at this time of year, but *Time Bandits* is no ordinary children's film. On the plus side, it carries its comedy to hilarious heights in a few scenes, while bringing in some unexpectedly deep themes—the nature of reality, the problem of evil, the relationship of God to mankind. Not that any deep conclusions are reached on any of these matters, but it's rare to see them even hinted at in an entertainment film. Indeed, one character (played by Ralph Richardson) is a so-called "Supreme Being" who shows up just in time to vanquish "Evil," slitheringly portrayed by David Warner.

On a less uplifting note, *Time Bandits* contains a share of violence though it's cartoonish rather than realistic, and there's less of it than in a *Star Wars* [George Lucas, 1977] or a *Superman II* [Richard Lester, 1980]. Also included are a few moments that kids would describe as "gross" (a hungry hero gnawing on a rat, for instance) that help account for the movie's PG rating. And the ending is downright bizarre for a children's film—an unexpected and unsettling twist that may disconcert younger moviegoers. While these elements have put off some viewers, Gilliam feels they add a kind of weight—comic and otherwise—that speaks to children more than their elders realize. "This isn't really a comedy," he said over lunch recently. "It's an adventure, and the comedy just springs from our approach. What we wanted to make was a decent kids' film, something that hasn't been done for years. Beyond that, we just followed our feelings, like we always do.' The trouble with adults, in Gilliam's opinion, is that they don't really look at children. "They look at their own romantic views of their own child-hoods," he says. "But actually, kids are very clear-minded. They don't have our prejudices, our structures, our pigeon-holed ways of looking at life. And they can be ruthless. Though they have less experience than adults, they are no less intelligent. Their minds are just as active—more so, in fact, because they haven't been limited and defined yet. To them, wonderful things can happen!"

In writing and directing *Time Bandits*, filmmaker Gilliam was reacting against the bowdlerized and "suburbanized" versions of fairy tales he ran across in reading to his own 4½-year-old daughter. Still, he acknowledges meeting with some studio opposition to the last scene, which has a downbeat feeling. "There were two arguments against our ending," he says, "the commercial and the paternalistic. The commercial one didn't interest me at all. But the other argument—that children might be disturbed—did concern me. I'm really pro-kid, you know! So we screened it for lots of people before it was released, and we found the kids weren't bothered at all. Anyway, at the very end the camera sweeps back from the action, which puts everything in a cosmic perspective. I like to take the large view. I think it's comforting."

The story of *Time Bandits* concerns a lad named Kevin, who finds a "hole in time" right in his own bedroom. Venturing through this mysterious tunnel, he emerges in different historical periods, teaming up with a band of comical time-traveling outlaws. There are strong echoes of *Snow White and the Seven Dwarfs* and *The Wizard of Oz*, and also of the *Chronicles of Narnia* novels by C. S. Lewis, which are among the few children's books to tackle questions usually regarded as food for philosophers rather than youngsters. Still, most of the action is blatantly boisterous, with flashes of Python sharpness among the more frivolous jokes and surprises. Gilliam seems aware that it's an odd duck of a film. But then, cheerful eccentricity has always been a Python stock in trade. According to Gilliam, the troupe's humor is invariably personal. "If it makes us laugh, that's the end of the discussion," he says. "We've never gone chasing after the audience, though we love having them along. The important thing isn't how many people come to see your work. The important thing is having to live with it for the rest of your life."

That's why Python comedy always seems so individualistic: It's based on "nothing but what pleases us," says Gilliam. "In fact," he continues, "it's all about us—or, in this case, about what's left of the kid in us." Hence the philosophical issues in his latest movie. "The 'big questions' are always there for us. Michael and I had solid religious upbringings, so we grew up believing and thinking about God and religion and good and evil. I can't get those out of my system; they're a part of me. The normal approach in a kids' film is to make the final character a wizard. But why not bring God into it? Why not stop fiddling around, and get right down to things? The cosmic view appeals to me. I like to think I'm not alone, that there's a whole structure around us…"

If his name and approach seem more familiar than his face and voice, it's because Gilliam is the Python behind the scenes— the nonperforming member of the popular troupe, the one who dreamed up the zany animations that filled in between comedy skits on their bygone (but frequently rerun) TV series. When the sextet moved toward the movies, it seemed natural that Gilliam (whose background is in magazine work as well as TV) should turn director. His first feature-filmmaking job was *Monty Python and the Holy Grail* [codirected by Terry Jones, 1975], followed by the less inspired *Jabberwocky* [1977]. Though the Python TV show is no more, the troupe remains loosely together, and will be putting a new movie together soon

Time Bandits is very much Gilliam's work, though it was co-written by Palin and features a brilliant appearance by Python stalwart John Cleese, as a hilarious Robin Hood. As a basically personal project, it reflects Gilliam's views. He leans away from some popular entertainment: "I enjoyed *Raiders of the Lost Ark* while it was on," he recalls, "but I couldn't remember it much afterward." And he favors some older forms of expression, such as classic fairy tales. "They put you through some rough experiences, but you come out a little more confident at the end," he says with emphasis. His values are visible in many details of *Time Banditsi,* such as the fact that the young protagonist is seen as a book reader, while his parents are hooked on TV. "The boy is a throwback," says Gilliam proudly, "while his parents are the wave of the future, and much less attractive." There's even a bit of international satire here, since Gilliam—an American who moved to Britain as a young man—considers the English youth of today (like Kevin in the film) to be more literate than their American counterparts. "British kids still read, and are still uncorrupted by a lot of the Americanization that's going on," he says.

Time Bandits is very much a British film, right down to its incredibly low budget of under $5 million, less than half the Hollywood average. Of Britain Gilliam says, "They have gone through disasters much worse and much more real than the apparent disasters in the States," he says, "and yet everyone gets along, and seems quite happy! That's why it's better in England, even with all the problems. The people have more sense of history, more perspective, and more resilience." Which sounds like a list of main ingredients in *Time Bandits*, a flawed and quirky movie, yet one that may be remembered after more expensive and more ephemeral entertainments have faded from the screen for good.

The place of the "civilized" movie on today's screen
Interview with James Ivory and Ismail Merchant, January 14, 1982

James Ivory and Ismail Merchant make civilized movies. That's a rare pursuit these days, and it has its drawbacks. Studios prefer to invest in big-budget blockbusters, which makes intimate pictures hard to finance. Moreover, today's audiences lean toward John Belushi and lost arks rather than Henry James and Jane Austen, to mention just a couple of names Ivory and Merchant have brushed against lately. Civilization is not all the rage at our neighborhood theaters just now.

Yet these enterprising artists have made a go of it. In fact, director Ivory and producer Merchant are celebrating their 20th year as a team, from *The Householder* in 1962 through *Quartet* and *Jane Austen in Manhattan*, which are currently opening across the United States. In between have come such respected titles as *Shakespeare Wallah* [1965] and *The Guru* [1969], *Roseland* [1977] and *The Europeans* [1980]. It's a long list—17 features in two decades—and an elegant one. Not all its entries have found audience applause, critical praise, or black ink on the ledgers. But as a body of work, they have earned enormous respect for Ivory and Merchant, even from viewers who quarrel with their approach.

And a distinctive approach it is. Ivory likes a leisurely style, letting a story take its time to unfold, with the burden of interest falling on character rather than plot. He also has a high regard for scenic design. The settings can seem as important as the actors and the actions. In all these strategies, he has willing collaborators in producer Merchant and screenwriter Ruth Prawer Jhabvala, who has been a third member of the team on nearly all their projects. Together they have invented their own brand of cinema: deliberate, contemplative, and, well, civilized.

As part of their 20th-anniversary celebration, Merchant/Ivory Productions is sending an extensive sampling of its work to theaters in various American cities. A complete Merchant-Ivory retrospective is due in New York at the Museum of Modern Art late this year or early in 1983, and similar programs are being prepared for London and Bombay. In addition, two Ivory-Merchant-Jhabvala films are now in first-run release. One is *Quartet*, based on a brooding Jean Rhys novel—in fact, it improves on the novel, especially at the end—about a young woman on the loose in Paris after her ne'er-do-well husband is jailed. The other is *Jane Austen in Manhattan*, a flawed but often fascinating yarn about a rare playscript by Austen that piques the interest of two rival theater groups which want to stage it—one as a traditional opera, the other as an avant-garde outburst.

Meanwhile, Ivory and Merchant have just headed for Europe to oversee their latest production, *Heat and Dust*, with Julie Christie as a woman who visits India to unravel the facts of a long-ago family scandal. When it is finished, the team will move on to *The Bostonians*, based on a Henry James work. The stars will be Christopher Reeve, Jodie Foster, and Blythe Danner. Anticipation for this one will be high, since the last James opus by Merchant and Ivory—*The Europeans*—is among their most successful productions.

Over the years, Merchant-Ivory movies have fallen into three categories. Their early films were heavily influenced by India— *The Householder*, *Shakespeare Wallah*, and *Autobiography of a Princess* [1975] among them. Equally respected are such literary adaptations as *The Europeans*, from James, and *Quartet*, from Rhys. And, a fact sometimes forgotten by Merchant-Ivory fans, there have been original screenplays having nothing to do with India or literary classics: *Roseland* [1977], for example, and the new *Jane Austen in Manhattan*. Controversy has followed all these films, and others by the Merchant-Ivory team. Many critics have objected to their halting pace; what's restful to one viewer may be lackadaisical to another. Ivory's intensely pictorial style has been accused of masking a lack of energy and imagination. Films hailed by some as bold and deliberate have been slammed by others as just plain boring. There is truth to some of these criticisms, especially with regard to some of the weaker Merchant-Ivory productions. It's easy to sympathize with viewers who have trouble staying awake during *Roseland*, for example, and even the ingenious ideas behind *Jane Austen in Manhattan* are weakened by too many dead spaces among the genuine dramatics and poetics. Other examples could be chosen without looking very far. In celebrating the Merchant-Ivory anniversary, though, the point is not to rehash old criticisms. Rather it's to cheer the integrity, the originality, and— not least in these dog days of cinema—the very existence of a team that has believed in something worthwhile, found a way to realize its vision, and stuck to it no matter what.

How does the Merchant-Ivory-Jhabvala team go about choosing its various projects, ranging about the globe and covering subjects as varied as dance halls and expatriates? Ivory and Merchant answered that query over lunch recently in New York.

"Our films reflect our lives—where we've lived, what we've done, who we know—and our interests," Ivory said. "Where else could they come from?'

Though he looks at life from a cosmopolitan viewpoint, that doesn't mean a new idea will appeal to Ivory just because it's exotic. "There are lots of places in the world, and even in the United States," he maintains, "where I couldn't just go and make a film arbitrarily. The place and the subject have to be something I know about and feel something about." Ideas for new projects usually begin with director Ivory. The other members of the team, Merchant and Jhabvala, generally concur. But there are exceptions: The highly regarded *Roseland*, for example, was a Merchant suggestion—and Ivory, by his own admission, "had to be dragged into it." In retrospect, of course, he is delighted that the dragging succeeded.

Do the filmmakers have a particular audience in mind when they embark on their projects? Yes, says Ivory. "It's the generally literate audience in this country—and England, and France, and anyplace. I'm talking about fairly mature, educated, sophisticated people. We don't really aim at any group, large or small. But I suppose the people we appeal to are the same ones educational television goes for. And I suppose that's why we survive." Merchant agrees, adding that "we do appeal to all ages, and not just segments of the audience." The important thing is the team's commitment "to film, and not just to blockbusters." That's what limits the number of its fans but ensures the maturity of the productions.

Not surprisingly, the insistence on personal and meaningful projects has prevented the Ivory-Merchant-Jhabvala team from sliding into the well-oiled Hollywood machine. They have always been something of an oddity in the movie world, working alongside but never quite within the system

This pattern began with their first film as a team, *The Householder*, based on Jhabvala's own novel. "We wanted to film it," recalls Merchant, "but we were told right away that Hollywood would never be interested. So we did it on our own." They have been working with similar independence ever since, though Ivory grants that "there's always been a tenuous link with the system." Indeed, on such pictures as *Shakespeare Wallah*, *The Guru*, and the new *Quartet*, they worked directly with Twentieth Century-Fox, a Hollywood mainstay if ever there was one. "But," Ivory insists, "we have never changed a picture so it would be more conducive to studio financing.'

To date, the most successful Merchant-Ivory pictures—measured by the number of viewers—are *Quartet*, *The Europeans*, *Shakespeare Wallah*, and *Savages* [1972]. Ivory's own favorite is *Autobiography of a Princess*, among the Indian films, and probably *Quartet* among the others. Merchant favors *Shakespeare Wallah* from the Indian batch, along with *The Europeans* and *Quartet*. Their most expensive project was *Quartet*, at $2.1 million—about 20 percent of the average Hollywood budget. At least one feature, *Bombay Talkie* [1970], apparently didn't even earn its costs back, though there is some disagreement about the details. Says Merchant, "It was made for under a million, and we sold it to TV for a million." Returns Ivory, "But they didn't make the second payment!" Such are the vicissitudes of the low-budget movie life. Moreover, says Merchant, "We have had the experience of making a movie other people wouldn't touch, and then having it bought by a major company when it is completed. They wouldn't gamble on the original novel or the talent, but they certainly would gamble on the finished product." What's the secret of achieving success with such an unlikely project? "Start with a good idea, then spend a minimum amount of money, putting it where it counts, not on frills. You can get a wonderfully opulent look that way."

The team of Ivory, Merchant, and Jhabvala is international in fact as well as in outlook. As producer Merchant describes it: "India is my country and America is my second home. Ruth is European and has adopted America. Jim is American, with an interest in India and Europe." Their meeting was as fortuitous as it was fortunate. Ivory, a budding filmmaker from Oregon, was breaking into the business with short documentaries on artistic subjects. While shooting a movie on Venetian painting, he saw Indian miniatures for the first time. "They were so beautiful and vivid," he recalls, "and they seemed to be telling some kind of story, though I didn't know what it was. I wanted very much to film them." To that end, he started reading about Indian history and art—and by a happy coincidence was hired for a film on Delhi, a chance to combine his various interests. He met Merchant while working on this project, and "it was natural that we team up."

Merchant, a film buff from Bombay, had always dreamed of "going to Hollywood and seeing how films are made." His idea was "to get an international cast and make movies for an international audience, not just for India"—unlike most pictures made by the huge Indian movie industry, which are intended for home consumption only. After deciding to work together, Ivory and

Merchant visited Jhabvala to discuss the possibility of filming her novel *The Householder*. They ended up with not only the rights to the book, but with the author herself as the writer of the screenplay. The three felt cozy together from the first. "She liked doing it," recalls Ivory, "and we liked working with a serious writer, not someone who just turns out screenplays for a living.'

Gradually they fell into their independent niche, not rejecting the establishment but not joining it, either. "At first," says Ivory, "we saw no reason why our projects shouldn't be financed in Hollywood. We felt they were viable films that ought to be made. It was only later on, after repeated troubles, that we realized the difficulty of paying for what we do." But after we had gotten a reputation for making good films," he continues, "we were able to interest box-office stars in working with us, even if the budget wasn't very big. And that made our films somewhat more appealing to conventional sources of finance. But it's always been a hard, hard struggle. We're almost always turned down."

The next Merchant-Ivory production will be *Heat and Dust*, a drama that shifts between 1923 and the present, with some scenes in between. Then will come *The Bostonians*. Other forthcoming items include *A Room With a View*, from the E. M. Forster novel, and a pair of projects called *The Courtesans* and *The Deceivers*. Clearly, this is a team that plans ahead, reflecting Ivory's confidence that movies have a healthy future despite the challenges of cable TV and other changing conditions in the show-biz world. "People go to the movies now in the same way they used to go to the theater," he says. "It's a special event. Audiences still want the impact of that big screen and that big sound. Also, they have to get out of the house once in a while, even if it's just once a month." Even big Hollywood films can have strong quality, Ivory continues, citing the work of Woody Allen. "When you do see a civilized mass-market movie," he says, "it makes you feel so good!"

Beyond immediate plans, what is the future of Merchant/Ivory Productions and its members? Like the producer he is, Merchant gives a practical answer. "I'm happy we got the rights to *A Room With a View*, and I want to do another film in New York, because I enjoy working here. Also, we want to start our own distribution company. We've taken almost 50 percent of the responsibility as producers anyway, so why not take it all, and succeed or fail on our own? It's vital for a producer to have a distributor who shares his own enthusiasm for the film. There's no point in giving it to someone who's halfhearted. You work for two or three years on a project, raising money and working with actors and getting people to believe in you. And then you put it in the hands of someone who wants to forget about it if it isn't a blockbuster in the first two weeks!' And like the director he is, Ivory gives a more visionary version of the team's future. "I hope we'll go in whatever direction our lives go," he muses. "I hope our films will continue to reflect ourselves and our feelings and thoughts. But who can tell how our lives and thoughts will develop? One never knows. And that's a big part of the adventure."

When Meredith Monk sings, the whole world understands. Her radical style taps many cultures
Interview with Meredith Monk, January 18, 1982

Meredith Monk is an uncommon artist. Though her main interest is music, her talent ranges over many fields, from stage directing to filmmaking. She brings her own unique sound style to each of them. Her latest theater piece, *Specimen Days*, was presented by the New York Shakespeare Festival in a production that will run again Feb. 16-28. And you can hear her latest compositions on a splendid new record, *Dolmen Music* (ECM-1-1197), which recently won a West German prize as best recording of the year. Or you can hear the works on that disc—and more—performed live during her major tour of the West Coast and Europe, that is just getting started. It's a busy time for Monk and her colleagues, which is good news for listeners who enjoy opening their ears to new and adventurous music. Listening to her music is always an ear-opening experience. Her solo works, such as those on Side 1 of *Dolmen Music*, are virtuoso exercises in mood and texture, calling on all kinds of vocal resources not usually found in Western composition, from glottal stops to wailing ululations. Her ensemble pieces extend her personal techniques to other voices, while allowing them room for their own expressions. The dominant effect is one of eerie loveliness.

Over lunch recently, Monk sounded like a composer even when discussing her activity as filmmaker or stage director. She said, for example, that her most recent theater work has been quite abstract. "It's not laden with content," she explained. "It's musical." The key word seems to be "musical." Even her stage work, she feels, has a musical structure. "You'd know right away it was a musician who did this," she says. "Even the images are musical. When I use images, I'm like an orchestrator."

Just as her theater work is musical, her musical compositions are inherently theatrical, even when they are sung and played "straight" on a bare stage. This is partly because of the exotic voice-sounds Monk uses instead of words for her songs. "I rarely use texts because voice itself is such a strong, rich language," she explains. "You hardly need another language on top of it. The syllables I use are extensions of the music. I don't think English is any more interesting." And there's another reason, recalling the old ideal of music as a universal language. "I can do my music all over the world," she says, "and people can respond directly, without having to go through language... I'm trying to approach a vocal music that's both primordial and futuristic, and this is my way." Futuristic? "Sure. Maybe there won't be language differentiation in the future."

Monk started on her adventurous pathways early. "I've always been singing," she recalls. "My mother and grandfather and great-grandfather were all singers. I began writing vocal music when I was a child. I was writing piano compositions by the time I was a teen-ager.' But following the family tradition wasn't enough. "I wanted to do something else," she says. "I wanted my own territory. This led me to dance, which will always be a part of my life.' It was her early dance experience that suggested the direction her music would take. "In modern dance," she explains, "it's taken for granted that a person develops her own style and vocabulary of movement. But I realized this had never been done, vocally. I wanted to create a very personal vocal style, to stretch the voice in as many ways as I could. I was interested in using the voice as an instrument, as a source of energy and impulse, to get different registers and kinds of texture.' This impulse came to her "in a flash" as she practiced the piano one day. "I suddenly felt the voice could be as flexible as the spine," she recalls. "I realized the voice could move in as many ways as a body can. From that time on, I started working on my vocal music. I have a wide range, so I could work with my own instrument."

From the beginning, her methods were radical. "A lot of it was learning how to sing a melody in a way that was separate from Western training," she says. "It involved stripping away. Not stripping away technique—this singing requires a lot of technique and strength—but stripping away the idea that you can only sing something in a certain manner. The whole Western tradition is based on certain tones and sounds. I had to throw a lot of that out, using a trial-and-error method on my own voice. I just tried things—I was already an artist, so I knew what I was doing—and after a few years I started going to other sources, too. For example, I began to realize that some cultures have a glottal break or ululation sound, and that I found this interesting. But it all stemmed from my personal experiments." Her approach to dance was similar. "I wanted to throw away all the trained responses and start from scratch," she recalls, "with a natural and organic style that was very much my own. I wanted to get to a very straightforward and truthful expression, and I knew I couldn't get this by training and being in class." Later, she applied the same ideas to work in theater and film.

Like many of today's leading young composers, Monk went through a "minimalist" phase early in her career. In her album *Key*, for example, "each song has one vocal quality." But there's more to it than that. "I was also dealing with range a lot," she says, "and I was very aware of how the voice is directly hooked up to the emotional palette. You can get to emotions you can hardly reach with any other medium, certainly not verbally. And I felt I was connecting with ancient traditions and roots, as well as futuristic ones. "At the same time, like many of her contemporaries, Monk is uncomfortable with the "minimalist" label. "I was always more of a maximalist, really. It wasn't very interesting to pare everything down to one element. But I was working in fairly simple ways. I wanted to get back to real basics." Though so-called "minimalists" generally squirm under that heading, it has been useful in describing a great deal of recent musical activity by composers as different as Monk and Philip Glass, Steve Reich and Jon Gibson. Why should that be? The answer says a lot about current musical impulses and ideas.

"The Western classical tradition of the '40s, '50s, and '60s got detached from any basic consciousness," Monk says. "When I hear that music—and I try not to hear it—it's all head, as if nothing existed beneath the chin. A lot of people started to feel there was nowhere to go in that direction—that a more human, more essential, more vital expression was needed.' Also, I have the feeling that rock-and-roll had a lot to do with it. I used to play in a rock band, and I still think about how strong it can be— how the beat is involved with heartbeat, pulse, feeling. I listened to jazz around the middle '60s, too. It's all connected."

So unusual and eclectic is the Monk approach that she encounters problems peculiar to her own work. For instance, it isn't easy to come up with a standard-style score for much of her music. "Phrases are scored, and I usually know the overall form," she says. "But in rehearsal, I work on the phrases right with the voices, as if they were bodies. It's very alive, like something from the oral tradition. In a work like *Tablet*, there are sections you can't write out at all, so you just put 'improvisation.' Also in *Dolmen Music*, there are parts that would take 15 years to notate completely." And there are places where the singers have room to play around within the set form, and these sections are different each time they're performed... So if someone wanted to learn the piece, they'd need a score and a tape recording. After all, how can you write out a timbre or a texture?" By the same token, a director restaging a

Specimen Days would need a videotape as well as a script, to get a complete idea of what the creator intended.

For the immediate future, Monk expects to immerse herself more completely in music, and perhaps in film, leaving aside the demanding and time-consuming process of conceiving and directing new theater pieces. She will never leave theater behind, but music is calling her very insistently these days and will probably claim most of her attention for the next few years. Most important of all, she says, is communicating with her audience in as pure and direct a way as possible. Sometimes she feels the temptation to popularize her music, incorporating it in a rock framework—or some such package—and getting rich from it. But she rejects that approach, just as she rejects the "anticommunication" she sees in "arty, deliberately difficult" work that "masquerades as avant-gardism." She isn't in that mold at all, she asserts, despite the challenging nature of her art. "I want to reach people's hearts," she says. "I want my music to be a heart thing, not just a mind thing."

Coppola savors breaking the moviemaking rules
Interview with Francis Ford Coppola, February 18, 1982

Hollywood is built on the great contradiction between art and commerce. Commerce holds most of the aces, though art peeps out often enough to make the game interesting Francis Coppola finds this stimulating. But it isn't complicated enough for him. So he started his own studio, Zoetrope, and set out to revolutionize the movie world—a bearded Napoleon armed with ambition, a vast love for film, and the latest electronic doodads. So far, his campaign has been inconclusive. Coppola and company have turned out a string of successful pictures, from *Apocalypse Now* [Francis Ford Coppola, 1979] to the *The Black Stallion* [Carroll Ballard, 1979]. They have also teetered on the brink of financial oblivion—almost plunging over the edge when their latest project, *One From the Heart* [Francis Ford Coppola, 1981] found itself millions of dollars in debt, and still far from finished. The money was found, the picture was completed, and it opened in 11 cities a week ago. But this hardly spells success for Zoetrope. Many critics found the film a dud, and $23 million is a hefty budget for a dud to recoup. If it fails, Coppola could lose the enterprise he has spent a dozen years building. If it posts a profit, though, Hollywood had better look out. Coppola has dreams he hasn't even started to realize. If he has his way, and if his skills are equal to his aspirations, he could give us a radical new electronic cinema that's different from anything we've ever seen.

Like fabled Hollywood itself, Coppola is contradictory. Meeting last week with a handful of journalists in New York, he tossed out a multitude of ideas that careened off one another like billiard balls rushing in opposite directions. A few samples:

On his own ability: "I probably have genius but no talent. I was never a talented kid."

On his own success: "I'm an extremely wealthy person who sometimes has trouble coming up with $500."

On his new movie: "Someday people may measure films by whether they came before *One From the Heart* or after it." Then, a few minutes later: "It's just a dumbbell valentine I made, so girls and little children would like me."

Coppola might not get too much argument on that last point. *One From the Heart* is yet another contradiction—a great big beautiful bore. Made with the latest film technology, crammed with theatrical magic, it wastes these resources on a trite story with dreary characters. It's all style, without a shred of substance. Despite its R rating and occasional nudity, Coppola sees it as an "innocent" romance full of charm and optimism. But he's wrong. Happy endings don't mean a thing if there's nothing to build up to them. And pretty packages are disappointing if there's nothing inside. Still, there is one very impressive thing about *One From the Heart*—its refusal to follow the usual movie patterns. With his cinematic know-how, Coppola could have ground out a more conventional version of the same story (about a couple who break up and get together again) with a lot less risk. Instead, he surrounded his simple plot with all kinds of visual innovations. The lighting design, for example, is more expressive than the performances. This says little for the actors, but it demonstrates Coppola's expertise in technical matters.

How does Coppola feel about all this? He disagrees with the critics of *One From the Heart*, insisting the film will be a financial success. But he also looks beyond the moment—this is just one movie, after all—and glows with enthusiasm about the future. "I believe in a cinema of many possibilities," he said last week, settling on a sofa in his New York hotel suite. "I want to work in different styles and be unpredictable, just to get interested again. I don't like going to the movies anymore. Years ago, you could choose from 20 kinds of films to see: swashbucklers, musicals, comedy, social drama, romance, Abbott and Costello. Now there's just three or four things you're allowed to make: screwball comedy, psychosocial stuff, and space opera. You don't have diversity anymore. It's like a 55-m.p.h. speed limit. But what if you want to go 2,000 m.p.h.? There are plenty of areas in life where you have to stick by the rules. In this field, it shouldn't be that way."

Significantly, the visionary Coppola isn't interested in small experiments—inexpensive projects designed to reach a limited number of people. Rather, he wants to work on a large scale, using all the resources of cinema and hitting as wide an audience as possible. That's why he feels so proud over *Apocalypse Now,* his epic about the Vietnam war. "That was an off-the-wall picture," he says, "a UCLA surrealistic film. Yet it was seen by the world, and made around $120 million. That's just what I want to do—make movies in a free way, yet do major works with all the elements of the medium. And I want to end up with a crazy film like *Apocalypse*, not just another *King Kong* genre picture."

Coppola is bursting with projects right now, and some of them sound promising. This season Zoetrope will release several films, including *Hammett*—about mystery writer Dashiell Hammett, directed by Wim Wenders—and *The Escape Artist*, directed by Caleb Deschanel, who photographed *The Black Stallion* not long ago. The famous horse will also be back, in *The Black Stallion Returns*. And the Zoetrope revival of *Napoleon*, the 1927 classic by Abel Gance, is still traveling to special engagements around the United States. For next season and beyond, Coppola plans four films in a row aimed at young people. The first, already in production, is *The Outsiders*, about four teen-age boys who try to make it on their own after losing their parents. The story comes from a novel (by a teen-age author) that was recommended to Coppola in a letter from students at a California high school. He says it's about youth, "and that special moment when you look at something beautiful and realize that it will change. It's about how teen-agers talk about life and death. And it's very idealistic, because youth is idealistic."

Beyond these projects, the future looks hazy but exciting—if Coppola and Zoetrope manage to prosper. Even in *One From the Heart* he has been using a whole new system for conceiving and developing movies, involving computer technology that allows the entire film to be "composed" on tape before the first set is built or the first actor is chosen. In coming years, he envisions a time when the filmmaker will be able to conjure up any conceivable image or sound, work with it and manipulate it, and perfect the whole movie before going near the camera. If this vision comes true, filmmaking could become a more intuitive, less linear process, which is exactly what Coppola would like. "When I do experiments while making a film," he says, "it's because I'm trying to learn and master what I'll need for my later work. For example, I'm very interested in combining music and film, but I don't know enough about it. I'm like the Madison Avenue guy who dreams not just about writing a novel, but being qualified to write it."

What lurks in Coppola's mind as he frets and experiments and learns? "I'd like to make the opera of the future in film," he says. "It would be long—in four parts—like a tapestry with many threads of character, theme, setting, lights, music, poetry. It would be about life and love and energy, as in physics. It would involve history, with Japan and America coming together like lovers. And I want the last 15 minutes to be the first electronic hologram. The whole theater would become—something I can't describe, but you'd be right there in it." Is this all idle fantasy? Maybe not. Coppola sounds serious about his ultimate movie. In fact, he has pinpointed the three stumbling blocks to realizing it. "First, I have to be good enough to do it. Second, I'd need a company of people who had been with me a long time. And third, I need to figure out where I'll get the money." Ideally, he says, Zoetrope will provide the financing for his most ambitious plans. But that depends on the success of *One From the Heart* this year, *The Outsiders* next year, and other movies after that. Can the Coppola company build such a string of successes? The auguries are good, if past performance is any indication. Zoetrope hasn't made a flop yet, and Coppola's pre-Zoetrope career includes the *Godfather* [1972, 1974] pictures, which also did all right

But success comes hard in the movie business. "For a dinky little company with no financing," says Coppola about Zoetrope, "we have had tremendous influence. We've had a string of hits and started a string of new styles. We've introduced new directors, new technical programs, international trends, unorthodox methods of release. And yet we're still struggling to be alive!" Why? Largely because Zoetrope is still a new kid on the block, an "American Motors of the movie world" that just isn't as big as its competitors. And then there's the Coppola penchant for personal projects. "I do a lot of things out of enthusiasm," he says, "and I will say yes to pretty much of anything if it feels good to me. I could end all my financing troubles if I just decided to make movies for other people, for a fee of a million dollars or so. But I want to own the rights to what I do. And I want to build my base for the future."

Looking at the movie world as a whole, Coppola puts the blame for many of its current troubles—poor films, money worries, et al.—on the major studios. "The corporations and the exhibitors, and even the critical press, want films to be more and more uniform, more of a product," he says. "How could film fare have shrunk so much in its possibilities, if everyone weren't in agreement on that. "But it isn't me who posts the 55-m.p.h. limit. It's a system of overlapping, vested interests which protect the way things are—because the way things are, they're on top. How can we compete with that?" Though faith in the future is a big part of Coppola's outlook, it can be hard to maintain. "Optimistically," he says, "I believe in the tremendous potential of worldwide cinema, and uses for cinema in education and other fields. But the companies and conglomerates feel this is too big for the show-business people to be in charge of, so they replace them. They organize it and make it into a product and erode its traditions. The enormous Hollywood machine is all but gone. The craftsmen and artisans are replaced by a kind of cynical professional who goes from job to job. Each film is packaged. Everyone is in business for himself, and the ensemble tradition of the old studios has vanished. And with that erosion of our capabilities is an erosion of the kinds of film we can make." Coppola feels this is not only a tragedy for the movies, but an ominous sign of our time. "I'm not just interested in film," he says. "I care about what's going to happen to all of us in the future. And the best people are not in the driver's seat. We need people who use not just analysis, but intuition. They're our best headlights to go forward."

In sum, Coppola says, we are downgrading our way of life along with our films. "It's obvious that movies are nothing more than technology and talent put together," he insists. "If we have an antique technology and no effort to develop talent, what's the future?' He tries to combat this by developing all sorts of new electronic technology at Zoetrope, while including as many bright young talents as he can find room for. He even has an apprentice program, involving an "adopted" junior high school across the street from his studio. "Zoetrope is doing the research and development for the whole industry," he says, "and yet we're in a tenuous financial position because we're supposed to be reckless… But in my opinion," he continues, referring to the other studios, "they're the reckless ones. It's risky to not take risks, especially at this point in history. This is not a time to hold back. Although things are deteriorating, we have the resources to make the world a pretty nice place." And that's the bottom line for this self-described "genius with no talent." Quoting Aldous Huxley, he maintains that "any society should use its energies for encouraging people to develop their desirable human potentialities.' What are those potentialities? "Intelligence, creativity, and friendliness," says Coppola. "Let's do all we can to encourage those three things."

Composer John Cage, master of notes—and sounds
Interview with John Cage, May 4, 1982

According to the *New Grove Dictionary of Music*, John Cage has had "a greater impact on world music than any other American composer of the 20th century." Author, philosopher, and all-around artistic guru as well as musician, Cage is as busy as ever. His activities range from writing and composing to printmaking and performing—and participating in preparations for his 70th birthday, considered a major anniversary in some musical circles. The following interview took place at Symphony Space in Manhattan, the afternoon before a massive 14½-hour concert called *Wall-to-Wall Cage*, devoted to seminal works by him, his colleagues, and his followers.

Despite the extraordinary length of the concert, I understand there will only be time for a sampling of your own music and of composers you admire. Doesn't this suggest the enormous range of contemporary music?

There are so many different directions one can follow. This comes from changes in technology and the interpenetration of cultures that were formerly separated. Also, there are larger numbers of people, so you have more ideas coming forth.

Your music has always been elusive when people try to record it. Do you agree

I like live music. I don't stop my music from being recorded, because other people like it. But I've always been opposed to records.

You often work with electronic equipment. It seems to me that the spontaneity and good humor of your approach helps to humanize such devices.

The piece we're setting up now uses electronics, but it also uses junk things that are part and parcel of everyday life. We have a complex situation with three performers, and objects with cartridges and contact microphones. We enter a situation that resembles people trying to get through the tunnel into New Jersey, in terms of sound, not in terms of what we have to do to produce the sounds. One person may be turning down the amplitude while someone else is playing something. Causes and effects get dislocated. The personal element seems to make the machinery not quite work properly.

Is a concert hall a good place for such an experience?

Yes. If we have a concert such as this, people can then listen when they go outside… and the noises won't seem as disagreeable as they'd thought.

Would it be good if the sounds of life eventually replaced the concert hall altogether?

Not altogether. In the future, it seems to me, we should want all the things we've had in the past, plus a lot of things we haven't had yet!

It seems to take a lot of work and trouble to achieve the randomness and spontaneity you seek. Is this a contradiction?

It's an attempt to open our minds to possibilities other than the ones we remember, and the ones we already know we like… Something has to be done to get us free of our memories and choices.

Were your early classical studies—your work with Schoenberg, for example—a necessary preliminary to this

At the time I did them they were necessary, or I wouldn't have done them. When I was young, all you could do was follow Schoenberg or follow Stravinsky—write 12-tones or write neoclassical. There was no alternative. Such studies are less necessary now. But they're part of my life. Still, they need not be a part of yours. The fact that I had to learn to ride horseback, so to speak, doesn't have anything to do with someone who wants to travel to the moon.

In the past—in your book A Year From Monday, *for instance— you have invoked the idea of the whole world becoming a single "global village" through communications technology. Has this come to pass?*

Not sufficiently, yet. We won't have a global village as long as we have the nations divided. We need the realization that we're all together in one place, and that we all have the same problems.

Your ideas have often reverberated beyond the world of art, into the realm of politics and society in general. Has there been a subtle effect, perhaps, on the general climate?

That's possible. But I think the first thing we have to do is embarrass the government out of existence… This year two magazines asked me about the nuclear threat. I sat down and spent a whole day answering them. That takes the place of voting, for me.

You have always advocated the mingling of different arts. That is happening a great deal these days. But there is little mingling of art and politics — or art and social communications, like advertising and TV. This seems discouraging.

But not sufficiently discouraging to stop us. [*laughs*] In a talk I gave at a school in Boston, I explained that I was less optimistic than formerly, due to current events. And they said, Oh, please remain as optimistic as you were

Will you?

I'll try.

Two more films from Spielberg, a one-man fantasy factory
Interview with Steven Spielberg, June 3, 1982

Steven Spielberg is a one-man fantasy factory. His hits include the adventurous *Jaws* [1975] and the kinetic *Raiders of the Lost Ark* [1981], with the charming *Close Encounters of the Third Kind* [1977] in between. All earned glowing reviews, huge audiences, and piles of money for their studios. Will the Spielberg winning streak continue? This month the young filmmaker has two otherworldly treats in store, and both have already generated excitement in the trade. One is *E.T. The Extra-Terrestrial* [1982], a grade-school version of *Close Encounters of the Third Kind* with a cuddly spaceman in the title role. The other is *Poltergeist* [Tobe Hooper, 1982], a phantasmic ghost story set in the California suburbs.

Of the two, *E.T.* takes the most risks. The main character is a young child, and the story is a perfect preteen fantasy: Imagine having your own alien living in your bedroom, with nobody—not even Mom—in on the secret. Later you introduce him to your brother and sister, and when Halloween comes, you dress him in a sheet and take him trick-or-treating. He's full of surprises and special powers. And all he asks is a little help contacting his home planet, so he can get back home after a while. It's quite sweet, really, and some of it is enormously funny. In fact, it would be an ideal family film if not for a few vulgar words, and a sci-fi medical sequence preceding the *Peter Pan*-style climax. What's commercially risky about *E.T.* is that—as Spielberg readily admits—the hero is a lot younger than the "core audience" of teens and young adults that Hollywood pursues so eagerly these days. And the action is gentle, with hardly a shred of violence or vehemence. What if teen-agers find *E.T.* too tame, and adults consider it too coy? It could be the first Spielberg flop since *1941* [1979]. But it probably won't be. Spielberg is a canny filmmaker, and he has given *E.T.* a sly wit that will probably pull the picture through. As for *Poltergeist* it's hard to imagine how this spook-filled romp could fail. The buildup is careful and deliberate, leading to an explosion of shockers from the *Raiders of the Lost Ark* bag of tricks, cleverly leavened with humor. While it's not for young children, and contains a few vulgarities of its own, its natural audience of *Raiders of the Lost Ark* fans will be captivated before the first reel has unspooled.

How has Spielberg managed to pull two major entertainments from his sleeve in a single season? There's no magic involved: He had a lot of help, that's all. Some of that help came from filmmaker Tobe Hooper, who is listed as director of *Poltergeist*, with Spielberg credited as producer. Unfortunately, this partnership has led to recriminations from Hooper, who apparently feels his contribution to the picture has been slighted. What does Spielberg want to accomplish in pictures like *Poltergeist* and *E.T.?* Discussing his work with a few journalists in New York the other day, he expressed a fondness for larger-than-life adventures in garden-variety surroundings. Both new films take place in suburban areas where dullness is the rule, recalling Alfred Hitchcock's preference for ordinary heroes and suspenseful adventures that strike in broad daylight. According to Spielberg, the suburban reality of *Poltergeist* and *E.T.* is the ideal background for a "battle between the fantastic and the mundane," which is what most of his films are all about.

Spielberg's movies have been criticized for frivolity—a just accusation when aimed at *Raiders of the Lost Ark* or *1941*, which lapse into old formulas instead of looking for new insights, deep meanings, or at least fresh cinematic thrills. But there's a streak of the sublime in Spielberg, along with his weakness for standard movie conventions. When he concocted *Close Encounters of the Third Kind* a few years ago, he proved himself capable of truly audacious filmmaking—combining lavish visual delights with a philosophical humor and a childlike awe that boldly ran against the contemporary grain. Anyway, says the young director, "Movies are frivolous, fantastic, unbelievable. The suspension of disbelief is the whole point. It's just a question of whether you're suspending your disbelief for an *Ordinary People* [Robert Redford, 1980]—accepting the idea that those histrionics occur in every family—or for a *Star Wars* [George Lucas, 1977]. It comes to the same thing." What is his own goal? "I want to make movies you can't tune into right away. I want to be more original than that. I loved *Chariots of Fire* [Hugh Hudson, 1981], and maybe I could make a picture like that in five years—maybe I'll move into a more human naturalism. But not today. Today I'm on a different track, and I can't tell where it's going right now."

Perhaps it takes a critic to tell Spielberg that his work is pretty "human" and "natural" already. For all the flash and fantasy of his latest films, they have a clarity, an everyday credibility, and a sense of family warmth that are often missing in more mundane pictures. Even when the poltergeists turn vicious and the E.T. unleashes his magical powers, these movies still revolve around the family closeness and parent-child love that are so carefully established in the opening scenes. The young hero of *E.T.* is a boy named Elliott who never looks quite at home in the world. "There's lots of me in Elliott and Elliott in me," says Spielberg. "I only regret I wasn't such a neat kid." What was Spielberg like as a child? "I was a weird little outsider," he says with a smile. "At 12 years old I was living in Arizona and making 8-mm movies, and the neighbors thought I was crazy. They couldn't understand why I was dressing their children in German and Japanese uniforms and staging battle extravaganzas." In later years, Spielberg found himself the only member of his freshman class who knew what he wanted to major in. "I wanted to be a movie director," he recalls, but his grades weren't strong enough for transferring to a school with a film program. So he made 16-mm experimental movies, learning and creating at the same time. Today he misses the "fraternal" experience that some other filmmakers had during their college years — the Coppola-Lucas-Milius crowd, for example, from the University of Southern California. "I never had that group feeling," he laments. "My college friends were all strange. I wished I could be around normal people like filmmakers!"

When casting a child to star in *E.T.*, Spielberg looked for two qualities: awkwardness and honesty. "That's the kind of kid I grew up with," he explains. But it wasn't easy to find these attributes. "I kept getting auditions from kids who looked like they'd been playing Las Vegas. At seven years old, they had more credits than I do! It's better to get a child who's lost and needs guidance — a shy kid who internalizes a lot. When I found Henry Thomas, I saw the chance for an adult performance to come from a child's body. He's very gentle, and very controlled. He was just what I needed." Thus prepared, Spielberg fashioned *E.T.* to be a movie he'd like to see, not a movie that would automatically thrill a huge audience. "I made *Poltergeist* for the young audience, and I made *E.T.* for myself," he says.

What's next for Spielberg? A whole list of projects. First will come *The Twilight Zone*, based on the memorable television series. It will comprise four stories — two originals, two remakes from the TV show — directed by four filmmakers. Spielberg's own episode will be a remake of the fantastic yarn about a little boy who can control people with his mind, written by veteran fantasist Richard Matheson. Other episodes will be directed by John Landis, Joe Dante, and George Miller. Next will come *Always*, a feature-length remake of the 1943 drama *A Guy Named Joe* [Victor Fleming], with Spencer Tracy and Irene Dunne. Spielberg says this will be his first "adult love story," but again there's a twist: "The leading man isn't alive. He's a ghost." Spielberg saw the original on TV when he was 14, and loves it dearly; there's even a clip from it in *Poltergeist*. And yes, movie fans, there will be a follow-up to *Raiders of the Lost Ark*, directed by Mr. S. himself. In fact, he says, "there will be a sequel if I have to break into the studio vault and steal the money." Why? "Because the kids won't leave me alone." Sounds like a very good reason.

Lively, enriching tale of the Chinese-American experience:
***Chan Is Missing* uses detective format for humor and insight**
Interview with Wayne Wang, July 1, 1982

Yes, there's a touch of Charlie Chan in the new movie called *Chan Is Missing*. But it's a wry touch—the mark of a Chinese filmmaker who has adopted America and loves both parts of his heritage so much he can't resist kidding them a little The filmmaker's name is Wayne Wang, and he grew up in Hong Kong before coming to the United States as a young man. In fictional form, *Chan Is Missing* tells what he found in the Chinatown district of San Francisco, where he did community work for a few years after finishing college. The main characters are a middle-aged cabdriver and his friend, a streetwise and sometimes foul-mouthed young man. They are searching for an acquaintance who has suddenly vanished. They look everywhere: in streets and shops, on the piers, and at the university. They meet a splendid cross section of humanity, and stumble on nooks and crannies they had never dreamed of. But they don't find Chan. What they do find is a scattered mosaic of clues to the Chinese-American experience—clues as rich and varied and messy and vibrant as life itself, and just as impossible to figure out.

As a commercial movie, *Chan Is Missing* is no more likely than its own wild-goose plot. Using local actors, borrowed equipment, and his own money—along with grants from a couple of generous institutions—Wang completed it on a staggeringly low budget of about $20,000. Despite its modest means and its grainy black-and-white look, it attracted wide attention. After winning high praise at a couple of festivals, it was picked up for release by New Yorker Films, an enterprising distribution company that is often willing to take a chance on a promising new thing. Result: *Chan Is Missing* is doing bang-up business in Manhattan, and wending its way to other cities as fast as its growing reputation will allow. Imminent openings include San Francisco on July 9, Los Angeles and Boston on July 28, and Chicago on Aug. 6, with more to come. That's a lot of exposure for a proudly personal project about a pair of amateur sleuths poking through the ethnic underbrush of California.

There are many ways to approach *Chan Is Missing*—as a detective story, a dark comedy, a light melodrama, or simply a portrait of a time and place. You might call it an existential mystery yarn with a broad sense of humor. Its heroes are Everymen, and its Chinatown setting seems quite universal once you get to know it. Most important, the theme is timeless. As the main characters plunge into their neighborhood and their city, they come to realize the complexity of even a vague and seemingly unimportant person like the missing Chan Hung. The movie is at its best when revealing the fragmented clues they find: a photograph, a newspaper clipping, an anecdote from a neighbor, a memory from a friend. The deeper they dig, the deeper the mystery becomes—and the funnier it gets, as facts become garbled and one incident blurs into another. In the end, the story simply dissolves, fading gracefully and enigmatically into its own background. It's like a trick out of a Thomas Pynchon novel, and European movies like *Eclipse* [Michelangelo Antonioni, 1962] and *Out One: Spectre* [Jacques Rivette, 1972] come readily to mind. But this disappearing act is no arty pirouette. It's the triumph of cinema over story, of poetics over plot.

Discussing his film in New York the other day, Wang said he first intended it to be more of a documentary. But he found the project becoming "too dry and academic," to the point where his own crew and actors had trouble understanding it. So he wrote a different script—more dramatic, more of a narrative, and centering on a Chinese character. The final screenplay reflects his wish to make a movie that would be accessible and meaningful to the Chinese-American community, while reaching non-Chinese audiences at the same time. "If 500,000 people see it," he says, "that would be 500,000 people with a slightly better understanding of Chinese-American life, and not just a Charlie Chan-style understanding." Though its initial audience has not been an ethnic one, Chinese viewers are being wooed through newspaper ads, and Wang would like to see a trial run in a Chinatown theater. But he hopes its Asian subject won't limit viewers to Asians and art-film patrons in big cities. Indeed, he sees no reason why *Chan Is Missing* shouldn't play as well in Iowa, say, as in New York—a peripatetic hit like *My Dinner With Andre* [Louis Malle, 1981] featuring Chinese food.

Wang considers the film "extremely realistic" as a portrait of Chinatown, from the settings and locations (and sometimes vulgar language) down to the news stories that weave around the main plot. But in making the picture, he says, "I wanted to question myself and never take this reality for granted." Gradually, he wants the audience to question its own attitudes, too. "It's important not to rely on stereotyped images or easy answers," he says, discussing the complexity of immigrant life in the 20th century. "Collisions between cultures are very real, and they're always changing. They're too complex for simple formulas. I even feel that way about myself. I grew up in Hong Kong. Then I came to America and became completely Americanized. Then I went back to Hong Kong and didn't feel Chinese anymore. Am I a Chinese or an American person? That's a complicated question. And it also goes for people who grow up in one region of America and then move to another that's very different. There are differences between cultures even within the United States. And I expect that'll be the theme of any film I ever make."

By training, Wang is an artist who studied commercial art, fine art, and painting in college. He switched to film in graduate school, worked for a while in the Hong Kong film and TV industry (where important developments are taking place, he says), and made some shorts in the San Francisco Bay Area. *Chan Is Missing* is his second feature. "A filmmaker can create very different kinds of work," he says. "I'd like to make an intelligent and abstract film on a low budget, and also do a commercial picture—on an important subject—for a major studio. Wang considers the movie to be a political gesture, despite the frequent whimsy of its approach. He hopes it will prompt audiences to think about immigrant realities, and about the problems he encountered during his social-work days in San Francisco. That's why he soft-pedaled the intellectual basis of *Chan Is Missing*, emphasizing the story and characters "so people could get involved with the movie, and understand things about Chinese-Americans that they can't find anywhere else." The result is "a compromise," he says, "but a good one: I did a little of everything I wanted to do."

Wang considers *Chan Is Missing* a means of educating Americans about Chinese immigrants not through complex theorizing, but through its own Asian qualities. "There is a special perspective in much Asian art," he says. "It's a bird's-eye view of things, a 'wide shot' that takes in a great deal all at once. And there's real cultural basis for that—a holistic view that sees things in a connected and continuous way. It's the opposite of the close-ups and isolated shots that most Western movies have. In ways, I'm very Asian. Like most Asian artists, I'm afraid of powerful and flashy visuals. I have a kind of minimal aesthetic, and *Chan* is very functional in that way. In other ways, though, *Chan* is not so Asian—it's full of bits and pieces. I'd like my next film to be smoother, in the old Chinese and Japanese manner. But then again, the bits and pieces in *Chan* do all connect, in one way or another, even when it isn't obvious. In a sense, it is very Asian. And I hope it communicates that quality to as many people as possible."

Multimedia man Altman plunges into... opera?
Altman stages Stravinsky, November 22, 1982

Ann Arbor, Michigan.

Hollywood's loss, it seems, is everyone else's gain. Stung by a series of box-office disappointments, director Robert Altman—of *M*A*S*H* [1970] and *Nashville* [1975] fame—stalked out of the movie world recently, determined to try his hand at other media. Since then, he has staged Broadway and Off Broadway plays and dabbled in cable television. He has also directed a non-Hollywood film with the unlikely title of *Come Back to the 5 and Dime, Jimmy Dean, Jimmy Dean* [1982], which has been well received in Europe and has now opened in the United States.

And now, opera. Altman has tackled a major contemporary work: *The Rake's Progress* by Stravinsky, a haunting mixture of modernist methods and Mozartian mannerisms, neoclassic nostalgia and Faustian fantasy. The results here at the Power Center for the Performing Arts were dazzling. Nestled in an academic setting— the show was sponsored by the University of Michigan School of Music—director Altman was free to soar above the "commercial" considerations that came to hamper his film career. It was clearly a liberating opportunity for him, and it may pay dividends back to the movie world, if a film is now made (as has been hinted) from the stage production. Today as ever, there can be little doubt that Altman is among our boldest and most imaginative directors. This bodes well for his next project, another musical extravaganza due early next year: a $3 million Broadway show, scheduled to open in the spring, based on the work of vintage American composer Louis Moreau Gottschalk. [*Note: This project never materialized.*]

What led Altman to take on the world of opera? "I don't know," he told me after a stunning performance of *The Rake's Progress* the other night. "It's an idea that's been bouncing around my head for a while," he added, smiling at his own vagueness. Part of his motivation may have been the chance to work on a scale as large as some of his biggest Hollywood projects. "I've always wanted to get this many people on a stage at the same time," he cackled, referring to scenes in which nearly 150 people swarm around the setting at once—scenes that would almost certainly be too costly outside the walls of academe in a conventional opera house or theater. Then too, Altman's film work has long had a certain musical structure. Some of his best pictures, such as *3 Women* [1977] and *A Wedding* [1978], are based more on developing themes than traditional storytelling techniques. The soundtracks of *Nashville* and *A Perfect Couple* [1979] resound with music almost as much as an out-and-out musical like *Popeye* [1980]. And don't forget that Altman is not the first filmmaker to invade the musical stage. Indeed, both Ingmar Bergman and Ken Russell have directed productions of *The Rake's Progress* itself.

In any case, Altman's edition of *The Rake's Progress"* showed a confident approach to the perennial challenge of matching images with sounds. Taking some cues from William Hogarth, who originated the "Rake's Progress" in his 18th-century paintings and engravings, Altman has carried the theme to its logical—and illogical—conclusions. Physically, the undertaking must rank with the grandest "grand opera" in recent memory. The stage creaked under a huge metallic cobweb of platforms and scaffolds. On it were draped scores of bizarrely costumed figures representing both the sublime and (more often) the phantasmagoric aspects of the story, which centers on an ambitious young man who strikes an unwitting deal with the devil. Inanimate objects took on unexpected life, as when a clock chimed in Stravinsky's score and suddenly its dial was spectrally embodied by a huge ring of performers. It was part circus, part reverie, part nightmare, part sleight-of-hand, and part sheer fun—all managing to serve the libretto (by W. H. Auden and Chester Kallman) rather than merely distracting attention.

Perhaps the most amazing thing about this production is that it seemed intimate, notwithstanding the hubbub that surrounded it. For all the fury of the staging, the musical personalities of the main figures were never neglected. Indeed, this would have been a strong and involving show if only the nine singers had been visible, so clearly did they enunciate the English text, and so vigorously did they attend to the acting chores that often seem an afterthought on opera-house stages. Altman the director was not upstaged by Altman the conceptualist. This *Rake's Progress* worked as theater as well as spectacle.

The importance of this imposing show lies not only in its theatrical success, though one hopes it's true that the production will soon reincarnate as a film available to viewers everywhere. [*Note: This didn't happen.*] What's most encouraging is its evidence that Altman has not given up his yen for excitement and experiment, in the face of his commercial reverses on the Hollywood scene. More evidence comes from his new independent film. Not long ago, Altman stood as one of the few truly independent voices in Hollywood, a lone explorer willing to put himself and his career regularly on the line for the sake of artistic adventure. His first non-Hollywood picture, *Come Back to the 5 and Dime, Jimmy Dean, Jimmy Dean*, suffers (like his original Broadway production) from an uneven and sometimes lurid script dealing with the reunion of a Texas fan club. But its one-set visual scheme works even better than it did onstage, shifting moods and tenses with a delicate precision that ideally suits its more intelligent impulses. Apart from its lapses in taste, it shows Altman in full command of his distinctive cinema style—and this at a time when he is moving like a powerhouse through other media, too.

A chat with veteran rockers about their film: Routine concert movie—on the very nonroutine Stones

The Rolling Stones, February 10, 1983

The Rolling Stones aren't exactly noted for hobnobbing with the press. So I replied with a quick "yes" when Mick Jagger and Keith Richards let it be known they would attend a reception in their honor at Tavern on the Green in Central Park.

The occasion was a celebration of their concert movie *Let's Spend the Night Together*, which opens nationally tomorrow. Not only did Mick and Keith make the scene, but they brought Ron Wood and Charlie Watts along, leaving Bill Wyman as the only no-show. Everyone seemed in fine spirits—Jagger acting a bit princely in his elegantly striped tie and turned-up collar, but Richards and Wood practically scrambling over each other to answer questions or exchange chitchat. Meanwhile, the elusive Watts huddled over a plate of hors d'oeuvres at a separate table, looking like he'd wandered in from some other band. Which is how he looks in performance, too, come to think of it.

For me, the reception was a chance to find out something I've always wondered: Do rock stars actually watch the concert films they make? I asked Jagger about *Let's Spend the Night Together*, and he said he's not only seen it, he likes it. Is it fun watching your face 20 feet tall on a giant screen, I continued? "Like any torture, it gets painless after a while," he answered, his elastic face twisting into something between a smirk and a grimace. And can you learn useful things about your act by seeing it from the outside, for a change? "Sure," said Jagger, making a snip-snip motion with his fingers. "You learn what to cut out."

Richards and Wood had different responses. In fact, both admitted they hadn't seen their own movie, and said that was fine with them. "Do you know how much we've worked with that material?" asked Richards, leaning over the back of his chair with a conspiratorial look. "Between the American tour, the European tour, the rehearsals, the album—we've worked two years on those 15 songs. Enough is enough. I don't want to hear them anymore!"

But wouldn't it be useful, I kept on, to see yourself as others see you for a couple of hours? "Yes," conceded Wood. "Usually the only one who sees the show is Mick, when he goes off the stage as part of the act. He comes back and tells us what we looked like. It's usually 'monkeys' or something like that."

While I pursued these deep aesthetic questions, my 11-year-olds collected autographs with a single-minded determination that even impressed a couple of the Stones, surely no strangers to the signature-hunter's wily ways. The youngsters also posed an interesting question of their own: Do you still have to practice on your instruments, or are you too good for that by now? Richards and Wood both admitted to having a practice session now and then—not composing or rehearsing with the group, but just sitting down with the guitar and learning to play it better. Wood added, though, that he doesn't practice Stones material much that way, because he "can't get the rhythms unless the group is there."

Who do the Stones admire on the current scene? "There are a few I like," said Richards, who couldn't seem to name many except the Pretenders and some reggae groups. He hemmed and hawed for a few moments, then gave up and proclaimed that his "real favorites" are "the old people: the Coasters, Chuck Berry, Fats Domino, Little Richard... That's who I like!" he grinned, showing a love for the golden age of rock 'n' roll—the fabulous '50s—that many Stones fans will heartily share.

As for *Let's Spend the Night Together* itself, it's fun without bringing anything new to the concert-film format. The Stones and their sidemen spend about 90 minutes strumming and strutting their way from "Under My Thumb" to "(I Can't Get No) Satisfaction," with detours into such memorable ditties as "You Can't Always Get What You Want" and "Brown Sugar." The best parts are the long close-ups of Jagger's face—looking downright sculptural in the throes of performance—as caught by expert cinematographer Caleb Deschanel (of *Black Stallion* [1979] fame) and partner Gerald Feil. Occasional rough language and lyrics account for the PG rating, but the music tends to drown out such lapses. The director was Hal Ashby, maker of such fine films as *Coming Home* [1978] and *Harold and Maude* [1971]. Though his personality rarely pokes through here, his wit does manage to shine now and then, as when the classic "Time Is on My Side" is accompanied by photos of the Stones at various stages of their lives and careers. It's a bright moment in an otherwise routine picture that thrives almost entirely on the energy of its subjects.

Max Roach's mixed-media "study in shapes and sound"
Interview with Max Roac, February 24, 1983

It's hard to discuss Max Roach without bringing in well-worn phrases like "jazz giant" and "musical legend." The labels apply—Roach has been called the most influential jazz drummer of all time—and it's a pleasure to give this towering performer, composer, and teacher his due. Like any giant, Roach likes to keep growing with the years, absorbing new ideas and reaching into new territory. Along with many younger artists, he has become fascinated lately with mixed-media work. Accordingly, he has collaborated with performers in various artistic fields, creating works that overlap the usual boundary lines between disciplines— lines he feels are disappearing, anyway. His latest exploration is a work called *Intuitive Momentum*, due to premiere tonight at the Brooklyn Academy of Music, which helped bring the piece together as part of its precedent-setting Next Wave series. Running just over an hour, the show was developed entirely from impro- visations involving Roach, pianist Connie Crothers—an associate of the late jazzman Lennie Tristano—and choreographers Bill T. Jones and Arnie Zane. Danced by a company of five, with the musi- cians onstage as well, the piece also includes sets by Robert Longo, lighting by Craig Miller, and costumes by Ronald Kolodzie for a full-fledged multimedia effect. Roach calls it "a study in shapes and sound"—or, with a smile, "a work arrived at by the democratic process."

Dropping into a rehearsal the other night, I found Roach looking as cool as the proverbial cucumber while he pounded an accompaniment to the jumping Crothers piano and the frenetic gyrations of the dancers. Sitting down later to talk with the two musicians, I was struck by the drummer's clear admiration for his partners, whose energy seemed to awe him a bit. Despite his senior status—in years and reputation—the openness, flexibility, and even humility of his attitude are as admirable as they are impressive. The idea for this collaboration first hit Roach as he watched Jones and Zane perform in Seattle a year or so ago. He's also the one who suggested Crothers for the piano part. Before the improvisations began, no aspect of the show had been settled on or even discussed. "If anyone came in with a preconceived idea," says Roach, "we shot it right down." In some ways, this wide-open approach was more suited to the musicians than to the dancers. "Choreographers are used to working in set patterns," says Roach. "But jazz musicians improvise all the time, calling on the knowledge and information they've gathered over the years." One challenge of *Intuitive Momentum* was meshing all the artists into a smoothly functioning creative unit.

Did they meet the challenge? "The dancers and the musicians all improvise," says Roach, "within the moods that have been established in our rehearsals. It turned out to work just fine." Crothers concurs, adding that the artists thought "conceptually," focusing on the deeper connective tissues of the work so as not to bog down in momentary details. As experimental as it seems, *Intuitive Momentum* can be seen as a logical extension of Roach's whole career. He is famous, after all, for being one of the first jazzmen to decide that drums could do more—much, much more—than just beat time. Decades ago he launched an innovative style that continually bore new fruit: exploring the delicate shadings of percussion instruments, calling on their melodic capabilities, moving into rhythms far removed from the four-to-a-bar of standard jazz. So it's no big surprise to find Roach on the multimedia route in his quest for new percussion possibilities. He clearly enjoys the challenge of interdisciplinary improvisation, of blending his sonic rhythms with the visual rhythms of dancers, costumes, and lights. If the result is as stimulating as he hopes, jazz and dance fans alike—not to mention the legion of Roach fans—will have yet another facet of his robust career to follow and assess. If not, he's sure to nose out another promising path before long. And however this show turns out, he feels its methods plug into some of the most tantalizing possibilities on today's artistic scene. "The different media, the different approaches to expression, are all around us today," he says. "That's one of the good things about this country. And it feels good to get involved with all of them."

Angelo My Love is brilliant, compassionate; It all started when Robert Duvall spotted a Roma boy...
Interview with Robert Duval, April 28, 1983

The movies have a middle ground that is rarely explored—the twilight zone between fiction and documentary. But occasionally a filmmaker comes along who's too inventive, audacious, or plain restless to respect the usual boundary lines. One is Robert Duvall—yes, the same Robert Duvall whose performance in *Tender Mercies* [Bruce Beresford, 1983] is one of the most finely wrought achievements to reach the screen in recent memory. Not content with being only an actor, he launched a directing career a few years ago with a documentary called *We're Not the Jet Set* [1974], a memorable study of a ranching family.

Now, working again behind the camera, he has created a small miracle called *Angelo My Love*—a colorful, witty, and relentlessly dramatic picture that boldly mixes fiction and truth in a strikingly unusual approach to capturing the human comedy on film. It all began when Duvall was strolling down the street in his Manhattan neighborhood and spotted a Roma boy—about eight or nine years old—whom he had noticed before. The boy was talking earnestly with a woman in her late 20s, and as Duvall came closer, he heard the lad's parting words: "If you don't love me no more, Patricia, I'm gonna move to Cincinnati!"

It's a story Duvall loves to tell, and it is now being used in advertisements to promote *Angelo My Love*, the movie sparked by this chance encounter. Struck by the boy's precocity, charm, and streetwise intelligence, Duvall befriended him and got to know his family. Soon he had a circle of Roma acquaintances he was eager to catch on film. But what method should he use? Would documentary or fiction best convey the essence of these fascinating individuals? Casting about for the answer, Duvall turned screenwriter and began work on a script about two families feuding over a stolen ring. The story was fictional, but he carefully included roles that would echo the personalities, looks, and talents of his new acquaintances—many of whom jumped at the chance to play themselves in the movie. Duvall then shot the picture over a 10-week period, altering the plot and characters to suit changing conditions: incorporating preparations for an actual wedding, for example, or eliminating a character when a Roma performer abruptly left town.

The result is fiction illuminated by the glow of truth. In real life, there was no stolen ring or feud between Greek and Russian clans, as fabricated by storyteller Duvall. But there truly is a boy of exuberant charm named Angelo Evans, and his brother did "buy" a bride before marrying, and his family and friends do share the kinds of joys, miseries, aspirations, and superstitions we see here — depicted so vividly that some aspects (including occasional harsh language and dissolute behavior) might have mandated an R tag if the independently produced film had passed through the rating process. As I watched *Angelo My Love*, parts of it felt almost like a science-fiction movie, so removed are the characters and their folkways from the paths I usually travel. Yet the film's compassion is clear in every scene; never does Duvall sensationalize or condescend to his material, although he often treats it with enormous humor.

I talked with Duvall about the film in his comfortable Manhattan apartment a few days ago. He was notably relaxed and good-humored, and seemed thoroughly satisfied with *Angelo My Love*, which — taking an unusual risk — he financed out of his own pocket. He is aware it's a "special" movie that won't easily rack up the box office grosses of an outer-space or adventure epic. But it clearly reflects his vision of the Roma community that so captivates him, and this makes it a rousing success as far as he's concerned.

Complimented on the sense of authenticity that runs through the picture, Duvall says there was no need to beef up or Hollywoodize his material, since his performers — all natural actors in a "con artist" sort of way — needed little encouragement to play their parts to the hilt. In fact, the director says, they brought in sly nuances and subtleties that no outsider could have invented. And, though amateurs, they had the knack of repeating scenes for the camera as readily as the seasoned professionals Duvall has worked with in Hollywood films. "They were already actors by necessity," Duvall says. "It's an ability they've picked up in daily life. It comes from having eight children but needing to convince a landlord you only have two, so he'll rent you a storefront you want — and going through a hundred other trials like that, all the time. Fooling people is a part of living for them." The brilliance of "Angelo" stems partly from Duvall's delicately balanced attitude toward his unconventional collaborators — never ignoring their sometimes drastic flaws and foibles, yet keeping sight of the inner dignity and emotional vulnerability that are also essential parts of their natures.

The filming of *Angelo My Love* had plenty of difficulties, according to Duvall and his wife, Gail Youngs, who served as associate producer. Operating with a vague sense of time, Roma cast members thought nothing of showing up three hours late for a "shoot," keeping dozens of extras and crew members waiting. Since most of the performers were illiterate, dialogue had to be improvised from lines supplied (sometimes in an off-camera whisper) by Duvall. And finances had to be watched closely, since the director was paying the bills with no help from studio sources. "I'm still catching up, taking roles I'd normally leave alone, working to replenish the till," he says, with the bemused tone of an artist who's not accustomed to spending on such a scale, but knows both time and money have been well used.

"The movie grew from his love for these people," says producer Youngs, underlining the affection that drew Duvall to the subject and kept him immersed in it for several years. Duvall himself seems most proud of the authentic behavior the movie depicts. In fact, he feels his main strength as a director—building on his long acting experience—is a skill in guiding performances and bringing out their nuances. *Angelo My Love* won't be the last Duvall-directed film. More and more, he feels the urge to develop projects himself, making worthwhile things happen instead of waiting for them to drop in from outside. He still expects to play plenty of roles in other people's movies—in fact, he says, good parts are coming his way in unusual quantities nowadays—but his filmmaking career is also here to stay. Judging from the strength and substance of *Angelo My Love*, that's mighty good news for the movie scene.

Opera on film is like two continents colliding
Interview with Franco Zeffirelli, May 5, 1983

Capturing an opera on film is a daunting task. Separately, both opera and cinema are complex and hybrid arts. Bringing them together is like watching two continents collide. The result may be a towering new mountain or a shattered archipelago.

The heart of the challenge is the fact that music and cinema each have rhythms of their own. Matching them, integrating sound and image so neither seems the slave of the other, is a delicate matter at best. Then too, sound has a relation to its source— a relation that's disrupted by such moviemaking practices as prerecording and post-dubbing. Yet some talented artists have brought off the feat, and at the moment, two fine opera films are on view. One is Hans-Jurgen Syberberg's adaptation of Wagner's *Parsifal*. The other is Franco Zeffirelli's new version of Verdi's *La Traviata*, starring Teresa Stratas, Placido Domingo, and Cornell MacNeil.

Both films reflect the love of splendor and scope that cinema and opera share. The screen *Parsifal*, for example, is mounted on huge settings and decked out with cinematic surprises, including rear projections and elegant camera angles. It's as big and bold as Wagner could have wished. And yet it doesn't surpass, for sheer grandeur, such a spectacular stage production as the *Parsifal* of the Metropolitan Opera. For all the extravagance of Syberberg's approach, he finds no visual treats to outdo the Met's vision of Klingsor's castle or of the "transformation scene" when a sylvan setting gives way to a gloomy interior right before our eyes. Nor does Syberberg come up with more delicate nuances than the Met—as when, in the stage *Parsifal*, knights raise their arms in prayer and the curved lines of their bodies match the bent patterns of the woods around them.

There's more amazement in the florid zeal of *La Traviata* as reworked on film, since we're used to more intimate treatments of this robustly romantic work. Zeffirelli pulls out every musical and cinematic stop, restraining his imagery for the more intense moments between the protagonists, but otherwise reveling in a sensuous torrent of sight and sound. It's a movie just as much as an opera, and it smacks as much of Zeffirelli as of Verdi, especially when it uses cinematic resources to enrich the action in specifically cinematic ways. No stage production, for example, could punctuate scenes so slyly—as when a dowager sneakily pilfers a knick-knack during the early banquet scene—and still be sure the small touches would be noticed. And of course no live version could swoop so freely from place to place or bring so many perspectives to bear on the story.

Ironically, though, Zeffirelli feels the movie is too small in scale! "I cut it down too much," he told me the other day in a Manhattan hotel suite during a visit here. When he showed the film at the Rome Opera, he says, "It didn't fill the place. The proscenium is so much larger than that little stamp of a screen. I should have given the picture more splendor, like *Ben-Hur* or the old D. W. Griffith movies." Zeffirelli feels opera must be far larger than life, whether heard live or on film. "This is the tradition of opera," he says in his melodic Italian accent. "Just look at the opera theaters. They were built to cradle these creations—splendid cathedrals of gold and crystal and chandeliers. And rightly so. After all, you're dealing with 100 instruments and glorious voices and ballet and grand passions. Opera must be large to sustain visually the splendor of it all." Film, he feels, is a fine tool for catching that essential richness. "Cinema can be anything you want," he says—"a great epic, an intimate story, something to make you laugh or cry." And opera is a valid subject, even a natural subject, for film treatment.

Zeffirelli grants that seeing an opera at the movies isn't the same as "really being there as the music happens." But there are advantages to the motion-picture format. One is subtitles, "which allow you to follow the drama line by line for the first time." Another is closeups. "They can show the thoughts and feelings of a human being," he says. "How different this is from the opera house, where the closest you can be is 36 feet, if you're lucky." On this subject Zeffirelli moves far from musical purists who insist on live opera. "They say it doesn't matter how far you are from the singers," he remarks, "because the music and singing will make you imagine everything. "But if that's true," he continues, "you might as well stay home and listen to records. What's the difference between a great interpretation and a poor one? The great singer acts, and this adds something to the interpretation. Cinema can bring the audience closer to this and help us know more about the character."

Until now, most opera films have been made by movie directors with little or no operatic experience. (An exception is *The Magic Flute* [1975] by Ingmar Bergman, which was a filmed version of a stage production.) Zeffirelli has long experience in both media, though, and treats them with equal respect. Indeed, the only surprise about him filming an opera is that it didn't happen sooner—and he's a little surprised about that himself. "They say my movies have always been operatic, and my operas have always been cinematic," he says with a smile. "The marriage had to happen." He chose *La Traviata* largely because he wanted an opera with a good plot. "The great success of 19th-century operas depended on the story, the drama," he says. He also feels his own best pictures—*Romeo and Juliet* [1968] and *Jesus of Nazareth* [1977]—were projects that didn't depend on an original script. "The structure was already there," he remarks. "We just built on it."

Zeffirelli is unruffled by the problems I see in the very nature of filmed opera. He grants that opera and cinema have rhythms and dynamics of their own, but maintains that careful handling—something he didn't always manage in *La Traviata* he admits—can merge the media satisfactorily. As for the split between image and sound caused by common filmmaking techniques, this is no problem for an audience willing to make a "leap of good will," says the director. In any case, he recognized such problems from the beginning and used a whole bag of tricks to assemble *La Traviata*. Sometimes the performers would lip-sync to music already recorded, sometimes they would return to the studio after filming to rerecord a scene, and sometimes the singing was captured live as the cameras rolled. This last technique will be the future salvation of opera films, he believes, though it's "devilishly tricky" to carry off.

La Traviata has been well received. Audiences in Paris made it the biggest hit after *E.T. The Extra-Terrestrial* [Steven Spielberg 1982], with 800,000 spectators flocking to it in less than two months, and American critics have been enthusiastic. If the momentum keeps up, and maybe even if it doesn't, Zeffirelli will pursue plans for more operatic movies—Verdi's *Otello* being a likely candidate along with Bizet's *Carmen* and Verdi's *Aida*.

One plan he doesn't have, though, is seeing the cinematic *Parsifal*. Says the opinionated expert, "I can hardly bear it on the stage. I don't want to imagine what the film must be like."

Getting down to the bedrock of dance
Interview with Lucinda Childs, September 26, 1983

As a dancer, choreographer, and thinker on the arts, Lucinda Childs loves order. You can see it in her work, with its strong sense of pattern and consistency. But she has a playful streak, and she enjoys a challenge. That's why her newest work, a full-length dance called *Available Light*, will move away from the marked symmetry of her earlier pieces. "The same precision is there," she told me recently. "But the look is different. Things aren't so obvious—it's like having two patterns at once, so you don't see any pattern at all. Usually it's quite apparent what the relationships with the music are, and they change gradually. Here the contrasts are stronger. It might even look disorganized at times, though it isn't."

Another thing Childs enjoys is a good partnership. Although she initiated and coordinated it, *Available Light* is a three-member project with music by John Adams and decor by architect Frank O. Gehry. With such a trio of talents, the result could be as memorable as her *Relative Calm*, with its Jon Gibson score and Robert Wilson decor, or her *Dance*, with Philip Glass music and Sol Lewitt film; or even Wilson's opera *Einstein on the Beach*, which she helped choreograph. *Available Light* will have its premiere performances this Thursday through Sunday at the Museum of Contemporary Art in Los Angeles. Then it will travel to New York for a four-day run (Oct. 27-30) in the "Next Wave" festival at the Brooklyn Academy of Music, sharing the bill with a new dance to Philip Glass' piece *Mad Rush*. The work's European bow is slated for Nov. 28-Dec. 4 at the Theatre de la Ville in Paris, as part of the Festival d'Automne. Also coming up is an eight-day Childs residency at the American Center in Paris beginning Nov. 21. And a Brooklyn Academy revival of *Einstein on the Beach* will tour the United States in winter of 1984-85.

How did Childs hit on her distinctive style with its elegant patterns, crystal-clear logic, and aggressive precision? I asked her recently in her lower-Manhattan loft, where she answered questions with a quiet, friendly, thoughtful tone that recalled some qualities of her dance work. Her quest began, she says, with rebellion from an older generation—"the people we associate with avant-garde music and conceptualization" who preached the anything-goes, art-is-where-you-find-it philosophy of John Cage and his cohorts. As a young member of the Judson Dance Theater, she had "explored and dabbled in that area" and been "very influenced by Cage." But after five years she felt she had exhausted the possibilities of this research. "There was a profound dead end in all of it," she remarks. "When this dead end began to be perceived in the late '60s, it affected all the arts—emerging first in the visual art of, say, Sol Lewitt and later in dance and music."

So she turned in exactly the opposite direction. "I moved into a new world of throwing out all the tricks, getting rid of all the objects and monologues—all the things that aren't dance—and seeing what was left. I started to work with very basic things like walking and turning. I went back to a very simple vocabulary and found a new world opening up for me. It felt infinite." This artistic journey is remarkably similar to that of composer Glass, who also turned away from modernist mannerisms and looked for a music that was all muscle and bone, as basic as it could possibly be. Not surprisingly, Childs has been drawn to his work and has choreographed to it more than once. "Yet we couldn't have made this kind of statement earlier," she says, "because we needed the other people to come first and insist on questioning everything, turning everything upside down. That school had a built-in mechanism of self-exhaustion, but it gave us the highway we needed." She also recognizes that the evolution is still going on. "People like John Adams are coming in," she says, "and reacting against what is sometimes called the rigidity or strictness of the Glass-associated style." This, she feels, could be another turning point. Though she finds "traces of the Glass sensibility" in Adams' score for *Available Light*, she also finds "dramatic, almost emotional moments" and "lots of variation." This has pulled her in different directions, and she says she likes the feeling. "It isn't always as compatible as music I've worked with before," she muses. "I've had to struggle with it in some ways. But I'm happy to do that. It's been a voluntary struggle," she concludes with a smile.

Adams' score is written for synthesizer and some instrumental sounds. The composer performs it "live" by mixing tracks and shifting levels on a preexisting tape. Working with him and architect Gehry has been tricky for Childs because she's based in New York and they in California. "One loses some momentum because of this enormous separation," she says, adding that Adams had never even seen her work before this collaboration began. But this posed no insoluble problems. Looking at today's dance scene, she finds it very invigorating "because of all the interrelationships that are taking place. Fifteen years ago, the modern dancers stayed on one side of the room, and the ballet dancers stayed on the other.

If you went to modern class you didn't talk about your ballet class. Now there's an exchange going on. Some people deplore it. But I find it extremely exciting.'

E. L. Doctorow's collaboration with the "enemy"
Interview with E. L. Doctorow, October 13, 1983

Sag Harbor, N.Y.

"I resent the impact film has in this culture. As a writer, I find it's the enemy. All the rigorous and passionate moviegoing… makes me very jealous. With its variations, like TV, it has probably done more than anything else to create a kind of profound illiteracy in the world today." Such sentiments wouldn't be surprising from a man of works like those of E. L. Doctorow, except that he has been collaborating with the "enemy" lately—writing the screenplay for *Daniel*, based on his novel *The Book of Daniel*. And he has "very mixed feelings" about doing this. On one hand, he fears some *Daniel* viewers will feel there's no need to read the novel, which treats the story—about the children of two radicals executed for espionage—in more depth and detail. It's also possible, he says, that his reputation as a serious writer will suffer. On the other hand, he knows the film will reach a large audience that would never read the book anyway. And he made sure it would reflect his ideas. He insisted on having a say in all matters from casting to the final cut, and he worked closely with director Sidney Lumet.

Critics and audiences have had mixed opinions about the movie, which keeps the novel's main themes while scaling down the plot and sanitizing some of the action. (The rating is R, reflecting vulgar language and a clinical execution scene.) Doctorow himself is pleased with it, preferring its condensed energy to the talkiness of *Ragtime*, the last film made from one of his books.

What prompted this noted novelist to tackle the movie world? Just an impulse. "When I have a choice between caution and recklessness," he told me recently at his modest Long Island summer home, "I'll choose recklessness. It was the more dangerous alternative—and therefore more interesting—to make the film rather than block it. All my life, I've done the most important things instinctively, without sufficient thought," he concluded with a smile.

From the start, Doctorow wanted *Daniel* to echo his book closely, even though he feels "most movies are short stories rather than novels in their content and linearity." Once into it, he found screenwriting a snap. "It's another language," he says, "but you pick it up quickly if you deal in language. The principles of composition are the same, and you worry about the same things: Does it work? Are you repeating yourself?… Once you learn the tech-talk they use, you just move right in." The only frustration, he said, was having to collaborate, an unfamiliar activity for most novel-ists. And he still seems awed by the expense of filmmaking , even though *Daniel* was a relatively cheap movie at $8 million, with many of the participants working for minimum pay. "I used to tease my friends about this," Doctorow remarks. "They said they brought in *Ragtime* for $32 million. I said I brought in my novel for $78—a few boxes of paper and some typewriter ribbons!" Now that he's an accomplice in the movie business, though, his teasing days are probably over.

A controversial aspect of the *Daniel* film and book is the resemblance of two characters to Julius and Ethel Rosenberg, who were executed in 1953 for stealing atomic secrets. Doctorow stresses that his characters are fictitious. "If I wanted to write about the Rosenbergs, I would have called them that. Anybody who knows me at all knows this," says the author, whose *Ragtime* put such people as Harry Houdini and Sigmund Freud into a fictional plot. "My interest was not in writing a documentary novel. I began not with the Rosenberg family, but with the extremity of their situ-ation, and the law that was applied in their case. I used this for my own imaginative responses…" Doctorow is surprised that his fact-fiction blending causes a flap. "Fiction and the imagination are another way of knowing," he says, "as opposed to empirical investigation, legal discovery, journalism. I've never believed this is life over here and art over there. They mix up, and always have. I'm against precious and aseptic ideas of literature having nothing to do with life. So many of the great masters have jumped in with both feet—Dostoyevsky, Dreiser, Tolstoy, Dickens… They were steeped to the eyebrows in what was going on."

The themes of *Daniel* are diverse, including a child's fear of abandonment, capital punishment, and the effects of idealism on a family. Many are related to political ideas or circumstances. Yet the writer doesn't see the movie or novel as essentially political. "What art does is to enlarge our own humanity," he says, "by allowing us to live vicariously the experiences of others—with whom we might not otherwise be in sympathy. We find ourselves living intimately with people we probably would not invite to dinner at our home, like Raskolnikov. A major function of all art is to keep us alive to each other. And that's not political at all… At its best, in the great works, it's almost a religious function."

Since some of its key events are rooted in politics, however, is *Daniel* the kind of work that could prompt social change? "Once an Englishman called me the Balzac of the petrol pumps," remarks the writer, "because I want people who work at gas stations and wait on tables to read my books... Of course, you want your work to have an impact. But I must admit my doubts about the efficacy of this..." These doubts are the same ones W. H. Auden had "when he said art didn't change anything, and all the antifascist poets of the '30s did nothing to stop Hitler... If a book or film can make any kind of change, it's usually quite slow. Art never quite catches up to outrageous reality. It's always lumbering behind history."

Sounds gloomy. Yet later, Doctorow agrees that culture includes "a process by which myth takes over from history. Today, a writer's function must partly be to investigate the myths of the past—the myths we've accumulated and live by—and contravene them with some kind of additional intelligence. Otherwise, they'll run rampant." Here, then, is the social role of *Daniel* and others of its ilk. "This film probes some very uncomfortable things," Doctorow says. "But if people stop examining their national myths—as they have in Russia—something monstrous happens, and true totalitarianism sets in." Isn't the movie itself, though, just another step in the mythmaking process? Doctorow listens to this suggestion and admits there is a built-in paradox. "But if enough people do this kind of work, he remarks, "things will be healthy and free-flowing, and no one vision will become entrenched. It's true, we add to the clutter, and use up some paper and trees in the bargain. But the alternative is silence. And I don't see how that's a more positive contribution."

Jimmy Stewart looks back at Hitch, Hollywood of old

Interview with James Stewart, October 20, 1983

The credits always call him James Stewart, but his fans know him as Jimmy, and so many moviegoers can't be wrong.

He came to Hollywood in 1935, getting his start in a Spencer Tracy mystery. His career has flourished ever since, and though he's not as busy as he used to be, he still jumps at a good TV or movie role. He has even kept his zest for hitting the road and "plugging a picture" in the old Hollywood tradition.

In a switch, the pictures he plugged during his latest New York visit are in the neighborhood of 30 years old: a quintet of Alfred Hitchcock classics that have gone largely unseen since their first release, because the director felt rarity would increase their value. As it happens, Stewart stars in four of them, making their reissue (by Universal Pictures) as much a Stewart festival as a Hitchcock retrospective.

Rear Window has already started its new run with strong results at the box office, indicating that viewers are still spellbound by the Stewart-Hitchcock chemistry: *Vertigo*, perhaps Hitchcock's greatest work, and "*Rope*, one of his most rarely shown, will follow soon, along with the colorful 1956 version of *The Man Who Knew Too Much*. Also due is *The Trouble With Harry*, one of the suspense master's lighter and lesser efforts, sans the great Jimmy.

The New York Film Festival previewed *Rear Window* recently, and Stewart met the press afterward, admitting that he hadn't seen the picture for more than 20 years. Some of the conference focused on Donald Spoto's insightful new biography of Hitchcock, called *The Dark Side of Genius*, which claims Sir Alfred was a sadder, less balanced, more desperate man than most people have thought. Stewart took issue with this idea on the ground that "if he had a dark side, it's not something he could have hid. And I just never saw it."

The next day I drove with Stewart from his hotel to a Manhattan restaurant and enjoyed a long talk with him over lunch. Pressing for more details about Hitchcock and his work, I mentioned another Spoto theory—that Hitchcock used Cary Grant as an idealized version of himself, while Stewart represented the director as he felt he actually was.

It's a provocative notion, contrasting the glamorous Grant of *To Catch a Thief*, say, with the troubled Stewart of *Vertigo*. The actor wants nothing to do with such stuff, though. "I can't help but feel this is overanalyzing," he says in the engaging drawl that's been his trademark for nearly five decades. "There could be some truth and logic to it, but I've never felt that way, and Cary's never mentioned anything in that vein." In sum, he'll trust his instincts and recollections before the musings of critics.

Whatever the final verdict on Hitchcock's personality, Stewart speaks without hesitation about his "tremendous admiration" for the director, listing his own quartet of Hitchcock collaborations among his proudest achievements. "The word genius is thrown around too much nowadays," he says, "but I truly believe there are touches of it in his work. He had his own special way of getting on the screen what he'd prepared so carefully. He knew what he wanted. To be a part of this creation was a tremendous privilege. And a tremendous education."

Stewart's show-biz "education" started young. He made his bow in a Boy Scout play and moved on to college shows. After graduating from Princeton University with an architecture degree, he joined such future luminaries as Margaret Sullavan and Henry Fonda in a theater group. Later he roomed with Fonda as they braved the Broadway scene and again when they hit Hollywood. Their careers were parallel to a degree, though today Stewart seems to have been the more expert actor, moving so easily from comedy to drama it's hard to say which mode suits him best.

During the 1940s, Stewart not only won an Oscar for *The Philadelphia Story*, but left the movies to fly bombing missions in World War II. He kept up his military connections after the war, becoming a brigadier general in the Air Force Reserve. Back on the set in the '50s, he struck up a long-term relationship with director Anthony Mann—and in the '60s, a similar one with John Ford.

As recently as the '70s, he reconquered Broadway with a revival of his hit *Harvey* and tried a couple of TV series with varying success. He's still at work today, appearing next month with Bette Davis in a cable-TV movie called *Right of Way* and preparing another project for early next year.

Of course, despite the versatility that has carried him through several media, Stewart is known mainly as the movie star who provided such memorable moments in pictures ranging from *Mr. Smith Goes to Washington* and *The Spirit of St. Louis* to *Anatomy of a Murder* and *The Man Who Shot Liberty Valance*. I asked if he's pleased that his career gravitated so strongly toward the screen instead of the stage.

"At this point in life... when you start looking back," he replied, "one of my regrets is that I didn't do more stage work. That's partly because it's a great, exhilarating, uplifting thing.

"But it's also because you never stop learning to act. It isn't that kind of a racket; you never have the thing licked. And the stage is great training for every part of it—timing, tempo, all your instincts about how to react without overdoing... It's funny, but projecting your voice to the last person in the second gallery is wonderful training for movies, where you talk like we're talking now."

Is there a typical Jimmy Stewart character? Stewart thinks there's something to the idea, as long as you don't push it too far. "People have said—and I've felt it at times—there's a certain vulnerability about a lot of my characters. Perhaps this creeps into so many of my pictures because I've tended to select this type of character, because of my feelings about life.

"Even in a Western, people say when I get in a fight they aren't sure if I'll win. But when John Wayne gets in a fight, they know, all right!"

He also feels his personal style—as a person and an actor—contributes to the notion of a "typical" Stewart character. "And I see nothing wrong with that," he says. "Someone asked Spencer Tracy if he got tired of playing himself all the time. He said, 'Who do you want me to play? Humphrey Bogart?' I feel it's all right to bring your own style to a character."

Yet he stresses that acting is a demanding art that allows no free rides. "People sometimes say the liked a performance because it was so natural," he remarks. "Well, there's nothing more unnatural than movie acting. It's a craft that has to be learned, like any other."

Looking at today's movie scene, Stewart feels there's too much "sameness" to pictures, both in theaters and on television. "I don't believe in saying 'Give me the good old days' in anything," he muses, "but I feel the old studio system was the best way to make movies. Whatever disparaging things have been written about them, the big moguls had tremendous love for the movies, and excellent judgement, and in a strange way, good taste. They didn't narrow themselves down."

Stewart is clearly nostalgic for the busy heyday of his career, when "you had a contract and worked every day, including Saturday—and when you weren't in a picture you worked out at the gym or took diction lessons." But his enthusiasm goes beyond his own experiences. "There was a period in the late '20s and '30s and a little bit after the war," he says, "when there was an exciting glamour about the movie business. It had to do with the stars and the studios and the MGM lion, roaring.

"I feel so fortunate I was a part of it. But I don't think it's here any more, and I don't know if it will ever return."

With some 80 movies under his belt, does Stewart have a favorite? He answers quickly: *It's a Wonderful Life*, the story of a small-town banker who learns the significance of even the most unassuming person, directed by Frank Capra in 1946.

Does he value that film for more than technical or dramatic reasons? Does it reflect something of his own beliefs and ideals?

Stewart sits back and thinks for a moment. Then he answers, quietly and slowly, "I think so. It might be a sentimental choice, being the first picture I made after the war, and knowing it's Frank's favorite, too. But it says some things that I think mean something to me."

Twyla Tharp: dancing offstage and onto the television screen
Interview with Twyla Tharp, January 9, 1984

Twyla Tharp has seen the future of dance—and it's on television. If she has her way, a revolution is just around the corner. She will be its leader. And her banner will be made of videotape. "I see video-tape as the salvation of dancers," she told me recently, speaking in bold, punchy words between prodigious bites of post-rehearsal pasta. "There's no alternative. Dance can't support itself theatri-cally. All the companies run deficits. Touring is too exhausting. The theaters don't hold enough people, and when they do, you can't see the stage very well. So cassettes aren't the wave of the future. They're a necessity and a reality right now. If you don't like it, start learning to live with it."

As performer, choreographer, and director, Twyla Tharp stands with the most popular and influential figures in today's dance world. Her fame is international, requiring a densely typed page just to list the awards and grants showered on her troupe. She didn't get there by playing it safe. Since forming her company in the mid-1960s, she has devised dances for groups and soloists, for ballet slippers and running shoes, for music by Bach, Frank Sinatra, Brahms, and the Beach Boys. One piece was danced on a hillside. Another used graffiti for scenery. Her movie work includes *Ragtime* [Miloš Forman, 1981] and *Hair* [Miloš Forman, 1979]. Her pieces are in the repertoires of other troupes. In short, she's been around. Now she would like to settle down a bit. She still has an endless appetite for hard work, and slowing the pace is not on her agenda. But touring, a key part of dance life, is sapping her time and energy. She's determined to do something about it—by bringing dance off the stage and onto the TV screen.

"The business of touring is basically fruitless, as far as I'm concerned," Tharp says. "It's a waste of time, and extremely costly. What interests me is making dances. I'm all in favor of killing tours, and I think cassettes can do it." This doesn't mean Tharp's dancers have vanished from the stage quite yet. Just back from some over-seas travel, they start a major season at the Brooklyn Academy of Music on Jan. 24, offering eight dances for three weeks, and then tour to several US cities. Also coming are two new Tharp works for the American Ballet Theatre, which opens at the Metropolitan Opera House on April 24. And the movie version of the Broadway hit *Amadeus*, choreographed by Tharp for director Miloš Forman. And she's working with the Brooklyn Academy of Music on a dance and video facility to be set up in a renovated building nearby, giving her a new home base.

It's a busy schedule, reflecting Tharp's vigor and popularity. She clearly has a lingering affection for stage work, and you can tell she looks forward to an event like her imminent Brooklyn season. But she would rather finesse most of her current commitments, trading all those tour dates for one well-equipped TV studio. Tharp hasn't yet made a TV-only dance, never to be performed onstage. But she's working on the idea. Meanwhile, video looms large in her recent work. *The Catherine Wheel*, for example, was devised "more with the camera than the audience in mind," and has been presented in a video version on PBS as well as live. In the newer *Bad Smells*, a TV projection unit shares the stage with dancers. "The camera work is built in," says Tharp. "It gives the continuity. It's excellent for narrative pieces, because that's what the camera is all about: It tells a story."

Not everyone shares Tharp's enthusiasm for video as a performance vehicle. Some object to the fuzziness and small size of the image, which makes art smaller than life, not larger. "I'm used to movies," counters Tharp, "so for me TV screens are symbolic of movie screens, which can have a scale bigger than anything in real life. Anyway, it's only a matter of time before TV screens will be as large as the ones in theaters." Another objection is that camera work and editing intrude on a performance, forcing events into an arbitrary mold. "Even in a theater," answers Tharp, "people choose certain things they want to look at. When I direct a TV show, I'm just suggesting how the viewer might view." In other words, control—arbitrary or not—is a good thing. "Art is about control. That's why one develops a discipline. That's what form is. Conventional concert artists are trained to control their performances, emotionally and technically. Everything in their lives is about control, in order to attain a performance they feel is authentic, that says what they mean it to say. So for a choreographer, it's not a question of 'getting to direct' or suddenly finding yourself with more control. It's part of the same job you've always had, the same responsibility to refine the art."

If she succeeds in replacing tours with video cassettes, will Tharp still keep up her own company, with all its management demands and complexities?

"I do a lot of work," she replies, "and these days I'm going double time, with always at least two projects. It's quite conceivable that were I willing to abandon my own tradition, I could keep busy doing things for other places, people, companies. I think it's clear to us all, however, that something has been established by this group of people, and it has to be maintained. It is, in fact, part of the culture." Tharp's video crusade reflects this loyalty to her company and her tradition, which she's bent on exposing as widely as she can. She is an aesthetic democrat, aiming at one broad audience in both her stage and screen work. "All I have in mind is how people think normally," she says. "But they're not used to doing that in theaters anymore. Theaters have become very foreign places, while TV screens are very comfortable places for most of us."

In the end, she feels, "It all comes back to communication." Her artistic ideas are nurtured by the bustle of everyday life— "every phone call, every letter, everything you see, everything your kid does, everything!" Thus her dances should reach out to the widest audience she and her video gear can find. "I think my work is accessible now, and reaching a fairly large audience. And the audience it could have meaning for is extremely large. I want to reach people. I've never liked the concept of the elite, the aristocratic, art for the few, art for the wealthy. Who says that's what art is all about? Not me."

Living Theatre's journey toward change
Interview with Julian Beck and Judith Malina, March 6, 1984

Stagecraft and spectacle are the Living Theatre's tools. But ideas are its foundation—relentlessly radical ideas that have swept up controversy and even outrage for more than three decades.

It was in the late 1940s that Julian Beck and his wife, Judith Malina, formed the Living Theatre. The idea was "to create a theater that was persistently artistic, divorced from all the commercial thrust," Beck recalled in a recent interview in the West Side apartment he and his spouse share with their teen-age daughter, Isha. For the past 15 years the Becks and company have worked in Europe, settling recently in France, where a government grant helps support them. Ideally, they would like to spend six months each year in the United States; but they may set down permanent roots in Paris, where they hope a theater will soon be provided them—an instance of strong public support which they feel Americans can't (or won't) match. Still and all, they have a high profile in their native country just now. They recently presented a repertory of four plays at the Joyce Theater in Manhattan; the Malina diaries, covering 1947 to 1957, are being published this winter by Grove Press; and a new film on the Living Theatre called *Signals Through the Flames* [Sheldon Rochlin, 1983] was released last month. On the side, Beck is playing a part in Francis Coppola's new epic, *The Cotton Club* [1984].

What sort of ideas is the Living Theatre based on? Pacifism, for one. "Nonviolence isn't just getting America to disarm its nuclear power," says Malina, who is coleader of the company with Julian. "It's what Gandhi called *ahimsa*, his principle of nonhurting. It's looking your enemy in the face and saying, 'You are not my enemy. Let me see if I can help you.' It's following this path no matter what." Activism and absolute personal freedom—to the point of license and chaos, detractors say—are also on the agenda. "We speak of a journey toward change," says Beck. "This involves both collective and personal activity—with the understanding that you can't change the world unless you change yourself, and you can't change yourself unless you change the world."

The journey's goal is "a world that's less authoritarian, more peaceful, more active in eliminating class abuses," adds Malina. "Awareness of this goal comes in cycles. We optimists think the cycles are spiraling upward. After all, everyone wants the same thing: to create a world without hunger or violence." Of course, far from "everyone" agrees with the Becks' antimilitary, anti-government, brashly libertarian views of how to reach the "same thing" we all want. But it never bothers the Becks to be accused of going too far. "They call it 'utopian' when they don't want you to do it," says Malina, quoting social critic Paul Goodman.

In starting the theater, "we... insisted that experimentation is one of the essences of art," Beck remarks. "That's what art is—an attempt to discover what is new, to create some sort of revelation. And we insisted on speaking out politically." These goals dovetailed neatly, since in Beck's view, experimentation is a political act. "Every experiment with form indicates that life could be different and still be effective," he said. Controversy attended such early offerings as Jack Gelber's *The Connection*, about society's outcasts, and Kenneth H. Brown's *The Brig,* about militarist thinking. The furor reached its peak in the 1960s with *Paradise Now*, a communal production that was never the same from one performance to another but encompassed nudity and hot rhetoric in its wild-eyed call for instant anarchism.

Although the troupe has kept its convictions and its penchant for strongly physical theatrics, today it speaks to audiences in a different way. "During the 1960s," says Beck, "we became more and more politically outspoken. We used shock techniques, trying to shake people up and arouse them. Now we're trying to instigate a fruitful reflection—on where and who we are, and what we can become." Today is a hard time for political theater, in his view. "There has been a certain recovery of the artistic impulse—it's acceptable to experiment even on Broadway now—but absolutely none of the political impulse," he says. "The door is closing to political theater in Europe, too. Brecht is very out of fashion, and when he is produced, it's for the sugar coating. It's the same with Shaw. The interest is always in the performance, how brilliant the actors are, how clever the text is, how diverting and amusing the production is. The public and producers extract the superficia from these two giants, washing out the essential political, social, or philosophical statements." Thus, he feels, "the struggle to make theater into an honest, truthful reflection of the world has become very difficult again. Yet such a theater must include commentary on the economic, social, and political conditions, or it's leaving out some of the essentials of life."

There is hope for the future, though, because alertness to political issues is growing. "I see us ever more in the grip of military domination on the whole planet," Beck says. "But at the same time there's an enormous growth in our moral and ethical awareness. I see a greatly enlarged peace movement. Minorities are more aware of their oppression. Workers know more about self-management. Children are reaching for more freedom at home and in school. So there's a consciousness of conditions. How to change things is less apparent, however! This is a period in which we're silently mulling, working, grinding away at what the solutions could be. The service of theater now is to study these problems—to learn how we can get out of the grip of a militarist culture and begin real action to stop the march toward nuclear catastrophe."

Rather than call for instant revolution, therefore, the Living Theatre now ponders how an evolution—a process of change—is best prodded along, hoping that what Beck calls "some new news from nowhere" will inspire an answer before long. "The form of change must be as pure and total as the goal of change," says Malina. "It's the old ends-and-means story. No change is valid if we don't understand Gandhi's beautiful principle, which was certainly not understood in the '60s." With such unusual ideas and uncommon ways of expressing them, is it probable the Living Theatre will affect no one but a radical fringe? Malina bristles at the term— not suggesting that a mass audience is around the corner, true, but feistily defending her company's fans. "Those people you call the radical fringe we consider the heart of reality," she says with a voice that's half velvet and half iron. "These are the people who are going to make the changes. They are the future."

Steve Martin is no fool—and makes films to prove it
Interview with Steve Martin, November 15, 1984

"I've always played an idiot," says Steve Martin. As if we didn't know. After all, this is the Jerk talking—the wild and crazy guy of *Saturday Night Live*, the star of *Dead Men Don't Wear Plaid* [Carl Reiner, 1982]. But don't count on more of the same. Yes, farces are hot nowadays, and the surest way to a fast buck is to peddle another *Bachelor Party* [Neal Israel, 1984] spinoff. Still, says Martin, "I just can't bring myself to do that anymore. I'm the wrong age, and my emotions are completely somewhere else."

Don't get him wrong. He isn't auditioning for *Long Day's Journey into Night*, at least not yet. But he sees his current role, opposite Lily Tomlin in the comedy hit *All of Me* [Carl Reiner, 1984], as a step in a new direction. "This man is not an idiot," Martin told me over lunch recently, describing his *All of Me* role as a lawyer whose body is invaded by the transmigrating soul of a rich, daffy woman. In fact, says Martin, this character is "a contemporary person with some brains. The movie is wildly comic, but he's not naive or a victim of circumstances. He's an intelligent man who happens to get caught in a disaster. That's a big difference between this role and any other part I've played. And believe me, I really liked it," he adds with a grin. "I liked not having to say, 'What's happening to me?' all the time. After a certain age you can't act adolescent anymore. I'd love to play James Bond!"

Besides giving him a well-rounded role for a change, *All of Me* showcased Martin's talent in a less chaotic setting than usual. "For the first time," he says, "I'm in a story with a beginning, middle, and end. It's old-fashioned and solid, like a drawing-room comedy. The hardest thing to do is tell a story straight. That's why I'm happy I made this little movie that works, not some extravaganza that overwhelms the senses. This movie was like going to school. I learned a lot about structure and character." *All of Me* pleases moviegoers as well as Martin, judging from the box office. Some may be drawn by the movie's raunchy moments and bathroom humor, which push the PG rating pretty far. Speaking before the film's premiere, though, Martin insisted that the solid story and characters were salable in their own right.

"People wonder how it'll fare in a market where there's nothing but guys peering through peepholes at naked girls," he said. "Yes, those films do well, but other kinds also do well: *Tootsie* [Sydney Pollack, 1982] and *Heaven Can Wait* [Warren Beatty and Buck Henry, 1978]. I don't want to call this 'adult comedy,' because I think *All of Me* hangs in with the younger people, too. It has what Lily calls a naughtiness about it. But there are rebels even in the huge 10- to 16-year-old market—kids who like something a little older, more mature…"

Even before his move to *All of Me* and "more mature" work, Martin took on some risky and interesting projects. *Pennies from Heaven* [Herbert Ross, 1981] may have been an artistic failure, but it's among the most experimental movies Hollywood ever made, mingling sober drama with bizarre comedy and surreal musical numbers. *Dead Men Don't Wear Plaid* might have been a flop, but its format—new comedy scenes intercut with clips from old detective pictures—is one of a kind for a feature film. Why has Martin tested such uncertain waters instead of basking in the tried-and-true success of ordinary farce?

"I did *Pennies from Heaven* because—in my mind—my career had sort of peaked with *The Jerk* [Carl Reiner, 1979] and a concert tour I did," Martin recalls. "I knew I couldn't go on being just a stand-up comedian, because there's a bell curve to this stuff. Pretty soon you aren't playing 15,000 seats anymore—you're playing 10, then 3, then none. You're back in the clubs and doing TV commercials. Even though I was at the top of things with my act, I knew that was over. I was at the end of my rope emotionally." So he made the "painful" decision to move fully into movie work. The big prize he wanted from Hollywood was "longevity"—the ability to "make a movie, lay off for three years, then make another one." His model was "someone like Warren Beatty. He's always around even when he doesn't make a picture for four years."

Martin thought that would be paradise after his years of stand-up work. "Doing my act night after night was like always going up in smoke," he complains. "You do it—and it might be great, it might be lousy, but it's completely gone. I don't know if this is an ego thing, but you wish it would stay around. You work so hard on something that you'd like to be able to visit it again, instead of having it be a vague memory." Since he had one successful film already behind him—*The Jerk*—he found he was "already a star" when he knocked on Hollywood's door. "It gave me an entree into the movies," he recalls. This felt good, but had its disadvantages. "It wasn't like I had 10 films to get my feet wet and understand how movies are made and what they're about," he says. With hindsight, he would have managed some things differently—such as making *Pennies from Heaven* after *Dead Men Don't Wear*

Plaid, not before it. Coming at the peak of an "increasing bizarreness" trend, he feels, the daring "*Pennies from Heaven* might have worked better commercially.

How does Martin choose his roles? He isn't quite sure. "All those questions are still being answered in my mind," he says. "I still don't have a total grasp." He's certain about one aspect, though: He enjoys variety. "I liked doing *All of Me*, but to go out and repeat it isn't tempting," he says. "I'd be just as happy making a warm movie like *It's a Wonderful Life* [Frank Capra, 1946]. That's the business I'm in—try to make 'em laugh and cry. I'm not in the art business."

Martin entered the entertainment world as a southern California teenager, doing a magic act "in folk clubs where anyone could get up on Monday night." Later he got a TV writing job for which he was "really ill-equipped," worked on material for *The Smothers Brothers Show*, went back to stand-up work, and finally joined the *Saturday Night Live* cast—which, along with a successful record and appearances on the *Tonight* show, launched him for good. Though television was important to his early career, Martin feels "TV is isolated—a place where you show off rather than learn." The transition to film was not smooth. "I had to learn how to calm down a little," he recalls, "because the screen's real big. You have to speak from your heart. When a character got mad in my act, I really exaggerated it. But when people in life get mad they sometimes get very quiet. There's a big process to learning these things." At the core of the process is "learning to use your own personality," he continues, naming Jack Nicholson as a master of that art. "He's a great actor whatever he plays," says Martin. "He's really an oddball, and that always makes him interesting. I'm not too much of an oddball in real life, but I am normal, and I think there's a place for normal people on the screen!"

How does he assess his movies so far? "There's not a great film in my background," he says with reasonable modesty, "but there's no clinker to be ashamed of. There are at least good moments or good intent in each one." This isn't a bad track record, Martin thinks, given the mediocrity of today's comedy. "A friend said recently that the old comedies—by Chaplin and Keaton— were really clever and funny and you really laughed," he muses. "I realized that was true. Those pictures didn't just skim along the surface with a funny situation every now and then. There's something we've forgotten, lost sight of."

The "furniture music" of rock star Brian Eno
Interview with Brian Eno, May 3, 1984

Rock star Brian Eno is a law unto himself. A leader of the popular group Roxy Music, he left the band in midstream to experiment with his own musical ideas. A celebrated performer in his own right, he has also poured much of his energy into behind-the-scenes work with such superstars as David Bowie and such groups as Devo and Talking Heads. An established rock soloist, he abandoned successful formulas to pursue a sort of high-art Musak he calls "ambient music."

In short, he breaks all the rules—and stirs up controversy. Tim Page, a *New York Times* music critic and classical disc jockey for public radio, calls Eno "a gifted and interesting primitive" who has done "some masterful, classic rock" but whose more daring experiments are just "tasteful and imaginatively done borrowings." But rock critic Lester Bangs, describing him in *Musician, Player & Listener* magazine as "a serious composer who doesn't read music" and "a rock star without a band who never tours," calls him "one of the true originals of contemporary music," a "unique" figure whose career has been as dazzlingly varied as the "colors and patterns on a lizard's back." This variety has now been brought together in a new set of his 11 solo albums called *Working Backwards 1983-1973*, released by Jem Records. An imposing retrospective, it helps explain why his records have been hugely influential even when sales have been modest. "I'm proud enough to trust my own judgment," says Eno. "And when it's time to follow a new thread, it always seems like fresh territory. That's what appeals to me. It's a feeling of: Can I find my way through this?"

Reached by phone in Canada recently for one of his rare interviews with the press, he spoke at great and unhurried length about a subject that currently interests him most: his development of ambient music. It began, he says, as he listened to the nonstop drone of pop tunes often piped into elevators and supermarkets. He liked the idea of music being part of the architecture, the decor of a place. And he liked being able to ignore the sound or to pause for a while and enjoy it. But he spotted a fatal flaw: If you did stop and really listen, you discovered it was terrible music—trite arrangements of too-familiar melodies. What if the music weren't terrible, he wondered? What if it were new and ingenious—yet still easy to ignore if you were busy or weren't in the mood?

Hence the concept of ambient music, which treads a thin line. It must be unobtrusive enough to become part of the background, to be what composer Eric Satie called "furniture music." Yet it must be subtly inviting. And for those who stop and listen carefully, it must offer genuine musical rewards. "The ambient records are similar to paintings," Eno says. "You don't gaze at a painting for hours each day. But you're aware of its presence, and occasionally you choose to go into it deeply—at a time when you're receptive and want it to affect your mood."

Explaining this new approach to composition, Eno calls it "total-immersion music." The idea isn't to sit and listen as you would to a symphony, but to live with the sound over a period of time. The notion bore fruit in 1975 with the release of *Discreet Music*, the first Eno album meant to be part of the listener's environment. Other ambient records include *Music for Airports* and *On Land*, which found Eno moving away from synthesizer effects toward the manipulation of natural "found sounds." All are repetitive and undramatic—which is what the composer wants.

"When I was a kid I discovered a woody place where I could hunt for fossils," he says. "After a while I got to know all the details of the spot. Even now, wherever I live I develop familiar walks that I like because they're familiar... The predictability is part of the excitement. Ambient music is like that woody place. The music offers many possibilities, and in time you recognize some and welcome them when you run across them. I like a music that doesn't use the narrative form with climaxes and surprises and tensions. Rather, the condition stays the same, with changes of balance inside it."

That, of course, requires a new set of expectations from the listener. "You can't expect to jump around to it," says the erstwhile rocker. Nor does Eno regard ambient music as a mere aesthetic exercise. Indeed, he feels it can be useful. "I got to thinking about *Music for Airports* while sitting in one," he recalls. "It occurred to me that airports could be wonderful places instead of horrid. And one helpful thing could be a music that didn't try to brighten you and be all sparkly, which can actually make people more nervous. What's needed is music that would calm you and help you enjoy sitting and waiting. That would encourage creative thinking, and lead to positive environments instead of neutral or negative ones."

Or, say Eno skeptics, it could lead to boring ones. "Eno is excellent at adding unexpected sounds to rock music," says critic Page. "But on their own, the sounds seem artsy and contrived. They just sort of lie there." Still, ambient music has shown commercial appeal, and while none of his records has been a runaway smash, the ambient albums—to Eno's own pleasant surprise—sell as strongly as his rock discs.

For all his fascination with sound, Eno didn't start out to be a musician. Raised in England, he went to an English art school at a time when "they were full of people who wanted to do something creative but didn't know quite what," he says. Unfortunately, the art of the period bored him—even fashionable Pop Art, which he felt had become "tedious and matter-of-fact, with no room for the spirit." He found music more stimulating and looked up to experimenters like John Cage and Morton Feldman. Eno played no instrument but found there was a niche for him. "Everyone was excited about synthesizers, tape recorders, and studio systems," he recalls, "and nobody knew how to play them! I fit right in. Manual skills weren't needed, but rather a knack for figuring out what those things did, how they could change music." Joining Roxy Music as an onstage sound mixer, he became a key member, but later decided that the large size and grueling schedule of the band were blocking its experimental urges.

Then, as time passed, "I lost interest in songs," he says. "I'd find one sound that was interesting, and I'd develop it, and it would turn into something that could never become a song... A certain type of musical feeling became more and more important to me."

Polish director finds there are "many forms of freedom"
Interview with Andrzej Wajda, December 7, 1984

Political commitment burns through the films of Andrzej Wajda, the leading Polish director. Examples include his *Danton* [1983], a study of the French Revolution with parallels to recent Polish events; *Man of Marble* [1977], about Poland during its Stalinist period; and *Man of Iron* [1981], containing footage of Solidarity agitation. Other works go back to the early '60s, when Wajda established his international reputation with a trilogy on Polish wartime struggles.

By contrast, his latest drama has a romantic slant. *A Love in Germany* [1983], now in American release, focuses on a German shopkeeper having a hopeless affair with a Polish prisoner while her husband is away fighting World War II. What attracted an urgently political filmmaker to such a tale? It was no whim, as I learned from him during a rare New York interview. He turned again to a bygone time because the past can illuminate the present. And he dealt with romantic passion because he feels that attitudes toward love can be profoundly revealing.

"In a totalitarian system," he explained through a translator, "everyone is terrorized, even if they accept the system. Individual love is always prohibited, because it gives a sense of freedom and self-worth. Everyone should love Hitler, not each other!" In his new drama, Wajda continued, the heroine's courage to love an "enemy" transforms her—giving her "an inspiration, a certainty, a self-sureness." Thus he sees the story as optimistic, despite the tragic ending of the affair. "It was most important for the film to say that love brings freedom," he feels. "The reason other people set out to destroy [the heroine] is that they envy her feelings."

The most respected and influential of all Polish filmmakers, Wajda has become a father figure for a generation of younger directors in Eastern Europe and elsewhere. In recent years he has worked both inside and outside Poland, according to the requirements of each new project. (*A Love in Germany* is a German-French coproduction.) Much of his artistic independence stems from this flexibility, he says, and he hopes to keep such "autonomy" for as long as possible. "There are films such as *Danton* that I could not make in Poland," he explains. "Yet there are films I can only make in Poland because of their subjects." He also credits two other circumstances for his relative independence as an artist. One is his ability to work in both film and theater. "Whenever I'm unable to make a film I work on the stage," he says, "and I derive a tremendous satisfaction from it. My third source of autonomy consists of the fact that I have made many movies already—so I can teach and help younger directors. There are many forms of freedom."

Can films with strong social and political views be produced in Poland today? "Neither my colleagues nor I have given up on the idea of making political films," Wajda replies. "That's not because we are maniacs for political film, but because other forms don't have as much meaning for us." One reason for this, he says, is that "the political films we are capable of making, no one else can make for us. This is because nobody else has the political experiences we have, and because Poland lies between the East and West. This experience is extremely valuable. Whenever we are able to exploit it, our films acquire a special role—they say something to the world that others are unable to say." At the moment, according to Wajda, such films are hard to launch in his country. "At a time of crisis even production aspects are difficult," he notes. "It's difficult just to make a film. Still, many are being made."

Can political films have a real effect on the people who see them? Wajda's answer reveals a lot about political attitudes in different parts of the world. "I waver from extreme optimism to extreme pessimism," he admits. "When I show a film in the West, I often think people look at it superficially. I could show it or not show it. It falls into some kind of black hole. But when I try to make a political film in Poland and I meet with all the obstacles," he adds with a wry smile, "I think there must be something tremendously important about what I'm trying to do. Otherwise, why would they set all these obstacles in my way? And then I'm optimistic. Something must be present, if one side is doing so much that these films not be made." Asked which he cares about most—exploring difficult ideas or reaching a very large audience—Wajda says that "it's always ideal to combine these things. I make films in Poland because it's my country and I get my important subject matters there. But to make films for a very, very broad audience has always been my dream."

Known to be a longtime Hollywood fan, Wajda sees no need for conflict between commercial moviemaking and serious ideas. In his view, "Many people want to say something original and interesting—for example, about the situation of women. And many people are making such films. But the best, most powerful, and most interesting is *Tootsie* [1982], a commercial film!" He credits the movie's excellence to "the fantastic precision and intelligence" of director Sydney Pollack, one of many "commercial filmmakers [who] set limits for themselves in order to reach broad audiences. This produces a kind of tension, which some directors are able to break through and make fantastic films."

Not all popular communications get Wajda's approval, however. Television displeases him. "The way of watching a film on television is unacceptable to me," he states flatly. "I think of a film as a unity — all the elements have a higher consistency, are integrated. It is not an excerpt from a serial. On television a film becomes a fragment of a larger reality which has no beginning or end." More generally, Wajda worries about audiences growing fragmented, and less serious about what they see. "When I began to make films 30 years ago," he recalls, "nobody asked about the level of the viewers. We were people who saw life at the edge of tragedy, and films were about that. The audience could laugh, could be moved—everything was possible. Today everything has become much more complicated." The chief problem is that "suddenly the audience has become very young," Wajda says. "Their life experience is alien to us. They don't understand directors my age and we don't understand them. It's not quite clear what we want to say to them, especially since we are convinced they have nothing to say to us. This is such a serious question today that we have to consider whether making movies at all makes sense. Should one look for another form of self-expression?" At self-questioning moments like these, Wajda finds the stage especially appealing. "Perhaps it's best to have a more direct influence — and therefore a more powerful one—on a small group of people," he says, noting the satisfactions of interacting with performers during a theatrical project.

Despite such musings, Wajda remains an active and energetic member of the film community, at least for now. He is especially animated when discussing his latest movie, granting its flaws as readily as he defends its methods. He owns that the flashback structure of *A Love in Germany* is "antiquated" and "ineffective" and wishes he had made one major character—a man of the '80s visiting the town of his boyhood—a Pole rather than a German. Yet he takes open pride in the picture's savage tone and the nightmarish humor of some scenes near the end. "I wanted to understand that country through its own art," he says. "Germans must be seen through expressionist cinema, because in the expressionist film and painting of the '20s there is somehow the actual soul of Germany. When I'm dealing with this subject I can't refrain from reaching for this material."

Above all, Wajda loves the filmmaking process that allows him to explore such ideas. "The two truly creative moments in the work of a director," he says, "are the selection of the subject—what this film should say—and the selection of the actors. That is where it all begins... the rest is craft. Yet it isn't good to invent a film entirely beforehand. The director must make a film as if he were telling a story to a live person."

Robert Wilson, master of experimental theater
Interview with Robert Wilson, March 7, 1985

Robert Wilson is a grandmaster of the imagination. No director has a more radical, more original, more visionary sense of theater. But ask this extravagant dreamer about the art of acting, and he may launch into his Jack Benny imitation. "There was a great actor!" he told me not long ago, his palm cradling his cheek in the timeless Benny manner. "He had perfect voice rhythms, his gestures were so precisely timed!" It was surprising to hear Wilson name a popular comedian as a favorite, given his own reputation for bold experiments in what has been dubbed "the theater of images"—such as his epic about human conflict and brotherhood, *the CIVIL warS*, onstage now through March 17 at the American Repertory Theatre in Cambridge, Mass. [*Note: This refers to the Cologne sections of the massive work.*] Nor did he stop at Jack Benny while extolling "the great actors" who have influenced him. He went on to name Buster Keaton and Bert Lahr and Charlie Chaplin, noting that all of them perfected their routines "by doing them over and over until they became totally mechanical—and then they could become totally free."

In that last comment lies the connection between Wilson's stylized, deliberately dreamlike art and the vintage entertainment he loves. What fascinates him about vaudeville-trained actors is their formal quality—their use of a carefully worked-out plan that glues each comic bit into a seamless whole. His own productions also blend the mechanical and the free, taking highly intuitive material (developed in workshops with performers) and placing it in rigorously designed visual settings, with obsessive care to the smallest details of lighting and composition.

So far Wilson and his sweeping, slow-motion spectacles haven't found the popular acceptance that his vaudevillian heroes achieved. Although he grew up in Texas and began his stage career in New York, he has worked most often in Europe during the past decade, finding production funds and adventurous audiences more easily there. His schedule still calls for much European work, but his compatriots are seeing a bit more of him lately. Besides his current work on *the CIVIL warS*, a revival of his *Einstein on the Beach* [created with Philip Glass] drew rave reviews and cheering crowds at the Brooklyn Academy of Music (BAM) last December, and he plans to stage a more modest piece, *The Golden Windows*, there next fall.

Wilson's crowded international schedule makes him a hard man for the press to get hold of, but I have managed to track him down for interviews a couple of times over the past few years — most recently during an *Einstein on the Beach* rehearsal break at BAM, where he answered questions in his usual quiet, ironic tone between bites from a sandwich that would see him through hours of extremely technical stage-lighting sessions. In all his work, including the new *CIVIL warS*, light is the key element that holds everything else in place and perspective.

`"What we see is as important as what we hear," said Wilson, explaining his endless fascination with light. "A gesture can be more beautiful than a sound. But how do you make a gesture? People never think about it. Light is what helps us see and hear — or prevents us from really seeing and hearing." In many productions, he continued, directors tend to light scenery more carefully than performers. This is a risky practice, because "if you can't see an actor or singer, sometimes it's difficult to hear them, too." It also distracts viewers by drawing the eye to arbitrary places just because they're bright. When treated as a visual element with its own importance, however, light can focus the viewer's attention in unexpected ways. "I could light this glass," Wilson says, holding up a tumbler he's been drinking from, "and the light would be like an actor then — a part of the text, a part of what we're saying."

These ideas grow from Wilson's conviction that every nuance of sight and sound can have a stunning theatrical effect. "There's no such thing as silence," he says, citing John Cage's theory of music. "And there's no such thing as stillness. There's always movement. Sometimes the less movement we make, the more aware we are of motion. Sometimes the quieter we are, the more aware we are of sound. It's always there." Wilson's work has been called "theater of images" because it relies on elaborate stage pictures rather than story and dialogue. These pictures evolve slowly and organically during the course of a show, with each gesture framed and choreographed to suit the theater where the work is being staged. "You have to measure to the back wall with your eyes, check where the exit lights are, and decide to fill that space," Wilson says. "Each gesture must have a different weight. But you can't really explain to an actor how to texture space to make it alive and interesting. The actor has to feel it. It's mysterious. There's something magical when Brando goes to pick up a hat. It's something you're born with or discover. Onstage you can feel whether you're relating to everyone in the house. It's a certain sense you have."

Wilson's theatrical ideas stem largely from his background in the visual arts. Trained as a painter and architect, he started putting on shows while employed as a social worker with handicapped clients, shaping his productions around patients and friends who wanted to be in them. He stayed with theater as an expressive medium because "the images in my head were so much richer than what I could get on the canvas," as he told an interviewer. His slate of future activities is crowded. Plans include *King Lear* workshops in California and Canada for a 1986-87 production in Hamburg; a show suggested by the life of Franz Kafka late this year in West Berlin; a production of Gluck's opera *Alceste*, with Jessye Norman, late next year in Stuttgart, West Germany; a production of Wagner's opera *Parsifal* in the spring of 1987; the start of his first film, a French production of Wagner's *Tristan und Isolde*, with soprano Norman, late in 1987; and a new opera with composer Philip Glass in 1989-90. He is also considering a Broadway musical tucked in somewhere along the way. And he maintains an active interest in video, after achieving brilliant results in *Deafman Glance* [1981] and *Stations* [1982], shown on PBS and cable TV.

With so many projects going on, does the round of fundraising and production details get in the way of simply being an artist? Yes, says Wilson, who has long handled business affairs through his own Byrd Hoffman Foundation. And even the hardest work can't solve every problem, as he found when he partly lost his battle to finance the complete 10-hour version of *the CIVIL warS: a tree is best measured when it is down*—a multipart epic created in several nations but never assembled for the 1984 Olympic Arts Festival, as intended, because there simply wasn't enough money. He has learned from this frustration, however, and is readjusting his methods. Portions of *the CIVIL warS* are being mounted separately, such as the three-hour Cambridge edition, which was originally staged in Cologne, West Germany, and Rome. And Wilson has ensured that his future works will be produced by outside agencies rather than his own foundation. If this now leaves him free to do the dreaming that's at the core of his art, both his work and his audience should be stronger than ever in time to come.

Merce Cunningham: dance's bold adventurer. Audiences used to throw things; now they love his unconventional moves
Interview with Merce Cunningham, April 19, 1985

"I never think of anything as definitive," says dancer and choreographer Merce Cunningham about his work. "It's like saying this is a definitive day, or a definitive breath. It just seems that way until another comes along!" This love of change and spontaneity has helped make Mr. Cunningham a giant of modern dance. In the 41 years since his first New York solo program, he has seen his unconventional ideas—as dancer, choreographer, and thinker—move from the margin to the heart of the performing world. Today his work remains alive, unpredictable, and more popular than ever. His tours and New York engagements are greeted not only with glowing reviews, but with large and enthusiastic audiences—unfazed by abstract steps, quirky gestures, and an orchestra pit filled with whirring and chirping electronic gear. He has also plunged into video, using it to create a new form of recorded dance.

Talking with him in a cluttered corner of his Manhattan studio, you wouldn't guess Cunningham is a giant. Or an iconoclast. He wears rehearsal fatigues and rests on a plain wooden bench. He speaks quietly, punctuating his favorite notions with soft, throaty chuckles.

What accounts for the wide appeal of his unconventional work? Cunningham offers the most modest of reasons. "We've been around a long time," he says simply, "and people have gotten used to us. Twenty years ago, when we first appeared in Paris, they threw things and complained. Now people talk about the same things but say how interesting they are."

On a deeper level, he feels that ideas like his "have become part of society," since art and life mirror each other. Take the complexity of his work. "We live in such a complex atmosphere that people can now accept it onstage," says the dancer, "and not feel it's out of their realm."

The same goes for the freewheeling noises—more like random sound than traditional music—of composer John Cage, his longtime collaborator. "It's all part of daily life," Cunningham says. "People hear it all day long when they go out."

Of the many ideas associated with his work, the one that still excites Cunningham most—judging from the ring of his voice—is his respect for the unexpected. "I'd rather find out something new than repeat what I know," he says. "I prefer an adventure to something that's fixed."

Audiences are invited to share the adventure, but Cunningham doesn't see himself as an aesthetic tour guide who must explain or justify each bend in the road. Asked about "communication," he looks down his nose at the word. "You can use a telephone for that," he says, "and I don't telephone very often. What we do is present an experience that can be different for everyone who sees it."

The kernel of this approach—and of life itself, says Cunningham—is constant change and renewal. He disagrees with the view that art should offer finished, polished works. "History provides that, not art," he says. "Someone decides that's the piece, but if they were around when the artist made it, they might have a totally different idea about it. What is it Shaw says in one of his plays? History will lie as usual!" Cunningham also rejects the thought that art must obey firm standards. "One person's standard is somebody else's junk," he says. "If someone makes a rule, someone else is bound to break it." His own guiding principle? "You present a situation. You accept what happens. Then you push on."

The same philosophy steers his video work. Cunningham got interested in TV during the mid-'70s, when he realized that more and more dance was bound to appear there. Instead of relying on nondancers to wield the camera, he decided to study the medium himself. What he found was "a new kind of visual medium with its own possibilities. Everything is different from the stage: dancers, movement, space, time, and the effects they make. Most dancers I talked to didn't like it for that reason. But I thought that was the interesting thing." Cunningham still delights in the oddities of TV technique, including the simplest aspects. "For someone to leave the stage," he says, "they have to go away. With video, you just move the camera!" As for skeptics, he dismisses them as old-fashioned. "Think of the first people who came in from the village green to dance on a stage," he smiles. "They must have thought it was terrible—you always have to come on from the side!"

Both live and on-screen, Cunningham's work continues to grow from ideas and methods he established years ago. One is the insistence that dance, music, sets, and costumes each has its own life—created separately by independent artists, then brought together to share a single span of time before an audience. This method has risks, but Cunningham feels the components of a work rarely get in each other's way. As proof, he recalls a dance accompanied by Cage reading stories to the audience. "One person came backstage and said he couldn't pay attention to the dance because of the stories. Someone else said, 'What stories?' It's different for everyone."

Affection for ambiguity is another Cunningham constant. You'll never hear a Beethoven work accompany one of his dances because, he says, "That has intention. And if the music has intention, it doesn't leave things free." He prefers music of the Cage variety, created through chance and intuition. "When the music is sound—not intended to mean something—it opens things out in a different way," he insists. This doesn't mean his dances are random affairs, though. While music allows for chance elements, dance must cope with "traffic problems" that call for careful order and design. "When you're dealing with real virtuosity," says Cunningham, "everyone has to know what they're doing at every single moment, or there's the danger of an accident."

Does this mean he has strict rules? "No food in the studio!" he replies with a grin. Then he adds more seriously, "It's not a matter of rules, really, but trying to find new ways for things to happen." He tries not to ride herd on his dancers too closely, because he wants their individual personalities to come out in their performances. He finds running his company like walking a tightrope. "On one side is a very clear idea of technique and how things are done. On the other is the idea of just dancing." As important as technique is in his work, it's the "just dancing" that has inspired Cunningham most since the start of his career. This explains his yen for ambiguity, which he sees as liberating rather than confusing. "Telling stories in dance, or being explicit about something, seems to pin things down," he says. "I prefer the multiplicity of *Finnegans Wake* to something that tells us what it's all about. One always comes into a work burdened with one's memories, but it's marvelous if you can get rid of them when you see or hear something. I feel it's enlightening if you don't even know what something is. When I first looked at abstract expressionist painting, there were no words to describe it—and that was fine! There are so many possibilities for dance, if you just don't get your head stuck." The Merce Cunningham Dance Company is appearing now through April 23 in Chicago, and it will also perform this spring in Italy, England, and France. Then it returns to New York (June 20-29) with the large-scale *Roaratorio*, bringing dance, music, and James Joyce to the Park Avenue Armory.

Novelist Mailer turns his latest book into a movie
Interview with Norman Mailer, September 4, 1987

Provincetown, Mass.

"I think a film should be as sinister and lively, as odd and riveting… as a dream," says Norman Mailer, novelist turned moviemaker. "A good powerful dream."

Mailer's own movie, *Tough Guys Don't Dance*, has the makings of a bad powerful dream. Based on his 1984 novel, it turns a murder-mystery plot into a melodramatic fandango so dark and delirious that it's hard to know whether he wants us to laugh, cry, or cringe. The answer is all three, of course. This is the kind of film that begs to be called controversial—and surely will be, by reviewers and publicists alike. Just as surely, the term will imply automatic praise in many cases, as if its meaning didn't include a critical "con" as well as a promotional "pro." Mailer has benefited from that careless use of "controversial" as much as any writer in memory, using it to build a feisty media presence that has rivaled— many would say outstripped—his accomplishments on the printed page. His most respected works (such as his 1948 first novel, *The Naked and the Dead*, and some highly praised nonfiction books) have made him a major figure whose influence must be acknowledged. Yet it's hard to imagine a third-rate book like *Tough Guys Don't Dance* getting a fraction as much attention if it weren't the product of a self-aware celebrity with—in addition to two Pulitzer Prizes and a literary ambition that seems as genuine as ever— a knack for turning the trashiest accomplishments into media-hyped gold.

The screen version of *Tough Guys Don't Dance*, written and directed by Mailer, serves up a string of weird variations on the book's sordid plot. It's about a lovelorn man (Ryan O'Neal) who finds two severed heads in his Cape Cod marijuana cache and can't figure out—his memory is too fogged by alcohol—whether he's a villain or a victim. In a printed statement on the film, Mailer says he wants it to embody a "strange and sinister fever" that he suspects is rampant among "the pleasure-loving classes." Interviewed in the attic studio of his Provincetown, Mass., summer home, near the locations where *Tough Guys* was filmed, an affable and talkative Mailer says that statement was "cooked up" as a promotional ploy—the kind of thing you write "to get people to read your script" and then forget about. Still, he doesn't disavow it. "It is a picture about America," he says in the gruff but friendly voice that's one of his talk-show and interview trademarks. "It's not a realistic picture," he adds. "These are not typical American citizens. But I do think there's been a kind of greed and irresponsibility loose in American life in the last four or five years... This is a vision of some of the worst things that are going on in America now, and what could possibly happen to us if we keep going."

No amount of cautionary intent will get many filmgoers to swallow the grisly episodes in the *Tough Guys Don't Dance* movie, even if it does slightly tone down the novel's hard-boiled sexuality. In any case, Mailer says the tale's cautionary aspect is only marginal. For this aspiring auteur, the purpose of cinema is dark and dreamlike, not enlightening and instructive. "I think fiction can intensify the moral consciousness of a time," Mailer says. "I think theater can enlarge one's emotional appreciation of social situations. (But) film doesn't work on our minds. It works on all the places that have never been worked on by other art forms — all the synapses between our memory and our emotions and our nerves and our sense of time." Hence the connection Mailer sees between film and dreams, which he calls "the interface, if you will, between life and eternity, between life and death... Dreams, to me, are a dialogue between your soul and your self. It's a way for the soul to say, 'Look, you're not living in the proper fashion at all. These are some of the disasters, metaphorically speaking, that attend you."

Mailer sees a "dream logic" at work in every film, good or bad. "If someone throws a hand up like this," he says with an appropriate gesture, "and the next (shot) is some birds taking off like that... there's a connection. You might not be able to name the connection. But somewhere in that deep, mysterious world of signs, portents, images, and hints, there is a connection that makes sense to us." Whether the signs, etc., of *Tough Guys Don't Dance* make sense to moviegoers will be known Sept. 18, when the picture has its theatrical premiere.

The best part of theater is what happens after you leave
Interview with Peter Sellars, December 15, 1987

Peter Sellars loves the stage. But he scorns the "agreed-upon clichés" that—in his view—make up most contemporary theater. To prove it, he has developed his own controversial approach to stage directing and earned an international reputation in the process. Two of his most recent achievements have been featured in this season's Next Wave festival at the Brooklyn Academy of Music. His production of *Nixon in China*, an opera by composer John Adams and librettist Alice Goodman, is at the Academy now through Thursday, after earning enthusiastic reviews in its Houston Grand Opera premiere. It was preceded by *Zangezi*, his restructured version of a Russian theater piece dating from 1923. Described as "a supersaga in 20 planes," it epitomizes Sellars' view of theater as a "vertical" experience in which metaphors and allusions, piled atop one another, are more important than a "horizontal" story line. Neither production is the sort of show that's likely to pop up on Broadway next season. Sellars is a rebel, and he admits that audiences are often "upset" by this and other works he has concocted in such important venues as the Kennedy Center in Washington—where he served as artistic director—and now the influential Next Wave festival.

What's so unsettling about his approach? Sellars says it's his refusal to provide neat, easily understandable experiences. "Most people have a sense that they have to answer 20 questions on their way out of the theater," he says ruefully. "If they get 19 right, then they had a good time." But, he continues, plays that give simple answers to life's questions are not true to experience. As he sees it, "the surface of life consists of a series of delusions and traps and whatnot, where basically the facts are not known. And humanly, they are unknowable." So he chooses to challenge spectators—and himself—instead of doling out easy gratification. "My productions are all about not being able to sum it up on the way out," he says.

While he knows his approach is radical, Sellars sees elements of it in the classics, including Shakespeare's plays. In them, he says, "Existence is construed poetically. You finally have to realize that a human life is a metaphor, in a way, and a play is a metaphor. It's not the thing itself." Sellars sees theater as a way of breaking through assumptions we hold about the world, and about ourselves. "Most theater is so materialistically oriented," he says with a frown. "A chair's a chair, a table's a table, and a character can be defined in a two-sentence Hollywood synopsis... What I do in my shows is take these material things and force them to come out of themselves… so the roof of an apartment can also be a temple on the Ganges… and 15 other things." If this is an unconventional aim, so much the better. "The point of drama, historically, is to turn the world on its ear," he says. Sellars' work represents a quest for expression that's "above and beyond" the mundane world. Yet this mustn't be considered a substitute for religion. "The purpose of art is to indicate that there's another level," he asserts. "The purpose of religion is to live on that other level."

In seeking to "indicate another level" of reality, Sellars' method is to work "very intensely with the surface of something" until he begins to sense new and unexpected meanings in it. He likens this process to "the way Albrecht Dürer draws a rabbit. By the time he's done, it's the most realistic rabbit drawing you've ever seen. But the drawing isn't about a rabbit. It has… an intense spiritual value, because of the time taken to render it in such detail. Moving into the detail is the only way you can then move past it." In keeping with his philosophical approach to the stage, Sellars says that "the least important part of the experience is what happens while the audience is in the theater. You're planting a seed there, and what matters is how it grows later… It's all the same to me if they love it or hate it, because one way or another it enters their lives, and it's something they won't forget." Sellars knows such ideas won't always endear him to audiences or producers. "I've been gnawing at the edge of theater for a while now," he says, describing his position. "Because of the way I work, I will constantly be [considered] either the most important director in the world, or not even able to get arrested."

Encountering his energy and enthusiasm firsthand, one senses that Sellars rather likes being an outsider. He shares this attitude with aesthetic gadflies like filmmaker Jean-Luc Godard and stage director Elizabeth LeCompte, who share some artistic traits with Sellars and recognize their position on the fringe of "mainstream" culture. Like them, he is committed to expressing radical ideas in radical ways. "People have this notion of rational comprehension of the world," Sellars says, "and a whole series of rational [concepts] have been set up to explain things away. But that's not really the way most people take in the world." What fascinates him are things "lurking just on the edge" of theater and of life—ideas suggesting that, in his words, "maybe there's another structure behind the structure in this world."

Bill Viola: Art demands creativity from viewers, too
Interview with Bill Viola, December 21, 1987

"Creativity is not the property of artists alone," says video artist Bill Viola. "It's a basic element of the human character, no matter what culture you're in, no matter where you are on Earth or in history. When we talk about art, it's not creativity that's the real question... It's the desire to express things to the public." Mr. Viola has felt that desire to communicate since he was a youngster with a talent for painting and music. Now he's an important artist, but he still feels creativity belongs as much to his audience as to himself. "I think you have to be creative to look at art," he says with conviction. "In my work I've made demands—almost unconsciously—for a certain level of creativity... I'm not handing out ideas on a silver platter when [people] look at my work. Energy in equals energy out!" What are the hallmarks of Viola's work? His videotapes rarely have stories or characters in the usual sense. They focus on people, places, and objects in the real world, gazing at them with a patience and intensity that transforms the ordinary into the visionary. His best videos are marked by persistent camera work and an imaginative way of ordering shots so that unexpected meanings and relationships emerge. Many examples are on view through Jan. 3 in a major retrospective at the Museum of Modern Art here, including three room-size installations and a generous selection of tapes.

Discussing his work in a wide-ranging interview at the museum, Viola confessed to an "ego battle" that breaks out sometimes in his mind. "Is it me that's doing this stuff," he asks himself at such moments, "or is this stuff being given to me, sort of? Is it really my personality being expressed, or are things just transmitted through me?" The question arises because Viola's artistic decisions grow from ideas and observations that everyone has access to. "For me," he says, "the process of making a work directly parallels a sort of life process that everyone shares, not just artists alone. It's a process of creativity, thought, and gradual realization. A lot of my works start from a kernel of an idea, like a seed... I know I'm ready to begin a work when I get the awareness that the seed contains the whole tree or the whole plant. I don't know how to describe how I know that. But some ideas—when you get 'em, they just won't go away. They kind of nag at you. And each time they come back, a little more is revealed. You see it branching out and connecting with other things. My works really begin in a very simple way. Sometimes it's an image, and sometimes it's words I might write, like a fragment of a poem."

Memory plays a part, as well—even in a long and complex work like *I Do Not Know What It Is I Am Like*, his latest videotape. It's a meditative study of the relationships between intellectual and visceral modes of experience, focusing on people and animals in settings far removed from the urbanized, modern world. One "seed" for this superb work was an event from Viola's childhood, when he accidentally fell into a lake. Nearby adults were alarmed by the mishap, he recalls, but he was enchanted by it. "I remember the amazing experience," he says, "of this world I had no idea existed. I just broke through to it. It was incredibly beautiful, and I wasn't scared at all. There was this emerald green light everywhere, filtering down, and I could see the sandy bottom, and plants moving back and forth, and fish. Then a big hand came down, and gripped me, and yanked me right out of the water," he concludes, still sounding a little disappointed that the adventure had to end.

Viola forgot about those underwater images until a few years ago. Then they surfaced in his memory and became an inspiration for *I Do Not Know What It Is I Am Like*, which has many fish images and begins with the camera leaping from a lake into the air. Viola is fascinated with the idea that our dry-land world must look very strange to a fish—or any "outsider" with a different mental and physical makeup—just as the undersea world looks exotic to humans. "There's another world out there," the artist says, turning memory into metaphor, "just beyond the world we're in. It's just on the other side of that translucent, semitransparent surface." This strongly felt idea, dating back to Viola's early years, helps explain his use of video to capture the world not in flatly realistic terms, but in a visionary way that suggests there's more to existence than common surfaces—and common ways of looking and thinking—reveal.

Viola turned to video after exploring art and music for many years. "I think video comes closer to expressing [transcendent material] because its foot is half out the door of the material world anyway," he says. Another of Viola's key interests is in "the power of the gaze." He's captivated by the idea that vision can transmit to us things "beyond and beneath language and the social dialogue" of everyday life. "I want to break the separation that vision imposes on the environment," he says. "We can sit here and look out the window at those buildings, but it's a whole other thing to go down the elevator, walk across the street, and lean against them and touch them with your cheek. Vision connects you. But it also separates you. In my work, and my life, I feel a desire to merge. Not in terms of losing my own identity... but there's a feeling that life is interconnected, that there's life in stones and rocks and trees and dirt, like there is in us." Hence the long animal shots in some of his videotapes, which reflect his forays into the world of nature. A visit with an animal is "sort of a meeting of two intelligences," he adds. "They're ordered very differently from each other, but the meeting point is the gaze."

In making his videotapes, Viola says he aims for an "internal consistency, which people can sense but maybe not literally read — or rather, which they can read in their own ways. I connect my work very strongly with poetry, and people... can use poems in their own personal ways, beyond what the poet might have specifically intended. The bottom line is that... the work has to be true to yourself and your own life."

Louis Malle and his artistic dilemma
Interview with Louis Malle, April 22, 1988

Louis Malle is the European filmmaker of the hour. His newest movie, *Au Revoir les enfants*, has become a major international hit—even nominated for two Academy Awards in the best original screenplay and best foreign-language-film categories; On top of this, Malle is now being honored by a major retrospective of his French films at the Museum of Modern Art here (through Sunday) in conjunction with a series of new works called Perspectives on French Cinema. One of the world's most versatile and popular filmmakers, Malle earned his reputation with such respected pictures as *The Lovers* [1958] and *Lacombe Lucien* [1974] in his native France. More recently he's directed hits like *Atlantic City* [1980] and *My Dinner with Andre* [1981] in the United States, where he's lived and worked for the past 10 years. For his latest film, Malle decided to return to France, where the events of the picture actually took place. *Au Revoir, les enfants* is based on his own memories of boyhood during the Nazi occupation of France in the 1940s. In the private school he attended, a few of the pupils were Jewish children hiding from the Nazis under false names. Malle became close to one of these boys, accidentally learned his true identity, and then had to stand by helplessly as his new friend was discovered and taken away by the authorities, never to be seen again. Malle recreates this episode from his childhood in a dramatic and revealing story that builds powerful emotions without ever falling into sentimentality.

I visited Malle recently in the New York apartment he shares with his wife, actress Candice Bergen, and their young son. He told me he had mixed feelings about turning his most painful memory into a film. "I've always been split between two completely opposite trends in my work," he said in his lightly accented English. "What's been pushing me mostly is an extreme curiosity about looking around, trying to understand what's going on around me. It's a sort of extroverted curiosity that has always kept me pretty enthusiastic about what I'm doing. The other side is more introverted. And this has not been easy, this looking into myself. Usually I find it depressing, and I've tried to stay away from it for a long time.' It took many years, Malle says, before he was able to combine his extroverted and introverted tendencies, putting both of them at the service of a childhood memory that still disturbs him. "It was difficult," he says about the process of exploring this memory on film. "It was very painful, because [the original event] was such a shock. It was hard for me to think of giving it to others, for years. I thought it was my own secret. This is a little irrational, because at some point I went to the opposite: I felt this is something I really should pass on. I had two motivations to make the film. One was to deal with it and sort of make my peace with it. And, after all these years, to send this message of love to the boy who had been taken away in front of me.

When novelists or painters use their personal experiences as raw material, they have the advantage of working privately until they're pleased with the results. Malle says one of the challenges of filmmaking is that he can't work alone. Collaborators and technicians are always part of the process, even when the subject matter is deeply personal to the director. "You think of a project," he says, "a film that you want to do. And you have this dream of the film as it's going to be once it's finished. Of course, when you dream it, it's wonderful! And then you have to go through a year [of] different phases: the writing, the preproduction, shooting, editing, talking about it. And this involves a lot of people. There's a public stance that you have to take. You have to explain to your actors, your crew, your collaborators. It's very hard. And when you're dealing with something that's as intimate as *Au Revoir, les enfants*, it's almost a contradiction... I think that's what makes the film medium so fascinating, and so difficult. It also explains why, in the history of cinema, there's been so few really personal statements which have stayed away from becoming spectacular or show business, or which haven't lost a part of their intimacy in the process."

In writing and directing *Au Revoir, les enfants*, Malle knew he was dealing with highly emotional subject matter. So he worked hard to avoid exaggerating the characters' feelings or letting the story fall into easy sentimentality. "I've been fiercely watching myself," he says, "not to ever push the spectators, telling them what they should feel. I've tried to have the spectator participate and be almost like part of the process—not only watching the film, but being completely involved. "I think you achieve that only if you stay away from anything that has to do with the tricks and gimmicks of the medium. And they're so easy, and so obvious, that it's hard sometimes not to manipulate. Film is a medium where manipulation is almost common ground. I see very, very few films where I feel that as a spectator I'm completely free in the choice of my emotions.'

Malle's career has taken him to many countries—including France, the United States, and India—where he's made a wide variety of films. These range from thrillers and love stories to documentaries and some, like *My Dinner With Andre*, that don't fit any of the familiar movie labels. "I've been a little experimental in my work," he says with a happy smile. "I've been always trying not to repeat myself, not to go in exactly the same direction twice. I would be attracted to something, and I would deal with it in a film, and then something else would attract my attention or my curiosity. I've really been doing it deliberately... I don't know if it's always been good for the spectators, but it's been really good for me!" Malle seems almost mischievous when he thinks about the scope of his career, and the curiosity that has taken him to so many different subjects and styles. "I have no shame," he says with a grin. "I have no principles. Nothing will stop me. Even when people tell me, 'But Louis, this is really not for you.' Usually that's a good reason for me to deal with it—because if it's not for me, I want to know more about it."

"New cinema" director sees different Rio. Diegues discusses his new film, *Subway to the Stars*

Interview with Carlos Diegues, May 16, 1988

Carlos Diegues became a filmmaker to reckon with during the 1960s, when he helped establish Brazil's influential cinema novo movement—a new wave of film activity dedicated to confronting Brazilian social and political problems. Although that movement is no longer an active force, Diegues has become one of Latin America's most internationally acclaimed directors, with such socially conscious movies as *Bye Bye Brazil* [1980] and *Quilombo* [1984], both of which have been critical successes in the United States. His latest film is a drama called *Subway to the Stars*, set in Rio de Janeiro. The main character is a young jazz musician named Vinicius, whose girlfriend mysteriously vanishes one night. Searching for her, Vinicius travels into the poorest and most dangerous parts of his city. His only helpers are a friend who'd rather go and live in New York, and a tough policeman who remembers Brazil's former military government with nostalgia. *Subway to the Stars* deals with harsh and unpleasant subject matter. But its hero is a musician—based on the mythical character of Orpheus—and the tone of the movie is determined in large part by the lively music on its soundtrack. Diegues says his film is concerned with art, poetry, and love—not as entertainments to make us forget about world problems, but as tools for helping us understand our world better.

"I don't think films can change reality," the director told me during a recent New York visit. "It's impossible. A film is not a machine gun! But I think we can change the conscience of the audience. In other words, we can change the way people see reality and understand reality." In making *Subway to the Stars*, Diegues wanted to give his audience an unusually realistic view of Rio de Janeiro. This explains why the film so insistently explores the slums and the unpleasant underside of the city. "We have the habit of seeing Rio de Janeiro on the screen like paradise," the filmmaker says. "It's [depicted] like a tropical city and beach where everybody's happy... I think in this film we see the real Rio de Janeiro. I shot it where maybe 70 percent of Rio's population lives really." Diegues hopes this will impress moviegoers with everyday Rio de Janeiro hardships—which are generally ignored, he says, by Brazilians and others who are "alienated" from unpleasant facts that don't affect them directly. This does not mean Diegues wants his movies to preach or talk down to audiences. He knows that an effective movie is a popular movie that lots of people want to go and see. "I know that the first social role of a film is to be entertaining," he says. "That's for sure. But after that, if you can at the same time keep a moral commitment with people who are seeing your film, this is very important. I was a kid when I started loving movies. Everything I know in my life I learned from movies, and mostly American movies. The American cinema made up our minds—not only mine, but my whole generation. We have been seeing American movies for so long that we are impregnated with them...

"I have my own idols in the American cinema," he adds, "like King Vidor and John Ford and Orson Welles... I mean the classics. Everything I know, I know from American movies first. Afterwards I went to books and to school." Even today, Diegues says, about 65 percent of films shown in Brazil were made in the United States. Only about 25 or 30 percent come from Brazil itself. "In every country in the world," he explains, "there are two national cinemas: the local cinema and the American cinema. You take France, nowadays. Fifty percent of the French market is being occupied by American movies. And it's like that everywhere in the world. The American cinema is very strong. It's not only a matter of economics. People like those films! I'm not very familiar with financial problems in the world, but they say that Japan is taking over the whole economic world and becoming the first financial power in the world. But Japan will never export its culture. Japan will always consume the American culture... There is something very deep and very strong in the American cinema."

Even though American films continue to dominate the world movie scene, Diegues feels the arts are entering a new period and that national art movements, in a traditional sense, may be disappearing. "A lot of things are changing in the world these days," he opines, "in a cultural sense... I think we are living in a world that's becoming a planetarian culture. For instance, African music is influencing American music, which influences Brazilian music. Somehow those things become finally not national but very international. Maybe we are in the eve of a new international culture. And in the cinema, of course, American cinema will be the leader."

Diegues doesn't think about such large issues when he's actually at work on one of his movies. He's a practical filmmaker who knows that each new project needs a fresh approach. "The main thing in my thoughts when I'm making a film," he reveals, "is to represent the state of mind—the spirit—of my time and the society where I'm living. That's the way I go into filmmaking." He does acknowledge, however, that certain key ideas run through all his films, tying them together. These ideas grow from his thoughts about the society he reflects, and studies, in his work. "I think that every human utopia has died, has been destroyed," he says, summing up these ideas. "We are living in very hard days, and people are looking for some sort of new way of living together. I believe that solidarity—really caring for others—will be very important in this eve of a third millennium. I'm going to make my films on this subject. *Subway to the Stars* is a film about friendship, about solidarity. That what it's all about."

Director with an optimistic viewpoint. Wenders explains angel's presence in his latest film

Interview with Wim Wenders, June 2, 1988

Like many other European filmmakers, West German director Wim Wenders has a strong affection for the United States and its busy movie industry. He worked here for several years on such movies as *Hammett* [1982] and *Paris, Texas* [1984]. Now he's returned to his German roots in a prizewinning film called *Wings of Desire*, starring Bruno Ganz and Peter Falk. At last year's Cannes Film Festival, it earned Mr. Wenders the best-director award. It has just opened in the US to some of the strongest critical acclaim Wenders has received in a long while. The movie's unusual hero is a guardian angel named Damiel, who spends his time invisibly roaming West Berlin and giving silent comfort to the people he encounters.

When Wenders visited New York recently, I asked him about the movie's offbeat subject. He said he's been fascinated by the idea of angels since childhood. "I remember what I thought about angels as a kid," he began. "I really believed in them, and my favorite prayer was about angels. It involved seven angels, every night, that were supposed to be around me—next to me, above and below, left and right, and everywhere. I also remember that, as a kid, I sort of felt pity for them. I thought, how boring this must be. I thought they had to sing all the time. And they'd be watching me. I felt they couldn't really have much fun!"

The angel in *Wings of Desire* isn't exactly bored. But he loves human beings so much that his secret ambition is to be one of them. His decision becomes final when he falls in love with a woman. This indicates the high value that filmmaker Wenders puts on romantic love—which he feels is treated much too negatively by most movies today. "I had this in mind when I went to make this film," he reports. "I was really sick and tired of a certain notion—that there's no future, that nothing works anymore between men and women—which we've been fed now for a long time. So in a way, I wanted to make a very positive love story, and very optimistic, to give a counterimage to a current one that I really think is totally unproductive." An optimistic view of life— and especially of love—is a key ingredient in *Wings of Desire*. In some of Wenders' earlier films, from *The Goalie's Anxiety at the Penalty Kick* [1972] to *The American Friend* [1977], his attitude was less positive. But this changed when he decided to give his last movie—the family drama *Paris, Texas*—an ending with upbeat, family-reunion elements. Wenders says he was inspired by the positive energy this decision gave him. "I felt encouraged to try out this positive, optimistic energy," he says. "So in a strange way, I adopted optimism almost like a method—with the most amazing result for myself and for my life. The method turned out to become much more than that. I really can say now that I'm one of the great optimists I know! So it wasn't a method anymore. It became something fundamental and structural. I can work with that, and I certainly do believe in it."

Another mark of the positive energy in *Wings of Desire* is its strong element of humor. Much of this focuses on the American actor Peter Falk, who's best known for starring in the TV series *Columbo* and some of John Cassavetes' films. Falk appears to be playing himself in *Wings of Desire*—according to the plot, he's making a movie in Berlin, where he meets Damiel. But it turns out in the story that Falk is a former angel himself. Wenders chose him for this role because his movie and TV work is so well known throughout the world. "I found Peter Falk by deduction," the film-maker says. "The part demanded somebody who'd be known to a lot of people and would have an authority. You very soon find out that the persons known to everybody in the world are actors. Not so much artists, or painters—or politicians, who are certainly not former angels! People in China and in Iceland really have one thing in common, which is American movies and especially American TV series. So you realize you have to look among American actors for a former angel. I really liked Columbo very much. He had this very human, very warm, friendly, and strange presence. That was the only thing I watched with my parents and my brother and that we all liked really a lot. So I called [Falk] up. Luckily he had seen *Paris, Texas*, so he knew who I was. I said, 'We're making a movie. We're shooting already. I have the part of a former angel...' And two weeks later, he was there!"

Wings of Desire ends when Damiel and his new human friend declare their love for each other. It's the kind of moment that would begin most romantic stories, and *Wings of Desire* concludes with the words "to be continued."

"Now that I've started this love story, I think I'm going to go on," Wenders says. "I think I'm going to try and define something really optimistic, or at least an optimistic view of what the future can become. Even though it might not seem so likely that it's going to be all that great, I think it's still more productive—and more interesting—to imagine it better." He sees *Wings of Desire* as the start of a new phase in his career. In his English-language films, he says, he dealt with a kind of mood (restlessness) and subject matter (rootlessness) that had specifically American connotations for him. Now he feels he has exorcised his fascination with those issues and wants to deal with characters who have (or sincerely want) strong relationships with particular places. Yet, he points out, his Berlin-based production company is called Road Movies, and he still loves to explore the endless possibilities in the wide world around him.

Film focuses on possible mishandling of criminal case
Interview with Errol Morris, August 26, 1988

Cannes, France.

Late on a cold November evening in 1976, two Dallas police officers stopped a car that was traveling with its headlights out. Approaching the vehicle, officer Robert Wood was hit by five shots fired at point-blank range. The case stayed unsolved for several weeks, partly because the other officer failed to note the make or license number of the killer's automobile. Then investigators learned that a 16-year-old named David Harris had boasted to friends about killing a policeman. Harris was arrested, but shifted blame for the crime to Randall Adams, a hitchhiker he had met by chance on the day of the murder. Harris, who had a substantial criminal record, was cleared of guilt. Adams, who had no record, was convicted and sentenced to death. He is still in prison, his sentence converted to life imprisonment.

A filmmaker named Errol Morris believes Adams is innocent, however. Hoping to convince the world—or at least the Texas criminal-justice system—that he's right, he has made *The Thin Blue Line*, a new movie about the Adams case. Part documentary and part reenacted drama, it's an unconventional film with a clear message: that justice has gone astray, and it's not too late to set things right. "On one level," says Morris about his movie, "it's the story of a miscarriage of justice. On another level—at least I like to think of it as such—it's a story about self-delusion and fantasy."

As a person and as a filmmaker, Morris is not addicted to causes. Discussing his new picture with me at the Cannes Film Festival this spring, he spoke with mild distaste of what he calls "public-affairs documentaries," and indicated that he wants his own movies to deal with philosophical ideas as well as facts and events. "I've been asked whether I believe in the subjectivity of truth," Morris says, "and of course I don't at all... Robert Wood is dead. There's nothing subjective about that. And he was shot by somebody. There's nothing subjective about that." The way to reach an understanding of such a situation, he continues, is to examine every aspect of it with careful, thoroughgoing attention.

Morris' filmmaking career has followed an unusual course. A thoughtful man with degrees in history and philosophy, he became a director 10 years ago with *Gates of Heaven* [1978], a documentary about two California pet cemeteries. Three years later he completed *Vernon, Florida* [1981], a study of a rural

Southern town. Both consist primarily of interviews with ordinary people whom Morris met during the filmmaking process. *The Thin Blue Line* is a project that took Morris by surprise. Working temporarily as a private investigator in New York, where he lives with his wife and young son, he obtained funding to make a film on a subject that had long interested him: the career of James Grigson, a Texas psychiatrist whose frequent testimony in capital-punishment cases has earned him the nickname "Doctor Death" in law-enforcement circles. Morris traveled to Texas and began interviewing prisoners whose sentences had been influenced by Grigson's courtroom testimony. He felt uneasy about the enterprise, though, because it didn't mesh with his philosophy of filmmaking.

"I have a motto," he says: "Whatever film is, it's not social science. In my mind, all this had the aura—worse than that, the taint—of social science. And at that point, I was not interested at all in miscarriages of justice. I wasn't looking for innocent people in the Texas prisons." Morris then met Adams, who was serving his sentence for the Woods murder. "I didn't believe he was innocent," Morris recalls. "I was simply looking for four or five people to put on film in the context of this interview I had done with Dr. Grigson... But I started finding out more and more stuff about the Randall Adams case [and] learning an unending number of things about the 1977 trial that—in my opinion—made that trial a caricature of justice." Two things fascinated Morris about the Adams case. One was his growing conviction that Adams was innocent. The other was his curiosity about why he'd been convicted. What mistakes and misunderstandings, the filmmaker wondered, led to such an unfortunate result?

The interviews in *The Thin Blue Line* represent Morris' attempt to answer this question by interrogating people who played key roles in the case: witnesses to the crime, criminal-justice officials, and the men who were accused of the murder. Morris believes many of them were influenced at key moments—in their thoughts, their actions, or both—by misperceptions rooted in their social and personal backgrounds. An interest in such matters is a thread that runs through all of Morris' films. "I think all my films have been... solipsistic films, on one level," Morris says. "They're films about people lost in strange, private worlds of self-delusion and fantasy... They're about characters who are suspicious and desperate about what's 'out there' in the world." Another thread running through Morris' films is an unconventional visual style. Many documentary filmmakers like to give the appearance of working on the run, using grainy film and shaky camera movements. Morris takes an opposite approach, seating his interviewees right in front of the camera and inviting them to say anything they want. The interviewer's role, Morris believes, is to keep the subject talking—and nothing more. Of all the interviews he has conducted, the one he speaks of most proudly is a three-hour tape on which his own voice is never heard.

Morris uses his unconventional methods because they serve his purpose as an investigator, and also because he considers them an antidote to the showy techniques of some documentary filmmakers, who flaunt the rough-hewn qualities of their footage. "We associate that [rough-looking] style with truth-telling or with the documentary form," he says critically. "But it's a mere convention... The zooming of an image in and out, a shaky camera, people's nervousness on film—none of this means it's more truth-laden than anything else. I like to think I've taken the conventions of cinéma-vérité and stood them on their heads. The camera, rather than being unobtrusive, is overwhelmingly intrusive in a definite sense. The people in these films are performing for the camera. They know the camera's there; they're looking right at it!"

Edo de Waart's baton is in the service of all kinds of serious music. The fine art of re-creation
Interview with Edo de Waart, September 20, 1988

Some conductors like the classics best. Others favor romantic or contemporary composers. Edo de Waart is one of the rare conductors who seem equally at home in all parts of the repertoire. His favorite composer is Beethoven. Yet one of his latest recordings is of the opera *Nixon in China*, by John Adams, a young and experimental composer with whom de Waart has been associated for several years. De Waart is a cosmopolitan musician, dividing his time between the United States and the Netherlands, in addition to guest-conducting orchestras around the world. Originally from the Netherlands, he has served as music director of such organizations as the Rotterdam Philharmonic and the Netherlands Opera. He has a longtime association with the San Francisco Symphony, and more recently the Minnesota Orchestra, in the United States. His credits also include a long list of recordings and guest-conductor appearances in cities as varied as London, West Berlin, and Monte Carlo.

Discussing his work during a New York visit not long ago, he expressed his feeling that it's important for musicians to expose themselves — and their audiences — to music of all kinds and all periods of musical history, including contemporary works that may be unusual and unfamiliar. He calls himself a "re-creator" of music. "After all," he says, "I'm not writing the music. I'm just trying to get under the skin of the person who wrote it and understand why he or she wrote it." Within the domain of "re-creation," however, de Waart wants to cover the broadest possible domain of activity. "We need to be able to do it all," he says. "As performers, we should not be content just trying to do an even more polished and wonderfully thought-out performance of the Beethoven Violin Concerto. It's important that we go head-on into the encounter with our own time."

One challenge in conducting 20th-century music is the great difference between the styles of various modern composers. On one hand is the difficult and highly cerebral music of people like Arnold Schoenberg and Elliott Carter. On the other hand are simpler, deliberately repetitive pieces by Philip Glass and John Adams. De Waart says his job isn't to choose one over another but to interpret each of them as best he can. "I'm not in the profession of judging," he says. "I'm a performer. I feel a performer — almost like a photographer — should record not only what has been in the past, but what is going on in his own time. You show these pictures of the moment: This is now. Three years from now, John Adams might write something tremendously crusty… There are all kinds of possibilities. But we just record. We give it our everything: We rehearse them well; we play them with our whole hearts and leave time to judge it. And the critics!"

Of all the composers he's interpreted over the years, de Waart says he feels closest to Beethoven—because Beethoven's character, as expressed in music, sometimes reminds him of his own. "He changes moods within a split second," says the conductor, "from being extremely happy to being rather violently upset, to put it mildly. Some symphonies—the way he ends is like someone kicking the door behind him, just shouting the last sentence into the room and then going boom. Finished!" When interpreting a classical composer like Beethoven, de Waart works hard to re-create the kind of mood and atmosphere that conductors and audiences might have experienced when the music was new. He uses the opening of Beethoven's Third Symphony, the "Eroica," as an example, and the vividness of his description conveys the intensity of his feeling for the music. Beethoven jolted contemporaries "Can you imagine at his time," says de Waart, "what an incredible impression that must have made: these two incredible chords ripping through the hall, and people just jumping out of their seats. They had never heard anything like this! We listen to that symphony with our ears [attuned to] Mahler or Stravinsky's *Rite of Spring*, and to us it's just: 'Boom boom—yeah, that's nice.' But if you try to re-create and to think back to the people of that time—with their wigs on, they had just barely sat down and were probably not too interested. And they suddenly have this wild guy [Beethoven] walking up there, hardly looking at the audience. He turned around to the orchestra and banged his fist down, and you got these two monster chords! I think it's very important for us to try and recapture what that music meant at that time."

De Waart started his professional life as an oboist, but he quickly changed to a conducting career—which allowed him a more total involvement in the music he loved. "The physicalness of conducting is terrific," he says happily. "I always was very sporty. I ran a lot and always played soccer in the street. I can't sit still very well for a long time. So showing what you have to say through gestures comes very naturally. I guess I'm naturally bossy, too, and that helps!" he adds with a smile. "I just want to be totally involved—and a conductor is about as totally involved as you can get!"

Eastwood and *Bird*
Interview with Clint Eastwood, September 30, 1988

People think of Clint Eastwood as the toughest hombre in town.
Dirty Harry and the Man with No Name are his most famous
alter egos. His recent characters range from the hard-boiled cop
of *Tightrope* [1984] to the hard-bitten marine of *Heartbreak Ridge*
[1986]. But other Eastwood images get overlooked in such a list.
There's the gentle Eastwood of *Bronco Billy* [1980], the comical
Eastwood of *Every Which Way But Loose* [1978], and—most
important—the cinematically sophisticated Eastwood who has
built a widely respected career behind the camera. That's the Eastwood who shines in *Bird*, the new biopic on the life and times
of Charlie Parker, perhaps the greatest jazz musician who ever
lived—and a favorite of Mr. Eastwood ever since 1946, when he
first heard Parker play.

"It made a lasting impression," Mr. Eastwood told me during
an interview in Manhattan, where he came to attend the New York
Film Festival premiere of his new picture. "I was sort of overwhelmed." Leaning back in a comfortable sofa and talking one on
one about his career, Eastwood seems closer to the good-natured
Bronco Billy than to Dirty Harry Callahan or other supermacho
characters. *Bird*, which opens its theatrical run today, is only the
second film he's directed without appearing in. (It features Forest
Whitaker in the title role.) Yet no starring vehicle has given him
more satisfaction. What fascinates Eastwood most about Parker
are the contradictions in his personality. He says the film is about
"a man who could have a disappointment in his life... and become
disenchanted. But he could also go into a room and play 24 hours
a day, until he became the greatest alto saxophone player. He could
be very charismatic and sweet, and he could be mean and very
undisciplined. His excesses were enormous, but when it came to
his music, he switched into another kind of mode."

These contradictions appeal to Eastwood because his films
always strive to avoid easy characterizations and neat philosophies.
Bird, he says, "is an impressionistic piece. You give these various
portraits of the man, so the audience can draw its own conclusions." Eastwood paints a realistic portrait of Parker's excesses in
Bird, including his drug and alcohol problems, without sanitizing
or sensationalizing them. He didn't want to make a "propagandizing" antidrug movie, he asserts. But he feels an antidrug message
emerges from Parker's own sad experiences. "I'm trying to pay

tribute to a man and his artistry," the filmmaker says, "by telling about his life." But he adds, "I also want to pay tribute, some-where along the line, to all those fabulous musicians who lived a normal life. Just because a Bix Beiderbecke or a Charlie Parker—people who are considered brilliant—go off and do these [addic-tive] things, does that make them any better? Not really!' This is why bebop trumpeter Dizzy Gillespie emerges as an important and "normal" character in the picture. "He's sort of the conscience of the movie," Eastwood says with a pleased smile.

The most controversial aspect of *Bird* is likely to be its uncon-ventional structure. It's a memory-struck and almost dreamlike film that shifts its story lines and rhythms—as well as its sense of time and place—as freely as a jazz combo in a freewheeling jam session. "There is a more 'documentary' approach that I suppose would have been more normal," says Eastwood, "but this is more like a jazz tune—it's here and there.' Not that movie directors can improvise like jazz musicians; their medium is too cumbersome and costly for that. "You may get the feeling of improvisation," the director says, "but you can't just improvise. This film had to be very structured in order to make everything fit." How will movie-goers like this style? "People who don't mind impressionism will enjoy it," he predicts. "But people who like a literal, figurative drawing may say: What happened?" The important thing, he adds, is to shake people out of passively watching the screen and make them think about the movie's subject. "Hopefully [this approach] will stir the imagination," Eastwood says, "and people will come to conclusions on their own.'

This is a key part of Eastwood's filmmaking philosophy. He knows that many films, including his own, have social or even political undertones. He says he doesn't purposely choose a project because of such considerations, looking more to "story value" and other practical matters. "But maybe as a subconscious thing you think, 'I'd like to analyze that for the public.' You don't necessarily say what's right or wrong. You just give several points of view. I love the audience to work with you. Rather than be conde-scending or just give 'em a story with an ending, I love 'em to think about it." He also realizes that a picture must be entertaining if it's to reach an audience at all. His respect for Parker seems connected with Bird's ability to grab his listeners with the very first note. "He had a great impact on the audience," says Eastwood in awed tones, "without doing anything physically. He just sort of stood and played. But he had great charisma, and the music was so powerful.

It was aggressive. He just came out and took over, and everything was doubled up: He played at a much higher rate than anyone had ever played before, yet it all seemed to work out all right! He could be extremely tender on certain numbers, but he could also be really hot. It was some sort of ultimate confidence he had… It was just different.'

Eastwood says his directing style draws on his acting experience. "Being an actor has an advantage," he says, "because you know their securities and insecurities. You know how it feels to walk on a set and be introduced to someone you don't even know, to play a scene where you've been married for 35 years. By and large, it's up to the director to set a comfort zone to work in, so these people feel they can relax. It's a very insecure business, acting." Since making the thriller *Play Misty for Me* in 1971, Eastwood has directed 13 films. He has also appeared in many pictures by other directors. Now that he's equally at home on both sides of the camera, how does he choose which projects to direct and which "merely" to star in? "I have no answer for that," he says with a modest grin. "It's strictly whimsical. With a certain script, I'll see myself directing it. With another script, I won't." Directing a movie like *Bird* allowed him to combine his love for music with his love for film — and to stretch his filmmaking talent in new directions. Musing on this, he quotes "a good line" from *Magnum Force* [1973], one of his own movies: "You gotta know your limitations.' Then he quickly adds, "But you can't be afraid to expand your horizons, too. Don't ever be satisfied with limitations. Always push them to the wire."

Mira Nair: Interview with Indian director whose new film stars street children from Bombay

Interview with Mira Nair, October 12, 1988

"I really, firmly believe that truth is stranger than fiction," says film-maker Mira Nair, whose new movie is an unusual combination of fictional and real-life elements. It's called *Salaam Bombay!* and it's an international film in the fullest sense—shot in Bombay by an Indian-born director who discovered filmmaking while at Harvard University and now lives in New York. Nominally an Indian production, it was financed with money from British and French television as well as the Indian Film Development Corporation and Nair's own Indian-American production company. The picture began its American theatrical run on Sunday, but it's already a hit on the festival circuit—winning prizes in Cannes and Montreal and scoring big with audiences at the noncompetitive Telluride and New York filmfests. I interviewed Nair between screenings in Telluride, where the fresh Rocky Mountain breezes seemed as congenial to her as the bustle she's used to in Bombay and Manhattan.

Salaam Bombay! tells the story of Chaipau, a 10-year-old boy who is forced to struggle for a living in the teeming streets of Bombay after his parents oust him from their home. It's not a gentle film, as Chaipau gets drawn into a sordid world of hustlers, prostitutes, and other low-life characters. He never loses his spirit, though, and ultimately the film can be seen as an affirmation of his resilience and resourcefulness. "I'm really interested in people living on the edge," says Nair, whose previous films are docu-mentaries on such topics as street life in Old Delhi and the use of high-tech medical procedures to accommodate traditional Indian preferences for male children. "I'm interested in marginal people," she continues in her lightly accented English, "or people who are considered marginal. I think that's because... I'm interested in capturing the complexity of people and the complexity of life."

After making four documentaries, Nair turned to fiction because she wanted "a lot more control over gesture and drama and faces" in her work.

At the same time, however, she was determined "to create the unpredictability of life," especially "the gray area that makes us all what we are, and not the 'blacks and whites' and 'goods and bads' that cinema is often relegated to. *Salaam Bombay!* was an effort to have that control and yet be open to the inspiration of documentary.

Nair came up with the idea for *Salaam Bombay!* about five years ago. "I was just struck by the spirit of the kids I used to see on every street corner," she recalls. "I knew that if I were ever to make this film, I would use the kids from the street. It couldn't be made with any other children—primarily because the inspiration that came from them was their spirit, their will to live in a situation where they had been given nothing but life. They really lived it, with a flamboyance that was very striking to me. Also, their faces and bodies were a kind of map of the journey that they had traveled. They had wisdom and childlikeness at the same time."

The project started when two of Nair's assistants "walked the streets of the inner city and spoke to a lot of children in the centers where they hang out—on bridges and platforms and so forth. [The assistants] were both women, and they said we were going to do a workshop on [children's] lives. It was purposely vague. They kept going back to the kids, and the kids got intrigued." The workshop took place in a small inner-city church. About 130 children showed up on the first day, and the filmmakers chose 24 of them—aged 7 to 18—for the activity. "We worked with those 24 for seven weeks, six days a week," Nair reports. "It was very disciplined, and yet a lot of fun... Basically it was an amalgamation of physical exercise, mime, dance, and improvisation." Later in the workshop, "as we got close to each other," attention turned to "themes that were important to the children—be it running away, or sex, or gangs, or violence, or your first day in Bombay. The kids really got used to us, and us to them.' Not until the fourth week did Nair bring up the film itself. "We brought in a video camera and spoke about the film and the story," she says. "And we introduced the idea of un-teaching them their notions of acting, which are totally fed to them by Indian cinema—an overblown, declamatory style." Working with the children was "a very careful and slow process," but it was also a successful one. "By the beginning of shooting, the children were the least of my problems!" Nair says, smiling.

Nair's sense of commitment to the children of *Salaam Bombay!* runs very deep—to the point where she was reluctant to "abandon" them after filming was completed. "We know this is a real responsibility," she says, speaking of her decision to draw street children into a specialized—and temporary—artistic project

"My assistant director, who's a child psychologist, has worked with the kids full-time since shooting," she continues. "Our attitude was not to give them any illusions: that we were going to be their mothers forever, or anything of the sort. Our whole attitude was to meet them halfway and help them realize their own self-worth and dignity—not to 'reform' them, or change them, or get them off the street, or any of that artificial stuff, because it really was too short a term. We said we realized they had come so far, and [after filming was over] we wanted to help them create opportunities they want for themselves. Some kids knew what they wanted: Some are now in school; some have gone home to their villages; some are doing jobs. And some are still on the streets." Nair is taking her responsibility a big step further, as well—committing money from the film itself to the well-being of Bombay's youngsters. "Now that the film is successful and there's a possibility we can make money from it," she explains, "we've set up a Salaam Bombay Trust, which is going to create a learning center for street children. It will open in November in Bombay and also in Delhi. We're using benefits and premieres in India to finance this. So it'll be totally self-financed by the movie, and I hope it'll be permanent."

A rare thing in the commercialized movie world, this willingness to make an altruistic commitment springs from the same interest and concern that led Nair to conceive *Salaam Bombay!* in the first place. "It's amazing how many kids like this exist," she says thoughtfully. "They've become almost invisible in India; when you see so many, they become invisible. It's like the way materialism—how much people want to own—is invisible in the United States. It's so normal, so natural, that you stop thinking how absurd it is."

Ophuls: Nazi period is his specialty
Interview with Marcel Ophuls, November 17, 1988

From the moment it appeared at the Cannes Film Festival earlier this year, *Hotel Terminus: The Life and Times of Klaus Barbie* has been one of the most celebrated documentaries in recent memory. Running about 4 hours, it focuses on a former Nazi who was convicted of war crimes—the killing and deportation of victims numbering in the thousands—and sentenced to life imprisonment in France last year. The picture was produced and directed by Marcel Ophuls, a renowned filmmaker who's made the Nazi period his specialty—although he's also made a film on problems in Northern Ireland and even, years ago, a French comedy with Jeanne Moreau.

Although he's best known for his exhaustive accounts of the Nazi era, Mr. Ophuls in person is an easygoing man with a healthy sense of humor—and irony—about his career. He says he'd love to make regular entertainment movies, if only someone in Hollywood would hire him. He even speaks of his massive documentaries in terms of "show business," and says he'd like to be more than just "the *Sorrow and the Pity* man" to movie audiences. That's a half-joking reference to his first major film, *The Sorrow and the Pity* [1969], about collaboration between French citizens and Nazis during Germany's occupation of France. Yet the subjects of Nazism and World War II evidently have an endless fascination for Ophuls, whose filmography includes not only *The Sorrow and the Pity* but also *The Memory of Justice* [1976], a 4-hour examination of the Nuremberg war-crimes trials.

Hotel Terminus finds him immersed as deeply as ever in similar issues. As its subtitle indicates, it centers on Klaus Barbie's role in the unspeakably sad chronicle of Nazi atrocities. Yet it goes way beyond the career of this particular war criminal, revealing the thoughts and feelings of many people whose lives were affected by his. It also asks whether, this long after the fact, the Holocaust is still a relevant subject for most people. In one of the film's many poignant interviews, Ophuls asks Elizabeth Holtzman, a New York City district attorney and social activist, whether "only Jews and old Nazis are still interested in Jews and old Nazis." She replies that the issue of Nazi war criminals—and their role in postwar American history—first came to her attention through the efforts of a non-Jew who was "horrified, as a human being, that... our [American] government could protect Nazi war criminals living here and allow them to stay here." This reflects Ophuls' own view and his special interest in links between Barbie and the US government.

Moviegoers who see *Hotel Terminus* frequently comment on two unexpected omissions. One is the absence of "atrocity footage" showing graphic evidence of the torture, degradation, and misery that took place in concentration camps and other Nazi strongholds. Ophuls deliberately left out such material on the ground that audiences have become inured to it through earlier Holocaust movies. He is also aware that Claude Lanzmann's epic *Shoah* [1985], a film that deals specifically with the effects of Nazism on European Jewry, similarly relies on newly filmed interviews rather than archival footage from the Holocaust itself. Also missing from *Hotel Terminus* is a prolonged look at Barbie, who is seen in the film for only a few scattered moments. This is partly because he avoided the public spotlight for much of his life. But it's also because Ophuls had no particular interest in Barbie—or, by this stage in his filmmaking career, in the Nazi phenomenon— when he started work on the project. Rather, he was interested in things about Barbie—especially the way such a monster was able to move and operate far beyond the sphere of Hitler's activities, even receiving aid from the United States government at one point in his life. Beyond this, Ophuls wanted to attack an even larger subject that he sums up in one word: networks. *Hotel Terminus*, he explains, is about "networks of complicities" between those branded as war criminals and others who have—wittingly or not—allowed their crimes to be perpetrated. This is, according to Ophuls, "the underbelly of modern conscience." Exploring it through film, he says, was an attempt to pinpoint "the link that Barbie provides between National Socialism and the Thousand-Year Reich and modern cynicism."

Ophuls had his own first encounter with Nazism when he was still a child and his Jewish family fled from Germany to France. During the Nazi occupation there, his father—Max Ophuls, a renowned movie director—moved the family again, to the United States. Marcel attended Hollywood High School in California, then served in Japan with the US Army. Later he returned home and went into the film industry like his father before him. After two previous films on the Nazi period, Ophuls would never have begun *Hotel Terminus* unless something about its subject had an urgency for him beyond historical importance alone. What drew him into the project was a conviction that Nazi immorality isn't buried in the past but still reverberates in today's world. This is why he brought interviews with Holocaust survivors into the dense and complex fabric of *Hotel Terminus*.

"The victims and survivors of Barbie's crimes are there," says Ophuls about his film, "to remind us... how ludicrous and how far removed from any kind of moral reality the [Nazis] were. And how far the world we live in is removed from rational, moral reality. And how much further we're getting from it. I think Barbie—and his career, and the way he was able to swim in cosmopolitan waters—is a classic example of that. And a very rare example, because usually they don't get caught; or they don't get caught that late [in their careers]; or they don't get caught in the limelight."

Hotel Terminus deals not only with Barbie's victims, but also with those who worked with him. Through on-screen interviews, the film tells how the American government employed him after World War II, and how he then lived comfortably in Bolivia for many years. To document these and other points, Ophuls filmed more than 120 hours of interviews that were ultimately whittled down to the "mere" 4-hour running time of *Hotel Terminus*. Ophuls says he could have made the film shorter by using a so-called omniscient or "voice-of-God" narrator. But he says movies with narrators manipulate their audiences. He's against this, and he quotes an old Hollywood picture to make his point. "It's what has given documentaries a bad reputation," he says about moviemaking with voice-over narration. It's gray, and it's too easy to do... It's illustrated editorials. It also lends itself to propaganda in wartime, and to the legitimizing of all kinds of 'isms.' As Lionel Barrymore said in *You Can't Take It With You* [Frank Capra, 1938], I don't like the 'isms.' I don't like voice-of-God commentary because I don't like ideology!"

Vanessa Redgrave: as Dazzling as Ever
Interview with Vanessa Redgrave, September 21, 1995

A Month by the Lake takes place on the shores of Lake Como, framed by exquisite Italian landscapes from beginning to end. This setting provides spirited competition for the film's performances, but the best of them shine brightly over their luminous surroundings. None is more dazzling than that of Vanessa Redgrave, clearly having a marvelous time in one of the frothiest pictures of her career. A review of Redgrave's screen credits—from *Blow-Up* [Michelangelo Antonioni, 1966] and *Julia* [Fred Zinnemann, 1977] to *Howards End* [James Ivory, 1992] and *Prick Up Your Ears* [Sephen Frears, 1987], among many others—provides a quick reminder that she's always been more celebrated for serious drama than for effervescent romance. Her versatility is as strong as her talent, though, and in a recent interview she told me she thoroughly enjoyed her plunge into sunstruck comedy. Films with a comic bent "have not been my speciality," she acknowledges. But she quickly adds that she considers herself "the kind of actress who can respond totally to a situation. If the subject contains a good deal of joy and merriment... you have a completely different mood than you do with another kind of subject. "It's a common phenomenon for actors that something in which you can be light of heart, which makes you light of heart, and which you hope will make an audience light of heart, gives you a completely different feeling as you work."

None of which means that filming *A Month by the Lake* was more a carefree vacation than a professional challenge. "It's just as hard to make something that is light of heart," Redgrave says, echoing many performers who have named comedy as one of the most difficult acting chores. "Your moods are affected, but just as much work goes into it." Redgrave has kept up a busy cinematic schedule lately, appearing in movies as different as the mournful *The Ballad of the Sad Café* [Simon Callow, 1991], the colorful *The House of the Spirits* [Bille August, 1993], and the gritty *Little Odessa* [James Gray, 1994] in recent times. But she also remains active in stage work, as an actress and a key figure behind the Moving Theater, a British acting company that hopes to make its American debut next year. "I think it's terribly important for actors to be able to do both film and plays," she says. Redgrave laments the fact that current political and economic trends are making this more difficult by cutting the resources of stage companies even in her native England, which has a stronger tradition of subsidized theater than the United States does. "I think I'm the only person I've ever heard say such a thing," she continues, "but I feel very strongly that a major source of my development as a theater actress has come from work in cinema, and not the other way round. Film requires living in the moment and creating in the moment, whatever that moment is—and doing it out of chronology, since films are made in the editing, not in the linear sequence of a classical play... For all of life's contradictions, the cinema is ace at showing it as it really happens."

Redgrave also puts a high value on the human interactions that are integral to good ensemble work. "Every day you're working with actors who are one day older," she says. "Your director is one day older, and you yourself are one day older. You've changed, however unapparent that might be. Since your starting point has to be who you're with, not 'me and my part,' there's a synthesis with the script, which has a life of its own anyway. Then the play and characters begin to emerge of their own accord, as it were—to have a life bigger than all the thoughts of the director and the actors combined." Redgrave takes an unusual position on the much-debated question of which acting style gives better results—the Method approach of drawing on one's internal emotions, or the "external" technique based on outward appearances. "They are two different approaches," the actress says, "but they can arrive at the same place. Some actors distinctly work one way or the other, and some would die rather than actually feel what they act feeling. I work dialectically, from out to in and from in to out, at the same time." In a similar vein, Redgrave prefers not to choose between "intellectual" and "intuitive" ways of preparing a role. "I tend to put in a lot of intellectual work," she says, "although sometimes I don't need to, or don't think I need to." To illustrate her thinking on this subject, she cites an early stage role that she approached on a "purely intuitive" level. Even though she acted "without thinking it through," she spent a large amount of time writing diaries that reflected the thoughts and experiences of her character "so I could see in my mind's eye all [the character's] life, not just the particular scenes that were in the play. This didn't change any of my actions or impulses, but it nevertheless deepened the work."

In past years, Redgrave has sometimes made more news for her fearlessly voiced political opinions than for her purely professional activities. While the press has lately paid less attention to this facet of her life, she remains heartily concerned with world events and shows a detailed knowledge of current situations—most notably the war in former Yugoslavia—that trouble her. She's as outspoken as ever, she insists, even if journalists have eased off their coverage of what she says. Still, it's clear that the core of her life remains her work as an actress. "Having got to the age I am," she says with a smile, "I still absolutely love the theater, I love cinema, and I love the work of performing, investigating, developing productions. I haven't lost any of my enthusiasm whatsoever. In fact, I've probably got more than I ever had."

The Personal Is Political for a Chinese Director
Interview with Zhang Yimou, January 24, 1996

When movies are at issue, China's government has a remarkable talent for embarrassing itself in public. And the country's most renowned filmmaker, Zhang Yimou, is often the figure at the center of the storm. The most recent incident was touched off when Zhang's old-fashioned mobster epic, *Shanghai Triad* [1995], was selected by the New York Film Festival for its coveted opening-night slot. Angered by the presence of a completely unrelated movie in the festival—a documentary called *The Gate of Heavenly Peace* [Richard Gordon and Carma Hinton, 1995], about China's democracy movement—the Chinese authorities revoked permission for Zhang to attend the gala screening of his film.

The result: more press coverage for *Shanghai Triad*, for Zhang himself, and for the documentary than would ever have happened otherwise.

Something similar happened when China kept Zhang from the Cannes Film Festival two years ago. His drama *To Live* [1994] was being honored with a slot in the official competition, irking authorities who found the movie too critical in its view of recent Chinese history. A press conference for the director went forward as planned—with a conspicuously empty seat at center stage, reminding the world that a towering artist would have been present if not for governmental petulance. *To Live* is still unreleased in China. And fans in the United States still remember when Chinese authorities tried to have Zhang's brilliant *Ju Dou* [1990] yanked from the Academy Awards race, simply because the film's sardonic melodrama struck them as too downbeat for international consumption.

Zhang didn't make it to New York in 1995, but he did make it to Cannes in May, and I seized the opportunity to continue an intermittent dialogue I've had with him since our first meeting eight years ago. Meeting with a handful of journalists on a sunny balcony of the Grand Hotel, he proved as outgoing and articulate as ever. Unlike most of his previous pictures, beginning with the rowdy *Red Sorghum* [1988] and continuing through works like the elegant *Raise the Red Lantern* [1991] and the ironic *Story of Qiu Ju* [1992], the new *Shanghai Triad* is a straightforward genre piece with few subtexts or complexities. Set in Shanghai during the 1930s, it centers on a teenage boy who becomes the servant of a *Godfather*-type crime boss and his mistress, a brassy cabaret singer. "There's not much politics in this film," Zhang acknowledged through an interpreter. "To be honest, after the *To Live* incident, I am a bit tired."

Still, the picture does make implicit comments on the current state of Chinese life through its portrait of Shanghai's excesses some 60 years ago. "In its depiction of the world the boy enters," Zhang explains, "the film has parallels with today's China—in terms of how materialistic society has become, and how this influences people's views of money and [their] chase after material goods, and how this affects human relations... If you go to China today and talk to people, they'll be telling you [only] how they want to make money and improve their livelihoods. We want to convey that in the movie." To carry this message, Zhang selected the *Godfather* genre rather than a format that might appear more neutral. The choice suggests that his views of current Chinese trends are not optimistic, and his conversation bears this out. "I think the country will become more and more materialistic," he says. "We're heading in that direction. I'm interested in asking the question: As our livelihood improves, how can we maintain our more human side? From this point of view, one can say [the film] is somewhat political."

Another timely issue raised by *Shanghai Triad* is that of violence—on the screen and in the world. "In the 2,000 years of [Chinese] history," Zhang says when asked about this, "there are many cruel tales of violence. It doesn't exist just today, or in the last 100 years. In the vision of [former Chinese leader Mao Zedong], violence is normal... Power struggle [in China] has been a normal way of power transition—to eliminate the enemy physically. In today's Chinese cities, this question keeps popping up—whether to eliminate one's enemy physically." All of which has led Zhang to a strong reaction against violence in his life and work, including *Shanghai Triad*, which contains some mayhem but treats it with more restraint than one finds in typical Hollywood productions. "I am someone who abhors violence," he says with conviction. "There's not much gangster violence in my own experience, but as I was growing up there was a lot of violence connected with politics... which turned family members against each other. I saw people beaten up for political reasons, and my family has repeatedly been struggled against. All this made an impression on me... I keep thinking about why violence exists in such a way, to tear people apart."

Zhang is also fascinated by the stories he's heard about real mobsters of the 1920s and '30s, whose activities went beyond the realm of crime and into the political arena. "My intention in the film is not to depict organized crime coming to China," he explains, "or how violence exists in gangster movies. I'm interested in violence and human relations—how violence affects the humanity behind the characters." These thoughts helped motivate Zhang's treatment of the gangster's girlfriend. She enjoys a superficially easy life but knows she can't trust any of the dangerous men who hover around her. Eventually she confides in a woman she meets when the gang is in hiding, and she starts to grow closer to the young boy at the center of the story. "They're not from the same class position," Zhang notes, "but there's the beginning of a relationship between them. What my movie wants to say is that it's important to build up understanding between people, to get rid of hostility and opposition." If such understandings do come about and flourish, the result could be an improvement in Chinese life. "I think the Chinese people have been thinking about this issue," Zhang says of social conflict and violence, "and are heading toward a more liberal answer. I think China will take some time to become a more liberal society, however, and it won't be as simple as Westerners might think, because [the nation] is carrying a big [historical] burden."

The character of the girlfriend is played by Gong Li, who has starred in all of Zhang's major films. She was also widely praised in 1993 for her work in the popular *Farewell My Concubine* [1993], directed by Chen Kaige, another member of the Fifth Generation group that revitalized Chinese cinema after the tumultuous Cultural Revolution period. Gong and Zhang ended their long-term personal relationship while *Shanghai Triad* was in production, and some observers feared this bad "chemistry" might sour the movie. But happily, most critics have applauded her for yet another rich performance, reconfirming her as one of today's most versatile actresses. "She is a very good actress," Zhang enthusiastically agrees. "We have a very successful collaboration, and without her, many of my movies would not be so good." Accordingly, he seems open to the idea of future teamwork with her.

"Any good director likes to work with a good actress," he says. "There's a Chinese saying: As long as there's the right time element and the right people are together, anything is possible."

Sensitive *Secrets & Lies* Reflects Creative Journey
Interview with Mike Leigh, September 27, 1996

Telluride, Colorado.

Mike Leigh is on a roll. His new movie, *Secrets & Lies*, is coming to American theaters after opening at the prestigious New York Film Festival and winning the highest prize at this year's Cannes filmfest, where it also earned the best-actress award for Brenda Blethyn. His previous picture, *Naked* [1993], did almost as well at Cannes, garnering the best-director prize for Leigh and best-actor honors for David Thewlis, before arriving in theaters in a blaze of debate over its searing story of wasted lives in contemporary England. Leigh's reputation soared when *Naked* became one of this decade's most talked-about British movies, and *Secrets & Lies* should boost his fortunes even more as audiences experience its sensitive story, superb performances, and compassionate approach to a potentially troubling subject. Leigh paved the way for its US debut at Colorado's respected Telluride Film Festival, where he was the recipient of a special tribute in celebration of his career, still going strong after a quarter of a century.

Secrets & Lies centers on Hortense (Marianne Jean-Baptiste), a young woman who was adopted as a baby and now wants to meet her biological mother. Her search doesn't take long, and it leads to some major surprises. Hortense is black, well educated, and a solid member of the middle class. By contrast, her mother, Cynthia (Brenda Blethyn), is white, meagerly educated, and firmly rooted in the working class. The women circle around each other warily at first, then grow into a warm and companionable friendship—which raises the question of how they'll break all this to Cynthia's family, which has no idea this member of the clan has ever existed.

Like all of Leigh's movies, *Secrets & Lies* was a fully collaborative project in which everyone from technicians to stars made meaningful contributions. Key members of his process are the performers. They invented their own characters and dialogue in conjunction with Leigh, who jotted down the sketchy screenplay only after five months of discussion, consultation, and improvisation with his cast. "Filmmaking is very much a creative journey that involves all of the craftspeople involved," he said in a Telluride interview, acknowledging that he embarks on each movie with only the "vaguest notion" of what it will eventually be about. "It's a question of getting together with a group of people... and discovering what the film is by making it," he added. "That consists of inventing the characters, creating their whole lives, doing a huge amount of discussion and research, and most particularly a vast amount of improvisation with the actors... going through the years of relationships, living through things, and arriving at a point— very much under my control—where [we have] the dramatic premise."

Leigh got "hooked" on movies as a child and made an early decision to become a filmmaker. "For a kid in Manchester in the 1950s," he recalls, "this was about the most unfeasible thing one could possibly think of, as I was repeatedly told." But he stuck to his plan, entered London's renowned Royal Academy of Dramatic Arts in 1960, and "acted in very bad movies" as a way of entering the cinema scene. He directed his first full-length film, the darkly comic *Bleak Moments* [1971], in the early 1970s, with backing from actor Albert Finney.

Since most movies are developed in a very different way— with performers memorizing their lines from a completely written script—how did Leigh hit upon his improvisatory method? "In the '60s," he replies, "there were all kinds of things floating about in the air... All of us who started to do things {then} grew up in a period of great repression and restraint, and we started to kick over the traces and question [established] ways of doing things." Among his inspirations were John Cassavetes' offbeat film *Shadows* [1958], the New Wave filmmakers in France, and Peter Brook's productions with the Royal Shakespeare Company, most notably of Peter Weiss' seminal drama *Marat/Sade* [1967].

Leigh is often pegged as a political filmmaker, since his movies often deal—directly or indirectly—with the problems of very real people living under very challenging conditions. He accepts the "political" label, but only with qualifications. "I don't do films that are agenda-driven," he insists, "and I don't do work that is... propagandist. But nevertheless, what I do is kind of political, in the sense that my characters are always identifiable, and I instinctively draw them in their social and economic contexts." Despite this, Leigh ironically notes, some observers have criticized him for not being more aggressive in the political arena. Since his movies have always told straightforward stories with recognizable characters, he had a "bad time" during much of the '70s because "this was unfashionable. People said it was a bit decadent, old-fashioned, square. It didn't look avant-garde, it wasn't abstract or surreal enough... I said I wasn't concerned with that. The art was there, and I didn't want to advertise it!"

In the end, Leigh says, his definition of "a political act" is "just to share with other people things that you feel, in a way that makes them feel in some way. What I'm concerned with is the way we live our lives, and what politics should be concerned with is the way we live our lives, and what our lives are about. It's terribly important there are filmmakers whose films have very direct, specific, political objectives, and it's terribly important that those films work and cause changes to happen... but I don't make films of that kind. I make films where I don't leave you clearly able to conclude what I'm asking you to think or feel. I make films that ask a great number of questions but... don't come up with too many answers. And I hope I make films where you walk away from the [theater] with work to do, arguments to have, things to worry about, things to care about. In that sense, I would regard what I do as political."

Director Ken Loach: Voice for More Than Popcorn and Profits
Interview with Ken Loach, July 2, 1998

World-renowned filmmaker Ken Loach has devoted his career to exploring serious cultural and political issues. But some things are even more urgent—so he wouldn't be available for his interview until the World Cup soccer match was over and he'd had a chance to digest the results! It's good to know that Loach has a hearty appreciation for the simple pleasures as well as the pressing problems of contemporary life, and the same good-humored personality shines through his answer to the interview's first question. Does he view himself the way many critics do, as one of today's most socially and politically conscious movie directors? "I wouldn't disagree," he replies. "But if you say that out loud, people leave the theater in droves."

Keeping moviegoers entertained hasn't been as much of a problem for Loach as he mischievously suggests. Although he has never approached Steven Spielberg or George Lucas in mass appeal, he has built an international following over the past 30 years with historical epics like *Land and Freedom* [1995], political thrillers like *Hidden Agenda* [1990], and heart-wrenching family tales like *Raining Stones* [1993] and *Ladybird Ladybird* [1994]. His latest picture, *My Name Is Joe*, won the best-actor prize at Cannes for star Peter Mullan, who plays a recovering alcoholic in love with a social worker. His previous movie, *Carla's Song* [1996], is now enticing American audiences with its unpredictable story of a quiet bus driver and a troubled Nicaraguan refugee.

Loach began his career in British television, where he pioneered the use of lightweight equipment that allowed off-the-cuff filming in actual locations. "When you film in the streets," he explains, "you film what people are actually doing, what their situation is, what their plight is. And that turns into 'social drama,' which is a leaden-footed term for simply the lives that people are living." Given the built-in fascination of reality-based subjects, why don't serious films sell as many tickets as special-effects blockbusters? "It's because the cinema has always seen itself simply as a branch of the fairground," Loach answers, "and this has limited the options of what it can be. Films could have a range as diverse as any library, but what you actually have is like a roomful of popular novels. Cinema has mainly been about making commodities, not communications."

Unlike pundits who accuse the mass media of a liberal bias, Loach sees movie politics the other way around. "The majority of films have a right-wing subtext," he says. "The individual with a gun, the lone rider, the solo heroic figure who takes on everybody—this is basically a very right-wing concept." He feels his own movies "pull a little bit in the opposite direction," suggesting that people may be able to solve their problems through collective courage and cooperation. Loach believes thoughtful, constructive movies can affect society for the better since "they contribute to what's in people's minds, and to the overall cultural climate." He also believes Hollywood's barrage of "fairground" movies can have less-helpful results. "I'm sure there's a negative effect from the delight in violence, the exploitative nature of relationships, the exploitative nature of feelings," he says. "What seems to characterize commercial cinema is a mixture of violence and sentimentality, and I think those two [things] are related. What's real [in human values] is compassion and understanding and intolerance of cruelty. If filmmakers indulge violence—putting it into slow motion and all that—they can't at the same time explore relationships or emotions. The only feeling this leaves you space for is a sort of crass sentimentality, souped up with music and so on. The kind of films that do this must contribute to a kind of cynicism, a coarsening of sensibilities."

Simplistic spectacles also hurt our capacity for sustained attention. "It's terrible if people can't follow a chain of thought because they've got a button that zaps them to the next channel," Loach says. "That seriously disrupts their capacity to follow a point through, or to think, or just to lead their lives at a pace that's human. Entertainment has become a constant bombardment of images." One outcome of this trend is the dehumanization of movie characters. "The sense of sharing something with the characters tends to be lost," he says. "People become objects, and objects of derision, and something you can keep at arm's length without caring whether they get their heads blown off in slow motion." Loach says this problem "came home" to him and his colleagues when they showed *Carla's Song* in the Nicaraguan village where much of it was shot. "The fact that [villagers] saw themselves on screen, and recognized themselves and their place and their own experiences, was a transforming experience," he recalls with a warm smile. "It made you realize that films should do this. Film is a way of holding the mirror up to nature— reflecting it, reflecting on it—and that's very exciting. The idea of the audience as real, not just something to exploit for money and popcorn, is what films could be about."

Innovator sees the creative amid the crass
Interview with David Byrne, September 17, 1999

Filmmakers and rock stars have formed some interesting partnerships, but few rock-concert movies have achieved classic status. Near the top of anyone's list is *Stop Making Sense*, the Talking Heads extravaganza directed in 1984 by Jonathan Demme, whose nonmusical pictures range from *Something Wild* [1986] to *The Silence of the Lambs* [1991]. Despite its great success with pop-music fans, *Stop Making Sense* has been out of circulation on both film and video for several years. Now it's back, in freshly restored prints nursed into mint condition by a team of skilled technicians. Its theatrical run begins this week, to be followed by release on DVD and videocassette. *Stop Making Sense* is celebrated partly for its collection of Talking Heads hits, such as "Once in a Lifetime" and "Burning Down the House," and partly for its creative approach to the concert-film format. Unlike most pictures in this genre, it focuses almost entirely on the band's performance, avoiding offstage interviews and providing only a handful of the excited-audience shots that most such movies thrive on.

Looking back on the film's production during a recent interview in his Manhattan office, Talking Heads leader David Byrne gave much of the credit for these innovations to Demme, even though Byrne himself designed the concert documented by the movie. "This particular show was kind of cinematic from the beginning," he says. "It has an arc. It starts with an empty stage, and during the first half [of the concert] the visual elements of the show are assembled onstage… and in the second half, those elements are put to use. There's also a psychological arc in my performance: It's the story of an uptight guy who's eventually shaken loose by all these rhythms. There's kind of a narrative… This is different from a lot of concert movies, which are basically one song after another… with no overall structure." Demme's great contribution was to recognize these arcs—even before Byrne himself was fully aware of them—and use them to shape the movie. "In my blinkered way," Byrne recalls, "I was thinking more about the staging and lighting and music, and not realizing that it's also a collection of human beings up there. But one of Jonathan's strengths as a director is that he manages to find the interesting human quirks in his characters. He saw this concert that way—as an ensemble piece of different individuals."

Ironically, the popularity of "*Stop Making Sense* had a very mixed impact on Talking Heads, which disbanded about four years after the movie's premiere. "In some ways, it was wonderful," says Byrne of the film's success. "It got the band to places we'd never gotten to before... and it cemented our reputation very nicely. But in other ways, it was kind of devastating. We hardly toured anymore. How do you compete with something like this? The answer is you can't, so you have to use it as a way of liberating yourself to do something completely different—which I eventually did when I went out [in concerts] with a Latin band." Byrne sees the heyday of Talking Heads in the '70s and '80s as a healthy period, when rock musicians could think about creativity as well as commercialism. "We never had lots of hits," he muses. "We were the sort of band that did what we wanted to do, and occasionally a song would connect with the public at large. We knew that a certain amount of our sensibility overlapped with the general public's sensibility, and occasionally we would tread into that area... I like music when I have a sense of the integrity of the people making it. Today everything's turned upside down, and it's a matter of pride to sell your song as a car commercial. But we felt that was a sign of selling out."

Looking at the current pop scene, Byrne laments that "a lot of the vocabulary of rock has become the thing it set out to overthrow. It's become a formula." But he still sees "a healthy percentage of experimenters who are messing around with music," finding new uses for "the driving rhythmic base" that gives rock its undying energy. "There's nothing wrong with [virtuosity] per se," he says, when asked if some musicians value expertise over expression, "but it's an easy substitute for having something to say. Sometimes a rapper, or a person with a sampler or a turntable, expresses something profound and moving with a very limited technical vocabulary. And it may be the limited vocabulary that makes him focus on what's most important for him to say."

Byrne is a many-faceted artist with serious interests in film-making (he directed *True Stories* in 1986) and painting. He also runs the Luaka Bop record label, which blends international influences with rock music. Yet today as in the past, he says, "music occupies a pretty big chunk of my time. I'm pretty passionate. That's the nature of music—it can arouse passions and frenzy. You don't see people screaming and yelling in front of a painting very often. I like to work in other areas, too, since I can't express everything I'm interested in through the kind of music that I'm able to do. Music can transport people, though, and I've never gotten tired of that."

Kidman revels in risky film choices
Interview with Nicole Kidman, May 25, 2001

She's standing alone in a corner of a Cap d'Antibes hotel room, a few miles from the Cannes filmfest where her latest movie, *Moulin Rouge*, had its world premiere two days before. And you know in an instant that Nicole Kidman is a movie star. Maybe it's her modest but radiant smile, or the elegant way she wears her casual clothes, or her self-assured friendliness as she greets the small group of journalists who've come to make her acquaintance and ask about her new picture. You also know there's nothing phony about her pleasure in being at Cannes, meeting new people, or talking about her work. In an age of hype and pretense, she's clearly genuine. She's also cool under fire, since *Moulin Rouge* got decidedly mixed responses here. One newspaper printed a summary of reviews including phrases like "dripping in camp" and "a complete load of rubbish." What does Kidman think? It's hard for her to be objective after spending 192 days before the camera, undergoing two on-set injuries and now helping to publicize the picture. But she seems to admire it as much as the most enthusiastic critics, like the French reviewer who called it a "fabulous ode to showmanship."

Kidman certainly has her career — and her image — in perspective. Asked about director Baz Luhrmann's description of her as a "screen goddess," she chuckles over this typical bit of Hollywood hyperbole, noting that Luhrmann has been cultivating this notion as part of his strategy for promoting the movie. "You can't take yourself too seriously," she adds, explaining how she maintains a balanced view of herself and her work. "You need to be able to laugh at yourself, and I enjoy people who are little off-kilter. In fact, my whole family is slightly mad. My dad tap-dances and also runs marathons and has a weird sense of humor. I grew up with him reading *Mad* magazine to me."

Kidman's ability to take things in stride is illustrated by her willingness to do something new for her *Moulin Rouge* role: enter a recording studio for her first "real" musical work. She did "a bit of singing" when she was 17, in a band called Divine Madness, but that was mainly for fun. "This was like being pushed off a cliff," she says of her *Moulin Rouge* crooning, "and Baz had to convince me I'd be able to do it." Working with Luhrmann, whose other movies are *Strictly Ballroom* [1992] and *Romeo + Juliet* [1996], was quite a switch for Kidman after her previous project for a world-famous director. That was the controversial drama *Eyes Wide Shut* [1999], in which she and husband Tom Cruise (from whom she is now separated) starred for Stanley Kubrick, a filmmaker with a serious, cerebral touch. "Baz is a participator," she explains, "whereas Kubrick was more of a voyeur. Baz never says 'less, less,' as a director or a person. He loves to talk. But he always watches and analyzes. He enjoys people and makes grand statements in his movies... Maybe next time he'll make a small, intimate, naturalistic drama—but I doubt it."

Kidman talks readily about the filmmakers she's worked with, because she considers the director's style to be the key element of a movie. She acknowledges that her admiration for forceful film-making runs against the view of many American-trained actors, who prefer the freedom allowed by less strong-minded directors. "I become very devoted to a director if I admire him," she says, "and I choose my projects based on the director... I like the idea of people who have really strong opinions about what they want, and I love being devoted to somebody and his vision, the same way I become very passionate about a particular novel I've read or a painting I've seen." She's also savvy enough about the motion-picture industry to know that movie stars can play a part in making or breaking a filmmaker's career. "I think that as an actor you have a duty to support certain directors," she explains, "because if you have some [industry] power you can help to finance a movie. That's how you find the next generation of Kubricks and [Kyzysztof] Kieslowskis and [Ingmar] Bergmans, who don't necessarily have a chance to flourish in the industry now, since the films that make the most money today are formulaic action films and thrillers. Those can be very good movies, but they're not necessarily changing cinema or challenging our idea of what cinema is."

Kidman means what she says, and any doubt is quelled by a look at her forthcoming projects. Her next release, due from Miramax this August, is *The Others*, a psychological thriller directed by Alejandro Amenàbar, the rising Spanish filmmaker. She's looking forward to shooting an "experimental movie" with Danish auteur Lars von Trier, whose *Dancer in the Dark* [2000] and *Breaking the Waves* [1996] broke strongly with cinematic conventions. She is also developing collaborations with her close friend Jane Campion, whose films include *The Piano* [1993] and *The Portrait of a Lady* [1996], and Stephen Daldry, whose *Billy Elliot* [2000] competed in this year's Academy Awards race. While this is a diverse list of directors, they share with Luhrmann an ability to pursue individualistic ideas while working within the world of mainstream movie-making. *Moulin Rouge* is unorthodox in many respects, from its kinetic editing to its cut-and-paste musical numbers. But it's also a product of Twentieth Century Fox, an old-line Hollywood studio that wants to attract the widest possible audience. "It's a studio movie," Kidman notes, "but Baz wasn't dictated to at all. He's quite uncompromising, which is great! And the [studio] has been very supportive of him. It's interesting when you get a director who can actually operate in the studio system—and so has access to financial support and distribution—yet still maintains his creative control completely… I also have admiration for someone [completely independent] like Lars von Trier, but directors ultimately want people to see their films."

These comments about art vs. commerce inevitably turn attention to the story of *Moulin Rouge* itself, which focuses primarily on Kidman's character. She is Satine, a nightclub can-can dancer caught between the love of a poverty-stricken poet and the lust of a wealthy count who could help her become the serious actress she's always wanted to be. "Satine's choice is about her future," Kidman points out. "Does she trust this [poet] who's telling her to believe in love? She has a [sense of] powerlessness, but she has to say, 'I'm willing… to give myself over to you, and I believe you're not going to hurt me, and this is real. On the other hand, Satine comes from the streets. She's always had to protect herself and take care of herself. She's a courtesan, and the Moulin Rouge is her home." Satine ultimately chooses sentiment over success, of course, clearing the path to a schmaltzy Hollywood ending. "I'm glad the choice she makes is one of love," Kidman says with a smile. Would she make the same decision if she were in the dancer's difficult shoes? The answer comes in a flash. "Absolutely!"

He lets intuition, not money, guide him
Interview with Woody Allen, May 24, 2002

Cannes, France.

You can take Woody Allen out of Manhattan, but can you take Manhattan out of Woody Allen? The reclusive director-writer-star has been prominent on the wide screen for the past 30 years. In person he's played hard to get, though, especially if traveling outside New York City is involved. He surprised the world by appearing on the recent Academy Award show from Los Angeles, and this month—after years of saying no—he showed up at the Cannes film festival. After walking up the red carpet to the European première of *Hollywood Ending*, his latest comedy, he stayed a couple of days to do media appearances and schmooze with journalists.

What's going on? Not a permanent vacation from his reclusive ways, says Allen, who seems as surprised as everyone else. "It's just a coincidence that both events fell in the same year," he told a press gathering here. "It looks like I've had some kind of religious conversion. I'm suddenly out of the house! But I'm not. I'll be back in the house in a few hours, and you won't have to put up with me anymore."

Everyone here in Cannes has been happy to put up with him. And no wonder, given Allen's huge output of movies over the past three decades. He's made a new one almost every year, becoming one of the most prolific directors in modern cinema. How does such a distinctive filmmaker manage to thrive in a movie world driven by moneymaking formulas? One answer is efficiency. He makes his films on relatively low budgets and surrounds himself with a team that disdains Hollywood's elephantine procedures just as he does. "The day I take a finished script out of the typewriter," he says over lunch after his press conference, "I make one phone call. The next day, we're in production on the picture." Another secret to his success is simple "good fortune," he says with a smile, wringing his hands in a characteristic Woody gesture while ignoring the tempting lunch on his plate. "From my earliest pictures on, people seem to think I know what I'm doing, and they let me do things any way I want. I can't explain it!"

Allen chose an interesting year for his first Cannes visit. He's a proudly Jewish filmmaker, and shortly before the festival a group called the American Jewish Congress asked attendees to speak out against an alleged resurgence of anti-Semitism in France. Allen disagrees with this charge, and he speaks pointedly about the recent French election, in which right-wing candidate Jean-Marie Le Pen scored surprisingly high during the first round of voting, then lost in a runoff. "One can be very proud of the way [the French people] responded," Allen says. "The country came out in a clear-cut public statement on how they felt about issues like the extreme right and totalitarianism and intolerance and discrimination. People who hadn't voted in years felt it was important to show that France is a democracy that has no patience with the terrible ideas of the extreme right."

That pleased Cannes mightily. So did *Hollywood Ending*, partly because its satirical plot—about a blind director making a big-budget film—ends with French critics praising his picture after US reviewers drub it. Festival audiences also liked its implicit critique of Hollywood's studio system, based on an obsession with commercialism, to which, ironically, the fictional filmmaker's blindness makes him immune. Allen says moviemaking should be an intuitive process that "proceeds from the unconscious." His belief that a film should grow from the creativity of its makers, not the calculations of a business office, explains why he's never been a full participant in the studio system, despite the power it wields in today's world.

This doesn't mean Allen's intuitive methods always work as well as he'd like. Only rarely does a movie come out on screen the way it originally played in his imagination, he admits. *The Purple Rose of Cairo*, his 1985 fantasy about a Depression-era film buff who falls in love with a movie character, is an exception. It's one of the few he's truly pleased with, but even there the going was tough, especially when he felt compelled to replace Michael Keaton with Jeff Daniels since Keaton seemed "too contemporary" for a 1930s story. Finding the right performer for a part is often difficult, he adds, revealing that he starred in *Deconstructing Harry*, his 1997 comedy, "by default" after seven other actors proved unavailable, unsuitable, or both.

But problems and all, Allen would rather work on his own than bow down to Hollywood, and he doesn't mince words about this. "Hollywood films are calculated in venality from the start," he says. "The idea behind the films is to make as much money as possible. They're happy when the film comes out good, but they'd be happier making a bad film that made a lot of money than a good film that made less money. That's why you get all those Hollywood films that are uninspired. Everybody was trying to figure out the formula to make the most amount of money with the least amount of risk."

Veteran's films teem with vitality: Now in his 90s, Portuguese director makes a movie a year
Interview with Manoel de Oliveira, August 16, 2002

Manoel de Oliveira isn't just a filmmaker; he's a force of nature. The 90-something Portuguese master is still making a movie a year, most of which première in the prestigious main selection at the Cannes Film Festival. De Oliveira got his start as an actor at the end of the silent-film era in the late 1920s and has directed 35 films over 71 years. His most recent film, *I'm Going Home*, opens in the US this week. It stars France's Michel Piccoli as an aging actor approaching the end of his career with mingled nostalgia and regret.

It's hard to characterize de Oliveira's films in a sentence, because some are traditional, like Abraham's Valley [1993] and *Voyage to the Beginning of the World* [1997], and some are very experimental, like the three-part Inquietude [1998] and the 4½-hour-long *Doomed Love* [1979]. What they share is a profound respect for visual beauty and real human emotion. "My films come from my voice, but I'm not telling stories about myself," de Oliveira said in a recent interview. He spoke through an interpreter, slipping between French and his native Portuguese, and looking a good 20 years younger than he is. The secret of his long career seems to be the sheer pleasure he takes in cinema, which he sees as a unique art form that incorporates elements of all the other arts as well. He loves every aspect of moviemaking and has worked not only as director of his films but also as writer, producer, editor, and cinematographer of many projects.

"Cinema is always a fiction," he continued, "a representation. Even the horrible facts that were shot by television cameras on Sept. 11 are not reality itself, they're the ghost of reality. Cinema is always the ghost of something that took place." De Oliveira is fascinated by the complex relationship between real-world authenticity and the larger-than-life images movies fabricate so easily. "Cinema is the phantom of the moment," he reiterates, "not life itself. And yet we feel we are living more [intensely] when we see a film. It's strange! This shows the importance of memory. Cinema is always memory, just as literature and history are memory. Without memory, we lose our identity."

De Oliveira loves watching films as well as making them, but he's not too fond of most present-day movies. "They're too artificial," he says, "like [much of] modern life. We no longer eat fish that come from the river or sea, they come from an aquarium. Vegetables don't have their roots in the earth; they grow in a fiberglass box. Man seems to have forgotten that he's a son of nature and that he can't live without it."

Talking about his favorite films, he mentions the work of Charlie Chaplin and John Ford, old masters who "really knew what's important in telling a story." This contrasts with most modern pictures. "All their artificiality and special effects are very interesting and extraordinary, but they're not something I appreciate. I appreciate things that are simpler and have a more direct access to life." Direct access to life is exactly what de Oliveira's movies give. He leaves for Costa Rica in a few weeks to begin his next one. He'll celebrate his 94th birthday during the shoot. [*Note: de Oliveira's last film was released in 2015, the year of his death at age 106.*]

PART 2
ARTICLES AND ESSAYS

Coppola, *Apocalypse Now*, and the Ambivalent '70s

The Chronicle of Higher Education/The Chronicle Review
August 3, 2001

Francis Ford Coppola's most popular contribution to American screenwriting is surely Marlon Brando's wry promise in the first *Godfather* film (1972): "I'm gonna make him an offer he can't refuse." There's another oft-cited line, in Coppola's 1979 *Apocalypse Now*, that crystallizes far more of the '70s American spirit, however, with a wit so ferocious that audiences have never quite known whether to laugh, gasp, or shudder. It comes when surfboard-toting Lt. Col. Bill Kilgore, played to the hilt by Robert Duvall, sniffs the warm Vietnamese air, flashes a contented smile, and expresses his satisfaction with the war he's so zealously fighting: "I love the smell of napalm in the morning!" Expect that line to be quoted countless times again now that Coppola's epic is returning to theaters 22 years later as *Apocalypse Now Redux*, a reedited director's cut with an additional 53 minutes of footage that had been left out of the original release.

The story hasn't changed. Martin Sheen plays Willard, a soldier sent to hunt down and "terminate with extreme prejudice" the renegade Colonel Kurtz (Brando), a brilliant officer who has gone insane and established a jungle kingdom that answers to no law but his own megalomaniacal will. Meandering as unpredictably as the river bearing Willard's boat, the film etches an episodic portrait of the Vietnam War as historical farce, geopolitical tragedy, and psychological catastrophe. Pundits have already begun analyzing the previously unseen material, which includes a longer look at Willard and company as they begin the upriver journey; a sexual encounter between Willard and Playboy playmates on a stranded helicopter; a scene where Kurtz dissects the lies in a *Time* article about the war; and a sequence on a French plantation hidden in the Vietnamese jungle, where Willard listens to a conversation about the history, morality, and futility of the war as seen by Vietnam's former colonial masters. What threatens to get lost in critiques of the added footage is a broader perspective on Coppola as a quintessential voice of 1970s filmmaking. Like others of his generation— including the director Michael Cimino, whose Vietnam epic *The Deer Hunter* opened a year earlier—Coppola spent the ambivalent '70s hovering between the flamboyant idealism of the radical '60s and the self-absorbed cynicism of the conservative '80s. *Apocalypse Now* mirrors that instability, oscillating between outrage at the gut-churning horrors of war and pleasure with the spectacle that war produces for the widescreen Technovision camera.

The ambivalence of *Apocalypse Now* grew partly from Coppola's collaborators, who channeled 1970s sensibilities in wildly different ways. At one end of the spectrum was the screenwriter John Milius, a military buff who had celebrated guns, guts, and glory in aggressively post-'60s, anti-flower-power movies like *Magnum Force* (1973) and *The Wind and the Lion* (1975). On the other was the actor Dennis Hopper, the *Easy Rider* (1969) hippie whose on- and off-screen image had become an internationally known emblem of strung-out psychedelia. In a Salon review of the *Apocalypse Now* DVD edition last year, Michael Sragow accurately summed up Hopper's portrayal of a combat photographer who worships Kurtz's mad power: "He knows his brain has exploded even though he claims it has been enlarged. He catches himself up with a single word — 'wrong' — that sounds out like his conscious mind's foghorn. Hopper may express more about the fallout of the '60s than anything else in the movie."

The heart of the film's ambivalence lies in Coppola's own creative personality, however. He was an ambitious artist in the '70s, eager to tackle large-scale subjects and willing to court a reasonable degree of controversy. But he was also a savvy businessman, seeing mass-audience success as the key to his ongoing artistic freedom and the survival of American Zoetrope, the cinematic fiefdom he had established in 1970 as an alternative to Hollywood. Many critics in 1972 hailed *The Godfather* as a brilliant meeting of artistry and commerce. To his credit, Coppola disagreed, seeing the movie's wide appeal as a missed chance to reach the public with ideas as well as entertainment. "What an opportunity that could have been," he said at the Cannes International Film Festival in 1974. And he meant it. Riding his *Godfather* success as exuberantly as Kilgore on a California wave, the Coppola of the mid-1970s was still enough of a '60s loyalist to want more social impact in his work. He proved that in *The Conversation* and *The Godfather: Part II*, two 1974 releases with forthrightly sociopolitical themes: high-tech corporate snooping in the former, the hazy line between capitalism and criminality in the latter. Coppola's business side made sure, however, that even his most high-minded projects took few commercial risks. *The Conversation* placed well-liked Gene Hackman in an art-thriller plot heavily influenced by Michelangelo Antonioni's breakthrough hit *Blow-Up* (1966). As for the eagerly awaited *Godfather* sequel, its cast bristled with favorites like Duvall and Robert De Niro; its story moved at a compelling pace despite an unconventional flashback structure; and its powerfully choreographed violence erupted frequently enough to keep crime-movie fans cheering whether or not they paid attention to the picture's deeper messages.

Apocalypse Now opened new ground for Coppola the director—it was his first war film and, more important, his first foray into a truly contentious topic. But it continued the *Godfather II* pattern by anchoring its sociopolitical themes in time-tested genre conventions. True, it refought the Vietnam conflict with an anguished ambiguity that couldn't be more different from the macho posturing of *The Green Berets* (John Wayne and Ray Kellogg, 1968), *Rambo: First Blood Part II* (George P. Cosmatos, 1985), and their appalling ilk. Still, it paid obeisance to many Hollywood traditions, from its suspense-laden narrative (it's a road movie on a river) to its combat-film action scenes. Coppola hoped intellectuals would appreciate his ideas, but his first priority was making everyday moviegoers line up at the ticket window. The commercial aspects of *Apocalypse Now* underscore a side of Coppola that would become increasingly visible in the less adventurous 1980s, when his projects ranged from the tame (*Gardens of Stone*, 1987) to the trifling (*The Outsiders*, 1983) to the woefully misbegotten (*The Godfather: Part III*, released in 1990). Those and other ventures seemed more interested in exploiting marketable material—how else to explain the half-baked mishmash of *Godfather III*?—than exploring ideas that genuinely engaged Coppola's intellect and imagination.

A more subtle quality of *Apocalypse Now* casts additional light on Coppola's essentially conservative desire to treat momentous themes without unduly disturbing his audience. Despite the political ramifications of its story, *Apocalypse Now* has less to do with the history and morality of the Vietnam tragedy than with the possibilities for motion-picture mythmaking that Coppola saw there. It's not about the Southeast Asian war in particular but about war in general, seen as a fundamental force of nature—no less inevitable than floods or famines, no less morbidly fascinating than the existential *Heart of Darkness* conjured up by Joseph Conrad in the 1902 novel that inspired Milius' screenplay. While the film can be read as a cry against the evils inflicted on Vietnam, it's more accurately seen as a humanitarian statement on the tragedy of war itself, as timeless and unspecific as the Homeric epic that some of its admirers likened it to. It's interesting to consider that Coppola had reached the Hollywood big leagues in 1970 by co-writing the Academy Award-winning script for *Patton*, which President Richard Nixon viewed repeatedly during the Vietnam conflict. It's hard to think of a subject more freighted with political import, especially in the Nixon era when warmongers and war protesters were at each other's throats. Yet the critic Peter Cowie notes in his authoritative *The Apocalypse Now Book* that Coppola was "never… a political animal," and Coppola's own comments don't contradict this. Nor do the books and films that directly influenced *Apocalypse*: Hard-hitting documentaries like Peter Davis' *Hearts and Minds* (1974) and Emile de Antonio's *In the Year of the Pig* (1969) were in the mix, but Werner Herzog's hallucinatory melodrama *Aguirre the Wrath of God* (1972) provided at least as many ideas and inspirations. No wonder Eleanor Coppola told Cowie that her husband's goal was less to analyze the Vietnam conflict than to weave "a kind of myth, an opera" around his larger-than-life subject.

Coppola's mythmaking ambition was in sync with Hollywood's ambivalence about how—and whether—to put Vietnam on screen. American forces had left the region about a year before he started shooting in his Philippines locations. Studios had been dithering over the subject through-out the '70s, however, showing remarkable timidity even by Hollywood standards. When a screenwriter proposed a Vietnam project in 1971, Cowie reports, one executive declared it five years too early and another proclaimed it five years too late. Coppola decided the time was right for *Apocalypse* after a Paramount executive told him the public wasn't ready for it. While his decision came partly from contrarian boldness—by the time the picture was finished, the public would be ready for it—there was another motivation too. After the intensity of *Godfather II*, he wanted to make an action picture that would be as much fun for him to direct as it would be exciting for audiences to watch. Little did he know how hard it would prove to be, plagued by everything from a Sheen heart attack to his own marital problems and a full-blown Philippines monsoon.

Although various qualities tie the film to the self-indulgent '80s era—its preference for myth over polemic, its avoidance of hot-button commentary—the '60s links of *Apocalypse Now* speak loudly too, through its anti-authoritarian spirit and its willingness (however mixed Coppola's motives may have been) to tackle Vietnam when conventional studio wisdom balked at the prospect. Both sides of this chronological coin are captured by the newly restored scene showing Willard's visit to the French plantation.

Coppola never explains how these French folks have managed to live undiscovered for years in the heart of their country's lost colony. But their long conversation in Willard's presence says more about the specifics of Southeast Asian history than the rest of the movie's scenes together. "We fight to keep what is ours," says the French patriarch played by Christian Marquand, summing up his argument that France has proprietary rights because it brought Vietnam into the modern economic world. "You Americans fight for the biggest nothing in history." Here we have Coppola in full '60s mode, diving into Vietnam's tormented past with depth and candor. Remember, however, that he excised this episode from the original cut, to shorten the picture and prevent too much talk from taxing Saturday-night moviegoers.

This brings us back to Coppola the studio exec, ready to scrap his film's most analytical sequence rather than risk offending audiences more interested in action and psychedelics than dialogue and historiography. Caught though it is in 1970s ambivalence, *Apocalypse Now Redux* looks fresher and healthier to my eyes than any war movie made since then, perhaps excepting Terrence Malick's *The Thin Red Line* (1998), which also bears the scars of a troubled production history. The competition is admittedly thin, with Steven Spielberg's strident *Saving Private Ryan* (1998) the reigning "classic" and Michael Bay's insufferable *Pearl Harbor* (2001) the latest debacle. Both deal in aggressive nostalgia, self-justifying spectacle, and a faux verisimilitude built on Hollywood clichés and the high-tech voyeurism embodied by TV coverage of the Persian Gulf conflict. All this makes a sorry contrast with the willingness of Coppola and company to enrich their audience-pleasing product with discursive elements ranging from literary allusion (citing Conrad and T. S. Eliot) to mass-culture critique (excoriating *Time* magazine) to apocalyptic mysticism (evoking the demonism of drug-dazed combat, the blood ritual of assassination, the ineffable horror whose invocation by Kurtz provides the film's indelible climax). Coppola has his shortcomings as a filmmaker and a thinker, but there's no denying the energy and resourcefulness that surge through *Apocalypse Now* at its most powerful moments, alternately helped and hindered by its 1970s sensibility. While he found no magic key to unlock Vietnam's heart of darkness, Coppola's intuitive grasp of what may now seem an old-fashioned brand of cinema—there's not a computer-generated frame in sight—carries a unique blend of insights into one of the past century's most troubled historical moments.

Views of Vietnam: *Platoon* **vs.** *Rambo.* **Why did films with very different images of war and heroism both become hits?**
The Christian Science Monitor, March 26, 1987

Except for the studios that turned *Platoon* down for more than a decade—saying it wasn't a "commercial" project—nobody has been more amazed by the film's wildfire success than Oliver Stone, who wrote and directed it. "We didn't expect anything like this," he told me in a recent phone conversation. Backed up by eight Academy Award nominations, the picture's popularity has become the season's hottest movie-news story. Behind the headlines, however, lies a deeper issue—the significance of *Platoon* as an answer to *Rambo: First Blood Part II* [George P. Cosmatos, 1985], the previous blockbuster about the Vietnam conflict. To some extent, Hollywood movies constitute a dialogue with the public and each other. Sometimes the dialogue amounts to a debate, with box-office figures measuring the response of moviegoers to each argument. Seen in this light, the flamboyant action of *Rambo* represented a radical turn away from the ambiguity and skepticism of earlier Vietnam films like *The Deer Hunter* [Michael Cimino, 1978] and *Apocalypse Now* [Francis Ford Coppola, 1979]. In the same way, the success of *Platoon* can be seen as a strong and perhaps surprising reply to the *Rambo* worldview, which was thought by some to augur a new flowering of aggressive anti-Communism and conservatism. *Platoon* also appears to have opened up a more searching kind of introspection among moviegoers than *Rambo* did—focusing not just on Vietnam and the longing to "win," but on the physical and psychological destructiveness of all combat. "Students are constantly bringing up *Platoon* and asking about the war," says the director of a university film department in the New York area. "And parents have come to me, wanting to talk about it with me and their children. They aren't just titillated by the violence. They're troubled by the film, and it's opening many doors to discussion."

It would be simplistic to suggest that *"Platoon"* has abruptly changed the hearts and minds of avid *Rambo* fans. *Platoon* may be achieving its success by simply attracting a different audience to the theater. And some filmgoers may be equally enthralled by both pictures—taking *Rambo* as a heroic fantasy and *Platoon* as a truthful experience that occupies a separate movie universe. Differing and even contradictory attitudes (such as the wish for *Rambo* simplicities and the urge to recognize *Platoon* realities) can coexist within a society or even within an individual. *Platoon* has proved that *Rambo* doesn't constitute Hollywood's most resounding comment on Vietnam, however. Audience fascination with the relative complexities of *Platoon* and its characters—each driven by different motives, each working out different approaches to life and war—indicates that Sylvester Stallone's make-believe represented more of a bumpy detour than a lasting new direction in contemporary thought as represented by popular films.

The most striking feature of *Platoon* is its insistence on a naturalistic and even nightmarish view of combat. Fighting near Vietnam's border with Cambodia, its soldiers work not as individual Rambo-style heroes, but as a tight and terrified unit that's torn by inner rivalries and hatreds as well as fear of enemy troops. Violence and death are everywhere, and the most well-meaning soldier may come psychologically unglued at any time. The soldiers don't even share a common view of what they're facing. The character played by Charlie Sheen, who stands for filmmaker Stone in the movie, begins as an idealist but soon finds accustomed beliefs and behaviors sliding from beneath his feet. By contrast, the Willem Dafoe character has acquired a seasoned and skeptical perspective—not without its own idealism about the importance of maintaining some sense of humanity—while the Tom Berenger character is apparently led by little but his own traumatized cynicism.

The most striking feature of *Rambo* is its preference for heroics over realism and complexity. Played by Stallone, who also wrote the film, the title character is a Vietnam veteran alienated by American society, which is seen as cold and uncaring toward those who fought an unpopular war. The military asks him to rescue a group of soldiers listed as missing in action but really held prisoner by Vietnamese and Soviet forces. Rambo does the job pretty much alone, like the hero of an old-fashioned Hollywood western. Also recalling the western genre are his Indian-like costume and his most picturesque weapon, a bow-and-arrow device with an explosive instead of an arrowhead.

For all their differences, *Platoon* and *Rambo* both dwell on hard physical confrontation between "free world" and "Communist world" forces. This sets them apart from earlier Vietnam-related films, if one ignores minor-league action pictures like *Missing in Action* [Joseph Zito, 1984] and a few others. *The Deer Hunter* shows only a few moments of battle, using Russian-roulette games as a symbol of wartime destruction and corruption. *Coming Home* [Hal Ashby, 1978] deals entirely with war's effect on veterans who have returned from combat. *Apocalypse Now* stresses psychology and psychedelia in its metaphorical screenplay based on Joseph Conrad's novel *Heart of Darkness*. The huge popularity of *Rambo* was widely felt to reflect American impatience with intellectual views of the Southeast Asia war and frustration with what some saw as indecisiveness and impotence on the part of the United States in the post-Vietnam period. The movie is a straightforward revenge fantasy. Its hero specifically sees his Vietnamese mission as a replay of the war and asks if the good-guy side will "get to win" this time instead of being hampered by its own commanders. Audiences flocked to see his single-handed victory over both the "yellow peril" and the "Red menace," represented by evil Vietnamese soldiers and sadistic Soviet officers. And they embraced the film's brazen lack of realism, manifested by romanticized violence and an extravagantly idealized hero.

At the height of the *Rambo* phenomenon, it appeared that many Americans might well have rejected probing and complicated views of the Vietnam war in favor of direct emotions and patriotic cheerleading. Now that moviegoers are flocking in similar droves to the dark and unromantic images of *Platoon*, however, it seems clear that Americans were not deeply or seriously seduced by the *Rambo* idea of Vietnam as an exotic arena for thrilling victories over a bestial enemy. This isn't to say flatly that the lust for victory and "revenge" has given way to unashamed loathing for war. But loathing for war is present in every frame of *Platoon*, which filmmaker Stone expressly designed as a cautionary statement, and moviegoers seem eager to absorb his message.

The triumph of *Platoon* realism over *Rambo* romanticism has a fascinating parallel in earlier film history. No sooner did the United States enter World War II than Hollywood, with a government mandate, started cranking out war-related movies intended to boost morale and support the war effort. The first wave of this activity produced, in the words of film historian David A. Cook, "a raft of fatuous, super-patriotic melodramas of the battlefield and homefront which glorified a kind of warfare that had never existed in the history of the human race, much less in the current upheaval." That sounds amazingly like *Rambo* in the present day. And like *Rambo*, those early-'40s pictures with titles like *Captains of the Clouds* [Michael Curtiz, 1942] and *Blondie for Victory* [Frank R. Strayer, 1942] were routed from the screen when audiences got a glimpse of the real situation in battlefront newsreels and information films. The harsh realities of war quickly made their appearance in subsequent Hollywood fictions.

Platoon isn't "the real thing," only a simulation of it shot in the Philippines with professional actors. But testimony from Vietnam veterans has verified the truthfulness of Oliver Stone's depiction, which grew from a determination to get his own Vietnam experiences on the screen as accurately and vividly as possible. The result isn't a pretty picture. It is serving a useful purpose, though—in reminding its public of wartime's horror, and in offering a corrective to the seductive fantasies of *Rambo*.

When the larger-than-life gets smaller-than-life
The Christian Science Monitor, February 20, 1987

The flap over "colorizing" old movies is obscuring deeper artistic issues built into the practice of watching films on videotape. Colorization is such an unfortunate process that I once hoped it would be nipped in the bud by responsible members of the movie-marketing business. Pandering to a "popular demand" that nobody knew existed a few short years ago, it wipes out the unique and long-treasured qualities of black-and-white cinematography. And it does this for no better reason than cheap, unthinking conformity with the aesthetics of color television—as if all manifestations of the moving image should be measured by a single electronic standard.

Still, colorizing is clearly on the rise. Technologies tend to generate their own momentum. Many a movie scene has been shot because some new gadget made it possible, not because a story line demanded it. The moment colorization was invented, it was inevitable that the entertainment world's equipment freaks and profiteers would latch onto it. Sadly, audiences are also latching onto it. Artificially tinted movies may soon be as common as monophonic LP records "rechanneled" into ersatz stereo. I deplore this, but I can't bring myself to ride quite so high a horse as many of my fellow movie loyalists. That's because I have deep reservations about the existence of video-transferred films in the first place. A lot of critics, scholars, and fans have welcomed the flood of films-on-tape as an invaluable resource. Video, they point out, gives viewers an unprecedented control over what they watch. They have a point. During most of film history, distributors and exhibitors controlled virtually all access to movies. The only way to see a picture was to catch it at a theater, and programming was dictated almost entirely by box-office considerations. By contrast, videocassette machines are at the spectator's command. I can choose the movie I want to see. And having done so, I can plumb its mysteries by using my slow-motion and rewind switches—dissecting scenes and shots in a way that no number of theatrical viewings could make possible. I won't argue with video as a research or educational tool.

But using VCR movies as everyday substitutes for projected movies is, in my view, a sure way to cheapen and falsify the cinematic experience—even when the added indignity of colorization doesn't enter the picture. There are several reasons. Chief among them is the quality of the TV image, which can't compete with the crispness and clarity of a projected 35-mm film. Not to mention a 70-mm film, or even a 16-mm or super-8 film in a setting where projector and screen are in close proximity. The usual answer to this argument is that high-resolution television (HRTV) is right around the corner, bringing images as sharp as any film projector can offer. Although that sounds great, I'm not holding my breath. HRTV systems I've seen offer an improvement over the standard TV image—but not a new order of quality. Image size is a related issue. Films are larger than life; video is smaller than life. True, you can magnify the video image—with a projection system or giant TV tube—to approximate the large size of a movie screen. But the results will be disappointing, because you've magnified the short-fall in pictorial precision, too. (Ditto if you move your chair closer to the tube.) More important yet is the aspect-ratio problem. That forbidding term simply means the relationship between an image's width and height. Before the 1950s, nearly all movies were shot in a ratio that's just slightly rectangular. Little harm is done when such an image is squeezed into the shape of a standard TV screen. But how about CinemaScope and other widescreen formats? How about a classic like *2001: A Space Odyssey* [Stanley Kubrick, 1968], made specifically for huge-screen Cinerama theaters and crudely dwarfed when reduced to television scale?

Two solutions to the widescreen dilemma are commonly used on television. One or both sides of the image may simply be lopped off. Or the broadcaster's camera may scan the image from side to side, imposing a new and artificial motion that was never intended by the filmmakers. Both solutions are appalling. Imagine a museum where the sides of paintings are chopped off to suit their picture frames. Or imagine a movie scene intended to be as calm and unmoving as a still life—only the broadcaster's lens is scurrying back and forth to show us the parts that won't fit on the screen. Some responsible TV stations take the trouble to show movies in their proper aspect ratios, stretching wide-screen images across the middle of the screen while leaving the top and bottom blank. This is a commendable effort, but it reduces the size of the overall picture more than ever. Add a line of subtitles across the bottom of the image, if it's a foreign-language movie, and you have a grotesque miniaturization of the film's originally intended form. In addition to the cry against colorizing, therefore, I'd like to see a new alertness to the degradation of motion-picture quality that's part and parcel of the films-on-video format.

Meanwhile, the colorization crowd should remember that not all moviegoers are panting for their product. True, color cinematography has been standard filmmaking practice for decades now. Yet during that time, some conscientious directors have deliberately chosen to work in the black-and-white format—and their movies have tended to be very successful, from *The Last Picture Show* [Peter Bogdanovich, 1971] and *Young Frankenstein* [Mel Brooks, 1974] to *Raging Bull* [Martin Scorsese, 1980] and *The Elephant Man* [David Lynch, 1980]. So moviegoers aren't a monochromatic bunch. What they want are dramatic visual experiences—and varied ones, decked out in the differing tones and hues and shapes and sizes that only theatrical screens can now offer. I'm certain that some brave new form of high-resolution video will eventually make today's film technology obsolete. And that will be all to the good: Few will miss the broken reels and sloppy splices and scratchy prints that plague film screenings all too often. Even then, however, it will be indefensible to exhibit films in visibly altered forms—colorized, for example. And the post-celluloid era won't begin to dawn until today's video technology has leaped to a new and lofty level in terms of size and pictorial quality. Until such a time, moviegoers should remember that films on cassettes, colorized or not, are sorry substitutes for the real thing.

The Press Gang: Writings on Cinema from New York Press, *1991–2011*
Cineaste, Summer 2021

New York Press was an alternative weekly that flourished from 1988 to 2011, giving lively competition to *The Village Voice*, its older and more distinguished rival. Among its staffers were three estimable film critics whose reviews, essays, interviews, and occasional rants are collected for the first time in *The Press Gang: Writings on Cinema from New York Press, 1991–2011*, edited by Jim Colvill, who calls the hefty volume "an act of resurrection," since much of the material has been unavailable since the paper ceased publication. The introduction, by memoirist and *Press* veteran Jim Knipfel, gives a brief anecdotal history of the publication and its movie department.

Godfrey Cheshire, described by Knipfel as a "hip, bespectacled Southern gentleman," was the first film critic to arrive, serving from 1991 until he was fired in 2000 for reasons that no one ever seems to have figured out. He was joined in 1995 by Matt Zoller Seitz, who continued until 2006, submitting his last review a few weeks after the tragic sudden death of his wife. The triumvirate's third member, Armond White, commenced in 1997 and wrote until the paper went defunct, becoming one of the few Black film critics to establish and maintain a major voice in this perennially white-dominated field. Colvill has chosen the articles according to the quality of the prose, the continued relevance of the films(s) under discussion, and how each piece "speaks to others" in the book. A major aim of the volume is to preserve worthy specimens of long-form criticism, a once-thriving genre that needs all the preservation it can get. Here are hundreds of pages of it, most of them commendable, a few of them risible, a handful of them superb.

I'll note at the outset that I've known each of these critics well for decades, and while I've long held them in high regard, my estimation rose steadily as I made my way through this book. (I read it from cover to cover, although others may prefer to dip into it here and there.) Most of the pieces are reviews of individual movies, interspersed with think pieces, festival dispatches, and interviews with filmmakers as different as Abbas Kiarostami, Edward Yang, and Robert Drew. Recurring themes include the aesthetic legitimacy of digital cinematography and exhibition, the interplay of art and commerce as driving forces of film culture, the rivalry between theatrical film and television, debates over cinephilia and the real or imagined death of cinema, and the ever-growing celebrity of superstar auteurs. In the latter category, all three critics have great esteem for Steven Spielberg, who receives more coverage than any other filmmaker. Other frequently mentioned figures include Martin Scorsese, Oliver Stone, Terrence Malick, Jean-Luc Godard, Paul Thomas Anderson, and Todd Haynes; missing are the Southern Hemisphere and avant-garde cinema. Every article responds in one way or another to the issues, controversies, and movie releases of the moment, but broader and more complicated issues produce thought-provoking crosscurrents throughout.

Cheshire gets the first of the chronologically ordered sections to himself, and he readily confirms his bona fides as a compulsively quotable writer. On Stone's *Natural Born Killers* (1994): "For me, hoping for Stone to be 'superb' is like wishing Elvis had been born Prince of Wales: this way lies the cemetery of good taste, devoid of menace and magic." On Rainer Werner Fassbinder's use of "conventional religious speech" in describing *Querelle* (1982): "nothing is more alien or disconcerting to the arbiters of our 'arts' and 'liberal public discourse.'... Which is why, if an artist wanted to hide something crucial in plain sight, this area of speech, imagery and thought would make an unbeatable encrypting tool, would it not?" On diversity at the 1996 Sundance festival: "It meant several really terrible films about this year's favored subgroups, lesbians and Native Americans. It did not mean... any films boosting the identity politics of Southern Baptists, polar explorers, insurance salespersons, Michigan militia men, *Playboy* centerfolds, Republican presidential candidates, Hare Krishnas or Richard Petty fans. Diversity being best, presumably, when it's not too diverse." I enjoy reading Cheshire even when an opinion is amazingly off base. While he shares my view that Haynes' *Safe* was the best film of 1995, he gets the concluding scene—which embodies the entire point of the movie—not just wrong but, according to me, absolutely and confoundingly backward. How can this be? Such are the conundrums of cultural give and take.

Seitz is also excellent, commenting pithily and trenchantly on both mass-audience pictures and works that take artistic and commercial risks. Aleksandr Sokurov's single-take *Russian Ark* (2002) "suggests that time can be suspended, or overlapped, or folded in on itself: that time can be timeless, that limits can be limitless." Spielberg's *The Terminal* (2004) is "like Capra doing Kafka."

In Peter Weir's *The Truman Show* (1998), "Seahaven is what New York City would look like if Giuliani's dreams came true. There are no squeegee men, pot dealers, porn shops, loud teenagers, cab-drivers, jaywalkers, hotdog vendors or... poor people or citizens who yammer about their constitutional rights: There's also no color, no wit, no excitement and no possibility of transcendence or escape." Tarantino's hyperreferential *Kill Bill: Vol. 1* (2003) makes Seitz wonder, "are archivist directors the cinematic equivalent of singer-songwriters with a sense of history, or has the unsuspecting viewer wandered into karaoke night?" Writing about critic Pauline Kael, who worked unsuccessfully with Warren Beatty in Hollywood in 1979 and then derided his 1981 *Reds* as a mass of "stale gags and bits of business," Seitz writes that her next sentence could have been, "And if you see him, tell him I want my records back." I certainly don't agree with all of Seitz's judgments; he dismisses Gaspar Noé's darkly intelligent *Irreversible* (2002) as a "95-minute rape," for instance, and his review of Barry Levinson's 1998 *Sphere* takes the form of a sci-fi pastiche that doesn't work as either criticism or wit. But when he's good, which is most of the time, he is very good indeed.

White has a well-earned reputation as a contrarian, and I was pleasurably surprised when these pages presented a much more complex and interesting body of work than I expected. His tastes are varied, sophisticated, and smart, with particular enthusiasms for auteurs as dissimilar as Spielberg, Altman, Godard, and André Téchiné, and he illuminates the merits of undersung movies—David Gordon Green's *George Washington* (2000), Whit Stillman's *The Last Days of Disco* (1998)—with skill and sensitivity. He is also a first-rate writer with a formidable intellect and a prodigious grasp of pop culture. But contrarian outbursts do arise, sometimes aggressively, as in his tendency to insult his readers. Moviegoers who skip over Godard's *For Ever Mozart* (1996) are "fools," for example, and those who like Daniel Myrick and Eduardo Sanchez's *The Blair Witch Project* (1999) are "dishonest or hopelessly ignorant." His contumely can even fall on whole countries: Australia and New Zealand are both denounced as "third-rate cultures."

But there's nothing like White's scorn for other film critics, which reaches withering heights in the volume's concluding piece, written in the aftermath of the New York Film Critics Circle awards ceremony that he chaired in 2011, making remarks from the rostrum that some interpreted as antagonistic and rude. Those remarks brought reproaches from J. Hoberman of *The*

Village Voice and Lisa Schwarzbaum of *Entertainment Weekly*, and White excoriates them in his article. Motivated by "racism," he fumes, they are "class oppressors" and "shills." Hoberman is a "real despot" with "sinister whims." Schwarzbaum is "shameless" and "indecent," with "a pathetic, vindictive need to manipulate film culture." And plenty more along those lines. All of which is pretty rich, coming from a critic who had written a few months earlier that "when film discourse becomes discourteous, mindlessness takes its revenge on reason."

I don't mean to diss Armond the way he disses those colleagues, but I think he rather does ask for it. He may feel very differently now about the episode, and I'm confident that all three critics in *The Press Gang* would be happy to retract some of the words they wrote in bygone years; among the book's other accomplishments, it has made me dread the idea that an act of resurrection could someday bring some of my own better-forgotten prose out of the obscurity where it belongs. Reviewing reviewers is a tricky business, and I hope my admiration rings out clearly for this dedicated trio, all of whom remain active players in the field. Their supple writing in support of thoughtful cinema is exemplary.

Solid (James) Ivory
Quarterly Review of Film and Video 39:7 (2022)

Some unimaginative commentators think of Merchant Ivory Pictures as an unexciting enterprise devoted to "heritage pictures" burdened with sentimentalized narratives and reactionary aesthetics. They are wrong. Of course, the company's principal talents—director James Ivory, producer Ismail Merchant, screenwriter Ruth Prawer Jhabvala—and their shifting array of collaborators have generated occasional misfires during more than four decades of creative activity, but nearly all of their work embodies three core values I've always applauded them for upholding: it is thoughtful, it is civilized, and, above all, it is literate. This goes for the movies centered on Merchant's native India, such as *Shakespeare Wallah* (1965) and *The Guru* (1969), and for their celebrated adaptations of classic novels, such as E. M. Forster's *Howards End* (1992) and Henry James' *The Golden Bowl* (2000), and for their portraits of modern American life, such as *Roseland* (1977), from Jhabvala's original story, and *A Soldier's Daughter Never Cries* (1998), based on Kaylie Jones' memoir of life with James Jones, her famous and cantankerous father. As for reactionary attitudes, skeptics should have a look at the sexual antics in *The Wild Party* (1975), the lesbian overtones of *The Bostonians* (1984), the capering male nudes in *A Room with a View* (1985), and the same-sex smooching in *Maurice* (1987), a movie with gay sympathies at its very heart. The treatment of sexual themes in the company's films is usually subtle and reserved, but this accords with the periods, places, and sources of the stories they are telling; they have never worshiped at the shrine of "good taste" for its own sake, as do so many pictures that actually *are* steeped in the tradition of picturesque heritage productions. In a video interview for a recent Blu-ray edition of *The Bostonians* (1984), Ivory maintained that the whole body of his work is marked by a "subversive" streak, and while that's an exaggeration, the movies are more complex and sophisticated than lazy critics often recognize.

The impressive range and overall quality of Ivory's films testify to his own complexity and sophistication as a person and an artist, and if there is any question as to the vigor of his sexuality, it is (so to speak) laid to rest by *Solid Ivory*, his consistently engaging and surprisingly candid memoir, named after a "little comedy routine" he performed as a teenager at high-school assemblies in Klamath Falls, Oregon, the town where he grew up. The book is about far more than sex and sexuality, but sharing the pleasures of very active sex life is high on Ivory's agenda. I say its frankness is surprising because during most of his career his remarks about such matters have been reticent and reserved; in bygone years I moderated quite a few onstage dialogues with him and Merchant, and even when discussing an outspokenly gay film like *Maurice* they never chose to connect the material on the screen with their private lives off the screen, notwithstanding the fact that their decades-long history as a couple was a thoroughly open secret. In the aforementioned video interview, Ivory attributes his restraint to consideration for Merchant during his lifetime, saying that many of Ismail's compatriots in India would never have understood or perhaps tolerated his homosexual identity. I'm skeptical about this statement, since if all interested parties in the United States took the longtime intimacy of Jim and Ismail as a matter of course, it's unlikely that Merchant's peers in the South Asian community would have been especially startled or scandalized by it. It's more probable that the discretion of both filmmakers was motivated less by worries about censure than by the taste for dignity and diplomacy that characterizes their films.

Different policies apply in the memoir department, however, and a volume with a sizable chapter called "Queer as Jack's Hatband" is clearly not interested in artful circumlocution. The book tells of Ivory's early crushes on boys he found handsome and stylish—he himself was voted Most Stylish in his 1946 high-school yearbook, although Most Witty was the title he wanted—and of his predilection for "star qualities" in friends he had as a youth as well as performers he prized as an adult. On the negative side, recalling college life at the University of Oregon leads him to say that he has "rarely mixed well in large groups of gregarious men," feeling "excluded from their physicality, expressed most often in roughhouse or sports," and here his sensibility comports well with the tony aesthetics of his filmmaking. Throughout the memoir he pursues a healthy array of recollections large and small: childhood experiences, his parents' unselfconscious approach to nudity, a visit to a prostitute with a group of collegians who never learned he was as much a virgin after the encounter as before it, and much more, including all manner of male friendships, some energetically sexual, others platonic, and a few intriguingly in between.

For cinephiles, the most compelling parts of the memoir are those focused on Ivory's filmmaking career, and while a great deal of that is spelled out, readers must connect the dots between episodes scattered through a largely discontinuous narrative.

Connecting those dots is a pleasure, even though Ivory is no completist, preferring the contingencies of free association to the logic of linear reconstruction; this is very much a meandering memoir, not a formal autobiography. A long section comprises verbal portraits of friends and collaborators—among them are Vanessa Redgrave, Susan Sontag, Kenneth Clark, Bruce Chatwin, and Lillian Ross, who merits two chapters—with sketches of Jhabvala and Merchant closing things off. For me, the most unexpected aspect of the book is Ismail's relatively small presence. His death at age 68, after surgery for abdominal ulcers in 2005, was obviously a key event in Ivory's life and a turning point in his work. More about Merchant, and about their hugely productive personal and professional relationship, would have been welcome.

Much of the fun in *Solid Ivory* comes from comments that seem offhand but are richly colorful. In an anecdote that draws a fascinating contrast with his own movies, Ivory recalls a childhood viewing of a newsreel in which a heavy statue was dropped onto a mob, and speculates that this may have inspired his lifelong "love of disaster movies, with all their disorder, physical destruction, and mass annihilation." The chapter on George Cukor, a great director and erstwhile benefactor who facilitated Ivory's early career, depicts him years later as a crank who enlivens a meeting in the late 1970s by ranting that "agents, lawyers, writers—all were best consigned to a special Fucking Hell," spewing this as he sat in "a sort of vexed heap" and revealed his hatred of a Hollywood where "all the beauty had gone, and where everything and everyone was ugly." (Paradoxically enough, Cukor overcame his loathing and did a bit more Hollywood directing before his death in 1983.) Recalling a chance encounter with Pauline Kael before she had reviewed any of his films, Ivory remembers having "friendly, even hopeful, feelings about her," and leaves us to imagine what happened later. On the subject of criticism writ large, Ivory tells an acquaintance that "all critics [are] a lesser form of life." And in a passage that does link the personal and the professional, he waxes quite eloquent: "If you are a very restless, energetic, and physically active male, you make a film that has those qualities naturally. Ismail's best scenes [in his occasional work as a director] reflect that side of him. If, on the other hand, you are relaxed, easygoing, and comfort seeking, are happiest when lolling about without a single thought in your head—or with perhaps many thoughts in your head, all more or less of equal importance, then maybe your films—that is, my films—naturally reflect those qualities."

Solid Ivory shows that this very solid filmmaker has many, many thoughts in his head, and well into his nineties he continues to work, mainly as a writer and producer. His memoir, some portions of which have appeared in other forms in books and periodicals, is an engaging, generously illustrated addendum to a career that has made unique and irreplaceable contributions to modern cinema. It is worth the attention of every cinephile.

Dietrich & von Sternberg in Hollywood
Cineaste 44:1, Winter 2018

Marlene Dietrich had boundless energy and a tireless work ethic, and one of the tasks she pursued most enthusiastically was singing the praises of Josef von Sternberg, the director who made her a star in the golden year of 1930, when *The Blue Angel* and *Morocco* had their German and American premieres. You see this in a note she sent after seeing *Morocco* for the first time: "You—Only you—the Master—the Giver—Reason for my existence—the Teacher—the Love my heart and brain must follow." The rhetoric eventually calmed down; the message stayed the same for years to come.

Von Sternberg reciprocated after a fashion, but being a congenital grump, his praise was faint to the vanishing point. Dietrich is "no ordinary woman," he mused in his 1964 memoir, *Fun in a Chinese Laundry*, describing her as a "frank and outspoken" person with impressive poise" and "uncommon good sense which approached scholarship." On the negative side, he complained at great length about her habit of giving him excessive credit, which he regarded as a passive-aggressive ploy for gaining more kudos for herself; once she saw the good impression produced by her humility, he claimed in grotesquely sexualized language, a "geyser of praise began to shoot, hot and steaming, on the hour and every hour."

As for the origin of Dietrich's complex and magnetic public persona, von Sternberg said his great contribution was simply to recognize and mold her innate qualities. "I gave her nothing that she did not already have," he wrote in his memoir. "What I did was to dramatize her attributes and make them visible for all to see; though, as there were perhaps too many, I concealed some." They both understood that a canny balance of the revealed and the concealed, the manifest artifact and the alluring mystery, is the essence of the seductive star image they constructed and refined in the seven films they made together between 1930 and 1935.

The arrival of *Dietrich & von Sternberg in Hollywood*, a six-disc DVD and Blu-ray set from the Criterion Collection, makes this an excellent time to revisit and reassess the duo's collaboration. Each of their American productions is present in a crisp digital edition, and an accompanying booklet contains three well-written essays about the actress, the director, and the shifting currents of American culture and Hollywood practice. The first three films—*Morocco*, *Dishonored* (1931), and *Shanghai Express* (1932)—parlayed Dietrich's charisma and von Sternberg's stylistics into an irresistible package that countered the shocks of the deepening Depression with far-flung exotica, hothouse romance, and ornate spectacle. The second, less financially fortunate half of the sextet—*Blonde Venus* (1932), *The Scarlet Empress* (1934), and *The Devil Is a Woman* (1935)—fell prey to the tightening Production Code, changing audience tastes, and the director's increasing boldness in "rejecting narrative coherence in favor of emotional truths," to quote Gary Giddens' booklet essay.

It's true that von Sternberg habitually favored excess over lucidity, but I think it's more accurate to say that he cared less about emotional truths than *esthetic* truths, synthesized reflections of an intuitive reality that could exist only on the movie screen. Commercially speaking, his quest produced diminishing returns, and his bankability never fully recovered from the declining popularity of his last three Dietrich pictures; although he completed several more films, he was largely "exiled from a Hollywood that had little patience for unorthodox talent, much less so when that talent had little ability to suck up," as Farran Smith Nehme's essay puts it. Dietrich's career had better luck, prospering on screen and stage for two and a half decades after *The Devil Is a Woman* closed out the partnership.

Since the Dietrich pictures followed and built upon von Sternberg's greatest silent films—*Underworld* (1927), *The Last Command* (1928), and *The Docks of New York* (1928)—a quick recap of his earlier career is in order. He hailed from Austria, settled in New York as a teenager, and entered the movie business as a low-level technician and assistant director, adding the "von" so his name would look more important. He made his directorial debut in 1925 with *The Salvation Hunters*, a no-budget exercise in poetic realism that prefigures the best aspects of his future work. The main characters—a man, woman, and child thrown together by homelessness and loneliness—find temporary shelter on the deck of a dredge scooping mud from the bottom of a harbor, a paradoxically unglamorous setting for the lofty artistic mission stated in an intertitle: "Our aim has been to photograph a thought." Von Sternberg isn't the only filmmaker to announce that agenda, but like others who have used such language (D. W. Griffith, Jean-Luc Godard) he gets high marks for ambition. *The Salvation Hunters* is a spare and introspective drama, and von Sternberg's career took off when Charles Chaplin publicly admired it. His subsequent films confirmed his ability to compensate for narrative flimsiness with expressive lighting and ingenious visual design. As film scholar Homay King observes in a Criterion video essay, seeing a movie like *Shanghai Express* for the plot would be like going to an action movie for the script.

Dietrich was a mildly successful stage and film performer in her native Germany when von Sternberg, visiting Germany to direct *The Blue Angel* at the behest of producer Erich Pommer, saw her in a revue titled *Two Neckties* and offered her an audition, whereupon she piqued his curiosity by her evident lack of interest in being discovered or even noticed. Plunging into his role as Pygmalion to her Galatea, he signed her, gave her diet, exercise, and locution programs to follow, and set about crafting her screen persona, mobilizing various traits—most notably a smoldering sexuality and an audacious gender ambiguity—that she made very much her own even though were already widespread in German entertainment of the day. On the night *The Blue Angel* premiered in Berlin she and von Sternberg were already en route to Hollywood and Paramount Pictures, where she was welcomed as a promising competitor to MGM's most luminous female star, Greta Garbo.

The duo's first Paramount production, *Morocco*, set precedents for the five movies that followed, starting with von Sternberg's eagerness to replace the actual look and feel of his narrative settings—Morocco, China, Russia, Spain—with lavishly construed images gleaned entirely from his imagination. The effect is less *un*realistic than *anti*realistic, marked by gratuitously ornamented decors, deliberate pacing, frugal dialogue, and pause-punctuated line readings. As film scholar Janet Bergstrom observes in a Criterion video, von Sternberg's soundtracks opt for direct and uncluttered verbal content complemented by off-screen music, sound motifs, and words visibly inscribed in the mise-en-scène, as when they're carved into a tabletop or scribbled on a mirror. Such devices were dictated in part by technical considerations—the bulky cameras were heavily blimped in the early sound-film era—and perhaps also by the way Dietrich's accent struck von Sternberg, whose memoir contains two cranky pages alleging her inability to pronounce "help" as a single syllable. But the cumulative outcome is an oneiric atmosphere that grows steadily more effective from one movie to the next.

At the center of it all is the Dietrich persona, at once distinctly individualistic and the collective product of numerous gifted artists. One was cinematographer Lee Garmes, who claimed to have invented "the Dietrich face" via lighting that "shadowed her cheekbones, highlighted the triangle of her eyes and nose, and gave her close-ups the quality of a painting," in Nehme's description. Another was makeup artist Dorothy Ponedel, who spent her evenings studying Rembrandt and Vermeer so as to understand the play of light on the human face. Costume designer Travis Banton worked with Dietrich on fittings that lasted late into the night, sometimes aiming at simplicity — the legendary tuxedo in *Morocco*, the ratty streetwalker clothes in *Dishonored* — and sometimes at radical strangeness, à la the gorilla getup in *Blonde Venus*, or fabulous over-the-topness, as with the outfits in *The Devil Is a Woman*, which was Dietrich's favorite of the Paramount films.

Dressing the star was a daring and exacting business; according to designer Deborah Nadoolman Landis, the length of her veil in *Shanghai Express* was adjusted up and down by centimeters until the ideal measurement was found. Beyond the crafting of the Dietrich look was the fabrication of the von Sternberg universe, abetted by several cinematographers — all strictly overseen by the director, who eventually abandoned pretense and shot *The Devil Is a Woman* by himself — and the invaluable art director Hans Dreier, who concocted environments like the *Morocco* desert where Dietrich kicks off her high heels as she schleps into the sand, the *Dishonored* prison yard where she puts on lipstick while facing a firing squad, and the *Scarlet Empress* palace where she schemes to seize the reins of imperial Russia.

Of all the issues discussed in the Criterion supplements, none crops up more often than Dietrich's fluid gender identity. Unabashedly bisexual, she maintained an open marriage, frequented gay bars, and wore the violet flower symbolizing lesbianism. Many others in the Weimar Republic did the same, but Dietrich made real change when she imported this libertine morality into her American career — most magically and innovatively in *Morocco*, where she plays a nightclub singer who caps off her act by kissing a female patron on the mouth, earning appreciation and applause from onlookers at adjoining tables. It's been said that Dietrich represents sex without gender, but what she really offers is sex *across* genders. She also serves up a potent challenge to simplistic versions of the "controlling male gaze" theory so fashionable in the Seventies and still influential today. The dominant gaze in *The Blue Angel* is emphatically that of Lola Lola, surveying her world with commanding eyes after reducing her male companion to a humiliated wreck, and as film scholar Gaylyn Studlar pointed out years ago, the dynamic is still at work in *Morocco*, where no less a he-man than Gary Cooper accepts a feminizing flower from the heroine and tucks it cheerfully behind his ear.

Turning to specific films in the Paramount cycle, it's hard to imagine a more imposing opener than *Morocco*, where the cast includes Cooper as a love-struck Foreign Legionnaire and Adolphe Menjou as one of the less-privileged lovers frequently paired with Dietrich, perhaps mirroring von Sternberg's role in her notoriously amorous off-screen life. Advance publicity aggressively promoted Paramount's hot new actress—"The Ravishing Rage of Two Continents!" "A New Star Is Born! The Woman All Women Want To See!"—even though she wouldn't become a true Hollywood celebrity until the opening of this picture and *The Blue Angel*, which Paramount released to American theaters at the same time. Chockfull of vintage pre-Code mischief—double entendres, Cooper bargaining with a hooker via hand signals, and of course the nightclub kiss—*Morocco* holds up marvelously today. As does *Dishonored*, a World War I drama starring Dietrich as a spy code-named X27 and Victor McLaglen as a roguish rival. The heroine's flawlessly convincing impersonation of a peasant girl should dispel any skeptic's doubt about the technical excellence of Dietrich's acting skills.

Shanghai Express contains a multitude of bogus ethnic types, as do other von Sternberg films; having played an Austrian traitor in *Dishonored*, for instance, the Swedish-born Warner Oland took a break from Fu Manchu and Charlie Chan pictures to play the mixed-race Henry Chang here. Yet it seems almost beside the point to complain about von Sternberg's indulgence in the age-old vice of ethnic stereotyping, since the characters and performances in his films are as stylized and artificial as the scenery and lighting schemes in which they operate. Equally to the point, the army of Chinese "coolies" is played by real Chinese extras, and King reckons that *Shanghai Express* has more speaking roles for Chinese performers than 99 percent of today's American movies. Then too, the pioneering Chinese-American star Anna May Wong plays a smart, powerful woman whose revenge against the evil Chang is both exquisitely justified and wholly successful. Von Sternberg's many stereotypes are regrettable, to be sure, but King is right to emphasize the fantastical nature of these films, which present us with non-places where the normal rules of time, space, and biology don't readily apply.

After playing fallen women in three straight films, Dietrich gave the format a baroque twist in *Blonde Venus*, where her character strays from the straight and narrow with a millionaire (Cary Grant) to finance the medical treatment that will save her husband (Herbert Marshall) from death by radium poisoning. Here the ever-ravishing star runs through a gamut of plot and costume twists—now she's swimming in the nude, now she's dancing in the gorilla suit—that make this a visual stunner even by von Sternberg standards. Still and all, my choice for the cycle's best movie is *The Scarlet Empress*, a not-very-historical epic in which the rise of Dietrich's gloriously devious princess entails the defeat of her feeble-minded husband (Sam Jaffe), her kvetchy mother-in-law (Louise Dresser), and other powers-that-be in a Russian palace rendered fairy-tale fabulous by colossal doorways, looming gargoyles, and sculptural furniture imbued with nightmarish visual clout. My candidate for the cycle's least successful entry is *The Devil Is a Woman*, the only one shot by von Sternberg without a pro-forma cinematographer also present. It looks terrific, but this time bravura stylistics don't bring a mannered narrative alive. The only Criterion extra accompanying it is an audio rendition of "If It Isn't Pain (It Isn't Love)," a song deleted from the soundtrack before the film's release. As with the movie itself, the content doesn't live up to the title.

Most of the Criterion extras are highly worthwhile, offering a generous amount of film-historical context and an array of comments by an engaging gallery of feminist critics and scholars. "Every moral universe needs a bad girl," says Amy Lawrence, characterizing Dietrich as a flexible, resourceful woman who can't overtly reject fan-magazine morality but can "play with it, toy with it" in ways conventionally good girls couldn't get away with. Making a related point, Mary Desjardins argues that sexuality in Dietrich films is a game where closely identifying with a particular gender identity is optional. Garbo and Dietrich were both linked with a "beautiful, narcissistic… sexuality," according to Patricia White, but Garbo's carefully curated image tapped into Twenties and Thirties images of suave nightlife and "sexology," whereas Dietrich fostered a more extreme version of "female masquerade," flummoxing standard gender expectations in everything from the sleek tuxedo to the noticeably low register of her voice.

In sum, the six discs of *Dietrich & von Sternberg in Hollywood* provide both a captivating Hollywood nostalgia trip and an absorbing survey of the most advanced practices of an utterly original director and the trailblazing star who was his muse, his instrument, and his most brilliant collaborator. Each brought out the finest qualities of the other for five irreplaceable years, and revisiting their unique achievements is an experience no cinephile should pass up.

Sokurov: Early Masterworks
Cineaste 38:2, Spring 2013

Few would disagree that Alexander Sokurov is Russia's most important living filmmaker, picking up the mantle from his mentor, Andrei Tarkovsky, who died in 1986. Tarkovsky left the then-Soviet Union in 1982, sick of tussles with Soviet authorities. Sokurov faced similar problems, and several of his early films were denied distribution until the mid-Eighties, when *glasnost* unlocked the vaults. But since then, he has created a large, diverse, and aesthetically radical body of work, earning near-universal acclaim for his greatest hits: the subdued and sentimental *Mother and Son* (1997), about a young man caring for his dying mother, and the prodigious *Russian Ark* (2002), in which a nineteenth-century writer ushers us through St. Petersburg's Herimitage Museum over the course of a phenomenal ninety-nine-minute sequence shot. Sokurov has also switched between fiction and nonfiction—or rather, he has dissolved the boundaries that supposedly divide them—more gracefully and frequently than anyone this side of Werner Herzog.

Sokurov: Early Masterworks, an invaluable three-disc set from The Cinema Guild, doesn't reach back as early as the title suggests: Sokurov's fourth feature, *Save and Protect* (1990), is the oldest in the collection, followed by *Stone* (1992) and *Whispering Pages* (1994). It's regrettable that the towering *Days of Eclipse* (1988) and *The Second Circle* (1990) aren't here, but the features that do make it into the program are every bit as brilliant, challenging, audacious, and ornery as when they were new.

Although only one film in the collection (*Stone*) has a commentary track, the remarks by critic and curator James Quandt cast light on all the selections. As he insightfully observes, Sokurov's creative personality is a rare combination of cultural conservatism and artistic experimentalism—he's reactionary and futuristic in roughly equal measures, you might say. He believes the essential function of art is to preserve cultural inheritances from bygone times, repeating and revitalizing indispensable truths that will otherwise be lost. Yet his own works are wildly innovative fusions of anamorphic imagery, collagelike sound, attenuated narrative, and eccentric acting, often by nonprofessionals. Sokurov reminds me of T. S. Eliot in the Twenties, writing avant-garde masterpieces like "The Waste Land" and "The Hollow Men" while making solemn commitments to a traditionalist religion (Church of England) and an adopted country (Britain), all within a mere five years. Sokurov turns a similarly Janus-like gaze toward both legacies from the past and possibilities of the future.

The three features in *Early Masterworks* demonstrate this vividly, although I recommend watching them in chronological order rather than the reverse order used in the Cinema Guild package. They amount to (among other things) a trilogy of meditations on the nineteenth-century roots of twentieth-century culture, tapping into elemental themes of Gustave Flaubert, Anton Chekhov, and Fyodor Dostoevsky with novel techniques that translate early-modernist literary qualities into quintessentially postmodern cinema. Sokurov's evident goal is to draw out what he would call the "spiritual voices" of authors who anticipated the aesthetics of the future as he himself understands them. (*Spiritual Voices* is the title of his massive 1995 documentary about young soldiers, made right after *Whispering Pages*.) These aesthetics imply a gutsy insistence on both exploring and interrogating cultural conventions and traditions, including concepts of social organization, individual liberty, and (close to Sokurov's heart) spiritual enterprise. Ferment attaching to such matters helped catalyze the demise of the strenuously modern, ostensibly collectivist, officially atheistic U.S.S.R., and it's not coincidental that Sokurov made *Save and Protect*—the title comes from a Russian Orthodox prayer—just as Mikhail Gorbachev's world-altering era of perestroika and glasnost was finishing its crucial contributions to transforming and advancing the nations of the Soviet bloc.

Save and Protect is freely adapted from *Madame Bovary,* Flaubert's 1856 novel about a romantically inclined Frenchwoman who kills herself after discovering that the combined gratifications of marriage, motherhood, illicit sex, and heavy-duty shopping are not enough to make life worth living in a tedious provincial town. Retaining the basics of Flaubert's plot, Sokurov punctuates the fast-moving action with touches of the grotesque and bizarre, from near-hysterical acting to scenes of nudity and copulation that have few equals for sheer unsexiness. Although the opening titles acknowledge Flaubert's novel, the characters don't have names and the film is hazy about its time and place; it often has a nineteenth-century look, but then a car comes along and all bets are off. The theme seems fairly clear, however, suggesting the inability of material resources (including the body itself) to fulfill humanity's inner needs.

Its considerable strangeness notwithstanding, *Save and Protect* was arguably Sokurov's last relatively straightforward fiction film. Two years later he took a momentous new step with *Stone,* based not on a Chekhov play or story but on the presence of Chekhov's enduring spirit in the earthly world. The setting is precise this time—everything happens in or near the Chekhov Museum in Yalta, which used to be the writer's house—but everything else is as shadowy, obscure, and spectral as the shade of Chekhov who reveals himself to the building's only inhabitant, a young security guard. The two spend a night in fitful colloquy about mostly mundane matters, their talk alternating with long semisilences in which footsteps, breaths, snatches of music, and outdoor sounds prevail. As museum movies go, *Stone* contrasts drastically with *Russian Ark;* where the Hermitage picture is sumptuous and accessible, *Stone* is dour, austere, and not an iota less exhilarating.

Stone has been called Sokurov's most dreamlike film, but for me it's tied in that department with *Whispering Pages,* which takes its cues from Dostoevsky's 1866 novel *Crime and Punishment,* wherein a young man commits a murder and suffers dire pangs of conscience. The film's settings—tumultuous streets, misty sidewalks, and yawning apartments, flattened out and photographed in faintly tinted monochrome—capture the novel's delirious atmosphere with stunning economy, ideally suiting the handful of characters who are recognizable from the novel. The opening shot, a lingering view of a grimy exterior wall hung with fire escapes to nowhere, is one of the most broodingly enigmatic visions in any Sokurov film.

All three of these features confirm Sokurov as an eloquent film poet, a fearless stylist of imagery and sound, and an unsurpassed exponent of so-called "slow cinema," an artistic path that Tarkovsky helped map out. More provocatively, Sokurov is also some kind of mystic—just what kind isn't clear, which tends to be the case when an artist takes on the counterintuitive task of communicating the incommunicable, especially in a completely commercialized medium. No serious discussion of Sokurov can shy away from the spiritual, even though the nature of his religion—if he even has one in the ordinary sense—remains a slippery area where few critics have gotten much of a foothold.

Tarkovsky was a Russian Orthodox believer who continually dealt with faith, salvation, redemption, and resurrection, directly in films such as *Andrei Rublev* (1966) and *The Sacrifice*

(1986), and obliquely in others such as *Solaris* (1972) and *Stalker* (1979). What can be said with some certainty about Sokurov is he that he too is magnetically attracted to the invisible, the ineffable, and the seemingly unfilmable, and that the traditional Orthodox icon is (by his own account) a foremost inspiration for one of his visual signatures: a flattening of the image by means of lenses designed to minimize the illusions of depth, volume, and perspective that conventional cinema shares with post-Renaissance art in general.

Filmmakers as different as Tarkovsky, Sergei Eisenstein, Pier Paolo Pasolini, and Stan Brakhage similarly tried to get beyond the linear perspective that dominates modern optics, but it doesn't necessarily follow that Sokurov has much interest in the particular Christian agendas that motivated some of them. Sokurov has asserted his independence even from the filmmaker widely assumed to have been his most decisive influence, saying that Tarkovsky was more important to him as an adviser and supporter than as an artist or philosopher. Yet while it's true that Sokurov has pushed further than Tarkovsky into narrative ambiguity, optical distortion, stylized acting, and so on, their mutual fascination with iconography reflects a likeminded desire not just to *evoke* spiritual feelings but also to *body forth* intimations of the divine that are as viscerally authentic as any experiences the screen can offer. Sokurov's stylized sounds and pictures seek to transcend cinema, and the material world that cinema commonly represents, via techniques not all that different from the ones Tarkovsky favored— hieratic mise-en-scène, off-kilter framing, "incorrect" editing, long takes that manifest the reality of time, and distanced camera placements that privilege externality over interiority, presence over psychology. These are sources of the numinous aura that makes the work of these directors so singular.

Among the shorter films in the Cinema Guild set, the most outstanding are two docufictions about Boris Yeltsin that only *seem* more worldly than the narrative features. *Soviet Elegy* dates from 1989, when the Soviet Union was crashing and Yeltsin was maneuvering for power. After an impressionistic prologue in a cemetery, we find him striding importantly through a building with briefcase in hand, then perched in front of a TV set tuned to a state function, looking as if he might be asleep. The film's centerpiece is a succession of official photos showing Soviet leaders from Lenin on, gazing at the camera with a cumulative repetitiveness that comes to seem hypnotic. The finale is a long, uninterrupted shot of Yeltsin asleep again, this time slumped at a kitchen table. The film is definitely an elegy for a disappearing past, not a glimpse of a promising future. Yet it seems to me that Sokurov is not accusing Yeltsin of somnolence, indifference, or lack of stamina. Rather, the sleeping shots anticipate the prolonged images of Chekhov and the guard sitting silently together in *Whispering Pages*—profoundly stirring images that connote not dullness or torpor but two souls engaged in the most primal of all human activities: simply and purely *being*.

That interpretation is borne out by the next film, *An Example of Intonation*, made just before Yeltsin became Russia's first democratically elected president in 1991. Much of it shows Yeltsin and Sokurov conversing with companionable ease, and Yeltsin's humility can seem a little faux when he says (for instance) that his troubles pale when he remembers the millions who live in poverty. But overall he sounds unguarded, truthful, and sincere as he muses on topics like his overcrowded schedule, the signs of age (he's sixty) that are starting to creep him out, the way he's started to make time for his long-neglected mother, and the things that a "civilized leader" must have but he admits he lacks—cultural knowledge, a second or third language, a decent grasp of history, control of negative emotions. The kitchen-table shot from *Soviet Elegy* recurs in this film, and by now it's clear (at least to me) that he deserves his rest.

All of this said, there's a lot about Yeltsin that Sokurov leaves out—the drinking, for one thing, which was serious enough to land him outside the White House in his underwear during a 1995 visit, trying to hail a cab so he could get a pizza in the middle of the night. Why does Sokurov minimize the unsavory stuff? He may be playing savvy politics, or being chivalrous, or indulging a taste for understatement, or throwing out hints with the assumption that we'll get the joke. It's just as possible, however, that he is honoring the sacred spark that glimmers within a globally famous, unimaginably powerful mortal who's also as frail, flawed, vulnerable, and worthy of salvation as any other sinner in our midst. That may sound paradoxical, but paradox is familiar territory for consecrated artists like Sokurov, and for holy fools like Yeltsin too.

Late Ozu
Cineaste 33:1, Winter 2007

Given all the half truths circulating about Yasujiro Ozu, it's a wonder his artistic reputation has flourished so vigorously. Even well-meaning critics have hung misleading tags on him, making his films sound esoteric and demanding. His stock has risen anyway, thanks to open-minded moviegoers willing to embrace films built on subtle insights and small epiphanies, at once wholly artificial— every detail is meticulously arranged by an artist of legendary patience—and as fully, deeply human as anything in cinema. Apart from the Criterion Collection's new release of "Late Ozu," only half a dozen of his fiftythree features are readily available on DVD, so there's a long way to go before he's a household name. But this is a marvelous contribution to the cause.

Before getting to the films, a word about those half truths. Ozu is the most Japanese of all Japanese directors, the story goes. His interests are fixated on family life and slow burning domestic conflict, and he cares little about social or political issues. His invariably static camera sits just off the floor, like a guest on a tatami mat, and his 360-degree camera positions are an interesting eccentricity. Ditto for his long delays before accepting technical innovations like sound and color. And while many directors have acknowledged making essentially the same movie throughout their careers, Ozu pushed the idea to its limits, rarely venturing beyond a constricted set of themes, storylines, and editing patterns. Even experts have been snookered by some of these notions, and when they "explain" the director along these lines, they reinforce the impression that his movies are austere, obses-sive, and definitely an acquired taste—wholesome and nutritious, maybe, but not tasty enough to try very often.

It's not hard to poke holes in most of the Ozu myths. Calling him the most Japanese director assumes we know what "Japanese-ness" is, and why Ozu's lifelong love of American film-makers—Ernst Lubitsch, Harold Lloyd, Frank Borzage, Orson Welles, John Ford—didn't dilute it. (Ozu had few qualms about learning and refining his craft through "extreme imitations" of American movies, according to Kiju Yoshida, his mentor.) Of course he was fascinated by domestic drama, but he also made nonsense comedies and gangster pictures; he depicts the work-place and the neighborhood saloon as well as the home; and he often examines family ideology under stressful conditions that

bring out its weaknesses more than its strengths. Ozu's recycling of storylines, themes, and so forth was prompted in part
by studio preferences and box-office returns, but also by his
aesthetic passion for rhythmic repetition, incremental change,
productive tensions between stasis and flux, and the endless possibilities of theme-and-variation structures. He was slow to accept
new technical resources because he was doing fine without them
and preferred to wait until the kinks had been worked out.
Regarding his idiosyncratic visuals, film scholar David Bordwell showed twenty years ago that Ozu used occasional camera
movements until the late 1950s and organized his 360-degree
space with exquisite care, angling shots at multiples of fifteen
degrees vis-à-vis the central point of interest. The camera is rarely
at eye level, despite countless claims to the contrary, but shoots
from low positions to about halfway up the height of the main
subject; so conversing characters don't look *into* the camera but
over it. All this may sound like technical trivia to some, but with
Ozu's work the angel is in the details.

Since the works in "Late Ozu" date from the director's last
filmmaking years, a bit of historical perspective is in order. Ozu
directed his first movie, the silent *Sword of Penitence,* in 1927. He first
impressed American audiences when his final film, *An Autumn Afternoon,* was shown in the first New York Film Festival in 1963, and he
became an arttheater favorite when his 1953 masterpiece *Tokyo Story*
played New York in 1972. Most critics divide his films into an early
period, ending with the unsuccessful *A Hen in the Wind* in 1948, and a
"mature" period, starting with the masterly *Late Spring* in 1949. This
oversimplifies the case, but generally speaking the post-1948 films are
more sober in tone and more minimalist in style, paring away fades,
dissolves, traveling shots, and such until they pretty much vanish. The
later works also mark the full blossoming of Ozu's collaborations
with Kogo Noda, his longtime coscreenwriter and drinking buddy,
and Yuuharu Atsuta, his frequent cinematographer from the early
Forties on. Critics of Noel Burch's stripe say Ozu's work went down-
hill after 1948, but the five films in "Late Ozu" make an argument
for the defense that I find irrefutable. Steeped in Ozu's distinctive
aesthetic yet amazingly varied in story, atmosphere, and tone, they
cry out for careful viewing by anyone with even a passing interest in
this utterly original artist.

Ozu made most of his movies for the Shochiku studio, which
specialized in "home dramas" about ordinary people facing
commonplace crises. By the time he started *Early Spring* (1956),

however, the realistic *shomingeki* was losing ground to more up-to-date fare like science fiction and pop-music romps. Eager to regain the leading position it had recently lost to the upstart Daiei studio, Shochiku encouraged its staff directors, including Ozu, to try more "modern" approaches. One result was an increased emphasis on melodrama—a development of special interest where Ozu is concerned, since commentators like David Desser have taken his statement that *Tokyo Story* was "one of [his] most melodramatic pictures" as a mildly self-deprecating remark. Be that as it may, *Early Spring* is melodramatic to its bones, and brilliantly so.

The story centers on Shoji (Ryo Ikebe), a married "salaryman" whose low-level job in a Tokyo office provides little satisfaction aside from the companionship of his colleagues. One of them, a secretary nicknamed Goldfish (Keiko Kishi), seduces him into an extramarital affair. They keep it secret for a while, but eventually Shoji's wife finds out about it (gossip, lipstick stains, the usual}, whereupon she and Shoji separate. In the story's remarkable denouement, Shoji accepts a transfer to a remote branch of his company; his wife returns to him; and the two stand at a window of their new home in Mitsuishi, trying to persuade themselves that living in this bleak industrial wasteland is just the thing to get their marriage back on track, and hey, Tokyo isn't that far away, and anyway, it's only for a few years.

This is a finale that the Douglas Sirk of *All That Heaven Allows* (1955) and *The Tarnished Angels* (1958) would have been proud of, and other elements of *Early Spring* also recall Sirk's pessimistic vision of modern life. An office worker named Miura does nothing in the film but sicken and die. Characters ceaselessly express dislike for their jobs, restlessness with their routines, and fear about their futures, and Ozu's severe *mise-en-scène* offers ample visual support for their complaints. His declared purpose in *Early Spring* was to show the dissolution of a salaryman's hopes as he realizes that "even though he has worked for years, he has accomplished nothing." (This film does for the Japanese "economic miracle" what various Fassbinder films do for the German one.) Ozu wasn't a political artist, especially in his postwar period of elliptically told middle-class dramas, but he wasn't entirely apolitical either; only a filmmaker with strong opinions could have Shoji's wife listen to the sappy reminiscing of over-the-hill military men and remark, "With soldiers like that, no wonder Japan lost the war!" Ozu's deeply critical portrait of contemporary Japan, industrialized and Westernized in ways that were unthinkable a decade earlier, is astringent and acute. *Early Spring* may not have jump-started Shochiku's fortunes as the studio hoped, but it certainly brought fresh relevance to the home-drama genre.

Ozu's next movie again focuses on young characters, and its overtones are even more darksome; if *Early Spring* is Sirkian melodrama, *Tokyo Twilight* (1957) is *film noir*, swept by philosophical shadows and haunted by implacable death. Ozu's favorite actor and almost exact contemporary, Chishu Ryu, plays Shukichi, the aging father of young Akiko (Ineko Arima) and married Takako, played by Setsuko Hara, whose ready smile and melancholy eyes are as closely identified with Ozu's films as Ryu's amiable features and expressive voice. Scuttling the leisurely exposition of most late Ozu films, the narrative quickly informs us that trouble is afoot: Takako is leaving her husband, a mild-seeming man who's taken to drowning himself in alcohol and taking out his frustrations on her and their infant child. Then unmarried Akiko learns she's pregnant and both sisters discover that their supposedly dead mother actually ran off with a lover years ago, and now runs a mah-jongg parlor not far from where they live. Recriminations, abortion, and suicide follow.

Commentaries like to point out that *Equinox Flower* is the only postwar Ozu film set during the dead of Japan's bone-chilling winter. Many of the film's elements are downbeat and dreary, from its frequent nighttime scenes and unpleasant characters to its pitiless view of a Japanese family riven by secrets, lies, and betrayals. In no other film does Hara look as careworn, unhappy, and beaten down by life as she does here. *Tokyo Twilight* was the first Ozu film in twenty-one years not to reach the top ten in the annual poll conducted by Japan's respected *Kinema Jumpo* magazine. Seen today, it emerges as one of Ozu's most profoundly modern works, sounding psycho-logical and sociological depths that he never probed so fearlessly before or since.

Equinox Flower (1958) is Ozu's first color film, and it's a stunning one. The gentle comedy's main character, businessman Wataru (Shin Saburi), is caught up in a string of marital dilemmas: His older daughter Setsuko (Arima) doesn't want the arranged marriage he's planned on; his male friend Shukichi (Ryu) is upset that his daughter has moved in with a musician; his female friend Hatsu (Chieko Naniwa) is pushing her reluctant daughter to wed a physician who's treating her; and so on. The story's big irony is that while Wataru thinks he's modern and progressive, his support of youthful independence crumbles when his own offspring are involved. The film's big joke is a mischievous (if implausible) ruse that tricks him into allowing Setsuko to marry as she pleases, however much he still dislikes the idea. Ozu's unerring sense of color is obvious from the moment we see Wataru's younger daughter decked out in a dazzling pink sweater, just the garment to complement her perky chitchat about love and marriage, postwar Japanese style. According to one of his camera operators, Ozu's preference for muted colors made him dislike Agfacolor's red and Eastmancolor's blue, although he decided he could live with Agfa in the end. Intentionally or not, his alluring use of red became a trademark of his last movies, and the appropriately titled *Equinox Flower* is where it started. If the film is less resonant than its two predecessors, it's because the aging matinee idol Saburi looks right as Wataru but speaks and moves like even more of a stiff than the uncool character is supposed to be. Still, anyone looking for Ozu's most charming side will do better here than with the overrated comedy *Good Morning* that followed it in 1959.

Late Autumn (1960) is a much-modified remake of *Late Spring*, the 1949 masterpiece that kicked off Ozu's late period. Again a young person (Ayako, played by Yôko Tsukasa) is encouraged by a widowed parent (Akiko, played by Hara) to get married, and again the parent talks about remarrying in order to cajole the youngster. *Late Autumn* gives more weight to the younger side of the equation, though, and allows more independence to the single parent of the story. Japan was roiled in 1960 by the scheduled renewal of the Japanese-American Security Treaty, which touched off controversy and violence; in this atmosphere *Late Autumn* was seen by Japanese critics such as Tadao Sato as blinkered, backward-looking, and out of touch. Yet while this isn't one of Ozu's most invigorating works, it offers a near-perfect balance between the persuasive pull of tradition and the unstoppable sway of Westernized modernity. Ozu's sociopolitical side surfaces again, subtly but surely, in this portrait of postwar realities rubbing uneasily against their prewar counterparts. And his cinematic skills are as strong as ever, not least in his brilliant casting of Hara, the daughter of *Late Spring,* as the deeply sympathetic mother here.

Ozu's penultimate film, *The End of Summer* (1961), is actually called *Kohayakawake no aki,* which means *The Autumn of the Kohayakawaka Family,* a more accurate title for one of his most far-reaching portrayals of a clan facing personal, professional, and historical change. Bordwell has observed that right after World War II, sixty percent of Japan's workers labored in middle-class family businesses; most of these were defunct by the time this film was made, and their disappearance split many extended families into small nuclear households, forcing new challenges on Japanese society. Coming to grips with such changes, *The End of Summer* stresses emotion over analysis in Ozu's usual manner, but this doesn't diminish the story's strength as psychological drama and social commentary. The central character is Manbei Kohayakawaka, a feisty patriarch who's ignoring economic threats to the family sake-brewing business, preferring to frolic and carouse in ways his relatives find anything but age appropriate. In a plot twist based on a real-life incident Ozu knew of, Manbei collapses and lies near death for a night, only to spring up the next morning as if nothing had happened. But like the stopgaps and excuses his relatives fall back on while hardships draw near, his well-being is precarious and doomed to collapse. Ozu doesn't indulge in scatological humor nearly as often as critics like Bordwell and Donald Richie claim, but this is one of the rare pictures where he does seem a trifle naughty at times. Far more important is his use of Manbei's declining sense of order as a metaphor for the morphing face of Japanese society.

Vastly more can be said about "Late Ozu," but there's no substitute for simply watching the films. Each of them is emotionally rich, psychologically true, intellectually exact, stylistically nimble, and as entertaining as can be, drawing on finely tuned strategies whose narrative punch—comic, tragic, dramatic, romantic, and every stop in between—is all the stronger for their bold refusal of standard movie conventions. Among the people who visited Ozu as he lay dying of cancer was Shochiku studio chief Shiro Kido, and it's said that Ozu murmured into the ear of his longtime supporter, "Well, Mr. President, after all, the home drama." Like that dark joke at that disquieting moment, Ozu's cinematic home dramas are at once engaging, challenging, and ultimately inexhaustible to the inquiring mind. A zillion thanks to the Criterion Collection for expanding its Ozu filmography with these wondrous late works.

John Farrow: Ingenious Filmmaker, Incorrigible Fabulist, Impossible Person
Cineaste 50:1, Winter 2024

John Farrow's hour may be coming around at last. Although he directed scores of features between *Men in Exile* in 1937 and *John Paul Jones* in 1959, the prolific and versatile director has been oddly overlooked since 1963, when he died from a heart attack at the young age of 58. Today he's best known as the father of movie star Mia Farrow and the grandfather of crusading journalist Ronan Farrow, who have kept the family name very much in view. But he made respected pictures in an array of genres, from *Five Came Back* (1939) and *Two Years Before the Mast* (1946) to *The Big Clock* (1948) and *The Sea Chase* (1955). Hollywood talents on the level of John Wayne, Alan Ladd, and Ray Milland worked with him repeatedly, and Maureen O'Sullivan, who acted in several of his movies, was his wife and the mother of their seven children. He earned an Academy Award nomination for Best Director with *Wake Island* (1942) and shared an Oscar for Best Adapted Screenplay with James Poe and S. J. Perelman for the 1956 epic *Around the World in 80 Days*, which he directed for a day or two until producer Mike Todd fired him and gave Michael Anderson the job. He also produced a few movies and wrote a number of fiction and nonfiction books.

Quite a career. So why doesn't Farrow have a spot in the usual lists of major American directors? One answer might be that Andrew Sarris, the chief American popularizer of auteurism, skipped clear over Farrow in *The American Cinema*, his (overly) influential book on the subject. A more important answer might be that a director this flexible is hard to tag with a signature style and a set of favorite personal themes. As with other conspicuously supple filmmakers—Louis Malle, Michael Curtiz—his mercurial interests and all-purpose skills don't fit into easy critical pigeonholes. Yet auteurists who pay attention can't miss meaningful throughlines in his best pictures of the Forties and Fifties, when he wove his religious interests into film after film and cultivated a camera style based on continually flowing action captured in some of the most bravura long takes of their era. He also believed in personal cinema after a fashion, saying he wanted to craft commercially successful movies in order to keep studio interference at bay. He saw pleasing the multitudes as a route to pleasing himself.

Whatever the reason, Farrow is a semi-forgotten figure, and *Directed by John Farrow*, a Blu-ray box set from the Australian label Imprint, aims to get him back into the limelight. The set comprises five major films—*Commandos Strike at Dawn* (1942), *The Hitler Gang* (1944), *Night Has a Thousand Eyes* (1948), *Submarine Command* (1951), and *Botany Bay* (1952)—plus a feature-length documentary by Claude Gonzalez and Frans Vandenburg, aptly titled *John Farrow: Hollywood's Man in the Shadows*. The discs amount to a welcome and worthy effort, but the collection would be more persuasive if some of Farrow's most remarkable films weren't absent. *Wake Island*, *The Big Clock*, *Five Came Back*, *Alias Nick Beal* (1949), and *Where Danger Lives* (1950) are among the missing, and no first-rate Farrow library should be without them. The organizers eliminated two strong movies, *Alias Nick Beal* and *Plunder of the Sun* (1953), because they're already in the Imprint catalogue; for their final selections they sought out high-quality films not readily accessible from other sources. A more generous compilation would make a better case for Farrow as the note-worthy auteur he certainly is, but on the upside, Imprint's digital transfers are mostly excellent, and all except one of the films are accompanied by well-done audio commentaries and other extras. As far as it goes, this is a fine release.

The eclecticism of Farrow's filmography is matched by the variety of his offscreen exploits, although he was such a fabu-list that it can be hard to tell what's real and what's invented in his personal history. He was an Australian from a suburb of Sydney, where he worked briefly as an accountant before heading to sea with the Merchant Marine, sailing in the southern Pacific and fighting in Latin American revolutions, or so he claimed. According to Gonzalez and Vandenburg's documentary, he got in trouble as a teenager for running around with a stethoscope and pretending to be a physician, and according to Marilyn Moss' biography *The Farrows of Hollywood*, his first wife described him as a "mysterious, monocled youth" who said he was the heir to a British earldom. A lot of this was bogus, but he had indeed been to sea, and when he eventually landed in California he parlayed his shipboard experience and knack for writing into gigs as a screenplay consultant and technical advisor, first for Cecil B. DeMille and then for the RKO and Paramount studios. Soon he was writing silent-movie intertitles—the same entry point used by Alfred Hitchcock—and writing and doctoring scripts, special-izing in so-called women's pictures. He also penned a novelization of George Fitzmaurice's 1930 melodrama *The Bad One*, a book in which Moss detects a "stunning prose style" (but take it from me, the prose is exceedingly prosaic). In 1933 he was arrested for violating immigration law—his visa had expired and the government was chasing down "aliens" in the film industry—yet he managed to remain in Hollywood, making his directorial debut in 1934 with *The Spectacle Maker*, an MGM short about magical eyeglasses, with glowing Technicolor that justifies the movie's title. While codirecting *Tarzan Escapes* (1936, credited to Richard Thorpe) he met and married O'Sullivan, remaining with her until his death while sleeping with so many other women that O'Sullivan had a separate door and stairway added to their house so she wouldn't have to hear his late-night entrances and exits.

After directing some competent B pictures and programmers—*West of Shanghai* (1937), *Broadway Musketeers* (1938), *The Saint Strikes Back* (1939), et al.—Farrow made a breakthrough with *Five Came Back*, an adventure yarn about travelers stranded in the jungle when their plane goes down; in an Imprint video interview, filmmaker Joe Dante accurately describes it as a B picture with an excellent cast (Chester Morris, Lucille Ball, John Carradine, Wendy Barrie) and superior production values. Farrow made it look considerably more expensive than it was, and its success opened the way to more meaningful projects with more substantial resources. During the war years he made exclusively war-related pictures: *Wake Island* was the first movie based on an actual World War II campaign, according to one of the Imprint audio commentaries, and Farrow followed it with *Commandos Strike at Dawn*, about Norway's resistance to Nazi occupation, *China* (1943), about the Japanese invasion of that country, *The Hitler Gang* (1944), a truly remarkable biopic, and *You Came Along* (1945), a lightweight dramedy, cowritten by Ayn Rand, about war bonds and romance. He closed out the Forties with the musical *Red, Hot and Blue* (1949).

His subsequent films took in pretty much every familiar genre. In the Fifties he made a 3D western (*Hondo*, 1953) and followed the fashion for expansive and expensive super-productions, doing uncredited work on the Cinerama documentary *Seven Wonders of the World* (1956), helming the Spanish sequences of *Around the World in 80 Days* before getting sacked, and remaking *Five Came Back* as *Back from Eternity* (1956). Then came *The Unholy Wife* (1957), a Diana Dors vehicle, and *John Paul Jones*, a disappointing epic shot in Technorama, a short-lived CinemaScope competitor.

After failing to achieve his decade-long dream of filming the life of Jesus—it eventually morphed into Nicholas Ray's *King of Kings* (1961)—he turned to television in the early Sixties, directing three episodes of *Empire*, a modern-day western series. As an author, Farrow pursued his Roman Catholic convictions in books about the papacy, Thomas More, and a nineteenth-century saint; he also compiled an English-French-Tahitian dictionary, the first of its kind, and penned a history of the Royal Canadian Navy, in which he had served on antisubmarine patrols before contracting typhus and being discharged from active duty in early 1942. Although he rarely took screenplay credit on films he directed, he regarded directing as a form of writing. He clearly had a very verbal mind.

Returning to the question of Farrow's relative obscurity since his death, another answer might be the personal abrasiveness that turned off many of the people in his orbit. He was a dictator on the set, a notorious womanizer after hours, and apparently a practicing sadist as well. Moss' biography identifies him as the unnamed villain in a report by show-business columnist Sheila Graham, who wrote about an aging star's call for help after suffering "little cuts all over her [made] with razor blades," inflicted by a well-known figure whose "particular hang-up" was slicing into female flesh, a practice he evidently indulged more than once. Coupling this nasty business with his hard-edged directing manner, it's possible that when Farrow died a lot of people were glad to forget him. In an Imprint video essay, critic David Cairns offers a few choice quotations: Robert Mitchum called him "an interesting man but a sadist," Jane Russell described him as "a smart man with an evil sense of humor, and Milland deemed him a "good director" but a "strange" person and "the most disliked man on the lot." Farrow once told his daughter Mia that he "never saw a happy actress," and Cairns wonders if they were unhappy because they were working with him.

The earliest film in the box set, and the only one unadorned with video extras, is *Commandos Strike at Dawn*, originally slated for 1943 but released at the end of 1942 in response to recent war developments. Irwin Shaw's screenplay, based on a minor C. S. Forester story, centers on stolid, softspoken Erik Toresen (Paul Muni), a widowed scientist raising his little girl in a Norwegian fishing village, where he also finds time to court the daughter of a visiting British admiral. The year is 1939, as the opening dialogue makes laboriously clear, and Nazi invaders duly barge in, taking over the town, ruling through fear, confiscating necessities from the helpless residents, imposing racist propaganda on the kids at school, executing a man for having a radio, and torturing another who dares to speak against them. Before long Toresen decides he's had enough and organizes his friends in acts of sabotage. After killing the chief German officer he's forced to flee the country, making it to England and then returning to Norway with a troupe of British commandos on a mission to destroy a Nazi airfield and rescue the little girl he left behind.

Its bellicose title notwithstanding, *Commandos Strike at Dawn* puts human drama over battlefield action, although commandos do eventually arrive and do eventually strike. While the fighting was shot in Canada, not Norway, it looks reasonably authentic thanks to planes, equipment, and troops supplied by the Canadian government to Farrow, whose standing as a Royal Canadian Navy officer clearly came in handy. He returns the favor in an opening text dedicating the film to "the armed forces of Canada, Great Britain and Fighting Norway," all of which assisted with the production.

God may have helped as well, at least in Farrow's opinion, since this is one of many films in which his highly religious mindset is plain to see; in her otherwise good audio commentary for *Night Has a Thousand Eyes*, critic Imogen Sara Smith says religion is a minor element in his movies, but *Commandos Strike at Dawn* is one of numerous films that refute this peculiar claim. More than one prayer is delivered at length; the modest fishing village has a surprisingly large church; the pastor meets with his flock to announce that he won't cooperate with the evil forces now running the town; and so on until the final scene, when Toresen's daughter and other women head for freedom on a ship while a voiceover quotes the New Testament, saying the battle underway isn't really against "flesh and blood," it's against "rulers of the darkness" and "spiritual wickedness in high places." Farrow firmly believed in such dogma, and it's an enduring mystery how this comported with his off-hours activities as a constant seducer and occasional tormenter of women.

Viewers watching the box-set films in order of release will find *Commandos Strike at Dawn* a striking introduction to Farrow's love for challenging long-take sequences, here facilitated by William C. Mellor, who had photographed *Wake Island* two years earlier. The opening shot moves gracefully across the village's main square, then picks up Toresen as he strolls to the waterside and chats with companions. The second scene is even more impressive, capturing a festive wedding with a gliding camera and impeccably choreographed character movements; in a video essay on Farrow's war movies, film historian Daniel Kremer says this six-and-a-half-minute take was rehearsed for four days before shooting. Farrow's single-take episodes never come across as cinematic showing off; they are deliberate artistic choices by a director with a unique visual aesthetic and a forceful creative personality. This alone makes a persuasive case for his auteur status.

He also knew how to get solid performances, whatever the actors may have thought of his manner on the set. Muni had been appearing in stage productions for the past couple of years, but he welcomed *Commandos Strike at Dawn* as a way of contributing to the war effort, and he gives Toresen a convincing blend of toughness, vulnerability, and even wistfulness at times. Lillian Gish had been concentrating on stage work for even longer, and her small role here didn't make for much of a screen comeback, but she's perfectly believable as the wife of the unfortunate villager (Ray Collins, fresh from his great Orson Welles roles of the early Forties) who undergoes Nazi torture. Sir Cedric Hardwicke is as wooden as ever, which at least suits his part as an English admiral; Anna Lee is lovely as his daughter; and Robert Coote, billed as Flying Officer Robert Coote, RCAF, is just right as his son. Kudos also for six-year-old Ann Carter, soon to be the youthful heroine of Gunther v. Fritsch and Robert Wise's 1944 gem *The Curse of the Cat People*.

Commandos Strike at Dawn opens the box set well, but the program goes into high gear with *The Hitler Gang*, starring Bobby Watson as the eponymous führer, who was still terrorizing Europe when the film premiered in 1944. In the audio commentary, Kremer deems this the most "earnest" entry in a cycle of "Hitlersploitation" films made in the Thirties and Forties, such as Edward Dmytryk's *Hitler's Children* and Douglas Sirk's *Hitler's Madman*, both from 1943. (Co-commentator Allan Arkush also mentions the 1942 Disney cartoon *Der Fuehrer's Face*, one of the wittiest propaganda pieces ever.) Farrow and his credited screenwriters, the distinguished team of Frances Goodrich and Albert Hackett, aim at both entertainment and education as they trace Hitler's rise to power; they signal their serious intentions in an opening text averring that the "episodes throughout are authenticated by documentary records, by the works of reputable historians, and in some instances by actual participants," guaranteeing a tale that sticks to the facts "insofar as decency will permit." A sense of authenticity can be hard to sustain in a Hollywood fabrication, even a high-minded one like this, but Watson's performance strikes a good balance between impersonation and interpretation, keeping the movie within hailing distance of historical plausibility. Watson played Hitler in almost a dozen movies, according to Cairns' video essay on the film, and he definitely looks the part here, especially after he snips off the ends of his sizable moustache to achieve the Chaplinesque toothbrush look. Kremer reports that Watson was asked not to eat in the Paramount commissary because other diners might lose their appetites. Der führer was the part he was born to play.

The Hitler Gang begins at the tail end of World War I, when Lance Corporal Hitler is lying in a hospital with blindness that a physician ascribes to mental instability rather than physical illness. He leaves his sickbed just as Germany is surrendering, and the first thing he does is squeal on fellow soldiers who oppose the country's new government. Following orders from Ernst Roehm, his new mentor, he joins the German Workers Party and soon becomes its boss, recruiting the repellant likes of Heinrich Himmler, Rudolf Hess, and Hermann Goering as deputies. This outfit becomes the National Socialist Party, and Hitler's iron leadership and fiery speechifying lead to swelling enrollments. The rest is history, as they say, and the movie depicts decisive turning points—the Beer Hall Putsch, the Reichstag fire, the Night of the Long Knives— as well as incidents in private life, such as Goering's drug addiction and mental breakdown, Hitler's reliance on astrology, and his infatuation with his half-niece Geli Raubal, whom he may have murdered in real life and does murder in the film. The story ends in the middle Thirties, when Hitler takes over the German army and starts implementing his most horrifying ideas. The Holocaust looms as the end credits roll.

The movie was the brainchild of Paramount production head Buddy De Sylva, who had been appalled by a well-crafted German propaganda film and wanted to counter it with a "documentary-propaganda" picture making an anti-Nazi case so realistic and compelling that both American and European audiences would respond to it. He had admired *Five Came Back* and *Wake Island*, so Farrow got the nod to direct, and they agreed not to dilute its realism by casting big stars. True to its title, it portrays Hitler and company as the equivalent of a crime syndicate; it's easy to imagine more recent tyrants (Don Corleone, Donald Trump) running this mob. The art directors were Hans Dreier and Franz Bachelin, frequent Farrow collaborators who did excellent work on every-thing from intimate settings to the enormous murals in the Nazi headquarters; the cinematographer was Ernest Laszlo, who fell in perfectly with Farrow's predilection for elaborate camera move-ments and long takes, most stunningly in the Munich beer-hall scene, which has a 360-degree pan shot culminating in a riot packed with chaotic violence. And speaking of violence, the Night of the Long Knives sequence uses blood squibs, a brand-new device in 1944. Farrow did have a yen for blood.

Even though Farrow entered the project as a contract director picked by De Sylva, once he was there he made sure to inject his theological notions into the mix, using Hitler's hostility to religion as a glaring example of his outrageous wickedness. "My quarrel is not with the churches," the führer rants to his top accomplices. "I'm against the whole Jewish, communist idea of Christianity itself, with its eternal ten commandments—*thou shalt not* and *thou shalt not*, as if nature did not say *covet, murder, kill*!" An aide suggests giving Christ a new image as an Aryan, but Hitler wants the messiah gone altogether, and soon it's resolved that crucifixes, Bibles, and pictures of saints will be swept off every altar and replaced with copies of *Mein Kampf*. Since indoctrination must begin in child-hood, the next scene whisks us to a schoolroom. Teacher: "Who reminds us most of Jesus and his love for humble people and his readiness for self-sacrifice?" Pupils: "Our führer!" Teacher: "And who are his loyal disciples?" Pupils: "Goering, Goebbels, Hess…" And a little later, when Hitler confronts a church official: "Jesus Christ was only a man, and a Jew at that… I shall cut out this cancerous growth of pity and brotherly love that eats into our manhood!" The furnishings of this scene include items of religious flotsam from Farrow's own collection. A personal touch.

In his video essay on *The Hitler Gang*, Cairns says a few words about the box set's next selection, *Night Has a Thousand Eyes*, saying that few noirs place the issues of free will and destiny so clearly at the center of their concerns. I agree. And while this film doesn't touch on religion per se, the supernatural and the uncanny permeate it throughout. It also ranks with *The Big Clock*, *Alias Nick Beal*, and *Where Danger Lives* as one of Farrow's purest excursions into the dark-toned psychology of film noir. Based on a middling-good novel by Cornell Woolrich, a presiding spirit in the noir cosmos, it centers on John Triton, a magician who pretends to be clairvoyant in his cheerfully phony stage act but learns to his astonishment that his powers are real, enabling him to discern the future with an accuracy he can't begin to fathom. The story commences when Triton (the superb Edward G. Robinson in peak form) has a conversation with scientist Elliott Carson (the anodyne John Lund) and Carson's wealthy girlfriend, Jean Courtland (the charming Gail Russell), whom Carson has just prevented from committing suicide. Flashbacks ensue, revealing (among other things) how Triton discovered his psychic abilities, how Courtland came into his life many years ago, how he predicted her father's death in a plane crash, and how he now foresees her own imminent death, which will happen near the feet of a lion under a sky filled with stars.

Eventually the police come along, steering this mostly fascinating film into a more routine mold as they scurry about for signs of skullduggery, argue about whether to believe anything Triton says, and ultimately kill the only person with some understanding of what's going on. The film culminates with an effectively bittersweet finale, but not before a ridiculous rush to tie up loose ends and provide some semblance of logical resolution. What makes *Night Has a Thousand Eyes* so bewitching isn't the plot, it's the overall atmosphere of mystery and dread, rendered with moody intelligence by Farrow, art directors Dreier and Bachelin, and cinematographer John F. Seitz, fresh from *The Big Clock* and on his way to such noir-adjacent classics as Billy Wilder's *Sunset Boulevard* (1950) and George Stevens' *A Place in the Sun* (1951). In her audio commentary, Smith rightly says that spiritualism and mentalism were popular topics in Forties cinema—Edmund Goulding's 1947 *Nightmare Alley*, Bernard Vorhaus' 1948 *The Amazing Mr. X*—and Farrow's movie merges this trend with the archetypal noir theme of a seemingly great thing turning out to be more a curse than a blessing. In a related observation, Smith notes that noir's penchant for flashbacks usually shows how the past can overshadow the present, whereas here it's the *future* that overshadows the present; it also overshadows poor Triton, who was happy as a faker and becomes miserable when his gift proves real.

This is astute analysis, and there's more of the same in a video interview with Moss about the film, which I found a pleasure to watch after being disappointed by the exceedingly careless writing in her Farrow biography. She sees this and similar Farrow films not as noirs but as studies in psychology—they're actually both—and she pithily sums up *Night Has a Thousand Eyes* as the story of a man whose terror stems from his inability to comprehend the frightening secrets hidden within the depths of his own mind and soul. And this, she continues, is self-portraiture by Farrow, who "spills himself all over [his] films," bearing out Rouben Mamoulian's contention that every movie is an autobiography of its director. Other examples of Farrow portraying himself include the serpentine décor in *Alias Nick Beal*, which resembles the long snake tattoo running from groin to ankle on Farrow's body, and the entire plot of *Alias Nick Beal*, a Faustian fable where the devil is a surrogate for Farrow and the devil damn near wins. Bringing out the unity of Farrow the man and Farrow the director, Moss' remarks are among the savviest in the Imprint set.

Submarine Command is another military drama with a title that makes it sound more action-oriented than it is. It begins with Naval officer Ken White (William Holden) reminiscing about his days on the *Tiger Shark*, recalling the grim day when he was forced to save the submarine and its crew by making an emergency dive while two men were on its outside deck. One of the men who drowned was the captain, and while Ken is blameless in the eyes of the captain's family, a crew member named Boyer (William Bendix) seethes with resentment over what he regards as a needless death. Ken considers leaving the Navy but decides to press on with his career despite guilt feelings he has never been able to shake. Long afterward, when he has married girlfriend Carol (Nancy Olson) and taken a desk job, he is reassigned to the *Tiger Shark* for service in the Korean War, and is present at another fatal incident, rekindling Boyer's rage and increasing the depression that has afflicted Ken since the opening scene. The climax involves a combat mission in North Korea, a reconciliation between Ken and Boyer, and a new baby in Ken's now-happy household.

The audio commentary here is a loose, movie-buff session with film historians Lee Pfeiffer, Tony Latino, and Paul Scrabo, who mention Holden's oft-repeated remark that he drank so much during the shoot that he hardly remembered making the picture. They also make the valid point that *Submarine Command* is essentially a story of post-traumatic stress disorder, with protagonist Ken struggling against inner demons bred by a profoundly disturbing event. Carrying their analysis a step further, they suggest that testy, difficult Ken is a stand-in for Farrow, and the character's belated recognition of his flaws might be Farrow's way of atoning for his own unpleasing qualities; if that's so, it makes *Submarine Command* another instance of directorial self-portraiture. On the technical side, the commentators praise the film's smoothly integrated rear-screen work, supervised by special-effects wizard Farciot Edouart, and commend its expertly done miniatures. I wish they'd also talked about Bendix, who appears in many Farrow films, providing the sort of regular-guy lovability that William Demarest contributed to Preston Sturges pictures. (Demarest shows up in *Night Has a Thousand Eyes*, incidentally, lending the police lieutenant his distinctively raspy-voiced appeal.)

Although he was Australian by birth and upbringing, Farrow hardly ever dealt with that country in his films, and *Botany Bay* is the only one to settle in for an extended stay. Based on a harrowing but enjoyable novel by Charles Nordhoff and James Norman Hall, writers best known for launching the *Mutiny on the Bounty* franchise, the movie takes place in the late eighteenth century, when England had begun shipping convicted criminals, and in some cases their spouses and children, to the Australian penal colony at Botany Bay, where hard labor, persistent hunger, and frequent illness awaited those hardy and lucky enough to survive the sea voyage that got them there. Much of the film chronicles such a voyage, with unjustly imprisoned Hugh Tallant, stiffly played by Ladd in his fifth and final Farrow production, undergoing insults and tortures from Captain Paul Gilbert, played by James Mason with a virtuoso blend of panache and hatefulness. The two continue sparring on dry land, where attacks by indigenous inhabitants and an outbreak of plague add further complications. Others present include the colony's governor (wooden Hardwicke, wooden character) and a female prisoner played by Patrica Medina, whose lipstick and hairdo remain gloriously intact no matter how many insupportable hardships descend on her.

In an informative audio commentary, Kremer and critic David Del Valle recall that Ladd, who was sick with flu during three weeks of shooting, was about to leave Paramount at the time, which may have led the studio to skimp on the resources for what could have been a swashbuckling excursion to faraway climes. This might well be true, although Seitz's ravishing Technicolor cinematography helps offset the manufactured sets and generally claustrophobic look of the picture, which largely lacks Farrow's usual bravura camerawork. The commentators also come down heavily on the film's violence—lashings, keelhauling, the slow death of a child—and speculate that Farrow and/or Paramount amped up the brutality to cover up storytelling problems, such as the thinness of Gilbert's backstory and the awkward fact that Tallant, the putative hero, constantly makes bad choices that cause grief and suffering for others. (The film's most likely audience was "boys and ghouls," a reviewer wrote.) On the plus side, Mason mostly transcends the movie's weaknesses—he always wanted to play Captain Bligh, and here he came close, although he fell short of Charles Laughton for some critics—and Farrow works in fleeting cameos for a kangaroo and a pair of koala bears. He also indulges his religious zeal with a burial-at-sea scene featuring a lengthy Bible recitation by Gilbert, who knows the text by heart. In all, *Botany Bay* is an okay place to visit, but you wouldn't want to live there, or to watch this movie a great many times.

Farrow was a knotty, complicated, sometimes impossible person and a gifted, disciplined, highly imaginative filmmaker. When writing his biography, Moss says, she could only "stand back and gape" at such a paradoxical, contradictory life. There's a good chance that the Imprint set will rejuvenate his reputation, which also has its share of contradictions: Sarris gave him short shrift, but Manny Farber mentioned him alongside Howard Hawks, Raoul Walsh, and Anthony Mann, calling him an "urbane vaudevillian" whose best pictures shore up their "eccentric characterizations" with "a fine motoring system."

Gonzalez and Vandenburg's documentary, featuring such well-qualified talking heads as John Farrow Jr. and critic Farran Smith Nehme, also calls attention to anomalies, such as Farrow's short-lived first marriage, which should have disqualified the Catholic convert from wedding O'Sullivan later. And while the film illustrates his long-take virtuosity with appropriate clips from *China* and other films, reinforcing the admiration that Gonzalez and Vandenburg clearly feel for him, the extras on this disc counteract any tendency toward hagiography, with Australian filmmaker Bruce Beresford and prolific biographer Charles Higham complaining that *Botany Bay* botches what should have been an Australia-set epic for the ages; something must have gone really wrong to produce such glaring artificiality, Beresford says, and it's hard to disagree. All told, the documentary and the five titles selected by Imprint open the way for fresh reassessment of Farrows' career, and I encourage cinephiles to find his dozens of other films, almost all of which can be tracked down in some form. Some are sensational, a few are dismal, and all are grist for stimulating critical conversation. Let's keep the opinions flowing and see where they take us.

Confounding the Plausibles: Louis Feuillade's Epic Crime Serials

Cineaste 38:2, Spring 2013

Former bookkeeper, journalist, editor, and wine merchant Louis Feuillade entered the Gaumont studio as the thirty-two-year-old screenwriter of the amusingly titled short *Stop My Hat!* The year was 1905, when the French were enjoying Alice Guy's *Five O'Clock Tea* and Ferdinand Zecca's *Scenes of Convict Life* and Americans were watching Biograph's *Tom, Tom, the Piper's Son* and Edison's *The Whole Dam Family and the Dam Dog*. Gaumont was the second largest studio in France after Pathé, and Feuillade felt immediately at home. He made his directorial debut (*A Gust of Wind*) in 1906 and became Gaumont's artistic director a year later, taking over from Guy, who was moving to America with her new husband, Herbert Blaché.

Swiftly manifesting his career-long affinity for serials and series, Feuillade directed scores of comedies about a little scamp named Bébé between 1910 and 1915 and dozens of comedies about a little scamp named Bout-de-Zan between 1913 and 1915. But he was versatile as well as prolific, and in 1910 he decided to compete with the prestige-minded Film d'Art studio by launching a franchise named "Le Film Esthétique," which quickly tanked. Next he spotlighted downbeat melodrama in a series called "Life as It Is," achieving distinctive results in eccentric pictures like *The Trust, or, The Battles for Money* (1911) and *The Dwarf* (1912).

In 1913 Feuillade directed *Fantômas: In the Shadow of the Guillotine*, initiating the first of the multipart melodramas that made him famous. Today viewers can see all of the *Fantômas* films (four more followed in 1913 and 1914) on a three-DVD set from Kino International, which also distributes the ten episodes of *Les Vampires* (1915-16) in DVD and Blu-ray editions. Add these to the twelve installments (plus lengthy prologue) of the even more sophisticated *Judex* (1916), presented on two DVDs by Flicker Alley, and you have almost eighteen hours of shamelessly addictive silent cinema.

The plots of Feuillade's serials are notoriously hard to summarize, and difficult just to *follow* unless you enjoy keeping track of mysterious events, multitudinous characters, ever-morphing disguises, and shifting locations, all complicated further by narrative ellipses and visual uncertainties. Feuillade's most ardent admirers include moviegoers who thrive on exactly that challenge. Others, however—including me, and I'm definitely ardent—value his pictures more for cinematic tone, texture, mood, and atmosphere than for the more earthbound pleasures of coherent storytelling.

Nor am I the first viewer to regard the ambiguities and slippages of Feuillade's serials not as flaws to be tolerated but as assets to be celebrated, amplifying the gnawing angst, gothic fear, and spectacular creepiness that seep into every frame of the serials' most transfixing scenes. My favorite images include the boa constrictor's nocturnal attack in *Fantômas*, the corrupt banker Favreau driven mad by a panoptical prison mirror in *Judex*, and the huge party group gassed into unconsciousness in *Les Vampires*, a chilling portent of what unlucky soldiers would experience in World War I, which erupted just as the last installments of *Les Vampires* were being released. The improbability and illogic of moments like these contribute to their disquieting power.

And lest we forget, the films can be very funny! Funny peculiar and also funny to laugh at, as if the old *Mad* comics catchphrase—"Humor in a Jugular Vein"—had taken hold way back in the 1910s. It's a hoot to see the title of *Fantômas Against Fantômas* (1914) literalized when multiple figures draped in Fantômas' mysterioso garb come face to face (mask to mask, actually) at a gala social event, adding fresh confusion to a situation that's plenty confused already. I'm amused in a different way when the title character of *Judex*, a relentless nemesis of his family's hated foe, gets dressed down by his *more* relentless mother for going soft.

Feuillade's humor is usually sly and wry, but at times it careens into outright slapstick. When the wily Fantômas finds himself caught by two lawmen, each with a vice-like grip on one of his arms, he escapes them by... running off without his arms, which were imitations all along. On a similar occasion, he gets away when his captors fall into strategically placed holes next to the path they're marching him down. Leveling things out by giving the gendarmes a break, an episode of *Les Vampires* ends with crooks tumbling through a hidden trapdoor into the clutches of the cops, who are waiting below with a great big bag to catch them in. Where did they get that great big bag? When did Fantômas dig those holes and put on those bogus arms? How did he know they'd work, or that he'd be needing them today? Alfred Hitchcock, another consummate orchestrator of sinister laughs, spoke disparagingly of people he called Plausibles, more concerned with spotting plot holes than surrendering to the story's spell. Plausibles will find much to complain about in Feuillade's twisty narratives, but if you insist on rationality you'll miss both the surrealistic genius and the crazy-house humor of his multifaceted art.

Daunting though they are to synopsize, it's not hard to sketch out the basics of Feuillade's plots. *Fantômas* took its cue from a string of thirty-two French novels by Pierre Souvestre and Marcel Allain, published monthly from early 1911 to late 1913. These were out-and-out pulp fiction with no pretensions to literary art; as horror and crime-film specialist David Kalat says on a Kino commentary track, the authors divided up the chapters—one writing the police-inspector parts, the other writing the journalist-sidekick parts—and stitched them together when they were done.

Feuillade's adaptation is a series of five movies rather than a serial per se. The films are *Fantômas in the Shadow of the Guillotine* (1913), *Juve vs. Fantômas* (1913), *The Murderous Corpse* (1913), *Fantômas vs. Fantômas* (1914), and *The False Magistrate* (1914), ranging in length from fifty-four to ninety minutes, for a total of about five and a half hours. Each begins with leisurely shots of characters in the disguises they'll assume during the story—seemingly a helpful hint to the audience but actually a crafty trick, since Feuillade surely knew how hard it is to keep these images in mind as the installments take unexpected turns, dart down strange detours, and sometimes wander off the road entirely.

Fantômas (René Navarre) is an archfiend with a brilliant mind and an evil soul, able to commit crime after horrifying crime without leaving the smallest clue to his identity or motives. His chief opponent is Inspector Juve (Edmond Bréon), a seasoned police officer dedicated to tracking down and apprehending this sublimely wicked antagonist. Juve's main helper is Jérôme Fandor (Georges Melchior), a young journalist who supplies him with information and assistance. Another key figure is the aristocratic Lady Beltham (Renée Carl), who has become Fantômas' mistress after losing her husband to one of his deadly schemes. Additional characters appear, disappear, take on false identities, and masquerade as one another throughout the five movies.

To give an idea of the series' flavor, the climax arrives in the last installment when Fandor disguises himself as Juve and the real Juve, disguised as Fantômas, enters a Belgian prison in order to get Fantômas, who's somewhere else disguised as a judge, extradited to France where capital punishment is practiced. Everything goes haywire for everyone except Fantômas, who eludes the minions of justice once again. All this happens after the most explosive scene in the *Fantômas* series, showing the villain's revenge on a henchman who has cheated him of jewels hidden in a church's bell tower: when next we see the unfortunate double-crosser, he is where the bell's clapper ought to be, getting hideously smashed as the bell rings for the funeral of Fantômas' latest victim. An astonished crowd looks on as "a rain of pearls, diamonds, rubies, and blood" falls from the dead man's pockets to the pavement below — where the loot is promptly pocketed by Fantômas, conveniently on the spot in his judge disguise. The wages of sin, *Fantômas* tells us, are generous.

Les Vampires is a serial in the usual sense, comprising ten episodes that add up to a fairly cohesive whole. The shortest is "The Ring That Kills" at fifteen minutes; the longest is the concluding chapter, "The Terrible Wedding," at sixty minutes; the whole runs about seven hours. This is the epic that made a major star of Musidora, who had appeared in several previous Feuillade films and worked with him again in *Judex* before becoming a screenwriter, producer, and director in her own right. Although her beauty is different from the kinds displayed by today's screen icons, her portrayal of the malevolent Irma Vep set a standard for *femmes fatales* that has rarely been surpassed; as film scholar Vicki Callahan notes in her (uneven) book on Feuillade's crime sagas, Musidora is "the one unambiguous force of evil across two of [his] most popular serials," and the sight of her black silk bodysuit can still produce a shivery *frisson* in sensitive spectators.

The title characters of *Les Vampires* are urban gangsters, not horror-movie monsters, and Irma Vep is not a real name but an anagram for "vampire." In line with Feuillade's enthusiasm for slippery personas and ambiguous appearances, she takes on all manner of false identities — female and male, rich and poor, aggressive and retiring — as the story unfolds. Disguises are also used by hero Philippe Guerande (Édouard Mathé), another of Feuillade's virtuous journalists, recalling the filmmaker's own youthful labors in that profession. A third key character is Guerande's sidekick, Oscar Mazamette (Marcel Lévesque), who injects comic relief and exercises the unique privilege of looking into the camera, silently signaling his (often exasperated) feelings the way Oliver Hardy used to do. Also on hand are Mazamette's little boy Eustache, played by René Poyen of Feuillade's long-running Bout-de-Zan series, and a rival gang boss named Moréno, armed with hypnotic powers to which even Irma falls prey. A good deal of the action involves kidnapping or killing the Grand Vampire, who always has a replacement waiting in the wings.

In contrast with the production circumstances of *Fantômas*, this time Feuillade had no preexisting plot and set of characters to work with, and the scenario was made up largely while the picture was being shot. Yet while *Les Vampires* is clearly discombobulated in spots, it's no harder (or easier) to follow than *Fantômas*, and again the jumbles and scrambles work to the film's advantage, enhancing its aura of dreamlike disorientation. On another level, *Les Vampires* was a transitional film for Feuillade, who was prodded by real-life authorities into taking a more conservative line on matters of crime and punishment. As in so many stories about transgression, the villains are far more interesting than the heroes, and Feuillade's critics accused him of glamorizing crime by parading the courage and creativity of his criminals.

One such critic was the Paris police chief, who put the serial out of commission for a couple of months, until Musidora used her charms to change his mind. The story had to change as well, however, and as commentator Jonathan Rosenbaum has noted, "the efficiency of the police takes a quantum leap over the last four episodes." Guerande is an amateur who makes his own rules as he goes along, and it's not the police but Guerande's new wife who finally gives Irma the *coup de grâce* she deserves. The cops get their act somewhat together, though, pulling off an effective raid in the last installment. The following year Feuillade directed *Judex*, in which lawfulness and integrity play even stronger roles. Still and all, he had a deep-down skepticism toward police, investigators, and sleuths. Master criminals like Fantômas and the Vampire leaders evade them easily and regularly, and even impersonate them—in *Fantômas*, for instance, where the American detective Tom Bob is actually the titular villain in disguise.

Feuillade's fresh twists on the detective genre partially account for his serials' immediate and enormous popularity, since detective fiction is deeply rooted in French culture. A good candidate for the ur-text of modern true-crime writing is the four-volume memoir published in the late 1820s by Eugène François Vidocq, who had founded La Sûreté Nationale, the investigative branch of the Paris police, in 1812. Since that chronicle was mostly fiction cooked up by ghostwriters, it helped originate the modern detective story, which became a distinct genre with Edgar Allan Poe's "The Murders in the Rue Morgue" in 1841 and gained lasting popularity with Arthur Conan Doyle's tales of Sherlock Holmes starting in 1887. Going further back, both Poe and Conan Doyle were probably influenced by Voltaire's 1747 novel *Zadig, or the Book of Fate*, about an ancient philosopher who systematically studies effects to learn their causes. Logic, observation, and what Poe called ratiocination are essential ingredients of this tradition, in which French authors (and Poe, who was more popular in France than in his own country) stand out time and again.

Feuillade drew some of his most important devices from this legacy, including the heavy use of masks, disguises, aliases, and false identities. All of these return with a vengeance in *Judex*, which takes its title from the Latin word for "judge" and has an (amateur) upholder of the law as its central character. The story begins with a baleful message delivered to the dishonest financier Favreau (Louis Leubas), ordering him to atone for his crimes— bankrupting, robbing, and murdering innocent people—by giving half of his fortune to the Public Assistance Bureau before ten o'clock the following night. Succeeding episodes reveal the whys and wherefores. A decent man was driven to suicide when Favreau refused him money in a time of need, and the dead man's widow, the Comtesse de Tremeuse (Yvonne Dario), then raised their sons to share her obsessive desire for revenge, making them swear never to rest until they have subjected Favreau to an awful death.

The elder son, Jacques (René Cresté), has created the Judex persona to serve this plan, and his younger brother, Roger (Mathé), functions as his assistant. They strike Favreau down at the appointed hour and immure him in their secret dungeon. But complications ensue when Favreau's grieving daughter, Jacqueline (Yvette Andréyor), turns out to be an upright woman who knew nothing of her father's malefactions; the moment she learns of them she surpasses Judex's order by donating the family's *entire* wealth to charity, giving up her little boy, and going to live in a boarding house. As time passes, Judex realizes that he doesn't have the hardness of soul to fulfill his oath of total revenge, and when he falls in love with Jacqueline terminating her father seems like a really bad idea. Musidora slinks through the story as Favreau's wicked mistress, Diana Monti a.k.a. Marie Verdier, and Lévesque does more Mazamette-style comic bits and camera glances as Cocantin, the hapless proprietor of a private-eye business. Poyen also returns, as a spirited urchin called the Licorice Kid who teams with Jacqueline's son Jean (Olinda Mano) for some winning proto-*Our Gang* interludes.

As the title character, Cresté has a grave-looking face and imposing demeanor that make it all the more ironic when Judex's dissatisfied mother repeatedly humiliates him, or when he leaves himself wide open to capture and needs to be rescued by Daisy Torp (Lily Deligny), an old flame of Cocantin who recently entered the story. Judex is certainly no superman, and his limitations lend the serial a humanistic undertone. I'm not sure this makes *Judex* superior to its predecessors—the icy tone of *Fantômas* and the crisp impersonality of *Les Vampires* are ultimately more effective for me—but it carves out a special niche for the picture.

The most rewarding pleasures of Feuillade's crime serials are aesthetic, and film scholar David Bordwell has beautifully described the subtleties of movement, architecture, and design that allow their images to flow so smoothly, gracefully, and articulately across the screen. The movies take some getting used to, since they rely far more on mise-en-scène, framing, and deep focus than on the montage-based kineticism so fashionable today; but once you're on Feuillade's wavelength you'll probably be hooked for good. I'll add that the décor in the serials is astonishingly rich and the acting is invariably superb, as realistic and expressive as almost anything the cinema has given us.

Aesthetics never stand alone, of course, and the sagas acquire still more resonance when you think about their cultural context. Feuillade's movie career began near the end of what Americans call the Gilded Age and French people remember as the *Belle Époque*. Like the twenty-first century so far, it was a time when business interests advanced, corporate greed soared, and inequity festered, bringing riches to the privileged and new kinds of malaise to what we'd now label the ninety-nine percent. While capitalists, industrialists, and robber barons in the United States poured their greatest energies into competition for worldly goods, in France the arts reaped considerable dividends from patrons with extra francs on hand. The system exploded when World War I broke out in 1914, but internal tensions and external pressures were already growing, and cultural developments reflected the rising anxieties of the prewar years. At least two trends strongly influenced Feuillade's serial masterpieces: the turn of Impressionist art toward Dada and Surrealism, and the turn of radical politics toward anarchism, individualism, and illegalism.

What those movements have in common is a penchant for liminal zones, the shadowy sectors hovering between and beyond society's established categories. Such zones were well known to the Impressionist painters—Claude Monet, Pierre-Auguste Renoir, Edgar Degas, Mary Cassett—whose careers overlapped with Feuillade's activities. All were fascinated by the ephemerality of time, the instability of light, the inseparability of perception and psychology, and the ceaselessness of change in a modern world moving faster and faster. Feuillade shared their passions and did as much as any of them to prepare ground for the French Impressionist filmmakers (Germaine Dulac, Louis Delluc, Jean Epstein) who created their most haunting works in the 1920s, when anti-art Dadaists like Marcel Duchamp and Hans Richter and dream-obsessed Surrealists like Man Ray and Salvador Dalí carried the ambiguity and obliquity of late Impressionism to unprecedented lengths. (Delluc and company didn't much like Feuillade, but I think professional jealousy was behind at least some of their animosity.) Watch the black-enshrouded villain stalking an unsuspecting victim in *Fantômas*, or the aptly named Satanas stinging a victim with a poisoned pin in *Les Vampires*, or the Tremeuse brothers condemning their enemy to everlasting torment in *Judex*, and you're seeing liminal visions that oscillate between Impressionist allusiveness and Surrealist uncanniness. "I am convinced that surrealism preexisted in cinema," the legendary archivist Henri Langlois remarked in 1965, citing *Les Vampires* as "an expression... of the universal subconscious." Precisely. Feuillade unveils images of the craziest, most archetypal, most enthralling kind.

The same unsettled modernity that led to Dadism and Surrealism brought about political ideas of a contrarian hue, and anarchism had a significant presence in the later years of the *Belle Époque*. Sundry critics have seen likenesses between Feuillade's super-villains and anarchism's illegalist camp, which stretched the credo of unfettered personal freedom (patented by the individualist camp) to include violence and criminality not as *justified* acts, exactly, but as acts that don't *need* justification since true individualism has no social or moral limits. The most infamous illegalists, the Bonnot Gang, terrorized French-speaking Europe in 1911 and 1912 with help from high-tech equipment that the gendarmes didn't yet have, such as rapid-fire guns and speedy cars. Fantômas and the Vampires fit this profile perfectly, right down to the absence of any ideology except an implicit notion that the bourgeoisie and aristocracy deserve anything the criminal elite might choose to inflict on them.

These and other cultural currents of the *Belle Époque* were roundabout influences on Feuillade, not direct shapers of his work. Yet seeing his films today opens fascinating windows on ways of life and forms of entertainment that held great sway a century ago. Although similar insights can be gleaned from old movies of all sorts, Feuillade's films have a prescience that, say, D. W. Griffith's rarely equal. Rosenbaum puts this difference in stark terms when he writes that Griffith's work "reeks of Victorian morality and nostalgia for the mid-19th century" whereas Feiullade gazes forward to the "global paranoia, conspiratorial intrigues, and SF technological fantasies" of the decades lying ahead. I wouldn't use a verb like "reek" in connection with the great Griffith, and Feuillade had his own investment in romantic attitudes, usually steering his stories to happy endings brought about by love, conscience, virtue, and tenacity. Bold imaginer and innovator that he was, he never fully escaped the sentimental streak that propped up popular cinema in his day as in ours.

Feuillade is a titan of world cinema nonetheless, and it would take a much longer essay to trace his lasting influence on other filmmakers. I'll just mention two remakes that partly succeed in reproducing his unique touch. Paul Fejos directed a feature version of *Fantômas* in 1932, which begins as a mystery yarn in the vein of James Whale's *The Old Dark House* (released in the same year) and then turns into a standard 1930s crime story. It has a couple of rapid-fire montage sequences that recall Fejos' 1928 masterpiece *Lonesome*, but it also has magical moments of Feuillade-style staging in depth. In the most striking, a man hunting Fantômas walks to the back of a room and goes through a door, whereupon an armchair near the camera *stands up and throws off its slipcover*. You guessed it: another fine Fantômas disguise. And in 1963 Georges Franju made a feature version of *Judex*, pushing surrealism daringly far—the opening scene is a costume party, for instance, where *everyone* wears an oversized bird's-head disguise. The screenplay, cowritten by Feuillade's grandson, Jacques Champreux, strips away the slender explanations that allowed the original *Judex* to make a bit of sense, joining with Franju's stylized visuals for an overall effect that's simultaneously austere, bizarre, and delicate, even lilting, in tone.

The DVD and Blu-ray editions of Feuillade's serials are very well produced, with tinted prints (except *Les Vampires*) and period-appropriate music. My one big complaint is that all three sets replace the original French intertitles with bland English ones, a needless and annoying alteration. Kino supplements the first two *Fantômas* installments with commentary tracks by Kalat, who is stronger on background information than on critical savvy, plus two Feuillade shorts and a brief documentary on the filmmaker that's really a commercial for Gaumont's preservation work. Flicker Alley packages *Judex* with a lively booklet essay by film historian Jan-Christopher Horak and a nicely done "featurette" about how Robert Israel went about creating his new music score.

So rejoice, silent-cinema aficionados: Feuillade lives on! And now let's clamor for even more: restoration and distribution of the magisterial *Tih Minh* of 1918, a seven-hour feast of outlandish characters, exotic images, extravagant emotions, and inimitable Feuillade inventiveness. It cries out for resurrection. Here's hoping.

The Wooster Group
Quarterly Review of Film and Video 35:2 (2018)

I once knew a theater director who didn't just accept but actually *liked* the way his productions vanished into thin air once their final performances were over. In his view, theater must exist entirely in the moment, imbued with the physicality and ephemerality that separate stagecraft from more readily reproducible arts. Each new project calls for inventing a new world, he believed, and old worlds have no business hanging around when their natural life spans are over. I once ran this notion past Elizabeth LeCompte, founding director and honcho of the Wooster Group, the hugely experimental, hugely influential New York theater company. How did she feel about the inescapable impermanency of live theater? Her reply: "It drives me *crazy*."

That was more than thirty years ago. Times and technologies have changed since then, and making records of theatrical creations is now as easy as it is commonsensical, even if the crucial qualities of materiality and immediacy make live production the most "authentic" medium for stage artists. Then too, Wooster Group productions are multimedia works down to their postmodern bones, blending video, manipulated sound, and live action into intricate, ingenious tapestries. Recording them via video is a logical extension of what the group has been doing for decades.

LeCompte is still devoted to live theater, and to see the Wooster Group at its inimitable best you still have to catch them at their lower Manhattan headquarters, the Performing Garage on Wooster Street, or track them down when they're on tour. But in recent years the options have opened up a bit, thanks to LeCompte's embrace of video as a means of capturing and disseminating the troupe's work. It is not quite a total embrace—as of now half a dozen DVDs are publicly available, institutionally priced between $250 and $400, plus four items available for streaming at $100 a session—and the quality varies. Perhaps for that reason, you don't hear much about these videos. But such is the importance, originality, and sheer brilliance of the group's best work that these audiovisual records, ancillary and reductive as they necessarily are, deserve to be far more widely known.[1]

---

[1] LeCompte directed all of the stage productions and has sole credit as director of the DVD editions except *The Emperor Jones*, which she codirected with filmmaker Ken Kobland, a long-time Wooster Group collaborator.

Some history is in order here. I have been following the Wooster Group since the 1970s, when it was a brand-new offshoot of the Performance Group, the revolutionary troupe set up by Richard Schechner in 1967. Then, as now, headquarters was the Performing Garage in SoHo, the neighborhood that was just beginning its rise to artist-colony prominence when Schechner and company went into business there. I saw the first Performance Group production—*Dionysus in 69*, a semi-improvised work based on *The Bacchae* of Euripides—soon after it opened in 1968, and I can testify to its importance as a radical intervention in just about every aspect of theatrical convention, from the relationship between actors and roles to the distribution of the audience through the performing area.[2] Less brilliance was evident in the 1970 production *Commune*, a collage-like exercise assembled from classic texts and pop-culture artifacts, but it earned a place in history by introducing LeCompte and Spalding Gray as new members of the company. LeCompte was Schechner's assistant director for *Commune*, and when Schechner went abroad in 1971 LeCompte restaged the piece with a new cast and became interim manager of the group. Gray was an actor who did not much like to act, preferring intensely personal expressions—talking to the audience, sharing idiosyncratic thoughts and memories—that Schechner was happy to encourage.

Gray and LeCompte were a couple both inside and outside the Garage, and when LeCompte started developing her ideas independently of Schechner, she turned to Gray's obsession with his childhood and adolescence as the basis for loose, mostly nonverbal improvisations by him and other colleagues. LeCompte observed, guided, edited, and organized these until they crystallized in a 1975 piece called *Sakonnet Point*, named after a vacation spot Gray visited as a boy. This dreamlike, nonlinear production became the first installment in the trilogy *Three Places in Rhode Island*, followed by *Rumstick Road* in 1977, *Nayatt School* in 1978, and the 1979 epilogue *Point Judith*, which brought Kate Valk and Willem Dafoe into the troupe. Valk has starred in the group's productions ever since, and Dafoe became the company's male lead when Gray departed in 1985 to concentrate on his career as a monologist and sometime movie actor.[3]

[2.] Brian De Palma, Robert Fiore and Bruce Rubin made a filmed version *Dionysus in 69* in 1970.

[3] Gray presented his first monologue, *Sex and Death to the Age 14*, at the Performing Garage in 1979. (As a critic and friend, I was in the sparse

The only part of *Three Places in Rhode Island* available on DVD is *Rumstick Road*, a physically modest work (performed in a room over the Performing Garage with the audience on low bleachers at one end) that I consider one of the greatest achievements of American avant-garde theater.[4] Although its mood is allusive and impressionistic, its ingredients are grounded in documentary fact, centering on the suicide of Gray's mother in 1967 and using relics from Gray's past—interviews he recorded with his father and grandmothers, slides from the family collection—along with purely expressive props such as a Halloween mask and a small tent pulsing with mysterious red light.

One example will illustrate the piece's power. As a slide of Gray's immediate family is projected on the rear wall of the stage, the actress (Libby Howes) representing his mother sits between the projector and the wall, producing a blacked-out void in place of the dead mother's face, a haunting metaphor for her absence; the mother's face is now visible on Howes' chest, and the actor (Ron Vawter) representing Gray's father adjusts the projector upward until the picture is superimposed on Howes' face, then snaps it into focus so that the mother's projected face and Howes' real face become a single phantasmal image, simultaneously actual and virtual. During this process Gray recites a letter his mother sent him from a sanatorium, echoing the letter's increasing anxiety with increasingly anxious vocal tones until the final words, "Love, Mom," turn into a shriek. It is an electrifying scene in a theater piece whose unique properties are suggested, although not fully conveyed, by the DVD edition, a video reconstruction assembled from original elements of the show: audiotapes, slides, music,

---

audience of about 10 people.) Their following quickly soared and many more followed, a few of which were also reworked as movies: Jonathan Demme's *Swimming to Cambodia* (1987), Thomas Schlamme's *Spalding Gray: Terrors of Pleasure* (1988), Nick Broomfield's *Monster in a Box* (1992), and Steven Soderbergh's *Gray's Anatomy* (1996). Gray committed suicide in 2004.

[4] Other experimental stage works at this high level include the 1976 opera *Einstein on the Beach* by Robert Wilson and Philip Glass, which I have seen many times in various incarnations prior to its recent arrival on DVD, and the 1968 opera *Elephant Steps* by Stanley Silverman and Richard Foreman, which I saw at its Tanglewood premiere. Although her pieces are far more kinetic than Wilson's and somewhat less elaborately deranged than Foreman's tend to be, LeCompte has tremendous admiration for both of those artists, and the Wooster Group has productively collaborated with Foreman and his Ontological-Hysteric Theater.

and most important, grainy but invaluable Super-8mm footage of Gray's intimate, irreplaceable performance.[5]

The group's major undertaking in the 1980s was a series of pieces with the umbrella title *The Road to Immortality*, extending LeCompte's core creative technique—the "layering" of multiple audiovisual elements atop one another—into ever more radical territory. None of those shows have DVD editions, which is especially regrettable since some of them sparked uproarious controversies when first performed. The 1981 production *Route 1&9 (The Last Act)* was attacked for deconstructing a disreputable old African-American comedy routine with white actors in blackface, and the estate of Thornton Wilder revoked the right to incorporate portions of his 1938 play *Our Town*, apparently piqued by the drastically postmodern context in which it appeared.[6] In a similar occurrence three years later, the curtain fell on the 1984 production *L.S.D. (…Just the High Points…)* when Arthur Miller objected to portions of his 1953 drama *The Crucible* being incorporated in the mix.

Subsequent works are better represented on the DVD list. The 1991 production *Brace Up!* is a revisionist take on Anton Chekhov's 1900 play *Three Sisters*, generating remarkable emotional power with its inspired juxtaposition of Chekhov's restrained, evocative dialogue and the artfully mannered, non-naturalistic acting that the Wooster Group has so thoroughly mastered. The disc contains two full-length recordings of the show. The main attraction is a version assembled from three 2003 performances, featuring Valk, Dafoe, Scott Shepherd, Ari Fliakos, Anna Kohler, and other mainstays, photographed with a somewhat distanced camera and enhanced by close-ups that come and go along the margins of the master shot. The other is a 1993 performance photographed from

---

[5] As always with the group, music is essential to this production. The leitmotif linked to Gray's anguished mother is a solo partita by Johann Sebastian Bach, and the motif for his generally clueless father is Nelson Riddle's theme from the CBS television show *Route 66* (1960–1964). A recent Wooster Group production, *La Didone*, juxtaposes Francesco Cavalli's eponymous 1641 opera with Mario Bava's characteristically bizarre 1965 science-fiction movie *Terrore nello Spazio*, aka *Planet of the Vampires*. Scoring another point for digital video, I found *La Didone* more impressive as a serial on the group's website than when I saw it live at REDCAT in Los Angeles.

[6] Other elements included a faux documentary about Wilder's play, live phone calls soliciting deliveries from faraway take-out joints, and a hardcore pornographic film featuring Dafoe, Howes, and Vawter, seen as a murky video on a television set.

a single position (unenhanced by closeups) with a cast including Valk, Vawter, Kohler, Marianne Weems, and Paul Schmidt, who translated Chekhov's text for this production. To my surprise, I found *Brace Up!* more moving in its DVD form than when I saw it at the Performing Garage. Of the disc's two versions, I prefer the earlier one, thanks largely to Vawter's superlative performance as Vershinin, which Dafoe ably builds on in the later version.[7] Most of the Wooster Group videos are photographed from the sort of back-row position that LeCompte has always favored for seeing live performances, but as a spectator who usually likes to sit up front, I often wish for more proximity to the stage (and more variety of angle) when watching the DVDs.

Another brouhaha about blackface erupted in 1993 when the group staged Eugene O'Neill's ever-controversial 1920 play *The Emperor Jones*, starring Valk in heavy makeup as the title character, an African-American worker who has become a West Indies tyrant and is chased to his death through a forest by his outraged subjects. Of all the group's DVD presentations, the "video reconstruction" of this show is the most effectively "through-composed," to borrow a musical term, weaving Valk's astonishing performance— comprising rhythms, textures, and gestures so vibrant that the stage and screen barely seem to contain them—into a sophisticated mosaic of sight and sound. Also on view are single-shot recordings of 2009 performances in Chicago and Hong Kong, plus excerpts from work-in-progress performances in 1992.

The most recent Wooster Group works available on DVD were originally staged between the middle 1990s and 2006. As the title obliquely hints, the 1997 show *House/Lights* layers the text of *Doctor Faustus Lights the Lights*, an antic and elliptical libretto written by Gertrude Stein in 1938, with clips from *Olga's House of Shame*, an otherwise unmemorable horror film made by Joseph P. Mawra in 1964. It is a courageous pairing, and the DVD offers assorted options for watching it: an "edit" view cut together from varied camera angles, a "wide" view shot from a single position, and a "TV" view giving the whole screen to the show's video elements. You can switch between the "wide" and "TV" views as you watch, and you can listen to an optional audio commentary titled *Zinger File*, which is fully as antic and elliptical as Stein's libretto. I rank this show among the group's less felicitous accomplishments.

---

[7] *Brace Up!* incorporates the first three acts of Chekhov's play; the fourth is reworked in the 1994 production *Fish Story*, not on DVD at this point.

The 2001 production *To You, The Birdie! (Phèdre)* is another instance of extreme layering. The core text is Jean Racine's still-marvelous tragedy *Phaedra* of 1677, translated by Schmidt and combined with intricately interwoven video images plus an extended bout of onstage badminton (!) that brings LeCompte's longstanding commitment to the aleatory and spontaneous to new heights.[8] Valk, Shepherd, Fliakos, Suzzy Roche, and others give the proceedings an energy that never quits even on the DVD edition, which also presents a 2002 performance with Dafoe and Frances McDormand, a frequent visitor to the group in recent years.

Lecompte's production of *Hamlet*, first performed in 2006 and shot on video in 2013, has a baroque history, even by Wooster Group standards. Back in 1964, Richard Burton starred in a Broadway production of William Shakespeare's tragedy directed by the illustrious John Gielgud, who dressed the performers in modern "rehearsal clothes," except for himself, since he played the Ghost as a disembodied voice. Hume Cronyn and Eileen Herlie led the supporting cast. Bringing the classic to the masses, the producers enlisted television director Bill Colleran to record three performances via the Electronovision process—pioneered in 1955-1956 by *The Honeymooners*, the immortal CBS sitcom—and to edit the material into a 131-minute movie for a two-day run in theaters. I saw the Burton production onstage during its original run, and I saw the Electronovision version years later. It is now readily available in sundry venues including YouTube, and I assure you that while the stage production was less than thrilling, the canned production—shot from 17 angles and promoted as the debut venture of Theatrofilm, the world's newest art form—is a very great deal less than thrilling, except as a record of Burton's performance, which is indeed commanding.

Be that as it may, the Electronovision version of *Hamlet* is the raw material of LeCompte's show, projected on the rear wall of the stage as a black-and-white background for the live performances. Shepherd portrays the title character, and before launching into the play he explains that the Wooster Group has digitally altered the audio of the 1964 film, eliminating all vocal pauses occurring within lines of Shakespeare's verse and moving those pauses to the ends of any lines not audibly end-stopped by the speaker's cadences. The original visuals have been similarly

---

[8] For another example, *Route 1&9 (The Last Act)* included physical maneuvers by blindfolded actors.

altered via the pause and fast-forward buttons, the icons of which are steadily in view, reconfirming LeCompte's inveterate passion for what the Russian Formalists called "laying bare the device." With the Burton production twitching away behind them, the live players (Shepherd, Valk, Fliakos, Greg Mehrten, and others) reproduce its visual and vocal contents with continually varying degrees of reverent fidelity, imaginative variation, emphatic irony, and outright caricature. Shepherd wryly describes the enterprise as Reverse Theatrofilm.

Hamlet is the Wooster Group's only digital production released as a DVD and Blu-ray combo, and while the superior Blu-ray image is obviously a plus, it does not lift this offering to the heights of the earlier items I have discussed. Among other problems, the rejiggering of the 1964 film strikes me as pointless and counterproductive, turning it into a nagging irritant rather than a wraithlike revenant from the cultural past.

So lofty are the ideas and attainments of LeCompte and her colleagues, however, that all audiovisual records of their work take on major cultural importance, and anyone lacking opportunities to see them in the flesh should seize on even the least imposing of these discs. There was a long spell in Wooster Group history when favorable reviews were so hard to come by that they stopped having official openings, keeping shows in perpetual "preview" with no critics allowed. Those days are long gone, and audiences have finally gotten the message that my friend Liz expressed to me in one of our interviews: "I consider myself an entertainer. I don't mean my work to be difficult or obscure. It's meant to be enjoyed."[9] Truth be told, her work *is* difficult and obscure at times, but it is also unfailingly bold, visionary, and — yes — entertaining. Now the group's engagement with digital reproduction is spreading the gospel a little farther. I strongly recommend giving it a try.

---

[9] David Sterrit, "Pioneering a new kind of stage magic." *The Christian Science Monitor*, December 14, 1981.

Grand Opera and the Silver Screen
Quarterly Review of Film and Video, 36:2 (2019)

Many an opera has found its way from stage to screen. Worthy specimens of the breed include Michael Powell and Emeric Pressburger's colorful *The Tales of Hoffmann* (1951), Powell's brooding *Bluebeard's Castle* (1963), Ingmar Bergman's limpid *The Magic Flute* (1975), Joseph Losey's sturdy *Don Giovanni* (1979), Franco Zeffirelli's flamboyant *La Traviata* (1982), Hans-Jürgen Syberberg's exquisite *Parsifal* (1982), and Penny Woolcock's muscular *The Death of Klinghoffer* (2003), the most politically controversial of the bunch. Video recordings of stage productions have also proliferated in recent years, a growing number of which can be acquired as DVDs or streamed at will via OperaVision, Metropolitan Opera on Demand, and similar services.

Not surprisingly, much can be lost when a genuinely grand opera is reduced to the size of a video screen; for one example, numerous moment-to-moment choices by video director Don Kent make the towering Philip Glass-Robert Wilson masterpiece *Einstein on the Beach* less impressive on DVD than in any of the live performances I have seen, going back to its American debut at the Met in 1976. At least one opera-film auteur believed that even the most generous movie-theater screen is dinky when compared with a first-rate opera stage. "The proscenium is so much larger than that little stamp of a screen," Zeffirelli told me when his sumptuous film of *La Traviata* opened in 1983. In retrospect, he said, "I should have given the picture more splendor, like *Ben-Hur* or the old D. W. Griffith movies." Still, the loss of opera-house immediacy and scale can be compensated for by increased availability to audiences outside the urban areas where most opera houses reside.

Lately a complementary trend has been gathering steam as composers, librettists, and opera companies turn to cinema for ideas and inspiration. The first important instances were Glass' stage operas based on Jean Cocteau films: *Orphée*, written and directed by Cocteau in 1950 and adapted by Glass in 1991; *Les Enfants terribles*, directed by Jean-Pierre Melville from Cocteau's screenplay in 1950 and adapted by Glass in 1993; and *La Belle et la bête*, written and directed by Cocteau in 1946 and adapted by Glass in 1994. The practice has continued with Jake Heggie's timely and moving 2000 adaptation of Tim Robbins' 1995 *Dead Man Walking* and Kevin Puts' multilingual *Silent Night*, a Pulitzer Prize winner of 2011 based on Christian Carion's 2005 film *Joyeux Noël.* The 2016 season brought Thomas Adès' oneiric *The Exterminating Angel*, based on Luis Buñuel's surrealist classic of 1962, and Missy Mazzoli's appropriately jagged adaptation of Lars von Trier's 1996 *Breaking the Waves*, complete with Ennio Morricone-esque electric-guitar sounds, a nod to the movie's own soundtrack.

(Parenthetically, it's worth noting that the challenges of promoting these new works in the ultraconservative world of grand opera has occasionally led to bits of Hollywood-style ballyhoo. When the Met mounted *The Exterminating Angel*, press reports trumpeted a historic event embedded in the performance: the singing of the highest pitch ever essayed by a diva on the Met's venerable stage. The event proved anticlimactic—more a vocal screech than a musical tone, and brief enough to be gone almost before it registered—but history in the making is always fun to experience.)

At this writing the most recent film-related opera is Nico Muhly's 2018 *Marnie*, the second Met production by this gifted and enormously versatile composer. (His first was the interestingly melodramatic *Two Boys*, which debuted in London in 2011 and at the Met in 2014.) To be precise, the elegant and engaging *Marnie* is not directly based on the flawed but indelible Alfred Hitchcock movie of 1964, but rather on the 1961 novel by Winston Graham that inspired the Hitchcock version. Muhly and librettist Nicholas Wright retained the novel's setting of England in the 1950s, partly for the excellent reason that however ingenious a 21st-century woman might be at stealing company funds, changing her identity at will, and eluding capture over a period of years, today's ubiquitous trails of electronic information would surely bring her down as soon as anyone noticed that something was amiss. This context still leaves the question of why Muhly and his collaborators chose to adapt Graham's novel instead of the very famous Hitchcock film, and Muhly told me that from his point of view the movie—like all Hitchcock movies—is simply too cinematic for a stage adaptation to be effective. You can have a great experience watching a Hitchcock film with the volume off, he says, whereas in opera the sonic dimension obviously reigns.

The music of Muhly's *Marnie* is as dramatic as the narrative and as mercurial as the heroine, embellished with unusual structures, including "links" in place of arias, meant to suggest Marnie's momentary state of mind; characters paired with specific instruments (Marnie with oboe, her mother with viola, Mark with trombone, his brother Terry with muted trumpet); and a quartet of Shadow Marnies in the cast, representing hidden aspects of the title character's personality. The large-scale production calls for eighteen soloists—one of whom (Terry) is a countertenor—and a sizable orchestra. Michael Meyer's production enhanced the Met production with artful projections enabling the frequent scene changes and facilitating such visually demanding material as the foxhunt where Marnie's beloved horse Forio breaks a leg. Like the Hitchcock movie, Muhly's opera has to leap an extra hurdle in the current climate of zero tolerance for male sexual aggression, and the production's dramaturg, Paul Cremo, told me that the Met worked long and hard to strike a proper moral tone in the ever-troubling scene where Mark tries to force himself on unwilling Marnie after their wedding. The solutions settled upon seemed satisfactory to me.

Thanks in large part to Meyer's visual contributions, *Marnie* is about as cinematic as a stage-bound opera can be, surpassed only by the aforementioned Glass productions, wherein (during full-scale performances) the live music is accompanied by screenings of the films themselves. There is no requirement for a film-related opera to mimic cinematic techniques, of course, but productions I've seen of operas mentioned here have combined solid musical values with solid visual aesthetics. I'm thinking of Heggie's *Dead Man Walking* at both the Washington National Opera and the Baltimore Lyric Opera, *Silent Night* at the WNO, and *The Exterminating Angel* at the Met, which I saw in a live theatrical HD transmission, a format that brings music and movie together in still another way. As divergent as their histories have been, opera and cinema are different yet complementary means of approaching the ideal of the *Gesamtkunstwerk* that Richard Wagner theorized more than a century and a half ago. Their occasional convergence is a fascinating phenomenon to ponder.

Psycho Analyzed: The Hitchcock classic at 50, still inspiring discussion and debate
Moving Image Source, March 2, 2010

First, the history. Fifty years ago this June, the redoubtable Alfred Hitchcock launched *Psycho* with pre-release showings at two of Manhattan's more respectable cinemas. A week later it moved to Boston, Philadelphia, Chicago, and other locations across the country, in order to saturate the market—in the pre-*Jaws* era, that meant hundreds, not thousands, of theaters—before its surprises were undercut by what we now call spoilers. Reviews were all over the map, but moviegoers lined up for blocks, lured by the first well-funded publicity campaign Hitchcock had ever personally supervised, complete with a global publicity tour, unusually droll trailers, and special instructions to exhibitors recorded by Hitch himself, admonishing them to keep the theater dark for half a minute after the end titles. "During these 30 seconds of stygian blackness," the disembodied voice intoned, "the suspense of *Psycho* is indelibly engraved in the mind of the audience, later to be discussed among gaping friends and relations. You will then bring up houselights of a greenish hue, and shine spotlights of this ominous hue across the faces of your departing patrons."

Most famously, Hitchcock policed the audience from afar, mischievously emulating Mrs. Bates, who polices her son from beyond the grave. "No one but no one will be admitted to the theater after *Psycho* begins," he ordered in trailers, teasers, and lobby cards. "Please don't tell the ending," a second message cajoled. "It's the only one we have." Patrons obeyed with pleasure, delighted to conspire with the world's most celebrated movie director. The publicity, the gimmicks, the buzz, and the movie's excellence combined to give Hitchcock the runaway hit of his career, earning $9.5 million in its initial runs and an additional $6 million in international grosses.[1] It also brought Hitch the last of his five Academy Award nominations, although neither he nor the film's other nominees—Janet Leigh for supporting actress, John L. Russell for cinematography, and Joseph Hurley, Robert Clatworthy, and George Milo for black-and-white art direction and set decoration—were winners on Oscar night.

---

[1] Stephen Rebello, *Alfred Hitchcock and the Making of Psycho* (Dembner, 1990), 164.

The entertainment industry and the knowledge industry have been capitalizing on *Psycho* ever since. The former has cranked out two sequels — *Psycho II* in 1983 and *Psycho III* in 1986 — and a prequel, *Psycho IV: The Beginning*, in 1990, all starring Anthony Perkins, who also directed the 1986 opus. A television pilot, *Bates Motel*, made a fleeting appearance in 1987. Gus Van Sant cooked up a not-quite-totally slavish remake in 1998, on the extremely dubious theory that color photography, masturbation noises, and Vince Vaughn would revitalize Hitch's vision for the post-boomer crowd. Meanwhile, an enormously wide bookshelf of Hitchcock studies has appeared, including whole volumes on *Psycho* alone. Among them are *Alfred Hitchcock and the Making of Psycho* (1990), by Stephen Rebello, which details the film's production history; *Alfred Hitchcock's Psycho: A Casebook* (2004), edited by Robert Kolker, aimed at academic readers; and *Psycho: Behind the Scenes of the Classic Thriller*, a 1995 memoir written (partly) by Janet Leigh, the ultimate insider.[2] Also noteworthy are *24 Hour Psycho*, a 1993 video installation by Scottish artist Douglas Gordon that shows Hitchcock's film at about two frames per second, and Don DeLillo's novel *Point Omega* (2010), which deals with themes of time and consciousness inspired by DeLillo's viewing of the Douglas work in 2006.

The run-up to the film's golden anniversary brought three more *Psycho*-specific volumes: *Psycho in the Shower: The History of Cinema's Most Famous Scene*, by Philip J. Skerry, a professor; *The Psycho File: A Comprehensive Guide to Hitchcock's Classic Shocker*, by Joseph W. Smith III, a journalist; and *The Moment of Psycho: How Alfred Hitchcock Taught America to Love Murder*, by David Thomson, a critic.[3] Of these writers, Skerry seems to

---

[2] Other such volumes are *Filmguide to Psycho* (1973), by academic critic James Naremore; *Alfred Hitchcock's Psycho* (1974), assembled by Richard J. Anobile, who reconstructs the film via frame blowups and dialogue captions; a three-issue comic-book series also called *Alfred Hitchcock's Psycho* (1992), written by Joseph Stefano, the film's screenwriter; and *A Long Hard Look at Psycho* (2002), by Raymond Durgnat, the respected British critic. More recent books touching on the film include *Alfred Hitchcock: The Icon Years* (2010), by John William Law, about Hitch's career in the 1960s and 1970s, and *The Girl in Alfred Hitchcock's Shower* (2010), by Robert Graysmith, a true-crime account of a serial killer who had an unhealthy interest in Marli Renfro, the model who stood in for Leigh when shower-scene shots required glimpses of bare skin.

[3] Philip J. Skerry, *Psycho in the Shower: The History of Cinema's Most Famous Scene* (Continuum, 2009). Joseph W. Smith III, *The Psycho File:*

have the most single-minded fascination with the film, having published a 409-page study called *The Shower Scene in Hitchcock's Psycho: Creating Cinematic Suspense and Terror* in 2005. His new book clocks in at a more modest 316 pages, and even that may seem like rather a lot, even for cinema's most famous scene. Despite the narrow focus of its title, however, *Psycho in the Shower* ranges beyond Marion's four minutes in the bathroom. Skerry discusses the movie as a whole; traces elements of its style to Soviet montage theory and German expressionism; locates antecedents for Marion's spectacular demise in a long list of earlier Hitchcock films, from *Blackmail* in 1929 to episodes of *Alfred Hitchcock Presents* in the 1950s; and more along these lines.

For those of us who've been taking long, hard looks at Hitchcock for as long as we can remember, much of Skerry's work is anything but new. More than a hundred pages in, you still collide with numbingly dull topic sentences like *"Psycho* is the culmination of Hitchcock's obsessive interest in crime, madness, and claustrophobia." And whole chapters are consumed with material that isn't exactly essential. Chapter 1, unpromisingly called "My Research Trip," gives a detailed account of how Leigh almost ignored Skerry and Stefano as she happened to walk past their table at a ritzy restaurant. (She noticed them at the last second and said hi. Whew.) The last chapter, wherein Skerry's friends and acquaintances tell how scary *Psycho* is, doesn't score even as trivia.

This stuff is easily skipped, though, and on the plus side, Skerry piles up an impressive quantity of pertinent facts, semirelevant factoids, zealously close analyses, and meandering flights of cinephilia. One section got me thinking again about the kinship between Saul Bass' title designs for *Psycho* and for *Vertigo* (1958), so different visually—the former with its frantic tempo and compulsive horizontals, the latter with its leisurely pace and lissajous spirals—yet linked by the way the gazing female eye at the beginning of the earlier film anticipates the blinded eye of the murdered Marion, which is accompanied by spirals of abjection, not allure. Skerry usefully deploys the concept of suspense-film *cataphora*—cues that point to information not yet incorporated by the text, shaping the horizon of possibility for subsequent events without

A Comprehensive Guide to Hitchcock's Classic Shocker (McFarland, 2009). David Thomson, *The Moment of Psycho: How Alfred Hitchcock Taught America to Love Murder* (Basic, 2009).

manifestly signaling these the way foreshadowing does.[4] (Think of the scene with the highway cop, which heightens our sense of a tightening trap but foreshadows nothing that ever materializes.) A chart summarizes the 34 shots in the knife-attack sequence; a production still shows the shot of Marion's bare backside (actually that of Marli Renfro, Leigh's stand-in) that Hitchcock couldn't get past the censors; and so on.

The book's obsessiveness adds to its entertainment value, as when Skerry resurrects an old *Psycho* question: is there or isn't there a shot showing Norman's knife penetrating Marion's flesh? In the days before home video, this kind of thing kept movie buffs awake at night. The question was settled years ago—there *is* a shot of that description, and it's been reproduced in various books—but high-level participants in the production have stated that there is *not*. Hitchcock: "Naturally, the knife never touched the body; it was all done in the montage." Leigh: "People swear they saw the knife go in, but they never showed that." Stefano: "Actually, it never touches the skin."[5] This drives Skerry crazy, so he sets out to prove the nonbelievers wrong, with amusing results. His interview with Hilton Green, the film's assistant director, includes this:

Green: We never did… anything where it penetrated.

Skerry: But where did that shot come from because it's in the film? I did a shot-by-shot analysis of the film.

Green: We never shot it.

Skerry: Where the hell did it come from?

Green: Hitchcock was very proud of that restraint. Maybe that was put in later by somebody, after the fact.

---

[4] For full discussion see Hans J. Wulff, "Suspense and the Influence of Cataphora on Viewers' Expectations," in Peter Vorderer, Hans J. Wulff, and Mike Friedrichsen, eds., *Suspense: Conceptualizations, Theoretical Analyses, and Empirical Explorations* (Lawrence Erlbaum Associates, 1996), 1-17.

[5] Hitchcock interviewed by François Truffaut in Truffaut, *Hitchcock* (Simon & Schuster, 1985), 277. Leigh interviewed by Tom Weaver, "The star of 'Psycho' relives her finest shower," *The Astounding B Monster Archive*, n.d. http://www.bmonster.com/horror19.html. Stefano interview in *E! Online*, quoted in "The Psycho Shower Scene Myth," *The Sewergator Sanctuary*, n.d. http://www.sewergator. com/gfz/psycho/.

Still determined to enlighten the benighted, Skerry sits Terry Williams, the film's assistant editor, in front of a DVD, hitting the pause button when the tip of the knife pierces Marion's skin. "See, there it is," Skerry exclaims. "It's clear as day." Peering at the same screen, however, Williams doesn't think the knife is actually "touching the flesh." *Still* determined to enlighten the benighted, Skerry assembles multiple copies of the film—a laserdisc, a DVD, a VHS cassette, a TV version—and subjects them to microscopic scrutiny, confirming the existence of the penetration shot with a certainty that Jacques Derrida couldn't argue with. But he also finds "minor differences" between the versions, converging on that very shot! And here even Skerry must let the matter rest. We all go a little mad sometimes. Haven't you?

Joseph Smith's *The Psycho File* also presents a lot of lore, some of it erroneous. The *Eroica* is Beethoven's third symphony, for instance, not his ninth. And while it's unclear why Hitchcock placed this particular record on Norman's phonograph—my theory is that "Eroica" resembles " erotica"—the idea that Hitchcock was playing on (a) the symphony's association with Napoleon, who hoped to " take over the world," and (b) Norman's remark that the house " happens to be my only world," strikes me as uproariously far-fetched. Smith also repeats the legend that Leigh "never took another shower" after watching her *Psycho* death, but in 2002 she told me this wasn't so—she just took to leaving the bathroom door open.

Smith's interpretations can be acute, however. Discussing the film's ambiguous sense of time, he remarks that as Marion drives forward while viewing the police car in her mirror, objects seem to move forward and backward simultaneously, making visible "the way so much of the story moves toward the past" even as it pushes relentlessly ahead. Calculating that Marion must be on the road for more than 20 hours before arriving at the Bates Motel, he notes that her thoughts have little to do with the most urgent matters facing her—her relationship with Sam and her moral culpability for stealing—and concludes that her impassivity bespeaks an ability "to distance herself from herself," revealing a "splitting of the personality" not entirely different from Norman's fragmented condition. Commenting on the film's symmetries and reversals, Smith poignantly connects our last view of Marion in death with her explanation of why she pulled her car off the road for a nap. I couldn't keep my eyes open," she told the highway cop. A few hours later, tragically and irremediably, she can no longer keep them closed. Observations like these make Smith's book well worth perusing.

The Moment of Psycho: How Alfred Hitchcock Taught America to Love Murder comes from the British-American critic David Thomson, who specializes in film-related biographies. There isn't much biography in this book, but there's more plot synopsis than you'll find this side of a well-stocked press kit. Thomson is a proudly "opinionated" pundit, which would be fine if his opinions were better grounded, his prose more disciplined, and his attitude less condescending to the art (and audience) with which he's chosen to engage. His outlook on silent film is a good example of his wrong-headedness, and it's very relevant to his Hitchcock criticism. In his 2004 book *The Whole Equation: A History of Hollywood*, he writes that "if there was an 'art' in silent film, it was too reliant on stilted dance, Victorian theatricality, and the beginnings of Soviet dynamism in composition and editing (the latter generally rejected by Hollywood in that they were too radically intrusive, too dialectical)." Even the greatest silent films, he declares, represent merely "a half-made medium."[6]

So much for the long list of masterpieces that period produced. I quote Thomson's nonsense because Hitchcock learned his craft in silent movies, and as Sidney Gottlieb has amply demonstrated, he remained committed to visual storytelling—the "pure cinema" he spoke about so often—throughout his career. *Psycho* is exemplary in this respect, most stunningly in the long stretch of wordless narrative that begins when Marion returns to her room after talking with Norman and ends with the cry of "Mother! Oh God, mother! Blood! Blood!" that rends the air after Norman has cleaned up the murder scene. Of course there is music during some of this, but there was music in silent-movie theaters too. Is a critic who looks down on silent cinema a good choice to opine about a film that communicates so richly through images alone?

I think not, and here are some Thomsonisms from *The Moment of Psycho* to back up my contention. On the protagonists: "The great difficulty facing *Psycho* is that our identifier in the film (Janet Leigh) is gone. The only real replacement is Norman Bates—and that isn't going to work." On the film's rationale: "I don't credit half a second of this rigmarole about Mother having taken over Norman." On the film's second half: "Hitchcock has lost interest, and he has known all along that his payoff in *Psycho* is a drab concession to the trashiness of 'slasher' horror movies."

---

[6] David Thomson, *The Whole Equation: A History of Hollywood* (Vintage, 2006), 152, 153.

On the film's place in Hitchcock's oeuvre: "He had achieved an international sensation and helped establish the power of the director as auteur. But he had also isolated films from the larger horizons of meaning." Now let's think for a moment. Thomson says Hitchcock conceded to the slasher-movie subgenre, when in fact he pretty much invented it with this very film;[7] that Perkins' Norman is insufferably dull, which makes you wonder how he became a near-universal icon of American culture; and that *Psycho* somehow cut off cinema's ability to connect with important issues, which disregards the myriad critics and scholars who have found its horizons of meaning to be very large indeed. All this reinforces my belief that Thomson's sensibility isn't so much scrappy and opinionated as insular and contrarian. This book was not one of his better ideas.

I've been concentrating on critics' responses to *Psycho*, but people who worked on it have also expressed interesting views, and sometimes puzzling ones, like the notion that there's no knife-penetration shot. Even reminiscences can be perplexing. Seeing the picture in Los Angeles on opening day, screenwriter Stefano told Rebello years later, he was astonished to see grownup moviegoers "grabbing each other, howling, screaming, reacting like six-year-olds at a Saturday matinee... I never thought they'd be so vocal. And neither did Hitchcock." Perkins reported a similar experience, saying that "after hearing audiences around the country *roar*, Hitchcock—perhaps reluctantly—acknowledged that it was OK to laugh at the film and that, perhaps, it was a comedy after all. He *didn't* realize how funny audiences would find the movie, generally... He was confused, at first, incredulous second, and despondent third." Hitch even petitioned Wasserman to remix the soundtrack with added volume in spots, according to Perkins, because "leftover howls from the previous scene" rendered the hardware-store meeting of Sam, Lila, and Arbogast "practically inaudible."[8]

I'm skeptical about these stories. If he actually saw what he describes, Stefano should have remembered (as I'm sure he did) that the film's pre-release publicity blitz had promised the kind of

---

[7] Michael Powell's *Peeping Tom* arrived in British and American theaters a month before *Psycho*, but had little immediate influence because of its initial failure both critically and commercially.

[8] Wasserman said no, citing the cost of the prints. For this and the Stefano and Perkins accounts, see Rebello, *Alfred Hitchcock and the Making of Psycho*, 162-3. Emphases in original.

nerve-jangling shocker that many moviegoers—especially the fans
and connoisseurs who line up on opening day—take as enjoyable
occasions for yowling and braying and clutching their companions
in make-believe fear and trembling. This in no way diminishes the
film; as critics have long observed, its deeper meanings are likely to
emerge only with multiple viewings, and *Psycho* soon accumulated
more return visits than any picture had before.[9] The first time
around, audiences usually find it to be exactly what Hitchcock
said it was in 1963: "a *fun* picture."[10] Perkins' story is even more
problematic. The "previous scene" that elicited long-lasting howls
of laughter was, of all things, the shower murder. Are we really
to believe that "audiences around the country" responded to this
brutal event and its gradual, near-hypnotic denouement with
guffaws that persisted for *more than 15 minutes*? Hitchcock may
well have asked agent and facilitator Lew Wasserman to fine-tune
the soundtrack—he wouldn't have been the first filmmaker to seek
adjustments at (or beyond) the last minute—but Perkins' account
of the circumstances rings hollow.

I'm also skeptical because I saw *Psycho* in the summer of 1960,
at a first-run theater in my Long Island town. I couldn't tell you
today how the audience responded to this or that scene, because
I immediately took to the movie as a *personal* experience and
ignored everything except the screen and my own thoughts. I am
dead certain, however, that no one but no one, including the casual
fun-seekers among us, acted remotely like the hooting mood-busters
described above. Even at 15 I would have resented and remembered
such behavior, especially at a movie by the director I regarded as the
greatest long before I was certain what a director did.

It's a truism that popularity says nothing about a film's
enduring worth, but the hypnotic pull of *Psycho* is reaffirmed
for me every time I screen it for university students. I do this as
often as I can get away with it, mostly because it generates unusually thoughtful discussions, but also because *Psycho* is among the
few films that never fail to engross virtually everyone, whether
or not they've seen it before. They certainly don't laugh in the
wrong places, and they're surprised when I tell them Hitchcock
considered it a comedy, until I add what he told me in 1972—that

---

[9] Patrick McGilligan, *Alfred Hitchcock: A Life in Darkness and Light*
(Regan, 2003), 601.
[10] Ian Cameron and V. F. Perkins, " Hitchcock," *Movie* 6 (January 1963),
4-6; reprinted in Sidney Gottlieb, ed., *Alfred Hitchcock: Interviews*
(Mississippi, 2003), 44-54, cited at 47.

if he'd wanted to tell this story in a truly serious way, he would have filmed it as a case study without "mysterioso" touches. Many cultural critics today place *Psycho* into the centuries-old tradition of "carnivalesque" art, and that gets it exactly right. Not because it's funny ha-ha or even funny peculiar, but because its ultimate purpose is to laugh disdainfully and sardonically in the face of decadence, dementia, and death. Hollywood cinema doesn't come more exciting, ingenious, or subversive.

Godard, Gorin, and Company
Quarterly Review of Film and Video 35:4 (2018)

On one of my trips to the Telluride Film Festival some years ago, I asked Jean-Pierre Gorin where in the world one could find any of the hyperpolitical films he made with Jean-Luc Godard and the Dziga Vertov Group between the late 1960s and early 1970s. His answer did not really surprise me: He had no idea.

But that was then. Now, a boxed set called *Godard + Gorin: Five Films 1968–1971* has been released by Arrow Films, an enterprising company for which this commercially unpromising venture will presumably be a loss leader at best.[1] The bulk of the Dziga Vertov Group's output is therefore more available than ever before, and neither Jean-Pierre nor I need wonder about its whereabouts any longer.[2]

Godard was the primary force behind the Dziga Vertov Group, named after the pioneering Soviet director who championed the supremacy of nonfiction cinema in the era of silent film. The breezy way to summarize Godard's ambition for the Group is to say that he aimed to make films completely divorced from capitalist systems of production, distribution, and exhibition, and succeeded so well that he became completely divorced from his audience too. Well, not *completely* divorced, since a limited number of likeminded viewers were on board with almost any experiment

---

[1] *Godard + Gorin: Five Films 1968–1971*. A boxed dual-format DVD/Blu-ray set (Zone 1/ Region A) released by Arrow Films, 2018.

[2] Arrow is actually not the first distributor to put these films on the video market. A more comprehensive boxed DVD set (Zone 2) called *Jean-Luc Godard y el Grupo Dziga Vertov 1968–1974* was released by the Spanish company Intermedio in 2008, containing every film in the Arrow collection plus several others: the densely edited *Pravda*, a study of Czechoslovakia's sociopolitical circumstances; the argumentative *Letter to Jane: An Investigation About a Still* (1972), which subjects a photograph of Jane Fonda to lengthy analysis; the fictional *Tout Va Bien* (1972), with Fonda and Yves Montand in a story about labor action and consumerism; the pivotal *Ici et ailleurs* (*Here and Elsewhere*, 1974, incorporating footage shot by Godard and Gorin for a never-completed Palestinian film), codirected by Godard and Anne-Marie Miéville, who became Godard's personal and professional partner immediately after the Dziga Vertov Group period; and the off-the-wall *1 P.M.*, a 1968 film also known as *One Parallel Movie* and *One Pennebaker Movie*, assembled by D. A. Pennebaker from footage abandoned by Godard when his planned *1 A.M.*, also known as *One American Movie*, failed to reach completion.

that Godard might try. His political and aesthetic activism had been tending toward extremes since at least 1967, the year that gave us the analytical *2 ou 3 Choses que Je Sais d'Elle* (*Two or Three Things I Know About Her…*), the prescient *La Chinoise, ou Plutôt à la chinoise,* the rage-filled *Weekend,* and the minimalist "Camera-Eye" segment in the anthology film *Far from Vietnam* (*Loin du Vietnam*). The deconstructive Rolling Stones study *One Plus One* (*Sympathy for the Devil*) in 1968 and the pedagogical *Le Gai Savoir* (*Joy of Learning*) in 1969 proved that Godard's effort to find a degree zero of activist cinema was there to stay, at least for the foreseeable future.

It was the 1968 sort-of-documentary *Un Film comme les autres* (*A Film Like Any Other*) that escalated Godard's dissidence crusade so drastically that only the fiercest partisans could respond with anything close to enthusiasm. The semidocumentary *British Sounds* (*See You at Mao*), made in 1969 for a British television outlet that predictably refused to air it, attracted a similarly minute following despite its relatively manageable running time of slightly less than an hour. Those two productions were claimed retrospectively by the Dziga Vertov Group, which took quasi-official form with the production of *Wind from the East* (*Le Vent d'Est*) in 1969 and *Lotte in Italia* (*Struggle in Italy*) in 1970, and then faded from the scene after *Vladimir and Rosa* in 1971. Godard and Gorin codirected all of the Group's films except *Un Film comme les autres,* which was mainly Godard's work, and *British Sounds,* which Godard directed with substantial input from Jean-Henri Roger, the group's other mainstay. A handful of additional figures—including cinematographer Armand Marco and actress Anne Wiazemsky, who was married to Godard at the time—also made key contributions.

The five pictures just mentioned (*Un Film comme les autres, British Sounds, Wind from the East, Lotte in Italia,* and *Vladimir and Rosa*) are the main attractions in the Arrow collection, whose arrival is cause for celebration by anyone interested in the most obscure and demanding phase of Godard's multipronged activity as filmmaker, theorist, and militant stirrer of the sociopolitical pot. These movies are not easy to take in and fully fathom, requiring as much active viewing and creative listening as almost anything to be found in other branches of the audiovisual avant-garde. But hefty intellectual rewards are available in the challenges and perplexities they pose.

I won't offer an in-depth discussion of the individual films, which vary somewhat in character if not very much in ideology. The earliest of them, *Un Film comme les autres*, is perhaps the most daunting of the lot, consisting of largely static and repetitive footage—the dominant image is of students hashing out leftist politics in a pleasant outdoorsy setting—and a soundtrack mingling several voices into a layered sonority that is often hard to understand (and equally hard for English subtitles to encapsulate). Beyond this the film defies verbal description, thanks partly to its unorthodox content and partly to its existence in more than one version; for its fleeting first run in the United States another layer of English-language voicing was added to the mix, famously muddying instead of clarifying the situation.

In part, *Un Film comme les autres* is Godard's response to the death of a young protester in a recent political action, and like other works by the Dziga Vertov Group, it would surely have acquired more viewers if the filmmakers had set forth that real-life backstory somewhere in the movie itself. Godard has always had a hankering for the cryptic, however, and people watching his films—apart from his earliest, most self-contained features, from *Breathless* in 1960 to *Weekend* in 1967—are pretty much on their own when it comes to social, historical, and interpretive context.

Newcomers to the Dziga Vertov Group should bear in mind that the films have two overriding purposes. One is to rejigger the relationship between image and sound in cinema. The other is to pitch a set of radical ideas, usually exemplified by a three-part cinematic structure based on Godard and Gorin's notion of Maoist doctrine: an opening exposition of ideas is followed by an auto-critique of that exposition and then by an analysis and auto-critique of the first two parts. A great deal of verbiage is present in all the films, couched in the leftwing idiom of a bygone era. The politically fraught words *revisionist* and *revisionism* are endlessly reiterated—although never defined or delineated—and the formula "concrete analysis of a concrete situation" is repeatedly trotted out in sequences that are more schematic and abstract than concrete in any practical sense.

Arrow obligingly supplements its selection of films with a pair of illuminating extras. One is a more than two-hour interview with Godard, conducted and filmed by Pierre-Henri Gibert and Dominique Maillet in 2010; clearly at ease with his interlocutors, Godard shares a generous number of anecdotes and reflections, none of them deeply insightful or sustained, but steadily interesting to followers of his creative exploits. Among other highlights, Godard repeatedly uses James Cameron's blockbuster *Avatar* as an example of the cinema he despises—released at the tail end of 2009, it was evidently sticking in Godard's craw at the time of the interview—and he chides Quentin Tarantino for naming his production company, A Band Apart Films, after Godard's crime comedy *Band of Outsiders* (*Bande à Part,* 1964), which Godard now professes to regard as his worst movie ever (and which, by the way, it definitely is not).

The other extensive extra is "Michael Witt on Godard, Gorin and the Dziga Vertov Group," a 90-minute video essay in which Witt, a first-rate English film scholar, traces Godard's artistic evolution from increasingly bold, contentious, and Bertolt Brecht-influenced maker of French New Wave art films to ornery ideologue of the post-May 1968 era. In the latter period he was a guerrilla participant in the samizdat *Cinetracts* project, a combative journalist publishing articles and photographs in *J'Accuse,* an organizer helping to conceptualize the Agence de Presse Libération in the early 1970s, and a Maoist revolutionary paying eccentric homage to Vertov in films in which ideology reigns supreme.

In that video piece and in "Godard and the Far-Left Press," a lucid essay in a booklet accompanying the Arrow package, Witt calls attention to Godard's intense focus on the politics and ethics of capitalist media, very much including television, during the Dziga Vertov Group phase of his career. Witt also acknowledges Gorin's important claim that all of the Group films basically grew from an unproduced screenplay called "Un Film Français," which Gorin wrote in 1968 for a 24-hour project called "Communications" that Godard planned but never managed to actuate. Illuminating but never sentimentalizing the Group's work, Witt is candid about its circumscribed sphere of influence; phrases like "It was received very poorly" recur more than once in his remarks on the initial showings of the films.

Its brief lifespan notwithstanding, the Dziga Vertov Group generated a secret history as intriguing and tangled as that accrued by the New Wave during its considerably longer heyday, and the Arrow extras provide tantalizing glimpses thereof. My quibbles with the collection as a whole are few and minor. There is some spotty editing and a bit of poor subtitling in the Godard interview, where U-Matic comes out "Hi-Matic" and Robert Rossen comes out "Robert Hossein," not once but twice, despite the clear context and Godard's reasonably clear enunciation. More significantly, not all of the Dziga Vertov Group films are present here; the most notable absentee is the rapid-fire essay film *Pravda* (1969), omitted "due to unforeseen circumstances," according to the Arrow booklet.

As densely packed and haunting as all the films in this collection are, I'll close by saluting my personal favorite, which is the minute-long television commercial for Schick aftershave lotion made by Godard and Gorin in 1971. It's as witty and mischievous a picture as either filmmaker ever produced, and after the rigors of the ultra-austere Dziga Vertov Group features, it comes as a revitalizing breath of brisk cinematic air. Bravo.

Mailer, Godard, and Company

from *The Cinema of Norman Mailer: Film Is Like Death*, ed. Justin Bozung (Bloomsbury, 2017)

The most fraught and famous encounter between writer-filmmaker-provocateur Norman Mailer and filmmaker-writer-provocateur Jean-Luc Godard took place when Mailer recruited Godard to write a 1987 adaptation of *King Lear*, featuring Mailer and his daughter as Lear and *his* daughter. Although the collaboration quickly disintegrated, it helped Mailer find producers for his 1987 film *Tough Guys Don't Dance*, based on his 1984 novel of that title. More broadly, Mailer's high regard for Godard was among the forces that shaped his overall approach to the film medium.

Their personal and creative differences notwithstanding, Mailer and Godard held each other in considerable esteem for reasons related to their aesthetic philosophies in general and their filmmaking practices in particular. Although he was not a systematic or painstaking reader, Godard loved literature and read Mailer over the years, quoting him several times in his 1983 film *First Name: Carmen* (*Prénom Carmen*), which has its own literary provenance, being a (fast and loose) adaptation of Prosper Mérimée's 1845 novella *Carmen*.[1] Mailer had a longstanding interest in Godard as well. "In a funny way," he remarked in 1970, "I think Godard approaches films in the same way that I do. Which is, he loves these myths. He grew up with these myths. They formed him."[2] Mailer doesn't specify just which myths he has in mind, but the great mythos of modern America clearly fascinated him as a Brooklyn-bred, Harvard-educated writer whose 1948 debut novel, *The Naked and the Dead*, became a critical and commercial smash in the postwar era of American cultural, economic, and ideological ascendency. And he is right about Godard, whose fascination with the American ethos—in itself, and as the power center of predatory Western values—was powerfully fueled by the Hollywood movies he voraciously took in as a critic and aspiring filmmaker in

---

[1] Colin MacCabe, *Godard: A Portrait of the Artist at Seventy* (Faber, 2003), p. 329. Godard's film pays reverse homage to the 1875 opera *Carmen*, replacing the music by Georges Bizet with string quartets by Ludwig van Beethoven and (briefly) a song by Tom Waits.

[2] Joseph Gelmis, "Norman Mailer," in J. Michael Lennon, ed., *Conversations with Norman Mailer* (Mississippi, 1988), pp. 155-175, cited at 173. Originally published in Joseph Gelmis, *The Film Director as Superstar* (Doubleday, 1970), pp. 43-63.

the 1950s. Godard has directed (and written, in most cases) many scores of feature films, short films, and video productions since 1960, when his widely acclaimed *Breathless* (*À Bout de souffle*) helped launch him and France's nascent New Wave movement to the forefront of European cinema. Mailer's energies went mainly into his writing, which produced about three dozen books and a good deal of culture-world celebrity in his lifetime, but he also cared deeply about the four movies he directed.

The first two, *Beyond the Law* and *Wild 90*, were made back to back in 1968.[3] *Beyond the Law*, released on the twentieth anniversary of the publication of *The Naked and the Dead*, takes place in a Manhattan police station where a handful of officers are interrogating, intimidating, and hassling a handful of suspects brought in on a variety of charges, all of which is intercut with a conversation between some cops and their wives or girlfriends in a nearby saloon. Mailer plays belligerent Lt. Francis Xavier Pope with a conspicuous Irish brogue, supported by Rip Torn as a lowlife called Popcorn and George Plimpton as the city mayor, who drops by to check on the discipline situation at the precinct. With all dialogue improvised by the cast, the film was shot over four nights that yielded eleven hours of footage, which Mailer and coeditor Jan Welt spent six months reducing to a final cut of 105 minutes. Mailer said the film was intended "to create the reality... below the reality, beneath the reality, within the reality of an evening in the police station," and title refers to his notion that "whether you're innocent or guilty, when you're in a police station you're treated as if you're a crook. So existentially you are a crook... You're now beyond the law."[4] Critical reception was mixed. *Chicago Sun-Times* critic Roger Ebert called it "outdated" and "pretty inept," while *New York Times* critic Vincent Canby found it "good and tough and entertaining" despite occasional lapses.[5]

Wild 90 presents an environment even more claustrophobic and entrapping. Billed as The Maf Boys in the opening titles, Mailer, Buzz Farber, and Mickey Knox play mobsters called Prince, Buzz Cameo, and 20 Years, respectively. Holed up together in a drab urban loft, they kid, taunt, deride, and berate one another by turns,

---

[3] *Beyond the Law* was filmed before *Wild 90* but premiered several months later at the New York Film Festival.

[4] Gelmis, "Norman Mailer," p. 159-60.

[5] Roger Ebert, "Beyond the Law." *Chicago Sun-Times*, November 4, 1969. Vincent Canby, "Norman Mailer Offers Beyond the Law." *The New York Times*, September 30, 1968.

visited by others in the second half of the film. "I didn't know what I was doing," Mailer said when reflecting on the production, which cost more than three times its original budget and emerged with a technically defective soundtrack that was close to incomprehensible.[6] In her thoughtful *New York Times* review, Renata Adler wrote that the film "faces a problem that now confronts Mailer's work as a whole. The frontier has shifted. The battle against dead forms, useless conventions, and pointless inhibitions is over, or no longer interesting; the breakthroughs are now in terms of limit, live forms, tighter economies. The very urgency that Mailer has always tried to communicate makes it impossible to wade through so much rambling for a little art."[7] Mailer acknowledged the film's shortcomings, although he felt the technical matter of the soundtrack was the worst of these.

The more ambitious *Maidstone*, completed in 1970 and published in screenplay form a year later, is Mailer's most notorious movie, thanks in part to its sizable scale—the action was filmed by seven cinematographers in spacious Long Island locations with a large cast—and in larger part to its climactic scene, wherein Mailer, portraying movie director and presidential candidate Norman T. Kingsley, is clobbered on the head by Rip Torn, portraying half-brother and hanger-on Raoul Rey O'Houlihan, out of the blue, with a very real hammer. Mailer immediately leaps upon Torn, biting the actor's ear and being nearly strangled in return; eventually Mailer's then wife, Beverly Bentley, portraying Kingsley's wife, Chula Mae Kingsley, breaks up the fight as Mailer children shriek with fear and horror on the sidelines, making the aftermath of the attack more harrowing than the attack itself. Canby was not much taken with *Maidstone*, deeming it "a very expensive, 110-minute home movie that has been edited... out of something like 45 hours of original footage" ; musing on this, the critic comes to think that "almost anybody should be able to get 110 minutes of something out of 45 hours of anything, even if it's simply the filmed record of a chic, chaotic, seven-day brawl in East Hampton, which is the [film's] raw, not-so-base material." The influential *New Yorker* critic Pauline Kael was more succinct, saying that as a movie director "Mailer didn't have much to retrogress from, but he managed."[8]

[6] Gelmis, "Norman Mailer," p. 158.

[7] Renata Adler, "Norman Mailer's Mailer: *Wild 90*, Another Ad for Writer, Bows." *The New York Times*, January 8, 1968.

[8] Vincent Canby, "Mailer's Maidstone Opens Whitney Series." *The New*

Mailer used his filmmaker character in *Maidstone* as a vehicle for some of his own ideas about the situation depicted in the film—a sort of three-dimensional chess game involving a presidential campaign, the extremely mixed motives of the political operatives and fellow travelers on the scene, and a plot to assassinate the candidate—as well as, more interestingly, his ideas about the filmmaking process. He speaks out most directly in the eleventh of the film's twelve numbered episodes, when he and others in the cast step out of character and speak as themselves. At one point, for instance, the actress Bianca Rosoff, who plays Princess Barome, says that the movie's harsh tone has frightened some of the participants. Mailer responds that he intended exactly that, and continues:

> You're still thinking of movies that are made where you very carefully structure them. You get the maximum out of each moment. But what I'm arguing for in this method is that you cannot make a movie that way and get anything even remotely resembling the truth. That way you just get a unilinear abstract of one man's conception of how something possibly might happen. But what I'm saying is that that's not the way anything happens. The way anything happens is that we have five realities at any given moment which then swing around [here Mailer twists like a skier doing little turns] to there, you see, or like this, do you follow?

Mailer continued his lecture in the book version of *Maidstone*, where a transcript of the screenplay is preceded by an account of the filming and followed by "A Course in Filmmaking" penned by Mailer, who refers to "the director" in the third person.[9] "Cuts were like words," he asserts at one point. "You could put many an ordinary word next to another word but you could not put them all... Godard made jump cuts in *Breathless* which no one had been able to endure before, did it all out of his experience as a cutter and from his artistic insight that the *verboten* had moved to the edge of the virtuoso. Yet, you may be certain the twenty precise cuts before the jump cut fed subtly into it, if indeed the jump cut

---

York Times, September 24, 1971. Pauline Kael, *5001 Nights at the Movies: A Guide from A to Z* (Holt, Rinehart and Winston, 1982), p. 354.

[9] The brief production history is assembled from articles by Sally Lucas, J. Anthony Lukas, and James Toback.

had not become the particular metaphysics of that film."[10] Mailer may be ascribing more calculation to the *Breathless* cuts than the hugely instinctive Godard actually brought to bear on them, but his invocation of metaphysics is right on the money for that film, that filmmaker, and that pivotal film-historical moment.

At least three interconnected factors helped generate Mailer's experimental films of 1968 and 1970. One was the blossoming of American avant-garde cinema in the postwar era, producing innovative films like Kenneth Anger's *Scorpio Rising* (1964), which Mailer found superb, and Andy Warhol's *Kitchen* (1965), which he found horrible as a film but inspirational anyway, teaching him that "an uncut piece of film [is] beautiful" and that one's own friends and acquaintances can furnish a perfectly good cast.[11]

A second factor was Mailer's his experience as a playwright, which transpired when he wrote a stage adaptation of his 1955 novel *The Deer Park*, about excess and decadence among the Hollywood set.[12] The cast included Knox and Farbar, with whom Mailer hung out and drank every evening. "And we began playing this game," he recalled later. "We began improvising, to take on parts." Pretending they were gangsters, they spent hours cooking up what they thought was "absolutely fantastic" repartee.[13] When the idea of filming the improvisations arose, Mailer ran with it, paid for it, and initiated his career as a movie director.

A third factor was the rise of cinéma-vérité documentary, enabled by the development of lightweight equipment and propelled by groundbreaking works like Robert Drew's *Primary* (1960), Frederick Wiseman's *Titicut Follies* (1967) and *High School* (1968), the widely hailed *Salesman* (1968) by Albert Maysles, David Maysles, and Charlotte Zwerin, the French ethnographic film *Chronicle of a Summer* (1961) by anthropologist Jean Rouch and sociologist Edgar Morin, and D. A. Pennebaker's *Don't Look Back* (1967), shot during Bob Dylan's concert tour in England in 1965. Pennebaker is a link between Mailer and Godard, since he was a cinematographer for all three of Mailer's experimental films and for Godard's never-completed 1968 production "One AM," aka "One American Movie," which Pennebaker ultimately edited into *One*

---

[10] Norman Mailer, *Maidstone: A Mystery* (Signet, 1971), p. 168.

[11] Mary V. Dearborn, *Mailer: A Biography* (Houghton Mifflin, 1999), p. 232.

[12] Norman Mailer, *The Deer Park* (Dial, 1967). It opened at New York's Theatre de Lys in 1967, directed by Leo Garen, and ran for almost four months, winning Rip Torn an Obie Award for his performance.

[13] Gelmis, "Norman Mailer," p. 157-58.

PM, aka "One Parallel Movie" or "One Perfect Movie" or "One Pennebaker Movie," finished in 1971. Godard's artfully mercurial films often contain elements shot directly from life—the hidden-camera street scenes in *Breathless*, for instance, or the interview with a teenager in *Masculine Feminine* (*Masculin féminin*, 1966)—and in 1965 he contributed a segment titled *Montparnasse-Levallois* to a French anthology film called *Paris vu par...* (*Six in Paris*), for which he prepared an amusing romantic story about a woman sends letters to a pair of lovers but gets the envelopes mixed up. He then brought in the cinéma-vérité pioneer Albert Maysles to photograph the scenes as they unfolded without having read the script, seen rehearsals, or even heard what the movie was about. What compelled Godard's attention in this project was "fluidity, being able to feel existence like physical matter."[14] The result was an "action-film" capturing a time "when chance enters into the elaboration of the film, presiding over the encounter with reality," in biographer Antoine de Baecque's words.[15] Mailer used different methods in his experimental films, but his proclivity for the spontaneous, the intuitive, and the improvisational ran along the same general lines.

Mailer's final film was the 1987 drama *Tough Guys Don't Dance*, based on his 1984 novel of that title.[16] The production's genesis was quite a story in itself. At the Cannes film festival in 1985, Godard and producer Menahem Golan signed a deal (on a napkin) to make a version of *King Lear* where the tragic hero of William Shakespeare's tragedy would be portrayed "as King Leone, as a sort of patriarch-gangster... like a godfather."[17] The agreement stipulated that Golan approve the screenwriter, and when Godard suggested Mailer, the producer concurred. Mailer was hesitant, having heard that Godard was "hell on writers," but changed his mind when Golan said he could write and direct *Tough Guys Don't Dance* in return. Meeting with Godard, who seemed frustratingly vague and "heavily depressed," Mailer was asked to

---

[14] Jean-Luc Godard, "Montparnasse-Levallois," in Narboni and Milne, eds., *Godard on Godard*, pp. 211-13, cited at p. 211. Originally published in *Cahiers du cinéma* 171 (October 1965), pp. 9-1.

[15] Antoine de Baecque, *Godard*. Biographie (Bernard Grasset, 2010), pp. 249-50. My translation.

[16] Norman Mailer, *Tough Guys Don't Dance* (Random House, 1984).

[17] This and subsequent quotations regarding *King Lear* are from Richard Brody, *Everything Is Cinema: The Working Life of Jean-Luc Godard* (Metropolitan, 2006), p. 492-97.

play the title role as well as write the script, and also to recruit his daughters to play the Goneril, Regan, and Cordelia characters. He completed a script (which Godard never read) and went to Switzerland with his daughter Kate Mailer to start the shoot. Conflict reigned. Mailer recalled to biographer Richard Brody in 2000:

> I was hardly playing *King Lear*. [Godard] said, "You will be Norman Mailer in this." And then he gave me some lines and they were really, by any confortable measure, dreadful... I said to him, "Look, I really can't say these lines. If you give me another name than Norman Mailer, I'll say anything you write for me, but if I'm going to be speaking in my own name, then I've got to write the lines, or at least I've got to be consulted on the lines."

According to Godard, the biggest problem between himself and Mailer was a clash in working methods. Mailer perceived that "above all, I wasn't very... that I don't know very well what I want to do," Godard remarked, "so he couldn't really have a discussion about it, he had nothing to do but obey, to have confidence in me." Such obedience was not to be, and the last straw came when Godard insinuated that Lear, played by Mailer, would be sexually attracted to his daughter, played by Mailer's daughter. "Is it a reasonable demand to ask someone to, in their own name, play that they have an incestuous relationship to their daughter?" a fed-up Mailer rhetorically asked Brody when recalling all this. He left Switzerland and the production soon thereafter.

Godard finished *King Lear* with a cast featuring Burgess Meredith as Don Learo and Peter Sellars as William Shakespeare Junior the Fifth, along with Molly Ringwald, Woody Allen, Leos Carax, and Julie Delpy in mostly brief appearances. Also present are Godard as Professor Pluggy, the sort of tragicomic oddball that he habitually plays when appearing in his own films, and Norman and Kate Mailer in a tiny bit of footage near the beginning. Critics have variously applauded and derided it, as often happens with a Godard film.

The happy ending for Mailer was the opportunity to make *Tough Guys Don't Dance*, which premiered at Cannes in 1987. Set in Provincetown on Cape Cod, where Mailer had a longtime home, the film stars Ryan O'Neal as Tim Madden, an obvious Mailer surrogate—he's a writer, a drinker, and a Cape Codder with a complicated romantic past—who wakes from a blackout and finds blood all over his car and a woman's severed head buried in in his marijuana stash; among the other characters are his father (Lawrence Tierney), his former girlfriend (Isabella Rossellini), his wife (Debra Sandlund), his wife's ex-husband (John Bedford Lloyd), and a police chief (Wings Hauser) who has gone murderously insane. Although it did not fare well with audiences or reviewers, Mailer stood by it, defending it as a "horror film" in Greg Carson's short documentary *Norman Mailer in Provincetown*, included on the DVD release in 2003. It is better described as a super-hardboiled crime picture or a hyperbolic film noir, and some of its components—Rossellini's performance, Angelo Badalamenti's music, scenes shrouded in chthonic fog or darkness—put one in mind of David Lynch's surreal brand of oneiric mystery. Godard's influence also shows, particularly in a sequence when a Rolls-Royce is trashed in jolting jump cuts. The film's generally hypomanic tenor also recalls crime-related Godard pictures like *Made in U.S.A.* (1966), *First Name: Carmen*, and *Détective* (1985).

In the 2003 documentary about *Tough Guys Don't Dance*, Mailer makes much of his decision to include a particular moment of over-the-top hysteria that all of his collaborators told him to excise or at least tone down: a lengthy swirling-camera shot of Madden on a dune, crazily howling "*Oh man oh God oh man oh God!*" over and over in a moment of intolerable mental distress. Although he had no use for organized religion, Mailer took God quite seriously, and he had highly developed theories about the relationship between God and humanity, believing that God and the Devil are continually at war in every person, and that despite embodying vast power, God makes errors, loses control of the creation at times, and needs human help just as humans need divine help. "[W]hat I believe—this is wholly speculative but important to me—is that we are here as God's work, here to influence His future as well as ours," he said in a dialogue published in 2007, the year of his death. And again, "Live in the depths of confusion with the knowledge back of that, the certainty back of that—or the belief, the hope, the faith, whatever you wish to call it—that there is a purpose to it all, that it is not absurd, that we are all engaged in a vast cosmic war and God needs us."[18] Why did Mailer insist on retaining Madden's heartrending cry ("*Oh God oh man!*") against all sensible advice to the contrary? Perhaps because it crys-

---

[18] Norman Mailer with J. Michael Lennon, "The Rise of Mailerism." *New York*, October 7, 2000). Excerpted from Norman Mailer with J. Michael Lennon, *On God: An Uncommon Conversation* (Random House, 2007).

tallizes his conception of the symbiotic God-human bond, forged in mutual necessity and beneficial to both parties in the long run of eternity.

Godard took God seriously as well, most notably in *Hail Mary* (*Je vous salue, Marie*, 1985), his modern-day retelling of the Virgin Mary story; released just two years before *Tough Guys Don't Dance*, it depicts Mary (Myriem Roussel) as a young Swiss woman who works in her father's gas station, plays basketball for relaxation, and puzzles over her sacred pregnancy in talks with Joseph (Thierry Rode), a taxi driver. For both Godard and Mailer, theological reflection is less a route to revealed truth or heavenly salvation than a means of opening up thought to possibilities that exceed and transcend customary norms; they share an inclination toward spiritually attuned moods in which they go beyond pondering the divine and identify their creativity as artists with the creativity of the divine itself. "Mailer's deity is much like Mailer," his literary executor and confidante J. Michael Lennon observes. "He or she is an artist—with the stipulation that God is the greatest artist—concerned most particularly with the human soul, but with much else besides." This is not a metaphorical position on Mailer's part. "It is," Lennon writes, "what he believes to be true... [H]e has worked to forge his beliefs into a coherent catechism."[19] Something like this, mutatis mutandis, goes for Godard also. God has long been an alter ego for him, film scholar Sally Shafto accurately notes, and he likes to think of himself as a "distant as well as omniscient creator," conjuring images out of light, which is both the material ground of cinema and a signifier of the divine.[20] The theologies of Mailer and Godard are far from orthodox, but they are not merely theoretical either.

Returning to the secular world, Mailer and Godard are profoundly skeptical about the ever-growing sociological and psychological sway of American culture. Taking it as their responsibility to counteract the juggernaut by means of art, they fight conformity and materialism by drawing out bedrock constituents of the psyche—mystery, fantasy, paradox—that we habitually repress in the names of practicality and common sense. The essayist and novelist Jonathan Lethem captures this attitude well when he describes Mailer's core belief that "the uncanny symbolic

---

[19] Mailer with Lennon, "The Rise of Mailerism."
[20] Sally Shafto, "Artist as Christ/Artist as God-the-Father: Religion in the Cinema of Philippe Garrel and Jean-Luc Godard." *Film History* 4 (2000), pp. 142-157, cited at pp. 144, 145.

life of our imagination resolutely [steers] the outward action of the legible world, no matter how much we might legislate it out of existence or deny its relevance in one realm or another." Two conclusions follow from this. On the level of group experience, "the pressure of the denied myths... invariably [makes itself] crucial." On the level of individual life, nourishing and cultivating "the realm of the symbolic, the self's own intangible dream stuff," becomes an essential task, if also a precarious one, always in danger of being abandoned or betrayed.[21]

Mailer pursued hidden myths, dreams, and symbols first through writing and then through film, testing the idea that the resources of cinema—especially montage, which links disparate images into suggestive new configurations—can tap more deeply than literature into the some areas of the imagination. "If someone throws a hand up like this," he told me in 1987, making an appropriate gesture, "and the next (shot) is some birds taking off like that... there's a connection. You might not be able to name the connection. But somewhere in that deep, mysterious world of signs, portents, images, and hints, there is a connection that makes sense to us."[22] Godard spoke similarly about montage as early as 1956, saying that a cut from a gaze to the object of the gaze can "bring out the soul under the spirit, the passion behind the intrigue, [and] make the heart prevail over the intelligence by destroying the notion of space in favor of that of time."[23]

Mailer's admiration for Godard had multiple sources, one of which is that both he and Godard have refused to privilege fiction over nonfiction or vice versa. Mailer published a dozen novels, but his Pulitzer Prizes were won by two of his many nonfiction books, and Godard has swung continually among narrative, documentary, and hybrid modes, believing that "great fiction films tend towards documentary, just as... great documentaries tend towards fiction... And he who opts wholeheartedly for one, necessarily finds the other at the end of his journey."[24] At the same time, both artists

---

[21] Jonathan Lethem, "Advertisements for Norman Mailer." *Los Angeles Review of Books*, October 3, 2011.

[22] David Sterritt, "Novelist Mailer Turns His Latest Book into a Movie." *The Christian Science Monitor*, September 4, 1987.

[23] Jean-Luc Godard, "Montage My Fine Care," trans. Tom Milne, in Jean Narboni and Tom Milne, eds., *Godard on Godard* (Da Capo Press, 1986), pp. 39-41, cited at 39. Originally published as "Montage, mon beau souci" in *Cahiers du cinéma* 65 (December 1956), pp. 30-31.

[24] Jean-Luc Godard, "Africa Speaks of the End and the Means," trans. Tom

have a near-mystical faith in montage and juxtaposition as portals to a rich, enigmatic netherworld, and both take pleasure in flummoxing and transcending linear narrative by means of distancing, interruption, and discontinuity; for Mailer this dates at least as far back as the "Time Machine" episodes punctuating the narrative of *The Naked and the Dead*, and for Godard it has been a constant ever since the jump cuts that energize *Breathless*. In this area Mailer and Godard have much in common with (while remaining less extreme than) the Beat Generation writer and painter William S. Burroughs, who uses disjointedness and semi-incoherence to wage mortal combat against what he metaphorically sees as language-borne viruses of social and psychological control dispatched by hegemonic powers to infect our bodies and minds. Mailer and Godard also share a mingled fascination and vexation with modes of expression (mainstream film, hardboiled fiction) that they drastically revise but do not radically reject.

Both also have a modernist penchant for valuing the primal, visceral, and intuitive over the sophisticated, temperate, and cerebral. In the late 1960s, when received ideas and conventional wisdoms were being challenged around the globe, Mailer and Godard felt licensed to express gut feelings of antiestablishment anger in exceptionally drastic ways. Godard's escalating rage at Western profligacy and injustice gathered momentum in the sociological critique of *Masculine Feminine* and the youth-culture parody of *La Chinoise* (*The Chinese Girl*, 1967) and then exploded with volcanic force in *Weekend*, his tour de force of 1987. It centers on Corinne and Roland Durand (Mireille Darc and Jean Yanne), a married couple who drive to the countryside intending to murder a relative and secure an inheritance, whereupon each plans to kill the other and grab all the loot. Their journey turns progressively darker and stranger as traffic clogs, car crashes multiply, historical and literary personages enter the real world, and pockets of revolutionary violence proliferate. In the last scene Roland is dead and Corinne is enjoying a feral picnic, eating a stew of human flesh in which Roland's remains are an ingredient. The film's final equation is savage and uncomplicated: capitalism = cannibalism.

Weekend reached American theaters about a week before *Wild 90*, so it would not have directly influenced the content of that film or *Beyond the Law*, which was shot earlier. Mailer loved Godard's

Milne, in Narboni and Milne, eds., *Godard on Godard*, pp. 131-34, cited at 132-33. Originally published as "L'Afrique vous parle de la fin et des moyens" in *Cahiers du cinéma* 94 (April 1959), pp. 19-22.

film à la folie, however, and this speaks vividly to his state of mind in 1967. "*Weekend* re-established my modesty," he told Canby, one of his most supportive critics. "*It just knocked me on my rear!*"[25] He curbed his enthusiasm with respect to a lengthy scene where three workers deliver political monologues into the camera, calling this sort of thing a recurring blemish in Godard's films. He reiterated the point in another interview: "It's like saying, 'You're happy... You're really enjoying my movie... Now you'll be bored for a while. You have to pay your price for my movie.' I'm against that." This notwithstanding, Mailer's analysis of *Weekend* is perceptive. "I think it was a tremendous theme," he said. "In a way, what he was talking about was the death of the twentieth century. And he was talking about the fact that we may all perish, that our salvation may be cannibalism. And I would have almost liked a more thoroughgoing treatment of the matter. The only fault I have to find in *Weekend* is that it isn't pretentious enough, isn't grandiloquent enough. The man has a vision. There are parts of that film that to me are like Hieronymus Bosch. I'd never been a Godard lover until I saw that film. It converted me."

Godard moved beyond *Weekend* in short order. Soon thereafter he formed the Dziga-Vertov Group with a couple of like-minded colleagues and set about making films like *Le Gai savoir* (1969) and *British Sounds* (1970), designed to exist wholly outside the systems of commercial film. (Which is pretty much where they stayed.) He made a partial return to the marketplace with *Numéro deux* in 1975, but he has long since settled in as a cinematic outsider, reasonably content to dwell on the margins and work on his own idiosyncratic terms. He has always been a fighter and he remains one, never budging from the profoundly personal aesthetic that he has championed and exemplified throughout his career,

Mailer's first three films proved to be as commercially unviable as most of Godard's pictures, but since his primary calling was literature, he was under no pressure to stay in the filmmaking game. He did no directing in the seventeen years between *Maidstone* and *Tough Guys Don't Dance* and has done no directing since. While it is hard to see *Tough Guys Don't Dance* as more than a minor genre piece, his first three films constitute a small but enduring legacy, and their rowdy intransigence is lasting evidence that he was no less a fighter than Godard when his distinctive vision was in play.

---

[25] Vincent Canby, "When Irish Eyes Are Smiling, It's Norman Mailer." *The New York Times*, October 27, 1968. Emphasis in original.

Indeed, he spoke of filmmaking in quasi-military terms, and in true 1960s fashion he placed more value on the activity than on its outcome. "I'm leading a commando raid," he declared, "on fixed positions in certain commercial-aesthetic territory... A commando raid is not measured by its aesthetic perfection. It's measured by the amount of life it generates, by the amount of stimulation it gives in military history and the amount of time professional soldiers will spend in discussing it afterwards." And more sweepingly, "I still get a lot of pleasure out of writing... But making a film is a cross between a circus, a military campaign, a nightmare, an orgy, and a high."[26]

Making a film was also a mysterious enterprise for him. "I think fiction can intensify the moral consciousness of a time," Mailer told me. "I think theater can enlarge one's emotional appreciation of social situations [but] film doesn't work on our minds. It works on all the places that have never been worked on by other art forms—all the synapses between our memory and our emotions and our nerves and our sense of time." Hence the connection he saw between film and dreams, which he called "the interface, if you will, between life and eternity, between life and death... Dreams, to me, are a dialogue between your soul and your self. It's a way for the soul to say, 'Look, you're not living in the proper fashion at all. These are some of the disasters, metaphorically speaking, that attend you.'"[27] Mailer saw those disasters, metaphorically speaking, and evoked them—along with attendant joys and triumphs—in films that are raw, flawed, and memorable.

[26] Gelmis, "Norman Mailer," p. 174, 161.
[27] Sterritt, "Novelist Mailer Turns His Latest Book into a Movie."

Heroes Are Something We Create: Eastwood's Biopics
from *Tough Ain't Enough: New Perspectives on the Films of Clint Eastwood* (Rutgers University Press, 2018).

Clint Eastwood has cultivated an offbeat relationship with the Hollywood biopic. Of more than three dozen films directed by the iconic auteur, ten can fairly be called biopics; yet only half of those films fully exemplify the possibilities of the genre by tracing the experience of a notable personality over a significant span of time with attention to both individual psychology and sociohistorical context. Eastwood's interest in biopics and quasi-biopics has grown over the years; he made twelve films before undertaking his first effort in the genre, then made two in the 1990s and two in the early 2000s and directed no fewer than four between 2011 and 2016. Although his public image will always be connected most closely with westerns and action pictures, his varied exploration of the biopic is a noteworthy facet of his career that deserves more attention than it has generally received.

Not surprisingly, given Eastwood's gifts as a jazz musician, his most widely acclaimed biopic is *Bird*, a 1988 study of saxophone legend Charlie Parker that fulfills all qualifications for the genre by focusing on a key period in the protagonist's life and fleshing this out with flashbacks and reminiscences. Eastwood's other biopic in the classic mode is *J. Edgar*, his 2011 portrait of Federal Bureau of Investigation chief J. Edgar Hoover, whose history unfolds when an agent prompts him to reflect on his long career for a biography. In the underrated 2014 film *Jersey Boys*, about the rise of the Four Seasons to pop-culture fame, Eastwood expands his conception of the biopic by combining it with the musical genre and by dealing with a group rather than an individual. On a very different note, the 2014 drama *American Sniper* taps into questions about the morality of war in general and the Iraq war in particular, but much of the film's emotional heft comes from its treatment of the protagonist's early years and emotional conflicts, and critics strongly disagree as to whether Eastwood appropriately balances the personal and political aspects of the narrative. His most recent film to date, the 2016 release *Sully*, again explores linkages between the public and private personae of its main character, a commercial pilot who safely landed his damaged plane in the Hudson River.

Those five films are Eastwood's true biopics, and another five are semi- or quasi-biopics centering on real-world protagonists in oblique or unconventional ways: *White Hunter Black Heart*

(1990), in which Eastwood's character is a thinly veiled version of John Huston, a Hollywood actor and director who made some quasi-biopics himself; *Midnight in the Garden of Good and Evil* (1997), which revolves around a reporter and a wealthy man charged with murder, both drawn from life; the great World War II diptych *Flags of Our Fathers* (2006) and *Letters from Iwo Jima* (2006), the former probing the experiences of the men pictured in the famous Iwo Jima flag-raising photo of 1945, the latter viewing the Battle of Iwo Jima through the eyes of the general who commanded the Japanese garrison; and *Invictus* (2009), in which the South African leader Nelson Mandela and the South African rugby captain Francois Pienaar are the main characters.

Celebrity

As early as the dawn of the talkie era, movie industries around the world started pursuing what film scholar Ian Christie calls "a concerted project of 'national biography' through cinema" (292). This undertaking flourished in the Hollywood studios, where biographical pictures—or biopics, a term dating from the middle 1940s—became a staple in the early sound-film era and have continued to thrive ever since, usually focusing on famous or infamous figures already embedded in the popular imagination via literature or other media. The nature and characteristics of celebrity have been steady preoccupations of the genre, which has repeatedly applied its energies to more or less heavily fictionalized accounts of the triumphs and travails traversed by national rulers, corporate titans, canonical culture heroes, and others with lives deemed dramatic enough to captivate audiences at home and abroad (Epstein 11). Given the longtime partnership between Eastwood and Warner Bros., it's worth noting that Warners became the studio most closely associated with the biopic during the genre's classic era (Christie 291).

It is also noteworthy that Eastwood's biopics invariably center on men, all of whom (the main characters of *Midnight in the Garden of Good and Evil* excepted) qualify as public personalities to one degree or another. Eastwood's own history as a world-class celebrity is a probable factor in his gravitation toward male-oriented biopics, and toward biopics in general, and it is telling that his involvement in the genre has become strongest in the latter decades of his career, when his iconic status has been most powerful. As film scholar Dennis Bingham points out, biographical movies about women tend to be burdened by "myths of suffering, victimization, and failure perpetuated by a culture whose films reveal an acute fear of women in the public realm," whereas those about male figures occupy a more varied spectrum ranging from "celebratory to warts-and-all to investigatory to post-modern to parodic" (10). Eastwood's male-oriented biopics fall easily into these categories. *Bird*, *Invictus*, and *Sully* are celebratory—it may not be coincidental that their single-word titles have the mnemonic snappiness of memes, mantras, or cheers—while both World War II films are investigatory and *J. Edgar* presents its subject with warts galore, as does *Bird*. Warts also abound in the parodic *Midnight in the Garden of Good and Evil* and *White Hunter Black Heart*, and the metacinematic reflexivity of the latter places it under the postmodern rubric as well. *Jersey Boys* and *American Sniper* are harder to label, but the former manages to combine warts with celebration and the latter might be called investigative if it weren't bound to a memoir that's a vanity publication at heart.

Casting

Effective casting is essential to effective cinema, and biopics arguably have an added responsibility in this area, for while a fictional character must be played more or less *persuasively*, a character drawn from life must be played more or less *accurately* as well, assuming that the filmmakers want to keep at least a modicum of grounding in the real world that their movie claims to represent. As a leading actor-director with a substantial record of box-office success, Eastwood has made good use of his ready access to the industry's A list, populating his biopics with Hollywood stars whose physical traits, behavioral mannerisms, and professional skills are well suited to the accuracy and persuasiveness required by the genre.

As film scholar James Naremore has observed, however, biopics tend to be "crucially dependent upon an interaction between mimicry and realistic acting that can become threatened when a major star undertakes an impersonation" (40). Eastwood has occasionally fallen afoul of this hazard, as with Leonardo DiCaprio's makeup-caked impersonation of Hoover in the old-man scenes of *J. Edgar*. Still, this has generally not been a big problem for him, in part because his biopics often deal with people whose exploits have achieved some renown—army sniper Chris Kyle and airline pilot Chesley Sullenberger, for instance—but whose faces and voices are not especially familiar to large numbers of people.

As a major star himself, moreover, Eastwood has refrained from playing the protagonist in any of his biopics except *White Hunter Black Heart*, where main character John Wilson makes a uniquely good match with his own looks, demeanor, and screen image. Naremore rightly regards *White Hunter Black Heart* as one of Eastwood's most underrated films but criticizes his decision to cast himself as the character based on John Huston, saying that his accurate imitation of Huston's slow, mannerly speech is "slightly disconcerting" because when "an iconic star in the classic mold" makes a "basic change in... voice and persona," the result is "bizarre, almost as if he had donned a wig or a false nose" (41). In a parenthetical aside, Naremore allows for the possibility that Eastwood might know exactly what he is doing here, deliberately using the dissonance between his own persona and that of Huston so create an "intentionally alienating" effect. Given the thematic sophistication of *White Hunter Black Heart*, an understated satire of show-business glamour and cosmopolitanism, it is indeed likely that Eastwood saw his performance as a conscious contribution to an enjoyably "alienating" conceptual mix. Usually, of course, the lead performances in Eastwood biopics are more conventionally conceived, and for the most part they strike artful balances between imitation and interpretation, producing reality-based portraits that are biographically plausible if not always as psychologically rounded or dramatically compelling as one might wish.

Style

By the time he entered the biopic arena, Eastwood's visual style had become more varied and expressive than was evident in, say, the relatively heavy pyrotechnics of the high-octane thriller *Play Misty for Me* (1971) and the allegorical western *High Plains Drifter* (1973). His approaches to montage and mise-en-scène in the period starting with *Bird* could still indulge the hyperbolic violence of *The Gauntlet* (1977) and the macho heroics of *Heartbreak Ridge* (1986), but they were also capable of bringing out the milder moods of a *Bronco Billy* (1980) and a *Honkytonk Man* (1982) via colorful, almost comic-bookish aesthetics in the former and dusty Depression-era drabness in the latter. Broadly speaking, Eastwood's first biopic marked the beginnings of his full maturity as an artist.

A major contributor to Eastwood's early style was director of photography Bruce Surtees, known by the Hollywood set as the "prince of darkness" because of his fondness for shade and shadow. Surtees' successor as Eastwood's most frequent cinema-tographer, Jack N. Green, brought similar skill with low-key tones and pools of dimly illuminated space. Green set the tenor for his collaboration with Eastwood in *Bird*, a movie full of nighttime scenes and smoky dives, and tempered variations on that visual theme enhanced the darker portions of their subsequent films together, including *White Hunter Black Heart* and *Midnight in the Garden of Good and Evil.*

Eastwood's other biopics have all been photographed by Tom Stern, and while Stern's flexible approach does not lend itself easily to generalities, the deliberately depressed tones of *Flags of Our Fathers* and *Letters from Iwo Jima* carry the legacies of Surtees and Green to Eastwood's later films. A largely subliminal factor in Eastwood's best work is the immediacy produced by his penchant for speedy shooting with minimum fuss, and Stern is clearly able to oblige. Film editor Joel Cox and production designer James J. Murakami have also worked on a large number of Eastwood films, enabling the director to develop and sustain his increasingly distinctive style. Since no particular visual stylistics are inherent to the biopic as a genre, the eclecticism of Eastwood and his most frequent collaborators has served these movies well.

Bird

> There's going to be a Birdland in every city one day…
> —Charlie Parker

Eastwood's first biopic was written by Joel Oliansky, who based the screenplay in part on *My Life in E-flat* (1999), a then-unpublished memoir by Chan Parker, the protagonist's common-law wife. *Bird* posed an interesting challenge insofar as Charlie "Bird" Parker was a toweringly brilliant and profoundly troubled African-American jazz artist whose tumultuous life "played out every cliché of the self-destructive-celebrity life," in the words of film critic Jay Scott, who nonetheless calls the film a "marvel that avoids every cliché of the self-destructive-celebrity biography" (C1). Eastwood solves the problem inherent in telling Parker's story—how to make a fresh, surprising narrative from a life that followed all-too-familiar patterns of jazz-world excess—by tempering biopic realism with offbeat structural maneuvers and touches of poetic, even dreamlike action, as in the opening scene, where a dramatic moment in Park-er's early career is related in a bravely nonlinear fashion.

Eastwood first heard Parker play in 1946, and he remembered the experience as an "overwhelming" one. His intention was to "pay tribute" to Parker via the biopic format, employing a seemingly intuitive yet carefully calculated style to capture the contradictions he saw as integral to an artist who "could be very charismatic and sweet, and… could be mean and very undisciplined." Parker's excesses were "enormous," he told me in a 1988 interview, "but when it came to his music, he switched into another kind of mode" (Sterritt 2005, 38). Blending its unusual elements with standard Hollywood devices, *Bird* chronicles the basics of Parker's career from start to finish, depicting his childhood love of jazz and his rapid ascent as a player and bandleader; his rapport with other musicians; his relationship with his white common-law wife; his alcoholism and addiction to heroin; and ultimately his death in 1955 at age 34, so devastated by liver disease, heart disease, and a bleeding ulcer that the physician inspecting his corpse initially estimated his age at 50 or more.

To reproduce the power of Parker's playing, Eastwood needed to consider both visual and aural matters. The former depended to a large extent on casting, and Forest Whitaker is a gifted actor whose resemblance to Parker makes him a persuasive surrogate. To convey the specific qualities of Parker's sound, Eastwood had to choose between recording a Parker imitator, which would diminish the authenticity quotient of the film, or putting Parker's own recordings onto the soundtrack, which was problematic because his studio recordings generally have longer durations and more audio-engineered sheen than his live performances. While pondering this dilemma, the filmmakers unexpectedly came upon a trove of Parker tapes that had never been transferred to disc and released. Since the piano, drum, and bass sounds came across poorly on the tapes, music supervisor Lennie Niehaus recruited a recording engineer to isolate and extract Parker's saxophone lines, whereupon new backup tracks were recorded with a top-flight jazz crew (including trumpeter Red Rodney, a character in the film) and string section. This was an ingenious solution to a problem that biopics about musicians (and about artists in other fields, mutatis mutandis) often face: how best to represent the work of the biographical protagonist when the work is unavailable in a readily employable form.

Critical responses to *Bird* as a biopic have varied. In his *Washington Post* review, Desson Howe wrote that Eastwood's respect for Parker "runs so deep it disappears underground; and only the faintest signature arises from those devotional depths" (Howe). The jazz-savvy film critic Jonathan Rosenbaum had a different view, asserting that despite "legitimate quibbles that must be made—about substituting new accompanists, short-shrifting the issues of racism, and muddling certain musical and biographical facts—the man and his music almost get the canvas they deserve" (Rosenbaum). The critical consensus on *Bird* inclines toward the latter view, consolidating its status as one of Eastwood's most broadly successful biopics.

White Hunter Black Heart

Hollywood is just a place where they make a profit.
—John Wilson

Eastwood made his second venture into biographical territory with his very next film: the 1990 quasi-biopic *White Hunter Black Heart*, based on Peter Viertel's 1953 novel about working with director John Huston on the screenplay of *The African Queen*, the 1951 classic starring Humphrey Bogart and Katharine Hepburn as an extremely odd couple surviving harsh conditions and personality clashes during a harrowing African journey. In one of his most audacious performances, Eastwood plays the semi-fictional Huston surrogate John Wilson, whose film-within-the-film doesn't get started until after Eastwood's actual film has ended. The reason for the delay is Wilson's obsessive wish to hunt and shoot an African elephant; and if puttering around in the bush looking for a target jams the gears of the film production that brought him to Africa in the first place, this is a price he is willing to pay. In his autobiography, *An Open Book*, Huston admitted that he never managed to kill an elephant when *The African Queen* was in production; the same happens in Eastwood's film, where he faces the elephant but doesn't pull the trigger. "I prefer... that the obsession come to an end" without the killing, Eastwood told an interviewer. "The obsession driving him to the brink [and causing the death of a guide] is bad enough to give him the guilts" (Perlez).

Eastwood portrays Wilson as a narcissistic bon-vivant and swaggerer. What injects uncommon boldness and novelty into his performance is the decision to make Wilson a grinning, garrulous, chain-smoking imitation of the real John Huston, whose voice and mannerisms are well-known to moviegoers (especially in 1990, only three years after his death) from his appearances in such major Hollywood productions as Roman Polanski's *Chinatown* (1974) and Otto Preminger's *The Cardinal* (1963), which brought him an Academy Award nomination. Eastwood surely realized that Huston's persona was distinctive and familiar enough to make a purely imitative portrayal seem derivative, unimaginative, and perhaps ridiculous. But a deeper strategy underlies his approach. The key can be found in Oscar Wilde's famous claim that he put only his talent into his art, putting his genius into his life. Although the swashbuckling, speechifying Wilson is ostensibly in Africa to put his talent to work on a movie, he is putting whatever genius he can muster into a self-appointed effort to be more of an adventurer and daredevil than his limited supplies of courage and concentration can ever allow. Eastwood's portrayal is a walking, talking metaphor for Wilson's ill-fated attempt to be what he clearly is not, a job he botches so badly that his art *and* life come perilously close to collapsing.

One of Eastwood's motivations for making *White Hunter Black Heart* was his longtime interest in obsessive characters, but he took the project's biographical properties no less seriously. The costumes draw on photographs published in Hepburn's book about the production; Wilson's crew members wear khaki outfits like those of the actual technicians; and their on-screen camera equipment is of authentic 1950s vintage (Perlez). These and other details confirm Eastwood's commitment to basic principles of the biopic, even in an obliquely constructed one where the spirit of the breed is respected but the laws are bent with abandon.

Midnight in the Garden of Good and Evil

> This place is fantastic. It's like *Gone With the Wind* on mescaline.   —John Kelso

Seven years elapsed before Eastwood returned to the biographical field with *Midnight in the Garden of Good and Evil*, based on a bestselling nonfiction novel by John Berendt, a journalist and editor. Berendt's book chronicles the murder trials of Jim Williams, an antiques dealer who became a leading light of Savannah, Georgia, by virtue of his successful business, his restoration of a historic house in the city, and his munificence as host of a Christmas party held annually in the refurbished manse. Although the narrative's dramatic impact derives chiefly from the legal process, both the book and Eastwood's screen adaptation—written by John Lee

Hancock, who had scripted *A Perfect World* for Eastwood in 1993—surround the main action with colorful and idiosyncratic characters. The primary figures are Williams (Kevin Spacey) and journalist John Kelso (John Cusack), a fictional visitor from New York who adds psychological warmth to the detached, observational tone of Berendt's account. Among the Savannah citizens are Billy Hanson (Jude Law), the druggy, bisexual murder victim; Minerva (Irma P. Hall), a voodoo priestess; Joe Odom (Paul Hipp), a house-sitter and party-giver; Sonny Seiler (Jack Thompson), a defense attorney; Lady Chablis (Lady Chablis), a drag queen; and Mandy Nichols (Alison Eastwood, the director's daughter), a Savannah woman who gets romantically involved with Kelso.

Eastwood was attracted to the project by its arresting title, its Southern setting, and his increasing realization that stories driven by plot, action, and sensation now held less interest for him as a director than "character studies" (Wilson, 173) centered on psychology and personality. Hancock's original draft pared away parts of the book that Eastwood asked him to replace, including an alternative account of the killing that Williams came up with in jail, contradicting parts of his initial statement. This reminded Eastwood of Akira Kurosawa's *Rashomon* (1950), a classic exploration of the slipperiness of truth. "I like that ambiguity," Eastwood said. "Williams tells us two different scenarios... It leaves Kelso in a quandary, but life is like that." Elusiveness and ambiguity are main concerns of the film, along with the importance of open-mindedness and acceptance. The movie is about "tolerating other lifestyles," Eastwood said in 1998, "learning to be less judgmental" (Wilson, 171).

Midnight in the Garden of Good and Evil is as much a courtroom drama as a quasi-biopic, but the latter aspect gains in importance through Eastwood's decision to condense the multiple trials that Williams actually went through into a single proceeding. Although streamlining the story in this way has the effect of downplaying bigotry and other factors that skewed the judicial process as described in Berendt's account, it sharpens the movie's narrative thrust and sharpens the focus on its biographically based protagonist. Since the city's moods and flavors are atmospherically captured by Jack N. Green's cinematography, and further evoked on the soundtrack via songs by local luminary Johnny Mercer, the film can also be seen as a quasi-biopic of Savannah itself.

Flags of Our Fathers and *Letters from Iwo Jima*

> Heroes are something we create, something we need. It's
> a way for us to understand what's almost incomprehen-
> sible, how people could sacrifice so much for us.
> —James Bradley

> A day will come when they will weep and pray for your
> souls.   —General Tadamichi Kuribayashi

Eastwood's two movies of 2006 are distinctive achievements
in every respect, including their approach to the quasi-biopic
subgenre. The first to be released was *Flags of Our Fathers*, a film
about war but not a film *of* war. The title alludes to the raising
of an American flag on the Japanese island of Iwo Jima by five
Marines and a Navy corpsman who became famous when the
federal government turned an Associated Press photograph of
the event into a public-relations tool, using it to rally Americans
in support of the war effort. Three of the men subsequently died
in combat. The others, who were brought home and sent on tour
to promote war-bond sales, are the film's central characters: John
"Doc" Bradley (Ryan Phillippe), the quietest and most equable of
the three; Ira Hayes (Adam Beach), a shy and vulnerable Native
American; and Rene Gagnon (Jesse Bradford), a jaunty and genial
type. A profound irony that sets the intellectual and emotional
tone of the picture is the fact that the six men in the photo were not
the first to raise an American flag on the Mount Suribachi site—
a smaller flag had been planted earlier by another team, then taken
by a souvenir-hunting naval officer—but were hailed as unique,
trailblazing heroes by a public under the thrall of a devious advertising ploy.

The screenplay by Paul Haggis and William Broyles Jr. is
based on a bestselling book by the corpsman's father, and Eastwood used it to develop the ideas about violence and mortality that
were increasingly on his mind. He also regarded the narrative as a
cautionary tale about the hazards of celebrity, a recurring concern
in the history of biopics. The famous flag raisers didn't feel heroic,
he noted, however brightly the unsought and unwanted spotlight
glared upon them. Treated like stars and courted by powerful
people, they were more dazed and confused than thrilled or
excited, as the film shows in harrowing detail. Such matters are

a world away from the Hollywood pyrotechnics of earlier military movies that Eastwood had starred in and/or directed. *Flags of Our Fathers* is an exemplary portrait of three overlooked historical figures.

Letters from Iwo Jima, made immediately after *Flags of Our Fathers*, focuses on Tadamichi Kuribayashi, the Imperial Army general who commanded the Japanese forces on Iwo Jima before and during the battle that ended with their utter defeat. Written by Iris Yamashita from a story she crafted with Haggis, the screenplay had two principal sources: *Picture Letters from the Commander in Chief*, a collection of letters written by Kuribayashi in the late 1920s and early 1930s, and a book by Kumiko Kakehashi about the Iwo Jima battle based on letters Kuribayashi wrote on the island. Eastwood recruited the samurai-film specialist Ken Watanabe to play Kuribayashi, a venturesome figure who inclines toward intuition and experience where others rely on protocol and tradition. The literate and introspective Kuribayashi is the story's biographical center of gravity, and the chief supporting character is Saigo (Kazunari Ninomiya), a rank-and-file soldier excruciatingly aware that fate is inexorably closing in.

Apart from sequences with explosions and the like, Eastwood and cinematographer Tom Stern shot both *Flags of Our Fathers* and *Letters from Iwo Jima* in starkly desaturated color, aiming to convey a "non-comfortable" sense of war (Gross, 211). More boldly still, Eastwood presented the Japanese-language dialogue in *Letters from Iwo Jima* in Japanese with English subtitles for English-speaking audiences. Since major American distributors regard subtitles as commercial poison, no filmmaker lacking Eastwood's industry clout could have managed this extraordinary feat. *Flags of Our Fathers* was Eastwood's least financially successful film in years, earning back only about two-thirds of its $90 million budget. *Letters from Iwo Jima* fared even worse in American markets, freighted as it was by subtitles, a color-drained appearance, and a reverse perspective on what Hollywood customarily depicts as a virtuous battle fought by a greatest generation of American warriors. But the latter's dismal domestic returns (less than $14 million on a $20 million investment) were outbalanced by almost $55 million overseas, most of it in the Japanese market. In the end, Eastwood's experimental war picture paid gratifying dividends in both aesthetic and financial terms.

Invictus

> People don't realize that I played rugby myself when I
> was a student... It is a very rough game, almost as rough
> as politics.   —Nelson Mandela

Invictus takes its title, a Latin word meaning "unconquered," from
the 1888 poem by William Ernest Henley that concludes with
the often-quoted couplet, "I am the master of my fate:/I am the
captain of my soul." During his 27-year imprisonment by South
Africa's notorious apartheid government, the revolutionary leader
and future president Nelson Mandela recited it to others incarcer-
ated with him. Eastwood's film begins with Mandela, played by
Morgan Freeman in a case of incontestably ideal casting, attaining
his long-delayed release from prison in 1990. From the window of
the car carrying him to freedom he sees South African racial divi-
sions personified by two everyday athletic matches alongside the
road: on one side, whites playing rugby on a carefully maintained
field; on the other, black children playing football on a patch of
uneven ground. The scene is a précis of the movie's main concerns,
racial separation and the power of sports to divide people in such
circumstances, to unite them in others.

The film then fast-forwards to 1994, when Mandela is elected
as South Africa's first black president, facing the task of amelio-
rating the country's seemingly intractable racial animosities. Sports
reenter the picture when he attends a rugby march and sees black
South Africans cheering for England instead of for the Springboks,
their own rugby union team. Meeting with Francois Pienaar (Matt
Damon), the Springboks captain, Mandela exhorts him to make an
all-out effort in the World Cup competition their country will be
hosting soon, reasoning that if blacks can be persuaded to overcome their hostility toward a team they associate with white privilege and domination, shared enthusiasm for victory on the rugby
field will spur healing and reconciliation throughout the land.
Pienaar and his players train for the tournament, reach out to black
communities, defeat the Australian and French teams, and prepare
for the decisive match with the All Blacks from New Zealand, their
arch-rivals.

Eastwood and Freeman had worked together well in *Unfor-
given* (1992) and *Million Dollar Baby* (2004), and Eastwood liked
the idea of Freeman playing Mandela in a quasi-biopic crystal-
lizing a decisive moment in the struggle to bring about black-white

rapprochement. It is likely that Eastwood's conservative politics were an additional factor when he took on the project. Barack Obama had become America's first black president a few months before shooting began, and although Eastwood said when the film opened that he "wasn't trying to sell any American politics in the thing," he added that Obama had not inspired him with confidence thus far. Obama was "a charismatic young man," he told an interviewer, "and he did talk about change and all this kind of stuff that sounded great... Whether he's able to deliver the goods or not is another thing" (Foundas 243). This comment lends piquancy to an early moment in *Invictus* when the newly elected President Mandela sees an Afrikaans newspaper headline reading, "He Can Win an Election but Can He Run a Country?" The thing might contain American politics after all.

Directorial touches aside, Anthony Peckham's screenplay for *Invictus* is based on John Carlin's 2008 book *Playing the Enemy: Mandela and the Game that Made a Nation*, an account that has been accused of treating Mandela too uncritically and deferentially. Rather than refute the charge, Carlin has pleaded nolo contendere: "It's difficult not to do a hagiography. Mandela is to politics what Mozart is to music. He is the Abraham Lincoln of our times. And the great good fortune of my working life has been to know him." (Cheshire, 102). Eastwood and Peckham fall into the same pitfall, if pitfall it is, and their consistently reverent film sparks less excitement than one might wish from a fact-based movie about sports and politics, the key competitive areas of our age (Sterritt 2014, 202). Its message of racial union and understanding is thoroughly sincere, however, and its heart is in the right place even when its art wanders elsewhere.

J. Edgar

> What's important at this time is to re-clarify the difference between hero and villain.   —J. Edgar Hoover

Eastwood's politics may also inform *J. Edgar*, his first full-fledged biopic since *Bird* almost a quarter-century earlier. Famous in all circles and infamous in many, longtime FBI chief J. Edgar Hoover was regarded by countless critics as the embodiment of clandestine power, conspiratorial maneuvering, ideological blackmail, and moral turpitude, the very forces that his public persona purportedly opposed throughout his seemingly interminable career. But moviegoers looking for a sensational exposé did not find it in East-wood's film. What they did find was a reasonably well-balanced account of Hoover's bull-in-a-china-shop tactics juxtaposed with his passionate friendship for deputy and companion Clyde Tolson (Armie Hammer), the sexual undertones of which rumble steadily in the movie's id. Melodramatics erupt when Hoover's fantasy of marrying a Hollywood actress elicits an overwrought response from Tolson, culminating in a knockabout fight, an unwelcome kiss, and a lingering fog of fiercely repressed yearnings. The men's situation is pitiable and inescapable save through growing estrangement, disharmony, and ultimately Hoover's lonely death.

As film scholar Douglas McFarland observes, Eastwood's right-wing views might have encouraged an aspiration to "restore Hoover's reputation," and the participation of screenwriter Dustin Lance Black, a prominent gay-rights advocate, opened the possi-bility of a "sympathetic perspective" on Hoover's compulsively closeted homosexuality. In the end, McFarland concludes, East-wood and Black steered between the overheated and the under-stated, examining "a life enmeshed in the interwoven complexi-ties of familial, ethical, social, psychological, and political forces" (146). This is a fair assessment. Eastwood's libertarian leanings had inflected his approach to homophobia and heteronormative hypocrisy in *Midnight in the Garden of Good and Evil*, and the same propensities are evident in *J. Edgar*, which limns an absorbing portrait of a top-grade Eastwood protagonist: a Dirty Harry who has a whole police force in his pocket, but is burdened to his depths by anger, shame, and desperately denied desire.

Jersey Boys

> They ask you, "What was the high point?" Hall of Fame, selling all those records… it was all great. But four guys under a street lamp, when it was all still ahead of us, the first time we made that sound, our sound… That was the best.   —Frankie Valli

Eastwood's next film was the second of four consecutive biopics. *Jersey Boys* is also the first out-and-out musical he has directed, leaving aside the music-laced melodramas *Bird* and *Honkytonk Man* (1982) and the documentary *Piano Blues* (2003). Again placing celebrity into the foreground, *Jersey Boys* is a lively ramble through the collective career of Frankie Valli and the Four Seasons, beginning with early iterations of their act, when they went by names like Frankie Valli and the Four Lovers, and passing through the usual pop-group succession of renown and riches, jealousies and rivalries, and disillusionments and breakups, ultimately yielding the nostalgic glory of induction in the Rock and Roll Hall of Fame, the 1990 event that climaxes the film.

The characters are standard-issue Joisey Boys one and all: lead singer Valli (John Lloyd Young), née Castelluccio; band mates Tommy and Nick DeVito (Vincent Piazza, Johnny Cannizzaro), Bob Gaudio (Erich Bergen), and Nick Massi (Michael Lomenda); Gyp DeCarlo (Christopher Walken), a mobster who serves as Valli's mentor; Bob Crewe (Mike Doyle), a gay recording entrepreneur and songwriter who fuels the group's success; and Norm Waxman (Donnie Kehr), a loan shark you wouldn't want to mess with. Even more familiar are the more-or-less golden oldies that pepper the soundtrack, ranging from the 1962 chart-toppers "Big Girls Don't Cry" and "Sherry" to the more mature "My Eyes Adored You" (1974) and "Grease" (1978), number-one hits for Valli as a solo performer.

Jersey Boys came into existence as a stage musical that opened on Broadway in 2005, with a book by Marshall Brickman and Rick Elice, music by Gaudio, and lyrics by Crewe, all of whom make the same contributions to Eastwood's adaptation. Like the theatrical work that inspired it, the film has an episodic structure and a presentational acting style, whereby characters periodically speak to the camera, passing the narration from one person to another in a relay-race manner that lends fresh life to an old convention.

As with *Bird* some twenty-six years earlier, Eastwood faced the question of how best to present the music so essential to the tale, and as before he took an unusual option. Normally music and vocals are prerecorded before shooting begins and the actors mime (or sing and play along) while the recordings are played back, aware that no sounds made on the set will be heard on the film's soundtrack. Eastwood made two unexpected choices. First, he decided not to replace the stage show's main performers with actors more experienced in movie roles, reasoning that they had "done 1,200 performances: How much better can you know a character?" (Setoodeh and Foundas). And second, he and his sound engineers recorded the vocal and instrumental performances live while the camera rolled. This is not a new methodology, but Eastwood uses it skillfully, producing a seamlessness and spontaneity that serve the biopic well.

Few suspected that the jazz-loving Eastwood harbored a yen for jukebox sounds, but his feel for the Four Seasons rings true, and he spices the story's well-worn ingredients with the spirited textures, tones, and moods that distinguish the period's best popular music. *Jersey Boys* is a worthy addition to the honor roll of rock-and-roll biopics.

American Sniper

> There are three types of people in this world: sheep, wolves, and sheepdogs.   —Chris Kyle

Eastwood's biopic of 2014 is based on *American Sniper: The Autobiography of the Most Lethal Sniper in U.S. Military History*, a memoir written by Navy SEAL Chris Kyle with Scott McEwen and Jim DeFelice; published in 2012, it stayed on the *New York Times* bestseller list for more than nine months and sold more than a million copies in its first three years in print. The popularity of the film, starring Bradley Cooper as Kyle, was no less phenomenal: racking up the highest worldwide earnings of any 2014 release, it became the biggest grosser of Eastwood's career and the highest-grossing war film (unadjusted for inflation) of all time. It also received Academy Awards nominations for best picture, best actor (Bradley Cooper), best adapted screenplay (Jason Hall), best film editing (Joel Cox and Gary Roach), best sound mixing, and best sound editing. A stellar showing indeed.

And a troubling one. Kyle's very personal, very action-packed book can be read as an avowal of patriotism, a celebration of self-sacrifice, and a candid memoir of what it's like to wage war in the Middle East when you could be living an ordinary, contented life. But it can just as easily be read as the self-justifying confession of an unreflective man who enlists in an elite military branch for valid personal and patriotic reasons, then discovers he has a natural talent for shooting and a deep-down taste for killing that finds an ideal outlet for expression amid the violence-ridden chaos produced by the American-led invasion of Iraq in the early 2000s.

Kyle's musings are invariably trite. On Islam: "The people we were fighting… wanted to kill us, even though we'd just booted out their dictator, because we practiced a different religion…" (80). On rules of engagement: "[P]icking apart a soldier's every move against a dark, twisted, rule-free enemy is more than ridiculous; it's despicable" (151). On the pleasure of killing: "[I]t was like a scene from *Dumb and Dumber*. The bullet went through the first guy and into the second" (289). "I had been trained to kill... And I liked doing it. A lot" (316). "I wondered, how would I feel about killing someone? Now I know. It's no big deal... They all deserved to die" (370-1).

The interesting thing about Kyle's book is not his hackneyed thinking but rather the fact that it attracted Eastwood, whose treatments of violence, vengeance, and death had been deepening with the passage of time, as the contrast between, say, the Dirty Harry films (1971-1988) and the clumsy yet humane *Gran Torino* (2008) illustrates. Here he bypasses nuanced thinking to produce a hard-fisted biopic organized mainly around action and suspense. After sketching out Kyle's all-American upbringing, youthful stints as a ranch hand and rodeo cowboy, and marriage to a (usually) patient wife, the movie depicts his military enlistment and training, multiple deployments to the Middle East, success as a sharp-shooter, temporary addiction to combat-induced adrenaline—a theme more powerfully explored in Kathryn Bigelow's *The Hurt Locker* (2008)—and finally his departure from the service and volunteer work with wounded veterans. The film ends with a brief, elliptical account of Kyle's death at the hands of a Marine veteran with post-traumatic stress disorder, who killed him at a shooting range where they had gone for an informal therapy session.

Critical opinions about Eastwood's film have been diverse, but the overall tone has been positive, with praise going to Cooper's acting, to Eastwood's success at humanizing the rifle-toting protagonist, and to the film as an extension of Eastwood's decades-long fascination with gunslingers and their guns. Eastwood himself says he makes war movies "because they're always loaded with drama and conflict," but adds that by showing the stresses undergone by veterans and their families, *American Sniper* "adds up to kind of an anti-war [message]" (Beaumont-Tomas). This writer is not convinced, finding *American Sniper* to be a guts-and-glory drama that adds no luster to Eastwood's filmography. What value it has derives from its credentials as a topical biopic, not as a study of war and its horrifying human consequences.

Sully

> Everything is unprecedented until it happens for the first
> time.   —Chesley Sullenberger

The protagonist of *Sully* is Chesley "Sully" Sullenberger, a US
Airways pilot who was hailed as a hero in January 2009 after taking
his abruptly disabled Airbus A320 from a height of some 2,800
feet to an emergency landing in the Hudson River, having made
an instant judgment that the nearest airports were too distant for
the incapacitated craft to reach. There were no significant injuries,
but Sullenberger was profoundly shaken by the experience, which
he kept reliving in flashbacks and nightmares. Todd Komarnicki's
screenplay takes an unexpected route into these events, organizing
the narrative around an investigation by the National Transpor-
tation Safety Board, which has data suggesting that Sullenberger
(Tom Hanks) and First Officer Jeffrey Skiles (Aaron Eckhart)
did have sufficient power for a return to New York's LaGuardia
Airport, whence the flight originated, or a landing at New Jersey's
Teeterboro Airport, fairly close and undoubtedly safer than setting
down on a river. Following a great deal of technical debate, ethical
discussion, and review of high-tech simulations executed by test
pilots, the inquiry concludes that Sully and Skiles made the only
decisions that could have worked under the circumstances, thereby
saving their reputations and careers.

The portions of *Sully* that show Sullenberger's private life—
learning to fly in the past, reassuring his wife in the present—
qualify the film as a biopic rather than a fact-based drama revolving
around a single headline-grabbing occurrence. Its main liability is
the by-the-numbers neatness of its construction, which proceeds
from thought-provoking questions—perhaps the lifesaving feat
was not a marvel of quick thinking under pressure but a potentially disastrous instance of bad judgment—to a series of excul-
patory scenes that hammer home the hero's professional purity
with diagrammatic precision, elbowing moral and psychological
complexity off the screen. On another front, the film's skeptical
take on the NTSB has been accused of propagandizing for Eastwood's anti-government politics, a plausible charge that seems
rather flimsy in this context.

The limitations of Komarnicki's screenplay are counterbal-
anced by Hanks' richly three-dimensional performance—his work
as chief of a hijacked ship in Paul Greengrass' biopic *Captain Phil-*

lips (2013) erased any hesitations about his ability to make vulner-ability and emotional damage seem achingly real—and by East-wood's directing, which is less surprising in cinematic terms than on the level of old-fashioned storytelling but is unfailingly fluid, eloquent, and engaging nonetheless. Again reaching an enormous audience and profits to match, it is another worthy milestone in his worthy career.

Epilogue

At this writing, Eastwood is 86 years old and still hard at work, with yet another biopic in the making. Trade publications report that the new project is based on *Impossible Odds: The Kidnapping of Jessica Buchanan and Her Dramatic Rescue by SEAL Team Six*, a 2014 memoir in which Jessica Buchanan and her husband Erik Landemalm recount the events of three months in 2011 when she and another American aid worker were kidnaped in Somalia and held captive in the desert while Landemalm worked with various agencies to effect a rescue. Freedom finally arrived when President Obama approved the engagement of a SEAL team that parachuted in, killed the land pirates, and extracted the prisoners. The screen-writer is Brian Helgeland, who penned Eastwood's *Blood Work* in 2002 and the stunning *Mystic River* a year later.

Eastwood's late-career stock in trade is primarily modern Americana, whether with a military political, or pop-culture twist. If and when *Impossible Odds* comes into being, six of his seven films since 2009—the exception is *Hereafter* (2010), made between *Invictus* and *J. Edgar*—will have been biopics, underscoring the importance of this supple, adaptable genre to one of Hollywood cinema's key chroniclers of the American scene.

[Note: *Impossible Odds* did not reach the screen, but since *Sully* most of Eastwood's movies have been biopics of one kind or another: *The 15:17 to Paris* (2018), *The Mule* (2018), *Richard Jewell* (2019), and *Juror #2* (2024).]

Works Cited

Beaumont-Thomas, Ben. 2015. "Clint Eastwood: *American Sniper and I are anti-war*." *The Guardian*, 17 March.
Bingham, Dennis. 2010. *Whose Lives Are They Anyway? The Biopic as Contemporary Film Genre*. Rutgers.
Cheshire, Ellen. 2015, *Bio-Pics: A Life in Pictures*. Wallflower.
Christie, Ian. 2002. "A Life on Film," in Peter France and William St. Clair, eds., *Mapping Lives: The Uses of Biography*, pp. 283-301. Oxford.

Epstein, William H. 2016. "Introduction: Strategic Patriotic Memories," in William H. Epstein and R. Barton Palmer, eds., *Invented Lives, Imagined Communities: The Biopic and American National Identity*, pp. 1-21. State University of New York.

Foundas, Scott. 1999. "Eastwood on the Pitch: At Seventy-Nine, Clint Tackles Mandela in *Invictus*," in Robert E. Kapsis and Kathie Coblenz, eds., *Clint Eastwood: Interviews*, pp. 234-244. Mississippi.

Gross, Terry. 1999. "Eastwood's *Letters from Iwo Jima*," in Robert E. Kapsis and Kathie Coblenz, eds., *Clint Eastwood: Interviews*, pp. 206-218. Mississippi.

Howe, Desson. 1988. "*Bird*." *Washington Post*, 14 October.

Kyle, Navy SEAL Chris, with Scott McEwen and Jim DeFelice. 2013. *American Sniper: The Autobiography of the Most Lethal Sniper in U.S. Military History*. Harper.

McFarland, Douglas. 2016. "*J. Edgar*: Eastwood's Man of Mystery," in Epstein and Palmer, eds., *Invented Lives, Imagined Communities*, pp. 145-159.

Naremore, James. 2012. "Film Acting and the Arts of Imitation." *Film Quarterly* vol. 65 no. 4 (Summer), pp. 34-42.

Perlez, Jane. 1990. "Clint Eastwood Directs Himself Portraying a Director." *The New York Times*, 16 September.

Rosenbaum, Jonathan. 1999. "The Ten Best Jazz Films (1999 List)." *JonathanRosenbaum.net*, 4 June.

Scott, Jay. 1988. "*Bird*." *The Globe and Mail*, Toronto (14 October), p. C1.

Setoodeh, Ramin, and Scott Foundas. 2014. "Should *Jersey Boys* Have Cast Movie Stars?" *Variety*, 19 June.

Sterritt, David. 2005 "Hollywood Players Who've Made a Difference: Cassavetes, Eastwood, Martin, Nicholson," in David Sterritt, *Guiltless Pleasures: A David Sterritt Film Reader*, pp. 31-49. Mississippi.

Sterritt, David. 2014. *The Cinema of Clint Eastwood: Chronicles of America*. Wallflower.

Wilson, Michael Henry. 1999. "Truth, Like Art, Is in the Eyes of the Beholder: *Midnight in the Garden of Good and Evil* and *The Bridges of Madison County*," in Kapsis and Coblenz, eds., *Clint Eastwood*, pp. 168-177.

Bad Mixings: *Dirty Harry*, Social Anomaly, and the Gospel of Healthy-Mindedness
Quarterly Review of Film and Video 3:4 (2015)

Clint Eastwood embarked on the middle period of his career in the eventful year of 1971, when he showed new sides of his acting talent in Donald Siegel's *The Beguiled*, made his feature-directing debut with *Play Misty for Me*, in which he also starred, and scored a pop-cultural bull's-eye in Siegel's *Dirty Harry*.[1] Firmly established as a star, a celebrity, and a quasi-studio chief running his own production outfit, the Malpaso Company, Eastwood went on to direct a half-dozen more pictures in the 1970s and appear in the same number of films by other directors. Most were very well received, and some—the comic "monkey movies" of 1978 and 1980—were phenomenal hits, but *Dirty Harry* became a box-office sensation, spawning five sequels between 1973 and 1988 and turning into a *cause de scandale* that critics and moralists chewed over for years to come.[2]

The Movie

> Five—count 'em, five—chances to wallow in the shoot-first, ask-questions later ethos of San Francisco cop Harry Callahan... You can't ask for much more firepower in one box than this. (Fine, "Editorial Reviews")

According to film critic Marshall Fine's Editorial Review of *The Dirty Harry Collection* (2001) for Amazon.com, the *Dirty Harry* ethos is grounded in straight-shooting fun, and the boxed five-DVD set of his adventures is cause not merely for rejoicing but for wallowing. Harry has also sparked a good deal of *thinking* since his advent in the 1971 thriller that bears his moniker, and "Dirty Harry" has become an immediately recognizable catchphrase referring to people who break the rules for reasons they find to be good, or—in some cases—for no real reasons at all. Indeed, the

---

[1] This article is based on a portion of my book *The Cinema of Clint Eastwood: Chronicles of America*, published in 2014 by Columbia/Wallflower in the Directors' Cuts Series. I gave a slightly different version in a presentation to Columbia's University Seminar on Cinema and Interdisciplinary Interpretation in September 2014.

[2] The monkey movies are *Every Which Way But Loose* (Dir. James Fargo, 1978) and *Any Which Way You Can* (Dir. Buddy Van Horn, 1980).

fabled Harry Callahan has become so familiar a persona that one might almost say he needs no introduction. For the record, he is a hard-working police inspector whose weapon of choice is a .44 Magnum revolver, which he calls "the most powerful handgun in the world," living as he does before the arrival of the .500 Smith and Wesson, the .480 Ruger, and other present-day champions, not to mention large-caliber hand cannons that shoot rifle cartridges.[3] After thwarting a bank robbery at the start of his first picture, *Dirty Harry*, he joins his new partner, Chico, in a hunt for one Charles Davis, also known as Scorpio, a psychopath on a murder spree. Harry has been in trouble with his superiors, including the mayor and his own lieutenant, for bending police tactics beyond the breaking point. But this trouble doesn't stop him from collaring Scorpio without benefit of mandatory procedures. As Harry reasons, had he spent time on bureaucratic details, Scorpio's latest prey—a 14-year-old kidnapping victim—would have died by suffocation. The girl dies anyway, and Chico is badly wounded during the arrest. As for Scorpio, the joke is on Harry: The killer walks, freed on legalities related to the manner in which he was captured. Vowing to catch him again, Harry starts dogging the psychopath's trail. Scorpio now arranges to get himself beaten up (paying a thug $200 for the job) and then tells the press that blame for his ill treatment rests with the San Francisco police in general and Harry Callahan in particular. Stealing a fresh gun, Scorpio now escalates his rampage, kidnaping a whole platoon of kids in a school bus. Harry heads him off, hops on the bus' roof, flushes Scorpio out, and shoots him dead after a final chase. Finally fed up for good with what Hamlet calls "the law's delay," he takes a last look at his badge and throws it away with disgust.

Beyond Professionalism

> If the law supposes that," said Mr. Bumble, squeezing his hat emphatically in both hands, "the law is a ass—a idiot. If that's the eye of the law… the worst I wish the law is, that his eye may be opened by experience—by experience.   — *Oliver Twist* (Dickens 436)

---

[3] After losing his Smith and Wesson M29 during a fistfight in *Sudden Impact*, his fourth film, Harry switches to an even deadlier .44 Auto Mag pistol.

District Attorney: This rifle might make a nice souvenir,
but it's inadmissible as evidence.
Harry: And who says that?
District Attorney: It's the law.
Harry: Well, then the law is crazy.

— *Dirty Harry*

Harry's exchange with District Attorney William T. Rothko occurs
when Rothko informs Harry that, no matter how solidly the ballis-
tics laboratory might match the bullet that Scorpio fired to the rifle
from which he fired it, the result would be irrelevant to a legal case
against the killer, regardless of other factors involved. In a similar
vein, in Dickens' work *Oliver Twist,* the exchange between Mr.
Bumble and Mr. Brownlow occurs when the latter tells the former
that "in the eye of the law" he is guilty of a peccadillo committed
by his wife, since "the law supposes that your wife acts under your
direction" (Dickens 436).Upon receiving these impromptu law
lessons, Mr. Callahan and Mr. Bumble are both confounded and
outraged at what they learn. The law is not misguided, misdirected,
or mistaken, in their view; according to Bumble it is naïve and
fatuous, and according to Callahan it is flat-out insane. Emotions
run high when people feel that the prescriptions, proscriptions,
and binding ideological systems of their time countervail their own
ideas and intuitions as to the fundamental qualities of right and
wrong.

Emotions certainly ran high when *Dirty Harry* debuted in
December 1971, directed by Siegel from a screenplay penned by
Harry Julian Fink, R. M. Fink, and Dean Riesner, based on the
Finks' original story.[4] Among critics, the movie's chief supporter
was *Time* magazine reviewer Jay Cocks, who admired Siegel for the
"closely calculated, irresistible momentum" of his films, adding that
the director "has an explosive talent for violence that turns his action
scenes... into set pieces that pummel the senses." His review, titled
"Outside Society," also lauded Eastwood for "his best performance
to date—tense, tough, full of implicit identification" with his character (33). Cocks later placed *Dirty Harry* on his list of the year's
10 Best Films, but he was an outlier on the picture; according to
Eastwood biographer Richard Schickel, who was also a *Time* film
critic, Cocks' review was "the only positive review in a major publi-

---

[4] Jo Heims assisted with the story and John Milius—whose writer/director
credits include the reactionary 1984 fantasy *Red Dawn*—contributed to
the script, receiving no screen credit.

cation."[5] Even the auteur-friendly *New York Times* critic Roger Greenspun had his doubts. He started his review with a reference to the "honorable and slightly anachronistic enterprise of the Don Siegel cops-and-crooks action movies," but went on to say, "the grim devotion to duty that has always been the badge of Siegel's constabulary is here in Clint Eastwood's tough San Francisco plainclothesman... pushed beyond professionalism into a kind of iron-jawed self-parody" (paragraph 1). The trade magazine *Variety* called the picture "a specious, phony glorification of police and criminal brutality" and a "well-made but shallow running- and-jumping meller" that features "a superhero whose antics become almost satire" and is inflated with "philosophical garbage" (paragraph 1). Finally, a review in *Newsweek* scorned the "lethal ugliness" of the picture, but added that neither good-spirited nor mean-spirited movies ever have much effect on the real world: "There is little chance that this right-wing fantasy will change things," the critic wrote, "where decades of humanist films have failed."[6]

In spring of 1972, the *New York Times* reprinted an essay from the *Harvard Crimson*, perhaps the most famous student newspaper in America, opining that *Dirty Harry* has "no pretensions to art; it is a simply told story of the Nietzschean superman and his sadomasochistic pleasures."[7] In summer of 2012, the *New York Times* published an article by Michael Cieply headlined "A Studio With Violence in Its Bones," timed to coincide with the opening of Christopher Nolan's *The Dark Knight Rises* (2012), starring Christian Bale and Eastwood's good friend Morgan Freeman, and the anticipated arrival of Ruben Fleischer's *Gangster Squad*, a January 2013 release with Sean Penn and Ryan Gosling in the leads. The studio with violence in its bones is Warner Bros., which has been Eastwood's home base in Hollywood through most of his career; the studio's long association with violent pictures is therefore worth noting. Cieply likens Warner Bros.' relationship with violence to Disney's focus on family films and Universal's long romance with monster movies. Warner Bros. forged a link with violence in such pre-Production Code pictures as *The Public Enemy* (Dir. William A. Wellman, 1931), *Little Caesar* (Dir. Mervyn LeRoy, 1931), and *I Am a Fugitive from a Chain Gang* (Dir. LeRoy, 1932) and reaffirmed it in the 1960s with the hugely influential *Bonnie and Clyde* (Dir. Arthur Penn, 1967) and *The Wild Bunch* (Dir. Sam Peckinpah,

[5] Quoted in McGilligan, *Clint*, 226.
[6] Quoted in Cieply, "A Studio," C5.
[7] Ibid.

1969). The studio released *Dirty Harry* just four days after Stanley Kubrick's ultraviolent *A Clockwork Orange*, which also sparked lasting controversy. Cieply adds that, by 1974, a *Variety* writer "had speculated on the supposed influence" of *Dirty Harry* in "a string of brutal incidents involving the San Francisco police."[8]

Roger Ebert was bothered less by the mayhem in *Dirty Harry* than by the ethical implications he discerned behind the mayhem. His review in the *Chicago Sun-Times* called the movie "a very good example of the cops-and-killers genre," with "lots of dynamite action and enough wry cynicism to keep the blood from getting too thick," but also said that its "moral position is fascist. No doubt about it." Explaining and defending this charge, Ebert was direct: "The movie clearly and unmistakably gives us a character who understands the Bill of Rights, understands his legal responsibility as a police officer, and nevertheless takes retribution into his own hands. Sure, Scorpio is portrayed as the most vicious, perverted, warped monster we can imagine—but that's part of the same stacked deck." Having said this, Ebert held back from damning the film outright, holding that movies should not bear the blame for the evils they depict. "If there aren't mentalities like Dirty Harry's at loose in the land," he concluded, "then the movie is irrelevant. If there are, we should not blame the bearer of the bad news."

Pauline Kael, a critic far more prominent than Ebert in the early 1970s, wielded the accusation of fascism more boldly and aggressively, calling *Dirty Harry* a work of "fascist medievalism," a "right-wing fantasy," and "a remarkably single-minded attack on liberal values" (191). Looking back on the film years later, J. Hoberman articulated a more nuanced view in the *Village Voice*, likening *Dirty Harry* to Siegel's earlier *Invasion of the Body Snatchers* (1956) in that "it offers a fabulous, multifarious political metaphor" capable of multiple, and even opposite, interpretations. As happened with the 1956 science-fiction film, Hoberman continued, "Siegel's own liberal interpretation was trumped by a more forceful hard-right reading [that celebrated] the figure of the Legal Vigilante that would prove so useful to Richard Nixon in the upcoming election year. Dirty Harry was a dirty man for a dirty time." Although fans of the film included the countercultural *Rolling Stone* magazine and—it turned out—the Soviet leader Leonid Brezhnev, the groundswell of appreciation was led by "the new Republicans of America's northern cities." The director and

---

[8] Quoted in Cieply, "A Studio," C5.

star were invited to speak at police gatherings, and a craze ensued for "the foot-long Smith & Wesson .44 magnum—a weapon whose use value," Hoberman wrote, "was less practical than magical."

The Sequels

> Go ahead. Make my day.
> —Inspector Harry Callahan (*Dirty Harry*, 1983)

> Go ahead. Make my day.
> — President Ronald Reagan (1985, 472)

Dirty Harry begat four sequels. *Magnum Force* arrived in 1973, directed by Ted Post, who had worked with Eastwood as early as the TV series *Rawhide*, which began its six-year run in 1959. *The Enforcer* was a 1976 release directed by James Fargo, and 1983 brought *Sudden Impact*, directed by Eastwood himself. Finally there was *The Dead Pool*, directed by Buddy Van Horn and unleashed in 1988 to mixed reviews and lackluster grosses. *Sudden Impact*, the fourth entry in the franchise, is notable for at least three reasons. In addition to being the only installment that Eastwood directed, it brought in the highest grosses of the five movies, although it slips to fourth place when ticket prices are adjusted for inflation.[9] Finally, *Sudden Impact* introduces the most famous catchphrase of the series, uttered by Harry to a criminal holding a hostage in the immediate aftermath of a robbery that Harry has foiled by killing the other crooks. He would love to have a reason for killing this one too, so he issues a famously ironic invitation to the cowering bad guy: "Go ahead. Make my day." The evildoer, knowing he cannot win, chooses not to.

Those words thrilled the franchise's countless fans in 1983, and three years later they acquired even more notoriety when President Ronald Reagan delivered a speech to the American Business Conference in which he declared, "I have my veto pen drawn and ready for any tax increase that Congress might even think of sending up. And I have only one thing to say to the tax increasers: Go ahead, make my day" (1985, 472). The line was so effective for Reagan that one year later he congratulated himself for having used it. He said in a 1986 speech to the conference:

---

[9] In inflation-adjusted dollars, *Magnum Force* leads the pack, followed by *Dirty Harry* in second place and *The Enforcer* in third. *Sudden Impact* comes in fourth, exceeding only *The Dead Pool* in ticket sales.

You know, it was last year before this group that I told the tax hikers in Congress that if they wanted to send me a tax increase, well, go ahead, make my day. [*laughter*] I got that line from Clint Eastwood [*laughter*] — although now that the voters of Carmel, California, elected him mayor, I suppose I should say, Mayor Eastwood [*laughter*]. I have to confess that I'm amazed that a Hollywood actor who costarred with a monkey could ever make it in politics [*laughter*].[10]

Not surprisingly, Eastwood himself recycled the *Sudden Impact* tagline in the aforementioned mayoral race, distributing bumper stickers reading "Go Ahead — Make Me Mayor," notwithstanding his complaint that he "must have heard [the endlessly repeated phrase] about 10,000 times."[11]

Sudden Impact was originally developed as a vehicle for Sondra Locke, who came on the Eastwood scene with *The Outlaw Josey Wales* in 1976 and had most recently costarred with him in *Bronco Billy* (1980) and *Every Which Way You Can*, both released in 1980. Transformed into a Dirty Harry story with Locke as the vengeance-crazed villain, it allowed both her and Eastwood to exploit the chemistry they had been cultivating on and off the screen. This film proved to be Locke's last with Eastwood, although their personal relationship lasted until she moved out of their home and filed a palimony suit against him in 1989. *Sudden Impact* was a high point in neither of their careers.

The movie's plot lurches into gear when the San Francisco homicide squad assigns Harry to investigate a string of grisly murders. The killer, whose identity is revealed (to the audience, not the inspector) at the beginning, is one Jennifer Spencer, a sociopath bent on slaying the men who viciously raped her and her younger sister a decade earlier, leaving the sister in a permanently

---

[10] Reagan concluded this part of his statement with an extension of the Eastwood citation: "Of course, the American Business Conference has helped make our year a — well, you've helped make more than my day — make it a banner year of entrepreneurship and innovation, laying the foundation for what I'm convinced can become a decade of vibrant economic growth." His mention of "a Hollywood actor who costarred with a monkey" refers to his own role in the comedy *Bedtime for Bonzo* (Dir. Frederick de Cordova, 1951), where he played a scientist experimenting with a chimpanzee, as well as Eastwood's two comedies with an orangutan.

[11] Quoted in Dawson, " Dirty Harry Comes Clean," paragraph 16.

catatonic condition and Jennifer craving revenge. Her modus operandi is to shoot each victim twice, in the genitals and then the forehead. The estimable Vincent Canby complained in his *New York Times* review that since the audience knows from the start who the murderer is, "there's not... any mystery in the movie." Canby is wrong to count this as a flaw—the film is hardly a purebred whodunit, and suspense might reside in other particulars, such as the progress of Harry's sleuthing or Jennifer's agility in eluding him. Nor is the critic entirely persuasive when he opines that the story sets Jennifer up as "a serious painter—sort of neo-Edvard Munch in style," whereas Locke's portrayal makes her look "as if she should be running a boutique at Big Sur" (*Impact*, paragraphs 1, 2). Those categories should not be mutually exclusive, in my view.

Canby is on stronger ground when he notes the film's strong resemblance to Michael Winner's *Death Wish*, a 1974 vigilante melodrama that tapped into the worst instincts of its increasingly crime-ridden era, making Charles Bronson an international star and bringing several sequels in its wake. Released three years after *Dirty Harry*, one year after *Magnum Force*, and nine years before *Sudden Impact*, the ostentatiously truculent *Death Wish* escalated Harry's brand of off-the-books justice from a matter of righteous personal crusading to one of commonsense moral principle. It is indeed a key intertext for *Sudden Impact*, playing on the same urban paranoia that drives all of the Dirty Harry films and anticipating—perhaps even inspiring—the story of *Sudden Impact*, focusing on a liberal-minded New York businessman who becomes an enraged vigilante after muggers kill his wife and leave his daughter in a state of catatonic muteness.

Canby detested *Death Wish*, deeming it "a despicable movie... that raises complex questions in order to offer bigoted, frivolous, oversimplified answers," and the echoes he found in *Sudden Impact* probably heightened his animus toward Eastwood's picture (*Death*, paragraph 10). In any case, Canby was disturbed by more in *Sudden Impact* than just the early revelation of the killer's identity and the shortcomings of Locke's boutique-proprietor appearance. Canby's review concluded: "The screenplay is ridiculous, and Mr. Eastwood's direction of it primitive... Among other things, the movie never gets a firm hold on its own continuity, [allowing various] "scenes of simultaneous action [to] appear to take place weeks or maybe months apart. Not that this makes much difference." Canby intended the last sentence as a putdown of the movie's irredeemable incoherence, but the poor continuity made no difference in another sense: audiences loved the picture, implausibilities and all.

The Gospel According to Callahan

Of the five Dirty Harry films, the first remains the most widely known and commented on, and the high emotions it has elicited comprise the best evidence that Siegel and Eastwood struck an especially sensitive and susceptible American nerve. Why does this picture stir such passionate responses in so many people? The title provides a clue. In his classic work *The Varieties of Religious Experience: A Study in Human Nature*, first published in 1902, the American philosopher William James presents a nuanced and skeptical view of what he calls "the gospel of healthy-minded-ness," to which he attributes "the interesting notion... of there being elements of the universe which may make no rational whole in conjunction with the other elements, and which, from the point of view of any system which those other elements make up, can only be considered so much irrelevance and accident—so much 'dirt,' as it were, and matter out of place." James' skepticism leads him to add that "most philosophers seem either to forget [the gospel of healthy-mindedness] or to disdain it too much ever to mention it," but he concludes, "we shall have to admit it ourselves in the end as containing an element of truth.

Dirt may be the key to *Dirty Harry*, who is viewed with partiality or repugnance depending on what version of "healthy-mindedness" a particular moviegoer embraces. The most readily available options are (simplified for the sake of discussion) the healthy-mindedness of liberals, which tends to reject rogue policing and vigilante justice, and the healthy-mindedness of conservatives, which may be sympathetic toward rough policing and vigilantism if they contribute to the maintenance of social order. *Dirty Harry* draws much of its appeal from the cleverness with which the filmmakers scramble these categories: by pitting a "sadist-with-badge" against a "sadist-without badge," in the *Variety* critic's hyperbolic words (1971, 3) they offer an unusually high number of discursive opportunities for spectators to inject the spectacle with the ideological meanings they prefer.

In an important extension of James' remarks on dirt, order, and matter out of place, anthropologist Mary Douglas describes dirt as "the by-product of a systematic ordering and classification of matter, in so far as ordering involves rejecting inappropriate elements." Thinking about dirt along these lines "takes us straight into the field of symbolism," Douglas continues. This is because all cultures must devise methods for dealing with anomalous or ambiguous phenomena that seem to contradict its assumptions, and symbols readily serve this function when organized into ritual, poetry, and mythology. Douglas does not write about cinema here, but I think it is reasonable to assert that going to movies is among the prime occasions we moderns have for making contact with the social rituals, demotic poetry, and (mostly) secular myths of our era. Like symbols of so-called primitive times and places, the ones that flash across our multiplex and plasma screens are often of the kind that Douglas calls "symbols of anomaly" (44), serving to "incorporate evil and death along with life and goodness... into a single, grand, unifying pattern" (50).

It is also true, however, that *negating* the anomalous or impure is not the same as *removing* it. This is especially so when the body is taken into account, since the body is ultimately the basis of all symbolic schemes, and the body must be affirmed in both of its essential forms—the physical and the symbolic—if life in the body is to continue. Looking at primitive cultures, therefore, Douglas does not find "consistent dirt-rejecting" but emphatic "dirt-affirmation" as well. Her observation is worth quoting at length:

> In a given culture it seems that some kinds of behavior or natural phenomena are recognized as utterly wrong by all the principles which govern the universe. There are different kinds of impossibilities, anomalies, bad mixings and abominations. Most of the items receive varying degrees of condemnation and avoidance. Then suddenly we find that one of the most abominable or impossible is singled out and put into a very special kind of ritual frame that marks it off from other experience. The frame ensures that the categories which the normal avoidances sustain are not threatened or affected in any way. Within the ritual frame the abomination is then handled as a source of tremendous power. (203–4)

The abomination that pollutes society in the *Dirty Harry* movies, and in *Death Wish* and its ilk, is sadistic violence, so arbitrarily chaotic that it seems as illogical and inescapable as a force of nature. This is the kind of violence that revels in murder and physical affliction, à la Scorpio, whose specialty is tormenting and killing children, or in manslaughter and psychological affliction, à la Harry, who in his first film taunts a criminal at gunpoint with another of his most famous lines:

> I know what you're thinking: 'Did he fire six shots or only five?' Well, to tell you the truth, in all this excitement I kind of lost track myself. But being as this is a .44 Magnum, the most powerful handgun in the world, and would blow your head clean off, you've got to ask yourself one question: 'Do I feel lucky?' Well, do ya, punk?

But if such things are the stuff of abomination—if they would shock or traumatize most of us were we to run up against them in reality—why do large numbers of moviegoers revel in watching them? The answer is that *these* abominations have been singled out by skilled practitioners of contemporary mythmaking (Directors Eastwood and Siegel, the Malpaso Company, Warner Bros. Pictures) and placed into a ritual frame known as the heavily publicized mass-audience melodrama. The film's purpose is precisely to single out anomalous behaviors (few murderers are as exotically horrific as Scorpio proves to be) and bad mixings (the title character is a law officer *and* a law breaker, a hero *and* a hothead, a guardian of society *and* an antisocial outsider) and to foreground them in ways that allow them to be vividly and memorably manifested without threatening the sense of safety, the desire for order, or the impulse toward condemnation and avoidance with which most of us stave off the prospect of confronting such evils in actual experience.

This is the sort of paradox that pivotal artistic events occasionally produce: *Dirty Harry*'s dirt protects and sustains particular kinds of complacent healthy-mindedness that modern societies cultivate as psychological and spiritual survival strategies. The film accomplishes its task by marking what we deem social anomalies—represented by Harry's self-righteous rage and violence, Scorpio's psychotic rage and violence—as subject matters out of place, familiar and entertaining on the screen but posing no threat to the systems by which we order and codify our lives. The result is exactly what Douglas describes: a heavily symbolic spectacle weaves evil and death, life and goodness into a grand, unifying pattern that simultaneously thrills, jolts, and soothes its audience. The controversies aroused by the *Dirty Harry* films also contribute to this effect, allowing different forms of healthy-mindedness (left-wing and right-wing attitudes of varying types and intensities) to fight it out on strictly rhetorical turf. Whether all of this contributes to social wellbeing or to the *illusion* of social wellbeing is a different question. To paraphrase another critic in another context, Eastwood and Siegel had a hit on their hands, and perhaps on their consciences as well.

Works Cited

Any Which Way You Can. Dir. Buddy Van Horn. Clint Eastwood, Sondra Locke, and Geoffrey Lewis. Malpaso Co., Warner Bros., 1980. Film.

Bedtime for Bonzo. Dir. Frederick de Cordova. Ronald Reagan, Diana Lynn, and Walter Slezak. Universal International Pictures, 1951. Film.

The Beguiled. Dir. Donald Siegel. Clint Eastwood, Geraldine Page, and Elizabeth Hartman. Universal Pictures, 1971. Film.

Bronco Billy. Dir. Clint Eastwood, Sondra Locke, and Geoffrey Lewis. Warner Bros., Second Street Films, 1980. Film.

Canby, Vincent. *Death Wish* Hunts Muggers: The Cast Story of Gunman Takes Dim View of City. *New York Times*, July 25, 1974.

Canby, Vincent. *Impact*, with Clint Eastwood. *New York Times*, December 9, 1983.

Cieply, Michael. A Studio With Violence in Its Bones. *New York Times*, 26 July 26, 2012.

Cocks, Jay. Outside Society. *Time*, January 3, 1972.

The Dark Knight Rises. Dir. Christopher Nolan. Christian Bale, Heath Ledger, and Morgan Freeman. Warner Bros., 2012. Film.

Dawson, Jeff. *Dirty Harry* Comes Clean. *The Guardian*, June 5, 2008.

Dickens, Charles. *Oliver Twist, or, The Parish Boy's Progress*. Penguin, 2002 [1838].

Dirty Harry. Dir. Donald Siegel. Clint Eastwood, Andy Robinson, and Harry Guardino. Malpaso Productions, 1971. Film.

The Dirty Harry *Collection*. Dir. Clint Eastwood. Clint Eastwood, Andrew Robinson, Liam Neeson. Amazon.com, 2001. DVD five-boxed set.

Douglas, Mary. *Purity and Danger: An Analysis of Concepts of Pollution and Taboo*. Routledge, 2002, 44, 49–50.

Ebert, Roger. *Dirty Harry. Chicago Sun–Times*, January 1, 1971.

Every Which Way But Loose. Dir. James Fargo. Clint Eastwood, Sondra Locke, and Geoffrey Lewis. Warner Bros, Malpaso Co., 1978. Film.

Fine, Marshall. Editorial Reviews. *Amazon.com* (n.d.) http://www.amazon.com/Complete-Enforcer-Magnum-Sudden-Impact/dp/6302186161

Gangster Squad. Dir. Ruben Fleischer. Josh Brolin, Ryan Gosling, and Sean Penn. Warner Bros., 2013. Film.

Greenspun, Roger. Dirty Harry. *New York Times*, 23 December, 1971.

Hoberman, J. *Dirty Harry. Village Voice*, March 28, 2006.

James, William. *Varieties of Religious Experience: A Study in Human Nature*. Arc Manor, 2008, 104.

Kael, Pauline. *5001 Nights at the Movies*, Holt, Rinehart and Winston, 1982.

McGilligan, Patrick. *Clint: The Life and Legend*, HarperCollins, 2002.

Murphy, A. D. "Dirty Harry." *Daily Variety*, December 22, 1971.

The Outlaw Josey Wales. Dir. Clint Eastwood, Sondra Locke, and Chief Dan George. 1976. Film.

Play Misty for Me. Dir. Clint Eastwood. Clint Eastwood, Jessica Walter, and Donna Mills. Malpaso Productions, 1971. Film.

Reagan, Ronald. Remarks at a White House Meeting With Members of the American Business Conference, April 15, 1986. In *Public Papers of the Presidents of the United States: Ronald Reagan, 1986, 2 vols*. Ann Arbor: University of Michigan Library, 2005. 472–4.

Red Dawn. Dir. John Milius. Patrick Swayze and Charlie Sheen. United Artists, 1984. Film.

Schickel, Richard. *Clint Eastwood: A Biography,* Alfred A. Knopf, 1996.

Sterritt, David. *The Cinema of Clint Eastwood: Chronicles of America*, Columbia, 2014.

Sterritt, David. *The Cinema of Clint Eastwood: Chronicles of America*. Wallflower, 2014.

Sterritt, David. "Presentation to the Columbia University Seminar on Cinema and Interdisciplinary Interpretation." New York. September 2014.

Sudden Impact. Dir. Clint Eastwood. Clint Eastwood and Sondra Locke. Warner Bros. and Malpaso Company, 1983. Film.

Thomas Hart Benton and the Hollywood Epic
Quarterly Review of Film and Video 32:7 (2015)

> Austen Barron Bailly, ed., *American Epics: Thomas Hart Benton and Hollywood* (Salem, MA: Peabody Essex Museum/Munich: Delmonico Books-Prestel, 2015). 239 pp., $60.

> *American Epics: Thomas Hart Benton and Hollywood*, an exhibition organized by the Peabody Essex Museum in Salem, Massachusetts, in collaboration with the Nelson-Atkins Museum of Art in Kansas City, Missouri, and the Amon Carter Museum of American Art in Fort Worth, Texas. On view at Peabody Essex Museum through September 7, 2015, and then at Nelson-Atkins (October 10, 2015–January 3, 2016), Amon Carter (February 6–May 1, 2016); and the Milwaukee Art Museum (June 9–September 5, 2016).

Near the beginning of George Clooney's wartime drama *The Monuments Men* (2014), about art experts recovering works stolen by Nazi pillagers during World War II, two curators played by Clooney and Matt Damon have a conversation in a Manhattan bar. Their chat gets the story rolling, but for aficionados of American painting, the scene's real action is on the wall behind them, where production designer Jim Bissell has placed *America Today*, a sprawling mural created by Thomas Hart Benton in the early 1930s. This touch is fictional, since the film takes place in the 1940s, when *America Today* still adorned a boardroom at the New School for Social Research, which commissioned it (and then neglected it by stacking chairs and blackboards against it, producing "very marked lines of abrasion" that Benton personally repaired in the 1950s and again in the 1960s[1]). The mural now resides at the Metropolitan Museum of Art, although more people will probably see it in Clooney's film, notwithstanding the movie's poor reception by critics and lackluster box-office returns. Bissell asked the Benton estate for permission to use it because for him it exemplifies American art with a European pedigree.[2] "This set was a pet project of mine," he told *Architectural Digest*, "and I felt the painting was very fitting."[3]

---

[1] Bailey, "Thomas Hart Benton and America Today," para. 15.
[2] Sluis, "*The Monuments Men* Designer Jim Bissell Re-Creates a Ruined Europe," para. 8.
[3] Whitlock, "Sets of *The Monuments Men*," para. 4.

It is also very cinematic, comprising 10 panels up to 7.5 feet high—the equivalent of a pretty big screen—and depicting a broad array of American people, places, and activities. Aluminum-leaf moldings divide it into thematic sections, evoking the diversity of machine-age America while tipping a hat to the Art Deco details of the New School's building, designed by Joseph Urban, an originator of the style. One admirer of the mural, cinematographer John Bailey, calls it "a kaleidoscopic portrait of working people and their entertainments," and so it is.[4] In addition, however, it is a deftly articulated montage, combining the stylized realism of Hollywood storytelling with the startling juxtapositions of what Sergei Eisenstein called "the montage of attractions," geared less to narrative logic than to psychological force and intellectual import.[5]

Modernism, Synchromism, Regionalism
The cinematic aspects of *America Today* are typical of Benton's style, and his affinity for the filmic is the focus of the book and exhibition aptly titled *American Epics: Thomas Hart Benton and Hollywood*. Born in Missouri in 1889, Benton began as a modernist in the European tradition, studying art in Paris, where his companions included the Mexican muralist Diego Rivera and the American abstractionist Stanton Macdonald-Wright, whose short-lived Synchromist movement attempted to orchestrate colors the way musicians organize tones. Benton moved to New York in 1913 and joined the motion-picture industry, thanks in part to entry-level jobs provided by his friend Rex Ingram, who had studied sculpture at Yale and then become a prolific movie director, actor, writer, and producer with dreams (never fully realized) of raising the young medium's artistic standards. Painting expansive sets and backdrops had a lasting effect on Benton's mural designs, although he eventually became cynical about the film industry's insatiable appetite for financial gain, suspecting that cinema's clutch on the American imagination was a death grip auguring "social and political disaster," according to the cultural scholar Erika Doss.[6]

After his stint in the movie business, Benton worked on camouflage for the Navy and then became a successful teacher, first at the Art Students League in New York City—where Jackson Pollock was among his students—and later at the Kansas City Art Institute in Missouri, from which he was fired for making

[4] Bailey, "Thomas Hart Benton and America Today," para. 1.
[5] Eisenstein, "Montage of Attractions," 230.
[6] Doss, "Artists in Hollywood," 14, 11.

homophobic remarks. By the early 1930s he had abandoned modernism and joined Grant Wood and John Steuart Curry as leaders of the Regionalist movement; Benton's self-portrait graced the cover of *Time* magazine in 1934. His generally leftist politics led him to paint subjects soft-pedaled or avoided by many artists, including the persecution of Native Americans and the enslavement of African Americans, and while his treatments can seem naïve or ambivalent today, they were progressive and even daring when new.

American Business Napoleons

The movies played a recurring role in Benton's work. A high point came in 1937 when *Life* magazine commissioned him to depict the filmmaking process—writing, casting, set design, shooting, editing, exhibition of the finished product—in a series of pictures and an essay. Benton ensconced himself at Twentieth Century-Fox, where the tentpole production of the day was Henry King's lavishly budgeted drama *In Old Chicago*, about feuding brothers (Tyrone Power and Don Ameche) whose mother (Alice Brady) owns the cow that overturns the lamp that ignites the legendary fire of 1871. Also under way were David Butler's musical fantasy *Ali Baba Goes to Town*, with Eddie Cantor in the title role, and William A. Seiter's comedy *Life Begins at College*, starring the Ritz Brothers and Joan Davis.

Benton observed everything he could, turning out hundreds of sketches, dozens of ink-and-wash drawings, and the essay "Hollywood Journey," commenting on his experiences.[7] He also painted *Hollywood*, a vast work (7 feet wide, almost 5 feet high) that evokes the making of the previously mentioned movies in images that flow across the canvas in a kinetic wave enhanced by the vivid colors that Fox had not bestowed on the films themselves. Dazzling as it is, *Hollywood* does not mythologize the movies any more than Benton's most penetrating history paintings mythologize the Western frontier; he told his *Life* editor that he wanted "to give the idea that the machinery of the industry, cameras, big generators, high voltage wires, etc., is directed mainly toward what young ladies have under their clothes."[8]

This was an idea that *Life* did not like. Keenly aware of Hollywood's popularity with the public, and loath to gamble with its

---

[7] Benton, "Hollywood Journey."
[8] Doss, *Benton, Pollock, and the Politics*, 199.

willingness to buy advertising space in its pages, the magazine chose not to print the artworks it had paid the artist to produce. Nor did it publish Benton's essay, which described studios run by "American business Napoleons" and "yes-guys" concerned only with the cash they can milk from a degraded art form that "sings and clowns in Rotary Club fashion" and evinces "a high regard for the status quo in everything."[9] When the iconic *Hollywood* painting finally did appear in *Life*, it accompanied a 1938 article about the Carnegie International art show in Pittsburgh, not the movie business. Benton was probably not surprised by the magazine's frowning response to his creations, which were evidently too true for comfort.

Fifty Thousand Smackers

Benton did return to Hollywood, however. The first occasion was in 1939, when studio chief Darryl F. Zanuck bought the rights to John Steinbeck's novel *The Grapes of Wrath*, fresh from the presses and already pushing buttons with its sexual candor and pungent New Deal politics. Zanuck recruited Nunnally Johnson to write the screenplay and John Ford—the screen's leading spinner of quintessentially American tales—to direct a cast led by Henry Fonda and Jane Darwell as impoverished sharecroppers on the road from Oklahoma to California, seeking respite from the Depression and Dust Bowl that have brought their family to its knees. Fox's publicity department hired Benton to create a group of lithographs that would promote the film by capturing its spirit in an accessible, audience-friendly manner. Benton, Ford, and Zanuck were well suited to this enterprise and to one another. Each was attracted to stories with meaningful messages and none were averse to mingling comfortably familiar imagery (a.k.a. stereotypes) with a mild aura of Hollywood-type realism. In an essay for the *American Epics* book, curator Margaret C. Conrads explores their collaboration and underscores Benton's influence not just on the advertising but on the film itself. As director Ford and cinematographer Gregg Toland prepared for shooting, art director Richard Day gave them production sketches imitating Benton's style, prompting them (according to Dan Ford's biography of his father) to "emphasize the contrasts, to go for a stark, almost documentary effect: murky silhouettes against light skies, and grim figures bent against the

---

[9] Benton, "Hollywood Journey," 24–25.

wind."[10] Benton's own lithographs included five portraits of key characters and a scene study called *Departure of the Joads*, all of which appeared on posters, in advertisements, and in oversized reproductions blazoned across the Rivoli Theatre when the picture had its New York premiere.

Benton's next Hollywood journey occurred in 1940, when United Artists and producer Walter Wanger summoned him and seven other American artists to observe the production of Ford's seafaring drama *The Long Voyage Home*, about rough-and-ready sailors played by a high-profile cast including Thomas Mitchell, Barry Fitzgerald, and Ian Hunter as well as John Wayne sporting an improbable Swedish accent. The artists' efforts appeared in ads and theater displays, and *Esquire* magazine used Benton's painting *No More Sea for Us* to illustrate a 1940 article by Harry Salpeter titled "Art Comes to Hollywood: Fifty Thousand Smackers for a Team of Artists to Paint the Take of *The Long Voyage Home*."[11] Benton returned to Twentieth Century-Fox in 1941 to make promotional images for *Swamp Water*, the first (and almost certainly the best) picture directed by the towering French filmmaker Jean Renoir during his brief Hollywood period. Some of the movie was shot on location in Georgia's famous Okefenokee Swamp, and Benton's rendering of the initial scene, *Swampland*, is a stunning entry in his lithograph series for the film. His last noteworthy Hollywood project was a portrait of Burt Lancaster as the eponymous hero of *The Kentuckian*, a western about a widowed frontiersman and his growing son. Lancaster directed the picture, which did not fare well with moviegoers despite a striking poster bearing a reduced version of Benton's enormous painting. Benton's meticulous working methods are limned in marvelous detail by the detailed treatment of the *Kentuckian* project in *American Epics*. Lancaster and United Artists expected him to work from photographs, but he insisted on access to Lancaster in person, and to prepare the ground he produced an extensive series of preliminary images, ranging from a cubist drawing to colorful sketches done with oil or tempera. Separately and together, they are beautiful to behold.

Conquering Deep Space

As disenchanted as he became with the movie business, Benton never stopped benefiting from his experiences as a young behind-

---

[10] Ford, "Life of John Ford," 143; quoted in Conrads, "*The Grapes of Wrath* in Pictures," 68.

[11] Cited in Chasse, "Benton, Hollywood, and History," 203.

the-scenes worker and a sometime observer of the industry's practices, personalities, and idiosyncrasies. As part of the Public Discussion Day that inaugurated the *American Epics* show, I had a public discussion with film scholar and historian Matthew Bernstein, who wrote the book's highly enlightening essay "Movie Culture in the Segregated Era" and curated the exhibition's film component, incorporating well-chosen excerpts from Maurice Tourneur and Clarence Brown's *Last of the Mohicans* (1920), William A. Wellman's *A Star Is Born* (1937), Stuart Heisler's *The Negro Soldier* (1944), Anthony Mann's *The Far Country* (1954), and other notable pictures. In this discussion we unpacked the word *epic* in the context of Benton's art, noting that while no single comprehensive definition exists for this term, Hollywood has always embraced elements—largeness of scale, bigness of budget, settings picturesquely removed from the here and now, casts of hundreds or thousands, whether filmed in the flesh or conjured on a computer—that have roots in millennia of epic literature and present-day iterations in hugely popular varieties of theatrical, televisual, and digital spectacle. The epic aspects of Benton's art derive from his absorption in American history and his fascination with American landscapes, industries, occupations, and personality types, all of which continue to loom very large in the American cinema.

Benton's interaction with film took many different forms, and was by no means limited to the Hollywood subjects he sometimes drew and painted. He traveled widely through the United States, exploring different environments and sounding out local personalities like a movie director scouting locations and acquiring a sense of the people who live in them. His observations behind the scenes spurred his proclivity for chiaroscuro lighting and kinetic compositional effects. Perhaps most revealingly, before putting brush to canvas he habitually modeled his images in three-dimensional clay and tested different lighting configurations on them, lending his painterly images the solidity and depth they would have in an expertly photographed film. His primary artistic concern, critic Jake Milgram Wien astutely argues in the *American Epics* volume, "was to conquer what he called 'deep space,' comparable to the lifelike quality of cinematic projection."[12] Benton was a painter through and through, but he never relinquished the lessons he learned from the movies.

---

[12] Wien, "Thomas Hart Benton and the Art, " 140.

Unique and Characterful

Benton did not always reach his audience as effectively as he might
have hoped, and certain attitudes and opinions in his paintings and
writings strike sour notes. His art was patriarchal and male-dom-
inated; his homophobia was stark enough to cause a scandal in
1941; and some of his individual works remain controversial to
this day. A good example of the latter is the 1942 painting *Negro
Soldier*, showing an African-American infantryman walking
toward hostile ground with rifle and bayonet at the ready. Benton
makes this figure look "apelike, animalistic, and non-human" as
well as "grotesque" and "emasculated," in the view of curator
Pellom McDaniels III, who links the picture with contempora-
neous Nazi claims that Black people are "half-human and half-
monkey" and with American fears that "an invasion... held the
potential outcome of a foreign power elevating the marginalized
Negro into the role of ally."[13]

This is a forceful interpretation of the image, but I must
disagree. Leaving aside the outlandish notion that the Black Americans vilified by Nazism might somehow become willing participants in Nazism, the intently focused gaze, lithe physique, and
manifest courage of the *Negro Soldier* seem to me a celebration
of African-American bravery, proficiency, and steadfastness in
the face of danger. The painting might indeed stir anxiety in those
misguided Americans who find the sight of an armed Black man
to be ipso facto a cause for alarm, but to my mind they misread
Benton's picture and the motives behind it. Discussing the 1931–
1932 painting *Romance*, wherein a Black man and woman stroll
down a quiet country road, the African-American art scholar
Richard J. Powell describes a very different Benton who believed
that White Southerners owe Black Southerners an immeasurable
debt for their role in elevating and sustaining a region where the
beautiful and the horrific are historically commingled.[14] Benton's
racial consciousness was multifaceted and complex, like that of
America in general and the South in particular. In his 1951 autobiography he forthrightly saluted the contributions made by Black
people to their land. "In your childhood they taught you the
language by which you express yourself," he wrote, addressing a
white Southerner of his acquaintance, "they made your songs, your
jokes, and all else that will stand in your civilization as unique and

---

[13] McDaniels, "Negro Soldier," 174.
[14] Powell, "'Dem Shoes,'" 86–87.

characterful. Nearly everything you have can be traced to their influence except your architecture, and that is borrowed."[15] Any number of Benton's works affirm the sincerity of that statement.

Benton has been denigrated or dismissed by critics as prominent as Clement Greenberg in the 1950s and Robert Hughes in the 1990s, but in his day he was a celebrity artist and a substantial force in American culture. Enthusiastic responses to *American Epics* suggest that his reputation is once more on the rise.

Works Cited

Bailey, John, "Thomas Hart Benton and America Today." *American Cinematographer*. February 9, 2015.

Benton, Thomas Hart. *An Artist in America*. University of Missouri Press, 1983.

Benton, Thomas Hart. "Hollywood Journey." In *American Epics: Thomas Hart Benton and Hollywood*, ed. Austen Barron Bailly, 22–27. Prestel, 2015.

Bernstein, Matthew. "Movie Culture in the Segregated Era." In *American Epics: Thomas Hart Benton and Hollywood*.

Chasse, Sarah N. "Benton, Hollywood, and History: A Timeline." In *American Epics: Thomas Hart Benton and Hollywood*.

Conrads, Margaret C. "The Grapes of Wrath" in Pictures." In *American Epics: Thomas Hart Benton and Hollywood*.

Doss, Erika. "Artists in Hollywood: Thomas Hart Benton and Nathanael West Picture America's Dream Dump." *The Space Between* vii, no. 1 (2011): 9–32.

Doss, Erika. *Benton, Pollock, and the Politics of Modernism: From Regionalism to Abstract Expressionism*. Chicago, 1991.

Eisenstein, Sergei M. "Montage of Attractions." In Sergei M. Eisenstein, *The Film Sense*, ed. and trans. Jay Leyda, 230–233. Harcourt Brace Jovanovich, 1947.

Ford, Dan. *Pappy: The Life of John Ford*. Da Capo Press.

McDaniels, Pellom III. "Negro Soldier: American Manhood Personified." In *American Epics: Thomas Hart Benton and Hollywood*.

Powell, Richard J. "'Dem Shoes': Thomas Hart Benton's Romance." In *American Epics: Thomas Hart Benton and Hollywood*.

Sluis, Sarah. "*The Monuments Men* Designer Jim Bissell Re-Creates a Ruined Europe." *The Credits.* February 6, 2014.

Whitlock, Cathy. "The Sets of *The Monuments Men*" *Architectural Digest*. 2014.

Wien, Jake Milgram. "Thomas Hart Benton and the Art of Painting Cinematically." In *American Epics: Thomas Hart Benton and Hollywood*.

---

[15] Benton, *An Artist in America*, 197–198.

Schizoanalyzing Souls: Godard, Deleuze, and the Mystical Line of Flight

from *A Companion to Jean-Luc Godard*, ed. Tom Conley and T. Jefferson Kline (Malden, MA: Wiley-Blackwell, 2014)

Originally published in the Journal of French and Francophone Philosophy *18:2 (2010). A different, somewhat condensed version titled "Godard, Schizoanalysis, and the Immaculate Conception of the Frame" appears in* Sonimage: The Legacies of Jean-Luc Godard *(Wilfrid Laurier, 2014).*

Subjectivity is never ours, it is time, that is, the soul or the spirit, the virtual.

—Gilles Deleuze[1]

Spirit… is volatile, whereas the soul is weighted, a center of gravity.

—Gilles Deleuze
and Félix Guattari[2]

Mary: Does the soul have a body?
Doctor: What do you mean, young lady, the body has a soul.
Mary: I thought it was the opposite.

—*Hail Mary*

In an article on montage written for *Cahiers du cinéma*, Jean-Luc Godard made an observation that has been quoted many times in many contexts:

If direction is a look, montage is a heartbeat… what one seeks to foresee in space, the other seeks in time… Cutting on a look is… to bring out the soul under the spirit, the passion behind the intrigue, to make the heart prevail over the intelligence by destroying the notion of space in favor of that of time.[3]

---

[1] Gilles Deleuze, Cinema 2: *The Time-Image*, trans. Hugh Tomlinson and Robert Galeta (Minnesota, 1989), 82-83.
[2] Gilles Deleuze and Félix Guattari, *A Thousand Plateaus: Capitalism and Schizophrenia*, trans. Brian Massumi (Minnesota, 1987), 366.
[3] Jean-Luc Godard, "Montage my Fine Care," in *Godard on Godard*, ed. Jean Narboni and Tom Milne, trans. Tom Milne (Da Capo, 1986), 39-41, cited at 39.

This passage appeared in 1956, almost three decades before Gilles Deleuze published *Cinema 1: The Movement-Image* and *Cinema 2: The Time-Image* in 1983 and 1985, respectively. Yet despite the distance between those dates, the young critic's remark anticipates key aspects of the philosopher's film-theoretical stance. The need to displace the notional bias toward space with a conception of time as a concrete and dynamic force is the single most vital element in the thinking of Henri Bergson, whose ideas about this subject—ramified into such areas as affect, memory, perception, language, and the ontological properties of mind itself—play indispensable roles in Deleuze's writings on cinema and allied areas of immanence, multiplicity, and difference.

Godard's statement also resonates with Deleuzian theory in its preference for the material (heart) over the abstract (intelligence) and in its praise of filmmaking that breaks the "link between man and the world," in Deleuze's phrase. When a technique of this kind detaches a film and its spectator from the "general system of commensurability" that habitually orders perception and action in space and time, cinema can perform its liberating function of bringing thought "face to face with its own impossibility and animating the "higher power of birth" that this encounter can catalyze. "The sensory-motor break," Deleuze declares, "makes man a seer who finds himself... confronted by something unthinkable in thought." Seeking cinematic expression of precisely this—the unthinkable in thought—through innovative and far-reaching means, Godard works the assemblages of montage and mise-en-scène into volatile folds that reveal, refract, and reflect upon their own rich mysteries. Above all he probes the potential of the irrational cut, which for Deleuze marks a limit or interstice between paradoxically "non-linked (but always relinked) images,"[4] producing structures more akin to the productive branchings of the rhizome than to the arborescent linearity of classical film.

In this essay I consider ways in which certain ideas developed by Deleuze and Félix Guattari, particularly in connection with the practice they call schizoanalysis, illuminate the 1985 film *Hail Mary (Je vous salue, Marie)*, which is actually two films in one—a molar ciné-assemblage, in Deleuzian terminology. The longer portion, written and directed by Godard, presents the biblical myth of the Virgin Mary translated to the present day, depicting Mary as a young Swiss woman who works in her father's gas

---

[4] Deleuze, *Cinema 2*, 169, 277, 168, 169, 278.

station, plays basketball for relaxation, receives the Annunciation when the angel Gabriel flies in on an airplane, and has a cab-driving boyfriend named Joseph who is understandably perturbed when she tells him she's pregnant. This is preceded by *The Book of Mary* (*Le Livre de Marie*), a shorter piece made by Anne-Marie Miéville that focuses on an adolescent girl coming to terms, psychologically and spiritually, with her parents' impending divorce. Sharing the collective title *Hail Mary*, the movies are connected by a splendid irrational cut: the Mary of Miéville's film is sitting at a table with a soft-boiled egg before her; a tight close-up shows her cracking off the egg's top with a knife; the severed portion falls onto the table; and an intertitle reading *At That Time* (*En Ce Temps La*) instantly appears, followed by a shot of light rain falling across windswept reeds on a country slope. This marks the start of Godard's film, which slides into existence so softly and subtly that one isn't sure it has begun until the opening credits appear shortly afterward.

I'll focus my attention on Godard's portion of *Hail Mary*, which I've chosen from his expansive oeuvre because it is one of his most intellectually and aesthetically adventurous works, and because its complex imbrications of narrative drama, theological speculation, Catholic iconography, and Protestant music are well suited to the themes I want to explore. One of these is the connection between Godard's highly intuitive cinema and the "transcendental unconscious" that Deleuze and Guattari speak of in *Anti-Oedipus: Capitalism and Schizophrenia*, where they declare that a materialist revolt against psychoanalytical strictures must rediscover the unconscious as an assemblage of desiring-machines, geared not to representation and meaning but to the production of desire and "libidinal investments of the social field."[5] Another is Godard's interest in the theologically informed psychoanalytical theories of Françoise Dolto, and how this relates to the schizoanalytically informed atheology that Deleuze and Guattari espouse. A third is the applicability of some central schizoanalytical tropes—deterritorialization, lines of flight, nonhuman becoming, and the body without organs—to *Hail Mary*, which deterroritalizes being in ways that are physical, metaphysical, astrophysical, or all three. And throughout the discussion I'll be following (sometimes tacitly) the notion of *soul* as it winds through Godardian cinema and Deleuzian theory, often using such aliases as *virtuality* and élan vital and *spiritual automaton*.

---

[5] Gilles Deleuze and Félix Guattari, *Anti-Oedipus: Capitalism and Schizophrenia*, trans. Robert Hurley, Mark Seem, and Helen R. Lane (Minnesota, 1983), 350.

My goal is less to arrive at a conclusive destination than to emulate the strolling schizo imagined by Deleuze and Guattari, scanning the horizon for intriguing desiring-machines, spiritual automata, flows of becoming, and breaths of fresh film-philosophical air.[6] Our guide for this excursion is Godard, who attempts in *Hail Mary* to achieve "an 'Immaculate Conception' of the frame,"[7] by which he means a mode of improvisational practice that eschews preconceived framing, selection, and organization so as to open fresh frontiers of intuitive perception. The most powerful way to experience his work is to follow its flows toward the non-place that Deleuze and Guattari describe, "a world created in the process of its tendency, its coming undone, its deterritorialization."[8] In other words: find the body without organs in Mary's enigmatic egg; apply the "schizoanalytic flick of the finger"[9] as decisively as she cracks its macrogametic shell; then watch as one story closes and another, surpassingly schizoid tale begins.

God/ard

Godard was interested in psychoanalysis when he started conceptualizing *Hail Mary*;[10] more precisely, he was interested in a particular species of Freudian thought, which he found in a book by Françoise Dolto, a French physician and psychoanalyst (1908-1988) who specialized in child psychology. A member of the Freudian School of Paris who worked alongside Jacques Lacan for many years, she developed the very Lacanian idea that beginning in the fetal stage, persons evolve an "unconscious image of the body" that constitutes the "symbolic incarnation of the desiring being."[11] By the late 1970s she was "the best known and most beloved psychoanalyst in France," according to psychoanalytic theorist Sherry Turkle, who summarizes her core contribution

---

[6] Deleuze and Guattari, *Anti-Oedipus*, 2.

[7] "Godard/Sollers: The Interview (Extracts)," trans. Pasquale G. Tatò, in Maryel Locke and Charles Warren, eds., *Jean-Luc Godard's Hail Mary: Women and the Sacred in Film* (Southern Illinois University, 1993), 123-124, cited at 124.

[8] Deleuze and Guattari, *Anti-Oedipus*, 322.

[9] Ibid., 321.

[10] In this essay the title *Hail Mary* refers to Godard's portion of the film unless otherwise specified.

[11] Eric Binet, "Françoise Dolto." *Prospects: The Quarterly Review of Comparative Education*, 29:3 (1999): 445-454. Reprinted at UNESCO: International Bureau of Education (2000), 1-8, cited at 1, 3,

thus: "*Where other psychoanalytic thinkers stressed childhood sexuality, Dolto insists on childhood lucidity.*"[12]

Most important for our purposes, Dolto was also a practicing Roman Catholic who wanted "to add a mystical foundation to her thesis of the body image," according to psychoanalytic historian Élisabeth Roudinesco; her reasoning was that the Incarnation and the Resurrection, through the Crucifixion, "pulled Christ out of a 'placenta' and a uterine world to accede to eternal life," allowing him to become "the very metaphor of desire that leads humankind… on a great identity quest."[13] Dolto believed that "psychoanalysis which seeks to substitute analysis for 'acting out' reinforces the Christian ethic just as the Christian ethic reinforces the psychoanalytic one."[14] One of Dolto's projects was a series of radio dialogues with Gérard Séverin, another Freudian School psychoanalyst. These were published in book form as *L'Évangile au risque de la psychoanalyse*,[15] the text that captured Godard's interest.

According to biographer Richard Brody, the roots of *Hail Mary* lie in an unrealized Godard project provisionally called *Fathers and Daughters*, a film "about incest" that would feature Godard playing the role of God, an "invisible and ubiquitous" presence, opposite the young actress Myriem Roussel, with whom he was infatuated. When he ran into resistance from Roussel, who was wary of the ticklish material he was coming up with, he looked for a more sensitive way of approaching the subject of forbidden desire. For a while he considered a story about Sigmund Freud and the early patient known as Dora, he said later. "Then, I looked at it with regard to God the Father. And I came upon the story of Mary."[16] He also came upon Dolto's work, or at least one corner of it.

---

[12] Sherry Turkle, "Tough Love: An Introduction to Françoise Dolto's When Parents Separate," PsicoMundo (1995). Emphasis in original.

[13] Élisabeth Roudinesco, "Françoise Marette Dolto," in Lawrence D. Kritzman, ed., *The Columbia History of Twentieth-Century French Thought* (Columbia, 2005), 508.

[14] Turkle, "Tough Love," n.p.

[15] Françoise Dolto and Gérard Séverin, *L'Évangile au risque de la psychoanalyse* (Paris: Éditions universitaires Jean-Pierre Delarge, 1977). Published in English as *The Jesus of Psychoanalysis: A Freudian Interpretation of the Gospel*, trans. Helen R. Lane (Doubleday, 1979).

[16] Richard Brody, *Everything Is Cinema: The Working Life of Jean-Luc Godard* (Metropolitan, 2008), 457-458.

I don't mean to suggest that Dolto's psychoanalytical work exercised no influence whatever on the evolution of *Hail Mary*. Godard was sufficiently interested in *L'Évangile au risque de la psychoanalyse*, or at least the introduction, to mention it in interviews about the film; a few of its phrases appear in the dialogue; and certain of its ideas are detectable within the movie's intellectual and affective matrices. But while Godard's limited Dolto reading influenced the early stages of his script, the finished film reflects little of her thought. (This isn't surprising. I find her book a naïve and superficial work marked by essentialism, nebulous language, and biblical hermeneutics that turn into flights of self-indulgent fantasy.) In sum, it is as clear as matters can be with a Godard film that *Hail Mary* was influenced very little by psychoanalytical ideas. On this score the authors of *Anti-Oedipus* can rest content.

...and ...and ...and...

Deleuze and Guattari state that the infinite series "and... and... and..." is the very fabric of the rhizome.[20] The additive is a concept long embraced by Godard, whose films and videos continually strive to erase boundaries and celebrate the productivity of paradox.[21] An endless "...and... and ...and..." would be the perfect subtitle for his oeuvre. One of Godard's closest affinities with Deleuzian thought lies in his insistence on a radically *intuitive* cinema that opens lines of escape *from* linearity, rationality, and organicity and *toward* the open-ended natural-historical-social multiplicities of the transcendental unconscious. This is the non-metaphysical unconscious that Deleuze and Guattari describe as

> material rather than ideological; schizophrenic rather than Oedipal; nonfigurative rather than imaginary; real rather than symbolic; machinic rather than structural—an unconscious, finally, that is molecular, microphysical, and micrological rather than molar or gregarious; productive rather than expressive.[22]

The transcendental unconscious radiates automatic desire, and the subject attached to its desiring-machines has "no fixed identity"

---

[20] Deleuze and Guattari, *Thousand Plateaus*, 25.
[21] For more discussion see David Sterritt, *The Films of Jean-Luc Godard: Seeing the Invisible* (Cambridge, 1993), 14, 141, 262.
[22] Deleuze and Guattari, *Anti-Oedipus*, 109-110.

but is "forever decentered, *defined* by the states through which it passes."[23] Although he does not use schizoanalytic language, Godard approaches the unconscious as the schizoanalysts do, not as a site for archeology (the psychoanalytic task) but as a plane of immanence that forever pulsates with positive desire, which can either be diverted into static *being* or liberated into boundless *becoming*. The idiosyncrasies, eccentricities, excesses, and paradoxes of his films are products of his instinctive urge to create a destabilized and destabilizing cinema that seeks to purge the sociopolitical unconscious of entrenched habits and beliefs. *Hail Mary* envisions a virtual, intensive realm, showing Mary's desiring-becomings as lines of flight toward the nonhuman sexualities of impregnation by spirit and production of intermingling Word and flesh, and Joseph's as matters of the social field, of the codings and stratifications that are flummoxed and then vanquished by his intimacy with Mary's deterritorializing flows. At the end of the film both characters are again enmeshed in quotidian reality, and the addition of their child to the household (…and …and …and…) indicates, as does Gabriel's valedictory appearance to Mary, that they are newly defined by the states through which their decentered becoming-souls have passed and are continuing to pass.

"Just as in the New Testament," critical theorist John E. Drabinski observes, "Godard's Mary is uniquely chosen to make a home *with* God in a world from which the true God has fallen away,[24] reconnecting by way of his soon-to-be son… The virginal space of Mary… extends to her a social economy in which she is an uncanny presence."[25] This is an important point, and all the more so because the uncanny in Godard, and in Deleuze, has been regrettably undertheorized to date. Exploring it is outside the scope of this essay, but I'll append two statements that I find illuminating in this regard. The first is Martin Heidegger's remark in *Being and Time* that "uncanniness pursues Da-sein and threatens its self-forgetful lostness."[26] The second comes from Robert Mugerauer's gloss of Heidegger's point: "[T]he uncanny is liberating for us

---

[23] Ibid., 20. Emphasis in original.
[24] Recall a remark made by Fritz Lang, playing himself, in Godard's film *Contempt* (*Le Mépris*, 1963): "Now it's no longer the presence of God, but the absence of God, that reassures man."
[25] John E. Drabinski, *Godard Between Identity and Difference* (Continuum, 2008), 91-92.
[26] Martin Heidegger, *Being and Time*, trans. Joan Stambaugh (State University of New York, 1996), 277.

because in it and through it we can be called to and find a way to recover what has gone missing, to come back into what is our own and to find a new ground in place of the groundlessness of the they."[27] This is the ground that Mary and Joseph are recovering at the end *Hail Mary*, and that their uncanny child is discovering in ways that are radically inflected by his uncanniness. "The big error, the only error," Deleuze has said, "would be to believe that a line of flight consists of fleeing life; a flight into the imaginary, or into art. But to flee [fly] on the contrary, is to produce the real, to create life, to find a weapon."[28] This is exactly what Mary and Joseph have done, and what their child will continue to do. As his counterpart in the Bible says, "Think not that I am come to send peace on earth: I came not to send peace, but a sword."[29] A weapon.

A Euclidean postulate

> There was a certain democracy in those great Protestant families that I come from and that left me the time to find, by myself, that in fact it is not the body that has a soul. And I found that line in Artaud, in which, by a simple play on words, he posits, like a theorem, a Euclidean postulate: "I want the soul to be body, so they won't be able to say that the body is soul, because it will be the soul which is body." —Jean-Luc Godard[30]

Turning to the above-quoted statement by Deleuze that subjectivity "is never ours, it is time, that is, the soul or the spirit, the virtual," and bearing in mind Deleuze's high regard for Godard, who explicitly addresses questions of soul in *Hail Mary*, we may ask whether the two film-philosophers have the same sort of thing in mind when "soul" comes into their discourse. Clearly neither is referring to conventional beliefs of traditional religions. "I'm not a religious person, but I'm a faithful person," Godard has said. "I believe in images."[31] Although the positions of Deleuze and Guat-

---

[27] Robert Mugerauer, *Heidegger and Homecoming: The Leitmotif in the Later Writings* (Toronto: University of Toronto Press, 2008), 42.

[28] Gilles Deleuze and Claire Parnet, *Dialogues II*, trans. Hugh Tomlinson and Barbara Habberjam with Eliot Ross Albert, second edition (Columbia, 2002), 49.

[29] Matthew 10:34, Authorized King James Version.

[30] "Godard/Sollers," 124.

[31] Quoted in Sally Shafto, program note for *Religion and Cinema: A Con-*

tari vis-à-vis the spiritual are complex, an indication of their attitude toward theology can be gleaned from their statement in *What
Is Philosophy?* that atheism "is not a drama but the philosopher's
serenity and philosophy's achievement. There is always an atheism
to be extracted from a religion."[32] One can take this as an affirmation
of philosophy's mission to demonstrate the emptiness of religion and
the fallaciousness of religious faith, but on this level it is uncharacter-
istically reductive, oversimplifying the philosophers' own contention
that every discipline necessarily interacts (as Jacques Derrida would
obviously insist) with its own negation; philosophy itself, they argue,
"needs a nonphilosophy that comprehends it... just as art needs
nonart and science needs nonscience."[33] More interestingly, one can
take it as an extension and expansion of Deleuze's earlier statement
in *Difference and Repetition* that philosophers have "too often been
invited to judge the atheist from the viewpoint of the belief or the
faith that we suppose still drives him — in short, from the viewpoint
of grace; not to be tempted by the inverse operation — to judge the
believer by the violent atheist by which he is inhabited, the Antichrist
eternally given 'once and for all' within grace."[34]

Deleuze yields to that temptation in a discussion of the
"adventure of faith," which would be a good alternate title for *Hail
Mary*. The believer who engages in this adventure has a dual identity, Deleuze asserts: on one hand, the seeker is a "tragic sinner"
bereft of grace, and on the other, the seeker is what Søren Kierkegaard would call a "comedian and clown" in contact with the paradoxical absurd. In a process supercharged with cosmic humor and
towering irony, Deleuze continues, the believer conducts a quest
for "a self rediscovered and a god recovered," failing to understand that Friedrich Nietzsche finessed those naïve ideals with
the teaching of the eternal return, which is not a faith, doctrine,
or belief, but rather "the truth of faith... the simulacrum of every
doctrine... the parody of every belief."[35]

---

ference, Princeton University, 2001.

[32] Gilles Deleuze and Félix Guattari, *What Is Philosophy?*, trans. Hugh
Tomlinson and Graham Burchell (Columbia, 1994), 92.

[33] Deleuze and Guattari, *What Is Philosophy?*, 218. Quoted in Patricia Pisters, The Neuro-Image: A Deleuzian Film-Philosophy of Digital Screen
Culture (Stanford, 2012), 14.

[34] Gilles Deleuze, *Difference and Repetition*, trans. Paul Patton (Columbia,
1993), 96.

[35] Deleuze, *Difference and Repetition*, 95-96.

Truths, simulacra, and parodies are complicated articles, however, bearing kinship with the nomadic, the minoritarian, and the powers of the false; and it is none other than Nietzsche, according to Deleuze, "who, under the 'will to power,' substitutes the power of the false for the form of the true," thereby resolving "the crisis of truth… in favor of the false and its artistic, creative power."[36] By replacing the escape into theology with the embrace of the eternal return and its tantalizingly ambiguous "belief and… doctrine eternally yet to come,"[37] Deleuze negates the counterfeit claims of religion while affirming the unbounded becoming held forth by infinite recursions of molecular vibration over the course of sempiternal time.

Sensation

Art responds to vibrations along the plane of immanence, the Deleuzian scholar Patricia Pisters reminds us, by contracting them to humanly accessible tempos; the results are what we call sensation, an intensity of material elements preserving the fullness of duration in modes of "quality" and "variety" that extend to every form of life, actual and virtual, organic and inorganic. "In this vitalistic conception of spirituality," Pisters writes, "when speaking of the soul or force of life that art can make us feel, the cosmic universe is full of microbrains that are constantly moving, acting and reacting, but that in sensations find a moment of pause, where all options are still open."[38] Decisions among the options must be made, and in this "spiritual choice," the alternatives are "not between terms (such as *good* or *bad*) but between modes of existence of the one who chooses." Making the "true spiritual choice" is a matter of faith, since one must choose whether to believe that one has choices in life or to believe that one has not. At stake here is faith in one's connection with the world, and the issue is a crucial one because so many in the modern world no longer try to find, work to forge, or manage to sustain faith in that connection. "This link must become an object of belief," Deleuze maintains: "it is the impossible which can only be restored with a faith… Only belief in the world can reconnect man to what he sees and hears." And seeing and hearing is where movies come in. "The cinema must film, not the world, but belief in this world… Whether we are Christians or atheists, in our universal schizophrenia, we need reasons to believe

---

[36] Deleuze, *Cinema 2*, 131.

[37] Deleuze, *Difference and Repetition*, 96.

[38] Pisters, Neuro-Image, 32, 154.

in this world."[39] Hence the need, Pisters adds, to explore not only illusions of reality but the reality of illusions as well.

The reality of illusions is a core concern of *Hail Mary*, which bodies forth cinematic intuitions of Mary's sensations, transmuting them into the artwork that is the character's (virtual) life and the artwork that is Godard's (actual) film. Like every film, it is a simulacrum of all that it depicts, and it is also a parody (in the musicological sense) of certain strains within the centuries-long history of Marian iconography.[40] Beholding it with receptive senses and responsive mind can bestow an aesthetic joy that feels very much like grace, and if an Antichrist lurks within this experience, it is less a glowering demon than an imp of the perverse, a metaphysical counterpart of the comedian and clown that dwells within Godard and inflects all of his movies.

Enter the body without organs

The essential point is that Godard and Deleuze and Guattari bring soul, spirit, and related terms into play when it suits their purposes, and this can't be written off as careless terminology. Godard has stated that while he doesn't practice the Protestant religiosity which with he was raised, he is "very interested" in aspects of Roman Catholic thought.[41] And no philosopher exercised a stronger influence on Deleuze than Henri Bergson, whose metaphysics of body, mind, and soul—of *corps, esprit,* and *âme*—leads him to say that, "giving the name of Idea to a certain *settling down into easy intelligibility,* and that of Soul to a certain *longing after the restlessness of life...* an invisible current causes modern philosophy to place the Soul above the Idea."[42] Some thirty years later he declares that if we are able to get beyond the brain's restrictive function of attentiveness to the instrumental and extensive, "there enters in something of a 'without' which may be a 'beyond.'... Suppose that a gleam from this unknown world reaches us... Joy indeed would be that simplicity of life diffused through the world by an ever-spreading mystic intuition."[43]

---

[39] Deleuze, *Cinema 1*, 114, 116. Quoted in Pisters, 32.

[40] For more on this, especially the tradition of Madonna lactans, see Sterritt, *The Films of Jean-Luc Godard*, 187.

[41] Shafto, program note, n.p.

[42] Henri Bergson, *An Introduction to Metaphysics*, trans. T. E. Hulme (Palgrave-Macmillan, 2007), 46-47. Emphases in original.

[43] Henri Bergson, *The Two Sources of Morality and Religion*, trans. R. Ashley Audra and Cloudesley Brereton with W. Horsfall Carter (Notre Dame,

These are not theistic statements, nor would it make sense to tie Deleuze or Guattari to them. What does make sense, I think, is to detect a connection between Bergson's conception of soul and the notion of the body without organs. Deleuze and Guattari discovered the BwO in Antonin Artaud's extraordinary 1947 radio play *To Have Done with the Judgment of God*, which concludes thus:

> Man is sick because he is badly constructed.
> We must make up our minds to strip him bare in order to
>   scrape off that animalcule that itches him mortally,
>
>> god,
>> and with god
>> his organs.
>
> For you can tie me up if you wish,
> but there is nothing more useless than an organ.
>
> When you will have made him a body without organs,
> then you will have delivered him from all his automatic
>   reactions
> and restored him to his true freedom.
>
> Then you will teach him again to dance wrong side out
> as in the frenzy of dance halls
> and this wrong side out will be his real place.[44]

Deleuze and Guattari limn the body without organs as the antithesis of the theological body whose unyielding organ-ization, imposed by God, is always already stopping up fluxes, draining off flows, squashing intensities, and blocking becomings at every pass. "[T]he system of the judgment of God," Deleuze and Guattari assert, "the theological system, is precisely the operation of He who makes an organism... because He cannot bear the BwO, because He pursues it and rips it apart so He can be first, and have the organism be first." The organism is "a phenomenon of accumulation, coagulation, and sedimentation" that strangles the BwO

1977), 315-317.

[44] Antonin Artaud, "To Have Done with the Judgment of God," in *Antonin Artaud: Selected Writings*, ed. Susan Sontag, trans. Helen Weaver. (California, 1976), 553-571, cited at 571.

with "forms, functions, bonds, dominant and hierarchized orga-nizations, organized transcendences."[45] The body without organs is a fundamental trope of schizoanalysis, and it has strong links to schizo-cinema. Films that connect the BwO with the view-er-screen assemblage can open up the latter (i.e., us) to becoming by engulfing us with affect that, as Anna Powell puts it, "under-mines spatial and temporal orientation and unravels symbolic hier-archies... Slumped in our cinema seat, or in front of the domestic screen, our customary mind/body maps become fluid and percep-tive BwOs."[46]

The body without organs is related to the theory of thought that Deleuze and Guattari encapsulate in *What Is Philosophy?* when they present a tripartite schema of disciplines and their productions—philosophy/concepts, art/affects, science/functives —whose criss-crossing interactions culminate at points where "[e]ach created element on a plane calls on other heterogeneous elements, which are still to be created on other planes: thought as *heterogenesis*."[47] This is a discursive way of expressing the concept of *chaosmos*, a portmanteau word borrowed originally from James Joyce and referring to the interchangeability of *cosmos* and *chaos*, order and disorder. The body without organs is surely a chaosmic being—a concatenation of plateaus, a "component of passage" that is "always swinging between the surfaces that stratify it and the plane that sets it free." It is "that which one desires and by which one desires." It is "nonstratified, unformed, intense matter, the matrix of intensity, intensity = 0; but there is nothing negative about that zero."[48] It is "the body without an image," on which "the proportions of attraction and repulsion... produce, starting from zero, a series of states in the celibate machine; and the subject is born of each state in the series, is continually reborn of the following state... consuming-consummating all these states that cause him to be born and reborn." And it is the "intense... tantric egg."[49]

---

[45] Deleuze and Guattari, *Thousand Plateaus*, 158-159. Emphasis in orig-inal.

[46] Anna Powell, "Off Your Face: Schizoanalysis, Faciality and Film," in Ian Buchanan and Patricia MacCormack, eds., *Deleuze and the Schizoanalysis of Cinema* (Continuum, 2008), 116-129, cited at 123.

[47] Deleuze and Guattari, *What Is Philosophy?*, 199. Emphasis in original.

[48] Deleuze and Guattari, *Thousand Plateaus*, 161, 175, 165, 153.

[49] Deleuze and Guattari, *Anti-Oedipus*, 8, 20; Thousand Plateaus, 153.

It is also a hazy, mysterious presence in *Hail Mary*, evoked in subtle ways that are all the more striking by virtue of the fortuitous nature of their congruity with schizoanalytic discourse. Perhaps it's the tantric egg, "the full egg before... the organization of the organs," that closes *The Book of Mary* and opens the chaosmos of Godard's film, in which Mary's indiscernible ovum plays a pivotal role. (Deleuze and Guattari: "There is a fundamental convergence between... the biological egg and the psychic or cosmic egg.") Maybe the non-negative zero is what we see in the 10 on Mary's basketball jersey, or maybe it's what we hear when Gabriel accosts Joseph with the words, "What's the common denominator between zero and Mary? Mary's body!" (Maybe we also sense it when he calls Joseph an "Asshole!") More substantially, it is surely the body without organs that pulses within the deterritorialized flows of soul-body-becoming when Mary endures a night of solitary schizo-orison before the birth of her child, wracked with delirium as her soul and body pass through the molecular deaths and micrological births of dis-organized desiring-machinic parturition. The schizoanalysts use Artaud's vision to exemplify a "destratified, decoded, deterritorialized" body, consisting exclusively of "connection of desires, conjunction of flows, continuum of intensities"[50] that escape the judgment of God across and upon the plane of immanence. Godard uses it to crystallize a cinema of frameless images, of immaculate signs, of the "process of making nature possible," and of the univocity of metaphor and actuality.[51] "Reason is always a region," Deleuze declares, "carved out of the irrational—not sheltered from the irrational at all, but traversed by it and always defined by a particular kind of relationship among irrational factors. Underneath all reason lies delirium, and drift."[52] Like him, Godard sees delirium and drift as entirely positive qualities that proffer our best hope for freeing our machinic flows from stifling cultural categories and liberating them into torrents of untrammeled love and productive desire.

---

[50] Deleuze and Guattari, *Thousand Plateaus*, 153, 164, 40, 161.

[51] Katherine Dieckmann, "Godard in His Fifth Period," in David Sterritt, ed., *Jean-Luc Godard: Interviews* (Mississippi, 1998), 167-174, cited at 170-171.

[52] Gilles Deleuze, "On Capitalism and Desire," in Gilles Deleuze, *Desert Islands and Other Texts: 1953-1974*, ed. David Lapoujade, trans. Michael Taormina (Semiotext[e], 2004), 262-273, cited at 262.

Conceptual personae

The particularities of style in *Je vous salue, Marie* are of course crucial in conveying the affects and ideas that Godard has on his mind. One of his starting points for the film was his wish to juxtapose "Catholic images and Protestant music,"[53] not as harmonious consorts but as contrapuntal elements in dialogue with each other and with the movie's larger deterritorializing objectives. "I knew that the only music that would work would be Bach," he said in 1985. "And it couldn't have been Beethoven, or Mozart, because historically Bach was the music of Martin Luther. And... Luther was attacking the Catholic church, specifically the way the church makes images."[54] Expanding on the theme of Bach's uniqueness, critic Charles Warren writes that the composer's music evokes "a grasp of the things of the universe in their essentials and essential relations, and as they may, on principle, be recombined... Bach is thus in accord not so much with law as with an unaccountable, personlike spirit at the heart of things."[55] Warren makes no mention of Deleuze or Guattari, but the "spirit" he alludes to sounds very like what they call the *conceptual persona*, the "something else, somewhat mysterious, that appears from time to time or that shows through and seems to have a hazy existence halfway between concept and preconceptual plane, passing from one to the other."[56] The sound and spirit of Bach in *Hail Mary* serve wonderfully as conceptual personae, as "fluctuating figures who... express qualities or perspectives that want to become-other, to deterritorialize towards another plane by constructing its concepts," in theorist D. N. Rodowick's words.[57]

Similar things can be said about the painterly impulses in *Hail Mary*. Filmmaking is "like painting," Godard told me in 1994, "but it's also different from painting, because you use not just

---

[53] Giuseppina Marin, interview with Godard in *Corriere della Sera* (April 25, 1985), quoted in David Sterritt, "Miéville and Godard: From Psychology to Spirit," in Locke and Warren, *Jean-Luc Godard's Hail Mary*, 54-60, cited at 55.

[54] Dieckmann, "Godard in His Fifth Period," 171.

[55] Charles Warren, "Whim, God, and the Screen," in Locke and Warren, *Jean-Luc Godard's Hail Mary*, 10-26, cited at 14-15.

[56] Deleuze and Guattari, *What Is Philosophy?*, 61.

[57] D. N. Rodowick, "Unthinkable Sex: Conceptual Personae and the Time-Image." *Invisible Culture* 3 (2000).

space but time."[58] Film scholar Sally Shafto points out that Godard has often presented himself as a cinematic painter, playing down the collaborative nature of filmmaking and thereby promoting the filmmaker's work as a "solitary and divine creative act." The painterly aspects of *Hail Mary* also mirror his respect for Renaissance Catholicism, which responded to Luther's faith in words by reaffirming the power of images; this inspired Godard's remark that Luther reformed not only the church but also the audiovisual domain. God has long been an alter ego for Godard, according to Shafto, who argues that he likes to see himself as a "distant as well as omniscient and omnipotent creator." Hence the special vitality of light in Godard's aesthetic, serving not only as the material ground of cinema but also as a symbol of and metaphor for the divine.[59]

Turning to the all-important subject of montage, *Hail Mary* may be Godard's most far-reaching essay in the irrational cut. Destabilizing edits occur constantly, and their disorienting effects are often intensified by unorthodox camera placements that blur conventional notions of foreground and background. The primary narrative, centering on Mary and Joseph, is intercut with subplots — Joseph's strained relationship with his former girlfriend Juliette, a Professor's relationship with a student named Eva — in such jaggedly interstitial ways that newcomers to the film often have trouble sorting out what's going on, much less sounding its deeper dimensions. These devices turn *Hail Mary* into a *planar* filmic entity, a mercurially shifting surface that eschews empirical logic and psychological depth, instead folding narration back upon itself through *faux raccord* cuts and radical relinkages that transform the arboreal protocols of narrative thrust, linear montage, figural representation, and naturalized mise-en-scène into a rhizomatic assemblage of ontological conundrums and epistemological ruckuses.

---

[58] David Sterritt, "Ideas, Not Plots, Inspire Jean-Luc Godard," in David Sterritt, ed., *Jean-Luc Godard: Interviews* (Mississippi, 1998), 175-178, cited at 177.

[59] Sally Shafto, "Artist as Christ/Artist as God-the-Father: Religion in the Cinema of Philippe Garrel and Jean-Luc Godard." *Film History* 14 (2002): 142-157, cited at 144, 145.

Sublimity

> [A] creator who isn't grabbed around the throat by a set
> of impossibilities is no creator." — Gilles Deleuze[60]

The issues I've raised and the examples I've adduced are far from
exhaustive; but I think they give a reasonable overview of the territory, so that we can now consider a central question: is it is justi-
fiable to claim that *soul* has connotations for the Godard of *Hail
Mary* and the Deleuze of schizoanalysis that go beyond the nega-
tional, skeptical, and metaphorical meanings often encountered in
materialist philosophy and art? I think the answer is yes, with the
obvious caveat that the soul of which I speak has nothing to do
with that of religious orthodoxy. In the essay "Nietzsche and Saint
Paul, Lawrence and John of Patmos," which appears in Deleuze's
last published book, he writes, "The soul as the life of flows is the
will to live, struggle and combat."[61] This idea and its ramifications
may not equal the visionary intuitions of a Saint Paul or a John
of Patmos, but Deleuze's reference to soul (not the only one in
this essay) reinforces the impression that his thinking has drawn
close to theological terrain, and may perhaps have entered it. If
this conclusion seems to go against the Deleuzian grain, the reason
might have more to do with modernist intellectual biases than with
the actual trajectory of the philosopher who said in 1980 that

> if philosophers have spoken to us so much of God — and
> they could well be Christians or believers — this hasn't
> been lacking an intense sense of jest. It wasn't an incred-
> ulous jesting, but a joy arising from the labour they were
> involved with... God and the theme of God offered
> the irreplaceable opportunity for philosophy to free...
> concepts... from the constraints that had been imposed
> on them.[62]

---

[60] Gilles Deleuze, *Negotiations, 1972-1990*, trans. Martin Joughin (Columbia, 1995), 133.

[61] Gilles Deleuze, *Essays Critical and Clinical*, trans. Daniel W. Smith and
Michael A. Greco (London: Verso, 1998), 36-52, cited at 52. Mary Bryden
compares different versions of this essay in "Nietzsche's Arrow: Deleuze
on D. H. Lawrence's Apocalypse, in Mary Bryden, ed., *Deleuze and Religion* (Routledge, 2001), 101-114, cited at 111.

[62] Gilles Deleuze, Seminar on Spinoza, 25 November 1980, trans. Timothy
S. Murphy. Quoted in Philip Goodchild, "Why is philosophy so compromised with God?" in Bryden, *Deleuze and Religion*, 156-166, cited at 156.

Deleuze may be jesting as well, but if that's so, the jest has the richly positive aura of which he speaks; if "atheism is the artistic power at work on religion," as he said in the same discussion, he has at times been a highly creative artist in this field. Godard jests a good deal in *Hail Mary* as well—at times Gabriel is almost a slapstick character—and as a comedian and clown of the paradoxical absurd, he does so in the same affirmative spirit. He too has known the elation of freeing concepts from the preconceptions and prejudices that have so long blocked off their flows of infinite becoming.

Some critics group *Hail Mary* with its immediate predecessors, *Passion* (1982) and *First Name: Carmen* (*Prénom Carmen*, 1983), as a "trilogy of the sublime;"[63] the sublimity of *Hail Mary* takes its most vivid form in exquisite nature imagery. Godard's growing fascination with sights and sounds of nature indicates a wish to bypass his individual ego so as to produce "virgin" percepts and affects in his films. (Deleuze: "The inalienable part of the soul appears when one has ceased to be an ego."[64]) The immersion of *Hail Mary* in the natural world extends to its lyric celebration of Mary's virgin body as a sublime substance, revealing Godard's urge to approach the spiritual not through *transcendence* of the physical but through a passionate *awareness* of materiality; this in turn reveals the ongoing influence of Godard's early mentor and teacher André Bazin, a devout Catholic who regarded cinema as the most privileged means of recording the glory of the physical world and thereby unveiling materiality as not the *representation* but the *embodiment* and *incarnation* of the holy spirit. Godard's nature images exploit the retinal reality-effects of cinema while simultaneously segmenting, fragmenting, and collaging those effects into a mosaic of discontinuous surfaces, aiming to penetrate the hard shell of material reality (perhaps as Miéville's young Mary shatters her enigmatic egg) and gain some glimmering of *invisible* realities beyond. Along with this eloquent fracturing of space comes a profound reconfiguring of time, within scenes and among them, transforming chronological-extensive time into durational-intensive time—the time of the Deleuzian crystal-image, "the indivisible unity of an actual image and 'its' virtual image," which uncovers "the hidden ground of time," the double flow of "presents which pass and… pasts which are preserved." By merging our

---

[63] See for example Marc Cerisuelo, "La Trilogie du sublime," in *Jean-Luc Godard* (Paris: Quatres-vents, 1989), 207-232.
[64] Deleuze, "Nietzsche and Saint Paul," 52.

spectatorial brains with the "peaks of present and sheets of past" on the crystalline screen, we find that memory, the virtual, "is not in us; it is we who move in a Being-memory, world-memory."[65] Absorbing this counterintuitive lesson is exactly as difficult (or easy) for us as it is for Mary to realize that the soul has a body, not the other way around.

Into the chaosmos

Another character in *Hail Mary* who strikingly manifests the Godardian-Deleuzian ethos is one I briefly touched on earlier: the Professor, an unnamed academic from Czechoslovakia who is having an affair with a student named Eva and working out a kind of chaosmic philosophy. We first meet him in a classroom, where he is explaining his theory that life on Earth could not have originated through random chemical reactions. He points to a scientific chart, showing a slender horizontal line bisecting a red bulge at the center, and says it "can only be explained by something… intercepting light at a specific wavelength." For him, this establishes the presumption that what we know as life originated "in space" and that we are extraterrestrials as much as we are Earthlings, perhaps even more so. "The astonishing truth," he continues, "is that life was willed, desired, anticipated, organized, programmed by a determined intelligence." He demonstrates this thesis by having a student named Pascal work a Rubik's Cube while Eva covers his eyes and verbally guides his choices. To solve the cube blindfolded would take 1.35 trillion years, the Professor says, but one move per second guided by the eyes and mind can do the job in two minutes.

There is nothing very impressive about the Professor's notions, which have the hollow ring of Erich von Däniken and "intelligent design" pseudoscience. Godard is not vicariously pitching theories, however. He is schizoanalyzing theory, not using schizo terminology but performing schizo operations, such as transforming commonsense instances of either/or reasoning—the Earth/space binary, the us/them duality, the difference between 1.35 trillion years and two minutes—into assemblages marked by rhizomatic intensity *and* radical multiplicity *and* indiscernible difference *and* crystalline consistency, mapping escape trajectories of the body without organs in all its deterritorializing virtuality. By saying we were born in the heavens, which could include Heaven itself, the Professor and Godard take us along lines of flight that

---

[65] Deleuze, *Cinema 2*, 78, 98.

are incomprehensible to the soul-as-body but radiantly clear to the body-as-soul.

Mary is swept by this clarity at the end of her transformative night of spiritual suffering; but as prelude to this outcome her organ-ized theological body must be therapeutically twisted, distorted, and wrenched way from the desiring-machines that have enchained her to the ordinary human sphere. We perceive traces of her becoming-soul in the words of her interior monologue, which zigzags rhizomatically between negative and positive poles:

> Earth and sex are in us. Outside there are only stars. Wanting isn't expanding by force. It's recoiling into oneself from level to level, for eternity. You don't need a mouthhole to eat with and an asshole to swallow infinity. Your ass must go in your head, and so descend to ass level, then go left or right to rise higher... I'm a woman, though I don't beget my man through my cunt.

And then suddenly, luminously, "I am not resigned. Resignation is sad. How can one be resigned to God's will? Are we resigned to being loved? This seemed clear to me. Too clear." And a bit later, after her child's birth, "How did He look? What was He like? There are no looks in love, no outward seeming. No likeness. Only our hearts will tremble in the light." Only now, and in the film's final scene, does Mary realize the promise she intuited at the beginning: "I wondered if some event would happen in my life. I've had only the shadow of love... in fact, the shadow of a shadow, like the reflection of a water-lily in a pond, not quiet, but shaken by ripples in the water, so that even the reflection is not yours..."[66]

The supreme act of philosophy, Deleuze and Guattari write, is "not so much to think THE plane of immanence as to show that it is there, unthought in every plane, and to think it in this way as the outside and inside of thought, as... that which cannot be thought

---

[66] Jacques Derrida cites Kierkegaard's biblical allusion to "your father who sees in secret" (Matthew 6:18, English Standard Version) in connection with three modes of invisibility that Derrida has outlined: "the invisible as concealed visible, the encrypted visible or the non-visible as that which is other than visible." For me, Mary's plainspoken "No likeness," like the phrase from Matthew, "echoes across the reach of these limits." See Jacques Derrida, *The Gift of Death*, trans. David Wills (Chicago, 1995), 90-91.

and yet must be thought." [67] Accordingly, the challenge each of us confronts is to discover, in Rodowick's words, the "thinker within me that is the unthought of my thought [and] is... the power to transform life by revealing new lines of variation in our current ways of thinking and modes of existence."[68] Godard comes amazingly close to visualizing this insight at the end of *Hail Mary*, when Mary hears Gabriel's last greeting ("Nothing. Hail, Mary!") and then gets into her car and lights a cigarette. She is simply having a smoke, like countless characters in countless New Wave movies; but sometimes a cigarette is not just a cigarette. Its smoke blurs the borderlines between inner (body) and outer (world) as it transubstantiates an ordinary herb into a vaporous essence, subliminally dis-organizing Mary's self in an act of *inspiration* that is both literal and metaphorical. She then draws a lipstick tube toward her mouth, almost as if she were testing the Professor's theories with her own tiny spaceship; and indeed, the Professor's diagram closely resembled the inverse of this image, a closed mouth with puckered lips. After a tentative touch or two she begins to apply the lipstick, and the film ends on an extreme close-up of Mary's open mouth, so large that parts of it don't fit within the frame, ringed by her red lips but dominated by the dark emptiness at its center.

One valid Deleuzian interpretation of this shot would lead in negative directions: we are looking at a black hole, the part of the white wall/black hole facial system wherein the latter element, modeled after light-trapping singularities in space, is a territorializing blockage, the upshot of a failed line of flight.[69] We may also interpret it in positive terms, however—as an instance of what Deleuze calls the "gaseous image, beyond the solid and the liquid," which seeks (like drugs) to *"stop the world"* and *"make one see the molecular intervals*, the holes in sound, in forms, and even in water" and to *"make lines of speed pass through* these holes in the world."[70] Or we can take it as film scholar Kevin Z. Moore does when he finds it the emblem of the 'virginal source" of Mary's power, to wit, her "belief in the body as an aspect of mind," the

---

[67] Deleuze and Guattari, *What Is Philosophy?*, 59-60. Emphasis in original.
[68] D. N. Rodowick, *Gilles Deleuze's Time Machine* (Duke, 1997), 200-201.
[69] Ronald Bogue, *Deleuze on Music, Painting, and the Arts* (Routledge, 2003), 89.
[70] Gilles Deleuze, *Cinema 1: The Movement-Image*, trans. Hugh Tomlinson and Barbara Habberjam (Minnesota, 1986), 64, 85. Emphases in original.

effects of which we can observe in physical action but can *see* only as "the black hole outlined by the film."[71]

I incline toward the second and third options, but I think a more productive, liberating, and intensive way of fathoming this quintessentially mysterious image leads beyond the realm of mystery to that of mysticism. Although this subject is more explicit in Bergson than in Deleuze, its resonances with Deleuzian film theory are articulately brought out by cultural critic Michael Goddard when he understands mysticism as a set of practices that actualize a "prediscursive seeing and hearing," which opens an ecstatic pathway to and through the crystalline regime of signs. Goddard notes that while hallucinatory and ecstatic experiences can be brought about by schizophrenia, drug consumption, and mystical practices, it is only through the latter that "processes of recollection can maintain and extend their sensory metamorphoses into sustainable processes of subjectivization," formulating time crystals whereby "experience of the unknown, of the virtual, can be reintegrated and redeveloped as spiritual experiences... without sacrificing their singularity." Goddard concludes that "the 'spiritual' or 'spirits'... can be conceived of as virtually inhering in the material world in the form of temporalities, or conversely the material world can be conceived of as existing in the spiritual or in God in the same way that it exists in time. The spiritual and the material are simply two distinct yet indiscernible sides of the same fold." He adds that a truly crystalline cinema must lead back out of the movie theater "into a re-spiritualization of life itself, through the transmission of [the] experience via the crystalline regime of signs to the spectator."[72]

Godard, the faithful filmmaker who believes in images, would surely agree; and so might Mary, who rejoins the quotidian world at the end of her story, bringing with her the knowledge of a singularity—a child, a soul, a thought, a virtuality, a body without organs, an unprecedented upsurge of the élan vital—that promises to deterritorialize the actual in literally inconceivable ways. "At the limit," Deleuze himself observed, "it is the mystic who plays with the whole of creation, who invents an expression of it whose adequacy increases with its dynamism."[73] In this play there

---

[71] Kevin Z. Moore, "Reincarnating the Radical: Godard's Je vous salue, Marie." *Cinema Journal* vol. 34 no. 1 (Autumn 1994): 18-30, cited at 24.

[72] Michael Goddard, "The scattering of time crystals: Deleuze, mysticism and cinema," in Bryden, *Deleuze and Religion*, 53-64, cited at 54-56, 62.

[73] Gilles Deleuze, *Bergsonism*, trans. Hugh Tomlinson and Barbara Hab-

arises the intense sense of jest—of joy—that brave philosophers have found by pursuing thinking toward the becomings-flows of the infinite. If we share this delight it is because, as Deleuze tells us, "the essence of art is a kind of joy, and this is the very point of art. There can be no tragic work because there is a necessary joy in creation: art is necessarily a liberation that explodes everything."[74] Mary too feels the gladness of creating, and never more so than at the end of her tormented night, when she climbs out from under the impenetrable judgment of an inexplicable God and says, softly and simply, "I am joy. I am she who is joy." At such a moment the unthought in thought, for Mary and Godard and perhaps us as well, is tremblingly close to being thought.

berjam (Zone, 1988), 112. Quoted in Ibid., 61-62.

[74] Gilles Deleuze, "Mysticism and Masochism," in *Desert Islands and Other Texts: 1953-1974*, ed. David Lapoujade, trans. Michael Taormina (Semiotext[e], 2004), 131-134, cited at 134.

Haunted by Godard: Welcome Revenants and Lively Ghosts

Quarterly Review of Film and Video 40:6 (2023)

> *I gave this essay as a keynote address to the Second International Conference on Philosophy and Film presented by the Philosophical Society of Macedonia in May 2023. I subsequently tweaked it for publication in QRFV, and I have made a few minimal alterations for the version below. Thanks to Viktor Jovanoski inviting me to the conference and for skillfully facilitating my participation via Zoom.*

Jean-Luc Godard was haunted by cinema. In his early films, he grappled with genres that had long possessed his thinking, as in the romantic melodrama *Contempt*, where ancient literature and a venerable filmmaker represent the tenacious shades of traditional narrative whose confines he was eager to escape. The haunting takes a theological form in *Hail Mary*, where engagements with the soul and the divine manifest his quasi-spiritual faith in painterly and cinematic images. And in his magnum opus *Histoire(s) du cinema* he conjures up cinema's ghostly lineage by means of images translated from the crisp materiality of film to the ectoplasmic pliancy of video. These three masterpieces support my proposition that *hauntology* is an admirable tool for illuminating Godard's body of work.

As posited by Jacques Derrida, hauntology displaces *ontology*, figuring the *specter* as an unfathomable intruder that is, in the words of philosopher Colin Davis, "neither present nor absent, neither dead nor alive," a state resembling cinema's dual nature, both immanently present and physically unreachable (Davis 2005, 373). Another sense of the term, developed in psychoanalytic theory, emphasizes the *phantom*, the metaphorical presence of "a dead ancestor in the living Ego, still intent on preventing its traumatic and usually shameful secrets from coming to light," which is pertinent to Godard's fear of an "end of cinema" wrought by capitalist exploitation and political cowardice (Davis 2005, 373). Speculating along similar lines, Fredric Jameson has posited "spectrality" as an awareness "that the living present is scarcely as self-sufficient as it claims to be [and] that we would do well not to count on its density and solidity," another concept applicable to Godard's anxieties about cinema's convoluted past, living present, and threatened future (Jameson 1993, 39). In its revolutionary reworking of film history, Godard's project exemplifies Derrida's idea of "an interpretation that transforms what it interprets" (Derrida 2006, 87).

A major reference point for Derrida's hauntology is Hamlet's complaint that "time is out of joint" (Shakespeare 2012, I:5). It is through temporal displacement, philosopher Liam Sprod contends, that "the past invades, or haunts, the present with its return and in this disjuncture makes possible a new aesthetic that is hauntology," marked by "a return of the ideas, images and ideals of a past age, which now grate and creak against the joints of the present" (Sprod 2012). This suggests an interesting entryway to Godard's filmography, beginning with its earliest titles; these are very different from the pictures he made in later years, but although they are narrative movies with relatively straightforward structures, they offer clear signs that he was already haunted by film history, stalked by the spirits of traditional genres that he set about deconstructing and reconfiguring in what could almost have been a systematically charted program. *Breathless* (*À Bout de souffle*) reshapes the romantic melodrama; *A Woman Is a Woman* (*Une Femme est une femme*) does the same with the musical comedy; *My Life to Live* (*Vivre sa vie*) takes on urban docudrama; *Le Petit soldat* (*The Little Soldier*) is a secret-agent story, *Les Carabiniers* a war picture, *Bande à parte* (*Band of Outsiders*) a gangster film, *Alphaville* (*Alphaville: Une E'trange aventure de Lemmy Caution*) a science-fiction fantasy, *Pierrot le fou* a lovers-on-the-run adventure, and *Weekend*, a road movie, while *Masculin féminin* (*Masculine Feminine*) and *La Chinoise* (*La Chinoise, ou plutôt à la Chinoise: un film en train de se faire*) give absurdist twists to the youth-market trend that swept through cinema in the 1960s era. And so on.

In each case Godard invokes, materializes, and perhaps exorcizes a particular set of spirits from cinema's past. The success of the exorcism is signaled by his willingness and ability to cease operations along these lines at the end of the 1960s, making the break that brought about the esthetic radicalism of *One + One* (*Sympathy for the Devil*) and *Le Gai savoir*, then the political-esthetic radicalism of the Dziga-Vertov Group films, and then the decades-long avant-gardism of pretty much every work he created until *The Image Book* (*Le Livre d'image*) rounded off his career in 2018. Each film and video evinces a hyperreal present haunted by a visionary past, and while his palimpsests take many different forms, from the generic revisionism of the early years to the multifaceted tapestries of *Histoire(s) du cinema* and the three-dimensional kinetics of *Goodbye to Language* (*Adieu au langage*), they always reveal shades of the rekindled past grating and creaking against joints of the inescapable present.

No early film better expresses Godard's fascination with spirits of the departed than his sixth feature, *Contempt*, based on Alberto Moravia's 1954 novel *Il disprezzo*, known as *A Ghost at Noon* in its English translation. This was almost literally a haunted project, created only a few years after Godard's mother died in a Swiss traffic accident, an event that appears to have made a bitter and long-lasting impression on the second-oldest of her four children, then in his middle twenties. I synopsized the film in a 2001 essay:

> *Contempt* centers on Paul Javal, a French screenwriter... who agrees to rewrite the screenplay of an Italian film production based on *The Odyssey* in order to pay for the Rome apartment where he and his wife want to settle down. Paul is troubled by taking a motion-picture assignment, since he sees himself as a serious writer more attuned to high-flown theater than to lowbrow movies. His intellectual side is soothed by the idea of working with legendary German filmmaker Fritz Lang, played in *Contempt* by Lang himself, one of Godard's longtime heroes. But he also has to work with Jerry Prokosch, a Hollywood producer who is less interested in Homeric poetry than in the naked women he gets to ogle when viewing the daily rushes. Jerry is instantly smitten with Paul's wife, Camille, and flirts with her from their first moments together. When he invites the couple for a drink in his villa, Paul unhesitatingly agrees to let Camille ride in Jerry's two-passenger roadster while he finds a taxi for the trip. Camille takes this as a sign of Paul's decreasing commitment to their marriage—she gathers that he is indulging the producer's lust as a way of currying his favor—and begins revealing her own anxieties and insecurities about their future.
>
> The situation grows more complicated as it proceeds, especially when the threesome move to an exotic villa on Capri, where the *Odyssey* production is being filmed. Camille endures and even encourages Jerry's continuing flirtation; Paul shows a casual romantic interest in Jerry's attractive assistant; and Lang maintains a philosophical air while trying to keep his movie on a reasonably high plane despite Jerry's interventions. At one point Paul places a loaded pistol into his pocket, clearly intended for use on

Jerry and/or Camille if her growing contempt for him (hence the film's title) erupts into a full-fledged refutation of their marriage. But fate intervenes before he can fire it, assuming that he could actually have brought himself to do so. Camille leaves Paul for a new life with Jerry; the producer's luxurious Alfa-Romeo is crushed in a crash that kills him and Camille instantly; and Paul prepares for his departure from Capri as Lang films a sweeping seaside shot that concludes *Contempt* on a note of intricately blended lyricism, melancholy, and resignation (Sterritt 2005, 177-8).

Contempt contains a host of ghostly presences, many of them linked to practices of traditional narrative that Godard wrestled with as fiercely as Jacob wrestles with a God-sent adversary in the Book of Genesis, an incident wittily reprised by Godard in *Passion*), the story of a Godard-like filmmaker who can't bring himself to tell a story. The most concrete of these presences is Lang, triply figured as an actor, a character, and an icon of classical cinematic practice whose days as an active director are now behind him. The most abstract of the presences is the spirit of Homeric epic, a template for narrative art of every subsequent millennium. Although the Lang of Germany and Hollywood never essayed an adaptation of Homer, the Lang of *Contempt* has taken on the challenge, as has his money-minded producer, who is evidently thinking of the profits racked up by Italy's long string of Hercules peplums, which were still being cranked out when *Contempt* was released. *Contempt* itself has clear Homeric echoes, frequently mentioning *The Odyssey*, vividly depicting Greek statuary, draping Paul in a sheet resembling a toga, and building to a climax with a jolting *deus ex machina* twist. Although some critics have attacked the latter device as arbitrary and outmoded, it is utterly appropriate in a film that makes continual reference to ancient Greek culture and is profoundly rooted in ideas of fate, destiny, and the mysterious power of godlike figures. Godard does not show the smashup that kills Camille and Jerry, but he does show their corpses in its aftermath, and the tableau is silent and still, a scene of horror rendered paradoxically peaceful by the precision of Godard's mise-en-scène, the gentle motions of Raoul Coutard's camera, and the calming texture of Georges Delerue's music. The *deus* who presides here is *Thanatos*, identified by psychoanalysis as the unconscious drive toward impassivity, stasis, and the death that obviates all sorrows and strivings. This god governs the climax and also haunts the denouement, where Godard and Lang are both shooting their final scenes. Lang's camera is filming a sword-wielding actor and Godard's camera films Lang's camera with the same lateral movement; but then its motion carries beyond the ostensible subject of the shot, leaving behind the human figures and embracing the sunstruck waters of the sea as Lang's assistant, played by Godard, calls out the film's last word, "Silence," recalling another line from *Hamlet*, the prince's own last words: "The rest is silence" (Shakespeare 2012, V:2).

Simultaneously filling the screen with plenitude and emptying it of detail, the sea here becomes a specter in one of Derrida's most interesting senses, representing "what one imagines, what one thinks one sees and which one projects—on an imaginary screen where there is nothing to see" (Derrida 2006, 153). Like the end of Michael Snow's *Wavelength*, the end of *Contempt* shows practically nothing and almost everything, rendering pictorial reality as both visually present and materially ungraspable. The sea presents, like Derrida's specter in Davis' words, "a deconstructive figure hovering between life and death, presence and absence, and making established certainties vacillate" (Davis 2005, 376). Established certainties are among Godard's greatest adversaries, and a chief weapon against them is the dislocation of time. *Contempt* is one of cinema's most striking architectural achievements, moving through a series of visually unique locations, and its ostensibly linear chronology is even more complex, most conspicuously on the three occasions when the narrative is surprisingly interrupted by flurries of flashback or flashforward shots that serve less to flesh out the narrative than to offer moments of rhythmic punctuation and poetic reflection. More broadly, *Contempt* educes a heroically vast time span encompassing the legacies of Homeric epic, the exigencies of classical cinema represented by the real *and* fictional Lang, and the innovations of the Nouvelle Vague in which Godard played a formative role.

Somewhat similar dynamics animate *Hail Mary*, a work haunted not by a small-g god of antiquity but by the capital-G God of Christianity, the religion in which Godard was raised; he has said that although he didn't practice the Protestant religiosity of his family, he became "very interested" in certain areas of Roman Catholic thought, and a starting point for *Hail Mary* was his impulse to place "Catholic images and Protestant music" into contrapuntal dialogue. "I'm not a religious person," he remarked, "but I'm a faithful person. I believe in images" (Shafto 2001). The chief temporal displacement in this film is the transposition of the biblical account of Mary and the Virgin Birth from the New Testament era to modernity, portraying Mary as a young Swiss woman who works in her father's gas station, plays basketball in her spare time, receives the Annunciation when the angel Gabriel arrives by airplane, and has a taxi-driving boyfriend named Joseph who has not slept with her and is understandably nonplussed when she tells him she is pregnant. Here again we find a hauntological aesthetic, a spectral mingling of temporalities in which the world of the present and visitations from the past are impossible to disentangle.

"There are several times of the specter," Derrida writes. "It is a proper characteristic of the specter... that no one can be sure if by returning it testifies to a living past or to a living future. For the *revenant* may already mark the promised return of the specter of living being" (Derrida 2006, 151). In the multidimensional *Hail Mary* the living past is embedded in the living present, and both point toward a living future when the film concludes with a seemingly unmotivated closeup of Mary's mouth. At first the mouth is closed, distantly recalling the shape of a diagram drawn by a professor in an earlier scene, meant to illustrate his theory that earthly life could not have originated through random chemical reactions; the very spuriousness of this notion points away from ordinary logic and toward a conception of science haunted by the mysterious and the mystical. But in the film's last seconds the mouth is open, recalling moments when Mary or another woman has widened her mouth in a gesture of astonishment and delight, the two emotions that constitute the film's ultimately triumphant and fundamentally mystical essence. The cultural critic Michael Goddard describes mysticism as a set of practices that actualize a "prediscursive seeing and hearing," by means of which "the 'spiritual' or 'spirits'... can be conceived of as virtually inhering in the material world in the form of temporalities, or conversely the material world can be conceived of as existing in the spiritual or in God in the same way that it exists in time" (Goddard 2001, 54, 62) *Hail Mary* displaces not only discrete temporalities but the concept of temporality itself; as I have observed elsewhere, this is cinema that breaks the "link between man and the world," in Gilles Deleuze's words, confronting the viewer with "something unthinkable in thought" (Deleuze 1989, 169).[1] This resonates

---

[1] See also Sterritt, " Schizoanalyzing Souls," 384.

powerfully with Davis' discussion of the hauntological specter, whose "secret is a productive opening of meaning rather than a determinate content to be uncovered," much as the secret of the ghost for Derrida is "not a puzzle to be solved" but rather "the structural openness or address directed towards the living by the voices of the past or the not yet formulated possibilities of the future... The ghost pushes at the boundaries of language and thought" (Davis 2005, 377-9). Like established certainties, determinate contents and boundaries of thought are foes Godard never tired of opposing.

   Histoire(s) du cinema, is Godard's most haunted and hauntological work; it doesn't simply allude to the cinematic history that preoccupied his imagination, it resurrects and reconfigures that history through a plethora of favored shots, sequences, and scenes that together constitute a chronologically displaced history of film as well as a stream-of-consciousness record of Godard's drastically intuitive thinking processes. It also demonstrates his view of video possibilities not yet explored; in my 1994 interview with him, he said that "television discovers nothing, even though it could, it should. I think I'm the only one interested in film and video this way—to sometimes make a show, but other times an experimentation" (Sterritt 1998, 177). *Histoire(s) du cinema* shows his double identity as modernist and postmodernist in unfiltered form. In his discussion of Godard's idiosyncratic *Introduction to a True History of Cinema and Television*, critic J. Hoberman notes that the Godard of *Histoire(s) du cinema* is "a quintessential twentieth-century high modernist—the author of an ongoing... project comparable in ambition to *In Search of Lost Time* or *The Cantos*, composed in an idiolect that, as with Joyce or Picasso or Gertrude Stein, effectively reinvented a medium." Yet at the same time, "high modernist is only one way to characterize Godard. As the first filmmaker to fully recognize not only that the classic period of movies was over but also that preexisting movies were a text that he was free to quote, rework and otherwise pillage, he may also be considered cinema's first postmodernist and, despite his disclaimers, a model for postmodernists in other disciplines" (Hoberman 2015). The film scholar Wheeler Winston Dixon captures the flavor of the massive *Histoire(s) du cinema* collage when he states that "all is *simultaneous*, endlessly overlapping, one image and another swirling together to create a hybrid construct which deconstructs... original images and adds something new to them. All is context, history, archival research, and speculation here… Godard is immersed in his images, which become phantoms haunting our combinatory consciousness" (Dixon 1997, 183; emphasis in original).

The artifacts that Hoberman calls "preexisting movies" are more than that, however; they are what Derrida calls *revenants*, the specters hovering ambiguously between a living past and a living future. The same goes for the work's sophisticated sonic elements, which comprise music, ranging from Gustav Mahler and Giacomo Puccini to Leonard Cohen and Rita Hayworth, and "spoken collages," in which Godard's treatment of the human voice as a musical instrument calls attention to "accent, intonation, diction, vocal color, and…the sound of human breath," to borrow Michael Witt's catalogue of ingredients (Witt 2013, 205). The film theorist Céline Scemama has written that by "returning to what has been forgotten, *Histoire(s) du cinema…* does not raise the dead," but while that may be literally true, Giles Fielke and Ivan Cerecina have responded that Godard's exorbitant montage techniques give the work a "necromantic prescience by elaborating the historical conditions for the memory of cinema" (Fielke and Cerecina 2022).[2] In various ways, they continue, it "points to the fact of the supposition of death in the cinema, proposing instead that an expansion of the narrative tradition can take place through the new [medium] of video, a moment where the 'undead' nature of the technology is revealed" (Davis 2005, 379).

The idea of cinematic necromancy aptly captures Godard's implicit vision of a cinema forever dying and being reborn, like the supranatural figures at the core of religious belief systems through the ages, and being repeatedly transformed and refashioned in this endlessly cyclical process. He proclaimed the end or death of cinema multiple times in the course of his career; within specific works, the closing title of *Weekend* proffers the pithiest statement of the theme and *Histoire(s) du cinema* delivers the most extensive elaboration, positing no fewer than five such deaths, which Daniel Morgan lists as "the demise of silent cinema; the failure of cinema to record or show the Holocaust; the end of the studio system in the 1950s; the May'68 call for the end of bourgeois cinema; and, from the 1970s on, the crisis stemming from newer media technologies (Morgan 2013, 203)."[3] Taken together, Godard's numerous alarums

---

[2] See also Scemama, *Histoire(s) du cinema de Jean-Luc Godard*, 221, cited by Fielke and Cerecina (their translation).

[3] Alifeketi Brown also gives a useful summary of turning points that Godard laments: "the abandonment of the creative and poetic possibilities

and perturbations bespeak a concern that the history of cinema harbors the phantoms postulated by psychoanalytical hauntology, dead forebears nested in the living ego, bringing corruption and decay that the apparatuses of show business must keep deeply hidden lest the driving powers of blind commercialism and socio-political ignorance come shamefully to light. Fears about cinema's dark substructures have been a motivating force throughout Godard's career, from the genre revisions of the 1960s through the tantalizing puzzles and audacious perplexities of the 2000s, but he was keenly aware that however often an end of cinema seemed imminent, none of its deaths, demises, and dissolutions has been fatal, as the existence of *Histoire(s) du cinema*, and a long list of subsequent Godard works, amply proves. When he announces the death of cinema, Morgan observes, "he generally does so within a film... and with the full intention of making more films." Nor does he seem to want the announcements to be taken all that literally. "The death of cinema?" he remarked in 1984. "For me, I say, not at all... That idea has always existed in French cinema... You find artists in 1910 who say that the cinema is in crisis (Godard 1984–1985; quoted in Morgan 2013, 204)."

Histoire(s) du cinema is not an obituary, then, but a history and a story, as its title plainly indicates. In many contexts the term "history" connotes some sort of linear chronology, but Godard obviously has the other meaning of *histoire* clearly in mind, and stories need rules of straight-ahead recitation less than histories do; asked if a film should have a beginning, a middle, and an end, Godard famously replied, "Yes, but not necessarily in that order (Tynan 1966, 24)." This stipulation applies many times over to *Histoire(s) du cinema*, which displaces, dislocates, and discombobulates linear time with a freewheeling abandon that unmistakably evokes the elusive temporality of the hauntological specter. Derrida writes:

---

posed by cinematic imagery of the silent era; the collapse of an American studio system of mass-production which indirectly fostered a range of visionary artists and popularized film as an art form; the failure of poetic, artistic and socially-engaged cinema to counteract the fascistic and capitalistic roles of cinema in history; and how the Hollywood model of Steven Spielberg and spectacle came to dominate internationally, curbing the survival and development of other models of film production and development." Brown, "*Histoire(s) du cinema*."

What is the time and what is the history of a specter? Is there a present of the specter? Are its comings and goings ordered according to the linear succession of a before and an after, between a present-past, a present-present, and a present-future, between a "real time" and a "deferred time"?

If there is something like spectrality, there are reasons to doubt this reassuring order of presents and, especially, the border between the present, the actual or   present actuality of the present, and everything that can be opposed to it: absence, nonpresence, non-effectivity, inactuality, virtuality, or even the simulacrum in general, and so forth. There is first of all the doubtful contemporaneity of the present to itself. Before knowing whether one can differentiate between the specter of the past and the specter of the future, of the past present and the future present, one must perhaps ask oneself whether the *spectrality effect* does not consist in undoing this opposition, or even this dialectic, between actual, effective presence and its other (Derrida 2006, 72).

A crucial factor in the spectrality effect of *Histoire(s) du cinema* is its conversion of a teeming succession of film images into a teeming flow of video images. This transfiguration has two crucial outcomes: it deemphasizes the plastic physicality of the film stock on which most of the motion-picture materials were photographed, and it places clips from narrative movies onto the same ontological plane as the television images, the reproduced paintings, photographs, and advertisements, and (less directly) the spoken narration and musical accompaniments that are coequal parts of the mix. This connects *Histoire(s) du cinema* with a pair of well-established artistic practices. One is sampling, which has its own cultural history in diverse forms including musique concrète, musical instruments such as the Chamberlin and Mellotron, and the digital borrowings that became a major force in popular music in the 1970s; the other is appropriation, a timeless modus operandi in art that will surely survive the largely ill-informed attacks often leveled at it nowadays. The hauntological aesthetic, according to Sprod, profits from "the anachronisms of… samples and appropriations, mainly through the maintenance of the distance from their origin and the decay that occupies that distance: as crackles and scratches, or faded colors and images that become almost literally ghostly. Instead of mere repetition, this distance provides a sense of loss and mourning, making the present the future of that past, and in turn providing the possibility of another future for the present…" (Sprod 2012) A sense of loss and mourning is indeed detectable in the visual content, first-person narration, and overall tone of *Histoire(s) du cinema*, as it is in less ambitious displays of aging footage compiled by archivists and preservationists, such as Peter Delpeut's *Lyrical Nitrate* (*Lyrisch nitraat*) and Bill Morrison's *Decasia*. These and similar instances of commingled deterioration and preservation evoke the lesson that Jameson finds in spectrality: a recognition that what we take as the dense and solid present is less self-evident and self-sufficient than we would like to think it is.

Yet while it is never difficult to find overtones of loss, mourning, decay, and ghostliness in *Histoire(s) du cinema* and other Godard projects, the exuberance, multiplicity, and superabundance of the works lead in exactly the opposite direction; even as his turn to video implies that the death of film may be at hand, the vibrancy and vigor of the funeral ceremony show that the ghosts of cinema have a thrilling life of their own, different in form and structure from their more tangible progenitors but no less robust and exciting in their impact. *Histoire(s) du cinema* is a festival of welcome revenants and lively ghosts, and it is also a farsighted exploration of how video expression might evolve in time to come. The logic of the ghost, Derrida wrote, "points toward a thinking of the event that necessarily exceeds a binary or dialectical logic," transcending the limits of actuality and effectivity in ways exemplified by "the fantastic, ghostly, 'synthetic,' 'prosthetic,' virtual happenings in the scientific domain and therefore the domain of the techno-media and therefore the public or political domain (Derrida 2006, 104)." The intricate logic of *Histoire(s) du cinema* is dialogical rather than dialectical, rhizomatic rather than binary, and all of Derrida's descriptors for developments in scientific, public, and techno-media territories—fantastic, synthetic, virtual, ghostly— readily apply to it. A hauntological account of Godard's achievement in choosing, assembling, interweaving, and integrating multitudinous components must reserve a place of honor for the word "spirit," in the sense that Derrida intends when the "spirit of Marxism" is under discussion: "*spirits* in the plural and in the sense of specters, of untimely specters that one must not chase away but sort out, critique, keep close by, and allow to come back." This calls for a selectivity that will "guide and hierarchize" the spirits that are chosen, and will also "exclude

[and] even annihilate, by watching (over) its ancestors rather than (over) certain others," thereby engendering "new ghosts... by choosing already among the ghosts, its own from among its own... (Derrida 2006, 136; emphasis in original)" Godard's towering summa is both a historiography and a metahistoriography that will be reborn and renewed as other cineastes follow in its path. So in the Godardian spirit of dislocated time, I close by returning to my starting point: Godard was haunted by cinema; cinema remains haunted by Godard; and cinephiles are haunted by them both.

Works Cited

Brown, Alifeleti. 2008. "Histoire(s) du cinema." *Senses of Cinema*, 46, March.

Davis, Colin. 2005. "Hauntology, Specters and Phantoms." *French Studies* 59 (3): 373–379.

Deleuze, Gilles. 1989. *Cinema 2: The Time-Image.* Translated by Hugh Tomlinson and Robert Galeta. Minnesota.

Derrida, Jacques. 2006. *Spectres of Marx: The State of the Debt, the Work of Mourning and the New International.* Translated by Peggy Kamuf. Routledge Classics.

Dixon, Wheeler Winston. 1997. *The Films of Jean-Luc Godard.* Albany: State University of New York.

Fielke, Giles, and Ivan Cerecina. 2022. "Metahistory on Video: Hollis Frampton in the Histoire(s)." *Senses of Cinema*, 100, January.

Godard, Jean-Luc. 2012. *Introduction to a True History of Cinema and Television.* Translated by Timothy Barnard. Montreal: Caboose.

Godard, Jean-Luc. 1984–1985. "Jean-Luc Godard: La Curiosit'e du sujet: Entretien avec Domonique Païni et Guy Scarpetta." *Art Press* 14 (special issue 4): 4–10.

Goddard, Michael. 2001. "The Scattering of Time Crystals: Deleuze, Mysticism and Cinema." In *Deleuze and Religion*, edited by Mary Bryden, 53–64. Routledge.

Hoberman, J. 2015. "Brother from Another Planet." *The Nation*, February 25.

Jameson, Frederic. 1993. "Marx's Purloined Letter." In *Ghostly Demarcations: A Symposium on Jacques Derrida's "Spectres de Marx,"* edited by Michael Sprinker, 26–67. Galilée.

Marin, Giuseppina. Interview with Godard in Corriere della Sera (April 25, 1985). Moravia, Alberto. 1954. Il risprezzo. Bompiani.

Morgan, Daniel. 2013. *Late Godard and the Possibilities of Cinema.* California.

Scemama, Céline. 2006. *Histoire(s) du cin'ema de Jean-Luc Godard: La force faible d'un art.* L'Harmattan.

Shafto, Sally. 2001. "Program Note for "Religion and Cinema: A Conference," Princeton University.

Shakespeare, William. 2012. *The Tragedy of Hamlet, Prince of Denmark*. Simon & Schuster.

Sprod, Liam. 2012. "Against all Ends: Hauntology, Aesthetics, Ontology." *3:AM*, May 11.

Sterritt, David. 1998. " Ideas, Not Plots, Inspire Jean-Luc Godard." In *Jean-Luc Godard: Interviews*, edited by David Sterritt, 174–178. Mississippi (cited at p. 177. Originally in *The Christian Science Monitor* (3 August 1994), p. 12).

Sterritt, David. 1993. "Miéville and Godard: From Psychology to Spirit." In *Jean-Luc Godard's Hail Mary: Women and the Sacred in Film*, edited by Maryel Locke and Charles Warren, 54–60. Southern Illinois.

Sterritt, David. 2014. " Schizoanalyzing Souls: Godard, Deleuze, and the Mystical Line of Flight." In *A Companion to Jean-Luc Godard*, edited by Tom Conley and T. Jefferson Kline, 383–402. Wiley Blackwell.

Sterritt, David. 2005. "Thanatos ex Machina: Godard Caresses the Dead." In *Guiltless Pleasures: A David Sterritt Film Reader*, edited by David Sterritt, 175–182. Mississippi. Reprinted in Mikita Brottman, ed., *Car Crash Culture* (Palgrave Macmillan, 2002), pp. 225-232. Also in *Senses of Cinema* 14 (June 2001).

Tynan, Kenneth. 1966. "Verdict on Cannes." *The Observer*, 22 May, 24.

Witt, Michael. 2013. *Jean-Luc Godard, Cinema Historian*. Indiana.

Images of Religion, Ritual, and the Sacred in Martin Scorsese's Cinema

from *A Companion to Martin Scorsese*, revised edition, ed. Aaron Baker (Malden, MA: Wiley-Blackwell, 2021)

> I've always taken that word—the idea of love—very seriously. It may not be a stylish thing these days to say you're a believer… But I really think Jesus had the right idea.—Martin Scorsese, 1988 (Corliss 117)

Martin Scorsese has always been serious about religion. Only two of his films have directly religious subjects—his 1988 epic *The Last Temptation of Christ*, based on the 1953 novel by Nikos Kazantzakis, and the 1997 drama *Kundun*, about the Dalai Lama's early life; but themes relating to religion, Christianity, and Roman Catholic lore and legend circulate throughout his body of work. This puts him at odds with most other modern filmmakers and with the American film industry at large, which has a powerful belief in genre, formula, and noncontroversial narrative as the surest routes to popularity and profit. The idea of investing time, money, and talent in a project as personal, idiosyncratic, and devotional as *The Last Temptation of Christ* would not occur to the great majority of Scorsese's cinematic peers, and Scorsese himself encountered such enormous difficulties in launching, developing, and completing it that its very existence, flawed and faulty though it is, may be considered a minor miracle. Beyond the case of this conspicuously religious film, moreover, Scorsese has injected signs and signifiers of his distinctive religiosity into a broad array of movies in a variety of genres. To name only a few: *Taxi Driver* (1976) and *Raging Bull* (1980) are melodramas with themes of ritual and suffering; *After Hours* (1985) is a comic allegory of damnation and salvation; *Shutter Island* (2010) is a horror film about a private hell; and *Hugo* (2011) is a family-friendly fantasy celebrating cinema as a route to transcendence.

Pinning down the precise nature of Scorsese's religious convictions is as unattainable a goal as teasing out every devotional thread woven into his body of work, which comprises about fifty features, shorts, and documentaries as of 2012. In any event, his fascination with spiritually themed subjects shows no sign of waning. At this writing he is in preproduction for *Silence*, based on the 1966 novel *Chimmoku* by Shusaku Endo, the noted Japanese Catholic author. Set in the seventeenth century, when Japanese Christians were persecuted under the Tokugawa shogunate, the novel tells the fact-based story of a young Portuguese priest dispatched to Japan on an investigative mission after his Jesuit superiors receive reports that his mentor, a devout Christian with a long history of service in Asia, has inexplicably renounced his faith.[1] The young missionary's quest is excellent grist for the filmmaker who has charted voyages into spiritually perilous worlds by innocents and quasi-innocents as different as Boxcar Bertha (Barbara Hershey) in *Boxcar Bertha* (1972), Danielle Bowden (Juliette Lewis) in *Cape Fear* (1991), Newland Archer (Daniel Day-Lewis) in *The Age of Innocence* (1993), Frank Pierce (Nicolas Cage) in *Bringing Out the Dead*, and Howard Hughes (Leonardo DiCaprio) in *The Aviator* (2004), among others. One cannot understand Scorsese's films without the keys provided by his idiosyncratic Christianity—not the rigorous religiosity promoted by his early Jesuit teachers but the more haunting and elusive kind that Flannery O'Connor called "wise blood," wholly instinctive and all the more indelible for that.

While an identifiable set of religious themes, tropes, metaphors, and symbols can be traced through Scorsese's entire body of work, the most fruitful way to illuminate his spiritual concerns is to focus on a few specific films, teasing out religious ideas that may be readily apparent when one looks for them, as in *Mean Streets* (1973) and *The Last Temptation of Christ*, or may be more subtly embedded in the story and style, as in *After Hours* and *Shutter Island*. The intersections of Scorsese's spiritual inclinations and artistic achievements are intricate and innumerable, as a growing body of scholarly and critical writing attests, and it's impossible to estimate how many more years (or decades) of study and hundreds (or thousands) of books, essays, and articles will be productively devoted to this subject in time to come. All of which makes Scorsese's religiosity a particularly exciting and rewarding field of investigation.

---

[1] The film version of *Silence*, adapted from Endo's novel by screenwriter Jay Cocks, is slated for production in 2012 and release in 2013; its long gestation period began in 2007. Scorsese's casting choices reportedly include Daniel Day-Lewis as Cristóvão Ferreira, the Portuguese priest under suspicion; Benicio Del Toro as Sebastião Rodrigues, the young missionary sent to investigate; and Gael García Bernal as Francisco Garupe, another priest involved in the mission. Dante Ferretti, a frequent Scorsese collaborator, is the production designer. [Note: *Silence* was released in late 2016; it stars Liam Neeson as Ferreira, Andrew Garfield as Rodrigues, and Adam Driver as Garupe.]

Precursors and contemporaries

While openly religious pictures like *The Last Temptation of Christ* and *Kundun* are unusual in American cinema, religious narrative has a considerable pedigree among filmmakers working outside the Hollywood mainstream, and a brief acknowledgment of this lineage is in order. Among its pioneers are two African-American filmmakers: Oscar Micheaux, whose works include *Within Our Gates* (1919) and *Body and Soul* (1925), and Spencer Williams, who made such movies as *The Blood of Jesus* (1941) and *Go Down, Death!* (1944), all produced, distributed, and exhibited outside Hollywood's studio system. Among filmmakers contemporary with Scorsese, the most notable is his occasional collaborator Paul Schrader, whose upbringing in—and complicated attitude toward—the conservative Dutch Calvinist faith is a well-known part of his biography. Schrader has written original or adapted screenplays for four of Scorsese's films: *The Last Temptation of Christ*, the signature works *Taxi Driver* and *Raging Bull*, and the lesser achievement *Bringing Out the Dead*, all of which explore explicitly or implicitly religious themes that gain added intellectual interest from the creative tensions between the writer's essentially Protestant perspectives and the director's deeply rooted Catholic sensibility.

Another filmmaker whose agenda overlaps with Scorsese's is the Italian-American director Abel Ferrara, who explores the ubiquity of evil in *The Addiction*, a metaphorical vampire story with references to the Holocaust, and *Bad Lieutenant* (1992), wherein issues of conscience, repentance, and sacrilege swirl through the story of a corrupt police officer in an urban milieu that seems hopelessly depraved. Ferrara also directed *Mary*, in which the spiritual presence of Mary Magdalene affects the lives of an actress, a filmmaker, and a television performer. Since some of the characters in *Mary* are making a movie about Jesus, some critics speculate that Ferrara is referring to *The Passion of the Christ*, a 2004 release directed by Mel Gibson, a Roman Catholic traditionalist. Gibson's blood-soaked account of the crucifixion became a *cause célèbre* for some Christians and a *cause de scandale* for other viewers, whether Christian or not, who detected anti-Semitic biases in its depiction of Jews and perceived sadomasochistic overtones in its detailed depiction of the agonies suffered by the eponymous messiah. Gibson's personal scandals in subsequent years, some involving racist and anti-Semitic rants, have lent further ammunition to critics who find his biblical film crude, distasteful, bigoted, or all three. Other independent directors with religious interests include Todd Solondz in *Life During Wartime* (2009), African-American auteur Spike Lee in *Malcolm X* (1992) and *Get on the Bus* (1996), feminist filmmaker Nancy Savoca in *Household Saints* (1993), Michael Tolkin in *The Rapture* (1991), Joel and Ethan Coen in *A Serious Man* (2009), and Terrence Malick in *The Tree of Life* (2011), to name some of the more prominent figures who have traveled down this path.

Early stirrings

Scorsese's interest in religion and his conflicted relationship with Roman Catholicism began early, when questions of sin and salvation stirred such curiosity and anxiety in his impressionable young mind that he took a tentative step toward entering the Catholic priesthood. This move was not entirely based on selfless spirituality. As he has acknowledged, he was seduced in part by the rich displays of icons, music, ritual, and sheer theatricality so deeply ingrained in Catholic tradition. He also suspected that as a priest he would have more of an "inside line" to divine pardon for succumbing to the usual adolescent urges of the flesh. "I think I wanted to be a priest out of ego," he said in 1998, "rather than understanding of what a priest is supposed to be" (Smith 246). At age fourteen he enrolled at a junior seminary school, only to flunk out a year later thanks to low grades, poor discipline, and compulsive thinking about girls, girls, girls.

Catholicism remained a powerful influence for him, however. Despite his guilt feelings about sexual thoughts and masturbation, he "constantly" felt he was "communicating directly with God" and "having spiritual experiences." After listening to somber Jesuit sermons during a religious retreat, for instance, he had what Robert Casillo, the most thorough chronicler of his inner life, describes as an episode of "guilt and mysticism." The country noises outside his room at night seemed like an "auditory hallucination," Scorsese recalled years later, and "smudges on the window become like the face on the Shroud" in his keyed-up imagination. Eventually he got out of bed and went to pray in a grotto on the premises, but he remained so distressed that a priest told him a visit to a Catholic psychiatrist might help him cope with what was clearly some sort of emotional crisis. Taking the cleric's manifestly sound advice, Scorsese started a psychotherapy regimen that went on for seven years. (Casillo 96) This and similar experiences had lasting effects on his intellect, his psychology, his aesthetics, and his artistic practice.[2]

Scorsese was increasingly disillusioned and disheartened by the church itself, however, and he left it during the first half of the 1960s. Among the reasons for his departure (gathered by Casillo from various sources) were his disappointment with the pride, desire, and violence at constant play in Little Italy, the Catholic community where he grew up; the hypocrisy of priests who routinely baptized the children of mobsters and murderers; the joyless and arbitrary nature of church teachings about sex; the enforcement of dogmas and strictures (keeping the Sabbath holy is one thing, keeping Fridays meatless is another) that have no biblical basis; the church's weak responses to intolerance and injustice; and the enthusiasm of many clerics for the horrors being perpetrated in Vietnam, where America was waging a "holy war," according to a sermon that was a tipping point in Scorsese's decision to let his Catholicism lapse. All this notwithstanding, however, Scorsese has insisted that he is a "Catholic layman" rather than an agnostic. He says he has relinquished faith only in "the man-made aspects of… religion," that for him "living the good life" is synonymous with "practicing the tenets of Christianity," and that his films explore the question of "how to live and find an honest, non-institutional faith." (Casillo 96-97; Kakutani)

The critic who best understands these aspects of Scorsese's cinema is perhaps Roger Ebert, also a working-class Roman Catholic born in 1942 and fascinated by movies all his life. Ebert wrote the first published review of Scorsese's first completed feature, declaring in 1967 that *I Call First*, which he saw at the Chicago International Film Festival a year before it reached theaters as *Who's That Knocking at My Door*, was "a great moment in American movies."[3] Some twenty years later, Ebert took keen interest in

---

[2] It is interesting to recall that Tony criticizes Charlie in *Mean Streets* for being too credulous, tracing this weakness as far back as a high-school retreat where Charlie believed everything the priests told him. Charlie is unfazed, however: " That's my charm," he responds. Lee Lourdeaux relates this to Charlie's conviction that religious judgments must work in the streets as well as the church. Tony indirectly validates the latter idea when he says the church is basically " a business, it's work, it's an organization." (Lourdeaux 243)

[3] Scorsese originally intended this film as the centerpiece of a trilogy. The first film, *Jerusalem, Jerusalem*, would have included a retreat at a seminary

Although the typical Godard film is liberally bestrewn with literary allusions and quotations, there is often a surprising murkiness about what Godard has actually read, since he is frequently content to cite a work on the basis of fleeting acquaintance rather than serious engagement. (No matter what appears within a movie, biographer Colin MacCabe writes, "it would always be a mistake to assume that Godard had read a particular book."[17]) This uncertainty extends to Dolto's work. Godard ran across her book, he recalled,

> and in her introduction—I didn't really read the rest of the book—she spoke of Mary and Joseph in a way that I never heard before. It seemed very cinematic: the story of a couple. And I'm very traditional. I've always made love stories and stories of couples. So that's how I got to the story of "God and his Daughter."[18]

This theme—a couple in love—sounds rather too conventional for Godard in the 1980s, and his account of its genesis sounds rather too neat, asking us to see him as a teller of tales whose unfettered imagination peers down all manner of challenging conceptual byways—incest and taboo, father Freud and daughter Dora, God and Godard himself—and ultimately returns with "the story of a couple" that is "cinematic" and "traditional." Is something wrong with this picture?

There certainly is. It will be obvious to anyone who encounters *Hail Mary* that not even Godard could have set out to make a traditional "story of a couple" and somehow ended up with the exfoliating schizz-flows of this eminently rhizomatic film. Here as elsewhere, Godard's statement of intent is a creative semifiction—a purposefully inchoate *supplement* to a cinematic experience that is irreducible to language and unrepresentable except by its own intensive singularities. Godard's films usually do tell stories, but his real business is forging a new kind of cinema— a cinema of *between* and a cinema of *and*, as Deleuze describes it, which "does away with all the cinema of Being = is" and makes visible "the indiscernible."[19] Whatever role Dolto's psychoanalysis, or anyone's psychoanalysis, played in the origin of *Hail Mary* is surely outweighed by these grander considerations.

---

[17] Colin MacCabe, *Godard: A Portrait of the Artist at Seventy* (Farrar, Straus and Giroux, 2003), 207.

[18] Brody, *Everything Is Cinema*, 457.

[19] Deleuze, *Cinema 2*, 180.

The Last Temptation of Christ, finding strong resonances between the difficulty of the production and the sense of purpose that kept Scorsese toiling away when all signs seemed to indicate that the project was a lost cause. Before reaching the screen the picture slogged through two Hollywood studios, years of planning and false starts, and a barrage of denunciation by mud-slinging Christian fundamentalists; all that was missing were the locusts.

Scorsese's refusal to slack off or slow down, much less give up and move on, was motivated by the dual nature of the project as he envisioned it. According to Ebert's sensitive analysis, *The Last Temptation of Christ* was not only about the Son of God—it was equally about the son of Charles and Catherine Scorsese, who was using Jesus' struggle with inner demons as a vehicle for uncovering and confronting his own psychological and spiritual conflicts, which were the opposite of theoretical, as we have seen. Scorsese was also intimate with losing hope, as are the Christ of Kazantzakis and the Christ of Matthew 27:46, who cries "My God, My God, why have You forsaken me?" (NASB) during his ninth hour on the cross. "In his films [Scorsese] performs miracles," Ebert wrote, "but for years could be heard to despair that each film would be his last." (17, 103).

These ideas open new perspectives on numerous Scorsese films, suggesting (for example) that the self-doubting savior played by Willem Dafoe in *The Last Temptation of Christ* is essentially the same presence that haunts J.R. in *Who's That Knocking at My Door* and Charlie in *Mean Streets*. It is no stretch to see J.R. and Charlie as stand-ins for Scorsese, especially since both are played by Keitel, the filmmaker's alter ego of choice in his early films. In his boldest interpretive move, Ebert uses Keitel's portrayal of Judas in *The Last Temptation of Christ* as the basis for speculating that this character is, surprising though it seems, another kind of Scorsese surrogate—the mortal man walking beside the Messiah, "worrying about him, lecturing him, wanting him to be better, threatening him, confiding in him, prepared to betray him if he must." Jesus is the film, in other words, and Judas is the director. (104). This is a smart and subtle insight.

---

and images linked with the stations of the cross; it was never made because potential producers found it "too involved with religion" (Ebert 12). The third film, *Season of the Witch*, turned into *Mean Streets*.

Saints and sinners

Scorsese is not alone along contemporary filmmakers in viewing the vicissitudes of human experience largely through an Italian-American lens. His most prominent and influential peers include Brian DePalma and Francis Ford Coppola, who likewise invest their works with what film theorist Leo Braudy calls "a Catholic way of regarding the visible world" (19). The word "visible" is important here, since as Braudy notes, Catholicism places much sacral and liturgical emphasis on iconography, costume, and the stagecraft of ritual, in contrast with Protestantism's partiality for a pared-down mise-en-scène that allows more prominence for the revelatory powers of the spoken and written word. One can easily imagine these Italian-American directors echoing the Swiss-French director Jean-Luc Godard, who was raised as a Protestant but developed an attachment to the great Catholic heritage of visual aestheticism: "I'm not a religious person, but I'm a faithful person. I believe in images" (Locke 1).[4]

Three qualities constitute the Catholic way of seeing: the importance of ritual narratives, the significance of ritual objects, and the conferral of ritual status. Scorsese is most closely connected with the third. Typically centering on "the saint in the streets" who both manifests and moves beyond the norms of cinema and society, Scorsese's films transfigure the marginality of the protagonist into "a kind of transcendence," often preceded by a mortification of the flesh that renders the protagonist's deliverance from doom all the more ironic. Braudy's examples include Travis Bickle in *Taxi Driver* and Rupert Pupkin in *The King of Comedy* (1983), both played by De Niro and both rescued from self-inflicted disaster in endings "presented as part real, part fantasy" (25, 27), with the media playing *deus ex machina* roles. Another such figure is Big Bill Shelly in *Boxcar Bertha*, a labor organizer whom Scorsese regards as a saint mingling with lowlifes, criminals, and common people in order to fulfill his mission, which ends when he is literally crucified on the wall of a boxcar that then rolls down the tracks, taking the message of his martyrdom to whomever might witness it and comprehend its meaning. Along similar lines, Johnny Boy in *Mean Streets* can be seen as a holy fool in the New Testament sense of "fools for Christ's sake," weak where others are strong

---

[4] Prefiguring the protests against *The Last Temptation of Christ* in 1988, the 1985 release of Godard's film *Hail Mary* sparked an international outcry from Catholics and others who believed that the movie (which most of them hadn't seen) was sacrilegious or blasphemous.

and without honor where others are distinguished, exemplifying Paul's teaching that "the wisdom of the world is foolishness before God" (I Corinthians 4:10, 3:19). *Mean Streets* also resonates with mystical ideas that are not intrinsic to orthodox Christianity but can serve as complements and supplements thereto, and we turn to these now.

Season of the witch

> You don't make up for your sins in church. You do it in the streets. You do it at home. The rest is bullshit and you know it. — *Mean Streets*

The opening words of *Mean Streets* come from Charlie, the character played by Harvey Keitel, but the voiceover is spoken by Scorsese during a few seconds of blank screen before the first images appear. Any doubts about the deeply personal nature of Scorsese's first major film should obviously vanish at this point. To call the movie personal is only a tiny step toward fathoming it, of course, and as always in the cinema, creative contributions came from many sources. One was Scorsese's sometime collaborator Jay Cocks, who talked him into replacing the film's original title — "Season of the Witch," referring to the tension-filled time period of the story[5] — with a phrase from Raymond Chandler's description of the ideal detective-story hero: "Down these mean streets a man must go who is not himself mean, who is neither tarnished nor afraid… He must be, to use a rather weathered phrase, a man of honor — by instinct, by inevitability, without thought of it, and certainly without saying it." The proper activity for such a hero is an "adventure in search of a hidden truth," and an authentically realistic writer will set this in "a world in which gangsters can rule nations and almost rule cities." (Casillo 181; Chandler 523)

New York represents that world in *Mean Streets*, but Scorsese's hero is a petty crook rather than a detective, and the hidden truth he seeks is a route to spiritual absolution, not a clue that will solve a crime. These divergences from what Chandler has in mind suggest that Scorsese, who came to consider the *Mean Streets* a

---

[5] The provisional title "Season of the Witch" was borrowed from a pop song written by Donovan Leitch for his album *Sunshine Superman*, a 1966 release on the Epic label. Scorsese favored a cover version by Al Kooper and Steve Stills on the *Super Session* album (also featuring Mike Bloomfield) released by Columbia in 1968.

somewhat pretentious title, should have stuck with his original idea, alluding as it does to witchcraft, the casting of spells, and the ill luck inflicted on enemies by those gifted with the *mal occhio* or *jettatura*, known in English as the evil eye. These phenomena are familiar in the Mezzogiorno region of Italy whence Scorsese's four grandparents hailed,[6] and while they may seem esoteric in the context of American movies by a director with Roman Catholic roots, they are keenly relevant to some of Scorsese's films, of which *Mean Streets* is the earliest.

The witches who loom largest in Southern Italian lore bear little resemblance to the hook-nosed broomstick riders of Halloween fame. They are humans (usually female, occasionally male) who take on animal characteristics, and their specialty is creeping into houses by night for purposes of theft and mischief. A witch's machinations generally operate against a single victim or antagonist, according to Casillo, whereas stratagems involving the *mal occhio* frequently involve three participants: a gazer, a gazee, and a patron whose sanctified symbol can, like the Christian cross in countless vampire tales, render the gazee invulnerable to this particular variety of harm. The evil eye can also be taken as a malevolent cousin of the dirty look, which southern Italians often connect with envy and jealousy.[7]

These and related quasi-religious traditions run deep in *Mean Streets*, which takes place entirely in Little Italy, the New York neighborhood where Scorsese came of age. The main characters are Charlie, a young gangster on the rise in the syndicate run by his Uncle Giovanni (Cesare Danova), and Johnny Boy (Robert De Niro), a totally loose cannon whose foolhardy exploits may well be signs of outright madness. Johnny Boy hates Manhattan in general and Little Italy in particular, and for Casillo the *mal occhio* is present in the "malignant gaze" that expresses this hate. It is also at work in the contemptuous, covetous gaze that the creditor Michael (Richard Romanus) casts on Johnny Boy when an outstanding debt goes unpaid; Johnny Boy then seeks protection from his esteemed uncle, turning to him as a patron with power to

---

[6] Southern Italy, which has intense sunshine around noontime, acquired the name Mezzogiorno from the word meaning " noon" or "midday." Il Mezzogiorno takes in Sicily and Sardinia as well as the southernmost part of the continental peninsula.).

[7] This discussion of the witchcraft theme in *Mean Streets* is indebted to Casillo's careful analyses (254, 487-490), as it the subsequent discussion of parody and priestliness in *Casino* (344, 356-358, 378-379).

counteract the *mal occhio*. Giovanni is also the implicit patron in a case involving Charlie, who casts a malignant gaze on the owners of an Italian restaurant that he covets for himself.

In both cases Giovanni refuses the protection asked of him, bringing unpleasant consequences to the vulnerable parties. He is not so much a male witch (*stregone*) as a sorcerer or wizard (*mago*) whose very cigar calls to mind a magic wand, symbolizing his command of a "controlled and expulsive violence" used to "keep deviants in line and thus to maintain social order," in Casillo's words. Other characters with witch-like traits include the epileptic Teresa (Amy Robinson) and the African-American dancer Diane (Jeannie Bell), two sexually tempting women with the kind of marginal status that has brought ill will to bear on many a southern Italian misfit accused of being a witch (*strega*) because she failed to fit the norms of a tight-knit community. Continuing the *mal occhio* theme, Tony (David Proval) has equipped his rearview mirror with a red *cornicello*, the "little horn" considered a standard safeguard against the evil eye in southern Italian tradition.

Scorsese's references to such traditions do not carry the full weight of conviction found in his use of Catholic tropes and symbols, but his films implicitly recognize a metaphysical spectrum with Christian beliefs at one end and folkloric superstition at the other, all of it resting on the proposition that the natural world is surrounded and pervaded by supernatural forces that we ignore, deny, or demean at our peril. Mercurial, unpredictable, and capricious, spirituality is the most emotionally charged category in Scorsese's cinema, and the highest imaginable stakes are in the balance when it touches an individual life. The pain of hell is like "the burn from a lighted match increased a million times, infinite," Charlie says, sounding like the priest who terrorizes Stephen Dedalus with a sulfurous sermon in James Joyce's *A Portrait of the Artist as a Young Man*. "You don't fuck around with the infinite," he continues. "There's no way you can do that. The pain in hell has two sides—the kind you touch with your hand, and the kind you can feel with your heart, your soul, the spiritual side. And... the worse of the two is the spiritual." The rest, we know by now, is bullshit.

The morality car wash
In the novel that inspired Scorsese's eponymous *Casino*, author Nicholas Pileggi describes Las Vegas as a place where "everyone takes care of everyone else," where "a $20 bill can buy approval,

a $100 bill adulation, and a $1,000 bill canonization," and where the average person has "a shot at a miracle," (83, 4). In the film, gambling magnate Sam "Ace" Rothstein (Robert De Niro) echoes the novel's description of the money-counting area as "the holy of holies" and "the most sacred room in the casino," and he calls the city a "morality car wash" that washes sins away, promising to do for expectant patrons "what Lourdes does for hunchbacks and cripples." Citing the priestly power to transform "profane violence into beneficent… through ritual," Casillo writes that Rothstein presents an analogical parody of a priest, in that he "saves gambling from corruption" by enforcing rituals of play and sternly punishing all infractions. He surveys his casino and its "idolatrous worshippers" as if he were a prelate who "alternately faces and turns his back to the parishioners," photographed from a low angle that evokes how "a priest would appear to someone kneeling at an altar rail, ready for communion."

Yet here as in other Scorsese films, "the quest for divinity proves to be self-destructive." Blown high into the air when an assassin's bomb explodes in his car, Rothstein's body "twists and turns through the frame like a soul about to tumble into the flames of damnation," as the screenplay describes the moment (3). Rothstein does not plummet into the Inferno, however, at least for now; he survives the attack by virtue of a design detail in his car that the would-be killers did not anticipate. Gambler that he is, he survives by sheer luck—or perhaps by the grace of God unpredictably, even undeservedly, bestowed on a man who resembles an irreligious priest and emulates, in Scorsese's words, the "grandeur of Lucifer being expelled from heaven for being too proud" (Christie and Thompson 207). In keeping with his dual sacred-secular nature, his flight is choreographed at first to the *St. Matthew Passion* of Johann Sebastian Bach, then to the pop vocalizing of Louis Prima, a veteran Vegas entertainer. In these and similar moments throughout *Casino* a tumultuous drama of crime, love, money, and violence becomes a heartfelt religious allegory.

Orpheus descending, or, Scorsese in Nighttown
The script for *After Hours*, penned by first-time screenwriter Joseph Minion, reached Scorsese at a time when efforts to put *The Last Temptation of Christ* into production had come to naught and there was good reason to believe this long-cherished enterprise would never get beyond the planning stage. Gravely disappointed and fearing that his whole career might collapse, Scorsese immedi-

ately warmed to the quicksilver blend of comedy and melodrama in Minion's screenplay; he also welcomed the prospect of trading the unwieldy logistics and doomed negotiations of the Kazantzakis project for a nimble, no-frills production shot entirely in New York, the milieu he knew best.[8] Scorsese has directed only two comedies — *After Hours* and its immediate predecessor, *The King of Comedy* — and both are nervous, jumpy films made during times of great uncertainty in his life and work. *After Hours* is the darker and more mythically resonant of the two.

The protagonist is Paul Hackett (Griffin Dunne), a word-processing clerk in a Manhattan office. The story begins when he strikes up a conversation with a woman named Marcy Franklin (Rosanna Arquette) in a restaurant one evening. Soon thereafter he visits her at the apartment of her sculptor friend Kiki Bridges (Linda Fiorentino) in SoHo, a lower Manhattan neighborhood favored by artists and performers. On the way to the downtown rendezvous he loses his small amount of ready cash when wind blows it out the window of a wildly speeding taxicab — a woeful mishap, since he will have trouble extricating himself from SoHo later.

Marcy proves to have extreme mood swings that disturb and bewilder Paul, so he decides to cut the evening's losses by returning home. Entering the subway, however, he learns that the fare has abruptly risen to more than he can pay. A bartender named Tom (John Heard) offers to bail him out with him a loan, but before accepting it Paul goes back to Kiki's apartment and finds that Marcy has killed herself, perhaps pushed over the line by his irritated reactions to her moodiness. Encounters with women named Julie (Teri Garr) and Gail (Catherine O'Hara) follow, but Paul remains stranded in SoHo and struck in his predicament. The situation gets worse when bartender Tom turns out to be the late Marcy's boyfriend, and it grows even worse when local residents mistake Paul for a burglar and form a rage-filled posse to hunt him down. He finally makes a getaway when another sculptor, June (Verna Bloom), disguises him as a papier-mâché sculpture that the actual burglars, Neil (Cheech Marin) and Pepe (Thomas Chong), then mistake for a work of modern art. Stealing the "statue" and

---

[8] Minion wrote the screenplay for a class at Columbia University taught by the Serbian filmmaker Dušan Makavejev, who gave it an A even though, in Scorsese's words, "It wasn't really a script, more like a novel." Scorsese rewrote it with Minion and others before filming started. (Christie and Thompson 97).

stashing it in their van, the thieves unwittingly take Paul back uptown. In a miraculous final touch, the back door of their rickety vehicle flies open at exactly the right moment for him to tumble out in front of his office building. Morning is at hand. Paul's dark night of the soul—and the mind, and the body—has finally come to an end.

Scorsese was unhappy with the lackluster ending of Minion's original screenplay, so the rewritten version substituted a magic-realist finale of considerable daring: in the basement with June while the vengeful mob pounds on the door, Paul shrinks drastically in size, "returns to the womb" by entering June's vagina, and then appears "born naked, curled up on the cobblestones in the middle of 57th Street," whereupon he "gets up and… runs like hell home" (Christie and Thompson 100). Anticipating a central trope in *Being John Malkovich*, the 1999 fantasy by director Spike Jonze and writer Charlie Kaufman, this bizarre birth scenario was rejected by entertainment mogul David Geffen, whose production company became the principal financial backer of *After Hours*. Its hallucinatory nature—one part Lewis Carroll, one part Bertrand Blier, several parts sheer fever dream[9]—does not precisely comport with the story preceding it, which presents no impossible events alongside its many improbable ones. Even as a mere hypothesis, however, its über-oedipal extravagance indicates how tenuous a line divides the real from the phantasmatic in this film.

A productive way to approach *After Hours* is to observe how interestingly its disoriented hero, urban setting, nighttime ambience, and oneiric mood resemble elements of the "Circe" episode in James Joyce's magisterial comic novel *Ulysses* of 1922. Circe is the witch-goddess or enchantress in Homer's *Odyssey* whom Odysseus confronts after she transforms his crew into swine by means of a sinister potion; armed with his own magic herb, he forces her to reverse the damage, and later he travels to the Underworld with the aid of her knowledge and advice. The parallel episode in *Ulysses* finds Leopold Bloom following Stephen Dedalus into Nighttown, a fantastical red-light district, where an extremely inebriated Stephen stumbles into a brothel, raises a ruckus, and gets into a fight, not unlike the obstreperous characters in some Scorsese films. Stephen and Bloom both fall prey to hallucinations

---

[9] The pertinent works are Carroll's satirical novel *Alice's Adventures in Wonderland* (1865), in which Alice swells and shrinks in size, and Blier's strange 1976 comedy *Calmos*, also known as *Femmes fatales*, which reaches its climax (so to speak) inside a cavernous vagina.

and chimeras, the most dramatic of which is Stephen's vision of his dead mother, a specter saturated with the guilt he feels for refusing to pray for her in her final moments. She appears to him in Nighttown as a rotted corpse, reaching out a withered arm that turns into a "green crab with malignant red eyes" and then "sticks deep its grinning claws" into his heart (579, 582).

While nothing in *After Hours* matches the nightmarish aura of this visitant, Paul's rising paranoia is exacerbated more than once by confrontations with bewildering women. The most daunting of them is Marcy, whose death is a critical event in Paul's nighttime odyssey, marking the point when the movie takes on mythic-religious trappings and Manhattan's lower extremity becomes an anarchic underworld where chaos reigns and frenzied enemies abound. Paul's trials are so great that at a particularly harrowing juncture he throws himself on his knees in the middle of the street and pleads to the heavens for help. When he finally makes it back to his office in the last scene, providentially deposited by the thieves' van exactly where he is ordained to be, he is greeted by name by the computer network that serves as the godlike spirit of the place. The end credits then appear, unspooling over a slow panning shot around the office as others arrive and take their places at their workspaces as Paul has done—but when the camera returns to Paul's appointed desk, he is nowhere to be seen. Perhaps the words of his word processing have pleased the deity who in the beginning was the Word, and He has rewarded Paul by sweeping him into the heavens that he prayed to in the street, as if Paul were a latter-day Enoch, who, Genesis 5:24 (NASB) recounts, "walked with God; and he was not, for God took him." It is conceivable, in other words, that Paul has received a one-person Rapture just for him.

Working from this interpretation, we can credit Scorsese with giving Paul a last-minute rescue from the terrible fate suffered by another archetypal figure he resembles: Orpheus, the poet, singer, and lyre virtuoso of ancient Greek mythology. In the best-known variants of the Orphic legend, Orpheus visits the underworld to reclaim Eurydice, his wife, after a viper's venom causes her untimely death. The gods release her on the condition that Orpheus not look at her until they reach the upper world. But for some reason he looks too soon—perhaps her beauty is literally irresistible, or tension muddles his mind, or he miscalculates the point where the upper world begins, or he is simply distracted and careless[10]—and the deal is off. Enraged by his dereliction, the maenads (female followers of the Dionysus cult) exact murderous revenge by ripping his body apart and throwing the pieces into a river.

Although it is not tied to this chain of events, *After Hours* moves along a roughly parallel track, sometimes converging with the myth, other times ignoring it or gesturing toward it from afar. Orpheus was a poet who descended to the underworld; Paul is a word processor who travels downtown. Orpheus is forbidden to look at his wife; Paul tells Marcy about a childhood incident when he was made to wear a blindfold, and later his vision is cut off by a papier-mâché armature. Orpheus' dereliction sends Eurydice back to the underworld; Paul's impatience and lack of sympathy may be the venom that causes Marcy's death. Orpheus is murdered by enraged maenads; Paul barely escapes from SoHo vigilantes. Orpheus is torn to pieces; Paul's papier-mâché disguise shatters when he tumbles out of Neil and Pepe's van, flinging bogus body parts around the area, and earlier we glimpse a newspaper report that a man has been ripped limb from limb in a SoHo street. And just as some versions of the myth credit Orpheus' sublime song with making the sun rise every morning, Paul ends his odyssey as a new day begins.

If the ancient Greek provenance of the Orphic myth seems far removed from the Judeo-Christian heritage that Scorsese privileges, note that two of the myth's most important elements—the husband-wife dyad and the proscription of seeing as a condition of escape from death—play somewhat similar roles in the Old Testament (Gen. 19: 17, 26, NASB) when God destroys Sodom and Gomorrah by raining fire and brimstone from the heavens: "Escape for your life! Do not look behind you," an angel of the Lord commands Lot and his wife; yet the woman, "from behind him, looked *back*, and she became a pillar of salt." Note also that multiple allusions to fire and burning infuse *After Hours* with near-subliminal hints of a Christian-style Hell à la Dante's Inferno, positioned ominously near the story's visible locations; as critic Vincent Canby wrote regarding *Taxi Driver* in 1976, "Manhattan is a thin cement lid over the entrance to hell, and the lid is full of cracks."

---

[10] Jean Cocteau favors the " distracted and careless" explanation. His play *Orphée* appeared in 1926 and his film adaptation premiered in 1950, altering the story so that Death falls in love with Orpheus, intercedes with the gods after his second loss of Eurydice, and sacrifices herself so that the couple can resume their earthly lives together.

Some considerations work against this hermeneutic trajectory, to be sure. It is not a disobedient woman, for instance, but Paul himself who becomes an immobile object in *After Hours*, inert and helpless in his papier-mâché shell; and he does not get burned by infernal flames or torn asunder by modern-day maenads. So it seems he is an ordinary movie character after all. Yet if the event that spirits him back uptown is the quasi-miracle that it appears to be, and if his ultimate disappearance from the diegesis is the quasi-miracle that *it* appears to be, then some kind of higher power may indeed be taking an interest in him. And not necessarily a benign interest. The many antic elements in Paul's escapade do not erase the awful fact of Marcy's death, which his self-centered attitude and impatient behavior may have caused and certainly did not prevent. Although he escapes punishment by immolation, dismemberment, and permanent paralysis, the outcome of his odyssey is not a new lease on life but a renewed entrapment in the eternal recurrence of the same. Pitched back into the tedium of processing other people's words—the incessant monotony that drove him to his hopeless, fruitless quest for adventure and romance—he seems less like a redeemed soul than a damned one, condemned not to the fiery horror of Dante's outer circles but the *icy* horror of the inner circles, where stasis and isolation deny even the solace of tears and lamentation to those whose wasted lives have brought them there.

After Hours taps into other narratives as well, including Franz Kafka's novel *The Trial*, especially as that 1925 masterpiece is filtered through the luminous gloom of Orson Welles' imperfect 1962 film adaptation. Like the guardian of the gateway to the Law in *The Trial*, for instance, a nightclub doorkeeper tells Paul that he might be admitted to the premises at some later time but cannot enter now, and then accepts a bribe so that Paul will feel he has left no means untried in his doomed effort to reach the sanctum within. *After Hours* is a whimsical and entertaining film, and also a surprisingly intricate one, orchestrating nuanced echoes of ancient Greek myth, medieval Italian poetry, modernist European novels, and additional sources into what is ultimately a contemporary Christian fable—perhaps a tad more gnomic than Scorsese's other crypto-religious tales, but no less fascinated by the perplexing places where forces from our world and the underworld overlap, commingle, and collide.

Hauntology

As noted earlier, Scorsese's films often project the idea that everyday people can achieve a measure of sainthood or transcendence as they go about their ostensibly commonplace lives, usually after undergoing a mortification of the flesh that prepares the way. An extreme example of this character type is the protagonist of *Shutter Island*, Teddy Daniels, whose trials by fire and water are simultaneously physical and metaphysical. In such films as *Mean Streets* and *Taxi Driver* and *The King of Comedy*, Braudy argues, stylized visual forms become "a kind of skin over the eruptions within, as if to demonstrate how much chaos the rituals of seeing and story-telling can actually subdue" (25). This skin is stretched to its utmost limit in *Shutter Island*. Its delusional main character is the Godlike creator (and Scorsese-like director) of his own nightmarish fugues, which are so incessant and all-embracing that redemption can only be achieved through psychosurgery, the invasion of his brain and the destruction (or deconstruction) of his mind. This is a savage fate, and it comes directly from a savage God, at least according to Teddy's tormented thought processes.

His ordeals take place on an island that is geographically located a short way off the New England coast but is introduced with such mysterioso grandiosity in the opening scene, looming from murky fog and translucent mist like an ultima Thule of midcentury America, that it might be transplanted with little alteration from the fiction of Arthur Machen or H. P. Lovecraft, although contemporary novelist Dennis Lehane dreamed up the place in his eponymous novel. The island's sole inhabitants are professionals, workers, and patients connected with Ashcliffe Hospital, an asylum and prison for the criminally insane. Teddy and his partner, Chuck Aule (Mark Ruffalo), are United States Marshals visiting Ashcliffe to investigate the disappearance of a patient who somehow got out of the carefully locked, conscientiously guarded, thoroughly escape-proof cell in which she lived. "It's as if she evaporated," says an Ashcliffe physician, "straight through the walls." The year is 1954, and when a tempestuous storm cuts off communication with the mainland, Teddy finds himself caught in a web of interwoven puzzles that grow stranger and more baffling with every passing hour.

No facet of *Shutter Island* better rewards attention and analysis than Teddy's colloquy with the warden of Ashcliffe, played by Ted Levine, late in the film. Their exchange stands with Scorsese's most radical forays into the dark dimensions of the sacramental sublime, rendered all the more uncanny by Levine's mimicry of the creepy grin and faux-hearty vocal inflections deployed by Robert De Niro in his most menacing Scorsese roles. Teddy and the warden are speaking in the warden's car after the hurricane that pounded Shutter Island the previous day. It is the first and only time we hear the warden speak, and the full implications of his words are apparent only to those who have seen the film before and know that while the warden himself may be an actual human presence, the things he says are products of Teddy's paranoid imagination:

Warden: Did you enjoy God's latest gift?

Teddy [puzzled]: What?

Warden: God's gift. Your violence. [pause] When I came downstairs in my home and I saw that tree in my living room, it reached out for me. A divine hand.

God loves violence.

Teddy [still puzzled]: I—I hadn't noticed.

Warden: Sure you have. Why else would there be so much of it? It's in us, it's what we are. We wage war, we burn sacrifices and pillage and plunder and tear at the flesh of our brothers. And why? Because God gave us violence to wage in his honor.

Teddy: I thought God gave us moral order.

Warden: There's no moral order as pure as this storm. There's no moral order at all: There's just this: can my violence conquer yours?

A moment later, as Teddy gets ready to leave the car, the warden (who is never named) leans toward him with a conspiratorial smile and asks, "If I was to sink my teeth into your eye right now, would you be able to stop me before I blinded you?" Teddy replies, with a show of bravado and a steady stare, "Give it a try." And the warden ends the dialogue on a delighted note: "That's the spirit!"

If references to film history are among Scorsese's primary means for making "his own authority and complicity" into a theme of the stories he tells, as Braudy argues (26), then we can take the warden's closing question as a direct allusion to Hannibal Lecter's attack on a psychiatric nurse, not shown but graphically described in *The Silence of the Lambs*, the 1991 megahit by Jonathan Demme that threw open the doors to insane criminals as charismatic movie antiheros. Like the cannibalistic psychiatrist in Demme's film, the warden embodies the mind's raging superego in both of the forms that psychoanalytic theorist Slavoj Žižek ascribes to it: with his uniform, arrogance, and air of command, he represents the law in its pubic and symbolic guise, upholding order and enforcing discipline; yet his unsettling demeanor and alarming words reveal him as an avatar of the "obscene superego agency," described by Žižek as "the mad-obscene law which is *incommensurate* with our well-being" since it "derails the psychic equilibrium" and decenters the individual from within. As a phantom of Teddy's imagination, the warden is a sort of evil twin or doppelgänger, a sinister double whose unbidden articulation of Teddy's most deeply buried fears is at once a bewildering shock and a seductive opening to "the 'impossible'/traumatic/painful enjoyment" that lies beyond the reality principle and pleasure principle alike (Žižek 106, 182). As a source of self-confident claims about God's creation (violence is a divine gift, moral order is illusory) the warden is also a priest, or rather an antipriest, preaching a bad-news gospel of chaos on earth, ill will to humankind.

The warden's position of authority on Shutter Island naturally aligns him with the Ashcliffe psychiatrists—practitioners of weird science whose project, according to rumor, is to create "ghosts." Ghosts certainly abound in Teddy's mind and heart: visions of the Holocaust victims he saw as a GI entering Dachau in 1945, the specter of a hideously wounded Nazi whose agony he sadistically prolonged, apparitions of his three drowned children, visitations from the wife he murdered after she drowned them, and assorted other phantasms who populate his heavily armored yet pathetically vulnerable psyche. *Shutter Island* stands with Stanley Kubrick's *The Shining* (1980) and Steven Spielberg's *A.I. Artificial Intelligence* (2001) as an inspired instance of cinema *hauntology*, using that term in two senses that critical theorist Colin Davis has ably summarized (373-374). In one sense, deriving from Jacques Derrida, hauntology displaces its near-homonym *ontology* (i.e., that which is grounded in presence and being) with the figure of the ghost as an incomprehensible intruder on our world, "neither present nor absent, neither dead nor alive," presenting possibilities of otherness that we are ethically bound to acknowledge and respect. A second approach, developed by the psychoanalysts Nicolas Abraham and Maria Torok, sees a haunting phantom as the metaphorical presence of "a dead ancestor in the living Ego, still intent on preventing its traumatic and usually shameful secrets from coming to light," and using lies and misdirection to that end.

In these ideas we find many elements familiar from *Shutter Island*—ghosts, intruders, beings that flummox the binaries of absence and presence, phantasms of the dead jamming consciousness with fictions, fabrications, and deceptions so as to obscure and occlude thoughts thought by the living to be unthinkable. Since the ambience of the film and its location are always threatening and often terrifying, we must entertain the possibility that God's creation is as violent, anarchic, and morally desolate as the warden claims. (Scorsese not only entertains the possibility that violence is essential to God's creation; he often casts himself as the locus and instigator of that violence, playing pivotal roles such as the shooter who kills Johnny Boy in *Mean Streets* and the hate-filled passenger who rants about guns and pussy from the back seat of Travis' cab in *Taxi Driver*.[11]) Yet in the final analysis Scorsese is not a cynic, much less a nihilist, and his hauntology is closest to the relatively conservative version outlined by Fredric Jameson, who paraphrases the message of "spectrality" in a pithy formulation: "that the living present is scarcely as self-sufficient as it claims to be [and] that we would do well not to count on its density and solidity, which might under exceptional circumstances betray us" (Jameson 39; Davis 373).

The people, places, and things of *Mean Streets* and *Goodfellas* (1990) and *Gangs of New York* (2002) and other Scorsese films are as dense and solid as any in American cinema, but the spiritually attuned skeptic in Scorsese keeps him from indulging romantic notions of a stable past, a foreseeable future, or a dependable, self-sufficient here and now. The thickness and firmness of his filmic worlds are paradoxically fluid, impermanent, and endlessly in flux—so much so that Jesus in *The Last Temptation of Christ* can pull his beating heart from his torso; evildoer Max Cady (De Niro) in *Cape Fear* can be impervious to pain and almost impossible to kill; medic Frank Pierce in *Bringing Out the Dead* can

---

[11] Scorsese frequently appears as an " inciting force" in his films, Braudy points out; in addition to the above-mentioned roles he plays the make-up man preparing Jake LaMotta for his stage act in *Raging Bull* and the assistant director who sarcastically tells Rupert to talk to the director in *The King of Comedy* (26).

commune with the spirits of people he failed to save; and so on in other Scorsese films, capped by Teddy's ability to live in a totally unmoored realm of fantasy and hallucination. Filmic worlds are phantasmal by definition, of course—they are made of nothing but light—and their hauntological properties help explain the profundity and longevity of Scorsese's attachment to cinema. Traumas, wounds, and dreams are pretty much interchangeable things, Dr. Naehring (Max Von Sydow) of *Shutter Island* says. Movies of the emotionally intense, often physically violent kind favored by Scorsese can be added to the list.

Shelter Island stipulates that Teddy's deliverance from traumas, wounds, and dreams can come only via transorbital lobotomy—an ice pick in the brain, as another character describes it, entering the cranium through the socket of an eye in a procedure that faintly echoes the entry of the movie through the eyes of its beholders. This means that Teddy's chronic spiritual crisis is moving toward a wholly secular resolution. Or so it seems until one considers the last words of the protagonist and the film: "Which would be worse—to live as a monster, or to die as a good man?" Neither option is allowed to Teddy, who will finish his days as a decerebrated "zombie" or "ghost," in the movie's terminology. But his ability to ask this not-so-rhetorical question suggests that sparks of humanity, and perhaps of the divine, still survive in his horrifically damaged psyche, and may continue to persist, however dimly and inadequately, even after 1950s psychiatry has done its worst. Seen as a secular narrative, *Shelter Island* is a hyperbolic variation on *Huis clos*, the 1944 play by existentialist philosopher Jean-Paul Sartre; in Scorsese's version the Hell that allows "no exit" is not *other people* but, vastly more terrifying, *the self*, populated only by phantoms of its own unconscious devising. At the same time, however, Teddy's morally concerned reference to dying as "a good man" reminds us of the film's spiritual interests, suggesting that the amorality and violence adduced by the warden are not the entire sum and substance of our fallen world. The movie's last aching expression of humanity's endlessly enigmatic position vis-à-vis redemption, transcendence, and grace comes not during the story but after it, when the closing credits roll and the music score[12] (supervised by Robbie

---

[12] Supervised by Robbie Robertson, famous from the Band and Scorsese's rock documentary *The Last Waltz* (1978), the *Shutter Island* score incorporates part of Gustav Mahler's unfinished Piano Quartet in A Minor (ca. 1876) and bits and pieces from an imposing roster of progressive twentieth-century composers including John Cage, Morton Feldman, Lou

Robertson, a longtime Scorsese friend) reaches one of its most stirring moments, combining Max Richter's string composition "On
the Nature of Daylight" (2004) with Dinah Washington singing
"This Bitter Earth," which contains this lyric:

> This bitter earth
> Well, what fruit it bears
> What good is love that no one shares
> And if my life is like the dust that hides the glow
>   of a rose
> What good am I?
> Heaven only knows.

Not the warden or the guards. Not the psychiatrists or the
nurses. Not even the suffering protagonist himself. What good is
Teddy? Heaven only knows.

Humility and pride

In one of the more charming paradoxes of Scorsese's career, his first
fiction feature after the grim *Shutter Island* was his most good-natured and family-friendly film to date: *Hugo*, a 2011 release
produced in 3-D, boasting a $170 million budget, marketed as a
year-end blockbuster, and nominated for eleven Academy Awards,
of which it won five.[13] The title character (Asa Butterfield) is an
orphaned boy who lives a fugitive life in an outsized clock located
in a Paris railroad station during the 1930s. His most precious

---

Harrison, Alfred Schnittke, John Adams ("Christian Zeal and Activity"), Brian Eno ("Lizard Point"), György Ligeti ("Lontano"), Krzysztof
Penderecki (the third symphony), Giacinto Scelsi (the third movement
of "Uaxuctum: The Legend of the Mayan City Which They Themselves
Destroyed for Religious Reasons"), the " expressivist" composer Ingram
Marshall, and the video artist Nam June Paik, as well as pop hits from the
1940s and 1950s, most notably Johnny Ray's 1951 recording of " Cry" and
Kay Starr's 1952 cover of " Wheel of Fortune," which have moods (and
titles) that accord well with Scorsese's interest in the woes of the human
condition and the seemingly capricious, ultimately unfathomable nature
of divine grace.

[13] Based on Brian Selznick's novel *The Invention of Hugo Cabret*, the film
was written by John Logan, whose many credits include the screenplay for
The Aviator. Hugo was released in the American market by Paramount
Pictures; its other sponsors were GK Films, which had produced several
earlier Scorsese movies, and Johnny Depp's interestingly named production company, Infinitum Nihil.

possession is an automaton handed down from his late father, and his search for the key needed to activate it leads to an eccentric old man (Ben Kingsley) who turns out to be Georges Méliès, the real-life pioneer of early cinema whose magical trick movies—the most famous include *A Trip to the Moon* (1902) and *An Impossible Voyage* (1904)—have influenced a large number of subsequent filmmakers, ranging from Charles Chaplin and Georges Franju to Terry Gilliam and Scorsese himself.

The finale of *Hugo* is less a conventional plot-resolving scene than a tribute to Méliès that can only be described as reverential. Scorsese has worshiped at two altars throughout his adult life: the altar of Christianity and the altar of cinema, which claim his faith, trust, and commitment in roughly equal measure. The moments in *Hugo* that recreate Méliès sequences in 3-D and modern color are not merely spectacles, they are acts of mingled humility and pride—humility because Scorsese is placing himself at the service of an originary figure whose legacy is at the heart of cinephilia, and pride because he is presuming to revivify that figure's magic by means of today's digital prestidigitation, which Méliès would surely have applauded.

To put this a little differently, Scorsese is revisiting a creation myth of cinema, transmuting works that dazzled the turn of an old century into bigger, brighter incarnations that can dazzle the turn of the new one in ways it can instantly understand; and he is also resurrecting Méliès himself, not so much through Kingsley's acting as through the homage he pays to the foundational works over which Méliès' spirit still presides. Its commercial allure and box-office millions notwithstanding, *Hugo* is devotional cinema of a very high order.

Not *nihil*

As noted earlier, Scorsese began work on his adaptation of Shusaku Endo's novel *Silence* in 2012. In ways this is a surprising choice, since Scorsese has directed only one prior movie with a predominantly Asian setting (*Kundun*) and most of his literary adaptations have come from books by American authors. Looked at more carefully, however, the theme signaled by the novel's title resonates strongly with one of Scorsese's most persistent and long-lived concerns— the ongoing struggle with problems of faith, doubt, and divine grace, including the question of why peaceful confidence in future redemption appears to be so arbitrarily dispersed (if not downright rare) among Christian believers and humanity at large.

According to analysis of the novel by the Japanese-American theologian Fumitaka Matsuoka, it pivots on the idea that the *silence* of God is in fact the *message* of God, being not the silence of *nihil*, or nothingness, but rather "the silence of 'accompaniment' for the forsaken and the suffering" and the concomitant silence of Christians quietly hoping for salvation (294, 297). Implicit here is what Matsuoka terms "an element of uncertainty" (298), a possibility that the *nihil* of emptiness, meaninglessness, and hopelessness will ultimately prevail. Uncertainty about the fate of the soul (or the self, for secularists) lies at the heart of human experience, injecting many a mind with the existential fear, trembling, and sickness unto death of which Søren Kierkegaard vividly wrote. Taken in a positive light, however, this same uncertainty (and its Kierkegaardian symptoms) can be a stimulating impetus toward states of awareness, alertness, attentiveness, even excitement—in a word, *suspense*, as a storyteller would call it. A gambler feels those sensations on a regular basis, and as we have seen, gambling is one of Scorsese's most intriguing metaphors (in *Casino* and elsewhere) for the chronic elusiveness and prospective ecstasy of God-given grace. He has staked everything on the idea that a life in cinema can be a good life, a fulfilling life, and a Godly life, or at least a godly one. It is an enormous bet, and one he is likely to win.

Works cited

Canby, Vincent, "*Taxi Driver*." *New York Times*, February 8, 1976.

Chandler, Raymond, "The Simple Art of Murder," in Raymond Chandler, *The Simple Art of Murder* (Houghton Mifflin, 1950). Originally in *The Atlantic Monthly* (December 1944).

Christie, Ian and David Thompson, eds., *Scorsese on Scorsese*, revised edition (Faber, 2003).

Corliss, Richard, "...And Blood," in Peter Brunette, ed., *Martin Scorsese: Interviews* (Mississippi, 1999), 113-123. Originally in *Film Comment*, September-October 1988.

Davis, Colin, "Hauntology, specters and phantoms." *French Studies* vol. 59, no. 3 (July 2005), 373-379.

Ebert, Roger, *Scorsese by Ebert* (Chicago, 2008).

Joyce, James, *Ulysses* (Vintage International, 1990).

Kakutani, Michiko, "Scorsese's Past Colors His New Film," *New York Times*, 13 February 1983.

Matsuoka, Fumitaka, "The Christology of Shusaku Endo." *Theology Today* v. 39 n. 2 (July 1982), 294-299.

Jameson, Fredric, "Marx's Purloined Letter," in Michael Sprinker, ed., *Ghostly Demarcations: A Symposium on Jacques Derrida's "Spectres de Marx"* (Galilée, 1993), 26-67.

Locke, Maryel, "A History of the Public Controversy," in Maryel Locke and Charles Warren, eds., *Jean-Luc Godard's* Hail Mary: *Women and the Sacred in Film* (Southern Illinois, 1993), 1-9.

Lourdeaux, Lee, *Italian and Irish Filmmakers in America: Ford, Capra, Coppola, and Scorsese* (Temple, 1990).

NASB: New American Standard Bible, Lockman Foundation, 1995.

O'Connor, Flannery, *Wise Blood* (Farrar, Straus and Giroux, 2007).

Pileggi, Nicholas and Martin Scorsese, *Casino* (Faber, 1996).

Smith, Gavin, "The Art of Vision: Martin Scorsese's *Kundun*," in Peter Brunette, ed., *Martin Scorsese: Interviews* (Mississippi, 1999), 236-256. Originally in *Film Comment* (January-February 1998).

Žižek, Slavoj. *Enjoy Your Symptom! Jacques Lacan in Hollywood and Out* (Routledge, 1992).

Spielberg, iconophobia, and the mimetic uncanny

New Review of Film and Television Studies 7:1 (March 2009)

Critical theorist W. J. T. Mitchell has suggested that 'images are like living organisms' with drives, desires, needs, and a tendency to behave, or appear to behave, as if they have lives of their own. Seen in these terms, the motion-picture mechas in *A.I. Artificial Intelligence* (2001) are examples of the 'living image' that artists, alchemists, and others have dreamed of creating since antiquity: a replica that is not a mere copy but a holistic simulacrum of a biological creature—what Mitchell aptly calls a 'work of art in the age of biocybernetic reproduction' (2005, 11, 309). Telling the *Pinocchio*-like story of a futuristic android 'mecha' who dreams of becoming a real boy, this fantasy amounts to Steven Spielberg's intuitive working-through of various philosophical issues related to the 'living image' and its discontents. Put into dialogical play by Stanley Kubrick when he conceptualized the film, these issues underwent further vicissitudes when he bequeathed it to Spielberg, a filmmaker with more humanistic and optimistic sensibilities (Friedman 2006, 46–9).

Notwithstanding the aesthetic and intellectual shifts caused by this changing of the guard, the film's most telling philosophical concerns remained fundamentally intact. At its core, *A.I.* represents a complex, acutely troubled, sometimes barely coherent reaction to uncertainties posed by the mimetic uncanny that contemporary science has brought forth. The protagonist, a mecha named David, embodies those uncertainties by way of his dual nature as an artificially manufactured creature and a virtual duplicate of a generic human being. Apprehensions sparked by the idea of such an entity are embedded in the very origins of the *A.I.* project. One reason why Kubrick decided not to direct the film himself, for instance, was his realization that, given his proclivity for photographing his movies over unusually long periods of time, the child star would visibly age during production, discombobulating the flow of cinematic time in the finished film. Anxiety over the palpable effects of time on the human organism therefore played a significant role in *A.I.* right from the planning stage. Indeed, given the abundance of mirrors and mirror images in some parts of the film, one wonders if Kubrick thought of a line Jean Cocteau wrote for the angel Heurtebise in *Orphée* (1950): 'I give you the secret of secrets…. All of you, look at your life in a mirror and you see Death at work.' As a marvel of technology that stands outside biological time,

David can look into a mirror and see nothing more disturbing than his immunity to temporality and its works; this is one source of his uncanniness in the biocentric world of ordinary mortals.

This paper discusses *A.I.* along these lines, making four major points. One is that the hostility of the human 'orga' characters toward the artificial mechas is related to terror of the paranormal doppelgänger—a sensation that Mitchell (2005, 310) describes as 'horror of… one's own mirror image rendered autonomous,' reflecting traditional fears of the uncanny double as a portent of death and an existential threat to the 'authentically' human. My second point is that David's abandonment by his 'mother' acts out this fear on two psychosocial levels: as the expulsion of an alien presence from the threatened body of the family, and the ejection of an anomalous intruder from the communal corpus. My third point is that the feral chaos of the Flesh Fair scene is no mere rebellion against technology but an orgy of *iconoclasm*, in which the public smashing of uncanny mecha-images is an act of 'creative destruction' (Mitchell 2005, 21) that transmutes obliteration itself into a potent form of iconography. And lastly I find that David's eventual transfiguration into an ambiguous new state of being, a sort-of-maybe-human state, is an uneasy attempt on Spielberg's part to exorcise the brooding fear of specular simulacra that made *A.I.*, as Kubrick originally conceived it, less a Spielberg-style fantasy than a thinly veiled sequel to a pair of Kubrick films—*A Clockwork Orange* (1971) and *The Shining* (1980)—that are, paradoxically for this master of cinematic iconography, forcefully iconophobic works.

Masterplot

A brief plot synopsis will refresh memories of *A.I.* In the not-so-distant future, global warming has melted the polar icecaps and flooded coastal cities. Migrating inland, humankind survives by reconfiguring its social rules—families are allowed only one child, for example—and producing new technological wonders, including ultra-realistic mechas. In a new breakthrough, the robot scientist Professor Hobby (William Hurt) develops the first mecha capable of being programmed to love the people who own it. The prototype is David (Haley Joel Osment), a preadolescent boy mecha.

David is purchased by Monica and Henry Swinton, a well-to-do couple whose son, Martin, has been cryogenically frozen after contracting a terminal illness. Monica activates David's ability to love, and before long he is a full-fledged member of the Swinton family, albeit one who can only mimic biological functions like eating and sleeping. Things change when Martin, unexpectedly cured, returns to the household and becomes David's rival for attention and affection. Psychologically stressed by the new fault lines in the family, Monica abandons David in a forest, where humans capture him and bring him to a Flesh Fair, a sadistic circus in which ownerless mechas are savagely destroyed. David escapes with help from Teddy, a toy bear that Monica let him keep, and a new acquaintance named Gigolo Joe (Jude Law), a sex-worker mecha framed for murdering a human. Wanting to become a real boy worthy of Monica's love, David searches for the roboticist who designed him, eventually finding Professor Hobby high in a Manhattan skyscraper. Traumatized by the sight of countless David-like mechas just off the assembly line — here the uncanny double of the human finds his own uncanny double, many times over — David plunges into the sea and begins a vigil before a Blue Fairy statue in the underwater ruins of an amusement park. After two millennia he is discovered by highly advanced supermechas, who revere him as an early-model mecha who knew human beings, now extinct. David craves reunion with Monica, and the supermechas give him a reasonable facsimile, presenting him with a Monica clone; the catch is that she can exist only for a single day. When the joyous and contented day is over, David lies in bed with Monica at his side, and falls asleep — like a real boy — for the first time.

Uncanny Valley

I begin my discussion about a hundred years ago, when German psychologist Ernst Jentsch wrote an essay called 'On the Psychology of the Uncanny,' arguing that uncanny feelings are a special kind of fear sparked by cognitive uncertainty in the face of a stimulus or experience too radically unfamiliar to be readily absorbed. In storytelling, Jentsch wrote, an excellent way to create uncanny effects 'is to leave the reader in uncertainty whether a particular figure… is a human being or an automaton and to do it in such a way that his attention is not focused upon his uncertainty…' (Freud 1919, 219–20). Thirteen years later, Sigmund Freud quoted this with approval in his essay 'The "Uncanny,"' but went on to identify two obvious weaknesses in Jentsch's account: not every encounter with the new and unknown produces fear, distress, or revulsion, and uncanny feelings can arise in situations where intellectual uncertainty is negligible or absent. These and other considerations led Freud to reverse a key element of Jentsch's hypothesis, describing the uncanny as a specific kind of dread rooted not in fear of the unknown, but rather in 'that class of the frightening which leads back to what is known of old and long familiar.' Freud also noted that the uncanny is a richly ambiguous concept—so much so that the words *Heimlich* and *unheimlich* actually switch places in different written works (1919, 220, 224–5).

All of which brings us to Uncanny Valley, a metaphorical lowland mapped by Japanese roboticist Masahiro Mori, who picks up where Jentsch and Freud left off. In a 1970 essay, Mori warns that advances in robotics and prosthetics may be undercut by their own success, since designs that are too humanlike produce feelings of uncanniness—or 'negative familiarity,' in Mori's words—and generate exactly the kind of dread described by Freud, fueled not by the *novelty* of, say, the android or mecha, but by its capacity for seeming *old and familiar* in strangely disquieting ways. Mori illustrates this concept with a diagram that traces two sweeping upward curves. The left-hand curve has modestly humanlike artifacts at the lower elevations— prosthetic limbs, theatrical puppets, and such—and real human beings at the summit. At the bottom of the right-hand curve are mere industrial robots, hardly resembling humans at all, and at the top are ingeniously made androids that please us with their convincing likeness to our own species. Between the pinnacles of these curves—one bearing a person, the other bearing what *Blade Runner* (Ridley Scott, 1982) would call a replicant—is the plunging abyss that Mori calls the Uncanny Valley, representing his finding that the more humanlike a robot appears, the more it pleases us, but if it becomes *too* humanlike, its very verisimilitude can produce feelings of strangeness, shock, even horror (1970).

Mori does not claim to know the mechanisms behind these responses, but one conjecture holds that when an object seems *partly or sort of human*, its humanlike traits are thrown into relief by their clearly nonhuman background, gratifying our all-too-human narcissism; yet when an object seems *almost or virtually human*, the nonhuman traits leap into the perceptual foreground, jolting our narcissism and perhaps touching off hostilities toward the anomalous Other implanted during the evolution of our

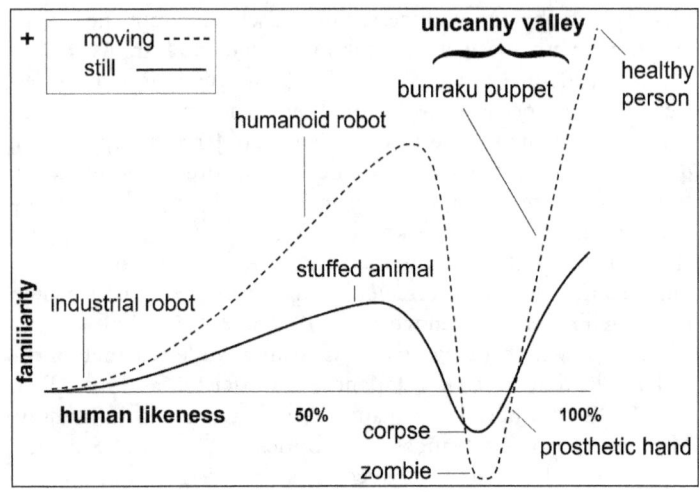

Masahiro Mori's Uncanny Valley, from his 1970 essay.
Karl F. MacDorman and Norri Kageki's translation appears in the
June 2012 issue of *Robots & Automation*.

species. Mori speculates that self-preservation instincts of a more
intimate kind may also be involved, pointing out that each of us is
fated to fall into the Uncanny Valley when we die, since then the
body itself becomes an anomalous Other—cold, pale, unfeeling,
unmoving, at once a human object and an inert parody thereof.
Mori concludes by encouraging us to be pleased that our final fall
is into the still valley of corpsehood and not the agitated valley of
'the living dead,' thus finishing his influential paper with something of a cinematic flourish (1970).

All this has clear implications for practices as different as
cosmetic surgery and video-game design. Discussing the Xbox
360 game *Peter Jackson's King Kong*, technology writer Clive
Thompson observes that its most frightening feature is not the
towering ape or the prehistoric monsters but rather Naomi Watts,
pictured on the game screen with 'lifeless eyes, plastic skin,
and weirdly slack mouth' (Mangan 2007). On this view, Kong's
companion has tumbled into Uncanny Valley, which is an occu-
pational hazard at a time when computer graphics have enabled
electronic media to erase the line between photographic reality and
digitized hallucination. To those who share André Bazin's respect
for the photographic image as an indexical representation of ontological reality (1967, 9–16), cinema's growing reliance on comput-

er-generated pixels is a sign of the medium's impending doom. But for those with more optimistic outlooks, the ability to blend digital *and* photographic images is giving us what film theorist Daniel Frampton calls "a new kind of fluid film-thinking," as in movies like *The Matrix* (Andy Wachowski and Larry Wachowski, 1999), which operates, according to Frampton, on 'one plane of film-reality: there are no "recorded" and "digitally animated" parts, just one level of film-world' (2006, 205). Among the trailblazers, innovators, and kung-fu masters of this metastasizing field, Spielberg stands with the most prominent—and nowhere is his fascination with simulacra more forcefully expressed than in *A.I.*

The living image

When he says that images are like living organisms, Mitchell means we can understand them in fresh and original ways if we hold onto our immediate, often visceral responses and take them literally for a change—not naively or permanently, but as useful heuristics rooted in the direct connection we feel with pictures and designs that move us. This connection, so strong that it seems like two-way communication, can be very pleasurable when it kicks in. But it can be disquieting when it gives rise to the uncanny, which Mitchell defines in Freudian terms as 'the moment when the most ordinary forms of disavowed superstition (monsters in the closet, toys coming alive) come back as undeniable truths' (2005, 7, 13). So we play it safe, like people of past eras, by approaching images with a kind of double consciousness, valuing their qualities of 'vitality' and 'energy' yet disowning their links with the actual living things they mimic, resemble, or evoke. The result is classic Freudian disavowal. We know they are not living, vital things, but all the same...

This mindset is especially prevalent in a media-drenched society where images proliferate exponentially, and it has profound consequences for what Mitchell calls our 'metapicture,' the image we have of images themselves—an über-image that arises from the ways certain pictures 'stage... the "self-knowledge" of pictures' and therefore the self-knowledge of beholders too (1995, 57, 48). The metapicture is both a source and a result of our double consciousness, and differing versions of it provoke image wars waged by antagonistic cultural factions, each committed to its own conception of how the current 'iconoclash' should ultimately play out. Some images are more caught up than others in this struggle, and at the turn of the twenty-first century it is hard to find more hotly fought-over examples than two that Mitchell singles out (2005, 10, 11, 18). One is the image of the World Trade Center, which was chosen for attack precisely because it was a ubiquitously recognizable icon, and was destroyed in such a way that its obliteration became an indelible icon in its own right. The other, far milder to look at but equally fearsome in many eyes, is the first mammal to be successfully cloned from a nonembryonic cell: gentle Dolly, the biogenetically engineered sheep.

As a living clone during her six-year lifespan, Dolly was the living image of the 'living image,' an organism that did not just resemble but actually re-embodied the parent whose cell had spawned her. Clones are controversial for various reasons: many religious conservatives regard them as unnatural entities, even if they are produced for purposes of research rather than procreation, and some secularists oppose cloning because it can generate malformed organisms unable to live properly, or to live at all. Even for sympathizers, moreover, clones have a powerful, sometimes unsettling mystique by virtue of their novelty, their origins in experimentation hard for nonscientists to understand, and uncertainties as to how advanced, widespread, and important to our ordinary lives they may become. In short, among 'living images' clones may be the uncanniest of all, dwelling in a corner of Uncanny Valley reserved for creatures whose similarity to authentic humans, already too close for comfort, is made still more disturbing by our knowledge of their not-quite-natural beginnings. Hence their significance in the contemporary image wars, where Dolly is still the poster animal for biogenetic derring-do, and hence the strong attention they receive from modern-day iconoclasts. It is interesting too that robot scientist Mori and art theorist Mitchell both use paradoxical formulations to capture the elusive nature of the phenomena at play here. As noted, Mori speaks of 'negative familiarity' to describe the uncanny feelings we get from close encounters with overly human replicas, while Mitchell sees iconoclasm as 'creative destruction' whereby 'a secondary image of defacement or annihilation is created at the same moment that the "target" image is attacked,' producing a new icon that is as tantalizing to idolaters as the icon so spectacularly smashed (2005, 18, 21). It goes without saying that the wide-screen extravaganza is one of the most efficient media in history for creating spectacles of creative destruction—moving-image icons, fetishes, and commodities for an emotionally numbed age.

An evening at the Flesh Fair

All the thinkers I have mentioned see the uncanny as a locus of uneasiness and disquietude at best, outright fear and loathing at worst. Looking at *A.I.*, we see those emotions doing especially hard work in the Flesh Fair episode. The purpose of this extended scene is to display in ferocious and frightening terms the raging hostility directed by orgas at the mechas who share their world; the action consists of tortures that would be considered outrageous even by the George W. Bush administration, with mechas being 'torn limb from limb, chainsawed in half, or melted by buckets of steaming acid' in vignettes 'recycling imagery from Inquisitional torture to African-American lynching,' as one critic describes it (Koresky 2003). The film partly rationalizes this spectacle: damage is inflicted only on mechas that have outlasted their usefulness; they feel no pain; and the lurid carnival is aimed at an audience of raving rednecks who may not have many other pleasures in life. Still, the brutality of the scene is jarring, especially compared with Spielberg's other movie fantasies; it is as if he were transfixed by the hellish vision of ordinary people thrown into sadistic tantrums by what psychoanalytic theorist Slavoj Žižek calls the 'obscene superego agency,' aka 'the mad-obscene law which is *incommensurate* with our well-being insofar as it derails the psychic equilibrium,' decentering the individual from within. Such a plunge into 'the "impossible"/ traumatic/painful enjoyment beyond the pleasure principle' (Žižek 1992, 106, 182) must be impelled by some psychic condition within the subject, and I see its operation in the Flesh Fair mob as, at least in part, a reaction to the existential terror provoked by dread of the doppelgänger, the unnatural double that uncannily mimics oneself or another authentically human subject. Seen in this light, the mechas of the world become humanity's evil twin, and if humans of the future carry the same folkloric unconscious as people of times gone by, the sinister dead ringers will be feared and hated as doppelgängers — and clones, for some people — traditionally are: as threats, ill omens, and harbingers of baleful things to come. The iconoclastic orga-orgy at the Flesh Fair is thus a feral celebration of paranoid hate's ability to make the *superannuated, annihilated* icon into the *transmuted, invigorating* icon through the very act of its obliteration.

To understand how fear-driven iconoclasm plays out more generally in *A.I.*, we must uncover one of the film's most crucial themes. The scientists who created David were motivated not by altruism or greed, but by their sense that humanity badly needed a new, mecha kind of love—a love that is manufactured, programmed, bought and paid for, but sufficiently obtainable and reliable to be longed for all the same. What fuels this need is the waning of humans' own capacity for authentic love, which is running out in ways so conspicuous that ordinary denial is wearing thin and stronger psychic defenses must be set in place. The declining power of human love is evident in the social and domestic life envisioned by the film (note the cool, sterile atmosphere of the Swinton home, for instance) in a technologized future that has preserved its physical existence at the expense of its spiritual strength. This spiritual void is symbolized by the missing children of Professor Hobby and the Swintons, as film critic Jonathan Rosenbaum recognizes when he notes that Professor Hobby created David partly to fill the aching emptiness left by the death of his own son; the film generalizes this by implying that 'all robots point to... lacks, absences, and failures in the people who make them' (2001). The movie's eagerness to pulverize mechas is thus a symptom of profound insecurity bred by human failures and inadequacies, of which the mechas are walking, talking witnesses—vivid simulacra of things the humans do not want simulated.

David in the bewilderness

A boy's best friend may be his mother, but David is not a real boy, and we discover before long that Monica is not a real friend. At first she seems relatively unscarred by the inadequacies and insecurities just mentioned. Or perhaps we see her that way because the film prods us into sympathy with her, showing how wounded she is by the catastrophic illness and virtual death of her son Martin, languishing in cryogenic suspension. Martin is also languishing in Uncanny Valley, since in his deathlike paralysis he is a (literal) embodiment of the terrifying Other hypothesized by Mori: the autonomous corpse, whose dreadful demeanor (cold, pale, unfeeling, unmoving) demonstrates the blurriness of boundary lines between the living image and the unliving twin that haunts it.

Simultaneously mourning the boy's moribundity and longing for his rebirth into the world, Monica and Henry have good reasons for acquiring a mecha as an outlet for their parental impulses; but their seemingly rational decision is destabilized from within by two inescapable considerations. The first: Martin is an intensely ambiguous being, caught in a liminal zone between the living and the unliving image; but so is David, *mutatis mutandis*, and this makes him a less-than-ideal surrogate for the frozen boy he is meant to replace. The uncanny aura hovers about each of them, bringing subliminal confusion to the human subjectivities that bond with them. The second: Martin recovers from his illness and returns to normal life, casting off the uncanny stain and offering the prospect of a household cleansed of that impurity for good. This change renders David superfluous in the family's balance of psychodynamic power; and worse, it makes his own uncanny stain more conspicuous and disquieting than before. Yesterday he was an indispensable place-holder for the family's procreational urge; today he is a surplus and an excess, the not-quite-living image of someone who has regained the power to live under his own steam.

Before this development, Monica had taken David to her heart, welcoming his presence and uttering the pseudomagic spell that transformed him from an emotion-free automaton to a loving and desiring one. Faced with his newly redundant status after Martin's return, however, Monica adjusts her allegiance in a heartbeat, channeling her maternal attentions to the biological child and making the fateful decision to abandon her uncanny humanoid in a forest 'so drear, so rank, so arduous,' as Dante called a similarly darksome wood (Alighieri 1954, 28). As suggested above, Monica's abandonment of David operates on two overlapping levels. Domestically, her casting out of David—a skewed reenactment of the Garden of Eden myth— represents her need to purge the body (here the body of the family) by expelling an alien structure that threatens its integrity and health; since this is a defensive need rooted in psychobiological instinct, it is as ineluctable for Monica as it is unknowable by her nonbiological quasi-child. Culturally, the banishment is an expulsion from the communal corpus (the body politic) of what anthropologist Mary Douglas would call an anomalous intruder (a telling phrase, since for Douglas the 'anomalous' and the 'ambiguous' are overlapping terms) that subsists between and beyond the socially useful categories of insider and outsider (2002, 47). When she discards David in the wilderness—or the bewilderness, to borrow psychoanalytic scholar Peter Swales' colorful word (Watson 1995, 13)— Monica acknowledges her son's escape from Uncanny Valley by exiling her mecha there. In keeping with Uncanny Valley law, she would have no need to banish David if he were a mere household appliance with arms and legs, or if he were *so* humanlike that his android-hood was undetectable. It is being *almost* a living image that makes him ambiguous, anomalous, and doomed.

As a venture in iconoclasm, Monica's expulsion of David is vastly less spectacular than the demolition derby at the Flesh Fair, which more conspicuously serves the creative-destructive function of transforming icon-smashing into iconography. The banishment and its aftermath serve that function nonetheless, however, since Spielberg makes up for their comparatively modest scale by injecting them with sure-fire emotional overtones snatched from preexisting myths, folklore, and fairy tales, some little known to average moviegoers (e.g. Gnostic tradition) but others as familiar as the Pinocchio and Garden of Eden stories. Supercharged with these ingredients, David's ordeal sustains a level of sentimental pull and specular appeal that compete reasonably well with those of major Spielberg hits like *Close Encounters of the Third Kind* (1977) and *E.T. The Extra-Terrestrial* (1982). (*A.I.*'s weaker box office performance is most likely due to other aspects of the film, including its notorious finale, which I will discuss presently.) Jettisoned in the wilds with no companions but faithful Teddy and the outcast Gigolo Joe, an almost-living image accused of killing a fully living one, David escapes destruction by the skin of his artificial teeth, but it is painfully clear that humanity has always already rejected him. He terrifies humans in ways that neither he nor they can understand, and Mitchell is right to call his story an 'extreme exaggeration of the uncanny,' limning a sentimental portrait of mother/son contentment that is blasted to bits by the 'horror of the double' coiled within it (2005, 310).

After surviving further tribulations, David topples into an ultimate Uncanny Valley beneath the sea. There he keeps vigil before the Blue Fairy for two thousand (biblical) years and then gains deliverance from the supermechas of the future, who treasure him as a quasi-living link to the fabled age when humans still walked the earth. As his story comes to an end, David apparently comes to life, becoming a truly living image at last—but in a crowning paradox, he is the living image of a dead original, a race that no longer exists. David is thus a loser once again, and despite Spielberg's decision to pull out the sentimental stops in the story's last chapter, there is little comfort in David's hopeless tryst with an image less alive than he is, the ghostly simulacrum of his long-dead mother. Monica has no more ontological authenticity for David now than he had for her when she abandoned him; and insofar as her one-time embrace of David was steeped in the self-deception of a desperately deprived mother, the final scene's inversion of their earlier relationship is best interpreted as a return of the repressed with a vengeance. It is also a revealing clue to the psychological game Spielberg is playing with his audience, as Rosenbaum (2001) observed in his review:

> One might say that the emotional conflicts experienced by Monica when she first encounters David implicitly remain our own conflicts throughout the film, but Spielberg is too fluid a storyteller to allow us to remember this ambivalence much of the time. He invites us to fool ourselves just as we always do with his films and just as Monica sometimes does with David—a deception based on primal emotional needs and repressed realities. This repression is generally sustained in most Spielberg films, but here the repressed knowledge and emotions periodically come back like icy waves lapping around our ankles.

We feel those icy waves acutely at the end, when Spielberg's legendary storytelling powers unexpectedly desert him, leaving the narrative, the characters, and us in a state of confusion that is, by virtue of its sheer contorted strangeness, as fascinating as anything in the film.

The key to existence?

'Many critics hated the ending,' writes Spielberg commentator Andrew M. Gordon (2008, 238), and it is remarkable how numerous and various were the reasons for their dislike. *Village Voice* reviewer J. Hoberman called the film's resolution a 'shamelessly milked miracle... replete with thunderous wonder, appropriate white light, and a symbiotic reunion so obliterating in its solipsism it could split your skull' (2001b). Roger Ebert deemed it a 'facile and sentimental' conclusion that 'has mastered the artificial, but not the intelligence' (2001), while a *Tikkun* magazine writer said that the sequence, 'bathed in morgueish blue light, borders on necrophilia, but Spielberg's treacly piety drains it of even that enjoyment' (Gordon 2008, 238). I wrote in *The Christian Science Monitor* that the film's last portion would provoke 'either cheering or jeering,' adding that Spielberg often 'energizes his movies by tapping into... religious impulses' but is 'a fundamentally earthbound filmmaker' who provides only the 'illusion of connecting with something greater than ourselves' (Sterritt 2001). Other critics praised the movie and its finale, but even some supporters lent ammunition to the detractors, as when a writer in the *Journal of Religion and Film* concluded an exhaustive analysis by discussing no fewer than nine interpretations of the ending, none of them definitive (Flannery-Dailey 2003). This is evidence of complexity for some, of muddle-headedness for others. I find it evidence of both, failing on narrative terms but succeeding as a polysemic manifestation of Spielberg's most interestingly conflicted attitudes toward life and art—a subject of no small interest, given his unquestionable status as the most powerful image maker in the world.

A good way to begin investigating the film's conclusion is by looking again at the Flesh Fair scene. As we have seen, this is driven in large part by abhorrence of the doppelgänger, traditionally a portent of calamity—and in this case an accurate portent, since at the end of *A.I.* mechas are still quasi-living their quasi-lives after humanity has vanished. To immediate hatred of mechas as a threat to human superiority fantasies, therefore, we can add long-term hatred of mechas as the winning contestants in the existential struggle to survive on a declining planet. Since one of Kubrick's abiding themes is the never-ending clash between humanity and the machine—between the orange and the clockwork—the human-free ending of *A.I.* joins the Flesh Fair episode, the abandonment scene, and other such forbidding moments as clear expressions of that filmmaker's moody pessimism rather than Spielberg's usual sunny outlook.

We have to modify this inference, though, when we recall that the story's hyperbolic mecha-hate has a very upbeat flip side: the loving, even reverential view of humans expressed by the future supermechas when David communes with them. Their access to moral and metaphysical truth is underwritten by their resemblance to the Giacometti-like space folks in *Close Encounters of the Third Kind*, who likewise manifested Spielberg's career-long case of messiah-itis. 'Human beings must be the key to existence,' one of them declares in awe-struck (telepathic) tones—and we feel the supermecha doth protest too much, since if humans were as excellent as all that, they would not have needed to cultivate near-psychopathic hate for their biocybernetic alter egos, who are physically harmless, after all. Spielberg himself may have felt he had gone out on a limb with such over-romantic praise for such a clearly flawed species, since he withholds it until the point in the story when the vaunted human race has perished and time has erased the evidence of its (our) capacity for gratuitous malevolence and reckless self-deception. Perhaps we are meant to take the human-worship critically and ironically, in which case Kubrick's sensibility is again asserting itself. Or perhaps we are meant to accept it at face value, in which case its exaggerated view of humankind's meritorious nature is at once an outbreak of characteristically Spielbergian idealism and, more interestingly, a sort of cinematic parapraxis that reveals—through its very effort to conceal—a specifically Spielbergian dread.

Spielberg is an artist who has devoted virtually his whole career to celebrating the essential goodness of human beings, making even the Holocaust of *Schindler's List* and the slave traffic of *Amistad* into arenas for benevolence and self-sacrifice. It takes only a smidgen of psychoanalytic thought to see Spielberg's energetic advocacy of intrinsic human virtue as a reaction formation geared to staving off a primal fear that just the opposite may actually be the case—that if aliens from outer space or future times ever did pay us a visit, for instance, they might not be the human-loving ego projections of *E.T.* or *Close Encounters of the Third Kind* or *A.I.*, but might rather be judgmental, unforgiving superego figures who find the essence of humanness in our contemptible proclivities for hatred, violence, and cruelty. Since this is not an ordinary reaction formation like mine and yours, but a top-of-the-line reaction formation that makes lots of money, it is fair to suggest that the vast number of people who buy tickets for Spielberg's films (including me) share similar forebodings, and welcome similar fantasies, for similar reasons.

However much the films may work as therapeutic or tranquil-lizing agents, I do not mean to suggest that Spielberg is particularly aware of such a function, much less that he designs his movies as high-minded exercises in pop-culture healing. He has dwelled for decades in the rarified sphere of certified media celebrity, and he appears to be quite comfortable about holding his legions of admirers at a distance, sharing their commonplace fears and aspirations more in theory—and movie fantasy—than in the everyday world of ordinary living. This gap between the artist and his audience may account for two specific aspects of the Flesh Fair's remarkable ferocity: the sharp delineation of its audience as proletarian rabble, exaggerated versions of the people who favor R-rated sex and violence over Spielberg's usually PG-ish entertainments; and the way its overkill makes the prevailing atmosphere of the earlier scenes, where the uninviting atmosphere of the Swinton home is bathed in a Spielberg-style glow of middle-class well-being, appear all the more idyllic by contrast. The brutal Flesh Fair episode thus emerges as a distinctively Spielbergian device, at once stoking inchoate fears and purveying avoidance mechanisms, all of which—fears and defenses alike—are rooted in a fantasy life that Spielberg has nurtured in his own unconscious and now imparts to others with unsurpassed skill.

David's day at the movies

Or unsurpassed in movies, at least. And still there are moments that simply do not work— with critics, as measured by unfavorable reviews, or with audiences, as measured by weak attendance. As noted, *A.I.* received mixed reviews (often pro and con within a single article) and was a box-office disappointment, especially in the American market, where its earnings dropped 50 percent in its second week and 63 percent in its third (Hoberman 2001a). As noted also, even many of the commentators who found much to admire in the film were puzzled by its finale, which seemed like a foray into Spielberg's longtime specialty—sentimentality calculated to the decimal point—that Spielberg had somehow managed to botch in all kinds of ways. I share this puzzlement. It is not even clear what is going on in the scene—has David really become real? If so, why now? And what will he see when he wakes up—his mother's body decaying like a vampire caught in the sun?

A plausible explanation for this confusion is that of all the episodes in the movie, this one was transplanted most directly from Kubrick's original scenario, in its prevailing spirit if not in its moment-to-moment content. I have found a trail of iconophobia running through many scenes and sequences of *A.I.*, and a deep suspicion of the visible is one of Kubrick's trademarks, rarely analyzed by critics but no less important for that. This is not the place to follow the thread of iconophobia throughout Kubrick's work, but the deceitfulness of visual representation can be found everywhere from the *trompe l'œil* masquerades of Peter Sellers in *Lolita* (1962) and *Dr. Strangelove or: How I Learned to Stop Worrying and Love the Bomb* (1964) to the antipsychological reverse-zoom shots of *Barry Lyndon* (1975) and the very title of *Eyes Wide Shut* (1999), his final film. (Remember too that when *A Clockwork Orange* was blamed in the UK for inciting off-screen violence, Kubrick pulled it from distribution rather than defend it as a work of art.) Its steady presence in *A.I.* culminates in the finale, when the gesture that confirms David's sort-of-maybe humanness turns out to be *shutting his eyes* and *losing his consciousness*, whereupon the movie fades from view like a dream at daybreak, taking with it the interminable trials it has visited on David for two and a half hours.

Kubrick found imagery to be a first-rate torture device, and thinking back on *A Clockwork Orange* and *The Shining*, one can imagine how grateful Alex would have been to *shut his eyes* while undergoing the Ludovico Technique, or Jack Torrance when the Overlook Hotel morphs into an Uncanny Valley of the animated, agitated dead. In those films, as in the ending of *A.I.*, a protagonist enters two-way communication with a set of private fetish images (Alex's ultraviolence, Jack's sadomasochistic demons, David's memories of the maternal) whose old, familiar nature conjures up inexorable uncanniness before their very eyes, and ours. Truly, pictures are untamable entities that can torment, persecute, and even kill. Such is the dark and lethal side of Mitchell's living-image metaphor, and of Kubrick's profoundly ambivalent engagement with the visual. In his cinema, the simple act of seeing—perhaps the oldest and most familiar of all human acts—is fraught with danger. For him a movie's vision is a shining, a clairvoyance, a glimpse beyond the veil, rendered real for the characters by the logic of their narrative, and made immediate for us by being caught within a frame, compressed to two dimensions, and reflected from a luminescent screen. Of the many ways to interpret the quasi-incestuous rendezvous at the end of *A.I.*, one of the most useful is to see the scene as David's day at the movies, with his own private star performing her old, familiar routines in the old, familiar space they used to share. Spielberg supplies the warm and fuzzy pictures, and Kubrick is the ghostly impresario behind the scenes. This was even more explicit in Kubrick's original plan (Bastian 2001), where the supermechas create not a clone but a hologram of Monica, so that when David reaches out to touch her, his hand passes through thin air.

Why would an artist as self-confident as Spielberg want to channel Kubrick's spirit so directly at the end of *A.I.*, one of the few films that Spielberg takes credit for as both director and screenwriter (Morris 2007, 299)? I can only speculate, but I am tempted to see the sequence's image-anguish as an expression (probably unwitting) of anxieties related to Spielberg's intermittent efforts to grow up as a filmmaker, to trade being a real boy for being a real man, to abandon the kid stuff of *Jurassic Park* and *Indiana Jones* for the grownup melodrama of *Saving Private Ryan* (1998) and *Munich* (2005) and the like. He backslides regularly—he is wrapping up *Indiana Jones and the Kingdom of the Crystal Skull* (2008) as I write—and even his smartest films, like *Schindler's List* (1993), imperfectly suppress his adolescent weaknesses for reductive plots and simplistic psychology. To the extent that Spielberg recognizes his limitations—and an artist this productive must have some degree of self-awareness—he may dimly feel that his facile knack for pumping out instantly endearing pictures is his curse as well as his blessing, and that his compulsion to make them so endearing has stunted his artistic growth.

Seen in this light, the uncanny ending of *A.I.* reflects Spielberg's deep-seated uncertainties about maturity and authenticity, and whether they are everything they are cracked up to be, and if they are even possible for him. In the end, *A.I.* is a Spielberg movie through and through. What his pictures want—what they desire and what they lack—is what David wants: to be real, and to love, and to be loved in return. The misfortune for his pictures and his mechas is that they are not quite the *living* images they so desperately wish to be.

Works Cited

Alighieri, Dante. 1954. *The Inferno*. Trans. John Ciardi. Mentor (Orig. pub. c.1309).

Bastian Jon 2001. "A.I. in depth." *Film Monthly*, July 13.

Bazin, André. 1967. "The ontology of the photographic image." In *What is cinema?*, Vol. 1. Trans. Hugh Gray: 9–16. California (orig. pub. 1945 in Problèmes de la painture).

Brakhage, Stan. 2003. "Artificial Intelligence: A.I." In *The Hidden God: Film and Faith*, ed. Mary Lea Bandy and Antonio Monda, 244–6. Museum of Modern Art.

Douglas, Mary. 2002. *Purity and Danger: An Analysis of Concept of Pollution and Taboo*. Routledge (orig. pub. 1966 by Routledge & Kegan Paul).

Ebert, Roger. 2001. *A.I. Artificial Intelligence*, RogerEbert.com, June 29.

Flannery-Dailey, Frances. 2003. "Robot Heavens and Robot Dreams: Ultimate Reality in *A.I.* and Other Recent Films." *Journal of Religion and Film* 7, no. 2 (October).

Frampton, Daniel. 2006. *Filmosophy*. Wallflower Press.

Freud, Sigmund. 2001. The 'uncanny.' Trans. Alix Strachey. In Vol. 17 of *The Standard Edition of the Complete Psychological Works of Sigmund Freud*, 217–56. London: Vintage (orig. pub. 1919 in Imago 5, nos. 5–6: 297–324).

Friedman, Lester D. 2006. *Citizen Spielberg*. Illinois.

Gordon, Andrew M. 2008. *Empire of Dreams: The Science Fiction and Fantasy Films of Steven Spielberg*. Rowman & Littlefield.

Hoberman, J. 2001a. The Dreamlife of Androids. *Sight and Sound* 11, no. 9 (September): 16–18.

Hoberman, J. 2001b. "The Mommy Returns." *The Village Voice*, June 25.

Koresky, Michael. 2003. Connective tissue. Reverse Shot. http://www.reverseshot.com/ legacy/aprilmay03/connective.html.

Mangan, John. 2007. "When fantasy is just too close for comfort." TheAge.com.au. http:// www.theage.com.au/articles/2007/06/09/1181089394400.html.

Mitchell, W. J. T. 1995. Metapictures. *In Picture Theory*, 35–82. Chicago.

Mitchell, W. J. T. 2005. *What Do Pictures Want?* Chicago.

Mori, Masahiro. 1970. *The Uncanny Valley*. Trans. Karl F. MacDorman and Takashi Minato. http://www.androidscience.com/theuncannyvalley/proceedings2005/uncannyvalley.html. (Orig. pub. in Energy 7, no. 4: 33–5.).

Morris, Nigel. 2007. *The Cinema of Steven Spielberg*. Wallflower.

Rosenbaum, Jonathan. 2001. The best of both worlds. *Chicago Reader*, http://www.chicagoreader.com/movies/archives/2001/0107/010713.html.

Sterritt, David. 2001. "A Tale of Two Directors." *The Christian Science Monitor*, June 29.

Watson, Steven. 1995. *The Birth of the Beat Generation*. Pantheon.

Žižek, Slavoj. 1992. *Enjoy Your Symptom!* Routledge.

Politics, Eternalisms, and the Mad Science of Ken Jacobs
Quarterly Review of Film and Video 39:6 (2022)

Perhaps the greatest benefit of digital cinema is the vast wealth of moving-image art—from all parts of the world and every period of film history—that has become available to cinephiles equipped with a modest array of electronic paraphernalia. No region of the movie cosmos has profited more from this development than the rarified realm variously called the avant-garde, the experimental, and the underground. Films of this ilk could be hard to see in bygone times, when new works by such towering visionaries as Stan Brakhage, Kenneth Anger, Su Friedrich, and Hollis Frampton were viewable only by those with access to museums, universities, and specialized showplaces like New York's fabled Anthology Film Archives and its counterparts in other big cities. But now a gradually increasing amount of avant-garde cinema can be seen by all interested parties, thanks to a handful of enterprising Blu-ray and DVD producers such as the Criterion Collection, Kino Lorber, and Milestone Films, current leaders in the field.[1]

No recent release is more welcome than the *Ken Jacobs Collection Vol. 1*, a two-disk compendium of major and minor works by the eponymous filmmaker. True, the title bestowed on it by Kino Classics is not entirely clear: Is there a Vol. 2? Or will there be a Vol. 2? Or is Vol. 2 actually *The Ken Jacobs Not on Blu-ray Bundle*, a group of seven works available on the Kino Now streaming platform? Be this as it may, both the Blu-ray set and the streaming package are invaluable for Jacobs aficionados and offer excellent points of entry for newcomers to his inimitable artistry.

It's slightly ironic that Jacobs' work has become so readily available, since he was a much an in-person performance artist as a filmmaker during a large portion of his career. His most radical and important innovation is the marvelously named Nervous System, whereby two analytic projectors cast nearly identical frames onto a single screen in rapid alternation produced by a spinning propeller that blocks off the light of each projector in turn.

---

[1] See for example the *Maya Deren Collection*, a Kino Lorber disc containing such classics as *Meshes of the Afternoon* (1943) and *At Land* (1944) as well as an hour of footage from Deren's unfinished *Divine Horsemen* project; Milestone's set *The Magic Box: The Films of Shirley Clarke*, three discs with more than eight hours of material; and Criterion's *A Hollis Frampton Odyssey* and two volumes of *By Brakhage: An Anthology*.

Jacobs developed and deployed this device from the early 1980s until about 2000, controlling the exhibition process as it happened. Among its other capacities, the Nervous System generates a 3D effect and plays into Jacobs' endless fascination with depth perception, which he has also explored through other methods, such as inviting audiences to watch projected images while holding a piece of darkened celluloid over one eye, throwing that eye into night vision, or crossing their eyes while viewing the double images taken by a stereoscopic movie camera. For me, the latter methods create much better 3D than the Nervous System does, but the Nervous System produces the most exhilarating spectacle, pulsing and throbbing with kinetic energy so vigorous that people with photosensitive epilepsy and similar conditions are advised to avoid it. For many years the only way to experience Jacobs' work was to attend screenings, but the advent of DVD convinced him that video was a viable exhibition format, and material started appearing on disk, a notable example being *Ontic Antics Starring Laurel and Hardy; Bye, Molly!*, a 2006 masterpiece that expands and explodes Lewis R. Foster's 1929 short *Berth Marks*, itself a masterpiece of comic-claustrophobic cinema. By now a fair amount of Jacobs' work is available via streaming on YouTube and Vimeo, and the Kino Lorber releases mark another big step forward in mainstreaming this extraordinary artist.

The selections on the Blu-ray disks provide a condensed history of Jacobs' evolution. His first film, *Orchard Street*, is a beautifully observed 1955 documentary about a beloved neighborhood in lower Manhattan, lyrically shot and gracefully edited. *The Whirled* is more fragmented, bringing together four individually made shorts: *Saturday Afternoon Blood Sacrifice* (1956), *Little Cobra Dance* (1956), *Hunch Your Back* (1963, incorporating footage of Ken improbably appearing on a television game show), and *Death of P'Town* (1961), with a great deal of screen time devoted to Jack Smith, the legendary filmmaker and performer with whom Jacobs had a longtime off-and-on professional relationship. Smith is also a central presence in two signature works of 1963, *Little Stabs at Happiness*, a multipart meditation on Lower East Side living, and *Blonde Cobra*, crafted by Jacobs from anarchic footage shot by Bob Fleischner, a likeminded filmmaker. More imposing is *The Sky Socialist* (1964–66), a feature-length sociopolitical fable in which real and imagined figures— the Jewish martyr Anne Frank, the writer and teacher Isadore Lhevinne, the hopeful Muse of Cinema, the whip-wielding Nazi Mentality, and others—caper about in the literal or figurative shadow of the Brooklyn Bridge, after which the film is named. The set also includes *The Sky Socialist: Environs and Outtakes*, a 1964–66 spinoff work presented, like the longer film that spawned it, in a definitive reworking from 2019. The grandest item on the second disk is another signature work, *Tom, Tom, the Piper's Son*, a 1969 extravaganza that stretches a fleetingly brief 1905 one-reeler into almost two hours of rephotographed, reedited, and drastically rejiggered structural cinema. Here again there is a spinoff film, *A Tom Tom Chaser*, from 2002, followed by two works that exemplify the uncompromising political concerns that directly or indirectly underpin all of Jacobs' activities: *Capitalism: Child Labor* and *Capitalism: Slavery*, a pair of 2006 shorts that translate mournfully revealing historical images into "eternalisms," Jacobs' term for the pulsating manifestations engendered by his idiosyncratic techniques. Also on the Blu-ray are *Window* (1964), *The Georgetown Loop* (1996), and *Movie That Invites Pausing*, a wholly abstract work from 2021 that rewards the eye when paused and also when viewed straight through. A video conversation between Jacobs and the astute film scholar Tom Gunning is appended as an extra.

Several of the films on the Kino Lorber disks are essential works in film history as well as Jacobs' own career. The lineup streaming on Kino Now is more recent and has therefore done less to shape the fortunes of avant-garde cinema, but much of it is equally enthralling, if not more so. The excitement starts with *Razzle Dazzle: The Lost World*, a 2006 feature that intersperses swirling amusement-park footage with nonfigurative designs ablaze with color and movement. *Return to the Scene of the Crime* (2021) does the seemingly impossible, actually improving on *Tom, Tom, the Piper's Son* with fresh editing choices, digitally enhanced imagery of superb quality, and violinist Malcolm Goldstein's characteristically amazing music. Here it's worth underscoring the point that few (if any) of Jacobs' works are purely aesthetic exercises; as rollicking as this picture is, a concluding text calls it an antidote to "the spectacle of our courts and politicians playing dumb while USA descends to Nazi levels..." *Seeking the Monkey King* (2011) makes the politics more overt, punctuating a stream of kaleidoscopic eternalisms with slogans and statements that are vastly less subtle than the cinema they interrupt. (Sample: "500 years of b.s. in an overnight collapse communist subversion never got its chance.") Subtlety vanishes completely in the tendentiously titled *Reich-*

stag 9/11: Some eyewitness images on the web, a 2016 montage of documentary materials from the internet transformed into eternal-isms that run the danger of aestheticizing the horrors of the September 11 attacks, a rare miscalculation on Jacobs' part. The semiautobiographical short *Failure* (2019) also lapses into strident verbiage ("Global warming remains denied by Republi-cans on orders of the American oligarchy...") that is fortunately overwhelmed by the splendor of the semi-abstract visuals. *Things to Come* is an elegant mélange of nonfigurative designs, historical footage, and protest of American racism. The concluding item, *The Whole Shebang*, employs bizarre footage from a 1930s novelty film, subsequently turned into a 1982 projection-per-formance and now computerized in a bravura act of digital magic.

In a booklet essay for the Blu-ray release, the redoubt-able critic J. Hoberman says that the Nervous System works are "un-DVD-able," and while there's some truth in that, Jacobs has transcended the problem by making ingenious use of new moving-image technologies as they have come on the scene. He has also benefited from a career-long partnership with his wife, Flo Jacobs, who has been crucial to his creative life, and from the contributions of their daughter, Nisi Jacobs, a major collaborator in recent years. (Their son, Azazel Jacobs, has become a flourishing narrative film-maker in his own right.) He has produced an enormous amount of cinema, and many interesting works not yet on disk—such as *Urban Peasants* (1975), *Perfect Film* (1986), and *The Doctor's Dream* (1978), all found-footage films—certainly deserve to be. Note also that *Two Wrenching Departures* (2006), an emotion-ally powerful Nervous System work initially performed in 1989, was revised for DVD in 2006. Most colossal of all is the magnum opus *Star Spangled to Death*, clocking in at around seven hours and available as a four-disk set on Jacobs' own Big Commotion Pictures label. It is as big and bold a venture as Jacobs has ever undertaken.

I have known Ken for decades— we were lower Manhattan near-neighbors for many years—and I have attended many a Jacobs screening, watched him experiment with shadow play, and seen the Nervous System with great pleasure in assorted venues. The variety of his work is prodigious, but pretty much all of it reflects an overarching goal he once described to me: "To see where [my mind] will take me, and where this technology will take me... And to exercise this power in a way that doesn't mean enslavement or subjugation to others" (Sterritt 2008).[2] Theorizing his aims some years ago, I formulated his "intuitive philosophical goal" in terms derived from Gilles Deleuze and Félix Guattari in *What Is Philosophy?* (Deleuze and Guattari):[3] Jacobs' aspiration is not to comprehend or explain the infinite field of existential possibilities, but "to show that it is there, unthought in every plane, and to think it… as the outside and inside of thought, as… that which cannot be thought and yet must be thought" (Sterritt 2013).[4] Jacobs read philosopher Henri Bergson as a young man, and his ideas are as sophisticated as his art. I regard him as one of the premiere mad scientists of the cinematic universe, and I am thrilled that his films, eternalisms, and unclassifiable whatsits are finding new outlets and audiences as he approaches his 90th year. My hat is permanently off to Ken and company, and to the thrilling eternalisms they have pioneered.

Works Cited

Deleuze, Gilles and Félix Guattari. 1994. *What is Philosophy?* Translated by Hugh Tomlinson and Graham Burchell. Columbia.

Sterritt, David. 2008. "Ken Jacobs." In *Exile Cinema*, edited by Michael Atkinson, 95–99. State University of New York.

Sterritt, David. 2013. "Wrenching Departures: Mortality and Absurdity in Avant-Garde Film." In *The Last Laugh: Strange Humors of Cinema*, edited by Murray Pomerance, 93–108. Wayne State.

---

[2] Sterritt, " Ken Jacobs," p. 99.

[3] Deleuze and Guattari, *What Is Philosophy?*, pp. 59–60.

[4] Sterritt, " Wrenching Departures," p. 105. Quotation on pp. 59–60.

Index